THE BIBLE AS IT WAS

THE
BIBLE
AS IT WAS

James L. Kugel

THE BELKNAP PRESS OF
HARVARD UNIVERSITY PRESS
CAMBRIDGE, MASSACHUSETTS
LONDON, ENGLAND

Second printing, 1998

Library of Congress Cataloging-in-Publication Data
Kugel, James L.
The Bible as it was / James L. Kugel.
p.   cm.
Includes bibliographical references and index.
ISBN 0-674-06940-4 (alk. paper)
1. Bible. O.T. Pentateuch—Criticism, interpretation, etc.—
History. I. Title.
BS1225.2.K84   1997
222′.106′09—dc21   97-3299

Once again, to R.

Contents

Preface

THIS BOOK was written for students and scholars alike. It is intended to be a new kind of guide for anyone interested in the Hebrew Bible (or Old Testament). Let me begin by saying why I think that such a guide is needed.

The Hebrew Bible contains the history, prayers, songs, laws, and prophecies of ancient Israel. These texts were written down over a long period of time, more than a thousand years. Recently, thanks in part to advances in archaeology, linguistics, and ancient history, scholars have been able to learn much about how the Bible came to be. We now know a great deal of the historical background of various biblical stories, as well as about how different parts of the Bible first came together.

When people study the Bible nowadays in schools and universities, it is often this "new knowledge" that is highlighted. Most standard guides and introductions to the Hebrew Bible discuss little else. Thus, people learn about the various stages in which the Bible was written, and about the work of different editors or redactors. They are told about the background history of Israel, and about other texts from the ancient Near East that shed light on biblical events. All this is extremely interesting information.

But it is really only half the story of the Hebrew Bible.

The other half has to do with what happened to these texts once they were written down. For, even before the Bible had attained its final form, its stories, songs, and prophecies had begun to be *interpreted*. From very early times, sages and scholars in ancient Israel had made a practice of looking deeply into the meaning of these sacred writings, and, with each new generation, their insights and interpretations were passed on alongside the texts themselves. As a result, as each new age inherited what were to become the Bible's various books from the previous age, it also inherited a body of traditions about what those texts meant.

The traditional interpretations were of all kinds. Some simply aimed at explaining the meaning of a difficult word or resolving an apparent contradiction. But others were more wide-ranging and imaginative. Interpreters sometimes felt themselves obliged to explain why a particular person in a biblical story should have behaved the way that he or she did, or to find some connection between what a particular prophet had predicted and some later event in history. Often, interpreters ended up actually adding to what the biblical text said, "deducing" whole incidents or facts that, the interpreters felt, were implied if not stated outright in the Bible's words.

More than anything, though, these interpretations tried to bring out the universal and enduring messages of biblical texts, for the interpreters considered Scripture to be a sacred guidebook for human existence. Interpreters therefore tried to look beyond the obvious content of what was being said to find some relevant, usable lesson, even if it was less than obvious at first glance. And so, whatever their particular form or purpose, these interpretive traditions all tended to *transform* the apparent meaning of biblical texts.

Such transformations were immensely important. As any reader of this book will see, chapter after chapter of the Bible took on a new, sometimes radically different, significance when its words were scrutinized in the characteristic manner of early interpreters.

The story of Adam and Eve, for example, only *became* the story of the Fall of Man thanks to a certain ancient interpretation of one of the verses in the story. The snake in the story came to be identified as the devil—but only by later interpreters, not by the story itself! And it was only because of another interpretation that the Garden of Eden (also known as paradise) came to be thought of as a *heavenly* garden, one in which the righteous would live eternally after their death.

Similar transformations occurred with other biblical narratives. Interpreters came to the conclusion that Abraham was the son of an idol-maker, that he was the first person to believe in one God, and that among his many virtues was an extraordinary generosity toward strangers. None of these things is stated outright in the Bible, though each of them *is* based on some slight peculiarity in the biblical text. Other creative interpretations helped to change the "images" of Sarah, Jacob, Rachel, and Joseph—what each of these biblical figures did and stood for took on an entirely different aspect when their stories were read and interpreted in the special fashion of these early interpreters. The shape and significance of the entire Bible came to be modified because of their work.

Then, gradually, as the centuries passed, these traditional understandings came to be *the* meaning. The historical circumstances in which a particular biblical passage might have originally been uttered were eventually forgotten or, in any case, considered irrelevant. What was important by, say, the third or second century B.C.E. (and, quite possibly, even somewhat earlier) was what was thought to be the text's deeper significance, that is, how it was explained by the traditional interpretations that now accompanied it. And this traditional, *interpreted* Bible—the Bible itself plus the traditions about what it really meant—was what was taught to successive generations of students, expounded in public assemblies and, ultimately, canonized by Judaism and Christianity as their sacred book.

The way in which these traditions of interpretation came to cling to the biblical text may be difficult for people today to comprehend. We like to think that the Bible, or any other text, means "just what it says." And we act on that assumption: we simply open up a book—including the Bible—and try to make sense of it on our own. In ancient Israel and for centuries afterward, on the contrary, people looked to special interpreters to explain the meaning of a biblical text. For that reason, the explanations passed along by such interpreters quickly acquired an authority of their own. In studying this or that biblical law or prophecy or story, students would do more than simply learn the words; they would be told what the text meant—not only the peculiar way in which this or that term was to be interpreted, but how one biblical text related to another far removed from it, or the particular moral lesson that a text embodied, or how a certain passage was to be applied in everyday life. And the people who learned these things about the Bible from their teachers in turn passed on the same information to the next generation of students.

And so, it was this *interpreted* Bible—not just the stories, prophecies, and laws themselves, but these texts as they had, by now, been interpreted and explained for centuries—that came to stand at the very center of Judaism and Christianity. This was what people in both religions meant by "the Bible." Of course, Judaism and Christianity themselves differed on a great many questions, including the interpretation of some crucial scriptural passages, as well as on just what books were to be included in the Bible. Nevertheless, both religions had begun with basically the same interpreted Bible. For both inherited an earlier, common set of traditions, general principles regarding how one ought to go about reading and interpreting the Bible as well as specific traditions concerning the meaning of individual passages, verses, and words. As a result, even when later Jews or Christians added on new interpretations—sometimes directed against each other or against other groups or ideologies within the world in which they lived—the new interpretations frequently built on, and only modified, what had been the accepted wisdom until then.

This book is essentially an attempt to reconstruct this traditional Bible, the Bible as it was understood in the closing centuries B.C.E. and at the very start of the common era. I have tried to assemble evidence of the things that scholars and ordinary people believed about the most important parts of the Torah or Pentateuch (that is, the first five books of the Bible).[1] But how does one go

---

1. While, for the period covered, the precise contents of the Bible—which books were to be part of the canon and which not—were still a subject of debate, all agreed that these first five books were Scripture *par excellence,* the very heart of the Bible and the essence of God's sacred teaching for the people of Israel.

about reconstructing this Bible-as-it-was? Unfortunately, there is no single text that contains, chapter by chapter, the commonly accepted interpretations of the Bible in the closing centuries B.C.E. Instead there is a mass of literature of various sorts—sermons, apocalypses, retellings of biblical stories, and other writings—in which these interpretations are mostly only hinted at or else taken for granted, assumed to be known to every reader. Trying to reconstruct the Bible as it was has thus been largely a matter of reading between the lines, figuring out interpretations that are rarely presented as such, from this mass of different sources.

Of course there is more to the Bible as it was than I have been able to include here.[2] But I hope that the present volume will give readers the essential, a view of the most important interpretive traditions that circulated during the crucial period of the Bible's emergence as such, when it was becoming the defined corpus of texts that would lie at the very heart of Judaism and Christianity.

I would like to thank the many colleagues and students who have helped me with various aspects of this book. In particular, I thank those who have consented to read through and offer suggestions on individual chapters: Professors Gary Anderson, Ellen Birnbaum, Robert Brody, Hanan Eshel, Jay Harris, Marc Hirshman, and Bernard Septimus. Throughout the stages of preparing the manuscript I have been aided by the comments and suggestions of Hindy Najman. My thanks go as well to Melissa Milgram, who helped at an early stage of the compilation, and to Luke Whitmore for assistance with the illustrations. I am grateful to David Kugel for his help with the index. I am also thankful for the assistance of Carol Cross and Rachel Rockenmacher of the Department of Near Eastern Languages at Harvard. Elizabeth Hurwit admirably edited the manuscript for publication, while Mary Ellen Geer and Margaretta Fulton helped it through production at Harvard University Press. I should also like to express my deep gratitude to my literary agent, Ellen Geiger of Curtis Brown Ltd., for her help and guidance at every phase of publication—I could not have managed it without her.

My gratitude goes as well to the Littauer Foundation, which generously helped to fund a leave in 1991 during which some of the work of this volume

---

2. To make this book as affordable (and widely available) as possible, I have included in it only the most important and influential interpretive traditions of the Pentateuch, and these have been presented largely without technical footnotes or bibliographical references. A considerably larger (and necessarily more expensive) selection of the Pentateuch's interpretive traditions, along with scholarly apparatus, is to be published separately by Harvard University Press.

was completed, and to the Alan Stroock Publication Fund at Harvard's Center for Jewish Studies for its support of the actual publication of this project.

A final note: Despite all the time spent assembling and checking the material presented herein, no doubt errors of commission and omission remain; moreover, texts now being published for the first time or yet to be discovered will likely provide further insights that might have enriched this study. And so I cannot but make a request of my learned readers: I will be most grateful for any corrections or additions that you might be kind enough to pass along, either via the publisher or to me by means of my Web page, http://www.fas.harvard.edu/~jlkugel/, where I intend to maintain a regularly updated information sheet about this book and related matters. I can also be reached directly by e-mail, at jlkugel@fas.harvard.edu or kugelj@ashur. cc.biu.ac.il. It is my hope that the age of electronic publishing may yet provide a release from the dire sentence of Eccles. 1:15.

THE BIBLE AS IT WAS

Note on Transcriptions

In transcribing Hebrew words and names, I have chosen not to confuse nonspecialists with the use of unnecessary diacritical marks and the like. Thus, biblical figures and places are generally rendered by their standard English equivalents (Joshua, Bethlehem); the same is true of the names of texts cited in this book (the Mishnah, *Yalqut Shimoni*) and certain other, fairly common, transcriptions (*halakhah,* the Shema). When a particular point has required more exact transcription, I have relied on that in current use in most scholarly journals.

I

The World of Ancient Biblical Interpreters

THE OLDEST PARTS of the Hebrew Bible go back very far into ancient times, some to before 1,000 B.C.E. These ancient texts may have been transmitted orally for a time, but soon enough they were committed to writing. Since the materials on which they were written were perishable, the texts eventually crumbled or wore out and had to be recopied. The stories, psalms, laws, and prophecies that have reached us today as part of the Bible must therefore have been copied many, many times even within the biblical period itself. (There were doubtless other texts, such as the "Book of Yashar" or the "Book of the Wars of the Lord" mentioned in the Bible itself,[1] which did not survive; for one reason or another, they ceased to be copied and so have been lost.)

The scribes who did the work of copying were not mindless duplicating machines, nor did they likely execute their copies so that the texts might then be put into some kind of "cold storage." If these texts were repeatedly copied within the biblical period itself, it was because they were *used;* they played some part in daily life. Some texts, especially the history of past events and of ancient heroes, were doubtless used in the royal court, perhaps for purposes of literacy instruction, royal propaganda, or simply record keeping. Other texts were just as certainly associated with temples and sanctuaries—songs and prayers and priestly instructions and the like. Still others—ancient statutes, prophecies, speeches, proverbs, and so forth—may have likewise had their place in court or temple, or they may have belonged to yet some other site. But wherever they were preserved, the very fact that they were attests to the role that these texts must have played somewhere in ancient Israelite society. No one would go to the trouble of copying texts for no purpose.

To say only this is virtually to assert that, from a very early period, the texts that make up the Hebrew Bible were *interpreted* texts. For, judges who seek to enforce written statutes have to do more than simply read the texts involved; they have to apply the law's general prescriptions to specific situations and, sometimes, adapt fixed formulations to new circumstances. (This is especially true with the laws contained in the Bible, which often function by describing

---

1. 2 Sam. 1:18, Num. 21:14. On this subject generally: Leiman, *Canonization of Scripture.*

a specific case while leaving to others the job of deriving from that case principles that might apply elsewhere.) The same applies to priests seeking to follow an established procedure for temple sacrifices or trying to diagnose a disease from a specific set of symptoms. Teachers, royal counselors, propagandists, or others who might make use of historical records doubtless did more than simply read them aloud: however much the records might have seemed to speak for themselves, even the clearest point in a text must sometimes be driven home to an audience through restatement, elaboration, and the like. And not all texts are clear. Writers often leave ambiguities in what they write, so that *all* the figures mentioned—judges, priests, teachers, and so forth—were of necessity also interpreters because of the simple fact that their work involved using texts.

Thus, it is probably safe to say that, at least in these ways, the interpretation of the Bible goes back virtually as far as the oldest texts within it. Indeed, evidence of this process is to be found within the Hebrew Bible itself. Later biblical books frequently mention or allude to things found in earlier books, and in so doing they often modify or change—sometimes radically—the apparent sense of the earlier text. The book of Daniel, for example, specifically interprets a prophecy of Jeremiah (Jer. 25:11–12, 29:10), in which Jeremiah's reference to "seventy years" is asserted to mean in reality 490 years (Dan. 9:2, 24). In somewhat less dramatic fashion, the entire book of Chronicles may be seen as a kind of commentary on (especially) the biblical books of Samuel and Kings, with numerous additions or modifications of the earlier material, plus a few blatant omissions.[2] Daniel and Chronicles are relatively late books in the biblical canon, but there is evidence of such interpretive activity far earlier, well before that "great divide" in biblical history, the point at which the Babylonians conquered Jerusalem and sent the Jews into exile (586 B.C.E.). Such ancient bits of interpretation, while generally less striking than later examples, nonetheless bear ample witness to the work of interpreters from very early times.

The Age of Interpretation

And yet, it would be wrong to conclude that interpretation proceeded at pretty much the same pace throughout the biblical period. On the contrary, the Babylonian conquest just mentioned seems to mark the dawn of a new age

---

2. See on this Seligmann, "Voraussetzung der Midraschexegese"; idem, "The Beginnings of Midrash in the Book of Chronicles"; Willi, *Der Chronik als Auslegung;* Japhet, *Ideology of the Book of Chronicles.*

with regard to Scripture and its interpretation. The Jews, exiled from their homeland for half a century, were suddenly informed in 532 B.C.E. that they were free to return home; this right was granted to them by an edict of the Persian king Cyrus following his stunning victory over mighty Babylon. Many Jews did indeed return home, and the society that they established in Judea was one in which—for reasons to be examined presently—the interpretation of ancient Scripture came to play a central role. As a result, a distinctive approach to interpretation began to develop, and in the ensuing centuries individual interpretations of biblical laws and stories and prophecies slowly accumulated and coalesced into a great body of lore that came to be known widely throughout Israel.

Some of the first fruits of this activity may be found among the latest books of the Hebrew Bible, but the great mass of ancient biblical interpretation appears in books that, for one reason or another, did not end up being included in the Jewish canon. These books—expansive retellings of biblical stories, first-person narratives put in the mouths of biblical heroes, pseudonymous apocalypses, the sayings and proverbs of ancient sages, plus actual biblical commentaries, sermons, and the like—were composed from, roughly, the third century B.C.E. through the first century C.E., although some of the interpretations of the Bible found in them doubtless go back still earlier. These old texts allow us to reconstruct in some detail how the Bible was read and understood during this crucial period. They are the focus of the present study.

The Need for Interpreters

As mentioned, almost any written text contains potential ambiguities. Normally, we ordinary readers deal with such ambiguities ourselves, so that there is no need for a special class of text interpreters. Perhaps it was so, for a time, in ancient Israel as well—although the job of being a judge, a priest, or a teacher certainly could imply some skill in interpreting texts. But the postexilic period marked (among other things) a time in which this interpretive function became a thing unto itself and in which, therefore, the interpreter of Scripture emerged as a figure in his own right.

Part of the reason for this figure's emergence had to do with the passage of time itself. For, however much *all* texts contain ambiguities, such ambiguities—and even out-and-out incomprehensibility—tend to increase with old texts, for the simple reason that language and culture are always in the process of changing. A word whose meaning may have been clear two or three hundred years ago may no longer be clear now; indeed, it may now mean something else entirely. Few speakers of English nowadays would understand that to call someone "lewd and silly" in Chaucer's day was hardly to criticize; the person was, in fact, being described as uneducated and defenseless.

In the same way, many Hebrew words had shifted their meaning by the end of the biblical period. Even such basic concepts as "get," "take," "need," "want," "time," and "much" were expressed with new terms; the old words had either shifted their meaning or dropped out of sight entirely. As a result, someone trying to read a text from the ancient past could not always make sense of it; an expert, someone acquainted with old texts and their meanings, was needed.

Words were not the only thing to change: ideas, social institutions, and political reality likewise shifted. Some of Israel's bitterest enemies of days gone by no longer existed, replaced by new foes unheard of in an earlier age. Old forms of organization and governance had likewise fallen from view. Successive waves of conquerors—the Babylonians, Persians, Greeks (subdivided into the Hellenized Ptolemies of Egypt and the Hellenized Seleucids of Syria), then the Romans—had introduced not only new words into the Hebrew language, but also new ideas and ways of thinking, indeed, whole new civilizations. Taken together, such changes had a way of distancing people from their own past: texts that had at one time been quite comprehensible might now appear to be an encoded mystery. There is little doubt that, for just such reasons, many of the particulars in the stories of Genesis or the laws of Exodus were no longer clear to readers as early as the time of the return from Babylonian exile. Henceforth interpreters of Scripture would increasingly be necessary.

Such interpreters were needed even more because of a curious feature in the transmission of ancient Hebrew Scripture. The Hebrew writing system was more than a little ambiguous. Like certain other Semitic languages, Hebrew was written down by recording the consonants alone: there were no letters to represent vowels. (Eventually, the consonants corresponding to our H, Y, and W came to be widely used as a way of indicating *some* vowels, but this was done only inconsistently at first and in any case still left many ambiguities.)

Of course, writing only the consonants in words would not work at all in English. The letters BRD, for example, could be interpreted as standing for "bird," "bard," "bared," "barred," "beard," "broad," "bored," "board," "brad," "bread," "bred," "breed," "braid," "by-road," "buried," "borrowed," and so on. In Hebrew, things are far easier: most words are built on a triconsonantal root and there are relatively few homonyms. The basic meaning of BRD, for example, is "hail." But even within the triconsonantal root structure, context alone will often determine whether a particular word is to be construed as a noun or a verb, or as belonging to one class of verb as opposed to another, or as being in the passive or active voice. Here, certainly, was plenty of room for ambiguity!

What is more, biblical texts were written without the use of capital letters, periods, commas, or any other kind of punctuation. Thus, even where a sentence began or ended was often a matter of opinion: it all depended on how you interpreted it. Indeed, even the separation between individual words was, in ancient times, frequently left ambiguous by author or scribe. And within the sentence, basic decisions about which words went together with which others and where, therefore, syntactic pauses were to occur—these too were a matter of interpretation.

Such ambiguities might at first seem rather minor, even trivial. However, especially when combined with other obscurities resulting from the passage of time, they created a significant barrier between text and reader. As a matter of fact, this ambiguous writing system was responsible for a great many of the interpretations charted in this book. The existence of such a writing system not only seemed to call forth interpreters to explain the biblical text, but soon enough, it furnished those interpreters with a flexible tool for tipping the interpretive scales in one particular direction or another. Carried to an extreme, the freedom of interpreters to read a single word in different ways or to break up a block of text into various syntactic combinations could at times allow them to make a text out to be saying exactly the opposite of its apparent meaning. The importance of the Hebrew writing system can thus hardly be overstated.

The Mode of Return

Many of the above factors, however, had existed from earliest times; while the passage of time may have heightened their effect, they alone are probably not sufficient to explain why it was the period following the return from Babylonian exile that inaugurated a new interest in the interpretation of Scripture. To account for this, a number of further historical considerations must be mentioned.[3]

The first might be called the "mode of return" in which the Jews found themselves after the return from the Babylonian exile. Not all those who had been exiled to Babylon did return; a number of them stayed in their new

3. I have discussed these factors at greater length in Kugel and Greer, *Early Biblical Interpretation,* 31–51.

home. Those who went back to Judah[4] doubtless did so for a variety of reasons, but certainly one of them was a straightforward desire to return to the place and the way of life that had been their ancestors' in days gone by. Yet here was a problem. For, while the physical places previously inhabited may have been clear enough, the way of life that had been followed in them was not. One could not interrogate the hills or the trees to find out how one's forebears had acted two or three generations earlier: that information depended on the restored community's collective memory, a memory embodied in (among other things) its library of ancient texts. Thus, the very mode of return—the desire to go back to something that once existed—probably made this community bookish to an abnormal degree.

Political differences among different groups within the returning exiles reinforced this tendency. To judge by the biblical evidence itself, some Jews at that time were bent on restoring the Davidic dynasty to full political leadership. (David's descendants had continuously ruled in Judah from the time of David himself, in the tenth century B.C.E., until the Babylonian exile.) Hopes eventually crystallized in the figure of Zerubbabel, heir to the Davidic throne. Many apparently looked to Zerubbabel to bring about drastic changes in the Jews' situation, perhaps through out-and-out rebellion against the Persian authorities; this hope is reflected in, among others, the writings of the biblical prophets Haggai and Zechariah (see Haggai 2; Zech. 4:6–7). At the same time, however, other Jews were more reserved in their political opinions. It is striking, for example, that the biblical books of Ezra and Nehemiah nowhere mention Zerubbabel's Davidic origins in their treatment of him; apparently, the author of these books saw the Persians as legitimate rulers.[5] Indeed, the author of Ezra begins by asserting that the emperor Cyrus had been commissioned by God Himself to rule "all the kingdoms of the earth" and to build a temple for Him in Jerusalem (Ezra 1:1–2).

Such political differences might exist at any time and in any place. But it is significant that the Jews of this period turned to their own ancient writings to

4. Here it might be appropriate to clarify a matter of terminology. Judah was one of Israel's original twelve tribes, eventually, the dominant one in the south. King David had united the twelve tribes into a single monarchy at the start of the tenth century B.C.E.; when this United Monarchy subsequently split in two under David's grandson Rehoboam, the southern part became the kingdom of Judah. The northern kingdom was subsequently conquered by Assyria in the eighth century B.C.E. and its citizenry dispersed; only the southern kingdom, Judah, continued to exist, still ruled by David's descendants. It was this kingdom that the Babylonians conquered early in the sixth century B.C.E. and to which the exiles returned at the end of that century. In Greco-Roman sources, the country is called Judaea (or Judea) and its people the Jews. However, the general term "Israel" also continued to be used as a name for the Jewish people.

5. Japhet, "Sheshbazzar and Zerubbabel"; see also her *Ideology of the Book of Chronicles*, 395–504.

legitimate their political views. Thus, when the prophet Haggai, a proponent of Zerubbabel, first prophesied about him,

> On that day, says the Lord of Hosts, I will take you, Zerubbabel my servant, son of Shealtiel, and make you **like a signet ring**, for I have chosen you, says the Lord of Hosts. —Hag. 2:23

his words had a somewhat "biblical" ring, perhaps intended specifically to evoke a dire prophecy of Jeremiah's from an earlier age:

> As I live, says the Lord, though Coniah the son of Jehoiakim, king of Judah, were a **signet ring on my right hand**, yet I would tear you off and give you into the hand of those who seek your life.
> —Jer. 22:24–25

The same prophet Jeremiah was evoked by members of the opposite camp—in the opposite sense, of course. The opening words of the book of Ezra, alluded to above, might be cited in full here:

> In the first year of Cyrus king of Persia, **in order to accomplish the word of the Lord uttered by Jeremiah**, the Lord stirred up the spirit of Cyrus king of Persia so that he made a proclamation. —Ezra 1:1

According to this source, not only was Cyrus a legitimate, divinely chosen ruler, but his deeds were nothing less than the fulfillment of a biblical prophecy uttered by the same Jeremiah.

So, more generally, the returning Jews used the stories, prophecies, songs, and prayers saved from before the Babylonian exile to bolster their own ideas on all manner of different issues. For example, the book of Chronicles has been shown to contain a detailed program for the restored Jewish community after the Babylonian exile: its author was a firm supporter of the Davidic monarchy; he was in favor of uniting the northern and southern parts of the country into a single polity, a state whose very existence was predicated on what he saw as the people's eternal (and, in his view, virtually uninterrupted) presence on its own land and loyalty to its God.[6] Yet how interesting, and typical, that this author sought to put forward his political program not as such, but in the form of a history of bygone times—specifically, a retelling of much of the biblical books of Samuel and Kings. It was no doubt the mode of return that led this author, like so many others, to present his ideas not as innovations but as a return to the glorious past. That is, by omitting some

6. These points are discussed at length in Japhet, *Ideology of the Book of Chronicles*.

things and adding others, this author reshaped the past and so made it into a more perfect model of what he himself wished to prescribe for the future.

The Centrality of Laws

Texts from the ancient past not only served as a general guide to how life had been lived before the exile. These texts—and in particular what is called the Pentateuch or Torah, the first five books of the Bible—contained numerous laws and commandments from an earlier day. Another result of the mode of return in which the Jews found themselves was the heightened importance of these laws.

Obeying laws is usually thought of in our society as a rather small and unimportant part of life. True, most people obey speed limits and traffic lights, stay off private property, and pay their taxes, but such acts of obedience hardly register in our daily consciousness. Ordinary citizens do not usually spend a lot of time in court. The whole subject of law seems rather specialized and marginal.

Among the returning exiles, by contrast, laws occupied a central position. According to the book of Nehemiah, the people at this time specifically took an oath "to walk in God's law which was given by Moses, the servant of God, and to observe and do all the commandments of the Lord our master and perform His ordinances and statutes" (Neh. 10:29). It was, apparently, crucially important that all members of the restored community do their utmost to conform to the divinely given statutes of old.

One reason was that they were *divine*, God's own commandments. If this divine provenance were not in itself sufficient to command the sustained attention of the community, the whole atmosphere of the postexilic period made it sufficient. The Babylonian conquest and exile had been *the* traumatic event in Jewish history. Not only had the defeat cost the Jews their freedom and homeland—as well as quite a few lives—but it had challenged the very foundations of Israel's understanding of its God and His ways with the world. The Jerusalem Temple, God's physical home on earth, had suddenly been razed by the enemy, and the daily Temple sacrifices, a centuries-old routine by which, in the common esteem, the divine will was appeased and made favorable toward mankind, had now been brutally put to an end. How could such events be understood?

The explanation offered by Jewish prophets and sages was that these events constituted God's punishment for the people's failure to obey the divine laws. When, in conformity to Jeremiah's prophecy (and in contradiction to all that common sense or political science might have predicted), the

Babylonians were in turn overthrown a few short decades after their defeat of the Jews, it certainly seemed as if the "punishment" explanation was indeed correct: God had used the Babylonians to show His people Israel the error of its ways but, once having done so, He in turn toppled the Babylonians from power lest anyone conclude that it was *their* military might, rather than God's will, that had brought them victory.

Back in their homeland, the Jews resolved to learn the lesson of history: henceforth they would be more careful, henceforth they would be sure to observe the divine statutes with punctilious zeal. But such resolve only heightened the interpretive crux of biblical law. How could one demand strict observance of laws that were frequently and notoriously short on particulars? For example, working on the Sabbath was forbidden—but what constituted "work"? Performing one's usual profession? Doing *any* work which was part of *a* profession, even if it was not one's own? Or perhaps something still more stringent? (For some answers, see Chapter 20.) Similarly, the book of Leviticus commanded that one not "take revenge or hold a grudge" (Lev. 19:18) against one's kinsman—but what did that mean? If "revenge" here implied actually harming him or killing him to recompense a wrong suffered, did the further prohibition of holding a grudge mean that one could not even resent him for the harm inflicted? Was this humanly possible? And did the continuation of this same verse—"And you shall love your neighbor as yourself"—mean that one was actually ordered by God to love someone whom one might otherwise be inclined to hate? How can love be *commanded?* (For answers given to these questions, see Chapter 22.) Like these, dozens and hundreds of other laws had to be understood precisely and thoroughly if another catastrophe was to be averted.

Quite apart from what we would think of as the "religious" importance of obeying biblical laws—the desire of the community to find favor with God and to head off another disaster—there may have been a more immediate spur to making sure that these laws were definitively interpreted and explained. It is likely that biblical laws were quite simply the law of the land in the restored community of Judah. Persian imperial policy under Darius I apparently consisted of giving the empire's stamp of approval to the old legal systems of its various subject peoples. Thus, in the year 518 B.C.E., Darius wrote to his satrap in Egypt to send him Egyptian scholars who might write down "the former law of Egypt." The scholars apparently complied, writing their laws "on one roll."[7] It seems likely that something similar happened with

---

7. Bickerman, *The Jews in the Greek Age*, 30. Bickerman elaborated on this theme in a paper presented at the Eighth World Congress of Jewish Studies in Jerusalem, 1981. (Unfortunately, he died

the Jews: the ancient laws, presented in definitive form, acquired the authority of the ruling powers. The words of Artaxerxes I (who reigned from 465 or 464 to 424 B.C.E.), cited in the book of Ezra, are eloquent in this regard:

> "I, Artaxerxes the king, make a decree to all the treasurers in the province Beyond the River: Whatever Ezra the priest, the scribe of the law of the God of heaven, requires of you, be it done with diligence . . . And you, Ezra, according to the **wisdom of your God which is in your hand**, appoint magistrates and judges who may judge all the people in the province Beyond the River, all such as **know the laws of your God**; and those who do not know them, you shall teach. Then, whoever will not obey the law of your God and the law of the king, let judgment be strictly executed upon him, whether for death or for banishment or for confiscation of his goods or for imprisonment."
>
> —Ezra 7:21, 25–26

Henceforth, the ancient Hebrew laws stood on a par with, or were equated with, the laws of the Persian rulers: the "law of your God and the law of the king" comprised the legal corpus by which daily life was to be governed, and not only the Jews but, as well, the Persian government officials in their midst were required to make sure that ancient biblical statutes were widely understood ("those who do not know them, you shall teach") and fully enforced as the law of the land.

The Rise of the Interpreter

For all these reasons, the interpreters of Scripture enjoyed an increasing prominence and authority in the period following the Babylonian exile. They were, first of all, the guardians of writings preserved from Israel's ancient past. With their bookman's skills, they could explain what that past was, what had been set down in writing by or about Israel's historic leaders; they could likewise look deeply into the words of ancient lore and traditions, the writings of divinely chosen prophets or sages from days gone by. Clearly, interpreting such ancient texts was a matter of more than merely antiquarian interest: the interpretation of Scripture could lend support for this or that political pro-

---

shortly after the conference and the paper was never published.) If it was similarly demanded of Jewish sages that they write down their "former law," this may have been an event of crucial importance not only to the ancient interpretation of biblical laws but to their very formulation in a final, fixed text of the Pentateuch.

gram or leader, and it determined as well the significance of divine law and its application to daily life.

Who were these interpreters? There is good indication that they came from within different groups and levels of Jewish society. Some of them were, like "Ezra the priest" (Ezra 7:21) just mentioned, priests or levites—people who, by birth, had a special association with the service of God—since part of their job had from earliest times involved not only interpreting divine statutes but promulgating and explaining them to the people. The book of Deuteronomy had said about the tribe of Levi (from which priests and levites were said to descend):

> They shall teach Your statutes to Jacob, and to Israel Your Torah.
>
> — Deut. 33:10

Elsewhere in the same book, the role of members of this tribe in interpreting the law is made specific (Deut. 17:8–13). So too in later times:

> "Thus says the Lord of Hosts: Ask the priests to decide this question."
>
> — Hag. 2:11

> True instruction was in his [Levi's] mouth, and no wrong was found on his lips . . . For the lips of the priest guard knowledge, and people seek instruction [*torah*] from his mouth, for he is an emissary of the Lord of Hosts. — Mal. 2:6–7

But priests and levites were hardly the only interpreters. We have glimpsed above the special association that judges, teachers, sages, and scribes probably had with the interpretation of ancient texts, and people from these walks of life as well served as Scriptural interpreters on into the Second Temple period and beyond. (Note that Ezra the priest is further described in the same verse as "the *scribe* of the law of the God of heaven"; Ezra 7:21). No doubt for a time at least, interpreting Scripture had merely been a function—one among many—associated with each of these various offices; indeed, certain areas of interpretation were probably long associated specifically with certain types of interpreters (for example, laws of sacrifices, purity, and impurity with priests). From the closing centuries before the common era, however, comes evidence of more "all-purpose" interpreters, people who held forth on every area of scriptural interpretation, and such continued to be the case in the centuries thereafter.

In explaining Scripture in their particular fashion, interpreters ultimately came to encroach on territory that had previously belonged to another, rather different figure: the biblical prophet. For centuries before the Babylonian exile, prophets had acted as divine spokesmen in Israel. They were seen, quite literally, as messengers of God, and the messages they brought—words of rebuke and announcements of divine judgment and punishment, as well as messages of hope and divine encouragement, or simply divine directives and commandments—compelled the attention of kings and commoners alike. Prophets, in short, were an intermediary link in communications between God and humanity. But then, in the period following the return from exile, prophecy began to fall into disrepute. Although we possess the words of prophets who existed at the time of the return itself, in the centuries that followed there is a void: apparently, prophecy was no longer regarded as it had been previously.[8] Perhaps the institution itself had fallen, or was falling, into disrepute:

> And if anyone again appears as a prophet, his father and mother who bore him will say to him, "You shall not live, for you speak lies in the name of the Lord"; and his father and his mother shall pierce him through when he prophesies. On that day, every prophet will be ashamed of his vision when he prophesies; he will not put on the hairy mantle in order to deceive, but he will say, "I am no prophet, I am a tiller of the soil." — Zech. 13:3–5

Later prophets sometimes alluded to, or interpreted, the words of earlier prophets, and these references in themselves may indicate a change in the air. Were not the words of the great prophets of the past turned to as a source of inspiration, or even information, about the present precisely because these words, now part of Scripture, outweighed anything that might be uttered by the latter-day prophets "in your midst"? God's word was increasingly thought of as a *written* word, given to Israel for all time, and it was therefore those who

---

8. This is not to say that prophecy itself ceased to exist as a phenomenon in postexilic times, although this was indeed asserted or implied in a number of ancient sources (1 Macc. 4:46, 9:27, 14:41; Prayer of Azariah 15; 2 Bar. 85:3; (perhaps) *Testament of Benjamin* 9:2; Josephus, *AgApion* 1:40–41; as well as in numerous rabbinic sources, e.g., *Seder Olam* 30, T. Soṭa 13:2, b. *Baba Batra* 12b, etc.). Elsewhere, however, is evidence of a different opinion: Wisd. 7:27, Philo, *Who Is Heir* 259, (1QH) *Thanksgiving Hymns* 4:16, 1 Cor. 11:4–5, 12:10, 14:4–5, etc., Josephus, *Jewish Antiquities* 13:311–13, 20:97, 169, etc. It seems not so much that prophecy ceased as that the prophet's very identity and role came to be redefined and significantly broadened, while at the same the conviction was spreading that the *great* prophets were a thing of the past (and, perhaps, the future). See further Urbach, "When Did Prophecy Cease?" idem, "Halakhah and Prophecy," 1–27; Vermes, *Jesus the Jew*, 69–82; Blenkinsopp, "Prophecy and Priesthood in Josephus"; Aune, *Prophecy in Early Christianity;* Horsely, "Like One of the Prophets of Old"; Greenspahn, "Why Prophecy Ceased"; Kugel, "David the Prophet"; Winston, "Two Types of Mosaic Prophecy"; Feldman, "Prophets and Prophecy in Josephus"; Brin, "Biblical Prophecy in the Dead Sea Scrolls"; and Milikowsky, "The End of Prophecy and the End of the Bible."

interpreted sacred texts from the past who were God's present-day messengers and spokesmen.

If the influence of prophets was on the decline, on the rise was that of another figure who had long existed in Israel, the sage or wise man. Sages in ancient Israel—and in the ancient Near East in general—were teachers and advisers, many or most of them no doubt attached to the royal court. They were often champions of a particular philosophy and way of life called "wisdom." Wisdom is not given to easy summary, but its basic tenet was that all of reality is shaped by a great, underlying pattern. This pattern, referred to in itself as wisdom, was of divine origin. Everything that happens in the world—the ways of nature and of human society, the course of history and of individual human lives—happens in keeping with this divine pattern. While it is not given to humanity to know all the particulars of the divine pattern, parts of it had certainly been grasped over the centuries by those who pursued wisdom, namely, the sages themselves. Their insights into the divine pattern had been "packaged" into little units, the pithy sayings or proverbs that were the sage's stock-in-trade. Such proverbs—whose overall message was one of patient self-control, treading the strait and narrow path—were often cleverly worded and required sustained contemplation to be fully understood. (Three biblical books that abound in such material are Proverbs, Job, and Ecclesiastes.) Sages taught this material to their students and sought to live by its teachings in their own lives.

These same sages became interpreters of Scripture. With the passage of time, the texts they contemplated and explained were no longer limited to ancient proverbs and sayings: laws and narratives and prophecies likewise came to be included in their repertoire. Soon enough, the writings they themselves produced encompassed more than old-fashioned proverbs: without quite abandoning these, they added pithily phrased expositions of Scripture to their words of wisdom.

The process by which such teachers of wisdom (in the sense described above) became teachers of Scripture is not hard to document: it happens before our very eyes in books like the Wisdom of Ben Sira (or Sirach, written around 180 B.C.E.) or the Wisdom of Solomon (late first century B.C.E.).[9] The sages who wrote these books are, in a sense, transitional figures. They are, on the one hand, traditional wisdom teachers whose mission it still is to put insights into the ways of God and men in little one-line proverbs, and the

---

9. An interpreter such as Philo of Alexandria might at first seem altogether free of any connection with the earlier wisdom heritage, yet even in his case has this connection been asserted: Mack, *Logos und Sophia;* Laporte, "Philo in the Tradition of Biblical Wisdom Literature."

proverbs they wrote and included in their books are no different in kind from the proverbs written by earlier sages, the authors of Proverbs, Job, and Ecclesiastes. On the other hand, Ben Sira or the author of the Wisdom of Solomon did something no sage had done before: they made Scripture part of the *subject* of their inquiry. It is a striking fact that nowhere do earlier wisdom collections—Proverbs, Job, or Ecclesiastes—ever talk about Abraham or Jacob or Moses, the history of the people of Israel or the messages transmitted by Israel's prophets. It is not that these things were unknown to the sages in question; of course they knew them. Rather, the universal nature of wisdom itself seemed to rule out any reference to such particulars, such local details: the great underlying pattern of the universe must, it seemed to them, apply equally to all of humanity and lie beyond any particularity of time or space.

But by the second century B.C.E., all this was changing: for the Jews Scripture itself had become God's great book of instruction—no longer merely the record of events from the distant past of one people, nor prophetic oracles delivered to a specific audience, but words of eternal validity that were relevant, therefore, to anyone in any age. In keeping with this view, Ben Sira devoted some of his wise sayings to the elucidation of biblical laws, since for him these laws embodied timeless principles of God's wisdom. Moreover, he addressed himself at length (chapters 44–49 of his book) to a review of the Bible's major figures, whose very lives and deeds seemed to him less history than moral example, tales told for the edification of readers in any age.

> Enoch pleased the Lord and was taken up [to heaven],
> he was an **example of repentance** to all generations.
>
> —(Greek) Sir. 44:16[10]

The biblical Enoch, mentioned in Gen. 5:18–24, appears in a long genealogical list of people who lived before the flood. As a figure from the shadowy past, he was of little historical significance to later generations of Israelites. Yet, by Ben Sira's time, biblical texts were being scrutinized for all their possible implications. In the case of Enoch, the fact that God was said to have "taken" him (Gen. 5:24) suggested to many that Enoch had been bodily taken *up*, transported into heaven while yet alive, very much as Elijah later was (2 Kings 2:11). Indeed, the idea of Enoch's heavenly sojourn found elaborate expression in such ancient writings as *1 Enoch*. (For more details, see below.) Just exactly

---

10. This verse is not found at all in the Masada manuscript or the Syriac version of Ben Sira, but it is present (in somewhat different form) in the Hebrew Geniza manuscript B as well as in the Greek. On the place of this verse in the development of the text of Ben Sira, as well as on the differences between the Hebrew and Greek versions: Reiterer, *"Urtext" und Übersetzungen*, 84–85; Skehan and Di Lella, *Wisdom of Ben Sira*, 499; Yadin, *Ben Sira Scroll from Masada*, 38.

what Enoch had done to be so "taken" by God the book of Genesis did not openly say. But Ben Sira, or at least the exegetical tradition being quoted above, found an answer to this question in the precise wording of the Enoch passage in Genesis:

> When Enoch had lived sixty-five years, he became the father of Methu-selah. **Enoch walked with God after the birth of Methuselah three hundred years,** and had other sons and daughters. Thus all the days of Enoch were three hundred and sixty-five years. Enoch walked with God; and he was not, for God took him. —Gen. 5:21–24

The passage says that Enoch "walked with God" *after* the birth of Methuselah; the clear implication is that before Methuselah's birth he did *not* walk with God. If so, it would seem that Enoch's great virtue, and the reason for God's taking him, was that he repented. Although he may not have been an exemplary youth, Enoch began to walk with God at age sixty-five and thus became, in the Ben Sira text cited above, "an example of repentance to all generations."

Enoch is only the first biblical figure treated in Ben Sira's category of heroes; after him come Noah, Abraham, Moses, and the others—all of whose lives are presented as models, embodiments of this or that divine teaching. It is in this sense that, for Ben Sira, Scripture itself is the great book of wisdom— so that, after having praised the figure of Wisdom very much in the fashion of earlier sages, Ben Sira can quite naturally add:

> All this [Wisdom] is the book of the covenant of the Most High, the Torah which Moses commanded us as an inheritance to the congregation of Jacob. —Sir. 24:23 (cf. Deut. 33:4)

In the same fashion, another sage, roughly a century later, could assert about Wisdom:[11]

> He [God] found the whole way to knowledge, and gave her to Jacob his servant, and to Israel whom he loved . . . She is the book of the commandments of God, and the law that endures forever.
> —Bar. 3:36–4:1

For a third sage of this period, the author of the Wisdom of Solomon, Scripture is likewise a great repository of wisdom; and very much in the fashion of Ben Sira, he also presents a catalog of biblical heroes and examples

---

11. Note in the same connection a wisdom text from Qumran that asserts that God has granted wisdom "to Israel, He gives her as a gracious gift," (4Q185) *Sapiential Work* 2:10.

(chapter 10). What is particularly remarkable in this author's catalog is the extent to which it is mediated by interpretive traditions. Thus, for example, in alluding to the exodus from Egypt, this text observes:

> She [Wisdom] gave to holy men the reward of their labors; she guided them along a marvelous path, and became a shelter to them by day and a starry flame through the night. She brought them over the Red Sea, and led them through the deep waters; but she drowned their enemies and cast them up from the depth of the sea.　　　—Wis. 10:17–18

The author is obviously referring to the events recounted in the book of Exodus—yet his account has been touched up a bit to clarify elements that might otherwise be troubling in that narrative. For example, the Israelites there are said to have borrowed silver, gold, and other precious items from the Egyptians before leaving, and so to have "despoiled" the Egyptians (Exod. 12:36). The Wisdom of Solomon is quick to explain that this was not thievery or even deception, but "the reward of their labors"; that is, it was only fair for the Israelites to take these items in recompense for all the years of slavery in which they had served the Egyptians without being paid. As for the pillar of cloud and the pillar of fire that accompanied the Israelites on their way out of Egypt (Exod. 13:21), the Wisdom of Solomon explains what the book of Exodus somehow had not, that while the nighttime pillar was made of fire in order to guide them in the dark, the purpose of the daytime pillar of cloud was to give *shelter* to the Israelites from the sun—hence two pillars were necessary. (See Chapter 17.) Moreover, this same author specifies that, after drowning Israel's enemies, Wisdom "cast them up from the depth of the sea." This is no gratuitous flourish but an attempt to resolve an apparent contradiction in the Exodus account, which at one point specifies that the Egyptians "were drowned in the Red Sea, the floods covered them, they went down into the depths like a stone" (Exod. 15:4–5) but elsewhere says that the Israelites "saw the Egyptians dead upon the seashore" (Exod. 14:30). Where were they, on the seashore or at the bottom of the sea? This author's answer is that they *at first* sank to the bottom of the sea but then were "cast up" to the shore again to be seen by the Israelites.

In short, it is not that teachers of wisdom began merely to include Scripture among their subjects; rather, the whole nature of their activity was changing. Where wisdom had previously consisted of contemplating the natural world and the social order and deducing from them the general plan by which God conducts the world, it was now more and more Scripture that was consulted to understand God's ways. As the examples from the Wisdom of Solomon show, consulting Scripture did not consist merely of finding the appropriate passage and repeating it, but of looking deeply into its words, for God's teachings were often not obvious. Thus, it happened that the sage, who had previously walked about the world or stood at his window looking out, now sat down at his table and opened the Book. For, the Book, even more than the world, was the place in which God's will and God's ways were expressed—but much thought and contemplation were needed if the sage was to understand fully God's sacred written messages.

In giving expression to these messages, sages—indeed, scriptural interpreters in general—did take over part of the ancient prophet's role. For, if the word of the Lord was no longer reliably spoken by chosen messengers sent directly to Israel, was it not because that word had already been set down in writing, in the great library of divine wisdom that Scripture had become? The interpreter, as mediator of that wisdom, was a bit like the prophet: it was he who could peer deeply into words from the ancient past and explain their present application—how this or that law was to be observed, what the present implications of some ancient narrative were, or even how, in the words of some prophet long dead, there nonetheless lurked a message directed to a later day.

The Four Assumptions

In Ben Sira and the Wisdom of Solomon, we have glimpsed some of the ancient interpreters' *modus operandi*. It might be well, before proceeding, to say something of a more programmatic nature about how interpreters interpreted.

To do so, we must begin with the interpreters' own understanding of Scripture: what was Scripture in their eyes, and *how* did it mean? At first this might seem like a foolish question. After all, why should one assume that so varied a group of interpreters as those treated in this book had any one view of Scripture? Surely what Ben Sira thought about Scripture was not what Philo of Alexandria thought, and their views in any case were hardly identical with those of the author of *Jubilees*.

This is to some extent true. And yet, the more one contemplates the whole corpus of ancient biblical interpretation, the more it becomes clear that, despite the great variety of styles and genres and even interpretive methods involved, underlying it all is a common approach, a common set of assumptions concerning the biblical text. Some of these have been alluded to in passing above, but it is appropriate here to set them out schematically. There are essentially four fundamental assumptions about Scripture that characterize all ancient biblical interpretation.

The first assumption that all ancient interpreters seem to share is that the Bible is a fundamentally cryptic document. That is, all interpreters are fond of maintaining that although Scripture may appear to be saying X, what it really means is Y, or that while Y is not openly said by Scripture, it is somehow implied or hinted at in X. The chapters that follow abound with instances of this assumption at work. Numerous interpreters seek to maintain, for example, that when Moses casts a tree or stick into the waters of Marah (Exod. 15:25), "the word *tree* here means divine teachings," or that when Dinah's brothers speak deceitfully to the men of Shechem (Gen. 34:13), "*deceitfully* really means 'with wisdom.'" Now it is hardly a natural thing to assume that a particular text is fundamentally cryptic or esoteric. Whether we are reading a history book or a newspaper editorial or a rousing hymn, we generally assume that what the words seem to say is what they mean to say. Yet ancient interpreters, when they read a piece of biblical history, or the urgings of a biblical prophet, or the hymns of an ancient psalmist, again and again tell us that in place of, or beyond, the apparent meaning of the text is some hidden, esoteric message. So, more generally, although the biblical text appears to be talking about a historical figure named Abraham, "Abraham is," according to Philo of Alexandria, "a symbol for the virtue-loving soul" in addition to being that historical figure, while for early Christian interpreters, "Cain's brother Abel is a foreshadowing of Christ."

It would be interesting, in another context, to try to trace the roots of this first assumption, which clearly go back to the Bible itself. To mention but one example cited earlier, the suggestion of the prophet-sage Daniel that the real meaning of the expression "seventy years" is 490 years is a classic case of "X really means Y."[12] The obvious question—If Jeremiah had meant 490 years, why didn't he say so?—is never addressed by Daniel; apparently even at the time of that book's composition it was already a well-known fact that Scripture often speaks indirectly or cryptically.

Whatever the origins of this first assumption, it was universally shared by ancient interpreters. Indeed, it had not a little to do with the interpreter's own standing in the community and with the authority that his interpretations enjoyed. The very fact that the Bible could be demonstrated time and again to contain some meaning other than the apparent one vouchsafed the necessity of specially trained interpreters who could reveal the Bible's secrets, and the interpretations that they put forward—precisely because they arose out of

---

12. For some literary connections to this passage, see Grabbe, "The End of the Desolation of Jeremiah." See also Grelot, "Soixante-dix semaines d'années"; Doukhan, "The Seventy Weeks of Daniel 9."

careful exegesis and would not appear to most readers at first blush—acquired an authority of their own.

The second assumption shared by all ancient interpreters was that Scripture constitutes one great Book of Instruction, and as such is a fundamentally *relevant* text. To appreciate the significance of this assumption, contrast it to the approach we normally take to the act of reading. If, for example, we were to open up *Gilgamesh* or the *Enuma Elish* or some other ancient Near Eastern text, we might find the stories moving, the language stirring, but no one would likely suggest that we ought to behave in keeping with what is written there, or that the characters are represented as acting in the way that they do so that we might emulate their example. Similarly, we might be drawn to read the prophecies of ancient sibyls in Greek, or read the writings of other makers of oracles, but no one would suggest that what these authors were *really* talking about was America in the twenty-first century. An ancient Roman law code might be of interest to a student of legal history; some of its laws might even serve as a model for new legislation in our own day; but scarcely any reader would think that, because such-and-such a law appears in this code, that fact alone is sufficient reason for us to regard it as currently binding upon ourselves. Songs, hymns, prayers, laments culled from centuries past would likewise have no automatic application to our present situation: we might find them moving, but the very fact of their existence would hardly constitute a reason for us to recite them in solemn assembly or obey their calls to celebrate or mourn.

Yet, it should be obvious, precisely these things were said about the Bible by ancient interpreters. As we have seen briefly in the case of Enoch, so Abraham, Jacob, Moses, and other biblical figures were held up as models of conduct, their stories regarded as a guide given to later human beings for the leading of their own lives. (Some interpreters saw the figures themselves as moral exemplars, others as allegorical representations of virtues to be emulated; it matters little, since the point in any case is that these historical figures are not merely historical but instructional.) Biblical prophecies were similarly read as *relevant* to the interpreter and his audience: one obvious effect achieved by Daniel's interpreting 70 years as 490 was to move the relevance of Jeremiah's prophecy four centuries into the future (rather close, in fact, to the time when, according to many scholars, this part of the book of Daniel was probably composed). Similarly, the Dead Sea Scrolls have yielded many examples of ancient *pesharim* ("actualized interpretations") whereby the prophecies of Habakkuk, Nahum, and other biblical prophets are explained as referring to the politics of Roman-occupied Palestine centuries after these prophets themselves had lived. The early Christian interpretation of the prophecies of Isaiah and other Old Testament figures are another well-known instance of making ancient works relevant. And, as will be seen in the following chapters, the same fundamental assumption was held to be true about *all* of the Hebrew Bible, the songs and psalms and prayers and laws and narratives it contained. Everything was held to apply to present-day readers and to contain within it an imperative for adoption and application to the readers' own lives. Paul's observation about the biblical narrative of the Israelites' wanderings in the desert,

> Now these things [that happened to the Israelites in the desert] happened to them as a warning, **but they were written down for our instruction**, upon whom the end of the ages has come   — 1 Cor. 10:11

is merely one formulation of an assumption that had long characterized ancient biblical interpretation. For Paul, as for all ancient interpreters, the Bible is not *essentially* a record of things that happened or were spoken in the past. That they happened is of course true; but if they were written down in the Bible, it was not so as to record what has occurred in some distant past, but "for our instruction," so that, by reading the sacred text whose material comes to us from the past, we might learn some vital lesson for our own lives.

The third basic assumption is that Scripture is perfect and perfectly harmonious. By this I mean, first of all, that there is no mistake in the Bible, and anything that might look like a mistake—the fact that, for example, Gen. 15:13 asserts that the Israelites "will be oppressed for four hundred years" in Egypt, while Exod. 12:41 speaks of 430 years, whereas a calculation based on biblical genealogies yielded a figure of 210 years—must therefore be an illusion to be clarified by proper interpretation.

But this third assumption goes well beyond the rejection of apparent mistakes or inconsistencies. It posits a perfect harmony between the Bible's various parts. Again, a comparison with other texts might be illuminating here. In an anthology of texts in English or Latin, for example, written by many authors over a period of more than a thousand years in diverse locales and under different political regimes and cultural norms, we would hardly expect to find absolute uniformity of views. One text would disagree with another not only in fundamental matters of orientation and belief, but even in its presentation of past events, since people's view of history tends to be colored by their own ideologies and, of course, to change radically over time. Yet with regard to Scripture—precisely because it was Scripture, a body of *sacred* writings—ancient interpreters adopted a different approach. They sought to discover the basic harmony underlying apparently discordant words, since all of Scripture, in their view, must speak with one voice. By the same logic, any biblical text might illuminate any other: Josh. 24:2–3 might provide some of the background information necessary for an understanding of God's words to Abraham in Gen. 12:1–3, and Prov. 10:8 might be a reference to Moses' meritorious deed in Exod. 13:19.

Taken to its extreme, this same view of Scripture's perfection ultimately led to the doctrine of "omnisignificance," whereby nothing in Scripture is said in vain or for rhetorical flourish: every detail is important, everything is intended to impart some teaching. While this doctrine finds its fullest expression in rabbinic writings, its traces can be found far earlier. Thus, the fact that Jacob is said to dwell "in tents" (Gen. 25:27) was used to support the notion that he, unlike his brother Esau, had had some sort of schooling—that is, the plural "tents" here is interpreted to imply at least two tents, one for a school and one for home. This understanding of the special significance of "tents" is openly stated in some rabbinic texts, but it probably underlies as well the assertion that Jacob "learned to read" in the book of *Jubilees* (19:14). In the same vein, the fact that Lev. 19:17 uses the emphatically "doubled" form of the word "reproach" suggested to Ben Sira that two different acts of reproaching were being urged, one before the misdeed occurs, and another afterward (Sir. 19:13–14). In similar fashion, all sorts of other, apparently insignificant details in the Bible—an unusual word or grammatical form, any repetition, the juxtaposition of one law to another or one story to another—all were read as potentially significant, a manifestation of Scripture's perfection.

Finally, it should be noted that this perfection of Scripture of course included the conduct of biblical heroes or the content of Scripture's own teachings. Thus, Abraham, Jacob, and other meritorious figures ought not to behave in unseemly fashion, and if at times they appeared to do so, ancient interpreters frequently saw themselves as obliged to come to the rescue. As just mentioned, when Dinah's brothers speak deceitfully to the men of Shechem (Gen. 34:13), "*deceitfully* really means 'with wisdom.'" This assertion reflects the belief not only that Scripture speaks, or can speak, cryptically, but that Scripture's very nature is such that it would scarcely seek to present Jacob's sons as a bunch of liars. Something else *must* have been meant, for Scripture is, in regard to its teachings as well, perfect. Similarly, although Rachel is said to have stolen her father's household gods (Gen. 31:19), she must not really have *stolen* them so much as taken them to protect her father from sin or for some other worthy purpose. Likewise, if a given interpreter believed (as the author of *Jubilees* did) that the moon has no role in determining the time of festivals or the duration of months, then all scriptural texts, even Gen. 1:14–18, had to be shown to conform to this view. Scripture's perfection, in other words, ultimately included its being in accord with the interpreter's own ideas, standards of conduct, and the like.

The fourth assumption is that all of Scripture is somehow divinely sanctioned, of divine provenance, or divinely inspired. Needless to say, much of Scripture itself asserts that its words come from God: "Thus says the Lord" is the introductory proclamation of many a prophet, and biblical laws in the Pentateuch are frequently introduced with "And the Lord spoke to Moses, saying . . ." Yet this very fact might have implied to ancient interpreters that the rest of Scripture was somehow of human fashioning—that, for example, the history of intrigue in David's court, or the corpus of supplications and praises directed *to* God in the book of Psalms, or many other texts within the canon could not have come *from* God in the same manner as divine prophecies or laws.

I have saved this fourth assumption for last because it is the one least frequently in evidence: particularly among the most ancient interpreters, the subject of the divine provenance of Scripture as a whole is hardly even addressed. What is more, the common practice of interpreters writing in Greek to refer to "Moses," "David," "Solomon," and others as the authors of this or that biblical composition—without further reference to them as mere conduits of the divine word—might suggest that, for such interpreters, the biblical compositions in question were fundamentally the product of human authors, however extraordinary the humans in question might be. But this is hardly so for a great many Greek-writing interpreters (as Philo of Alexandria, for example, makes clear), and evidence of the contrary view is occasionally explicit. In particular, a certain explanation of Gen. 34:7 found in the book of Judith (see Chapter 13) gives clear testimony that its author believed the divine authorship of Scripture to extend to the ordinary narrative fabric of biblical books: God was, according to this author, the omniscient narrator of Genesis. The author of *Jubilees* similarly believed all of the Genesis narratives to be of divine provenance—as much so as the laws of Exodus through Deuteronomy that are specifically attributed to God. Indeed, *Jubilees* likewise maintains that later scriptural books (apparently including, among others, Isaiah and Psalms) were inscribed in the "heavenly tablets" long before the human transmitters of these texts had even been born. A text from among the Dead Sea Scrolls, 11QPs.ᵃ, similarly asserts that David's songs and psalms were "given to him from the Most High," and this belief is reflected as well in Philo of Alexandria and Acts 2:30–31.[13]

If this is so, it would nevertheless be a mistake, in my opinion, to assume that this fourth assumption stands behind the other three—that, in other words, first it was assumed that all of Scripture is of divine provenance or inspiration, and then out of this first assumption developed the others sur-

13. Kugel, "David the Prophet."

veyed above, that all of Scripture is perfect, fundamentally relevant, and cryptic in its form of expression. To begin with, these things do not *necessarily* follow from the assumption of divine provenance (although I admit that, with regard to Scripture's perfection, a certain logical connection exists). But, more to the point, I do not believe that the interpretive texts themselves suggest such a sequence of events. As noted, the divine provenance of all of Scripture is a notion specifically addressed only rather late in the history of ancient interpreters, and it even seems to be contradicted here or there by some ancient writers, whereas the first three assumptions are attested across the whole spectrum of ancient interpreters, early and often. This is not the place to elaborate such a hypothesis, but my own belief is that the first three of the assumptions named are evidenced within the Hebrew Bible itself, indeed, they extend back even to parts of the Bible written before the Babylonian exile. If the fourth assumption is plainly stated about *some* parts of Scripture, it apparently did not come to be extended in homogeneous fashion to Scripture as a whole until a relatively late period. Therefore, I must reject the notion that assumptions 1, 2, and 3 developed out of assumption 4.

How Interpreters Interpreted

Bearing in mind these four assumptions will help in understanding why interpreters say what they do about the biblical text. Convinced that Scripture was a fundamentally cryptic document, they scrutinized its every detail in search of hidden meaning. That meaning was to be, by definition, relevant to the situation of the interpreter and his listeners—not some insight into the historical circumstances in which the text was originally written, but a message of immediate value and applicability, either a timeless moral truth or a law to be observed in one particular fashion or something bearing in some other way on the present or the immediate future. In searching for such a message, the interpreter could rest assured that no detail in Scripture's manner of speaking was insignificant, nor would there be any inconsistency between what is said in one place and what is said in another, nor any lesson that contradicted right thinking. For that reason, any apparent contradiction, or unnecessary detail or repetition or even an emphatic turn of phrase, seemed to be an invitation to the interpreter to look deeply into the text's words and so discover its *real* meaning, the hidden, relevant, perfect truth that only befit the word of God.

Indeed, the examples of interpretation already glimpsed in the Wisdom of Ben Sira and the Wisdom of Solomon may serve as a ready illustration of these ideas. Thus, the brief mention of Enoch in Gen. 5:18–24 says nothing about repentance, and a normal reader of the text nowadays would probably assume that Enoch's particular virtue had simply been omitted by the Bible; it says that Enoch "walked with God" without giving any further details. But an interpreter convinced of our first assumption, that Scripture is fundamentally cryptic, would be moved thereby to look more deeply—leading him, as we have seen, to Ben Sira's conclusion that Enoch's virtue was, specifically, repentance. And what greater expression of the second assumption than Ben Sira's own assertion that Enoch is not merely some obscure figure from the distant past but "an example of repentance *to all generations*"? As for the third assumption, we saw how the Wisdom of Solomon sought to resolve the apparent contradiction in Scripture with regard to the drowned Egyptians: first they sank to the bottom of the sea, then they were vomited up again onto the shore. Underlying this piece of exegesis is the conviction that Scripture does not contradict itself or even exaggerate: if the song of Exodus 15 says that the Egyptians sank "like a stone" but the preceding narrative has them "dead upon the shore," then both statements must be shown to be true. With regard to the fourth assumption, Ben Sira's assertion that the "book of the covenant of the Most High" is nought but divine wisdom (Sir. 24:23) is, while not an utterly unambiguous statement of the divine provenance of all Scripture, rather representative of the sort of programmatic formulations of this assumption that survive from our most ancient interpreters.

Clues from the Text

One aspect of the way interpreters interpreted needs to be highlighted. It is frequently said that these ancient writers played fast and loose with the Bible, twisting the plain sense of the text to fit their own ideology or the events of their own day, creating all manner of imaginative additions to what the Bible itself says. This is true, but to say only this is to miss the point about how ancient interpreters worked.

The formal starting point for ancient interpreters is always Scripture itself. An interpreter may be eager to assert that, for example, the Platonic doctrine of ideal forms is found in the Bible, or that Israel's prophets predicted the fall of the Roman empire, or that Jacob did not really deceive his father into giving him a blessing intended for his brother, Esau, or that the crucifixion of Jesus is an event foreshadowed in Hebrew Scripture centuries earlier. Interpreters did claim all these things, and more, but they did not simply claim them: they anchored their claims in some detail, however insignificant, found in the biblical text itself. That is to say, no matter how far-reaching or inventive the assertions of ancient biblical interpretation, they are formally a kind of exegesis. The Platonic doctrine of ideal forms is therefore evidenced in the Bible via a particular feature of the text, the fact that God created a "heavenly man" in Genesis 1 who was somehow different from the earthly one in Genesis 2. Similarly, Rome's fall is amply foretold by the prophet Obadiah, if only one understands—on the basis of Gen. 27:40 and other texts—that the words addressed to "Edom" in Obad. 1:4 are really meant for Rome. As for Jacob, he certainly would not lie to his father—and he doesn't, so long as his words in Gen. 27:19 and 24 undergo a radical repunctuation. That the crucifixion had been foreshadowed of old was supported through a reading of the Genesis account of the binding of Isaac, wherein even Jesus' crown of thorns was present in the text's reference to a "thicket" at the place of the offering (Gen. 22:13).

The foregoing are all examples of what one might call, broadly speaking, ideologically motivated interpretations—the interpreter clearly wishes to get the text to say something that accords with his own ideology or outlook. Yet it would be wrong to imply that interpreters were *always* motivated by ideology or some outside interest, that they were always seeking to import some extrabiblical doctrine or political stand into the world of the Bible. Very often their primary or sole motivation appears to be making sense out of the biblical text—but making sense out of *all* of it, its little details, chance juxtapositions, everything. For, once the rules of interpretive procedure had been established, the biblical text seemed virtually to invite the interpreter to try his hand at seeking out its fullest possible meaning. In so doing, interpreters were indeed quite free, reconstructing conversations never reported by the biblical narrator, recounting whole incidents somehow omitted in the narrative itself, connecting this with that in the most creative fashion. But if interpreters were, in this sense, free, it was because the text had granted them this freedom by including some unusual turn of phrase or repetition or unexplained ellipsis. By the rules of interpretation implied in the Four Assumptions, such creative turns are simply part of the business of interpreting. They could be used for some ulterior motive, but often they were not.

This point is important because many modern studies of the texts that talk about biblical figures or biblical stories have focused on their "ideological" side. Scholars have tended to assume that if an ancient author deviated from the biblical narrative in his retelling of it, that deviation must somehow have been motivated by the reteller's political allegiance or religious agenda or some other matter of ideology, or it must at least have been an attempt (if only an unconscious one) to retroject the realities of the reteller's own time back to the time of the biblical narrative. Such factors certainly did affect the way biblical stories were retold. But to these factors should be added another extremely significant one, the desire to explain the biblical text, to account for its particulars in one fashion or another.

In general, the attempt to distinguish between "pure" exegesis among ancient interpreters and exegesis that is ideologically or politically motivated is doomed to fail for any large sampling of texts. On the one hand, "pure" exegesis as such does not really exist. The ancient interpreter *always* had an axe to grind, always had a bit of an ulterior motive: at the very least, this interpreter wished to convince listeners or readers that the text means something other than what it might seem to mean at first glance, that his clever way of explaining things reveals the text's true significance. Sometimes that "true" significance does indeed turn out to correspond to something current in the interpreter's own world, some part of the political or religious or intellectual backdrop. Often, however, it does not: the interpretation is just that, an attempt to make sense of the text, albeit in keeping with the freewheeling methods suggested by the Four Assumptions charted above. Moreover, even in the case of blatantly ideological interpretations, it is usually quite difficult to decide whether a given interpreter set out to patrol all of Scripture in search of a place to "plant" an expression of his own ideology, or whether, on the contrary, faced with a particular exegetical stimulus in the biblical text—an unusual word, an apparent incongruity, or the like—the interpreter came up with an explanation that, in one way or another, also reflected his own ideology or the issues of his day.[14] For these reasons, it seems best to leave aside any distinction between "pure" and other forms of exegesis.

The Heritage of Wisdom

I should add that, in everything that has been said thus far about the methods of ancient interpretation, the heritage of wisdom is clearly visible. For, as was mentioned earlier, wise men of old had packaged their insights in clever proverbs that often demanded sustained scrutiny by later sages and students of wisdom in order to be fully understood. Schooled in these techniques, sages quite naturally brought them to bear on Scripture: were not *its* words just as likely to be cryptic, esoteric, in need of sustained contemplation in order to be fully understood? Likewise, the very conception of Scripture as a great corpus of divine instruction whose lessons, therefore, are relevant to every age—is not this also a projection of the sage's assumptions about wisdom literature onto *all* of Israel's variegated corpus of ancient writings? The treatment of

14. I have tried to illustrate some of the difficulties involved in making such a distinction in *In Potiphar's House*, 248–251.

various biblical figures as examples, models of proper conduct, is similarly a sagely construct. Indeed, it is certainly significant, in the light of wisdom literature's polarized division of humanity into the righteous and the wicked, the wise and the foolish, that a similar polarization takes place in ancient exegesis: biblical heroes are altogether good, with any fault air-brushed away, whereas figures like Esau or Balaam are altogether demonized—as if their neither-good-nor-evil status in the Bible itself was somehow intolerable. (The most persuasive instances of such polarization occur with figures like Lot or Enosh, simultaneously demonized by one group of interpreters while pronounced altogether righteous by another. Apparently they could go one way or another, but not remain in the intolerable ambiguity of the middle.)[15] On another occasion it might be profitable to explore the "wisdom connection" in ancient interpretation in greater detail.[16]

Where Is Interpretation Found?

In the past, the quantity of surviving ancient biblical interpretations has frequently been understated. This is because of a peculiar feature of the way ancient interpreters presented their material; with a few exceptions (Philo of Alexandria, some Dead Sea Scrolls texts), they did not write commentaries as such, mentioning a biblical verse and then offering their own interpretation of it. Instead, they followed the practice of *substitution:* in place of the element to be explained, X, the interpreter simply substituted his explanation, Y. This practice can operate on the level of a single word, whereby, for example, a difficult term no longer widely understood is replaced by a word in common use, or—as was glimpsed earlier—an ideologically difficult word (like "deceitfully" in Gen. 34:13) is replaced by a more acceptable term ("with wisdom"). But substitution can go well beyond a single word: as will be seen in Chapter 4, interpreters inserted, as the direct object of the verb "say" in Gen. 4:8, a whole conversation between Cain and Abel not found in the Bible itself, and in place of a cryptic reference in Gen. 49:24 they inserted a little story to the effect that Joseph was saved from sinning with Potiphar's wife because of the sudden appearance of his father's face at the critical moment. But the point is

15. See below, Chapter 10; see also Loader, *Tale of Two Cities;* Fraade, *Enosh and His Generation.*

16. Particularly suggestive in connection with this topic is Otzen, "Old Testament Wisdom Literature and Dualistic Thinking." "Dualistic thinking" in his definition includes not only the polarization of humanity into good and evil or wise and foolish, but as well such dualisms as the "sons of light/sons of darkness" and "two spirits" found at Qumran. See also such texts as Sir. 15:14–20, *Testament of Asher* 1:3–5, Philo, *The Worse Attacks the Better* 82–84, and Baer, *Philo's Use of the Categories Male and Female.*

that these explanations were simply inserted in a re-presentation of the biblical text: they were not labeled or specifically presented as interpretation or commentary.

Because interpreters tended to substitute for, rather than comment upon, difficulties in the text, there emerged the genre of writing known to modern scholars as "The Rewritten [or "Retold"] Bible."[17] The Rewritten Bible is really the interpreted Bible: an ancient interpreter—the author of *Jubilees* or the Wisdom of Solomon or the *Book of Biblical Antiquities*—retells a biblical story or group of stories *with the interpretations already inserted in the text.* Sometimes, as in the case of *Jubilees,* the retelling is a calculated, highly self-conscious attempt to explain Scripture (and, in this particular case, to explain it in keeping with a definite political and religious program). Other retellers of Scripture seem less self-conscious: sometimes the reteller himself may not even be aware where the biblical text leaves off and the interpretation begins, since he is simply passing along what he has heard or learned as a child is the meaning of a biblical text. In either case, however, the Rewritten Bible (whether one is talking about an extended retelling of whole biblical books, or the "retelling" of a single verse) should be recognized for what it is: the most popular transmitter of biblical interpretation among ancient writers.

This being the case, the first step in studying ancient biblical interpretation is to identify it, to sift carefully any restatement of a biblical law or any retelling of, or allusion to, a biblical narrative or prophecy or song, in order to isolate the interpretive elements. Often, this is not easy. An ordinary reader, unschooled in the ways of ancient interpretation, would probably not recognize as such *any* of the interpretations examined above: "a model of repentance," "reward for their labors," "cast them up from the depth"—these would doubtless strike most readers as simple restatement, not interpretation. It is therefore necessary to scrutinize all potentially interpretive texts with great care. The best guide in such scrutiny is the Bible itself: any deviation from its words, no matter how slight, may conceal an ancient interpretation of those words. (To be sure, some deviations are quite innocent; this too makes difficult the job of isolating interpretive material.)

The Exegetical Motif

Ancient biblical interpretation is an interpretation of verses, not stories.[18] Precisely because they focused their attention on the little details of the

---

17. This term was apparently first used by Vermes; see his *Post-Biblical Jewish Studies.*
18. At greater length, see Kugel, "Two Introductions."

biblical text, interpreters tended to pass on their insights in the form of verse-centered comments: "The word 'water' here means divine learning," "What the brothers told Shechem [in Gen. 34:13] was actually true." It is not that the overall significance of a particular story was neglected: Ben Sira, for example, sums up in a single phrase the whole significance of Abraham's offering up of his son Isaac, "He [Abraham] was found faithful when tested" (Sir. 44:20), and does the same for numerous other biblical narratives in the same catalog of biblical heroes (Sirach 44–49). But such summary treatment could hardly be regarded as *insightful:* any fool could figure such things out! The true insight was to realize that, for example, the opening verse of the story of the offering of Isaac, "And it came to pass, *after these things*" (Gen. 22:1), was actually an allusion to the previous tests that Abraham had undergone or, alternately, to certain "words" that had been spoken against Abraham in heaven (on both, see Chapter 9). And so it was such localized insights as these that tended to circulate, passed from one sage to another or from teacher to pupil. (Again, the heritage of wisdom here is clear.)

Thus, interpreters frequently explained biblical texts by retelling them, explaining in their own words not just what Scripture said but what Scripture meant. In the process, several, or even many, little, verse-centered explanations—either those created by the reteller himself, or someone else's explanations that the reteller had learned—became incorporated into an overall rewording of the text in question. Such retellings are found in a variety of ancient documents: in a brief prayer made by the heroine of the book of Judith; in Josephus' multivolume retelling of all of biblical history; in Abraham's first-person account of his trip to Egypt in the *Genesis Apocryphon;* and so forth.

How does one go about studying the biblical interpretation found in such retellings? Precisely because they tend to incorporate a number of separate, discrete insights into particular verses, the smooth-flowing unity of these retellings is deceptive. All too often in the past, scholars have dealt with things like "Josephus' Version of the Exodus" as if it were all of a piece, the sustained reflection of a single interpreter contemplating a large chunk of the biblical text. This is misleading on two counts. First, Josephus—like all his predecessors—had his eye on individual verses or even single words or phrases within individual verses. When, therefore, in retelling the story of the exodus or any other biblical narrative, he deviates from what the Bible itself seems to be saying, it is usually because he is expanding upon some little particularity in the narrative. True, these insights are strung together into a continuous narrative, Josephus' retelling of the exodus. But from the standpoint of biblical interpretation, it is most important not to lose sight of the trees for the forest:

Josephus' "interpretation" consists of *interpretations,* little insights—selected, to be sure, molded into a seamless narrative stamped with his own personal seal, but nonetheless capable of being broken down into its constitutive elements and connected with specific verses or even words. For this same reason "Josephus' Version of the Exodus" is misleading on a second count as well: it is not Josephus' alone. Many of the little insights that Josephus passes along are ones attested a century or more earlier in the writings of other people. It is highly unlikely that Josephus and these earlier figures all arrived at their interpretations independently (although this *may* happen every once in a while). After all, Josephus himself recounts how, as a youth, he was educated in traditional religious instruction (*Life* 7–12)—indeed, he was uniquely well acquainted with different schools of interpreters in his day— and he otherwise shows a broad awareness of exegetical traditions and even individual authors (he refers by name on one occasion to Philo of Alexandria, *Jewish Antiquities* 18:259–260). In a great many instances, therefore, Josephus' retellings of biblical stories are most likely an amalgam of things he has learned from different sources—indeed, at times he himself may not always be aware that what he is telling *is* interpretation and not, or not necessarily, a straightforward duplication of the biblical text alone.[19]

When I first began working on this book, I did not appreciate the extent to which the foregoing was true. I began by assembling long passages from different ancient authors relating to a given biblical story, and I dealt with each retelling as a unit, comparing, for instance, Philo's version of Abraham's departure from Ur with that found in the book of *Jubilees.* After a time, however, I realized that this was the wrong way to proceed: even the briefest allusion to a biblical story in an ancient writer may sometimes involve two or three quite distinct bits of traditional interpretation. Take, for example, Augustine's opening sentence in his discussion of the binding of Isaac:

> Among **other things, the sum of which it would take too long a time to mention,** Abraham was tested with regard to the offering up of his beloved son Isaac, in order to prove his obedience to God and **make it known to the world,** not to God.   —Augustine, *City of God* 16.32

The indicated phrases actually refer to two quite distinct interpretive traditions about the offering of Isaac, neither of which originated with Augustine. The first is a tradition mentioned earlier, to the effect that Abraham had undergone *other* tests prior to that of the offering of Isaac (which is specifically

---

19. See Feldman, "Use, Authority, and Exegesis of Mikra in the Writings of Josephus," esp. 471–476.

labeled as a test in Gen. 22:1). The notion that Abraham had undergone a series of tests is found as early as the book of *Jubilees,* six hundred years before Augustine—indeed, *Jubilees* specifies, as do later, rabbinic sources, that the total number of tests undergone by Abraham was ten (see Chapter 9). Augustine does no more than allude to this tradition here,[20] apparently because he felt it would be known to at least some readers; in any case, he is clearly recycling earlier interpretive material. The other bit of traditional interpretation in this sentence is the idea that God put Abraham to the test not in order to discover whether or not he would pass—for certainly an omniscient deity knew the answer to that question in advance, and besides, according to the first tradition Abraham's faith had already been amply tested on prior occasions—but in order to make Abraham's faith "known to the world." Again this is an ancient tradition—attested in *Jubilees* and, somewhat later, in Pseudo-Philo's *Book of Biblical Antiquities*—which is ultimately based on the reading of the Hebrew phrase "now I know" *(yāda'tî)* in Gen. 22:12 as if it read "now I have made known" *(yidda'tî).* (Augustine knew the tradition, though he certainly did not know this textual justification, since he did not know Hebrew.)[21]

The composite nature of such retellings or reflections on Scripture is the rule among ancient interpreters, not the exception—and such composites are sometimes found even in our earliest sources, like *Jubilees* or *1 Enoch.* The following representative passage from a slightly later text, *The Testament of Levi,* concerns the revenge taken by Jacob's sons Levi and Simeon in Genesis 34:

> [Levi recalls:] And after this I counseled my father and Reuben my brother **to bid the sons of Hamor not to be circumcised**; for I was zealous because of the abomination which they had wrought on my sister. And **I killed Shechem first, and Simeon [killed] Hamor.** And after that **the brothers came and smote the city** with the edge of the sword. And father heard of it and was angry and distressed, because they had accepted the circumcision and had been killed after that, and in his blessings he did otherwise [that is, he cursed Simeon and Levi instead of blessing them: Gen. 49:7]. And we had sinned in going against his opinion, **and he became sick** on that day. But I saw that **God's verdict upon Shechem was "Guilty"**; for **they had sought to do**

20. Unless his use of the phrase "other things" is intended to invoke the biblical phrase "After these *things*" (Gen. 22:1) to which this tradition was attached.

21. The basis of these traditions was certainly known to Eastern Christianity: see Brock, "Genesis 22 in Syriac Tradition."

the same thing to Sarah and Rebecca as they had [now] done to Dinah our sister, but the Lord had stopped them. And in the same way they had persecuted Abraham our father when he was a stranger, and **they had acted against him to suppress his flocks** when they were big with young; and they had mistreated Ieblae, his homeborn slave. And **in this way they treated all strangers**, taking their wives by force and banishing them. But the anger of the Lord against them had reached its term. So I said to my father: Do not be angry, lord, because through you the Lord will reduce the Canaanites to nothing, and he will give their land to you and your seed after you. For **from this day on Shechem will be called a city of imbeciles**; for as a someone mocks a fool, so we mocked them; because **also they** had wrought folly in Israel in defiling our sister.   — *Testament of Levi* 6:3–7:3

Each of the indicated phrases refers to a different interpretive tradition surrounding this biblical story. Some of them, such as the assertion that Jacob became sick as a result of the revenge attack, add details beyond what is explicitly said in the biblical narrative itself. Others, such as Levi's claim that he had counseled his father and brother *not* to tell the Shechemites to undergo circumcision, or Levi's assertion that he and Simeon had killed only one man apiece and that the other Shechemites had been killed by his other brothers, actually seem to contradict what the Bible says. *All* of these traditions, however, are rooted in some peculiarity in the biblical text, justified, as it were, by a particular turn of phrase in the narrative. More to the point, however, even by the time that the *Testament of Levi* was written, much of this interpretive material was traditional, and a good deal of it is attested in sources still earlier than this testament. Indeed, in one matter the above passage contains (again, not atypically) two quite contradictory traditions. The first maintains that the collective slaughter of the Shechemites was justified since all of them had somehow participated in the rape of Dinah; this tradition is alluded to in the very last clause of the above passage. (The same tradition is found elsewhere—for example, in Jth. 9:2–4.) Another interpretive tradition, however, maintained that the collective punishment was justified because of the city's criminal past, its history of previous outrages. This tradition is set forth in the group of three sentences beginning "But I saw that God's verdict was: 'Guilty.'" Since both traditions arose to solve the same difficulty—the apparent unfairness of a collective punishment for crimes committed by one man alone—a single explanation would have sufficed. Indeed, a careful reader might ask, If the Shechemites were killed because they had all participated in the rape of Dinah, then why had God pronounced them guilty even before the rape occurred? But precisely because this author has heard two traditional explanations each of which he regards as authoritative, he incorporates them both, even when the result is redundancy or internal inconsistency.

Such is the nature of ancient biblical interpretation. Once propounded, interpretations circulated widely, passed on largely by word of mouth. Presented by authoritative teachers as insights into the particulars of the biblical text, these interpretations soon acquired an authority of their own: they were repeated and repeated, often combined with other bits of interpretation, sometimes modified in the process, sometimes misunderstood by later transmitters, and passed on further.

This being the case, it eventually became clear to me that talking about large units of text, "Josephus' Version of the Exodus" and the like, was the wrong way to proceed. The first task was to identify and discuss each and every component of larger units, each of the individual bits of interpretation out of which the larger retellings were made, and to try to identify the same or similar bits of interpretation in the retellings of other ancient authors. So it was that I came to focus this book not on large blocks of texts nor on their authors as such, but on *exegetical motifs,* the individual pieces of interpretation that circulated far and wide and found their way into the writings of different authors of that period.

Simply put, an exegetical motif is an explanation of a biblical verse (or phrase or word therein) that becomes the basis for some ancient writer's expansion or other alteration of what Scripture actually says: in paraphrasing or summarizing Scripture, the ancient writer incorporates the exegetical motif in his retelling and in so doing adds some minor detail or otherwise deviates from mere repetition or restatement of the Bible.

To return to the examples given above: an ancient interpreter, scrutinizing Gen. 5:21–24, came to the conclusion that Enoch was a penitent sinner. Thus was born the exegetical motif that we might refer to as "Enoch the Penitent." In alluding to the story of Enoch, the book of Ben Sira incorporates this motif: Enoch "was an example of repentance to all generations."[22] Who was the originator of this motif? The fact that it appears for the first time in the book of Ben Sira does not necessarily mean that *that* is where it was first created. After all, the same motif is found not too much later in the writings of Philo, and it may be hinted at as well in the Wisdom of Solomon (4:14). Perhaps, then, even before Ben Sira, "Enoch the Penitent" was a motif that circulated widely. Similarly, an ancient interpreter scrutinizing the drowning of the Egyptians in the Red Sea came to the conclusion that after they sank to the

---

22. This is one form of the text; see above, n. 10.

bottom of the sea, the Egyptians were lifted up again and deposited on the shore. Thus was born the exegetical motif that we might call "Ups and Downs of the Egyptians." This motif first appears in the Wisdom of Solomon and subsequently in the writings of Philo, Josephus, and later interpreters. Again, its original author is a matter of speculation.

As these examples imply, exegetical motifs circulated widely and soon acquired an authority of their own. They were the very fabric of ancient biblical interpretation. Individual authors may have put their own stamp on the motifs that they inherited, and even the choice to include or not include a given motif may reflect the tastes, ideology, or other particulars of a specific author. But the motifs themselves constituted the raw material out of which most ancient retellings and commentaries were made. For that reason I present the material in this book motif by motif, seeking to demonstrate in each case how different authors in different periods explained individual verses or episodes in similar fashion.

There are, of course, some things that are lost by focusing on these individual units of interpretation. Identifying common exegetical motifs does not tell us much about the specific authors who pass them along, about the particular "spin" that a certain author may seek to put on a given piece of Scripture, nor about how that spin may be attested elsewhere in his writings. Indeed, the individuality of a given text is somewhat submerged by focusing solely on the traditional motifs found within it. Moreover, merely identifying motifs common to different sources does not tell us anything about the history of their transmission—who borrowed what from whom. (Often it is impossible to piece such things together with any certainty, but sometimes we can do so, or at least make an educated guess.) And if, as may have happened in some cases, two interpreters came to the same conclusion quite independently, there is something misleading about treating both under a single rubric, as if both are attestations of a common tradition.

In recognizing these limitations, I hardly seek to belittle them. (Indeed, I myself have elsewhere spent some effort in, for example, trying to trace the development of specific motifs over the centuries, or charting the relationship between one ancient interpreter and another, or characterizing the overall exegetical approach of a single author.) But given the purpose of this book—to offer a detailed look at how the Bible was interpreted in antiquity, to show what the Bible essentially *was* in that period—I found it necessary to focus on motifs in and of themselves, both because such motifs were the actual building blocks of all larger retellings of biblical stories and passages, and because these building blocks are also the only sure guide to common elements found among different ancient authors.

Scripture or Interpretation?

Who were the ancient writers in whose books these exegetical motifs are found? For the most part, we do not know their names or their biographies, and often it is difficult to determine even approximately when or where they lived. Nevertheless, by examining their writings carefully we can determine some basic facts, and sometimes an illuminating detail or two will go far in helping us to understand what motivated these largely anonymous writers to say what they say.

Before discussing any individual authors or works, however, it is necessary to spell out an important truth: one man's interpreter is another's Scripture. For example, we have seen briefly that the biblical books of Chronicles and Daniel sometimes interpret Scripture, say, a verse from the book of Genesis or Jeremiah. From the standpoint of the authors of Chronicles or Daniel, these interpretations must have seemed just that. But to a biblical interpreter of, say, the first or second century C.E., Chronicles and Daniel were, no less than Genesis and Jeremiah, part of Scripture. For such an interpreter, the fact that Chronicles talks about something found in Genesis hardly makes Chronicles an *interpretation* of Genesis: both books were part of the great sacred corpus of Scripture, that seamless body of divine instruction that was held to be perfect and perfectly harmonious. Similarly, Ben Sira may have started out by attempting to (among other things) interpret Scripture, but for those ancient Jews and Christians who subsequently came to view Ben Sira's book as part of the Bible, the things that Ben Sira says about Enoch, Abraham, and other ancient figures simply became part of what *Scripture* has to say about Enoch, Abraham, and the others, that is, they became part of the corpus of things *to be interpreted.* Likewise, while the New Testament frequently interprets (or reflects earlier interpretations of) the Old Testament, for later Christians the New Testament is every bit as authoritative as the Old, and what it says about the heroes of Genesis is thus quite on a par with what Genesis says.

In other words, the corpus of what constitutes "Scripture" and is therefore the object of interpretation changed over time and varied from one group of readers to the next.[23] In compiling this book, I wanted to create a snapshot, or a portrait at least, of the Bible as it was interpreted for a specific period—

---

23. A further complication is presented by such books as *1 Enoch* or *Jubilees,* books that arguably were at one time considered by some readers to be as scriptural as Genesis or Exodus, but that later in the course of their transmission came to be viewed as less authoritative or altogether irrelevant. If so, then—for a time, at least—the interpretations contained within them must not have been viewed as interpretations at all: they were no less scriptural than the interpretations found in Chronicles or Daniel. Did not the books' subsequent change of status mean that these same interpretations reverted

roughly speaking, from about 200 B.C.E. through the first century or so C.E. This required defining, in somewhat arbitrary fashion, what "Scripture" would or would not include (since even within this period its content varied over time and from group to group).

The dividing line I have decided to adopt for this purpose is that of the so-called Jewish biblical canon (though this name is not particularly accurate, since only *some* Jews in the period covered accepted its boundaries). In other words, books like Chronicles, Ezra-Nehemiah, Psalms, and Daniel, even though they all contain here and there what is clearly interpretation of earlier biblical books, are considered for the purpose of this study to be Scripture, since they were all probably complete, or virtually complete, by the start of the period covered by this book, and were already considered by many to be Scripture. By contrast, books like *Jubilees,* Ben Sira, the Wisdom of Solomon, and the New Testament are used herein as witnesses to the state of biblical interpretation during the period covered, since these books were all apparently written within that period rather than before it; while all of them would eventually be treated as Scripture by one group or another, for purposes of this study they are not yet Scripture.[24]

Meet the Sources

The present volume contains ancient biblical interpretations culled from hundreds of different sources—far too many to present individually here. (The Terms and Sources section at the end of this volume contains a brief characterization of each work or author cited herein, along with an approximate dating of the work and related information.) Nevertheless, it might be useful at this point to introduce a few of these sources in order to provide some overview of the sorts of books in which ancient interpretive traditions are to be found. The following, then, are some of the most important ancient texts I used in compiling this book.

1 Enoch: There circulated in antiquity a number of works focusing on or attributed to Enoch—the same Enoch mentioned in Gen. 5:21–24 and dis-

---

back to their original state, that is, turned from Scripture into interpretation (thereby reversing the path traced by the interpretations canonized in Chronicles and Daniel)?

24. Having taken care of this matter of definition, I must add that I have been careful to breach it in the honoring whenever I judged it worthwhile. That is, in tracing what "the Bible" has to say about a particular matter, I have been careful to include, in addition to the Pentateuchal material itself, later reflections or elaborations found elsewhere within the Jewish canon. While I have necessarily treated such reflections and elaborations as Scripture, the alert reader will certainly recognize in many of them an earlier stage of biblical interpretation.

cussed above. The very fact that this passage apparently asserted that Enoch had been "taken" by God while he was still alive seemed to imply that he continued to exist in heaven—indeed, that he exists there still. From such a vantage point, Enoch could presumably not only observe all that was happening on earth, but was privy to all the secrets of heaven, including the natural order and God's plans for humanity's future.

A number of anonymous writers who wished to discourse on such subjects attributed their writings to Enoch, and eventually a composite "Book of Enoch"—and then *Books* of Enoch—began to circulate. Our present *1 Enoch* is composed of a number of different works. Most or all were apparently originally written in Aramaic, and parts of these Aramaic texts have turned up among the Dead Sea Scrolls (on which see below). The most ancient manuscripts found—drawn from the "Book of Luminaries" section (that is, chapters 72–82) of our present *1 Enoch,* and the "Book of the Watchers" (*1 Enoch* 1–36)—have been dated to the late third or early second century B.C.E.[25] Since these manuscripts are apparently only copies of a still earlier work, the date of at least these Enoch writings can be pushed back even earlier. They thus seem to be the oldest Jewish writings that have survived outside the Bible itself. New sections were eventually blended in with the old, and the entire Book of Enoch was subsequently translated into Greek and from Greek into ancient Ethiopic (Ge'ez), in which language alone the book survived in its entirety.

Scriptural interpretation was hardly the major concern of most of *1 Enoch.* The very figure of Enoch in this book may be modeled on that of a Mesopotamian sage, and the astronomical learning and other materials presented likewise bespeak the transmission of ancient, eastern lore.[26] Nevertheless, Enoch, Cain and Abel, Lamech, Methuselah, Noah, and other figures from the Bible, as well as incidents mentioned in biblical history, also appear, and in what is said about some of them it is possible to see the outline of some very ancient interpretation, in particular, a grappling with difficulties associated with the story of Noah and the flood.

Septuagint: Starting in the third century B.C.E., Hebrew Scripture began to be translated into Greek, apparently for the use of Greek-speaking Jews in Hellenistic centers like Alexandria, Egypt. A legend eventually sprang up about this translation to the effect that seventy, or seventy-two, Jewish elders were commissioned to do the translation of the Pentateuch, each in an isolated cell; when the translations were compared, they all agreed in every detail,

---

25. The implications of this dating have been explored by Stone, *Scriptures, Sects, and Visions,* 37–47; idem, "Enoch, Aramaic Levi, and Sectarian Origins."

26. Grelot, "La légende d'Hénoch dans les apocryphes et dans la Bible"; idem, "La géographie mythique d'Hénoch et ses sources orientales"; Neugebauer, "Astronomy of the Book of Enoch."

for the translators had been divinely guided. As a result, this translation came to be known as the *Septuaginta* ("seventy"). (Subsequently, the name "Septuagint" also came to include the old Greek translation of the other books of the Hebrew Bible, a translation made in stages from the third to the first century B.C.E.)

Any translation by nature contains a good bit of interpretation: ambiguities in the original text can rarely be duplicated in translation and, as a result, the translator must take a stand and render the ambiguity one way or another. Moreover, translators aware of this or that traditional interpretation will sometimes incorporate it (consciously or otherwise) into their translation. For both these reasons, the Septuagint, although a fairly close rendering, can frequently provide information about how a particular verse or single word or phrase was understood by Jews as early as the third century B.C.E.

Jubilees: This book purports to contain a revelation given to Moses by the "angel of the Presence," one of the angels closest to God, at the time of the Sinai revelation. It takes the form of a retelling of the book of Genesis and the first part of Exodus: the angel goes over the same material but fills in many details, sometimes shifting slightly the order of things and occasionally skipping over elements in the narrative. The book was originally written in Hebrew, and fragments of it have been found among the Dead Sea Scrolls. From Hebrew it was translated into Greek (parts of this translation still survive in quotations from Greek authors) and from Greek into Latin and Ge'ez. The (almost) complete text exists only in Ge'ez, though a substantial section is extant in Latin as well. Many scholars date the book to the middle of the second century B.C.E., while a few (myself included) favor an earlier date, perhaps at the beginning of the second century B.C.E. or even a decade or two before that.

The author of *Jubilees* is one of the heroes of the present study. This writer was a bold, innovative interpreter in his own right—one might say, without exaggeration, something of a genius—and subsequent generations valued highly, even venerated, his book's insights into Scripture. In seeking to retell the book of Genesis and the beginning of Exodus, this author had a definite program: he wished to claim that this initial part of the Pentateuch, although it consists mostly of stories and does not contain any law code as such, had nonetheless been designed to impart legal instruction no less binding than the overt law codes found in the rest of the Pentateuch. In other words, by reading the stories of Genesis carefully, one could figure out all kinds of binding commandments that God had, as it were, hidden in the narrative. Reading in this fashion, the author of *Jubilees* was able to find a set of rules strictly defining what is permitted and forbidden on the Sabbath, regulations forbidding marriage between Jews and non-Jews, strictures against various forms of "fornication," and other subjects dear to this writer's heart. One interesting feature of the book is its claim that the true calendar ordained by God consisted of exactly 52 Sabbaths (364 days) per year and that the moon, whose waxing and waning determined the months and festivals for other Jews, ought rightly to have no such role in the true calendar. The author sought to show that this calendar, too, was implied by the stories of Genesis.

Apart from these pet issues, *Jubilees'* author ended up presenting a good deal more in the way of biblical interpretation. Some of these other interpretations may likewise have been of his own creation, but others were certainly widespread traditions at the time of his writing. One way or another, the book is a treasure of ancient thinking about the Bible. The Dead Seas Scroll sect adopted the same calendar as that prescribed by *Jubilees,* and it is clear that the members of that group held this book in high esteem.

Wisdom of Ben Sira[ch]: Yeshuʻa ben Elʻazar ben Sira is one of the rare Hebrew authors of this period known to us by name. He was a sage who wrote his book toward the beginning of the second century B.C.E., around the year 180 or so. From Hebrew the book was subsequently translated into Greek (by Ben Sira's own grandson) and became part of the Greek Bible of early Christianity; other ancient versions were made into Syriac and Latin (in which language it came to be known as "Ecclesiasticus"). Ben Sira's book was particularly beloved among the founders of rabbinic Judaism, but apparently because his identity was well known and the book was not attributed to some ancient worthy from the biblical past, they felt that it could not be included in the rabbinic canon of Scripture, and the original Hebrew version of it was therefore eventually lost. The book survived for centuries only in translation. Substantial fragments of the Hebrew text were recovered at the end of the nineteenth century from five medieval manuscripts that had been stored in a Cairo synagogue; subsequently parts of the Hebrew original have turned up in ancient manuscripts discovered among the Dead Sea Scrolls and at nearby Masada.

Ben Sira was, as we have glimpsed briefly, a traditional sage who, characteristically for his period, saw in Scripture a great corpus of divine wisdom; he therefore made broad use of Scripture in writing his own book, including the lengthy catalog of biblical heroes mentioned earlier. But Ben Sira was a conservative in all things—a "classicist," one might say—and this catalog contains relatively little that is not explicitly stated in Scripture itself. He certainly was aware of many interpretive traditions, which, for one reason or another, he chose not to include in his book. This conservatism notwithstanding, the book does contain a number of interpretations from a relatively early stage of development.

Dead Sea Scrolls: This is the name popularly used for a group of manuscripts found in the general area of Khirbet Qumran, a site along the shores of the Dead Sea, starting in 1947. Justly described as the greatest manuscript find in history, this collection of biblical manuscripts and other writings seems to have belonged to a group of ascetic Jews who retreated to this desert locale perhaps in the second century B.C.E. and who continued to exist there until 68 C.E. The group may be identified with the Essenes, a religious sect described by Philo of Alexandria, Pliny the Elder, and Josephus; these Essenes may in turn be the same sect as the "Boethusians" known from rabbinic literature.

The Dead Sea Scrolls have provided a wealth of information about the history and development of the biblical text itself, about first-century Judaism and the roots of Christianity, and about biblical interpretation as it existed just before and after the start of the common era. The Dead Sea Scrolls texts cited in this book include the *Genesis Apocryphon,* the *Community Rule (Serekh Hayyaḥad),* the *Damascus Document,* the *Temple Scroll,* a *Genesis Pesher* (4Q252), the *Halakhic Letter* (4Q394-399), and others.

Wisdom of Solomon: This book was written in Greek, probably late in the first century B.C.E. or early in the first century C.E. by a Greek-speaking Jew from, most likely, Alexandria. The book presents itself as the wise writings of the biblical king Solomon; it contains a lengthy praise of, and exhortation to follow, the path of wisdom. As already mentioned, it also summarizes a good bit of Scripture in brief, gnomic sentences that reflect many of the interpretive traditions then current. The author may have inhabited Egypt, but he was well versed in interpretive traditions otherwise known to us in Hebrew or Aramaic, traditions that seem to stem, in other words, from the Jewish homeland.

The Wisdom of Solomon, or Book of Wisdom, was part of the Greek Bible of early Christianity and has remained, along with Ben Sira, Judith, and other books, as part of the Old Testament in many churches (although these books are classified by some as biblical Apocrypha or "Deutero-canonical" works).

Writings of Philo of Alexandria: Philo was another Greek-speaking Jew; he lived in Alexandria from sometime before the start of the common era to around 40 C.E. He is the author of a multivolume series of commentaries on the Pentateuch. Philo inherited an already existing tradition of interpreting the Bible allegorically, a tradition that appears to have flourished in Alexandria. Philo championed this approach; for him, although biblical stories recounted historical events, they likewise had an "under-meaning" *(huponoia)* by which Abraham, Jacob, and other biblical figures were understood to represent abstractions or spiritual realities whose truth applied to all times and places. Philo explained many biblical texts in keeping with then-current Greek philosophical ideas.

Philo's allegorical explanations of Scripture were known to (for example)

Josephus and perhaps as well to some rabbinic exegetes; his commentary may even have found a brief echo in the rabbinic work *Genesis Rabba*.[27] Apart from that, however, his works played almost no role in the later history of Jewish biblical interpretation.[28] They were, however, extraordinarily important to Alexandrine Christianity and, through the writings of Clement of Alexandria, Eusebius, and other Christian scholars, gained a place for his ideas and methods in much Christian biblical interpretation.[29]

New Testament: The varied writings that make up the New Testament were not conceived principally as an exposition of Scripture; nevertheless, in numerous places these texts set forth interpretations of Hebrew Scripture that were to prove (or already had proven) critical to the new church. Moreover, New Testament texts everywhere bear witness to exegetical traditions current among Jews in the first century C.E. or earlier and, as well, show just how important was the interpretation of Scripture within the early Christian movement. In addition to the expositions of Scripture found in Paul's letters and the frequent references to the Hebrew Bible scattered throughout the four Gospels, particularly significant for the present study is Stephen's speech in Acts 7 and the Letter to the Hebrews.

Incidentally, the New Testament is only part of the library of early Christians relevant to a consideration of ancient biblical interpretation; along with them, the writings of the Apostolic Fathers (particularly *1 Clement,* the *Didache,* and the *Letter of Barnabas*), Justin Martyr, Origen, Eusebius of Caesarea, Ephraem Syrus, Aphrahat, and various later writers supply much of the material cited in the present study.

[*Flavius*] *Josephus:* Josephus was a Jewish writer who lived from c. 37 C.E. to c. 100 C.E. Born of a priestly family in Jerusalem, he was, by his own account, a gifted student who acquired a broad exposure to the different Jewish schools of thought existent in his own time. He served as a general in

---

27. See on this Runia, *Philo in Early Christian Literature,* 74–78.

28. Winston, "Philo's *Nachleben.*"

29. A lively debate continues over the extent of Philo's acquaintance with biblical interpretation as it existed among his Jewish contemporaries in Judaea. See (inter alia): Siegfried, *Philo von Alexandria als Ausleger;* Bousset, *Judischchristlicher Schulbetrieb in Alexandria und Rom;* Heinemann, *Philons griechische und jüdische Bildung;* idem, *Altjüdische Allegoristik;* Ginzberg, *Legends of the Jews,* 5:viii–ix; Stein, *Philo und der Midrasch;* Wolfson, *Philo;* Belkin, *Philo and the Oral Law;* idem, *Philo's Midrash;* Sandmel, *Philo's Place in Judaism;* idem, "Parallelomania"; Nikiprowetzky, *Le Commentaire de l'Ecriture;* Bamberger, "Philo and the Aggadah"; Rokeach, "Philo of Alexandria, Midrash, and Ancient Halakhah"; Grabbe, "Philo and Aggada." Even the last author, highly skeptical of certain others' claims, is prepared to concede that Philo knew "a modest amount" of aggadic traditions from elsewhere. My own feelings on this question are not given to easy summary, but in the end they are somewhat analogous to Kafka's words to the Jews of Prague: "You know more Yiddish than you think." (On the last, see Brod, *Franz Kafka,* 113.)

the great Jewish revolt against the Romans but was defeated and taken prisoner. (Josephus recounts that he prophesied that the Roman commander, Vespasian, would be made emperor; Vespasian spared Josephus' life and when, two years later, the prophecy came true, freed him.) After the war Josephus moved to Rome and composed, among other books, his multivolume *Jewish Antiquities*. This work, which purports to set forth the history of the Jews, begins by retelling much of the Hebrew Bible. Josephus' account is, as we have briefly seen, an amalgam of the biblical text itself and numerous interpretive traditions that accompanied it. This book is thus a valuable source of information about how Jews interpreted Scripture in the first century C.E.

Targums: Targum is a general name for a translation of the Hebrew Bible, or parts thereof, into Aramaic, a Semitic language related to Hebrew and spoken widely throughout the ancient Near East from the eighth century B.C.E. onward. Targums are not only interpretations in the sense already mentioned with regard to the Septuagint; some of them, notably *Targum Neophyti*, the *Fragment Targum*, and *Targum Pseudo-Jonathan* (all targums of the Pentateuch), contain frequent exegetical expansions of the biblical text, from a few words to entire paragraphs, not found in the original.

It is difficult to date targums with any certainty. *Targum Neophyti*, frequently cited on the following pages, may go back to the early second century C.E. (or perhaps slightly earlier); it is replete with ancient exegetical traditions. *Targum Onqelos* belongs to roughly the same period; while it sticks more closely to the actual text of the Pentateuch, it nevertheless supplies valuable insights into early biblical interpretation.

Composition and Aims of This Book

These brief sketches may give the uninitiated reader some idea of the sources used in this book, and with them this brief survey of the world of ancient interpreters is complete. Before, however, proceeding to the body of this book, I should perhaps add a final word about my intentions in compiling it, as well as some account of how I hope it may be used.

I did not get far into the present work before I began to worry about its eventual size. There was so much potential material that any one of its twenty-six chapters might in itself be turned into a book-length study. Indeed, some of the overall topics of various chapters—and even, in a few cases, a single exegetical motif therein—had already been the subject of someone else's whole book or monograph. Moreover, I soon began to amass a great deal of material which was altogether new and which, I felt, for that reason alone deserved to be published. All this would mean a book of considerable size—

without even counting the space to be taken up by scholarly footnotes and references to the research of others. Not only might such a volume end up being rather large and costly, but it would probably prove to be a difficult one for the nonspecialist to read and use: the more motifs I covered, the more the average reader was likely to get lost among them, unable to distinguish important, widespread interpretations from interesting but less crucial ones. What to do?

From an early stage, I began to think in terms of two different editions of the book. One would seek to present only the most important, most influential motifs—the sorts of things that a broad spectrum of Jews and Christians in the period covered would have heard or read about various biblical stories and figures. (These same motifs, not coincidentally, were by and large the ones which were transmitted to subsequent generations and which continued to shape people's ideas about the Bible for centuries and centuries afterward.) To keep this first edition reasonably small and reasonably simple, I also decided to avoid wherever possible technical discussions of Hebrew or Aramaic, and to eliminate almost all references to other works of scholarship (apart from the few references included in the present introductory chapter), saving these—along with more detailed discussion of some of the complications involved in the motifs set forth here, and the presentation of quite a few minor motifs not found here at all—for the larger, more technical edition I was preparing simultaneously.[30]

Even this larger edition has required a lot of pruning and judicious selection in order to be kept to publishable size. Such being the case, I should perhaps state from the beginning what this book, in either edition, is *not*. It is not a presentation of the whole of ancient biblical interpretation of the Pentateuch—far from it! Even the larger, annotated version falls considerably short of that goal. Within the time frame established for this book, the available material far exceeded what could be included. This book therefore represents a *selection* of some motifs from among many, and a *further selection* of some attestations of a given motif from among many. In deciding what material to include, I have been guided by three or four different principles.

In general, I have tried to favor the oldest attested motifs within the designated period. In fact, I have tried wherever possible to allow the oldest texts to determine my agenda. That is, I began by surveying the most ancient sources available—*1 Enoch, Jubilees,* the Septuagint, Ben Sira, and so forth—to

---

30. This plan of two separate editions has indeed gone forward: publication of the present volume is to be followed by that of a longer version, designed for specialists in the field, containing additional motifs and extensive notes discussing some of the more technical aspects of the subjects covered.

find out which interpretive motifs are attested there; then I sought to trace the presence of the same motifs in later sources, while at the same time surveying these later sources for new motifs or new wrinkles in the older ones.

This goal of favoring the oldest may seem to run counter to another aspect of the book: here and there I have also tried to include attestations of some of the motifs selected found in sources at the end of, or even well beyond, my stated cutoff time of the late first or early second century. That is, while I tried to choose the motifs themselves on the basis of the earliest sources, I also sought to show in some cases how these same motifs survived into later Judaism and Christianity, specifically, into rabbinic and patristic writings. Of course, not all motifs did survive, and their survival or nonsurvival was not a factor in my selection of motifs. But where I was aware of a later attestation or echo of an ancient motif in a rabbinic or patristic text, I tried to include it.

In adducing these later, rabbinic or patristic, attestations of earlier traditions, I have made no effort to be inclusive, and even where I have mentioned such later parallels I have usually contented myself with a single reference from either group. These references are generally taken from the most popular or influential parts of those literatures—books like *Genesis Rabba* or the Babylonian Talmud, on the one hand, or references from Augustine or Jerome or (in the Eastern Church) Ephraem, on the other. I have also from time to time cited from two other late sources, the *Cave of Treasures* and the Slavonic *Paleya*, since these works often embody exegesis of a far earlier period and sometimes preserve what appear to be unique, ancient traditions.

In addition to all the above, one final principle has operated in my selection of materials. That principle is what might be called, broadly, "interest." All other things being equal, I have tried to include in this selection some of the most interesting motifs, or interestingly stated attestations of a motif, or some of the material that was to prove particularly influential in later times. I admit that this quality of interest is hard to define—I will not define it beyond what was just said—but I must in candor make mention of it in any explanation of how I went about including what I included.

Another disclaimer: This book is not about *influences*. As mentioned above, I have not set myself the job of tracing relations among the various sources listed or speculating about which text may or may not have been known to which authors. Of course, such things can sometimes be determined with certainty, and even when they cannot, an educated guess can sometimes be offered. But that is decidedly not the purpose of the present volume. What I wish to do here is to show how the Bible was interpreted in ancient times and what conclusions individual interpreters drew about the meaning of individual texts. The fact that two sources present the same or similar interpretations may in some cases be quite coincidental; in others it may represent a direct borrowing from source A on the part of source B; in others, a common source was shared by A and B; and in yet others, A's and B's conclusions, although arrived at quite independently, reflect not so much a coincidental resemblance as the fact that both interpreters had been "programmed" with the same set of instructions about *how* to go about interpreting—including, prominently, the four assumptions listed earlier—and moreover had approached the text in question equipped with a common stock of other interpretations that served as models of proper procedure.

It is sometimes possible to decide among these various alternatives, but that is not the purpose of this book: I have attempted simply to assemble the things that ancient interpreters said about different verses or episodes and, to the extent possible, try to reconstruct the exegetical thinking that stands behind their assertions.[31] However, I would be less than candid if I failed to say that the material collected on the following pages is such as to persuade me, at least, that there indeed was a great common store of interpretations in antiquity, one that was widely known to interpreters and their audiences.

Having said all that this book does not do, let me now state briefly what it does seek to provide. The main purpose of this book is to present a detailed look at how the Bible was interpreted in the centuries just before and after the start of the common era—to show what the Bible essentially *was* in that period—and to do this by seeking to isolate and identify the principal interpretive traditions of, specifically, the Pentateuch as they are preserved in various ancient writings outside the Hebrew Bible itself. To be sure, any such reconstruction is bound to provide a somewhat distorted and only approximate picture. Community X or Group Y, or individual interpreters, certainly would have differed with this reconstruction on particular points: however much individual interpretations circulated and were held in common by different people, there was no single, universally accepted set of interpretations. But in choosing and organizing the material as I have, I hope that I have been able to provide an overall feeling for what Scripture as a whole meant for most Jews and Christians in the period covered, as well as to present in detail some of the most significant and widespread bits of interpretation known from that period.

I perhaps should make explicit here what some readers will have already

---

31. Despite this disclaimer, I fear that some may fail to understand this book's format (or even to read this introductory chapter) and consequently find me guilty of the sin made famous by Sandmel, "Parallelomania." It may therefore be appropriate here to repeat his definition: "We might for our purposes define parallelomania as that extravagance among scholars which first overdoes the supposed similarity in passages and then proceeds to describe source and derivation *as if implying a literary connection* flowing in an inevitable or predetermined direction" (p. 1, emphasis added). It is precisely that possible literary connection that I have not addressed in this book.

understood, namely, my reason for focusing on the particular three centuries or so that I have. It was in these three centuries that Israel's ancient library of sacred texts were becoming *the* Bible. From the standpoint of scriptural interpretation, then, there could hardly have been a more crucial time than this one, and the overall interpretive methods, as well as a great many individual interpretations, that were developed in this period did eventually become "canonized" by Jews and Christians no less than the scriptural texts that they explained. Interpretations of course continued to be developed and elaborated in later times; yet it is certainly no exaggeration to say that the main lines of approach, as well as an enormous body of specific motifs, continued to be transmitted by Jews and Christians from this crucial period on through the Renaissance and beyond. In short, the period covered is the formative period for the interpretation of Scripture.

A second purpose, no less important than the first, is to show in detail the *how* of ancient biblical interpretation. As we have already glimpsed briefly, Scripture itself was the formal starting point for ancient biblical interpretation: the motifs that ancient interpreters created and transmitted addressed specific points in the text. All too often in the past this (broadly speaking) exegetical function has been neglected; to cite but the most illustrious example, Louis Ginzberg's *Legends of the Jews* programmatically submerged the exegetical aspect of these motifs in order to turn them into a kind of folk literature, the *legends* of the Jews. But they are not legends, they are ways of explaining the biblical text.

Of course, the legends approach is not wrong in one respect: originally exegetical creations eventually did become *legendized.* Time and again in the history of the motifs' transmission, their particular connection to the biblical text came to be forgotten. The very genre of the Rewritten Bible encouraged this: one had to know the text and its problems virtually by heart in order to hear their solution in the rewriting. Doubtless many listeners and readers did, but eventually, the precise connection between text and motif sometimes came to be lost. Indeed, even in *pesharim,* commentaries, *quaestiones,* and the like—genres, that is, in which the biblical verse itself is first cited and then commented upon—one often finds that the original biblical site out of which a given motif arose has been lost and the motif attached to another verse.[32] Once they became separated from their original biblical sites, these exegetical motifs did in effect become something like legends, free-floating additions to biblical stories that were asserted to be true even though their textual justification had been lost. For just that reason, trying to figure out the relationship

---

32. Again, I have presented several detailed examples in *In Potiphar's House.*

between an individual motif and the precise verse or word in Scripture upon which it depends is often a difficult, challenging task: a good bit of detective work and mental reconstruction are sometimes necessary. But figuring out this relationship is absolutely crucial, since it is the connection between text and motif that is the key to all ancient biblical interpretation. And so, a second purpose of this book has been to reconstruct, to the extent possible, the thinking that lies behind the ancient interpretive motifs collected herein.

Another purpose of this book—connected with its focus on motifs, as explained above—is to show the traditional nature of ancient biblical interpretation. I have set forth the reasons for which it seemed important to focus on motifs rather than on the individual documents in which these motifs are found, or on those documents' authors as individual shapers of the traditions. For the same reasons, I hope that by setting out clearly the way in which motifs are passed on and elaborated from generation to generation, the altogether traditional nature of ancient biblical interpretation will be apparent.

It might be said of Jews and Christians—in line with the well-known witticism about the English and the Americans—that they are divided by a common Scripture. This is certainly true, and in trying to restore the Bible As It Was and so trace interpretive elements common to both religions, I am in no way attempting to paper over the great differences that separate these two faiths, including, prominently, many matters of scriptural interpretation. Yet I must confess that a fourth purpose I have had constantly in mind in preparing the present volume is frankly ecumenical. What I wish to show is that, the history of Jewish-Christian polemics aside (and along with it the sad story of church-supported anti-Semitism), rabbinic Judaism and Christianity emerged out of a common mentality including, prominently, a common set of beliefs about the Bible. In other words, it is not only Scripture itself, the written word, that Jews and Christians share. Both groups received, along with the written texts that make up the Hebrew Bible, the same set of attitudes about how the Bible ought to be read and explained, what it was meant for and how it was to be used. Moreover (as any reader of this book will see), both carried forward a substantial body of common explanations of individual words, verses, incidents, stories, songs, prayers, laws, and prophecies in Scripture. Of course, none of this is to suggest that the differences between Judaism and Christianity are somehow minor—they are not—nor is it my intention in pointing out communalities to encourage the wrongheaded efforts of those who, even as these lines are being written, have announced their renewed intention to bring about the "conversion of the Jews" by creating some strange hybrid of Christian teaching and traditional Jewish practices. Rather, it is simply my hope that in the present age, when many thoughtful Jews and

Christians are trying to turn a dark page of history and seek out what, despite their distinctness, nonetheless unites them, this book may make some small contribution to an awareness of common beginnings.

How Each Chapter Is Organized

Ancient interpretations are best broken down into individual interpretive motifs. In the chapters that follow I have therefore presented the material in this fashion, motif by motif. (Sometimes I have grouped together under a single rubric two or more related motifs that are nonetheless distinct; in so doing I have sacrificed a certain technical accuracy to my desire to present things in as straightforward and readable a fashion as possible.)[33] To each motif or group of related motifs I have given a brief title: "The Punishment Was Mortality," "The Garden in Heaven," "Abraham Saved from Fire." The titles appear as subheadings in the body of the chapter.[34]

In presenting each motif, I first seek to reconstruct why and how the motif may have developed; I then illustrate its existence with brief excerpts from ancient writings. I have kept these excerpts short, since all that I wish to show is that a particular way of understanding the biblical text is attested in ancient documents X, Y, and Z. I have generally stayed away from questions like "Did Y's author learn this interpretation from reading X?" or "Did the authors of documents Y and Z arrive at this interpretation independently, or did they have some common source?" As noted earlier, these are interesting, even fascinating questions, and answers to them sometimes can be put forward with reasonable certainty. In some cases, we can state unequivocally that Z's author read the book X; in other cases, we can just as unequivocally state that Z's author would have sooner died than open up X or be thought to have used it. In quite a few cases, it is reasonable to assume that the authors of X and Y drew on an earlier interpretive tradition known to both; in a few instances, a resemblance between X and Y seems utterly coincidental. As fascinating as this subject may be, however, it is somewhat beside the point here: my main goal is to investigate how these traditions arose and came to be widespread, not to reconstruct the specific steps involved in that transmission.

I have generally tried to present attestations of a particular motif in

---

33. In such cases I have generally tried to distinguish the individual subgroups by inserting some commentary—sometimes only the word "similarly"—between citations.

34. Sometimes I have grouped together quite different motifs whose only common element is that they all address the same difficulty within the biblical text. In such cases, I have phrased the title of the section as a question: "Why Did Joseph Put It Off?" "Whose Bad Idea?" "Which Ten Commandments?"

(rough) chronological order. However, when a later source seems to contain an earlier or more complete form of a motif, I do sometimes put the later source first. Likewise, I sometimes violate chronological order when a later source sets forth a particular motif more clearly or understandably than earlier sources. Since sources cited are all described and dated (to the extent possible) in the Terms and Sources section at the back of the book, I trust that this arrangement will not prove to be a source of confusion.

To make perfectly clear the transformative effect of traditional interpretation upon the biblical text, I decided to begin and end the body of each chapter with a brief summary, in italics. The opening italicized summary attempts to restate what an ordinary reader, knowing nothing but the words of the Bible itself, might think about the meaning of the biblical story or section in question. Then, at the end of the chapter—having surveyed some of the most important traditions of ancient interpreters—I summarize the story or section once again, this time with the ancient traditions included. The difference is of course striking: new details, sometimes whole new incidents, and a great deal of new "spin" now accompany the bare narrative. Although these summaries are necessarily somewhat simplified, comparing the one at the beginning of the chapter with the one at the end illustrates vividly how ancient traditions of interpretation changed utterly the meaning of the Bible.

2

The Creation of the World

(GENESIS 1:1–2:3)

*God and someone else
(top) divide light from darkness, then (bottom)
create the sun, the moon, and the stars.*

The Creation of the World

(GENESIS 1:1–2:3)

❖　❖　❖

The Bible begins with an account of God's creation of the world in six days: on the first day, light was created and separated from darkness; on the following days the sky and the earth were made, then plant life, heavenly lights, fish and reptiles, the animals and, lastly, humankind. Once the work was completed, God rested on the seventh day—the first Sabbath in the world.

THE BIBLE opens with the words "In the beginning God created the heavens and the earth." But did this mean the *very* beginning? Many interpreters believed that it did not. They arrived at the conclusion that God's work must have begun even before He created heaven and earth. One reason for this belief was the Bible's discussion of the creation in a few places other than Genesis; in one of these, a passage from the book of Proverbs, Wisdom (here personified as a female figure) says the following:

> The Lord made me the **beginning** of his work, the first of his acts of old.
> Ages ago I was formed, before the establishment of the earth . . .
> When He made the heavens, I was already there, when he drew a
> circle on the face of the deep. — Prov. 8:22–27

These words clearly state that God had created wisdom even before the heavens and the earth were made. (The idea that "wisdom"—that is, the great plan underlying all of reality—was of divine origin was in any case widespread in the ancient world.)[1] There was thus every reason to believe that the creation of wisdom had come at the very beginning of things; this fact was plainly stated in the book of Proverbs.

Wisdom Came First

And so, when ancient interpreters spoke about God's creation of the world, many mentioned specifically that wisdom existed even before the creation itself:

1. See Chapter 1.

One of our ancestors, Solomon [the reputed author of the biblical book of Proverbs], said more clearly and better that wisdom existed before heaven and earth, which agrees with what has been said [by Greek philosophers].

—Aristobulus, Fragment 5 (cited in Eusebius, *Praeparatio Evangelica* 13.12.11)

[Wisdom says:] From eternity, in the beginning, He created me.

—Sir. 24:9

Wisdom is older than the creation . . . of the whole universe.

—Philo, *On the Virtues* 62

Two thousand years before the world was created, [God] created the Torah [that is, divine wisdom].   — *Targum Neophyti* Gen. 3:24

But if Scripture said that wisdom was created before all things, was this not because wisdom actually was to play some role in the creation of the rest of world? Such an idea made good sense, and it was also suggested elsewhere in Scripture:

But the Lord God is true . . . who made the earth with His power, established the world with His **wisdom**, and by His understanding stretched out the heavens.   —Jer. 10:10, 12

Oh Lord, how great are your works, with wisdom You have made them all.

—Ps. 104:24

The Lord by wisdom founded the earth, establishing the heavens with understanding.

—Prov. 3:19

Many ancient interpreters therefore felt justified in asserting that wisdom was "present at the creation" or even had some part in creating the rest of the world:

With you [O God] is wisdom, who knows your works and was **present** when you made the world, and who understands what is pleasing in your sight, and what is right according to your commandments.

—Wisd. 9:9

And who is to be considered the daughter of God but Wisdom, who is the firstborn mother of all things.   —Philo, *Questions in Genesis* 4:97

Blessed is He who created the earth with his power, who established the world with His wisdom.

— (11QPs^a) *Hymn to the Creator*

God looked into the Torah [that is, the corpus of divine wisdom] and created the world. — *Genesis Rabba* 1:1

For reasons to be seen presently, wisdom was associated in particular with the creation of humanity on the sixth day:

Having given order by your Wisdom, You created, saying, "Let us make man according our image and likeness."

— Hellenistic Synagogal Prayer, *Apostolic Constitutions* 7.34.6

And on the sixth day I commanded my wisdom to create man.

— *2 Enoch* 30:8

The "Beginning" Did It

But if wisdom was the first thing that God had created, and if God had in fact used it to create the rest of the world, then biblical interpreters had to wonder: why did the book of Genesis leave out this crucial detail? Why didn't the first verse in the Bible read: "In the beginning God created *wisdom*, and afterwards, the heavens and the earth"?

In looking for an answer, interpreters noticed a striking coincidence. In Prov. 8:22, wisdom says, "The Lord made me the *beginning* of his work," while the Genesis account opens, "In the *beginning* God created the heavens and the earth." Perhaps this was not just a coincidence. Perhaps the word "beginning" in the Genesis verse was in fact a subtle hint, an allusion, to wisdom. For, if wisdom is called the beginning of God's work in Proverbs, then (one might argue) the word "beginning" itself might be used elsewhere in the Bible as a kind of nickname for wisdom, a shorthand reference to the very first thing that God created. If so, then the first verse of Genesis could now be understood as meaning not "At the *start* God created the heavens and the earth" but "In [or "with"] *wisdom* God created the heavens and the earth." This is precisely how that verse was translated in two ancient translations of the Bible:

With wisdom did God create and perfect the heavens and the earth.

— *Fragment Targum* Gen. 1:1

In the beginning with wisdom did God create . . .[2]

— Targum Neophyti Gen. 1:1

Similarly:

> By using different names for it, Moses indicates that the exalted, heavenly wisdom has many names: he calls it "**beginning**," "image," and "appearance of God."   —Philo, Allegorical Interpretations 1:43

And so, interpreters came to the conclusion that not only was wisdom the first thing God created, but the phrase "In the beginning" in Gen. 1:1 was intended to imply that it was *by means of,* or with the help of, wisdom that God had created the world.

Now of course a modern reader might well object to this kind of interpretation. Was not the fact that the word "beginning" was used in both Gen. 1:1 and Prov. 8:22 really just a coincidence? And doesn't "In the beginning" in Gen. 1:1 mean just that, *at the start of* the creation of the world?

There is no single answer to this type of question, which comes up again and again with ancient biblical interpretation. It often happens that interpreters pass up what seems to us to be the more likely sense of a text in favor of some rather improbable meaning. Sometimes they do so because they *want* to read the text in that fashion—there is some doctrine or idea of their own (or some idea that they have inherited from elsewhere, from ancient Near Eastern tradition or Greek philosophy or some other source) for which they would like to find support in the Bible. Sometimes they depart from the straightforward meaning because they feel they *have to:* the text as is appears to them illogical or seems to contradict something found elsewhere in the Bible. And sometimes, they take an apparent pleasure in willful, even playful, distortion—as if the interpreter were saying: "Look, read the text my way and you will see that this or that surprising conclusion can be derived from it."

But behind any of these sorts of interpretations is the fundamental conviction that the Bible's precise wording is both utterly intentional—that is, nothing in the Bible is said by chance or said in vain—and infinitely significant.[3] This meant that almost every aspect of the biblical text *ought* to be looked into, and that almost any sort of interpretive subtlety was justified in explaining it. The slightest unusual feature in its manner of expression—even a coincidence like the appearance of the word "beginning" in both Gen. 1:1 and

---

2. This is an example of a "double translation," in which the original word is translated twice (here, both "in the beginning" and "with wisdom") to fit two different understandings of the text.

3. This fundamental assumption of ancient interpreters is treated at great length above, in Chapter 1.

Prov. 8:22—could not be dismissed as mere accident. Thus, ancient interpreters had a large task before them, but they also had enormous freedom as interpreters. For, once it was understood that Scripture required deep investigation in order for its full sense to be revealed, the groundwork was laid for interpretations that sometimes departed drastically from what the text seemed to be saying. In this way, it became possible to conclude that by the word "beginning" in Gen. 1:1 the Bible had really meant "wisdom."

A Special Light

God says on the first day, "Let there be light" (Gen. 1:3). But the light created on the first day could not have been sunlight or the light of the moon or stars, since these heavenly bodies were not created until the fourth day. Many ancient writers therefore said that it was a special light that enabled God to see as He created the world:

> Then You commanded that a ray of light be brought forth from your treasuries, so that your works might then appear.   — 4 Ezra 6:40

If so, then perhaps it was a light unlike any other, one that illuminated all of creation at once:

> . . . the first [day], the one in which the light was born by which **all things** are seen together.
> — Aristobulus, Fragment 3 (cited in Eusebius, *Praeparatio Evangelica* 13.12.9)

> God commanded that there should be light. And when this had come about, He considered **all of matter.**   — Josephus, *Jewish Antiquities* 1:27

> [After summoning light, God says:] And I was in the midst of the light. And light out of light is carried thus. And the great age came out, and it revealed **all the creation** which I had thought up to create. And I saw that it was good.   — 2 Enoch (J) 25:3

> God said: Let there be light to illuminate the world, and at once there was light.   — *Targum Pseudo-Jonathan* Gen. 1:3

> Said R. Eli'ezer: With the light that God created on the first day one could see from one end of the world to the other.   — b. Ḥagigah 12a

Another possibility was that the light that was later to come from heavenly bodies was created, or conceived, on the first day, even though the heavenly bodies themselves were not created until the fourth:

> And [He created] the abysses and darkness—both evening and night—and light—both dawn and daylight—which He prepared in the knowledge of His heart.
>
> — *Jubilees* 2:2

> It is said that from this [primal] light, [now] diffused, and from fire—both of which were created on the first day—the sun was fashioned, which was made in the firmament, and likewise the moon and the stars, it is said, were made from that same first light.[4]
>
> — Ephraem, *Commentary on Genesis* 9:2

Similarly:

> Now that invisible light, perceptible only by mind, was created as an image of the God's Word [Logos], who made its creation known. It was a light higher than the stars, the **source** of the starlight that can be seen.
>
> — Philo, *On the Creation* 31 (also 55)

The Angels Were Also Created

The creation account in Genesis purports to tell how everything in the universe came to be. But this account apparently omits a number of details (besides the creation of wisdom). For example, where were the angels? Although all sorts of other biblical texts (and texts from outside the Bible) make mention of angels, nothing is said here about when they were first created.

The Bible contained at least one indication for ancient interpreters that the angels had in fact been created *sometime* during the first six days. For, after the sixth day is completed, the Bible says,

> Thus, the heavens and the earth were finished, and all their **hosts**.
>
> — Gen. 2:1

The phrase "*hosts* of heaven" is frequently used in the Bible for angels (see, for example, 1 Kings 22:19). This verse thus seemed to imply that the creation of these "hosts of heaven" had been *finished* by (at least) the end of the sixth day. What is more, the book of Psalms mentioned the angels along with other things created by God in the beginning:

> [God,] who has stretched out the heavens like a curtain, roofed
>   His upper chambers with the waters,

---

4. Ephraem's overall view is that this first day's primal light was created to serve until the sun and other luminaries could be made and take over.

who has made clouds His chariot and walks about on the wind's
    outskirts,
who makes the winds His **angels** and flaming fire His servants,
He established the earth on its foundations, so that it shall
    never be displaced.

                     — Ps. 104:2–5

In mentioning the angels in the context of the creation of the heavens, waters, and earth, this psalm seemed to be saying that God had created the angels at the same time as these other things. As a result of such passages (see also Job 38:7), a number of ancient interpreters included the angels among the things that God had created during the first six days—even though the book of Genesis made no mention of them.

When during the six days were the angels created? With no clear hints from the text, there was no unanimity among ancient interpreters. It seemed likely, however, that their creation preceded that of mankind and the other creatures created at the end of the six days:

When God created his created ones [that is, the angels][5] in the
    beginning, their portions He allotted to them:
He established [their] activities for all time, and their dominions
    forever:
So that they not hunger nor grow weary, nor cease from their
    labors, And so that one not interfere with another, and never
    might they rebel.
Afterward the Lord looked down at the earth and He filled it with
    His stores;
He covered its face with the breath of all life, and to it they shall
    return.

                     — Sir. 16:26–30

Dividing light from darkness, he established the dawning in His
    mind's decision;
When all His **angels** saw [it] they exulted, for He showed them what
    they had not previously known.

---

5. The Hebrew word *maʿăsim* ("created ones") frequently refers to people rather than things: see Pss. 8:7, 103:22, 104:24; Prov. 31:31; Job 14:15, etc. It seems likely that the "created ones" mentioned here are the angels in heaven. Ben Sira's wording paraphrases Deut. 32:8, which was understood to refer to angels being allotted their "portions"; what is more, the idea that these celestial creatures never need food or rest and do not interfere or overlap with one another in their heavenly missions—all these are elsewhere frequently asserted to be true of angels. A similar usage appears in *Odes of Solomon* 16:13.

He crowned the hills with crops, abundant food for all the
    living.

                   — (11QPsᵃ) *Hymn to the Creator*

These are the holy angels, who were created first . . .

                   —*Shepherd of Hermas* Vision 4:1

Some ancient interpreters pointed specifically to the first day as the time
of the angels' creation. Perhaps they did so because of the mention of the
"spirit of God" in Gen. 1:2, since "spirit" was one term commonly understood
to refer to angels:

For on the first day He created the heavens which are above and the
earth and waters and all the spirits which serve before Him—the
angels of the presence, and the angels of holiness, and the angels of the
spirits of fire and the angels of the spirits of the winds, and the angels
of the spirit of the clouds, and of darkness, and of snow and of hail and
of frost, and the angels of the sounds, the thunders and the lightnings,
and the angels of the spirits of cold and of heat, and of winter and of
spring and of autumn and of summer, and of all the spirits of His
creatures which are in the heavens and on the earth.   —*Jubilees* 2:2

When Scripture speaks of the creation of the world, it does not indicate clearly whether, or in what order, the angels were created. But if
they are alluded to at all, it is perhaps in the word "heavens" when it
says, "In the beginning God created the heavens and the earth" [Gen.
1:1] or, more likely, in the word "light" [in the phrase, "Let there be
light," Gen. 1:3].   — Augustine, *City of God* 11:9

In the beginning, on the first day . . . God created heaven and earth, the
angels, and the archangels and thrones and dominions and principali-
ties and authorities[6] and cherubs and seraphs, all the heavenly hosts of
spirits.   — *Cave of Treasures* (W) 1

Other sources saw the second day as the time of the angels' creation (because
that was the day when the "firmament"—deemed to be part of heaven, where
the angels lived—was created):

Then evening came, and morning, and it was the second day. And . . .
[on the second day] I created the ranks of the bodiless armies—ten

6. These are different ranks of angels; this list is apparently based on the New Testament, Col.
1:16; cf. Eph. 1:21, *2 Enoch* 20:1, *Testament of Levi* 3:7, *Book of the Bee* ch. 5.

myriad angels—and their weapons are fiery and their clothes are burning flames. — *2 Enoch* (J) 29:3

And God said to the angels who serve before Him and who had been created on the second day of the Creation . . .
— *Targum Pseudo-Jonathan* Gen. 1:26

[On the second day,] after separating off the waters He created the *er'elim* and angels and *ophanim* and *seraphim* and *ḥashmalim* [different classes of angels] and He blew upon the fire and ignited the seven bonfires of Gehenna. — *Midrash Konen*

On the second day God created the firmament and the angels . . . The angels, who were created on the second day, when they are sent by His word they become winds, but when they serve before Him, they are made of fire, as it is written, "Who makes His messengers the winds, and flaming fire his servants" [Ps. 104:4]. — *Pirqei deR. Eliezer* 4

There were yet other possibilities:

When were the angels created? R. Yoḥanan said: they were created on the second day . . . R. Ḥanina said: they were created on the **fifth** day, as it is said "[on the fifth day God created] birds to fly about above the earth across the firmament of the heavens" [Gen. 1:20], and it says elsewhere [speaking of an angel], "with two wings it would fly about" [Isa. 6:2]. — *Genesis Rabba* 1:3

God and Someone Else

After the heavens and the earth had been created, and the earth stocked with fish and birds and animals, God finally created mankind. But the precise way in which this event is related in the Bible aroused the curiosity of ancient interpreters:

Then God said, "Let **us** make man in our image, after our likeness; and let them have dominion over the fish of the sea, and over the birds of the air, and over the cattle, and over all the earth, and over every creeping thing that creeps on the earth." So God created man in His own image, in the image of God He created them; male and female He created them. — Gen. 1:26–27

Ancient readers were struck by a number of things in this passage, perhaps most of all by the fact that God starts speaking here in the plural, "Let *us* make man . . . *our* image . . . *our* likeness." What did this mean? (The "royal we" is less common in biblical Hebrew than in English, so such an explanation was not necessarily obvious.)

Many ancient interpreters concluded that God was indeed addressing some other being or beings—though they did not necessarily agree on whom:

> O God of my fathers and Lord of mercy, You who have made all things by Your word and by Your wisdom have formed man. —Wisd. 9:1–2

> Thus it was fitting and right that when man was formed, God should assign a share in the work to His lieutenants, as He does with the words "let *us* make men," so that man's right actions might be attributable to God, but his sins to others. For it seemed to be unfitting to God, the ruler of all, that the road to wickedness within the reasonable soul should be of His making, and therefore He delegated the forming of this part to His inferiors. —Philo, *Confusion of Tongues* 179

> And on the sixth day I commanded my wisdom to create man.
> —2 *Enoch* (J) 30:8

> Having given order by your Wisdom, You created, saying, "Let us make man according to our image and likeness."
> —Hellenistic Synagogal Prayer, *Apostolic Constitutions* 7.34.6

> R. Joshua b. Levi said: He consulted with the heavens and the earth . . . R. Ḥanina said: . . . When God set out to create the first human, He consulted with the ministering angels. He said to them: "Let **us** make man." —*Genesis Rabba* 8:3–4

Among Christians, the plural "Let *us*" suggested another interpretation:

> And furthermore, my brothers: . . . He is lord of the whole world, to whom God said at the creation of the world, "Let us make man according to our image and likeness." —*Letter of Barnabas* 5:5 (also 6:12)

> The Father commanded with His voice; it was the Son who carried out the work.
> —Ephraem, *Hymns of Faith* 6:13 (also *Commentary on Genesis* 1:28, etc.)

Other interpreters vigorously denied the idea that the phrase implied more than one Creator:

> When all His angels saw [it] they exulted, for He showed them what **they had not previously known.** —(11QPsª) *Hymn to the Creator*

O sovereign Lord, did you not speak at the beginning when You created earth—which You did **without help**—and commanded the dust[7] and it gave you Adam.   — 4 Ezra 3:4

These [the world and its contents] God created not with hands, not with toil, not with assistants, of whom He had no need; He willed it, and so they were made in all their beauty.

— Josephus, *Against Apion* 2:192

R. Samuel b. Naḥman said in the name of R. Yonatan: When Moses was writing down the Torah, he would write down what was created on each day [in the creation account]. When he got to the verse, "And God said, 'Let *us* make man . . .'" he said, "Master of the Universe! Why should you give support to the heretics?" He answered: "Let anyone who wishes to go astray go astray!"   — *Genesis Rabba* 8:8

Completed on Friday

The traditional Hebrew text at the end of the creation narrative contains a slight ambiguity:

And God **ended** on the seventh day His work which He had done, and God rested on the seventh day from all His work which He had done.
— Gen. 2:1

The word "ended" here is somewhat enigmatic. Does it mean "finished off," in which case, presumably, at least *some* work was done on the seventh day? Or does it mean "ceased," in which case the last bit of work was presumably done before the seventh day actually started? One would certainly think that the latter was the case, but the wording left room for misunderstanding.

Some ancient versions and retellings—perhaps in an attempt to clarify things, or perhaps reflecting a different form of the Hebrew text—specify that God had actually finished His work on the sixth day:

And on the sixth day God finished His works which He had done. And God ceased [or "rested"] on the seventh day from all of His works which He had done.
— Septuagint, Vetus Latina, Samaritan Pentateuch, and Peshitta, Gen. 2:1

7. Here God's words "Let *us* make man" are deemed to have been spoken to the dust of the earth from which the first human was made (Gen. 2:7).

And He finished all His work on the sixth day—everything in heaven and on the earth, and in the seas and in the depths, in the light and in the darkness, and in every place. And He gave us a great sign, the Sabbath day, so that we should perform work for six days, but keep the Sabbath on the seventh day from all work.   —*Jubilees* 2:16–17

Now, when the whole world had been brought to completion in accordance with the properties of **six**, a perfect number, the Father invested with dignity the seventh day which comes next, extolling it and pronouncing it holy.   —Philo, *On the Creation* 89

❖   ❖   ❖

In short: Early interpreters transformed the opening chapter of Genesis in several significant respects. The very first thing that God had created was wisdom. When He said "Let there be light" God was referring to a special light unknown to human eyes. God created the angels, either on the first, the second, or the fifth day. God's words in Gen. 1:26, "Let us make man," were understood to mean that He had received aid or advice in creating man. Finally, some translations and retellings of the creation story differed from the traditional Hebrew wording of Gen. 2:1 by making it clear that the creation was entirely finished by the end of the sixth day.

3

Adam and Eve

(GENESIS 2:4–3:24)

*God created humanity with the help of angels, but then the humans
went astray: was it the woman's fault?*

Adam and Eve

(GENESIS 2:4–3:24)

❖   ❖   ❖

Adam and Eve were the first human beings created by God. They were put in the Garden of Eden and told that they could eat any of the fruit in the garden except that of the "tree of the knowledge of good and evil." A certain serpent in the garden tempted Eve to disobey and she did, eating the forbidden fruit and giving it to Adam to eat. As a result, Adam and Eve were punished and expelled from the garden forever: henceforth, he was to earn his bread by the sweat of his brow, while Eve was condemned to bring forth children in pain.

THE STORY of Adam and Eve and their life in the Garden of Eden fascinated the Bible's earliest interpreters, since it seemed to concern the very nature of the human species. This biblical story was probably written about more than any other. Not coincidentally, readers today are likely to have great difficulty looking at this story "without blinders." For the importance of this episode to the Bible's ancient interpreters has given their interpretations of it a unique staying power. Who nowadays, for example, does not automatically think of the story of Adam and Eve in the Garden of Eden as telling about some fundamental change that took place in the human condition, or what is commonly called the Fall of Man? And who does not think of the "serpent" in the story as the devil, or paradise as the reward of the righteous after death? Yet a careful reading of the Bible itself shows that none of these things is said explicitly by the text—they are all a matter of interpretation.

Death in a Day

No doubt many factors influenced the way ancient interpreters came to understand the Adam and Eve story. But certainly one of the most important was a glaring inconsistency in the story itself. When God first put Adam into the garden, He said to him:

> You may freely eat of every tree in the Garden. But of the tree of the knowledge of good and evil you shall not eat, for **on the day that you eat of it you shall die.** —Gen. 2:16–17

The trouble is that Adam didn't die, at least not right away. After eating the fruit, he went on to live to the age of 930 (according to Gen. 5:5). Eve presumably had an equally impressive lifespan (we are not told exactly when she died). So what did God mean by saying, "for *on the day* that you eat of it you shall die"? Was this just an idle threat?

One way of resolving the situation was to claim that the "day" being referred to here was not an ordinary day. And indeed, the Bible itself provided support for this idea. A verse from the book of Psalms asserts:

> A thousand years in your [God's] sight are **like yesterday**.
>
> —Ps. 90:4

In context, this verse seems to mean that for God, centuries and centuries of past history are no more remote than yesterday; since He is eternal, a thousand years pass as quickly for God as a single day for us. But if so, interpreters reasoned, then perhaps there is an actual unit of time, a "day" of God's, that lasts a thousand years:

> But do not ignore this one fact, beloved, that with the Lord one day is as a thousand years, and a thousand years as one day. —2 Pet. 3:8

> . . . for with Him a "day" signifies a thousand years. And He himself bears witness when he says, "Behold, the day of the Lord will be as a thousand years." —*Letter of Barnabas* 15:4

> One day of God's is a thousand years long, as it is said, "A thousand years are in your sight as yesterday" [Ps. 90:4]. —*Genesis Rabba* 8:2

Here then was a possible solution. If Adam lived to the age of 930, then he actually lived less than a single one of "God's days"—and so, from God's standpoint at least, he did die *on the day* that he ate the fruit:

> Adam died, and all his sons buried him in the land of his creation, and he was the first to be buried in the earth. And he lacked seventy years of one thousand years [that is, he died at the age of 930]; for one thousand years are as one day in the testimony of the heavens [that is, according to Psalm 90], and therefore was it written concerning the tree of knowledge: "On the day that you eat thereof, you shall die."
>
> —*Jubilees* 4:29–30

It was said to Adam that on the day in which he ate of the tree, on that day he would die. And indeed, we know that he did not quite fill up a thousand years. We thus understand the expression "a day of the Lord is a thousand years" [as clarifying] this.

— Justin Martyr, *Dialogue with Trypho* 81:3

He [God] did not specify to Adam if it would be a day of his [own days] or a day of God's, which lasts one thousand years, since "a thousand years in your [God's] sight are like yesterday" [Ps. 90:4].

— *Pesiqta Rabbati, Baḥodesh ha-shebiʿi* 40 (similarly *Genesis Rabba* 19:8)

The trouble with this explanation, however, is that it skirts the issue of punishment. After all, Adam and Eve had done what they were specifically warned not to do. Shouldn't the threatened punishment, death, have come right away? Why did God wait?

The Punishment Was Mortality

There was another possible explanation, and it answered the same question in a better way. It understood the Bible's words "you shall die" not as "you shall immediately cease to exist," but "you shall become a person who dies," you shall become mortal. This explanation assumes, in other words, that God had originally created Adam and Eve to be immortal: they would continue to live in the garden forever and ever, so long as they obeyed the rules. But God also warned them from the beginning: If you disobey, I will take away your immortality on the very day of your disobedience, and you will from then on be subject to death, mortal—even though you will, of course, still have a normal (for those days, at least) lifetime of nine hundred years or so.

If this was indeed the meaning of "you shall die," then the sentence was in fact carried out. Adam and Eve lived a long time after their disobedience, but eventually they did die—which was, by this interpretation, exactly the punishment God had intended by the words that He uttered. And so the *real* punishment meted out to Adam and Eve was not the sweat of agriculture or the pains of childbirth but mortality itself.

How early was the story understood in this fashion? We have little way of knowing, but it is witnessed in a number of very early texts:

From a woman was sin's beginning, and because of her, we all die.

— Sir. 25:24 (also 15:14)

For God did not make death, nor does He take delight in the destruction of the living.

For God created man for incorruption [immortality], and made him in the image of his own eternity, but through the devil's envy death entered the world. —Wisd. 1:13, 2:23–24

Giving up immortality and a blessed life, you [Adam] have gone over to death and unhappiness.
— Philo, *Questions and Answers in Genesis* 1:45 (also *Creation* 152; *Virtues* 205; etc.)

For men were created no different from the angels, that they might remain righteous and pure, and death which destroys everything, would not have touched them; but it is through this knowledge of theirs that they are being destroyed. — *1 Enoch* 69:11

. . . you shall be mortal. —Symmachus Gen. 2:17

Adam said to Eve, "Why have you brought destruction among us and brought upon us great wrath, which is death gaining rule over all our race?" — *Apocalypse of Moses* 14:2

But that man transgressed my ways and was persuaded by his wife; and she was deceived by the serpent. And then death was ordained for the generations of men. — Pseudo-Philo, *Biblical Antiquities* 13:10

But a very horrible
snake craftily deceived them to go to the fate
of death . . .
The Immortal [God] became angry with them and expelled them
from the place of the immortals.
— *Sibylline Oracles* 1:39–41, 50–51

And you set one commandment on him [Adam], but he violated it; as a result you established death for him and his descendants.
— *4 Ezra* 3:7

What did it profit Adam that he lived nine hundred and thirty years and transgressed that which he was commanded? Therefore, the multitude of time that he lived did not profit him, but it brought death and cut off the years of those who were born from him.

Adam sinned, and death was decreed against those who were to be born. — *2 Baruch* 17:2–3, 23:4 (also 48:43, 54:15–19, 56:6)

And while he was sleeping, I took from him a rib. And I created for him a wife, so that death might come [to him] by his wife.

— 2 Enoch (J) 30:17

When God created Adam He created him so that he might live forever like the ministering angels [as it is written] "And God said, Behold man has become like one of us" [Gen. 3:22], just as the ministering angels do not die, so will he not know the taste of death . . . But since he did not abide by His commandments, death was consequently decreed for him.

— Pesiqta Rabbati 41:2

Sinfulness Is Hereditary

Thus, Adam and Eve were punished by becoming mortal. But this explanation raised another question: is the rest of humanity also mortal because we are being punished for Adam and Eve's sin? This hardly seemed fair. Why did not Adam and Eve's children get the same chance their parents had had and go back to being immortal as long as they obeyed God?

Some interpreters clearly did believe that Adam and Eve's punishment had been transmitted to all subsequent generations. Others, however, came to the conclusion that it was not their punishment, but their *sinfulness,* that was passed on. Yes, these interpreters said, death was decreed for Adam and Eve. But if we, their descendants, also are mortal, it is because we, in some fundamental way, are just like Adam and Eve. We inherited from them (just as children always inherit traits from their parents) their defective heart, with its predisposition to sinfulness; or they introduced sin, and it has existed ever afterward; or else, the banishment from Eden meant the end of the possibility of a sinless existence. In any case, we, too, are given over to sinning, and it is for that reason that we will die like them.

For the first Adam, burdened with an evil heart, transgressed and was overcome, as were also all who were descended from him. Thus the disease became permanent.

For a grain of evil seed was sown in Adam's heart from the beginning, and how much fruit of ungodliness it has produced until now, and will produce until the time of threshing comes!

O Adam, what have you done? For though it was you who sinned, the fall was not yours alone, but ours also who are your descendants.

— 4 Ezra 3:21–22, 4:30, 7:118 (also 4:30–32, 7:48)

And Adam said to Eve, "What have you done? You have brought upon us a great wound, transgression and sin in all our generations."

—(Latin) *Life of Adam and Eve* 44:2

By this interpretation, the narrative of Adam and Eve is indeed the story of the Fall of Man: human beings have ever afterward been condemned to a life of "transgression and sin in all our generations." Although this idea occurs in Jewish texts of (probably) the first century C.E., it came to be championed by Christians, while later Jews by and large abandoned it. Thus, this teaching is found in the New Testament:

Therefore as sin came into the world through one man and death through sin, and so death spread to all men **in that all men sinned**.

—Rom. 5:12

For Christians, this interpretation of the Adam and Eve story also suggested a certain correspondence between that story and the Resurrection: the latter seemed to answer, and set aright, the Fall of Man. Paul thus saw a relationship between the "first Adam" of the Old Testament and the "second Adam" of the New:

For as by a man came death, by a man has come also the resurrection of the dead. For as in Adam all die, so also in Christ shall all be made alive.

—1 Cor. 15:21–22

And so, thanks in part to the problem raised by God's threatened punishment, "on the day that you eat of it you shall die," interpreters came to see the true significance of the story as relating to human mortality and, perhaps, a human predisposition to sinfulness. Ultimately, Christianity developed the doctrine of original sin, whereby Adam and Eve's sinfulness was transmitted (in the view of some, through the act of sexual intercourse) to all subsequent generations.

The Serpent Was Satan

The identity of the serpent in the story was certainly tied to the overall meaning of the story. Who was he? In the text itself, the serpent (or snake) appears to be merely a clever animal who leads the humans astray. But this also struck interpreters as strange. To begin with, snakes are *not* particularly clever: they can be dangerous or annoying, but they are hardly distinguished by their intelligence. Why, then, did the Bible flatly assert that the serpent "was cleverer than any other beast of the field that the Lord God had made" (Gen. 3:1)? And why was he a *talking* serpent?

A number of ancient interpreters maintained that this snake was simply a snake, albeit an unusual one. If he talked, it may have been because snakes, or perhaps *all* animals, originally knew how to speak:

> On that day [when Adam and Eve were expelled from the garden], the mouth of all the beasts and cattle and birds and whatever walked or moved was stopped from speaking because all of them used to speak with one another with one speech and one language.   — *Jubilees* 3:28

> It is said that, in olden times, . . . snakes could speak with a man's voice.
> — Philo, *On the Creation* 156

> At that time all living things spoke the same language.
> — Josephus, *Jewish Antiquities* 1:41

Similarly, if the snake was ultimately condemned to slither about on his belly (Gen. 3:14), this merely implied that snakes originally had legs like dogs or horses. None of these details necessarily meant that the snake had any supernatural qualities. After all, did not the Bible plainly say that the serpent was one of the "beasts of the field" (Gen. 3:1)?

Other interpreters, however, saw the snake as Satan (or Satan's agent), or some other devil-like figure in disguise. This identification not only explained why this particular snake talked and was smarter than all other creatures, but also was reinforced by God's words to the snake at the end of the story:

> I will put enmity between you and the woman, and between your seed and her seed; he [mankind] shall bruise your head, and you shall bruise his heel.   — Gen. 3:15

It seemed most unlikely that the Bible here was really concerned with future relations between humans and snakes. (Moreover, how was this "enmity" between humans and snakes different from the enmity that exists between humans and lions or bears or tarantulas, none of whom had done anything to Adam and Eve in the garden?) Instead, many interpreters concluded that these words were addressed to the eternal Tempter with whom humanity would forever after be pitted in an unending struggle.

> [The angel Michael explains:] "And the name of the third angel is Gadreel: this is the one who showed all the deadly blows to the sons of men, and he led Eve astray, and he showed the weapons of death to the children of men."   — 1 *Enoch* 69:6

> The devil said to him [the serpent]: "Do not fear, only become my vessel, and I will speak a word through your mouth by which you will be able to deceive."

[Later, Eve recalls:] "The devil answered me through the mouth of the serpent." — *Apocalypse of Moses* 16:4, 17:4

[A woman recalls:] . . . nor did the Destroyer, the deceitful serpent, defile the purity of my virginity. — 4 Macc. 18:7–8

The devil is of the lowest places . . . and he became aware of his condemnation and of the sin which he had sinned previously. And that is why he thought up the scheme against Adam. In such form he entered paradise and corrupted Eve. — *2 Enoch* 31:4–6

And the great dragon, the ancient serpent, who is called Devil and Satan, was cast out, he who deceives the whole world.

And he [an angel] seized the dragon, the ancient serpent, who is the Devil and Satan, and bound him for a thousand years.

— Rev. 12:9, 20:2

The tree is sinful desire which Satanel [a wicked angel] spread over Eve and Adam, and because of this God has cursed the vine because Satanel had planted it, and by that he deceived the first-formed Adam and Eve. — *3 Baruch* (Slavonic) 4:8

Satanel, when he took the serpent as a garment . . .

— *3 Baruch* (Greek) 9:7

The devil . . . whom Moses calls the serpent . . .

— Justin Martyr, *Dialogue with Trypho* 103

[God says:] However, he [Adam] disobeyed my commandment and, having been deceived by the devil, he ate from the tree.

— *Apocalypse of Sedrach* 4:5

And the woman said, "The serpent is the one who instructed me." And He cursed the serpent and called him "devil."

— *Testimony of Truth* 47:3–6

And the woman saw Sammael [a wicked angel] the angel of death and was afraid. — *Targum Pseudo-Jonathan* Gen. 3:6

Perhaps also:

Through the devil's envy death entered the world, and those who are on his side suffer it.[1] — Wisd. 2:24

---

1. Some have suggested that this verse refers to the incident of Cain and Abel (see below, Chapter 4), but it may actually refer to the sin of Adam and Eve.

God's announcement of the serpent's punishment ("I will put enmity between you and the woman, and between your seed and her seed") thus
came to have a new meaning. It now appeared really to be a statement about
the fight against the devil that all subsequent human beings would have to
wage. And this view in turn strengthened the conclusion that the true subject
of the story was the Fall of Man, how humanity gained its susceptibility to
sinfulness. That susceptibility meant that the devil would henceforth be humanity's eternal enemy, always playing on people's weakness in the face of
temptation.

Blame It on the Woman

Another question occurred to interpreters: whose fault was it? A great deal
hung on the answer. If Eve was mostly to blame, then this first female was
responsible (according to the line of reasoning we have been following) for
nothing less than sin and death, and women ever after could be blamed for
these human ills. But if it was primarily Adam's fault, then the opposite was
true.

What does the Bible itself say? It is Eve who is persuaded by the serpent to
try the fruit, and she in turn gives it to Adam—so the evidence does seem to
support blaming Eve somewhat more than Adam. What is more, when God
details the punishments to be given out to the various principals (Gen.
3:14–19), He first announces the serpent's punishment, then Eve's, then
Adam's. To interpreters this seemed to suggest a descending order of guilt: the
serpent was certainly the most guilty, since he instigated the crime. If Eve came
next and only after her Adam, did this not imply that she was more guilty than
Adam but less guilty than the serpent? For both these reasons, many of the
sources mentioned earlier specify that Eve bore the primary responsibility:

> From a woman was sin's beginning, and because of her, we all die.
>
> —Sir. 25:24

> Woman becomes for him [Adam] the beginning of blameworthy life.
> For so long as he was by himself, as accorded with such solitude, he
> went on growing like to the world and like God . . . But when woman
> too had been made . . . love [erōs] enters in . . . and this desire [pothos]
> likewise engendered bodily pleasure, that pleasure which is the begin-
> ning of wrongs and violation of law, the pleasure for the sake of which
> men bring on themselves the life of mortality and wretchedness in lieu
> of that of immortality and bliss.   —Philo, Creation 151–152 (also 165–166)

But the woman first became a betrayer to him [Adam].
She gave, and persuaded him to sin in his ignorance.

— *Sibylline Oracles* 1:42–43

Adam said to Eve, "Why have you brought destruction among us and brought upon us great wrath, which is death gaining rule over all our race?"

"Oh evil woman! Why have you wrought destruction among us?"

— *Apocalypse of Moses* 14:2, 21:6

But that man transgressed my ways and was persuaded by his wife . . . And then death was ordained for the generations of men.

— Pseudo-Philo, *Biblical Antiquities* 13:10

Thereupon God imposed punishment on Adam for having yielded to a woman's counsel . . . Eve He punished by childbirth and its attendant pains, because she had deluded Adam, just as the serpent had beguiled her. — Josephus, *Jewish Antiquities* 1:49

I permit no woman to teach or to have authority over men; she is to keep silent. For Adam was formed first, then Eve; and Adam was not deceived, but the woman was deceived and became a transgressor.

— 1 Tim. 2:13–14

I [God] created for him a wife, so that death might come [to him] by his wife.

In such a form he [the devil] entered paradise and corrupted Eve. But he did not contact Adam. — 2 *Enoch* (J) 30:17, 31:6

An Extra Proviso

There was, however, one detail in the text that supported Eve's side in the debate. It might at first appear to be a minor discrepancy. When God first told Adam the rules of the garden, He did so in these terms:

And the Lord God commanded the man, saying, "You may freely eat of every tree in the garden; but of the tree of the knowledge of good and evil you shall not eat, for in the day that you eat of it, you shall die." — Gen. 2:16–17

But when the serpent asked Eve about the same rules, she had a slightly different answer:

> And the woman said to the serpent, "We may eat of the fruit of the trees of the garden, but God said, 'You may not eat of the fruit of the tree which is in the midst of the garden, **neither shall you touch it**, lest you die.'"
>
> —Gen. 3:2–3

Why should this additional proviso, "neither shall you touch it," have been added? It could hardly have been an accident. Here, then, was another question interpreters *had* to answer:

> Why, when the command was given not to eat of one particular tree, did the woman include even approaching it closely . . . ? First, because taste—and every sense—functions by means of contact. Second, [because] if even touching [the tree] was forbidden, how much greater a crime would those have done who, in addition to touching it, then ate of it and enjoyed it? Would they not therefore have condemned and brought punishment down upon themselves?
>
> —Philo, *Questions and Answers in Genesis* 1:35

Later interpreters, however, saw in the extra words "neither shall you touch it" a very subtle hint in the text—a hint, first of all, about how the serpent managed to trick Eve into eating the forbidden fruit and, as well, a clue as to who was ultimately responsible:

> The text says, "And God commanded Adam, saying, 'Of the tree of the knowledge of good and evil you shall not eat, for in the day that you eat of it you shall die' [Gen. 2:17]." But Adam did not choose to tell God's words to Eve exactly as they had been spoken. Instead he said to her, "God said, 'You shall not eat of the fruit of the tree which is in the midst of the garden, neither shall you touch it, lest you die' [as per Gen. 3:3]." Whereupon the wicked serpent said to himself, "Since I seem to be unable to trip up Adam, let me go and try to trip up Eve." He went and sat down next to her and started talking with her. He said: "Now you say that God has forbidden us to touch the tree. Well, I can touch the tree and not die, and so can you." What did the wicked serpent then do? He touched the tree with his hands and feet and shook it so hard that some of its fruit fell to the ground . . . Then he said to her, "[You see? So likewise] you say that God has forbidden us to eat from the tree. But I can eat from it and not die, and so can you." What did Eve think to herself? "All the things that my husband has told me are lies" . . . Whereupon she took the fruit and ate it and gave to Adam and he ate, as it is written, "The woman saw that the tree was good to eat from and a delight to the eyes" [Gen. 3:6]. —*Abot deR. Natan* (A) ch. 1

The extra proviso, according to this interpretation, did not come from Eve. She did not change God's words *because she did not hear them in the first place.* When God spoke to Adam about the tree in chapter 2 of Genesis, Eve had not even been created yet. (God's words appear in Gen. 2:16–17; Eve is not created until Gen. 2:22.) So it must have been Adam who, in telling Eve about God's prohibition after she was created, added the words "neither shall you touch it." Perhaps he did so to make sure that she would not even come close to eating the fruit. But if so, the plan backfired. The serpent came to her and first touched the tree himself. Then he invited Eve to touch it as well and so see for herself that nothing bad would happen. Then the serpent actually took a piece of fruit and ate it, and urged her to do the same thing. At this point she began to doubt the truth of everything that Adam had told her: "All the things that my husband has told me are lies." And so she decided to take a bite.

The Earthly Paradise

After their sin, Adam and Eve were banished from the garden, and God placed cherubim and a flaming sword at its entrance "to guard the way to the tree of life" (Gen. 3:24)—presumably, to prevent Adam and Eve, or later human beings, from reentering the garden. This very fact seemed to indicate that the garden had been located somewhere on earth. And the Bible had elsewhere said as much: God had planted the garden "in the east" (Gen. 2:8), and at least two well-known rivers, the Tigris and the Euphrates, are said to originate from a river that flowed from inside it (Gen. 2:14).[2] So the garden was indeed an earthly one. Those writing in Greek might refer to the garden as "paradise," but this word was, at first, only the regular term for an enclosed garden or orchard.[3]

But why had God, after expelling Adam and Eve, placed cherubim and a flaming sword at the entrance to this elegant garden, rather than simply destroying the whole thing or letting it revert to wilderness? Some interpreters doubtless concluded that God must have had some further plans for the garden after Adam and Eve's stay there.[4]

Ideas about the garden at a very early point joined speculation on other, broader issues—life after death, and the reward to be given to the righteous.

---

2. Eden is also found as an apparent place-name elsewhere: 2 Kings 19:12 (=Isa. 37:12), Ezek. 27:23, Amos 1:5.

3. "Paradise" had been used by the Septuagint translation for "garden" in Gen. 2:8–10, 16.

4. Note the references to the "garden of God" and the like in Gen. 13:10; Isa. 51:3; Ezek. 28:13, 31:9, etc.; and Joel 2:3. Though all these places might refer to a garden that *had* existed but was no more, this was hardly the only possible reading, and thus the very profusion of such references might be taken as an indication that the garden was still in existence and still of importance.

For centuries, different religions and civilizations had taught that people continue to exist in some fashion after their death, or that at some time following death a dead person's bones might be joined together and reshaped into a living being again. This life after death was sometimes thought to be God's reward to the righteous for having lived a good life. The Bible here and there seems to suggest as much.

It certainly must have struck some ancient readers that God's closing off of the garden was a clear indication that it was the intended dwelling place for the righteous after their death. After all, this garden did contain a tree called the "tree of life" whose fruit would allow people to "live forever" (Gen. 3:22)—might this not be precisely what the righteous would eat after their first existence? No wonder the Bible had said that the cherubim and flaming sword were there specifically to guard the way to the *tree* (Gen. 3:24).

And so, many ancient readers assumed that the Garden of Eden still existed somewhere on earth as the intended resting place for the righteous after their death. "Paradise" now came to mean more than an ordinary garden—it was the garden of the righteous (or of "righteousness" or "truth"), the place of their final reward:

> And from there I [Enoch] went over . . . far away to the east, and I went over the Red Sea and I was far from it, and . . . I came to the Garden of Righteousness, and I saw . . . many large trees growing there, sweet-smelling, large, very beautiful, and glorious, and the tree of wisdom from which they eat and know great wisdom.
>
> —*1 Enoch* 32:2–4 (=[4Q206] *Enoch*ᵉ fragments 2 and 3)

> [Noah says:] . . . the garden where the chosen and the righteous dwell, where my great grandfather [Enoch] was received, who was the seventh from Adam . . . All these things I saw toward the Garden of Righteousness.   —*1 Enoch* 60:8, 23 (also 61:12, 70:4, etc.)

> But those who honor the true eternal God
> inherit life, dwelling in the luxuriant garden
> of Paradise for the time of eternity,
> feasting on sweet bread from starry heaven.[5]
>
> —Fragment 3 from *Sibylline Oracles* (cited
> in Theophylus, *To Autolycus* 2.36)

[God says to Adam:] But when you come out of Paradise, if you guard yourself from all evil, preferring death to it, at the time of the resurrec-

---

5. That is, manna; see Chapter 19. The description "*from* starry heaven" may imply that this author felt the garden to be an earthly one.

tion I will raise you again, and then there shall be given to you from the **tree of life**, and you shall be immortal forever.

And both [Adam and Eve] were **buried** according to the command of God **in the regions of Paradise,** in the place from which God had found the dust [from which Adam was formed, Gen. 2:7].
— *Apocalypse of Moses* 28:4, 40:6 (also 6:2, 9:3, 13:1–4)

And I saw there the earth and its fruit . . . and the garden of Eden and its fruits, and the source and the river flowing from it, and its trees and their flowering, making fruits, and I saw righteous men therein, their food and their rest. — *Apocalypse of Abraham* 21:3, 6

[An angel tells Baruch:] "When God caused the flood over the earth . . . and the water rose over the heights 15 cubits, the water entered Paradise and killed every flower." — *3 Baruch* 4:10

The Garden in Heaven

Other interpreters, however, were troubled by the idea that the garden might be anywhere on the earth. Was not heaven the abode of God and the angels, that is, of beings who live forever? Indeed, did not the righteous Enoch and Elijah ascend *into* heaven (Gen. 5:24, 2 Kings 2:11)? So the prophet Isaiah had alluded to the reward of the righteous in these terms:

He who walks righteously and speaks uprightly, who despises the gain of oppressions, who shakes his hands lest they hold a bribe, who stops his ears from hearing of bloodshed and shuts his eyes from looking upon evil—he will **dwell on high,** his refuge will be craggy fortresses; his food will be given him, his water will be sure. Your eyes will behold the **King** in His splendor, they will see the **earth from afar.**
— Isa. 34:15–17

Considering such evidence, some interpreters found it only reasonable to suppose that the true garden was in heaven, perhaps presided over by God Himself:

Michael turned the chariot and brought Abraham toward the east, to the first gate of heaven.⁶ And Abraham saw two paths. The first was

---

6. The phrase "toward the east" betrays this author's desire to reconcile his own idea of a heavenly paradise with the biblical tradition that Eden was an (apparently) earthly garden planted "in the east."

strait and narrow . . . [and] this strait gate is the gate of the righteous, which leads to life, and those who enter through it come into paradise.

— *Testament of Abraham* (A) 11:1,10

If I had asked you how many dwellings are in the heart of the sea . . . or which are the exits out of hell, or which are the entrances of Paradise, perhaps you would have said, "I never went down into the deep, nor as yet into hell, neither did I ever **ascend into heaven**."

— *4 Ezra* 4:7–8 (also 7:36, 8:52)

[God says:] It [the likeness of the temple] is preserved **with Me, as also paradise.** — *2 Baruch* 4:6 (also 51:7–11)

And I saw a chariot like the wind and its wheels were fiery. I was carried off into the paradise of righteousness, and I saw the Lord sitting and His appearance was unbearable flaming fire.

— *Life of Adam and Eve (Vita)* 25:3 (also 42:4)

Take him up to paradise, to the third heaven.

— *Apocalypse of Moses* (also Georgian and Slavonic) 37:5 (see also 29:6, 40:1)

Fourteen years ago [I] was caught up to the third heaven . . . caught up into paradise, whether in the body or out of the body I do not know.

— 2 Cor. 12:2–3

And those men took me from there, and they brought me up to the third heaven. And they placed me in the midst of paradise . . . And I said, "How very pleasant is this place!" The men answered me: "This place has been prepared for the righteous, who suffer every kind of tribulation in this life and who afflict their souls, and who turn their eyes from [looking upon] injustice [Isa. 33:15], and who carry out righteous judgment to give bread to the hungry, and to cover the naked with clothing, and to lift up the fallen, and to help the injured, who walk before the face of the Lord, and who worship Him alone— for them this has been prepared as an eternal inheritance."

— *2 Enoch* (A) 8:1–9:1

Other references to this garden do not specify exactly where it was, but it was, in any case, the place where the righteous were to find their eternal repose:

And He shall open the gates of paradise; he shall remove the sword that has threatened since Adam, and he will grant to the righteous to eat of the tree of life. — *Testament of Levi* 18:10

[In the coming time] the saints will refresh themselves in Eden.

— *Testament of Dan* 5:12

And he [Jesus] said to him, "Truly I say to you, today you will be with me in Paradise." — Luke 23:43

To him who conquers I will grant to eat of the tree of life, which is in the paradise of God. — Rev. 2:7 (also 22:2, 14, 18)

And God took him [Sedrach] and put him within Paradise with all the saints. — *Apocalypse of Sedrach* 16:6 (also 12:2)

> Enoch pleased God and was transferred **into paradise**,
> so that he might give repentance to the nations.
>
> — (Vulgate) Ecclus. (Sir.) 44:16

And so, the garden of delights in which, the Bible said, God had placed the first man and woman was understood by interpreters to have had a further purpose. It was the reward and final resting place of the righteous after death, located either in some obscure corner of earth or, perhaps, in heaven.

❖   ❖   ❖

In short: Although the Bible spelled out the punishments that Adam and Eve would suffer for their transgression—the toils of agriculture and pains of childbirth—ancient interpreters found a different meaning implied by the story. The real punishment of Adam and Eve, many thought, was the mortality implied in God's words, "for on the day that you eat of it you shall die." This same punishment was passed on to all later human beings, either because mortality is hereditary, or because sinfulness has been transmitted to each successive generation of humans. The serpent, who brought about this catastrophe, was identified with Satan or some other wicked angel. As for the question of guilt, most interpreters seem to have blamed Eve, but there were also good grounds for saying that what happened was ultimately Adam's fault. The garden that God had planted still exists, either on earth or in heaven; it is to be the final reward of the righteous.

4
Cain and Abel
(GENESIS 4:1–16)

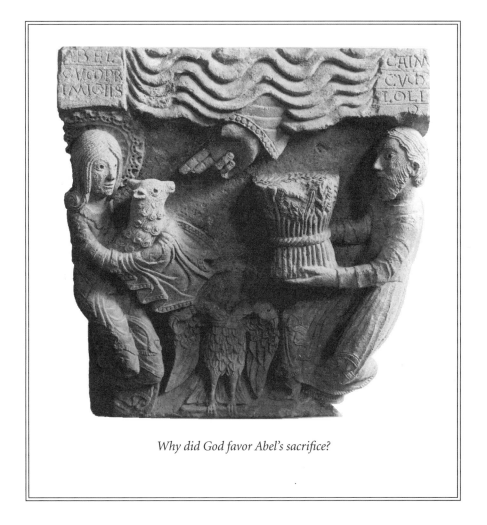

Why did God favor Abel's sacrifice?

Cain and Abel

(GENESIS 4:1–16)

❖   ❖   ❖

After they were expelled from the garden, Adam and Eve had two sons, Cain and Abel; Cain was a farmer and Abel a herdsman. The two sons decided to bring sacrifices to God—Cain from his agricultural produce and Abel from his herds. God received Abel's sacrifice with favor, but not Cain's. For this reason, Cain became angry at his brother and killed him. He thus was the world's first murderer, and God banished him from the settled land and condemned him to a life of wandering.

CAIN'S MURDER of his brother Abel raised many questions: Why had one brother's sacrifice been favored by God and the other's not—are not all offerings acceptable to God? And what was it that led Cain to murder Abel—should not his anger have been directed against God rather than his innocent sibling? How was the murder accomplished, and with what weapon? And what was the real nature of Cain's punishment?

Interpreters searching for answers to these major questions were ultimately led back to the story's very beginning, the one-sentence account of Cain's birth. Here was a rather minor question about the text, but one that had potentially great consequences for the other, larger questions:

> Now Adam knew Eve his wife, and she conceived and bore Cain, saying, "I have gotten a man with the Lord."   —Gen. 4:1

The minor question was this: why did Eve, as she contemplated her just-born son, refer to him as a "man"? The word "man" in Hebrew does not simply mean "male person," and certainly does not mean "male child"—there are other words for that. Man means man, a grown-up male. But what could Eve have meant by calling her baby that?

Some interpreters apparently understood that the baby Cain was born with abilities well beyond his years:

> And she bore a son and he was lustrous. And at once the infant rose, ran, and brought in his hands a reed [in Hebrew, *qaneh*] and gave it to his mother. And his name was called Cain [*qayin*].
> —*Life of Adam and Eve (Vita)* 21:3

85

If the newborn baby could walk, nay, run and carry something, here was a good reason for Eve to say, with only a little exaggeration, that he was a "man." And as for him being born "with the Lord," the apparent meaning was that he was born through God's direct intervention, "with the help of the Lord," since such an unusual child could not have been produced in the usual way.

Son of the Devil

But another explanation existed. In view of the wicked turn that his life was to take, some interpreters thought Cain might have been *evil from birth*, in fact, an offspring of the devil or some wicked angel. Indeed, this might be the cryptic point of the very beginning of Gen. 4:1, "And Adam knew his wife Eve"—Adam did not "know" his wife in the biblical sense, he knew something *about* her:

> By this it may be seen who are the children of God and who are the **children of the devil**; whoever does not do right is not of God, nor he who does not love his brother. For this is the message which you have heard from the beginning [that is, the book of Genesis]: that we should love one another and not be like Cain, who **was of the Evil One** [that is, the devil] and murdered his brother.   —1 John 3:10–12

> Having been made pregnant by the seed of the devil . . . she brought forth a son.   —Tertullian, *On Patience* 5:15

> First adultery came into being, afterward murder. And he [Cain] was begotten in adultery, for he was the child of the serpent. So he became a murderer, just like his father, and he killed his brother.
>   —(Gnostic) *Gospel of Philip* 61:5–10

> And Adam knew about his wife Eve that she had conceived by Sammael the [wicked] angel of the Lord, and she became pregnant and gave birth to Cain. He resembled the upper ones [angels] and not the lower ones, and she [therefore] said, "I have acquired a man, indeed, an angel of the Lord."   — *Targum Pseudo-Jonathan* Gen. 4:1

> The serpent came into her and she became pregnant with Cain, as it says, "And the man knew his wife Eve." What did he know? That she was already pregnant [from someone else].   — *Pirqei deR. Eliezer* 21

The idea that Cain was the offspring of Eve and the devil may also be reflected elsewhere:

[A heroic mother recalls:] I was a pure virgin and did not go outside my father's house; I guarded the rib that [Eve] was built [from] . . . nor did the Destroyer, the deceitful serpent, defile the purity of my virginity.   —4 Macc. 18:7–8

If Cain's true father was the devil, this would provide another explanation for Eve's cryptic words at the baby's birth, "I have gotten a man with the Lord." For, if Cain had in fact been engendered by one of God's angels—however wicked that particular angel might have been—then "with the Lord" could be a shorthand way of saying "with *an angel of* the Lord." Likewise, this divinely begotten child could appropriately be called a *man* (rather than a "baby") because angels are frequently called "man" in the Bible (see Gen. 18:2, 32:24, and elsewhere). Thus, some ancient interpreters concluded that Cain had in fact been a half-human, half-angelic creature begotten by the devil.

Cain's Sisters

We know that Adam and Eve had two sons, Cain and Abel, but the Bible tells us nothing about any daughters. If no daughters were born, how did the human race ever continue to propagate? Faced with this dilemma, some ancient interpreters simply supplied the missing female(s):

And in the third "week" [that is, period of seven years] in the second jubilee, she bore Cain. And in the fourth she bore Abel. And in the fifth she bore Awan, her daughter.   —*Jubilees* 4:1

In the beginning of the world Adam became the father of three sons and one daughter: Cain, Noaba, Abel, and Seth [born in Gen. 4:25].
                                     —Pseudo-Philo, *Biblical Antiquities* 1:1

Two male children were born to them; the first was called Cain, whose name may be translated "Acquisition," and the second Abel, meaning "Nothingness." They also had daughters.
                                     —Josephus, *Jewish Antiquities* 1:54

And she additionally bore from Adam her husband his [Cain's] twin sister and Abel.   —*Targum Pseudo-Jonathan* Gen. 4:2

"And additionally, she bore his brother Abel . . ." (Gen. 4:2). This word *additionally* supports [the idea that daughters were born; it means] *in addition* to the birth [of Abel] were other births in the same pregnancy.   —*Genesis Rabba* 22:3

If Adam and Eve had had two daughters, that would have provided a wife for both Cain and Abel. But what if only one daughter had been born (as some of the above sources suggest)? It occurred to some interpreters that this might have been the real reason for Cain's killing his brother:

[Adam says to Seth:] . . . A flood is coming and will wash the whole earth because of the daughters of Cain, your brother, who killed your brother Abel out of passion for your sister Lebuda.

— *Testament of Adam* 3:5

Said R. Huna: An extra twin was born with Abel. [Cain] said, "I shall take her [as my wife]," [Abel] said "No, I shall take her." The former said, "I should get her, since I am the firstborn," while the latter said, "I should get her, since she was born with me."   — *Genesis Rabba* 22:7

And she [Eve] became pregnant and bore Cain and Lebuda along with him; [some texts: "then she became pregnant again and bore Abel and his sister Qelima"]. And when the children had grown Adam said to Eve: "Let Cain take Qelima [as a wife], since she was born with Abel, and let Abel take Lebuda, who was born with Cain." Then said Cain to his mother Eve: "I will take my own sister, and let Abel take his own," for Lebuda was very beautiful.   — *Cave of Treasures* (W) 5:20–22

Professions Decided

Cain's devilish ancestry might indeed explain why he ended up as a murderer. But it hardly explained why God did not accept his sacrifice at the beginning of the story. Presumably both Cain and Abel offered sacrifices in good faith. Surely it was not the case that God preferred meat offerings to vegetable ones. So why did He accept Abel's sacrifice and not Cain's?

One line of interpretation suggested that the brothers' two professions, farmer and shepherd, determined the fate of their sacrifices. God's apparent preference for the shepherd's offering over the farmer's may really have reflected something of the differences involved in the two professions:

One of them labors and takes care of living beings . . . gladly undertaking the pastoral work which is preparatory to rulership and kingship. But the other occupies himself with earthly and inanimate things.

— Philo, *Questions and Answers in Genesis* 1:59
(also *The Sacrifices of Cain and Abel* 14, 51)

Now the brothers enjoyed different pursuits. Abel, the younger one, was concerned with justice, and, believing that God was present at every action that he himself undertook, he made a practice of virtue: he was a shepherd. Cain, however, was altogether wicked, and on the lookout only for his own profit: he was the first person to think of plowing the earth.

Now he killed his brother under these circumstances: They had decided to offer sacrifices to God. Cain brought the produce of the tilled earth and plants, while Abel brought the milk and the firstborn of the flocks. This latter was the sacrifice that God preferred, who is paid homage by whatever grows on its own and in keeping with nature, but not by things brought forth by force and the scheming of greedy man. —Josephus, *Jewish Antiquities* 1:53–54

Plowing the earth . . . is inferior to pasturing sheep . . . Quite rightly, then, when the brothers are born, the chronological order [of their birth] is preserved in Scripture [that is, Cain is mentioned before Abel, Gen. 4:1–2]. When, however, their way of life is mentioned, [that of] the younger comes before the older [that is, shepherding comes first, showing its superiority; Gen. 4:2]. —Ambrose of Milan, *Cain and Abel* 1.3.10

Defective Sacrifices

Another line of interpretation held that there was some problem with Cain's sacrifice. For example, the Bible states that Abel brought the *firstborn* of his flocks—the first part is indeed normally reserved for God—whereas Cain's sacrifice seems pointedly *not* the first part of his harvest. Moreover, Cain is said to have offered his sacrifice "in the course of time" (Gen. 4:3). Did not both specifications imply that Cain's offering was in itself flawed?

"And it came to pass after some days that Cain brought to the Lord an offering of the fruit of the ground" (Gen. 4:3). There are here two indictments of this self-lover [Cain]. One is that he made an offering to God "after some days" and not right away; the other that it was "of the fruit" but not "of the first fruit." —Philo, *The Sacrifices of Cain and Abel* 52

Abel chose and brought for sacrifice from the firstborn and the fattest, but Cain brought [merely] the fruits he found at the time . . . He [God] chose not to accept his sacrifice from him in order to teach him how it was to be offered up. For Cain had bulls and calves, nor did he lack other animals and fowl that he might sacrifice. But these he did

not bring on the day of the first fruit offering, but brought the fruit of
his land.   —Ephraem, *Commentary on Genesis* 3:2

"And Cain brought to the Lord an offering of the fruit of the ground"
(Gen. 4:3)—from the leftovers.   —*Genesis Rabba* 22:5

"And Cain brought to the Lord an offering of the fruit of the ground"
(Gen. 4:3)—what does this imply? The ordinary fruit [rather than the
first fruits reserved for God].   —*Midrash Tanḥuma* 9

The Problem Was the Sacrificer

There was yet a third, slightly different, explanation for God's preference.
Could it not have been the *past history* of the two sacrificers that caused God
to accept Abel's sacrifice but not Cain's? That is, if Cain had a long history of
sins and evil deeds while Abel had always been an exemplary human being,
perhaps that would have given God a reason for accepting only Abel's sacrifice:

And while indeed from Abel, as from a **righteous man**, you received a
sacrifice with favor, from the brother-murderer Cain you turned aside
the offering as from an **accursed person**.

— Hellenistic Synagogal Prayer, *Apostolic Constitutions* 8.12.21

[After the incident of the sacrifices] Cain said to his brother Abel,
"Come, let us both go out into the field," and it came to pass that when
the two had gone into the field Cain cried out to Abel, "It is my view
that the world was not created with divine love and is not arranged in
keeping with people's good deeds, but justice is corrupted—for why
else would your sacrifice have been accepted with favor and mine
not?"

Abel said to Cain: "No, it is my view that the world was indeed
created with divine love and is altogether arranged in keeping with
people's good deeds. But it was because **my deeds** have been better
than yours that my sacrifice was accepted with favor and your sacrifice
was not."   — *Targum Neophyti* Gen. 4:8

Having Abel contrast his own past deeds to those of Cain not only explained
why one sacrifice was accepted and the other not. It also gave a good reason
for Cain's killing of his brother. Now jealousy was not the only thing that
pushed Cain to murder Abel: there was also the fact that Abel had so matter-
of-factly pointed out that his own past deeds were much better than Cain's.

This may have been true, but Abel's saying it so bluntly might well have caused Cain to fly into a blind rage.

The Good and the Bad

Thanks in part to such explanations as these, the whole character of the story was altered by ancient interpreters. In Genesis, Abel is neither good nor bad—in fact, we really know nothing about him. He seems to be little more than a prop, the victim of his brother's rage. As for Cain, if he ends up being bad, he certainly did not start out that way; it was only the incident of the sacrifices that drove him to murder.

But ancient interpreters subtly turned the story into an elemental conflict between good and evil. As we have already seen, Cain was now believed to have been wicked from birth (according to some, the offspring of the devil), while Abel, despite the lack of biblical evidence, came to be thought of as fundamentally good, *righteous*, Cain's diametrical opposite:

> Even though the righteous man [Abel] was younger in time than the wicked one . . .   —Philo, *Questions in Genesis* 1:59

> And while indeed from Abel, as from a righteous man, you received a sacrifice with favor. . . .
> —Hellenistic Synagogal Prayer, *Apostolic Constitutions* 8.12.21

> And in his nine hundredth year he [Cain] was destroyed in the Flood on account of his righteous brother Abel.   — *Testament of Benjamin* 7:4

> Thus the Lord will bless you with the first fruits, as he has blessed all the saints, from Abel until the present.   — *Testament of Issachar* 5:4

> Abel, the younger one . . . made a practice of virtue . . . Cain, however, was altogether wicked.   —Josephus, *Jewish Antiquities* 1:53

> . . . so that upon you may come all the **righteous** blood on earth, from the blood of innocent Abel to the blood of Zechariah son of Barachiah.   —Matt. 23:35

> By faith Abel offered to God a more acceptable sacrifice than Cain, through which he received approval as righteous, God bearing witness by accepting his gifts; he died, but through his faith he is still speaking.
> —Heb. 11:4 (also 12:24)

> And why did he murder him? Because his own deeds were evil and his brother's righteous.   —1 John 3:12

This is the son of Adam, the first-formed, who is called Abel, whom Cain the wicked killed. He sits here to judge the entire creation, examining both righteous and sinners.   — *Testament of Abraham* 13:2

And there I saw the holy Abel and all the righteous . . . And Adam and Abel and Seth and all the righteous approached.

— *Martyrdom and Ascension of Isaiah* 9:8, 28

God had made a distinction between the two men's sacrifices, having respect for the one but not for the other . . . because the works of the one were bad, while those of his brother were good.

— Augustine, *City of God* 15.7

Since Abel was a righteous man, his death took on a new coloring as well. In an age when many Jews were called upon to sacrifice their lives for their beliefs, Abel became one more biblical example of the martyr who willingly submits to suffering and even death:

He read to you about Abel slain by Cain, and Isaac who was offered as a burnt offering, and of Joseph in prison.   — 4 Macc. 18:11

Meanwhile, Cain became more than one bad individual. He became the very symbol of evil, and his progeny (though technically all his offspring were thought to have perished in the flood at the time of Noah) were considered responsible for human wickedness in subsequent generations:

This is the spirit which had left Abel, whom Cain, his brother, had killed; it [continues to] pursue him until all of [Cain's] seed is exterminated from the face of the earth.   — 1 *Enoch* 22:7

But these men revile whatever they do not understand, and by those things that they know by instinct as irrational animals do, they are destroyed. Woe to them! For they walk in the way of Cain.

— Jude 1:10–11

From Cain sprang all the generations of the wicked.

— *Pirqei deR. Eliezer* 22

Killed with a Stone

How did Cain kill Abel? The Bible doesn't say. But since it does say that the murder occurred "when they were in the field" (Gen. 4:8), some interpreters saw in this detail a hint concerning the weapon: it must have been something likely to be found in a field, namely, a stone:

He [Cain] killed Abel with a stone. — *Jubilees* 4:31

He took a stone and drove it into his forehead and killed him.
— *Pirqei deR. Eliezer* 21

How did he kill him? He made many wounds and bruises with a stone on his arms and legs, because he did not know whence his soul would go forth, until he got to his neck. — *Midrash Tanḥuma, Bereshit* 9

God Knew Where Abel Was

After he killed Abel, Cain buried him in the earth, but God soon arrived on the scene:

Then the Lord said to Cain, "Where is Abel your brother?" He said, "I do not know; am I my brother's keeper?" And the Lord said, "What have you done? The voice of your brother's blood is crying to me from the ground. And now, you are cursed from the ground, which has opened its mouth to receive your brother's blood from your hand."
—Gen. 4:9–11

This passage was likewise troubling to interpreters, since God's question—"Where is Abel your brother?"—seemed to imply that He did not know. Still worse, God's further assertion that "your brother's blood is crying to me from the ground" seemed to imply that, were it not for hearing this sound, God indeed would never have known where Abel was. But if God does not know everything that happens on earth, then how can He be a just judge?

For that reason, many interpreters stressed that God in fact knew all along what had occurred; His question to Cain was merely a way of proving the murderer's evil intentions:

Why does He who knows everything ask of the fratricide [Cain], "Where is Abel your brother?" He wishes that man himself shall confess of his own free will . . . for he who killed through necessity would confess . . . but he who sins of his own free will denies it.
— Philo, *Questions in Genesis* 1:68

Abel, the younger one, was concerned with justice, and, believing that **God was present** at every action that he himself undertook, he made a practice of virtue . . .

[After the sacrifices:] Thereupon Cain, incensed at God's preference for Abel, slew his brother and hid his corpse, since he thought that the matter might thus remain a secret. But God, **aware of the deed**, came to Cain and asked him where his brother had gone, since He had not seen him for many days, although previously He had always seen him together with Cain. Cain was thus cast into difficulty and, having nothing to reply to God, at first said that he was likewise surprised at not seeing his brother. But then, exasperated by God's persistent, inquisitive meddling, he finally said that he was not his brother's baby-sitter or body-guard responsible for whatever happened to him. At this, God accused Cain of being his brother's murderer.[1]

— Josephus, *Jewish Antiquities* 1:55–56

It was not for lack of understanding on God's part that He asked Adam where he was, or Cain where Abel was, but to convince each what kind of a person he was, and so that the knowledge of all things should come to us through the [sacred] Scripture.

— Justin Martyr, *Dialogue with Trypho* 99:3

God **tested** three and found them all [deficient, namely, Cain, Hezekiah, and Balaam]: Cain, when God said to him, "Where is your brother Abel?" sought, as it were, to lead God astray. He ought to have said, "Master of the Universe! Things both hidden and revealed are known to You, yet You are asking *me* about my brother?!" Instead, however, he said, "I do not know, am I my brother's keeper?" God said to him: "Such is your answer [when] your brother's blood is crying out to Me?"

— *Numbers Rabba* 20:6

Cain's Sevenfold Punishment

For his crime, Cain was punished with exile and a life of wandering. When Cain protested that his punishment was too severe, since anyone who happened upon him in his wanderings might kill him, God said, "Not so![2] Anyone who slays Cain will suffer vengeance sevenfold" (Gen. 4:15).

The idea of God threatening a sevenfold revenge on Cain's murderer bothered a number of interpreters. They therefore sought to find in God's

---

1. In the Bible, Cain answers God's question "Where is Abel?" with the words "I do not know—am I my brother's keeper?" To Josephus, this looks like *two* answers. He therefore supposes that some time gap separated them. Thus, at first Cain simply said, "I do not know." But later (and the very fact that Cain ends up giving a second answer implied for Josephus that God had kept asking the same question again and again) Cain became exasperated and blurted out, "Am I my brother's keeper?" thus showing his true colors.

2. Or, "Therefore . . ."

words some further elaboration of *Cain*'s punishment (although they disagreed on the particulars):

Because sevenfold has it been avenged from Cain . . .
— Septuagint Gen. 4:24

For according to the law, a sevenfold punishment was given [to Cain]. First, upon the eyes, because they saw what was not fitting; second, upon the ears, because they heard what was not proper; third, upon the nose, which was deceived by smoke and steam; fourth, upon the [organ of] taste, which was a servant of the belly's pleasure; fifth, upon the [organs of] touch, to which by the collaboration of the former senses in overcoming the soul are also brought in addition other separate acts, such as the seizure of cities and the capture of men and the demolition of the citadel of the city where the council resides; sixth, upon the tongue and the organs of speech, for being silent about things that should be said and for saying things that should be kept silent; seventh, upon the lower belly, which with lawless licentiousness sets the senses on fire. This is what is said [in Scripture], that a sevenfold vengeance is taken on Cain.   — Philo, *Questions in Genesis* 1:77

It is for this reason that Cain was handed over by God for seven punishments, for in every hundredth year the Lord brought upon him one plague. When he was two hundred his suffering began and in his nine hundredeth year he was deprived of life. For he was condemned on account of Abel his brother as a result of all his evil deeds, but Lamech was condemned seventy times seven.
— *Testament of Benjamin* 7:3–5

Other interpreters believed that Cain's just punishment—death—was somehow suspended by God for seven generations:[3]

He [God] made him [Cain] accursed and threatened to punish his posterity in the seventh generation.   — Josephus, *Jewish Antiquities* 1:58

For seven generations punishment was suspended for Cain.
— *Targums Onqelos, Neophyti, Pseudo-Jonathan* Gen. 4:24

3. Indeed, the same idea underlies the passage just cited from the *Testament of Benjamin* 7:3–5, for if Cain is punished with seven punishments spaced at one hundred year intervals, until he is finally killed off in his nine-hundredth year, then the death penalty will have been suspended for seven centuries or (by a certain understanding) "generations."

[Cain's punishment] was delayed by the most merciful God for seven generations.   —Jerome, *Epistle 36 to Damasus* 164

Cain's Repentance

Strange to tell, Cain's protest to God, "My punishment is too great to bear" (Gen. 4:13), might also be translated "My sin is too great to forgive." Now, this is clearly *not* what Cain was saying. But ancient interpreters, who were fond of preaching the virtues of repentance, seized on this opportunity to claim that the world's first murderer was overcome with his own guilt after the deed was done. Even after God had pronounced a severe sentence upon him, Cain still cried out: "My sin is too great [for You] to forgive." (If, as just seen, Cain's sentence was suspended for seven generations, was it not in consideration of these heartfelt words?)

> And Cain said to the Lord God: My guilt is too great for me to be forgiven.   —Septuagint Gen. 4:13

> My sins are too great to bear . . .   —*Targum Neophyti* 4:13

> My iniquity is too great for me to merit forgiveness.
>   —(Vulgate) Gen. 4:13

> Whence do we know that he [Cain] repented? "And Cain said to the Lord, 'My sin is too great to forgive.'"   —*Pesiqta deR. Kahana Shubah* 11

❖   ❖   ❖

In short: Cain was not really Adam's son but the offspring of Eve and the devil or some other demonic angel. His hatred for Abel was in part inspired by their long-standing rivalry over their sister. As for God's preference for Abel's sacrifice, this was caused by the moral differences reflected in the sacrifices the two brought, or by the past history of the two sacrificers. For Cain had always been altogether sinful and wicked, while Abel was just the opposite, righteous in all his deeds. Cain murdered Abel in the field by striking him with a stone. When God later asked him where Abel was, the question was intended to trip Cain up and so reveal his true character. Despite his wicked reply, there is some evidence that Cain was later sorry, since he said to God, "My sin is too great to forgive."

5
Noah and the Flood

(GENESIS 6–8)

The fallen angels: a bad match.

Noah and the Flood

(GENESIS 6–8)

❖   ❖   ❖

After the death of Abel, Adam and Eve had another son, Seth, and the human race continued to grow. But as the generations multiplied, God came to be displeased with how humanity had turned out. At length He resolved to destroy it once and for all. "But Noah found favor in the eyes of the Lord" (Gen. 6:8). He therefore ordered Noah to build an ark big enough to hold himself and his family as well as a large number of animals, so that this remnant might survive the destruction. Then He brought a flood upon the earth for forty days and forty nights. After it was over, the waters began to recede, until finally Noah was able to leave the ark and settle on the dry land.

EARLY READERS of the Bible wondered why there had been a flood at all. The Bible says that it was humanity's "wickedness" (Gen. 6:5) that made God resolve to annihilate life on earth. But really, what had human beings done that was so bad?

Cain Was the Worst

The one truly wicked deed recorded from the era preceding the flood was Cain's murder of his brother Abel. Some interpreters therefore singled out Cain as a crucial factor in God's decision:

> When an unrighteous man [Cain] departed from her [that is, from Wisdom] in his anger, he perished because in rage he slew his brother. When the earth was flooded **because of him**, Wisdom again saved it, steering the righteous man by a paltry piece of wood.   — Wisd. 10:3–4

> [Seth is told:] A flood is coming and will wash the whole earth because of the daughters of Cain, your brother, who killed your brother Abel.
> — *Testament of Adam* 3:5

Here, apparently, Cain's crime is specially mentioned because his wickedness, passed on to his descendants, was thought to have been an important cause of the flood.[1] Were it not for the "righteous man" (Noah), the world would indeed have perished.

But to most interpreters it seemed that even if Cain had something to do with bringing about the flood, his crime could not have been the *only* thing involved—for otherwise, why had God waited so long after the murder before destroying humanity? There must have been another reason.

The Immortal Enoch

Some supposed that the human beings who came after Cain had been almost as bad as Cain himself, and that the flood was thus the result of *all* the evil that had piled up from the time of Adam and Eve to that of Noah. Accordingly, this period, the ten generations from Adam to Noah, eventually came to be regarded as a time of increasing corruption.

> There were ten generations from Adam to Noah. This demonstrates how patient God was, for all these generations brought God to anger, until He brought upon the waters of the flood. —m. *Abot* 6:2

In other words, it was only after God had patiently delayed punishment over these ten evil generations—waiting for some sign of goodness—that He finally visited on Noah's generation the deserved punishment.

But such an explanation was difficult to accept. Certainly *some* of the people who lived during the ten generations were thought to have been good, notably Adam's son Seth, or later, Enosh and Enoch. Enoch in particular struck most ancient interpreters as the very model of virtue and piety.

Enoch is mentioned among the descendants of Seth in Gen. 5:18–24. In spite of this brief "cameo appearance" in Genesis, a great deal of speculation surrounded Enoch—in particular because of a few peculiarities in the biblical description of him:

> And Enoch lived sixty-five years and he became the father of Methuselah. And Enoch **walked with God** after he became the father of Methuselah for three hundred years; and he fathered sons and daughters. And all the days of Enoch were three hundred and sixty-five years. And Enoch **walked with God**; and he was not, for **God had taken him**. —Gen. 5:21–24

---

1. That is not to say that Cain's sin was all that was involved, even for the author of the Wisdom of Solomon. See below.

One thing interpreters concluded from this passage was that Enoch must have been especially righteous, since he is twice said to have "walked with God," whereas the same phrase is only used once of the righteous Noah (Gen. 6:9). (The Septuagint version rendered "walked with God" as "was pleasing to God," and this may have seemed to underline Enoch's virtue to readers of the Greek text.) As for the cryptic phrase "he was not, for God had taken him," this was interpreted to mean that Enoch had *not died*—his death is, after all, not mentioned—but that he had instead ascended bodily into heaven while still alive, a notion detailed by such texts as *1 Enoch*, which recounted at length Enoch's heavenly journey:

> And Enoch was pleasing to God; and he was not, for God had **transferred** him. — Septuagint Gen. 5:24

> And the vision appeared to me as follows . . . : winds caused me [Enoch] to fly and hastened me and **lifted me up into heaven**.
> — *1 Enoch* 14:8 (also [4Q204] *1 Enoch* col. 6:21)

> Few on earth were created like Enoch, and he was likewise **taken within**.[2] — Sir. 49:14

> And the Lord said to [the angel] Michael: Go and extract Enoch from his earthly clothing. And anoint him with my delightful oil, and put him into the clothes of My glory. — *2 Enoch* (J) 22:8

> [Noah] lived longer on the earth than [other] people, **except Enoch** because of his righteousness in which he was perfect; for Enoch's work was something created as a warning to the generations of the world, so that he should report all deeds of each generation on the day of judgment. — *Jubilees* 10:17

> He [Enoch] was "transferred," that is, he changed his abode and journeyed as an emigrant from the mortal life to the immortal.
> — Philo, *Change of Names* 38

> He [Enoch] lived three hundred and sixty-five years and then returned to the divinity, which is why nothing is recorded concerning his death.

> However, concerning Elijah and Enoch, who lived before the Flood, it is written in the sacred books that they became invisible, and no one knows of their death. — Josephus, *Jewish Antiquities*, 1:85, 9:28

---

2. "Taken within"—a somewhat obscure phrase—seems to mean taken bodily inside heaven. Ben Sira says "likewise"; he had earlier mentioned Elijah's ascent into Heaven (Sir. 48:9–10).

> By faith was Enoch taken up **so that he should not see death**; and he
> was not found, because God had taken him. Now before he was taken
> he was attested as having pleased God.[3]   —Heb. 11:5

Enoch was thus held to be similar to the prophet Elijah, who, the Bible later
implies, likewise entered heaven alive. Indeed, Scripture uses the same word in
both cases: God "took" Enoch and Elijah (Gen. 5:24, 2 Kings 2:1). However, in
some later texts Enoch was presented as less than righteous and his immortality was sometimes denied:

> And Enoch walked in the fear of the Lord, and he was not, for the Lord
> **had killed him.**   — *Targum Onqelos* Gen. 5:24

The Heavenly Scribe

Having—according to many interpreters—entered heaven alive, Enoch was
naturally assumed to have continued living there, and, in the process, to have
acquired a unique knowledge of "heavenly things"—not only the ways of God
and the angels, but also of natural phenomena on earth as observed from
above. It is in part upon this (very old) assumption that there arose an early
body of writings attributed to Enoch: several ancient authors, speaking
through the figure of Enoch, set forth their own ideas as well as ancient
traditions about the world and future history.

In so doing, these writers—and other ancient interpreters who followed
them—frequently referred to "Enoch the [Heavenly] Scribe": he had to be a
scribe in order for his esoteric knowledge to have been transmitted back to
human beings in written form. Some ancient writers therefore also stressed
Enoch's connection with the art of writing, specifying as well that his information had come to him from the angels he encountered in heaven:

> And I, Enoch, was blessing the Great Lord and King of Eternity, and
> behold the Watchers called to me, Enoch the **scribe**, and said to me:
> "Enoch, scribe of righteousness, go inform the Watchers of heaven
> who have left the high heaven and holy eternal place, and have cor-
> rupted themselves with the women."
>
> And the Lord called me with His own mouth and said to me, . . . "Hear!
> Do not be afraid, Enoch, scribe of righteousness. Come here and hear
> my voice."   — *1 Enoch* 12:3–4; 14:24–15:1

---

3. This last part may reflect the Septuagint translation of "Enoch walked with God" (Gen. 5:22),
namely, "Enoch *was pleasing* to God."

And he [the angel] said to me: O Enoch, look at the book of the tablets of heaven and **read what is written** upon them and note every individual fact. And I looked at everything in the tablets of heaven and I read everything which was written and I noted everything.

—*1 Enoch* 81:1–2

And he called him Enoch. He was the first of mankind born on earth who **learned writing** and instruction and wisdom from [among] the sons of men the signs of the sky in accord with the fixed pattern of their months, so that mankind would know the seasons of the years according to the fixed pattern of each of their months. He was the **first to write** a testimony. He testified to [that is, warned] mankind in the generations of the earth: the weeks of the jubilees he related, and made known the days of the years; the months he arranged, and related the sabbaths of the years, as **we** [angels] **had told** him.

And he was therefore with the angels of God six jubilees of years, and they showed him everything which is on earth and in the heavens, and the rule of the sun, and he **wrote down everything**.

For the work of Enoch had been created as a witness to the generations of the world, so that he might report every deed of each generation in the day of judgment.   —*Jubilees* 4:17–18, 21; 10:17

. . .E]noch, after **we** [angels?] **taught him**[. . .
. . .]six jubilees of years[. . .
. . .ea]rth, to among the sons of men, and he testified against [that is, warned] them about all things[. . .
. . .]and also about the Watchers, and he **wrote everything down**[. . .
. . .]the heavens and the ways of their hosts, and the mo[nths. . .
. . .S]o that the ri[ghteous?] not go astray[. . .

—(4Q227) *Pseudo-Jubilees*

. . . in the writing of Enoch, the excellent **scribe** . . .

—(4Q203) *Book of Giants*ᵃ, fragment 8

[God says:] "Apply your mind, Enoch, and acknowledge the One who is speaking. And take the **books** which you yourself have written . . . and go down to earth and tell your sons all that I have told you . . . and give them the books in your handwriting . . . and let them distribute the books in your handwriting, children to children and family to family and kinfolk to kinfolk."

And he remained in heaven for sixty days, writing down all [those] notes about all the creatures which the Lord had created. And he wrote **three hundred sixty-six books** and he handed them over to his sons.

— *2 Enoch* (J) 33:5–9; 68:1–2

[In the heavenly court] the one who produces the evidence is the teacher of heaven and earth and the **scribe of righteousness**, Enoch.

— *Testament of Abraham* 11:3

And Enoch served faithfully before God and behold he was not with the inhabitants of the earth, for he had perished and ascended to heaven and He called his name Metatron **the great scribe**.

— *Targum Pseudo-Jonathan* Gen. 5:24

In line with his scribal functions as presented in some of the passages cited above, Enoch was also held to have written things down as a legal scribe or officer of the court:

And they asked me [Enoch] to **write out** for them the record of a **petition** that they might receive forgiveness, and to take the record of their petition up to the Lord in heaven . . .

And behold a dream came to me . . . and I saw a vision of wrath, that I should speak to the sons of heaven and **reprove** them.

The book of the words of righteousness and **reproof** of the Watchers . . . As He has created and appointed men to understand the word of knowledge, so He created and appointed me to **reprove** the Watchers, the sons of heaven.

— *1 Enoch* 13:4, 8; 14:1, 4 [≅ 4Q204 *Enoch*ᶜ col. 6]

He was the first to write a **testimony**. He testified to [that is, warned] mankind in the generations of the earth . . . And behold he [Enoch] is there [in heaven] writing down the condemnation and judgment of the world, and all the wickedness of the children of men.

— *Jubilees* 4:18, 23

Words of "reproof" or "reproach," as well as words of "testimony" or "witness," were warnings that the law required to be administered before sentence could be imposed (see Chapter 22). Other Qumran fragments seem to refer to the same motif:

And he [Enoch] **testified against** [that is, warned] them about all things[. . .

— (4Q227) *Pseudo-Jubilees*

Did not Enoch **accuse**[. . .
. . .]and who will bear the guilt[. . .
[if] not I and you, my children. Then you will know[. . .
— (4Q213) *Aramaic Levi*ᵃ fragment 5, col. 3.6–7

Enoch the Sage

Of a piece with "Enoch the Heavenly Scribe" are the still more numerous references to him as a wise man and, in particular, an astronomer. After all, any Jewish scribe of late antiquity was almost by definition also a sage. Moreover, the fact that "Enoch's" writings came to include an entire treatise on astronomy and related phenomena (*1 Enoch* 72–82) caused him to be thought of as a master of astral sciences and to be presented in terms redolent of ancient scholarship:

And in those days [the angel] Uriel answered me and said to me: "Behold I have shown you everything, O Enoch, and have revealed everything to you, that you may see this sun, and this moon, and those who lead the stars of heaven, and all those who turn them, their tasks, and their times, and their rising."   — *1 Enoch* 80:1

And he [Enoch] wrote in a book the signs of the heaven according to the order of their months, so that the sons of man might know the [appointed] times of the years according to their order.   — *Jubilees* 4:17

Abraham . . . explained astrology and the other sciences to them [the Egyptian priests], saying that the Babylonians and he himself had obtained this knowledge. However, he attributed the discovery of them to Enoch. Enoch first discovered astrology, not the Egyptians.
        — [Pseudo-]Eupolemus (Eusebius, *Praeparatio Evangelica* 9.17.8)

[Enoch was] a sign of **knowledge** forever and ever.
        — Sir. (Hebrew) 44:16

. . . since he [Enoch] is beloved and since [with the holy ones] is his lot apportioned and **they inform him of everything**.
        — *Genesis Apocryphon* 2:20–21

It was of these also that Enoch in the seventh generation from Adam prophesied, saying, "Behold the Lord came with his holy myriads to execute judgment . . ." [a quotation from *1 Enoch* 1.9].   — Jude 14–15

This accumulated learning Enoch passed on to later generations through his son Methuselah:

> And now, my son Methuselah, all these things I recount to you and write down for you; I have revealed everything to you and have given you books about all these things. Keep, my son Methuselah, the books from the hand of your father, that you may pass [them] on to the generations of eternity.
>
> — *1 Enoch* 82:1

> The Greeks say that Atlas discovered astrology. However, Atlas is the same as Enoch. The son of Enoch was Methuselah. He learned everything through the angels of God, and so knowledge came to us.
>
> — [Pseudo-]Eupolemus (Eusebius, *Praeparatio Evangelica* 9.17.9)

> and now I [Enoch] say to you. . .and to you I make known [. . .
> Go, say to Lamech, your son [. . .
> And when Methuselah heard [. . .
>
> — *Genesis Apocryphon* 5:9–10, 24

Enoch the Penitent

Another important aspect of Enoch's image also emerged from the brief biblical passage cited above:

> And Enoch lived sixty-five years and he became the father of Methuselah. And Enoch walked with God **after he became the father of Methuselah** for three hundred years; and he fathered sons and daughters.
>
> — Gen. 5:21–22

The text says that Enoch walked with God (Septuagint: "was pleasing to God"—see above) *after* Methuselah's birth. The clear implication is that before Methuselah's birth he did not walk with God (or was not pleasing to Him). From this interpreters concluded that Enoch had repented—he may have done evil at the beginning of his life, but after his son's birth he changed his ways:

> Enoch pleased the Lord, and was taken up; he was an example of repentance to all generations.
>
> — Sir. (Greek) 44:16

> There was one [Enoch] who pleased God and was loved by him, and while living among sinners was taken up. He was caught up lest evil change his understanding, or guile deceive his soul . . . Being **per-**

NOAH AND THE FLOOD ❖ 107

fected in a short time,[4] he fulfilled long years; for his soul was pleasing to the Lord, therefore he took him quickly from the midst of wickedness.

What is the meaning of the words, "Enoch was pleasing to God after he begot Methuselah . . ."? [Scripture] legislates about the sources of all good things at the beginning of Genesis . . . For not very long after the forgiving of Cain it introduces the fact that **Enoch repented**, informing us that forgiveness is wont to produce repentance.

— Philo, *Questions and Answers in Genesis,* 1:82

Moses next mentions [Enoch], who changed from the worse life to the better; he is called in Hebrew "Enoch," which in Greek means "recipient of grace." — Philo, "On Abraham," 17

And Enoch lived after he became the father of Methuselah for 200 years, and he was the father of five sons and three daughters. However, Enoch pleased God **at that time** and he was not found, for God had transferred him.[5] — Pseudo-Philo, *Biblical Antiquities* 1:15–16

In short, Enoch was a righteous man, or at least a righteous penitent. It seemed unlikely to most interpreters that, after such a person, God would nonetheless punish the world for a sin that Cain had committed generations before Enoch. Instead, they looked to the events immediately preceding the flood.

A Bad Match

The Bible says little openly. One rather cryptic passage, however, seemed to interpreters to imply that one truly evil thing had occurred just before the flood episode:

When people began to multiply on the face of the earth, and daughters were born to them, the sons of God saw that the daughters of men

4. If Enoch was sixty-five when Methuselah was born, and *after that* he "walked with God," then it must be that he became "perfected" at the age of sixty-five, a relatively short time in the view of the author of the Wisdom of Solomon. Incidentally, where the traditional Hebrew text puts Enoch's age at sixty-five here, the Septuagint says that he was *one hundred* and sixty-five.

5. The phrase "at that time" is not found in Gen. 5:24; its addition appears designed to reflect the motif "Enoch the Penitent." Note also that both the "200 years" and "transferred" here agree with the Septuagint against the traditional Hebrew text.

were fair; and **they married such of them as they chose**. Then the Lord said, "My spirit shall not abide in man for ever, for he is flesh, but his days shall be a hundred and twenty years." The Nephilim were on the earth in those days, and also afterward, when the **sons of God came in to the daughters of men**, and they bore children to them. These were the mighty men that were of old, the men of renown. Then the Lord saw that the wickedness of man was great on the earth.

—Gen. 6:1–5

It is hard to know what to make of this strange passage even today. In any case, ancient readers saw in these words a hint that the immediate cause of the flood (and perhaps of other ills) had been the mating of the "sons of God" (generally interpreted to mean some sort of angel or heavenly creature)[6] with the "daughters of men." The flood must have come about, directly or indirectly, as a result of this union. Perhaps it was because of some sort of sexual profligacy implied in this passage, or because the mating of these two groups brought about a new race of beings who were given over to sinfulness, or because, through their contact with the humans, the angels had passed along a knowledge of secret things that led to the humans' corruption. All three traditions are found intermingled even in the most ancient writings of the period.

And the angels, the sons of heaven,[7] saw them and desired them. And they said to one another: Come, let us choose for ourselves wives from the children of men, and let us beget for ourselves children.

And they took wives for themselves and everyone chose for himself one each. And they began to go in to them and were promiscuous with them. And they taught them charms and spells, and showed to them the cutting of roots and trees. And they became pregnant and bore great giants, whose height was three thousand cubits. These devoured all the [products of the] toil of men, until men were unable to sustain them. Then the giants turned against them in order to devour men. And they began to sin against birds, and against animals, and against reptiles, and against fish, and they devoured one another's flesh and drank the blood from it.

6. Some ancient writers refer to these as the "Watchers." This term (the Aramaic 'irin) is used of a type of angel in Dan. 4:11, 20 (some versions, 4:13, 23) and was employed specifically with regard to Gen. 6:1–4 in 1 and 2 *Enoch, Jubilees,* and other writings.

7. That is, the "sons of God" spoken of in Gen. 6:1.

And the women bore giants, and thereby the whole earth has been filled with blood and iniquity.[8]

— 1 Enoch 6:2–7:5, 9:9 (≅ [4Q201] 1 Enoch col. 3)

And it came to pass that when the children of men began to multiply on the face of the earth and daughters were born to them, that the angels of God saw . . . that they were beautiful to look upon. So they [the angels] married of them [the human females] whomever they chose. They gave birth to children for them and the[se] were giants. Wickedness increased on the earth. All flesh corrupted its way—from people to cattle, animals, birds, and everything that moves about on the ground. All of them corrupted their way and their prescribed course. They began to devour each other, and wickedness increased on the earth. Every thought of all mankind's knowledge was in this way continually evil. The Lord saw the earth, and behold it was corrupted, and all flesh had corrupted its prescribed course, and all that were upon the earth had acted wickedly before His eyes. And He said that He would destroy man and all flesh upon the earth which He had created. But Noah found favor in the eyes of the Lord.

— Jubilees 5:1–5 (also 7:21–25)

In examining these and other ancient traditions about the flood, it is difficult to judge how much of their contents arose exclusively out of a contemplation of the biblical material and how much may have been influenced by outside factors. (This is particularly so in the case of 1 Enoch, which, because of its great antiquity and its overall connection to Mesopotamian lore—which had itself preserved the memory of a great flood—may well have passed on traditions originally unrelated to the biblical text.) Whatever their origins, however, these traditions, transmitted to later readers, suggested that the flood narrated in Genesis had, in one of the three ways mentioned, resulted from the disastrous union of human females with the angels.[9]

8. In this part of 1 Enoch, the act of the "sons of God" in mating with the "daughters of men" is interpreted as a rebellion against God, a "great sin" (1 Enoch 6:3). The "giants" (see below) apparently result from this forbidden union. Even though the Bible seems to praise them as "men of renown," our text presents them as a race of tyrannical and oppressive creatures who terrorize humanity, deplete the earth's resources, and spread violence and death everywhere.

9. 1 Enoch was itself undoubtedly considered by many to be sacred Scripture—it is cited, for example, in the New Testament, Jude 14—and its contents were themselves interpreted and passed on as authoritative teachings supplementing the Genesis narrative.

The Wicked Giants

In particular, attention came to be focused on the offspring of the angels ("sons of God") and the humans. On the one hand, the Bible describes these hybrid offspring as "mighty men of old, men of renown" (Gen. 6:4)—which certainly makes them sound good. On the other hand, since the very next verse speaks of the "wickedness" of humanity, most interpreters were inclined to see these divine-human creatures in a less than positive light.

One clue as to their true nature lay in the sentence cited earlier, "The Nephilim were on the earth in those days, and also afterward, when the sons of God came in to the daughters of men, and they bore children to them" (Gen. 6:4). It was not clear to interpreters if these Nephilim *were* the divine-human hybrids, or if they merely were around at the time when this mating took place. Nor was the meaning of the word "Nephilim" crystal clear to them. However, this word does occur in one other place in the Bible, in the report of the Israelite spies whom Moses sent to scout out the land of Canaan:

> [The returning spies said:] The land through which we have gone to spy it out is a land that devours its inhabitants, and all the people that we saw in it are men of **great stature**. And there we saw the **Nephilim** (the sons of Anak, who come from the Nephilim), and we seemed to ourselves like grasshoppers, and so we seemed to them.
>
> —Num. 13:32–33

This passage implies that Nephilim were giants, "men of great stature," in comparison to whom the spies "seemed to ourselves like grasshoppers, and so we seemed to them." Here, then, was an indication from elsewhere that the word "Nephilim" meant "giants." This identification of the Nephilim in Gen. 6:4 is attested early:

> The **giants** were on the earth in those days, and after that, when the sons of God went into the daughters of men.   —Septuagint Gen. 6:4

If the Nephilim were giants, then it did make sense that *they* were the offspring of the "sons of God" and human females—where else would giants come from but such a divine-human union? And if they were described as "mighty men of old, the men of renown," this was probably just a reflection of their great physical size, not of their moral standing.[10] Indeed, they must have been bad if the Bible mentions them just before God resolves to bring the flood.

---

10. In keeping with this view, the Septuagint version has for the Hebrew phrase "mighty men of old" the Greek "*giants* of old," using the same word for "giants" as it had for the Nephilim mentioned at the beginning of this verse.

Thus it seemed that these giants were fundamentally wicked. Did not the very fact that they were described as "mighty" imply that they were arrogant rebels whose great size led them to challenge God's authority?

> He [God] did not forgive the princes of yore, who in their might
> **rebelled** of old.[11]
>
> — Sir. 16:7

> The giants were born there, who were famous of old, great in
> stature, expert in war.
> God did not choose them, nor give them the way to knowledge,
> so they perished, because they had no wisdom, they perished
> through their folly.
>
> — Bar. 3:26–28

Abraham traced his ancestry to the giants. These dwelt in the land of Babylonia. Because of their impiety, they were destroyed by the gods.

— Anonymous tradition cited in Eusebius, *Praeparatio Evangelica* 9.18.2

The interpretation [*pesher*] concerning Azazel and the angels wh[o went in to the daughters of men and b]ore them giants, and concerning Azazel [who turned them astray to deceit, to the love of] evil and to pass along wickedness . . . — (4Q180) *Pesher of the Periods* 7–9

For even in the beginning, when **arrogant** giants were perishing, the hope of the world took refuge on a raft. — Wisd. 14:6

You did destroy long ago those who did injustice, among whom were the giants trusting in their strength and **arrogance**, bringing upon them a boundless flood of water. — 3 Macc. 2:4

[Hear me] so that you are not taken in by the designs of the inclination to evil and by lustful eyes . . .

The Watchers of Heaven [that is, the "sons of God"] fell because of this; they were taken because they did not keep the commandments of God. And their sons—as tall as cedar trees and whose bodies were like mountains—[likewise] fell. All flesh on dry land perished, they were as though they had not been, because they **did their own will** and did not keep the commandments of their Maker, so that his anger was kindled against them. — *Damascus Document* 2:16–21

---

11. The Hebrew text of Sirach makes it clear that this is a reference to the Nephilim, the "mighty men that were of old," both by its use of the word "might" and, in one surviving manuscript, the same expression "of old" that appears in Gen. 6:4.

For many angels of God had consorted with women and brought forth wanton children, children who were disdainful of all good because of their **overweening** trust in brute strength.

— Josephus, *Jewish Antiquities* 1:73

From them were born the giants who walked about **haughtily** and indulged themselves in all manner of theft and corruption and bloodshed.

— *Pirqei deR. Eliezer* 22

In short, the union of the "sons of God" with the "daughters of men" had, either by itself or because of the hybrid giants who resulted from this union, caused God to bring about the flood.

But then another question occurred to interpreters: Why did God decide to spare Noah and his family? What had Noah done to be so singled out? There is not a *single* good deed of Noah's that is told about before the flood. Why then should Scripture have said that "Noah found favor in the eyes of the Lord" (Gen. 6:8)? Interpreters were also anxious to know why God had not at least warned the other human beings of impending doom before the flood actually occurred. Certainly it was not in the nature of divine justice to impose a penalty without prior warning. Should not God have given them some opportunity to repent?

One Hundred and Twenty until Punishment

A possible answer to this second question (and, eventually, to the first as well) was spotted by interpreters in the biblical passage already seen above. For there, it will be recalled, God had reacted to the deeds of His "sons" with a particular pronouncement:

When people began to multiply on the face of the earth, and daughters were born to them, the sons of God saw that the daughters of men were fair; and they married such of them as they chose. Then the Lord said, "My spirit shall not abide in man for ever, for he is flesh, but **his days shall be a hundred and twenty years.**"

— Gen. 6:1–3

These words spoken by God were not taken by most interpreters at face value, that is, as if God were now decreeing that humans could not live more than a hundred and twenty years each. How could such an interpretation be correct, when so many later biblical figures lived considerably longer? (Noah himself lived to the age 950, while his son Shem lived to 600, his grandson Arpachshad to 438, his great-grandson Shelah to 433, his great-great-grandson Eber to 464, and so forth.)

And so, these words were instead interpreted as a warning: if human beings don't improve, I will destroy them *a hundred and twenty years from now.* Alternately, what God might have meant was, I will destroy the wicked people of this generation at an early age (for those days, at least), namely, when they are one hundred and twenty years old. In either case, God's words did not announce a fundamental change in human longevity but warned of an impending punishment of the *flood generation alone.* Such an understanding is attested as early as the Septuagint translation of the Bible:

> And the Lord God said: "My spirit will not abide **with these men** forever, because they are flesh, but their days shall be one hundred and twenty years." —Septuagint Gen. 6:3 (also Symmachus Gen. 6:3)

Where the traditional Hebrew text reads, "My spirit shall not abide *in man*"— apparently a general pronouncement about all of humanity—the Septuagint specifies that God was talking only about a particular group of humans, the generation of the flood. The same idea was stated or implied by other interpreters:

> In the four hundred and eightieth year of Noah's life, their end-time was made known to Noah, for God said: My spirit will not abide in man forever. Let their days be cut short, one hundred and twenty years, until the time of the flood.[12] —(4Q252) *Genesis Pesher* col. 1:1–3

> And God said, "This evil generation shall not endure before me forever; for they are flesh and their deeds are evil. I will grant them an extension of one hundred and twenty years, [to see] if they repent. —*Targum Onqelos* Gen. 6:3

> And the Lord said: None of the generations that is to arise will be judged according to the judgment of the generation of the flood. In truth, the judgment of the generation of the flood is sealed before Me, to have it destroyed and blotted out from the midst of the world. Behold, I have given my spirit to the sons of man because they are flesh and their works are evil. Behold, I have given you the space of a hundred and twenty years [hoping that] they might repent, but they have not done so. —*Targum Neophyti* Gen. 6:3

> For you gave an extension to the generation of the flood in order to repent, and they did not repent; as it is said, "My spirit shall not abide in man." —*Mekhilta deR. Ishmael, Beshallaḥ* 5

12. Here, the 120 years are clearly the time until the flood, since Noah's age at the time of this supposed warning, 480, plus 120 equals his stated age at the onset of the flood, 600 (Gen. 7:6).

God established for them a time after one hundred and twenty years in case they should repent, but they did not.

— *Abot deR. Nathan* (A) 32

In the time of Noah, He also gave the wicked a period of one hundred and twenty years, but they were unwilling to repent.

— Aphrahat the Persian (cited in Funk, *Die Haggadische Elemente*, 27)

They had one hundred and twenty years [in which] to repent. This does not mean, as many erroneously believe, that human life was to be shrunk down to one hundred and twenty years. But to that particular generation, one hundred and twenty years were given until the punishment.

— Jerome, *Questions in Genesis* 6:3

When God said "Their days will be one hundred and twenty years," this certainly is not to be understood as if it were foretelling that henceforth human beings would not live more than one hundred and twenty years, since even after the flood we find that [some] exceeded five hundred . . . But the one hundred and twenty years predicted here are [what remain of] the lives of the peoples who were to perish: after these [years] had passed, they were destroyed in the flood.

— Augustine, *City of God* 15.24

Here, then, was proof that humanity had been given an opportunity to repent and stave off disaster.

Noah Warned of the Flood

As for Noah's (unspoken) good deeds before the flood, they came to be connected to this idea of a warning prior to the flood. For if Noah had "found favor in the eyes of the Lord," was it not merely logical that he himself—by his example, or perhaps by actual exhortation—had tried to turn his fellow human beings away from sin and so save them from destruction? Support for this idea was found, once again, in the passage cited above:

Then the Lord **said**, "My spirit shall not abide in man for ever, for he is flesh, but his days shall be a hundred and twenty years." — Gen. 6:3

Said to whom? If the reference to one hundred and twenty years was indeed a warning, then this warning must have been spoken to some human being(s) in the hope of being heeded. Since Noah is later singled out as *the* righteous man of his time, it seemed only natural to interpreters that the divine warning was spoken to him—and that he must have immediately passed it along to his contemporaries, perhaps trying to get them to mend their ways and so be saved. Thus emerged the figure of Noah the preacher:

> To him God Himself spoke as follows from heaven:
> "Noah, embolden yourself, and proclaim repentance
> to all the peoples, so that all may be saved.
> But if they do not heed, since they have a shameless spirit,
> I will destroy the entire race with great floods of water . . ."
> [Then Noah] **entreated the peoples** and began to speak such words:
> "Men, sated with faithlessness, smitten with great madness,
> what you did will not escape the notice of God."
> — *Sibylline Oracles* 1:127–131, 149–151

> But Noah, displeased with the deeds [of his contemporaries] and finding their intentions to be odious, sought to persuade them to [adopt] a better way of thinking and to change their ways.
> — Josephus, *Jewish Antiquities* 1:73

> [God] preserved Noah, a **herald** of righteousness.
> — 2 Pet. 2:5 (see also 1 Pet. 3:19–20)

> Noah preached repentance, and those who obeyed were saved.
> — *1 Clement* 7:6 (also 9:1)

> [Noah recalls:] "And I did not cease proclaiming to men, 'Repent, for behold, a deluge is coming.' But no one heeded."
> — *Revelation of Paul* 50

> Noah preached repentance.   — Clement of Alexandria, *Miscellanies* 1, 21

> The righteous Noah used to warn them [his contemporaries] and say to them: Repent, for if you do not, God will bring a flood upon you.
> — b. *Sanhedrin* 108a

> But the greatness of the light of the foreknowledge informed Noah, and he proclaimed [it] to all the offspring which are the sons of men. But those who were strangers to him did not listen.
> — *Apocryphon of John* 29:1–5

> And he [Noah] preached piety for one hundred and twenty years. And no one listened to him.
> — *Concept of Our Great Power* 38:25–28 (also 43.17–20)

Noah the Righteous

This tradition of Noah the preacher helped to explain why God had saved him. Noah had gone about trying to get others to repent—certainly this was one good deed to his credit. Perhaps this was why Scripture had called him "righteous" (Gen. 6:9, 7:1; see also Ezek. 14:14). In any case, Noah's righteousness was elaborated by many interpreters:

> And in those days the word of the Lord came to me [Noah], and He said to me: Noah, behold your lot has come up before me, a lot without reproach, a lot of love and of uprightness.   — *1 Enoch* 67:1

> On account of his righteousness, in which he [Noah] was perfected, his life on earth was more excellent than [any of] the sons of men except Enoch.   — *Jubilees* 10:17

> The righteous Noah was found to be perfect, in time of
>   destruction he was a ransom [for humanity].
> Because of him a remnant was left, and by his covenant floods
>   ceased.   — Sir. 44:17

> When the earth was flooded . . . wisdom again saved it, steering the righteous man by a paltry piece of wood.   — Wisd. 10:4

> [The name] "Noah" means "righteousness."
>   — Philo, *The Worse Attacks the Better* 121 (also *On Abraham* 27;
>   *Questions and Answers in Genesis* 1:87)

> Noah alone among all was most upright and true,
>   a most trustworthy man, concerned for noble deeds.
>   — *Sibylline Oracles* 1:125

> God loved him [Noah] for his righteousness.
>   — Josephus, *Jewish Antiquities* 1:75

> God used a most righteous man to be the father of all born after the flood.   — Origen, *Contra Celsum* 4:41

Only in His Generation

This opinion was not unanimous, however. Some interpreters felt that Noah was hardly a model of righteousness: apart from his heeding (and perhaps passing on) God's warning, he does not seem to have done anything remarkable before the flood—and even afterward, his conduct seemed hardly exemplary. In particular, the incident of Noah's drunkenness (Gen. 9:20–27) did not seem to speak well of him. Perhaps he was not so righteous after all.

For this opinion as well Scripture seemed to offer some support. When Noah is first introduced, the text says, "Noah was a righteous man, blameless *in his generation*" (Gen. 6:9). The last words seem to be some sort of qualification or reservation. And in the next chapter, God says to Noah,

> Go into the ark, you and all your household, for I have seen that you are righteous before Me **in this generation.** —Gen. 7:1

Here again is the same qualification. No wonder, then, that some interpreters expressed doubt about Noah's righteousness:

> However, having praised that man [Noah] with regard to these virtues, [the text] adds that he was "perfect in his generation," indicating that he was good not in absolute terms, but in comparison with the people who were living at that time. —Philo, *Abraham* 36

> "Noah was a righteous man, blameless in his generation" [Gen. 6:9]. R. Judah and R. Nehemiah disagreed on this verse. R. Judah said: In *his generation* he was righteous; had he lived in the generation of Moses or the generation of Samuel, he would not have been considered righteous . . . R. Nehemiah said: if even *in his generation* he was a righteous man, had he lived in the generation of Moses or Samuel, how much more of a righteous man would he have been!
> —*Genesis Rabba* 30:9

> It says specifically "in his generation," so as to show that he was not just according to perfect justice, but that by the standards of justice of his generation was he just. —Jerome, *Questions in Genesis* 6:9

In other words, Noah's somewhat shaky credentials as a righteous man are to be understood in the context of his times. If his virtues were not always conspicuous, the fact is that those around him were so depraved as to make his conduct look exemplary by comparison.

The Animals Also Sinned

Many interpreters were troubled by the fact that the flood killed animal life as well as people. That people were somehow guilty might be figured out from the mention of the "daughters of men" as well as the crimes with which the earth was filled. But what did the animals do wrong? Perhaps they were merely guilty by association:

In the first place, just as when a king is killed in battle, his military forces are also struck down together with him, so [God] decided now that when the human race was to be destroyed like a king, other beasts should be destroyed together with it . . . Second, just as when the head is cut off, no one blames nature if the various other parts of the body also die together with it, so also no one will now condemn [this] . . . Third, the beasts were made not for their own sake, but for the service and needs and honor of man. It is right that when those are taken away for whose sake they [the beasts] were made, they too should be deprived of life.   —Philo, *Questions and Answers in Genesis* 2:9 (also 1:94)

Some, however, felt that the destruction of the animals in the flood must have been deserved. It seemed only reasonable to suppose that they had somehow participated in the corruption that had previously filled the earth.

And they began to sin with[13] birds, and with animals, and with reptiles, and with fish . . .   —*1 Enoch* 7:5 ([4Q201] *1 Enoch* col. 319–320)

And lawlessness increased on the earth and all flesh corrupted its way, alike men and cattle and beasts and birds and everything that walks the earth—all of them corrupted their ways and their orders.

And afterwards they sinned against beasts and birds and everything that moves or walks upon the earth.   —*Jubilees* 5:2, 7:24

The generation of Noah was plunged in wantonness and used to have sexual relations with those who were not of their kind. For it is written about them, "And the sons of God beheld the daughters of men . . ." [Gen. 6:2] and for that reason they were destroyed. And even animals were so corrupted with those not of their species, horse with donkey and donkey with horse and snake with bird, as it says, "For all flesh had gone astray . . ." [Gen. 6:12]. It does not say "all humans" but "all flesh," therefore, "And He destroyed all of creation which was on the face of the earth, from man to beast . . ." [Gen. 7:23].

    —*Midrash Tanḥuma, Noaḥ* 12

The Purifying Flood

God could have destroyed humanity in any manner He desired. Why did He bring a flood, first drenching all of creation and then waiting for the world slowly to dry out? The process suggested to interpreters a sort of enormous,

13. The Aramaic text reads *mn qwbl*, that is, "with regard to" or, in this context, "by means of."

purifying bath. And since such baths played a crucial role in everyday life, having been prescribed in the Bible as the means for cleansing priests and ordinary citizens from physical impurity, it was only natural to suppose that God had chosen the flood as a means not only of destroying life on earth but of purifying the very land of the abominations that had been committed upon it.

[God says to the angel Michael:] Destroy all wrong from the face of earth . . . and **cleanse** the earth from all wrong, and from all iniquity, and from all sin, and from all impiety, and from all uncleanness which brought about on the earth; **remove them** from the earth.

— *1 Enoch* 10:20

When the Creator took it to mind to cleanse the earth by means of water and decided that the soul [symbolized by the earth] should be purged of its unmentionable ill deeds and have its uncleanness washed away in the manner of a sacred purification . . .

— Philo, *The Worse Attacks the Better* 170

You have heard, my son Seth, that a flood is come and will wash the whole earth. — *Testament of Adam* 3:5

For this reason, [God,] having forewarned a certain righteous man [Noah] along with his three [sons] and their wives and remaining [family] to find refuge in an ark, sent a deluge of water, so that, after all had been destroyed, the world, having been **purified**, might be given over clean for a second beginning of life to that same person who had been saved in the ark. — *Pseudo-Clementine Homilies* 8.17.4

For some unknown reason he [Celsus] thinks that the overthrow of the tower [of Babel] had a similar purpose to that of the flood, which, according to the doctrine of Jews and Christians, **purified** the earth. — Origen, *Contra Celsum* 4.21

The idea of the cleansing flood was adapted by some early Christians, who saw in it a typological foreshadowing of the sacrament of baptism:

God's patience waited in the days of Noah, during the building of the ark, in which a few, that is, eight persons, were saved through water. Baptism, which corresponds to this, now saves you, not as a removal of dirt from the body but as an appeal to God for a clear conscience.

— 1 Pet. 3:20–21

Elsewhere in the New Testament, the story of the flood was presented as a model or prefiguring of the end of days:

> As were the days of Noah, so will be the coming of the Son of man. For as in those days before the flood they were eating and drinking, marrying and giving in marriage, until the day when Noah entered the ark, and they did not know until the flood came and swept them all away, so will be the coming of the Son of man. — Matt. 24:37–39

> [Scoffers] deliberately ignore this fact, that by the word of God heavens existed long ago, and an earth was formed out of water and by means of water, through which the world that then existed was deluged with water and perished. But by the same word the heavens and earth that now exist have been stored up for fire, being kept until the day of judgment and destruction of ungodly men. — 2 Pet. 3:5–7

❖   ❖   ❖

In short: The flood came about at least in part because of the mating of the "sons of God" (generally understood to be angels) with the daughters of humans, which produced a race of violent and corrupt giants. God gave people warning one hundred and twenty years in advance of the flood, but it did no good. God's decision to spare Noah in the flood came about in part because of Noah's zeal in trying to persuade others to repent of their sinful ways. Noah himself was outstanding against the background of his own time's iniquity, "righteous in his generation." Even the animals in Noah's time were sinful. The flood not only killed the wicked but purged the earth like a purifying bath.

6

The Tower of Babel

(GENESIS 11:1–9)

God and angels (right) went down to thwart the builders.

The Tower of Babel

(GENESIS 11:1–9)

❖   ❖   ❖

After the flood, Noah's three sons, Shem, Ham, and Japhet, all had children, and humanity increased and prospered. At this time "the whole earth was of one speech and one language" (Gen. 11:1). The people came to the land of Shinar and there they set out to build a great city with a high tower in it. God, however, was displeased with the idea and came down to frustrate their plans. He confused their speech, so that they could no longer understand one another, and they left off building the city and were scattered across the earth. The city was called Babel.

THE BRIEF STORY of the tower of Babel raised a number of questions in the mind of interpreters, but perhaps the most troubling was that of God's reaction to the project. After all, what was wrong about what the builders had tried to do? Their plans did not seem to have anything particularly wicked about them:

> Then they said, "Come, let us build ourselves a city, and a tower with its top in the heavens, and let us make a name for ourselves, lest we be scattered abroad upon the face of the whole earth." — Gen. 11:4

Ancient interpreters felt obliged to find something in these words that might justify the divine punishment that followed.

They Tried to Storm Heaven

Building a city certainly was not objectionable in itself. The only suspicious detail seemed to be the mention of the proposed tower, especially one so tall that its top would reach the heavens. And so the "city" part of this building project receded into the background: for interpreters, the tower seemed to be the whole point (that is why we still refer to the whole story as "the *tower* of Babel"), and its very height was assumed to be its offensive feature. The purpose of the tower came to be understood (although this is nowhere stated in the Bible itself) as the storming of heaven, an attempt by human beings to build a structure so tall that they could use it to climb up to the sky. A number of early sources reflect this tradition:

For they [the descendants of Noah] had emigrated from the land of Ararat [where the ark had landed] toward the east, to Shinar, and . . . they built the city and the tower, saying, "**Let us ascend on it into heaven.**" — *Jubilees* 10:19

They were all of one language
and they **wanted to go up to starry heaven.**
— *Sibylline Oracles* 3:99–100

[Later, the angel says:] "And they [these builders of the tower] had taken an auger, and **sought to pierce the heaven**, saying, 'Let us see whether the heaven is made of clay, or of brass, or of iron.' When God saw this He did not permit them, but smote them with blindness and confusion of speech." — *3 Baruch* 3:7–8

They said: Let us build a tower and climb to the firmament and **strike it with hatchets** until its waters flow forth. — b. *Sanhedrin* 109a

A War against God

Some saw the purpose as, more specifically, the storming of heaven as part of a war against God:

He who is zealous for earthly and corruptible things always fights against and makes **war** on heavenly things and praiseworthy and wonderful natures, and builds walls and towers on earth **against heaven.** — Philo, *Questions and Answers in Genesis* 2:82

[An angel said to Baruch:] "These are the ones who built the tower of the **war against God**, and the Lord removed them." — *3 Baruch* (Greek) 2:7

And they said: Come, let us build ourselves a city, and a tower whose top will reach to the heavens, and let us make for ourselves at its top an idol and we will put a sword in its hand, and it will **make war** against Him. — *Targum Neophyti* Gen. 11:4

If they [the builders] **waged war** with the Height, how much more shall they conquer him whose warfare is on earth?
— Ephraem, *Nisibene Hymns* 41.2

They built a tower and said, "Come, let us split the firmament to make **war** against it." — (Anonymous) Day of Atonement 'Abodah

Nimrod Built It

Of course, it is no mean feat to build a tower that reaches all the way to heaven. If God even took their plan to reach heaven seriously, the builders themselves must have been extraordinary people. Unfortunately, the Bible does not say who these builders were. But it contained one clue for ancient interpreters: it said *where* the tower was built, "in the land of Shinar," and that the particular place of the tower was later called Babel because there "the Lord confused [*bālal*] the language of all the earth." Now the names of both Shinar and Babel are in fact mentioned in the previous chapter, just in passing, in connection with the descendants of Noah's son Ham:

> The sons of Ham: Cush, Egypt, Put, and Canaan . . . Cush was the father of Nimrod; he [Nimrod] began to be a mighty man on earth. He was a mighty hunter before the Lord; therefore it is said, "Like Nimrod a mighty hunter before the Lord." The beginning of his kingdom was **Babel**, Erech, and Accad, all of them in the land of **Shinar**.
>
> —Gen. 10:6–10

The fact that this passage not only mentions Shinar but says that the "beginning" of Nimrod's kingdom was Babel, seemed indisputably to connect Nimrod with the building project. Indeed, it was only reasonable to suppose that Nimrod was something like the leader or sponsor of the project, for why else would the city be called the "beginning of *his* kingdom"? And why else should Nimrod have gone on to found *other* cities, like Erech and Accad, mentioned in the same verse, or Nineveh and the other cities mentioned in Gen. 10:11–12—why else but that he had been forced to abandon Babel because God had frustrated his plans there?

Thus, interpreters determined that Nimrod must have been the one who conceived or commissioned the tower. And precisely for that reason, the rest of the above passage now seemed particularly interesting. For what was the Bible trying to say when it called Nimrod a "mighty man," a "mighty hunter," indeed, "a mighty hunter before the Lord"? These might sound like praiseworthy titles. But two things caused interpreters to view them with suspicion. One was Nimrod's very name. To speakers of Hebrew "Nimrod" seems to come from the root meaning "rebel." A biblical figure named Rebellious was likely to be some sort of villain. And the second, of course, was the now-established "fact" of Nimrod's involvement in the building of the tower—for the tower had obviously met with God's disapproval. Both the story itself and the name suggested that Nimrod was some sort of rebel against God, a challenger of divine authority, a "mighty hunter *before* [and perhaps a would-be snarer *of,* a hunter *against*] the Lord." A number of sources there-fore make Nimrod out to be a wicked character, distinguished by his arro-gance and challenging attitude toward God, some specifically in connection with the tower-building project:

> But those things that are here [on earth] are against those things which are there [in heaven]. For this reason it is not ineptly said [that **Nimrod** was] "a giant *before* God" [Gen. 10:9] which clearly [means] *in opposition* to the Deity.   —Philo, *Questions and Answers in Genesis* 2:82

> He began to be violent before the Lord.   —Symmachus Gen. 10:8

> Now Cush became the father of Nimrod. He began to be **arrogant** before the Lord.[1]

> And Fenech and **Nimrod** said to Joktan [Iectan], "Where are the men whom you locked up [for refusing to build the tower]?"
> —Pseudo-Philo, *Biblical Antiquities* 4:7, 6:13

> Nimrod, the grandson of Ham the son of Noah, an **audacious** man endowed with innate force, incited the people to insolence and con-tempt toward God . . . Lest God seek once again to flood the earth . . . he would build a tower higher than the water would be able to reach up to, and so seek to avenge the destruction of their ancestors.[2]
> —Josephus, *Jewish Antiquities* 1:113–114

> He was mighty in sinning before the Lord; therefore it is said "like Nimrod, a mighty man in sinning before the Lord."
> —*Targum Neophyti* Gen. 10:9

> He was a mighty man, powerful in hunting and mighty in sinning before the Lord. He used to entrap human beings through their speech and say to them: Abandon the [religious] statutes of Shem and adopt the statutes of Nimrod. For this reason it is said "Like Nimrod the

---

1. This is Pseudo-Philo's "translation" (a reinterpretation, really) of Gen. 10:8, "Cush was the father of Nimrod; he [Nimrod] *began to be a mighty man* on earth." Interestingly, in Pseudo-Philo's account, Nimrod seems to play some role in the building of the tower (*Biblical Antiquities* 6:13–14), but the leader there is named Iectan (who may be identical with the Joktan of Gen. 10:25–29).

2. The tradition presented by Josephus is obviously trying to find some connection between the story of the tower and the story of the flood that preceded it. And it does: Nimrod builds the tall tower as protection against God's bringing another flood. In this way, humanity will not need to fear further divine punishment.

mighty one"—mighty in hunting [people] and mighty in sinning
before the Lord.[3]   — *Fragment Targum* Gen. 10:9

[God said:] "There were three kings who became emboldened before
Me [until] I revealed Myself in My judgments and set their names at
nought. Nimrod, when he became emboldened with the army of the
Cushites, from the beginning of his boldness I revealed Myself and
killed him."   — *Tibat Marqa* 218b–219a

Nimrod the son of Cush was the first to seize tyrannical power, [pre-
viously] unused, over the people and he ruled in Babylon, which was
called Babel because there the speech of those who were building the
tower became confused.   — Jerome, *Hebrew Questions in Genesis* 10:8

It is humility that builds a safe and true path to heaven, raising aloft
the heart towards God—not *against* God, in the way that that same
giant [Nimrod] was said to be a hunter "against God" [Gen. 10:9] . . .
He and his people thus erected a tower against God, by which is
signified irreligious arrogance.   — Augustine, *City of God* 16.4

Nimrod said to his people: Come, let us build for ourselves a great city
and let us settle therein, lest we be scattered over the face of the whole
earth as the earlier people, and let us build a great tower in its midst.
We will ascend to heaven, for God's power is only over water [to bring
a flood], and we shall thus gain great fame in the land.
                                            — *Pirqei deR. Eliezer* 24

The Builders Were Giants

If Nimrod was indeed behind the building of the tower, then there was a
further point of interest in the biblical description of him in Gen. 10:6–10
(cited above). Some interpreters thought that the Bible's calling Nimrod
mighty in the phrases "mighty man" and "mighty hunter" was intended to
suggest something more than mere physical strength: it seemed to be implying
something about his size as well. As a matter of fact, the same word, "mighty"
(*gibbor*), had been used of the offspring of the Nephilim in Gen. 6:4. If the
Nephilim were giants,[4] and if the word "mighty" is used to describe both their

---

3. The idea that the victims of Nimrod's "hunting" were actually human beings whom he
deceived may be borrowed here from a similar motif about Esau. See Chapter 11.

4. See Chapter 5.

offspring and Nimrod, then perhaps indeed this word meant something like "mighty in size," gigantic. This was just how the ancient Greek translators rendered these phrases:

> And [Cush] begot Nimrod; he began to be a **giant** upon the earth. He was a **giant** hunter before the Lord God.   — Septuagint Gen. 10:8–9

If Nimrod was a giant, one can better understand how a tower built by him could be a real threat and could have brought about the divine response that it did. For a giant, or a group of giants, might indeed build an enormous tower, perhaps even one reaching all the way to heaven:

> The Assyrian city of Babylon was first founded by those who escaped the flood. They were giants, and they built the tower well known in history. When the tower was destroyed by God's power, these giants were scattered over the whole earth.
>
> — (Pseudo-)Eupolemus (cited in Eusebius, *Praeparatio Evangelica* 9:17:2–3)

Apparently their great height had not only enabled these giants to build a very tall tower, but it had previously enabled them to "escape" the great flood without having recourse to Noah's ark—presumably, they were simply tall enough to keep their heads above the waters. Similarly,

> While these giants were living in Babylonia, they were destroyed by the gods because of their wickedness. One of them, Belus, escaped death and came to dwell in Babylon. There he built a tower and lived in it. It was named Belus, after Belus who built it.
>
> — "Anonymous writings" (cited in Eusebius, *Praeparatio Evangelica* 9:18:2)

The Tower Lies in Ruins

There remained only to ask what finally happened to the tower, which, according to verse 5, had not only been started but perhaps even completed ("And the Lord came down to see the city and the tower, which the sons of men *had built*").[5] The Bible says nothing of its fate. God makes the speech of the builders unintelligible and scatters them over the face of the earth, but the tower itself is not mentioned again, and one might presume from the text that God left it standing where it was.

But, surely, God would not have simply left a serviceable tower undis-

---

5. The same phrase, however, might equally well be understood as "were building" without indicating whether it was in fact complete. See below.

turbed, ready for the next group of sinners to use! Considering this question, interpreters noted God's own words just before stopping the project:

> And the Lord said, "Behold, they are one people and they all have one language, and this is what **they have begun** to make." —Gen. 11:6

The indicated phrase implied that the tower had only been *started*. Interpreters thus concluded that the tower was left as an unfinished monument, a view that seemed to confirm the claim of some that this or that half-destroyed or unfinished structure in the ancient Near East was in fact the abandoned tower. Indeed, if the tower now lay in ruins, perhaps it had not merely been abandoned, but destroyed:

> And the Lord sent a wind against the tower and overthrew it to the ground. It is now between Asshur and Babylon in the land of Shinar. He named it the Collapse.[6] —Jubilees 10:26

> But immediately the Immortal One imposed a great compulsion
> on the winds. Then the winds **cast down the great tower**
> from on high, and stirred up strife for mortals among themselves.
> Therefore humans gave the city the name Babylon.
> But when the tower fell, and the tongues of men
> were diversified by various sounds, the whole
> earth of humans was filled with fragmenting kingdoms.
> — Sibylline Oracles 3:101–107

> The tongues
> of all were loosed, but on them came the wrath
> of the Most High God, hurled down, and the wondrous tower fell.
> — Sibylline Oracles 11:10–13

> Said R. Ḥiyya bar Abba: Of the tower that they made, one third was burned, one third was swallowed up, and one third is still standing. Anyone who climbs to its top can see the date trees of Jericho [and they look] like grasshoppers. — Midrash Tanḥuma, Noaḥ 18

6. This seems to reflect a play on the name "Shinar," apparently here interpreted as "shake, overthrow." Similarly, Philo, *Confusion of Tongues* 68, explains the name as "shaking out"; see also b. Talmud *Zebaḥim* 113b, and cf. j. *Berakhot* 4:7b (bottom). Origen says "a shaking of teeth," an explanation representing two distinct Hebrew words, *šn* ("tooth") and *n'r* ("shake").

❖   ❖   ❖

In short: The real crime involved in the building project was the tower itself, which was intended for the purpose of "storming heaven" or some related evil desire. For this plan and the arrogant attitude underlying it the builders were punished. Their leader was Nimrod. He himself was a wicked giant and a rebel against God; he may have been aided by other giants. As a result of this deed, the people themselves were scattered and their great tower was cast down to the ground.

7
Abraham Journeys from Chaldea
(GENESIS 12)

Abraham turns his back on astronomy.

Abraham Journeys
from Chaldea

(GENESIS 12)

❖   ❖   ❖

Abraham, a descendant of Noah through his son Shem, lived with his family in the city of Ur in Chaldea. God promised to bless Abraham and make his descendants into a great nation. Having left Ur with his father, Terah, his wife, Sarah, and his nephew Lot, Abraham stayed for a time in Haran and then continued his travels into the land of Canaan. Once there, however, he discovered that there was famine in the land, and he and his wife, Sarah, continued on to Egypt. After an eventful stay there, they returned to Canaan.

ALTHOUGH Abraham's name[1] is mentioned in passing in Gen. 11:27–31, his story really begins with the opening words of chapter 12:

> Now the Lord said to Abram, "Go forth from your country and from your kindred and your father's house to the land that I will show you. And I will make you into a great nation, and I will bless you; and I will make your name great, so that it will be a blessing. And I will bless those who bless you, and whoever curses you will I curse, and all the families of the land will be blessed because of you."　　—Gen. 12:1–3

So begins this biblical figure's great adventure—his journey to Canaan, his stay in Egypt, and everything that ensues.

Yet readers of these opening words were doubtless disturbed by them. For the Bible has just now begun Abraham's story, and suddenly God is promising him that he will be blessed, he will found a great nation, and so forth—what had Abraham done to deserve these things? Moreover, if God was so pleased with Abraham, why did He begin by telling him to leave his homeland? To leave one's homeland meant leaving the security of family and friends and becoming a defenseless wanderer. If God had truly wished to bless Abraham and grant him all manner of good things, would He not have at least allowed him to stay where he was?

---

1. At the beginning of the story his name is Abram and his wife's Sarai; only later (Gen. 17:16) are they changed to Abraham and Sarah. Except when citing the biblical text, however, I refer to them consistently by their later names, as ancient interpreters generally did.

In searching for an answer to such questions, early interpreters of course took into account Abraham's overall "image" in the Bible. For throughout the rest of his story in Genesis, Abraham is presented as God's devoted servant, someone who obeyed every divine commandment (note, in this regard, Gen. 26:5). In particular, God singles out Abraham elsewhere as one "who loved Me" (Isa. 41:8; in some translations, "my friend")—as if, of all the people mentioned in the Bible, Abraham was the one who loved God the most. In keeping with this, 2 Chr. 20:7 also speaks of "Abraham *who loved You.*" Thus, it seemed to interpreters that the promises made by God at the beginning of Genesis 12 must have had something to do with Abraham's great love of, and devotion to, God.

But there was one part of the Bible that seemed to shed special light on these opening words of Genesis 12. It was a passing reference to Abraham's departure from his homeland found later in the Bible, at the end of the book of Joshua. Though the reference there is brief, to ancient interpreters it seemed to supply precisely the information that was missing in Genesis itself:

> And Joshua said to all the people, "Thus says the Lord, the God of Israel: 'Your ancestors lived of old beyond the Euphrates, Terah, the father of Abraham and of Nahor; and they served other gods. Then I took your father Abraham from beyond the River and led him through all the land of Canaan.'"   —Josh. 24:2–3

It struck ancient interpreters that God says here, "I took your father Abraham," setting him apart, as it were, from Terah and Nahor, who are mentioned along with him in the previous verse. Why single out Abraham?

Ancient interpreters concluded that Abraham must somehow have been . different from Terah and Nahor—that is why he is singled out. And surely it was significant that the previous verse, after mentioning Terah, Abraham, and Nahor, adds: "and they served other gods." Who "they" refers to here is not clear; but if Abraham is singled out in virtually the next breath, "Then I took your father Abraham," it seemed that the reason must be that "they" refers to Terah and Nahor and the others, *but not to Abraham! They* served other gods, but Abraham did not, and for that reason "Then I took your father Abraham."

Such a conclusion could only be bolstered by another biblical verse that mentions Abraham:

> Consider Abraham your father, and Sarah who bore you: **him alone did I call**, and bless him and and make him many.   —Isa. 51:2

If God called Abraham *alone,* is this not another way of saying that Abraham was quite unique among his family members? He—and not his father, Terah, or his brother, Nahor—was summoned personally to God's service.

Abraham the Monotheist

Out of this basic insight—arrived at by reading the beginning of chapter 12 of Genesis in the light of Josh. 24:2–3—arose an interpretive tradition that held Abraham's great virtue (never mentioned in Genesis itself, nor even stated explicitly in the Joshua passage) to have been his refusal to worship other gods. *They* served other gods, but not Abraham. And so Abraham came to be thought of in more general terms as the great opponent of polytheism (the belief in the existence of many gods), in fact, as the person who, in the midst of a nation that worshipped many gods, had become convinced that in truth there is only one God.

How far back this line of thinking goes we do not know, but it is certainly present very early. For example, it is found in a part of the book of Judith that some scholars date to the second century B.C.E. (if not earlier). And it may be significant that the theme of Abraham's recognition of the existence of only one God is presented in Judith in a somewhat offhand manner—Abraham himself is not even mentioned there by name. One might conclude that the author of Judith thought (or wished to claim) that it was simply common knowledge that the ancestor of the Jews had left his homeland because of his belief in the existence of only one God:

> [A foreign general explains:] This people [the Jews] is descended from the Chaldeans. At one time they lived in Mesopotamia, because they would not follow the gods of their fathers who were in Chaldea. **For they had left the ways of their ancestors, and they worshiped the God of heaven, the God they had come to know**; hence they [the Chaldeans] drove them out from the presence of their gods and they fled to Mesopotamia, and lived there for a long time. Then their God commanded them to leave the place where they were living and go to the land of Canaan.　　　　　　　　　　　　　—Jth. 5:6–9

It is interesting that this passage presents an answer to our second question as well, namely, why along with promising Abraham all sorts of blessings God had told him to leave his homeland. The text in Judith suggests that this is in fact related to Abraham's belief in the one true God: Abraham and his family had to leave Chaldea "because they would not follow the gods of their fathers who were in Chaldea . . . hence they [the Chaldeans] drove them out from the presence of their gods."

This same idea—that Abraham rejected the worship of many gods and their idols and believed only in the one true God—is found in other ancient sources as well:

And the child [Abraham] began to realize the errors of the land—that everyone was going astray after graven images and after impurity.

And he began to pray to the Creator of all so that He might save him from the errors of mankind . . . And he said [to his father], "What help or advantage do we have from these idols . . . ? Worship the God of heaven." . . . And his father said to him: ". . . Be silent my son, lest they kill you."

—Jubilees 11:16–17, 12:2, 6–7

He [Abraham] grew up with this idea and was a true Chaldean for some time, until, opening the soul's eye from the depth of sleep, he came to behold the pure ray in place of the deep darkness, and he followed that light and perceived what he had not seen before, One who guides and steers the world, presiding over it and managing its affairs.

—Philo, On Abraham 71

You are the One who delivered Abraham from ancestral godlessness.

—Hellenistic Synagogal Prayer, Apostolic Constitutions 8.12.22

And when all those inhabiting the land were being led astray after their [idols], Abraham believed in Me and was not led astray with them.

—Pseudo-Philo, Biblical Antiquities 23:5

He thus became the first person to argue that there is a single God who is the creator of all things . . . Because of these ideas the Chaldeans and the other people of Mesopotamia rose up against him, and having resolved, in keeping with God's will and with His help, to leave his home, he settled in the land of Canaan.

—Josephus, Jewish Antiquities 1.154–157

And so both questions now seemed to have the same answer: God promised Abraham all those things in Genesis 12 because Abraham, unique among the people in Chaldea, had come to know the one true God and so had refused to worship the Chaldean gods, "the gods of their fathers"; and for precisely this reason, the Chaldeans would no longer allow Abraham to dwell in their midst, which is why God begins by saying, "Go forth from your homeland."

Terah, Priest of Idolatry

"They served other gods," it says in Josh. 24:2, presumably referring to Abraham's father, Terah, and his brother, Nahor. Since Scripture says so (and so matter-of-factly), interpreters seeking to understand the full meaning of Abraham's story must have returned again and again to this striking statement to consider all its possible implications. Indeed, perhaps this reference to his father and brother serving other gods explained not only *why* Abraham ended up being the one to whom God promised great things in Genesis 12, but also *how it was* that Abraham came to know that there is only one God in the first place and that all the "other gods" are simply false. Now, elsewhere in the Bible the worship of "other gods" is frequently described—caricatured, one might say—as bowing down to "gods of wood and stone," that is, idols, mere human creations. And so, ancient interpreters and retellers of the story of Abraham enjoyed depicting at length Terah's ministering and tending to such idols. Terah became not just an idol worshiper, but a priest of idolatry, or a manufacturer or seller of idols. With such a father, Abraham must in his youth have gotten a close-up view of the folly of worshiping idols, and it was this exposure that might ultimately have led him to realize that these "other gods" are simply an illusion:

> And he [Abraham] separated from his father so that he might not worship the idols with him.

> And it came to pass . . . that Abram said to his father, "O father," and he said, "Yes, my son?" And he said: "What help or advantage do we have from these idols before which you worship and bow down? For there is no spirit in them, because they are mute, and they are an error of the mind . . ." And his father said to him, "I also know that, my son, but what shall I do to the people who have ordered me to serve before them [that is, the idols]. If I speak to them truthfully, they will kill me because they themselves are attached to them [the idols] so that they might worship them and praise them."   —*Jubilees* 11:16, 12:1–3, 6–7

> When I was watching over the gods of my father Farah [Terah] and my brother Nahor, I was experimenting [to find out] which god was truly the strongest. Then, at the time when my [priestly] lot came up and I was to finish the service of my father Farah's sacrifice to his gods of wood and stone, of gold and silver and copper and iron, I, Abraham, having entered their sanctuary for the service, found a god named Marumat,[2] which had been carved out of stone, fallen at the feet of an iron god, Nakhin. And it came to pass that, when I saw this, my heart was troubled, and I thought to myself that I, Abraham, would be unable to return it to its place all by myself, since it was heavy, [carved] out of a great stone; so I went to inform my father, and he went in with me. And as we both were moving it to return it to its place, its head fell off of it in such a way that I was left holding on to its head. And it came

---

2. There have been many suggestions for the underlying sense of this apparently Hebrew or Aramaic name. One possibility is *mar 'umot*, "lord of nations."

to pass, when my father saw that the head of his god, Marumat, had fallen off of it, he said to me, "Abraham," and I replied, "Here I am." And he said: "Bring me a chisel from the house." And I brought it. Then he carved another Marumat, without a head, out of another stone, and [placed on it] the head that had been broken off from [the first] Marumat, and then smashed that [first] Marumat.

Then I said to myself, "What are these useless things that my father is doing? Is he not rather a god to his gods, since it is by virtue of his sculpting and shaping, by his skillfulness, that they come into being? It would be more fitting for them to bow down to my father, since they are his handiwork. Yet what is my father's reward from his labors? Behold, Marumat fell down and was unable to get up in his own temple, nor could I lift him on my own, until my father came and then we lifted him together. And even so we were unable, and [Marumat's] head fell off of him, and [my father] placed it upon another stone of another god which he had made without a head . . ." And I said to myself, "If it is thus, how then can my father's god Marumat, having a head made from one stone and [the rest] being made from another stone, save someone or hear a person's prayer and grant him any-thing?"

— Apocalypse of Abraham chs. 1, 3

R. Ḥiyya said: Terah was an idolator. Once he went off somewhere and left Abraham to sell [idols] in his place. A certain man came wishing to buy. [Abraham] said to him: "How old are you?" He said: "Fifty." He said: "Fifty years old and you are going to bow down to something only one day old [that is, this idol]?!" The man went off in embarrass-ment. Later, a woman came bearing a container of flour. She said to him, "Here, offer this before them [the idols]." He took a stick and broke them [the idols] and then put the stick into the hand of the biggest of them. When his father came he said to him, "What hap-pened to these?" He said to him: . . . "One [idol] said, 'Let me be the first to eat,' another said, 'No, let me be the first to eat,' then the biggest one took a stick and broke them [the others]." [Terah said:] "Why are you mocking me—do these idols know anything?" [Abraham] said: "Cannot your ears hear the words coming from your own mouth?"

— Genesis Rabba 38:13

Abraham the Astronomer

In the ancient world, Chaldea was famous for one thing in particular: it was the home of astronomy and astrology. So great was the association between

Chaldea and the study of the stars that the very word "Chaldean" came to mean "astronomer" in both Aramaic and Greek. Many interpreters therefore naturally assumed that Abraham the Chaldean must himself have been something of an astronomer. And so a number of early sources present Abraham as both a learned astronomer and a teacher of this occult lore to others:

> Abram sat up during the night on the first of the seventh month, so that he might observe the stars from evening until daybreak so that he might see what the nature of the year would be with respect to rain.
>
> — *Jubilees* 12:16

> [Orpheus tells Musaeus about God, that no one can]
> see Him; for around [Him] a cloud has been fixed . . .
> Except a certain unique man, by descent an offshoot
> of the Chaldeans. For he was knowledgeable about the path of the
>   Star,
> and the movements of the spheres around the earth,
> in a circle regularly, but each on its own axis.
> [This Chaldean, Abraham, understood]
> how He guides the winds [that is, spirits, subsidiary forces] around
>   both air and water.   — *Pseudo-Orphica* (Recension B) vv. 21, 27–31 (cited
>
>   in Clement of Alexandria, *Miscellanies* 124)

> Abraham excelled all in nobility and wisdom; he sought and obtained the knowledge of astrology and the Chaldean craft, and pleased God because he eagerly sought to be reverent. At God's command, he traveled to Phoenicia and dwelt there. He pleased the Phoenician king by teaching the Phoenicians the cycles of the sun and moon, and everything else as well . . . [Later, when he was in Egypt,] Abraham lived in Heliopolis with the Egyptian priests and taught them much: He explained astrology and the other sciences to them.
>
>   — [Pseudo-]Eupolemus (cited in Eusebius, *Praeparatio Evangelica* 9.17:3–4, 8)

> Abraham . . . came to Egypt with all his household to the Egyptian king Pharethothes and taught him astrology.
>
>   — Artapanus (cited in Eusebius, *Praeparatio Evangelica* 9.18:1)

> He [Abraham] introduced them [the Egyptians] to arithmetic and transmitted to them the laws of astronomy. For before the coming of Abraham the Egyptians were ignorant of these sciences, which thus traveled from the Chaldaeans into Egypt, when they passed to the Greeks.   — Josephus, *Jewish Antiquities* 167–168

And He said to him [Balaam]: Did I not speak to Abraham in a vision concerning this people, saying, "Your descendants shall be as numerous as the stars of heaven" [Gen. 22:17], at the time when I lifted him above the firmament and showed him the arrangement of all the stars?
— Pseudo-Philo, *Biblical Antiquities* 18:5

In those days, Abraham was born and was given over by his father to study astronomy.   — *Historical Paleya* (Popov, p. 21)

Tipped Off by the Stars

At the same time, interpreters had to ask: was there not some connection between astronomy/astrology and Abraham's devotion to God? Surely it was not just chance that Chaldea—Astronomyland—was the place in which Abraham had discovered that there is only one God. And so interpreters found an alternate explanation for how Abraham came to know that there is only one God: they connected his refusal to worship "other gods" (implied by Josh. 24:2–3) with his knowledge of the stars. Somehow, Abraham came to understand that it is not the stars but God who controls human destiny:

And he was sitting alone making observations [of the stars] and a voice came into his heart saying, "All the signs of the stars and the signs of the sun and the moon are all under the Lord's control. Why am I seeking [them out]? If He wishes, He will make it rain morning and evening, and if He desires He will not make it fall, for everything is under His control."   — *Jubilees* 12:17–18

The Chaldeans exercised themselves most especially with astronomy and attributed all things to the movements of the stars, believing that whatever is in the world is governed by forces encompassed in numbers and numerical proportions. They exalted the existence of what is visible, and took no thought for what is perceivable to the mind and [yet] invisible. But seeking out the numerical arrangement according to the cycles of the sun, moon, the planets and the fixed stars, as well as the changes of the yearly seasons and the overall connection of the things of heaven with what happens on earth, they supposed that the world itself was god, sacrilegiously making out that which is created to be like the One who had created it.

   He [Abraham] grew up with this idea and was a true Chaldean for some time, until, opening the soul's eye from the depth of sleep, he came to behold the pure ray in place of the deep darkness, and he followed that light and perceived what he had not seen before, One who guides and steers the world, presiding over it and managing its affairs.

— Philo, *On Abraham* 69–71 (also *Questions and Answers in Genesis* 3:1)

He [Abraham] left Chaldea at the age of seventy-five, having been told by God to move to Canaan, and he settled down in that [land] and left it to his descendants. He was skilled at understanding all things, and persuasive to those who listened to him; nor was he mistaken in what he conjectured. For that reason his conception of virtue surpassed that of other people, and he came to have a new understanding of, and to modify, the idea of God then adhered to by all.

He thus became the first person to argue that there is a single God who is the creator of all things, and that whatever any of these other things contribute to the good of the world, they are enabled to do so at His command, and not by any inherent force of their own. He was able to figure this out by the changes which land and sea undergo, and those that are connected with the sun and the moon, and from all those occurring in the skies. For if these bodies had any power over themselves, they would surely have arranged for themselves to be regularly ordered; but since this is not so, it is clear that they come together for our benefit not by any authority of their own, but by the power of the One who commands, to whom alone it is proper to give honor and thanks.

Because of these ideas the Chaldeans and the other people of Mesopotamia rose up against him, and having resolved, in keeping with God's will and with His help, to leave his home, he settled in the land of Canaan. — Josephus, *Jewish Antiquities* 1:154–157

And so, the motif "Abraham the Astronomer"—based on the simple fact that the Bible names Chaldea as Abraham's birthplace—led to a new motif, one that explained *how* Abraham came to be a monotheist: it was Abraham's knowledge of astronomy and observations of the heavens that led him to discover that there is only one God.

Abraham Rescued from Chaldea

Whether Abraham was an idol maker's son who rebelled, or an astronomer whose researches led him to conclude that there is only one God, interpreters could safely conclude that Abraham's new ideas about God would not have been acceptable to the Chaldeans. *That* was why God began by telling Abraham to "go forth from your country and from your kindred" (Gen. 12:1).

Yet there was another side to this tradition. It held that Abraham did not just casually leave his homeland, but that God had in fact *rescued* him from the hands of his own countrymen. Support for this idea was found elsewhere in the Bible:

> Therefore, thus says the Lord, who **redeemed Abraham**, concerning
> the house of Jacob . . .   — (traditional Hebrew text of) Isa. 29:22

"Redeemed" means not only "bought back," but "ransomed" or "rescued from captivity." These words of Isaiah might thus be seen to suggest that, in telling Abraham to leave Ur, God had in fact *rescued* him, taking him out of some difficult or dangerous situation. It was not hard for ancient interpreters to imagine such a scene (especially since many Jews in later times—including the interpreters' own days—had found themselves in just such a position): Abraham, having proclaimed that there is only one God and that the official religion of his homeland was mere foolishness, must have soon been pursued by an angry mob of Chaldeans or hounded by a regime that felt Abraham's assertion undermined its very authority. Indeed, such a scenario is implied in a number of passages seen earlier:

> For they had left the ways of their ancestors, and they worshiped the
> God of heaven, the God they had come to know; hence they [the
> Chaldeans] **drove them out** from the presence of their gods and **they
> fled** to Mesopotamia, and lived there for a long time. Then their God
> commanded them to leave the place where they were living and go to
> the land of Canaan.   —Jth. 5:8–9

> And his father said to him, "I also know that, my son, but what shall I
> do to the people who have ordered me to serve before them [that is,
> the idols]. If I speak to them truthfully, **they will kill me** because they
> themselves are attached to them [the idols] so that they might worship
> them and praise them."   —Jubilees 12:6–7

> Because of these ideas the Chaldeans and the other people of Mesopo-
> tamia **rose up against** him, and having resolved, in keeping with God's
> will and with His help, to leave his home, he settled in the land of
> Canaan.   —Josephus, *Jewish Antiquities* 1:157

> You are the One who **delivered** [that is, saved] Abraham from ances-
> tral godlessness.
>
>   —Hellenistic Synagogal Prayer, *Apostolic Constitutions* 8.12.22

Abraham Saved from Fire

This reasonable supposition (backed up by Isa. 29:22) that the Chaldeans might have sought to harm Abraham because of his beliefs soon took on a new form. For, the city in which Abraham and his family lived was called Ur. But the word *'ur* in Hebrew had another meaning as well: "fire" or "flame." Ancient readers of the Bible could not help concluding that this was no mere coincidence. And so, when God later says to Abraham:

> "I am the Lord who took you out of [the] *'ur* of the Chaldeans . . ."
>
> —Gen. 15:7

many interpreters found in these words a hidden meaning, a hint about some fire or burning that had taken place in Ur and from which God had in fact saved Abraham, *taking* him from the midst of the flames. In one version, the fire comes down from heaven:

> And it came to pass, while I was considering such things with my father Terah in the courtyard of [his] house, that the voice of the Almighty came down from the heavens in a **stream of fire** saying aloud "Abraham, Abraham!" and I said, "Here I am." And He said, "You are searching in your mind and the thoughts of your heart for the God of gods and the Creator: I am He. Leave Terah your father and go forth from his house [compare Gen. 12:1] so that you will not be killed because of the sins of your father's house." So I went out. And it came to pass, when I went out, that I had not even gotten as far as going beyond the doors of the courtyard when the sound of great thunder came forth and **burned** him and his house and everyone in the house to a distance of forty cubits. — *Apocalypse of Abraham* 8:1–6

In another, widely diffused version of this motif, the fire was a fiery furnace prepared by the Chaldeans to burn Abraham for his heresies:[3]

---

3. A similar incident is recounted in the book of Daniel, in which three youths in Babylon are cast into a fiery furnace by the Babylonian king and saved by God (Dan. 3:19–23). The tradition that understands the "fire" of the Chaldeans as a fiery furnace seems clearly to be based on the narrative in Daniel. No doubt the fact that God says to Abraham, "I *took you out* of Ur," instead of something more like "I told you to leave," only further encouraged interpreters to identify the "Ur" in question as a great fire from which Abraham had been rescued. (Indeed, interpreters must have wondered why God should say, "I am the Lord who took you out of [the] *'ur* of the Chaldeans" in the first place. Did not Abraham *know* who God was? These words therefore seemed to be intended more as a reminder to Abraham of God's previous beneficence—*saving* him from the fire of the Chaldeans.)

And Teraḥ took his son Abram and his grandson Lot and his daughter-in-law Sarai, Abram's wife, and [he] went out with them from the Chaldeans' **fiery furnace** to go to the land of Canaan. [Later, God said to Abraham:] "I am the Lord who took you out of the fiery furnace of the Chaldeans to give you this land to inherit."

— Targum Neophyti Gen. 11:31, 15:7

[The Levites prayed:] "It was you yourself, O Lord God, who chose Abram and led him **out of the fire** of the Chaldeans."

— (Vulgate) Neh. 9:7

[Nimrod said to Abraham:] You are speaking foolishness. Let us worship fire and [if not] I will cast you into its midst—then let your God whom you worship come and save you from it.　　— *Genesis Rabba* 38:13

In yet another variant of this motif, the fire turns out to be none other than the one found in the tower of Babel story, which the builders had proposed to make in order to prepare the bricks for the tower ("Come, let us make bricks *and burn them thoroughly*," Gen. 11:3). Abraham, along with others of similar conviction, refuses to help make these bricks to build the tower:

And those men answered saying, "We will not contribute bricks [literally, "stones"] to you, and we will not be associated with your plan. We recognize the one Lord, and He is the one whom we worship. Even if you were to cast us into the fire with your bricks, we would not agree [to join] with you." And the leaders [of the builders] were angry and said, "As they have spoken, so do to them. If they do not agree to contribute the bricks, let the fire consume them along with your bricks."

[Later, God says:] "And when all those inhabitants of the land were being led astray by their erroneous ideas, Abraham believed in Me and was not led astray with them. And I snatched him from the **flame** and took him and brought him over all the land of Canaan."

— Pseudo-Philo, Biblical Antiquities 6:4–5, 23:5

Abraham Was Upset

After staying in Haran for a time, Abraham continued on his journey to Canaan. When he arrived there, however, he found the land stricken with famine, and he and Sarah continued on to Egypt in order to get food.

This journey to Egypt certainly troubled interpreters. For one thing, as the couple was preparing to cross the Egyptian border, Abraham instructed the beautiful Sarah to tell the Egyptians that she was his sister rather than his wife, lest they kill him in order to take her for themselves. "Say you are my sister," he says, "so that it may go well with me because of you, and so that my life may be spared on your account" (Gen. 12:13). These hardly sounded like heroic words! To make matters worse, the Bible records that Sarah acted on Abraham's advice and that, as a result, she was taken by Pharaoh to his palace for an unspecified period of time (until God "afflicted Pharaoh with great plagues" and he discovered the truth). If Abraham was upset by her departure, the Bible does not mention it—in fact, it implies at one point that Abraham's silence actually caused him to profit by this interlude (Gen. 12:16).

Interpreters were understandably disturbed by Abraham's apparent cowardice and subsequent silence. But the fact that the Bible narrated the whole incident so quickly—in less than a dozen verses—certainly left room to suppose that Abraham's true feelings, and even some of his actions, had simply been omitted in the Bible's telegraphic account. Many ancient writers, in retelling the story, thus felt entitled to add in what the story had somehow left out, an account of Abraham's deep distress at these events. (Some also simply skipped over what Abraham had said to Sarah, implying or stating that she had been taken to Pharaoh's palace by force.)

> So Abram went to Egypt [and] lived in Egypt five years before his wife was taken from him **by force** . . .[4] When Pharaoh took Abram's wife Sarai by force for himself, the Lord punished Pharaoh and his household very severely because of Abram's wife Sarai.　　*— Jubilees* 13:11–13

> He [Abraham] had a wife distinguished greatly for her goodness of soul and beauty of body, in which she surpassed all the women of her time. When the Egyptian officials saw her and admired her beauty . . . they told the king. He sent for the woman and, seeing her extraordinary beauty, paid little regard to decency or the laws enacted to show respect to strangers . . . [He] intended, he said, to take her in marriage, but in reality merely to dishonor her. She who in a foreign country was at the mercy of a licentious and cruel-hearted despot and had no one to protect her—for her husband was helpless, menaced as he was by

4. Not only does this account omit Abraham's words to Sarah, but the words "taken . . . by force" are intended to make it clear that Abraham in no way cooperated with Pharaoh's deed. Moreover, the fact that Abraham had been in Egypt for five years before Sarah was taken from him may further be intended to suggest that she was not taken as a result of anyone being under the mistaken (first) impression that the two were not married.

the terror of stronger powers—joined him [Abraham] in fleeing for refuge to the last remaining championship, that of God.[5]

— Philo, *On Abraham* 93–95

I, Abram, **wept greatly**, I and my nephew Lot as well on the night that Sarah was taken away from me **by force**. On that night I prayed and begged and pleaded, and in great suffering, as the tears went forth, I said: Blessed are You, God Most High, Master of the whole universe. For You are master and ruler over all, You rule over all the kings of the earth, meting out justice to all of them. Now I lodge my complaint with You, Lord, against Pharaoh Zoan, king of Egypt, that my wife has been taken from me **by force**. Execute justice upon him for me and show forth Your great hand against him and his house, and do not allow him to defile my wife this evening, so that I may know about You, my Lord, that You are master of all the kings of the earth." And I wept.

— (1Q20) *Genesis Apocryphon* col. 20:10–16

When Abraham saw what had happened, he **began to weep** and pray before God, saying, "Master of the universe! Is this what comes of the faith I have placed in You? But now, act in accordance with your mercy and faithfulness and do not disappoint my hope." Sarah likewise wept and said, "Master of the universe! I had no prior inclination, but when you said 'Leave your homeland,' I believed your words. Yet now I am left all alone, without father or mother or husband—shall this wicked man [Pharaoh] now come and abuse me? Act in keeping with Your great name and the faith that I placed in your words." Said God to her: "By your life, nothing ill will happen to you or your husband."

— *Midrash Tanḥuma, Lekh Lekha* 5

Abraham's Dream

One retelling of the biblical story, found among the Dead Sea Scrolls, reckoned with the problem of Abraham's apparent cowardice in another way, suggesting that there had been a good reason for Abraham to tell Sarah what he did ("Say you are my sister"). It all came about because of a dream that Abraham had:

---

5. Philo omits all mention of Abraham's request of Sarah that she say she is his sister. Pharaoh is presented as acting in violation of the laws of the land and solely out of lust. Philo says that Pharaoh claimed he "intended" to marry Sarah in order to account for Pharaoh's words in Gen. 12:19 ("I took her as my wife"). However, Philo says that this was merely a ruse, and that it was only as a result of God's intervention that "the chastity of the woman was preserved" (*On Abraham* 98).

And I, Abram, dreamt a dream on the night that I entered the land of Egypt, and I saw in my dream a cedar tree and a beautiful, tall, palm-tree. Then some people came and sought to cut down and uproot the cedar and to leave the palm-tree alone. But the palm-tree protested, "Do not cut down the cedar, for both of us are from the same root." So the cedar was spared for the palm-tree's sake, and it was not cut down.

That night I awoke from my sleep and I said to my wife Sarah, "I dreamt a dream and I am frightened by this dream." And she said, "Tell me your dream so that I may know." And I began to tell her the dream, and I made known to her the meaning of the dream.

— (1Q20) *Genesis Apocryphon* col. 19:14–19

In the dream, the cedar is Abraham and the palm tree is Sarah. What the dream says, therefore, is that Abraham's life is in great danger, and he can only be saved if Sarah says the right thing. Now if Abraham had indeed had such a dream, it would have virtually constituted a divine *commandment* for Sarah to tell the Egyptians that she was Abraham's sister, since dreams in the Bible are generally messages from God. Abraham's conduct would therefore have been an instance not of cowardice but of obedience to God.

But did he really have such a dream? It may be that the author of this text found a tiny bit of support for the dream in the Bible itself. For, in the biblical version, when Abraham starts his instructions to Sarah, he says, "Behold, *now I know* that you are a beautiful woman; and it will come to pass that, when the Egyptians see you . . ." (Gen. 12:11–12). These are strange words for Abraham, Sarah's husband of so many years, to be saying to her—especially since "I know" in Hebrew often carries the connotation of "I have [just] found out," and joined with "behold *now*" it could easily seem to be implying that Abraham *now* knows something that he did not know previously. But surely he knew before now that his wife was beautiful. What then could the text mean?

If Abraham's words are read in the Hebrew in a slightly different way, they convey a striking difference in meaning: "Behold, now I know [or "I have just found out"]—since you are a beautiful woman—that it will come to pass that, when the Egyptians see you . . ." In this way what Abraham knows, or has just found out, is not simply that Sarah is beautiful, but that, given Sarah's great beauty, the Egyptians will try to kill him and take her for themselves. This does indeed make Abraham's "Behold I know" seem a bit more reasonable. But this approach would have raised a further question for interpreters: how could Abraham *know* that the Egyptians would try to kill him, indeed, how can anyone *know* for certain what is going to happen in the future? Unless, of course, Abraham had been told as much by God. It was apparently such reasoning as this that led the author of the *Genesis Apocryphon* to suppose that God had informed Abraham of what was to happen through a prophetic dream.[6]

❖   ❖   ❖

In short: There was good reason for God to promise Abraham manifold blessings. For Abraham had, even in his homeland, been a dogged opponent of idol worship. Through his study of the stars and/or his exposure to the idols worshipped by his own father, Abraham had come to understand that there is only one true God. That was why the Chaldeans, who worshipped the stars and bowed down to idols, sought to kill Abraham, even, in one interpretation, casting him into a fiery furnace in Ur. God saved Abraham and ordered him to leave his homeland. When he found Canaan in the midst of a famine, he journeyed to Egypt, and a prophetic dream warned him of coming danger.

6. God in fact goes on to refer to Abraham as a "prophet" in Gen. 20:7, after Sarah has been taken to the house of Abimelech under similar circumstances. That such a title was given to Abraham *in that context*, where the narrative itself provides scant justification for calling him a prophet, may have led interpreters to suppose that it was some sort of *prophetic vision* that had led Abraham in both incidents to tell people that Sarah was his sister. And what better place to locate such a prophetic vision than in connection with Abraham's "Behold I know" in Gen. 12:11? Incidentally, it may be that Sarah's words in the *Genesis Apocryphon* passage cited, "Tell me your dream *so that I may know,*" reflect this understanding of Abraham's words as implying a prophetic vision. He says, "Behold I know," and she says, "Tell me your dream so that I will know too!"

8
Melchizedek

An uncircumcised priest?

Melchizedek

(GENESIS 14:17–20)

❖   ❖   ❖

After his return to Canaan, Abraham suddenly found himself drawn into a great war: Lot, Abraham's nephew, had been taken prisoner, and Abraham intervened to save him, taking a band of men with him. They succeeded in freeing Lot; afterward Abraham returned home. It was then that he encountered a certain Melchizedek, the king of Salem. Melchizedek brought out bread and wine; he was "a priest of God Most High." Melchizedek blessed Abraham, and he gave him a tithe (tenth) of his possessions.

MELCHIZEDEK is something of an enigma in the Bible. We are not told the name of his father or his mother, or anything about his family. He is not mentioned anywhere in the various lists of Noah's descendants. We are not told *when* he was born—nor even *that* he was born—and the Bible is equally silent about his death. Nor, for that matter, is the location of his kingdom, Salem, known for sure. Thus, almost everything about him was mysterious for ancient interpreters. His encounter with Abraham certainly seemed designed to impart some lesson—but what exactly was it? Nothing really happened in this meeting, save that Melchizedek brought out food and then blessed Abraham (as priests were later to bless people who came to the Jerusalem Temple). Abraham then apparently[1] gave him a tithe (as people were also to bring tithes to the temple). But these very details were what was most intriguing in the story. For Melchizedek thus seemed to be a priest. But how could that be? The priesthood itself had not yet been established, nor had the Jerusalem Temple been built. Yet here was Melchizedek, bluntly described as a "priest of God Most High." Not only that, but Melchizedek apparently had not the slightest connection to the priesthood that would eventually be established in Israel—for that priesthood was hereditary, and its family line went back through Abraham, not Melchizedek! Who was this so-called priest?

---

1. The text says simply "*he gave him* a tithe" without specifically identifying who the giver or the recipient was. Since Melchizedek is a priest, however, he (like later priests and temple personnel) would normally have been the recipient and Abraham therefore the giver.

A Generous Host

Many ancient interpreters supposed that, if the Bible had gone out of its way to describe this puzzling (and apparently inconsequential) episode, it must be that Melchizedek had nevertheless done something significant. The main thing that he did, according to the biblical account, was to "bring out bread and wine," although the text does not say for whom. Perhaps, in characteristically understated fashion, the Bible here was alluding to an extraordinary act of generosity, the providing of food and drink (and wine at that!) to Abraham's entire army. In any case, a number of writers specified what the Bible did not, that the food and drink were given to Abraham's whole company:

> And Melchizedek the king of Salem brought out food and drink to Abram and **to all the men** who were with him; and he was a priest to God Most High. And he blessed Abram and said: Blessed is Abram to God Most High, master of heaven and earth; and blessed is God Most High, who has given over your enemies into your hand. And he [Abraham] gave him a tithe from all the possessions of the king of Elam and his confederates.   — (1Q20) *Genesis Apocryphon* col. 13:14–17

> He [Melchizedek] stretched his hands to heaven and honored him [Abraham] with prayers on his behalf and offered sacrifices of thanksgiving for the victory and feasted handsomely **those** who had taken part in the contest, rejoicing and sharing their gladness as though it were his own.   — Philo, *On Abraham* 235

> Now this Melchizedek hospitably entertained Abraham's **army**, providing abundantly for all their needs, and in the course of the feast he began to extol Abraham and to bless God for having delivered his enemies into his hand. Abraham then offered him a tithe of the spoils, and he accepted the gift.   — Josephus, *Jewish Antiquities* 181

Righteous King and Priest

Other things, however, suggested that Melchizedek must have been a noteworthy figure in his own right. To begin with, *Melchizedek* seems to mean something like "king of righteousness" or "king of justice" in Hebrew.[2] It occurred to some that this might be not his real name but—like "king of

2. One of the peculiarities connected with this name is that, in the traditional Hebrew text, it is written with a space between its two parts, *malki ṣedeq*—as if it were actually two different names or

Salem" and "priest of God Most High"—a title, one that might hold the key to his real importance. Perhaps he was an extraordinarily just and righteous king.

> [Jerusalem's] first founder was a leader of the Canaanites, called in his native tongue "righteous king"—for so indeed he was.
>
> —Josephus, *Jewish Wars* 6:438

> He is first, by the translation of his name, king of righteousness.
>
> —Heb. 7:2

Moreover, since "Salem" corresponded to the last part of the name "Jerusalem," some interpreters concluded that Melchizedek had been Jerusalem's first king and founder. Indeed, if he was a "priest," perhaps he had also founded some sort of sanctuary in Jerusalem, a forerunner of the great temple to be built there centuries later:

> For this reason he was the **first to serve as a priest before God** and, having been the first to build the temple, gave to the city previously called "Salem" the name *Jerusalem* [understood in Greek as "Holy Salem"].　　　—Josephus, *Jewish Wars* 6:438 (also *Jewish Antiquities* 1:180–181)

> And Melchizedek, the king of **Jerusalem** . . . was a priest serving in the high priesthood before God Most High.
>
> — *Targums Onqelos, Neophyti* Gen. 14:18

> He was made king by reason of his greatness . . . and moreover was a high priest, which office he had received from Noah in succession.
>
> —Ephraem, *Commentary on Genesis* 11:2

> The Jerusalem temple was built in his [Melchizedek's] domain, as it says, "And Melchizedek, king of Salem . . ." [Gen. 14:18], and "Salem" means Jerusalem, as it says, "His [God's] abode has been established in Salem, his dwelling place in Zion" [Ps. 78:3 (some texts: 2)].
>
> — *Midrash ha-Gadol* Gen. 11:10

Divinely Appointed High Priest

There was, however, another factor that bore on Melchizedek's true identity. The name "Melchizedek" appears in one other place in the Hebrew Bible, in a

---

two separate words. The first word might thus appear to mean "my king," while the second part would be "justice" or "righteousness."

passing reference in Psalm 110. The language of this psalm is somewhat obscure in Hebrew; here is one modern translation of its opening lines:

> The Lord says to my lord: "Sit at my right hand, until I make your enemies your footstool."
> The Lord sends forth from Zion your mighty scepter. Rule in the midst of your foes!
> Your people will offer themselves freely on the day you lead your host upon the holy mountains. From the womb of the morning like dew your youth will come to you.
> The Lord has sworn and will not change his mind, "**You are a priest forever, after the line of Melchizedek.**"
>
> —Ps. 110:1–4

Ancient readers of the story of Abraham and Melchizedek in Genesis looked to this psalm to help clarify its significance. But that meant first of all deciding to whom these words were addressed and what they meant. Here, the potentially ambiguous writing system of biblical Hebrew played a crucial role: the Hebrew words that correspond to those highlighted above could in fact be read and understood in two radically different fashions. This led to the development of two different schools of thought on the identity of Melchizedek among the Bible's ancient interpreters.

One way of understanding the highlighted words in Ps. 110:4 was: "You are a priest forever by my order [or "on my account"], O Melchizedek." If this is the right translation, then it is Melchizedek who is being addressed throughout the psalm, and everything else in the psalm that refers to "you" must therefore be talking about Melchizedek. The psalm would thus seem to recount that Melchizedek had been appointed to the priesthood by God Himself (since the whole of verse 4 would now be: "The Lord has sworn and will not change his mind, 'You are a priest forever by my order, O Melchizedek'"). This would of course correspond to his description in Genesis as a "priest of God Most High"—indeed, a priest who was personally appointed by God must have been no ordinary priest but an ancient forerunner to the exalted office of high priest:

> When the **high priest** of God Most High saw him [Abraham] approaching and bearing his spoils . . .   —Philo, *On Abraham* 235

> You [O God] are the one who **appointed** Melchizedek as a **high priest** in Your service.   —*Apostolic Constitutions* 8.12.23

And Melchizedek, the king of Jerusalem ... was a priest serving in the **high priesthood** before God Most High. — *Targum Neophyti* Gen. 14:18

The Heavenly Melchizedek

But interpreting Abraham's encounter with Melchizedek in the light of Psalm 110 led to other, more radical conclusions. After all, the Melchizedek described in the psalm seemed in some ways superhuman. His royal scepter had come from God Himself ("The Lord sends forth from Zion your mighty scepter"). In fact, Melchizedek is apparently the "lord" referred to in the first line, who was commanded by God to "sit at my right hand" like some sort of angel or divine being.

It is from this interpretation of Psalm 110 that there emerged the figure of a heavenly Melchizedek, an angelic being who sits next to the divine throne.[3] Such a Melchizedek is found in the Dead Sea Scrolls, where (in a text going back to the early first or second century B.C.E.) he is said to be ready to punish the guilty and save the righteous in the great day of reckoning:

> Melchizedek will carry out the vengeance of the laws of Go[d on that day and he will sa]v[e them from] Belial and from all his k[indred spirits,] and to his aid will (come) all the "gods"[4] of [justice and] he [Melchizedek] is the one w[ho will stand on that day over] all the sons of God and will ord[ain] this [asse]mbly.
> This is the Day of P[eace, a]bout which [God] spoke [of old in the words of] the prophet [Isai]ah, who said "[How] beautiful on the mountains are the messen[ger]'s feet, [pr]oclaiming peace."[5]
> — (11Q13) *Melchizedek Text* 2.13–16

It may be that the interpretation of the name "Melchizedek" had a role in the understanding of this angel's precise functions: he is the "king of justice" in the sense that he "will carry out the vengeance of God's laws." This understanding also corresponds to the psalm's assertion that "he will execute judgment among the nations" (Ps. 110:6). Some identified this angelic Melchizedek with the archangel Michael.

In a liturgical text among the Dead Sea Scrolls are further possible refer-

---

3. If so, the description in Gen. 14:18 as "king of Salem" had to be reinterpreted; the same letters could be read as "king of peace."

4. Apparently used in the sense of "angels."

5. Here as well, apparently, Melchizedek's title in Genesis, "king of Salem," is understood as "king of peace."

ences to Melchizedek the angel; unfortunately, the text here is quite fragmentary:

>] priest[s
> G]od of knowledge and [
> Melchi]zedek, priest in the assemb[ly of God[6]
>
> —(4Q401) *Songs of the Sabbath Sacrifice* 11.1–3

>] holy ones of [
> holine]ss [?] consecrate [
> Mel]chizedek [
>
> —(4Q401) *Songs of the Sabbath Sacrifice* 22:1–3

Although both passages are fragmentary, if the restoration of the name Melchizedek is correct, it would seem from the overall context (namely, a hymn describing the service of God performed by the angels in the heavenly temple) that Melchizedek is, here as well, an angel, indeed perhaps the highest of the angels serving God in heaven.

Another crucial ambiguity found in Psalm 110 also contributed to the identification of Melchizedek as an angel or heavenly being. It is the verse translated above as, "From the womb of the morning like dew your youth will come to you." This could be translated in a radically different way—and was. The old Greek ("Septuagint") translation of this verse reads:

From the womb, before the morning star, **I have begotten you.**

> —Septuagint Ps. 110:5

If these words were spoken by God to Melchizedek (as they seemed to be in context), then they meant that Melchizedek is God's "son." Now, "sons of God," as we have seen, was a phrase elsewhere understood as referring specifically to the angels.[7] If so, then this "son of God" who sits at God's right hand, must have been an angel charged with executing divine justice on earth, the angelic "king of justice."

A somewhat related Melchizedek appears in the work called *2 Enoch*, which may go back to the early first century C.E. In this text, Melchizedek

6. The phrase "assembly of God" may be a reference to Ps. 82:1. Interestingly, the lines just prior to those cited above from 11Q *Melchizedek* also refer to this psalm: "He [God] has decreed the year of favor for Melchizedek . . . as it is written about him [apparently, Melchizedek] in the songs of David, where it says, '*Elohim* [st]ands forth in the asse[mbly of God], in the midst of the gods he rules'" (col. 2, ll. 9–10). It seems that the divine name "Elohim" here is interpreted as a reference to Melchizedek, while the "gods" in the same line refer to the angels, thus eliminating any polytheistic implications from this psalm.

7. See above, Chapter 5, "A Bad Match."

seems to be born to Sopanim (or "Sothonim"), the wife of Noah's (mythical) brother Nir, without any prior act of sexual intercourse (2 *Enoch* 71:2). The idea that Melchizedek was so conceived may be in keeping with the interpretation of Ps. 110:5 just seen: God's words "I have begotten you" meant that Melchizedek was begotten without any human progenitor. In any case, God promises Nir that, although a great flood is coming to destroy the earth, Melchizedek will be safe:

> Behold, I plan now to send down a great destruction onto the earth. But concerning the child [Melchizedek], do not be anxious, Nir, because I in a short while shall send my archangel Gabriel. And he will take the child and put him in the garden of Eden, and he will not perish with those who must perish . . . And Melchizedek will be my priest to all priests, and I will sanctify him and I will change him into a great people who will sanctify me.   — 2 *Enoch* (A) 71:27–29

However much this Melchizedek had a human mother, he nonetheless seems to have acquired superhuman traits: miraculously saved from the flood, he is actually permitted to reenter Eden, and will go on to become some sort of "priest to all priests"—in keeping with Melchizedek's title in Genesis, "a priest [directly] to God Most High."

The Christian "Order of Melchizedek"

But there was a second way of reading the crucial verse Ps.110:4. Instead of indicating the person being spoken to (that is, "You are a priest forever by my order, *O Melchizedek*"), the word "Melchizedek" could be understood as part of the previous phrase; then the verse would read, "You are a priest forever, after the order of [or "for the sake of," "on account of"] Melchizedek."[8] If so, then the psalm was addressed *not* to Melchizedek but to some undefined "you," a "you" who is also being referred to in the first line of the psalm as "my lord."

Early Christians interpreted this "you" as Jesus. (Indeed, the fact that Psalm 110 began "The Lord said to my lord" was offered as proof that there were indeed two heavenly "Lords"; see Mark 12:35–37 and parallels, Acts 2: 34–36). Consequently, the psalm seemed to be saying that Jesus was in fact a priest:

> Christ did not exalt himself to be made a high priest, but was appointed by Him who said to him, "You are my Son, today I have

8. This is the translation of Ps. 110:4 in the old Greek (Septuagint) version.

begotten you," as it also says elsewhere [in the same psalm], "You are a priest forever, after the order of Melchizedek." In the days of his flesh, Jesus offered up prayers and supplications . . . and he became the source of eternal salvation to all who obey him, being designated by God a high priest after the order of Melchizedek.

For this Melchizedek, king of Salem, priest of the Most High God, met Abraham returning from the [war] and blessed him, and to him Abraham apportioned a tenth part of everything. He is first, by translation of his name, king of righteousness, and then he is also king of Salem, that is, king of peace. He is without father or mother or genealogy, and has neither beginning of days nor end of life, but resembling the Son of God, he continues a priest forever.[9]

—Heb. 5:5–10, 7:1–3

For the author of Hebrews, it was certainly important that the Melchizedek of Gen. 14:17–20 was a "priest to God Most High" without having been from the traditional priestly line. For, this meant that the "you" of Psalm 110—by this interpretation, Jesus—could likewise be appointed a high priest without being of priestly descent (see Heb. 9:11–12). That is what "You are a priest forever, *after the order of Melchizedek*" meant to this author—a priest directly appointed by God.

It was not a big step to interpret the person of Melchizedek as a foreshadowing other elements of Christianity, including the Eucharist:

"Salem" means specifically "peace," of which our Savior is said to be king. For concerning him does Moses say, "Melchizedek, king of Salem, priest of God Most High." He offers him "bread and wine" [Gen. 14:18], holy food, as a prefiguring of the eucharist. It is true that the name "Melchizedek" means "just king," but justice and peace are synonyms.   —Clement of Alexandria, *Miscellanies* 4:161, 3

An Uncircumcised Priest?

At the same time, the fact that Melchizedek was a priest without the usual genealogy, and that he had apparently not undergone circumcision nor fol-

---

9. It is interesting that, according to the second line of interpretation described above, all the supernatural traits in Psalm 110 should belong to the "you" addressed in the psalm and *not* to Melchizedek, who could simply be an ordinary priest so designated by God. Yet in the excerpt from Hebrew 7, Melchizedek seems to have retained some of his supernatural traits from the first line of interpretation described: he is "without father or mother or genealogy, and has neither beginning of days nor end of life, but resembling the Son of God, he continues a priest forever."

lowed other Jewish laws and practices, was taken by Christians from an early period as a biblical proof that such things were not important.

> For if [circumcision] were necessary, as you think, God would not have formed Adam uncircumcised, nor would He have looked with favor upon the gifts of Abel, who offered sacrifices but was not circumcised, nor would Enoch, who was not circumcised, have pleased him . . . The priest of God Most High, Melchizedek, was without circumcision, and he had tithes given him by Abraham as offerings. Abraham was the first to receive circumcision in the fleshly sense, and yet he was blessed by Melchizedek [the uncircumcised], after whose order God has announced by David [for example, in Psalm 110] that He would establish the eternal Priest.
>
> —Justin Martyr, *Dialogue with Trypho* 19:3–4 (also ch. 33)

> Likewise Melchizedek, priest of God Most High, was not circumcised and did not keep the sabbath, yet he was chosen for the priesthood of God. —Tertullian, *Against the Jews* 2

Others maintained the opposite:

> Likewise, [Melchizedek] was born circumcised, as it says "And Melchizedek, king of Salem" [interpreted as the king who was *šālēm*, "complete" or "perfect," hence, circumcised]. —*Abot deR. Natan* (A) 2

> He was righteous and he was born circumcised. —*Genesis Rabba* 26:3

Melchizedek in Samaria

As we have already glimpsed, Jewish sources generally held that Melchizedek's kingdom, Salem, was simply a shortened form of the name "Jerusalem":

> And the king of Sodom heard that Abram had given back all the captives and all the booty, and he went up to meet him; and he came to **Salem, which is Jerusalem.** —(1Q20) *Genesis Apocryphon* col. 22:12–13

> There he was received by the king of Solyma, Melchizedek . . . Solyma was in fact the place called thereafter **Jerusalem.**
>
> —Josephus, *Jewish Antiquities* 180 (also *Jewish War* 6:438)

> And Melchizedek, **king of Jerusalem**, brought out bread and wine.
>
> —*Targum Onqelos* Gen. 14:18

> And Melchizedek, the **king of Jerusalem** . . . was a priest serving in the high priesthood before God Most High. —*Targum Neophyti* Gen. 14:18

Some interpreters, however, thought otherwise. A tradition existed that identified "Salem" as a site at or near Shechem, the capital of Samaria (formerly
the northern kingdom of Israel). A fragment attributed to (Pseudo-)Eupole-
mus (who may or may not have been a Samaritan) actually mentions Melchizedek in retelling the story of Abraham. However, this text says that Melchizedek served as a priest in a temple on the Samaritan mountain, Mt.
Gerizim, near Shechem:

> He [Abraham] was accepted as a guest by the city at the temple of
> *Argarizin* [that is, Mt. Gerizim] which means "mountain of the Most
> High." He also received gifts from Melchizedek, who was a priest of
> God and king as well. — (Pseudo-)Eupolemus, *Fragment One* 5–6

Elsewhere, as well, Salem is identified as a place in its own right:

> And Jacob came to **Salem, the city of Shechems**.
> — Septuagint Gen. 33:18

> And . . . Jacob went up to Salem, **to the east of Shechem**, in peace.[10]
> — *Jubilees* 30:1

> And Jared became the father of Enoch and he built a city and called it
> Salem the Great. — *al-Asaṭir* 2:5

The idea that Salem was at or near Shechem would have been very useful to
the Samaritans. For in later times, too, they considered Mt. Gerizim to be
sacred and, indeed, the *real* site intended by God for His temple (not Jerusalem). If Melchizedek had been a priest of God in their territory way back in
the time of Abraham, here was biblical proof that their claims for the sanctity
of their own temple and its priests were truly valid.

Melchizedek Was Shem

Many Jews must have found such uses of the story of Melchizedek disturbing.
No doubt the situation was eased somewhat by a contrary tradition that held
that "Melchizedek" was simply an honorific name of Shem, Noah's son.

> About Shem['s being a prophet] it says, "Upon My word, Mel-
> chizedek" [Ps. 110:4].[11]
> — *Seder Olam* 21

10. Here is a double translation of the Hebrew *šlm*, understood as both "to Salem" and "in
peace."

11. I have translated the verse in this fashion to reflect the apparent interpretation of *Seder Olam*
here: Melchizedek [Shem] was a "priest to the Lord Most High *upon My word*"—that is, one whose
mission it was to communicate the divine word, a prophet. (With this understanding of "priest" *Seder
Olam* goes on to cite Gen. 14:18.)

And Melchizedek, the king of Jerusalem, **who was the great Shem** . . .

— *Targum Neophyti* Gen. 14:18

Likewise Shem was born circumcised, as it says, "And Melchizedek, king of Salem . . ." [interpreted as the king who was *šālēm*, "complete" or "perfect," hence, circumcised]. — *Abot deR. Natan* (A) 2

This Melchizedek was Shem. — Ephraem, *Commentary on Genesis* 11:2

The [Jews] say that he [Melchizedek] was Shem, Noah's son, and counting up the total years of his lifetime [eight hundred years, according to Gen. 11:11] they demonstrate that he would have lived up to [the time of] Isaac [and so certainly could have encountered Abraham in Gen. 14:18–21]. — Jerome, *Questions in Genesis*, Gen. 14:18

This identification—while probably of ancient origin—must have helped to "domesticate" Melchizedek in the face of some of the claims made regarding his true identity. For if Melchizedek was indeed Shem, a distant ancestor of the Jews, and if his high priesthood was associated with the very site on which the great temple was to be built (Salem, understood as Jerusalem), then here was really only another indication that Jerusalem had always been God's chosen spot for His sanctuary and that the Jewish people, even in the time of their remotest ancestors, had already been chosen by God to supply that sanctuary with its priests.

Services No Longer Needed

Nevertheless, a later rabbinic tradition proposed a rather different understanding of Abraham's meeting with this mysterious figure. According to this interpretation, the whole significance of the biblical story can be grasped only by considering the wording of the blessing that Melchizedek offers. He says:

Blessed be Abram to God Most High, maker of heaven and earth; and blessed be God Most High, who has delivered your enemies into your hands. — Gen. 14:19–20

In these lines the Rabbis saw a crucial mistake on Melchizedek's part: he blessed Abraham *before* blessing God, which was a great sacrilege. As a result, they concluded, God must have decided that Melchizedek was not a very good choice for the priesthood after all:

R. Zechariah said in the name of R. Ishmaʿel: God at first wished to have the priesthood come from Shem [that is, Melchizedek], as it is written, "and he was a priest to God Most High" [Gen. 14:18]. But when he [Melchizedek] put Abraham's blessing before God's own, God resolved to have the priesthood descend from Abraham instead . . . And thus it says, "The Lord has sworn and will not change his mind, 'You are a priest forever, after the order of Melchizedek' [Ps. 110:4]." ["After the order," *'al dibrātî*, should be interpreted as] "because of the words [*'al dibbûrô*] of Melchizedek." Likewise it says "and **he** was a priest to God Most High"—*he* was a priest, but not his descendants.

—b. *Nedarim* 32b

According to this interpretation, the words in Psalm 110, "You are a priest forever, after the order of Melchizedek," were not spoken to Melchizedek but to his *replacement,* who was to found the priestly dynasty in Israel. Melchizedek himself had proven to be an unsuitable priest: if the Bible says, "he was a priest," it means to imply by this "he alone": his descendants would not inherit the job from him.

❖   ❖   ❖

In short: Melchizedek provided bread and wine to Abraham and all of his troops. He was king of Jerusalem and perhaps its founder; his name meant "king of righteousness" (or "justice"). He served there as a priest, perhaps a divinely appointed high priest. Indeed, some interpreters concluded that Melchizedek was in reality an angel or semidivine being. Early Christians further saw in him a foreshadowing of Jesus—a priest by divine appointment rather than through priestly pedigree, whose gift of bread and wine foreshadowed the Eucharist and whose uncircumcised state demonstrated that circumcision was not necessary. Another tradition, however, held that "Melchizedek" was simply an honorific title for Noah's son Shem, who had inherited the priesthood from him; the priesthood was taken away from him because of his defective blessing.

9

The Trials of Abraham

(GENESIS 15–22)

Isaac offered as a sacrifice (hands unbound).

The Trials of Abraham

(GENESIS 15–22)

❖   ❖   ❖

God appeared to Abraham in Canaan, once again promising him the land for his offspring in a solemn agreement. He also revealed to Abraham that his descendants would be slaves in Egypt; after four hundred years they would be freed and return to Canaan. But Sarah, Abraham's wife, had been childless for many years; where would his descendants come from? At Sarah's urging, Abraham took her maidservant Hagar as a concubine and she soon bore him a son, Ishmael.

Some years later, God told Abraham that he and his descendants had to be circumcised as part of God's covenant. Abraham acted at once: he and his son Ishmael and all the males of his household were circumcised the same day. Afterward, three angels in human form appeared to Abraham with good news: Sarah would at last bear Abraham a son of her own. And so it was. In due time she gave birth to Isaac, though she and Abraham were quite advanced in age.

When Sarah later saw Ishmael mocking her little son, she told Abraham to banish Ishmael and Hagar, and he reluctantly complied. Isaac was now the only son in Abraham's household. But then Abraham received a horrifying commandment from God: Take your beloved Isaac and offer him up to Me as a sacrifice. Once again, Abraham unhesitatingly obeyed. However, as he was about to kill his son upon the altar, an angel called out to him to stop. Abraham offered up a ram, miraculously caught by the horns in a thicket, in place of his son.

GOD'S COMMANDMENT to Abraham to offer up Isaac as a sacrifice is presented in the Bible as a test. The episode begins, "After these things God *tested* Abraham" (Gen. 22:1), and after it is over, the angel who tells Abraham to stop says, "Now I know that you fear God, since you have not withheld your son, your only son, from me." The test has been passed.

But surveying the whole of Abraham's life as it is narrated in Genesis, ancient readers could not help thinking that the incident with Isaac was not the first time that Abraham had been tested. In fact, his whole life seemed to be one long series of divinely instituted challenges. From the very start, when

165

God had first told Abraham to leave his homeland, it was to go "to the land that I will show you" (Gen. 12:1). Why did not God say "to the land of Canaan"? This order sounded as if it was deliberately worded to test Abraham's faith, as if God were saying, "Follow me! I will not even tell you where we are going."[1]

And then there was all the rest. As we have seen, no sooner had Abraham arrived in Canaan than he found himself in the midst of a famine and was forced to go down to Egypt. Once in Egypt, Abraham's wife, Sarah, had been taken from him by Pharaoh. Were *these* the "blessings" promised to Abraham? More difficulties followed: Abraham's nephew Lot was captured, drawing Abraham into a war in order to secure his safe return. Then there was the matter of Sarah's barrenness itself, and the troubles that ensued when Hagar, Sarah's maidservant, gave birth to Abraham's son Ishmael. And so on and so forth. In the eyes of many interpreters, Abraham's life seemed to be full of tests, and noticing the precise wording of the sentence that begins the incident of the offering of Isaac, "After *these things* God tested Abraham" (Gen. 22:1), some interpreters concluded that the unspecified "these things" referred to all Abraham's previous trials and tribulations—that, no less than the commandment to sacrifice his own son, the previous incidents in Abraham's life were also tests.

In line with this view, it struck interpreters as significant that, in a prayer uttered centuries after Abraham's death, the biblical hero Ezra had summed up Abraham's life in these words:

> You are the Lord God who chose Abram and brought him out of Ur of the Chaldeans and changed his name to Abraham, and You **found his heart to be faithful** to You and made a covenant with him to give to his descendants the land of the Canaanite.   —Neh. 9:7–8

The highlighted words seem to refer to God's testing of Abraham—for what did God's *finding* Abraham's heart to be faithful mean but that, after having caused him to be sorely tried, He had become convinced of the man's loyalty and steadfastness? But if so, then it was perhaps significant that God's covenant with Abraham in Genesis 15 seems, according to Ezra's prayer, to have come about *after* Abraham was tested and found faithful. That could only

---

1. In fact, these words of God in Gen. 12:1 even *sounded* strikingly similar to His words at the start of the story of the sacrifice of Isaac: in the latter incident God likewise did not reveal the name of the place, but instead told Abraham to offer up his son "as a burnt offering on one of the mountains *of which I shall tell you*" (Gen. 22:2). The two incidents thus seemed verbally linked, and if the latter was specifically called a "test" in Gen. 22:1, then the former had perhaps likewise been a test, although Scripture did not say so explicitly.

suggest to later interpreters that God had begun testing Abraham even before the covenant of Genesis 15. Here was a further indication in the Bible that the earlier trials in Abraham's life had indeed been divinely sent tests.

Abraham the Tested

And so, for ancient interpreters, Abraham's "image" was primarily that of "Abraham the Tested," the one who had been tried repeatedly by God:

> In spite of everything, let us give thanks to the Lord our God, who is **putting us to the test** as he did our forefathers. Remember what He did with Abraham, and how he tested Isaac . . . For He has not **tested** us with fire, as He did them, to search their hearts, nor has He taken revenge upon us; but the Lord scourges those who draw near to Him, in order to admonish them.   —Jth. 8:25–27

> Abraham was the father of a multitude of nations, his glory was untarnished.
> He kept the commandments of the Most High, and entered into a covenant with Him.
> He established His covenant in his flesh, and when **tested** he was found faithful.
> Therefore He established by oath to bless nations by his offspring,
> To cause them to inherit from sea to sea, and from river to the ends of the earth.[2]
>   —Sir. 44:19–21

> Remember the deeds of the fathers, which they did in their generations; and receive great honor and an everlasting name. Was not Abraham found faithful when **tested**, and it was reckoned to him as righteousness?[3]   —1 Macc. 2:51–52

> [Even before the offering of Isaac] the Lord knew that Abraham was faithful in every affliction which he had told him, for he had **tested** him with regard to [leaving his] country, and with famine [in Canaan], and had **tested** him with the wealth of kings, and had tested

---

2. The phrase "was found faithful" seems to deliberately echo Neh. 9:8, cited above.

3. Again, "was found faithful" echoes Neh. 9:8. The phrase "and it was reckoned to him as righteousness" comes from Gen. 15:6 and pertains to a part of the Abraham narrative entirely separate from the offering of Isaac. Thus perhaps here too is an early indication that Abraham's "tested" status had spread out from the one explicit test with Isaac to include other incidents of Abraham's life.

him again through his wife when she was taken forcibly, and with circumcision; and He had **tested** him through Ishmael and Hagar, his maid-servant, when he sent them away. And in everything in which He had **tested** him, he was found faithful; he himself did not grow impatient, yet he was not slow to act; for he was faithful and one who loved the Lord.[4]

— *Jubilees* 17:17–18

The list in *Jubilees* above mentions seven tests specifically, but elsewhere it is asserted that Abraham underwent no fewer than ten such trials:

And she [Sarah] died in Hebron. When Abraham went to mourn over her and bury her, we [angels] tested him to see if his spirit was patient and if he was not rash with the words of his mouth; and he was found to be patient in this and was not disturbed . . . This was the **tenth test** by which Abraham was tested, and he was found faithful, patient in spirit.

— *Jubilees* 19:2–3, 8

Abraham our father (may he rest in peace) was tested **ten times** and he passed them all. This is an indication of how great was Abraham's devotion.

— m. *Abot* 5:3

Abraham's many tests soon became a commonplace:

Among other things—it would take too much time to list them all— Abraham was tested through [the incident of] the offering up of his beloved son Isaac.

— Augustine, *City of God* 16.32

Abraham Saw a Dire Future

One incident that might at first seem to have little to do with "Abraham the Tested" is the covenant that God made with Abraham in Genesis 15. Through this solemn agreement God officially granted the land of Canaan to Abraham and his descendants. Here, surely, was a positive note in Abraham's story.

Yet along with this grant of land came a solemn warning:

As the sun was going down, a deep sleep fell on Abram; and lo, a dread and great darkness fell upon him. Then the Lord said to Abram: "Know that your descendants will dwell in a land that is not theirs and will be slaves there, and they will be oppressed for four hundred years. But I will mete out justice to the nation for whom they slave, and

---

4. Here as well, the word "faithful"—appearing no fewer than three times in two sentences—is intended to echo Neh. 9:8. "One who loved the Lord" reflects Isa. 41:8.

afterward they will come out with great wealth. As for you yourself, you shall die in peace; you shall be buried in a good old age. And they shall come back here in the fourth generation, for the iniquity of the Amorites is not yet complete." —Gen. 15:12–16

These words of God hardly foretold a happy future—slavery, oppression, four hundred years . . . No wonder "dread and great darkness" fell on Abraham! And so this covenant (sometimes called the "covenant between the pieces" because it was solemnized between the pieces of sacrificial animals, Gen. 15:10, 17) also turned out to be a trying event, another difficulty confronted by Abraham.

Considering this passage as a whole, however, interpreters came to a further conclusion: what was particularly trying about this incident was the fact that God had actually shown Abraham *far more* than the period of slavery in Egypt to be endured by his descendants. To begin with, if God had shown Abraham four hundred years of future history, it seemed logical to interpreters that He would have shown him the rest as well, including the punishment to be meted out to the later "nation[s] which they serve." Such a notion could only be supported by the text's mention of the "dread and great darkness falling" on Abraham (Gen. 15:12)—for certainly such dread ought not to have been caused merely by the sight of his descendants' sojourn in, and exodus from, Egypt. Interpreters therefore came to view this incident as a fully prophetic apocalypse in which Abraham was afforded a view of all of human history, of heaven and hell, and other things normally hidden from the sight of mere mortals.

> "As the sun was setting, an ecstasy fell upon Abraham . . ." [Septuagint Gen. 15:12]. This is what is felt by those who are [prophetically] inspired and suddenly possessed by God . . . For indeed, the prophet, even when he seems to be speaking, in reality is silent, and his organs of speech, mouth, and tongue are wholly in the employ of Another, to show forth what He wishes. —Philo, *Who Is Heir* 258, 266

Then a voice came to me saying twice to me: "Abraham, Abraham." And I said, "Here I am." And He said, "Behold, it is I. Fear not, for I am before the universe and the mighty, the God who created at the first, before the light of the universe. I am a defense for you and your helper [Gen. 15:1]. Go get Me a three-year-old heifer, a three-year-old she-goat, a three-year-old ram, a turtledove, and a pigeon, and make me a pure sacrifice. And in this sacrifice I will place the ages. I will announce to you **guarded things** and you will see great things which you have not seen, because you desired to search for Me, and I called you one who loves me [Isa. 41:8]." — *Apocalypse of Abraham* 9:1–6

And when they [the inhabitants of the earth] were committing iniquity before You, You chose for Yourself one among them whose name was Abraham. You loved him and to him alone did You reveal the end of the times, secretly, by night, and with him You made an everlasting covenant, and promised him that You would never forsake his descendants. — *4 Ezra* 3:13–15

Simeon b. Abba said in the name of R. Yoḥanan: [God] showed him [Abraham] four things: Hell, the foreign kingdoms [that would dominate Israel], the giving of the Torah, and the future temple. He said to him: so long as your descendants busy themselves with the latter two, they will be saved from the former two. — *Genesis Rabba* 44:21

He [God] showed him [Abraham] that his offspring would sin, and that they would be saved by the prayers of their righteous ones.
— Ephraem, *Commentary on Genesis* 12.3

This prophetic revelation no doubt unnerved Abraham; however, despite the dire future awaiting his offspring, he never wavered in his faithfulness to God.

As we have seen, interpreters saw subsequent events of Abraham's life—Sarah's infertility; the banishing of Ishmael and his mother, Hagar; Abraham's circumcision; and so forth—as additional tests. In these as well, Abraham showed himself to be God's faithful and obedient servant. Yet certainly the greatest of the tests to which Abraham would be subjected was yet to come: God's commandment that Abraham offer up his beloved Isaac on a sacrificial altar. That he was willing to give up the son for whom he had so long waited and hoped was indeed a testimony to Abraham's faith in God.

But even this inspiring narrative raised questions for early interpreters. Why, to begin with, should God *want* to test Abraham? Certainly not in order to find out whether Abraham was worthy. For, as we have just seen, Abraham had already proven himself worthy many times in the past. Why yet another test now, and this one (lest there be any doubt about its purpose) specifically designated as a test ("And it came to pass after these things that God tested Abraham," Gen. 22:1)? Moreover, why in general should God *need* to test people? Does not an all-knowing God know in advance who is worthy and who is not, indeed, who will pass and who will fail? What good was served by putting Abraham through an ordeal whose results were known to God in advance?

Challenged by Angels

In seeking the answer to these questions, interpreters looked to other parts of the Bible, in particular, to the book of Job, another biblical figure whom God had tested. In his case, however, the test was initiated not by God but by Satan, who in effect challenged God's high opinion of Job: "Do some harm to him, indeed, afflict all that he has, and then see if he does not curse You to Your face" (Job 1:11).

To ancient interpreters it seemed plausible that, with regard to Abraham as well, God may have received a challenge from Satan or some other angel(s). The opening sentence of the episode, "After these things God tested Abraham," seemed to offer interpreters confirmation for this theory. For in Hebrew, the word for "things" can also mean "words." If this sentence is understood as meaning "After these *words* . . ." could not Scripture be hinting that certain words had been spoken to God (by Satan or the other angels) and that *after* them, and as a result of them, "God tested Abraham"?

> There were **words** in heaven regarding Abraham, that he was faithful in everything that He told him, [that] the Lord loved him, and in every difficulty he was faithful. Then the [Satan-like] angel Mastema came and said before God, "Behold, Abraham loves Isaac his son, and he delights in him above all else. Tell him to offer him as a sacrifice on the altar. Then You will see if he will carry out this command, and You will know if he is faithful in everything through which You test him." Now the Lord knew that Abraham was faithful in every affliction which he had told him, for he had tested him with regard to [leaving his] country, and with famine . . . And in everything in which He had tested him, he was found faithful; he himself did not grow impatient, yet he was not slow to act; for he was faithful and one who loved the Lord.
> — *Jubilees* 17:15–18

> And He gave him [Abraham] a son in his extreme old age and brought him forth from a sterile womb. But all the angels were jealous of him and the heavenly hosts hated him. And it came to pass, since they hated him, God said to him [Abraham] "Kill the fruit of your womb for Me and bring him before Me as a sacrifice offered by you to Me."
> — Pseudo-Philo, *Biblical Antiquities* 32:1–2

"And it came to pass, after these things [words] . . ." After what words? Said R. Yoḥanan in the name of R. Yosi ben Zimra: After the words spoken by **Satan**. For the text earlier relates, "and the boy grew up and was weaned, and Abraham made a great banquet on the day that Isaac was weaned" (Gen. 21:8). At that time Satan said to God: "Master of the Universe! You have blessed this old man at the age of one hundred years with offspring. Yet amidst all [the bounty of] this banquet that he prepared, was there not one pigeon or fowl for him to sacrifice before You?" He replied: "All that he did he did only for the sake of his son. Still, were I to say to him, 'Sacrifice your son before Me,' he would sacrifice him at once." Hence it says thereafter, "And [after these words] God tested Abraham."

—b. *Sanhedrin* 89b

According to this tradition, then, God was well aware of Abraham's faithfulness long before this test and knew in advance that Abraham would pass it. If He went ahead with it anyway, it was to prove Satan wrong.

God Made It Known

But in interpreting in this way, these writers seemed to contradict what the Bible itself says explicitly later on. For in the biblical account, after Abraham has demonstrated his willingness to offer up his beloved Isaac, God says to him: "Now I know that you fear God, since you have not withheld your son, your only son, from me" (Gen. 22:12). "Now I know" seems to imply "I did not know before." How then could the author of *Jubilees* and other interpreters maintain that God *did* know all along?

The answer lies in yet another ambiguity in the Hebrew. For the same consonants that spell the Hebrew word "I know" (*yd'ty*) can also be read in such a way as to mean "I have made known" or "I have notified." This is apparently how some interpreters chose to understand the text:

[God tells Abraham:] "All the nations of the earth will be blessed through your descendants because of the fact that you have obeyed my command. I have **made known to everyone** that you are faithful to Me in everything that I have told you. Go in peace."[5]

—*Jubilees* 18:16

[God says:] "For now **I have made it known** so that you may be seen by those who do not know you, and I have shut the mouth of those [angels] who are forever speaking against you.

—Pseudo-Philo, *Biblical Antiquities* 32:4

5. The same "I have made known" also appears earlier, where *Jubilees* restates Gen. 22:12 as "For now I have made known [or "shown"] that you fear the Lord." (This is so at least in the Latin version of the text. The Ethiopic version has "Now I know," but this probably represents a "correction" of the translated *Jubilees* text by some later copyist who wanted it to conform exactly to the words in the Bible as they were, by then, commonly translated).

For now I have made known . . .   —Peshitta (some versions) Gen. 22:12

[For the words] "now I know . . ." [in Gen. 22:12, read instead] "now I have made known" to everyone that you are one who loves me, and so "you have not withheld your son" [Gen. 22:12].   —*Genesis Rabba* 56:7

Abraham was tested through [the incident of] the offering up of his beloved son Isaac to prove his pious obedience and so make it known to the world, not to God . . . It says "Now I know" for "Now I have made known"—for certainly God was not ignorant [of this] previously.   —Augustine, *City of God* 16.32

Thus, God's great test of Abraham took place in response to a challenge and was carried out in order to prove Abraham's virtues not to God, but to others—Satan, the other angels, or the world at large.

But there was another troubling question arising out of the story, and it concerned the role of Isaac. Isaac is spoken of in reverential terms in the Bible: indeed, God is more than once called the "God of Abraham, *of Isaac,* and of Jacob," and along with these other two, Isaac is specifically referred to as God's "servant" (Exod. 32:13). And yet, while the virtues of Abraham and Jacob are recounted in detail in the Bible, relatively little is said about Isaac. Apart from this glimpse of him as the near-victim of God's command to Abraham, the main incidents of Isaac's life reported in the Bible are his encounter with Abimelech in Genesis 26 and his blessing of Jacob instead of Esau in Genesis 27. Neither of these incidents involves any conspicuous display of Isaac's virtues.

And so, interpreters anxious to discover what *was* praiseworthy in Isaac's life were naturally drawn back to the story of his being bound on the altar and prepared for sacrifice by his father. It certainly seemed that his willingness to be sacrificed was no less heroic or praiseworthy than Abraham's willingness to carry out God's commandment to sacrifice him. Was this not Isaac's great and heroic act—the fact that, on that fateful day, he offered himself willingly to the sacrificial knife?

The trouble is, that is not what the Bible says. There is no indication in the biblical narrative that Isaac willingly consented to anything—he seems rather to be an unknowing victim, virtually a prop. On the way to the place of the sacrifice there is an exchange between father and son that proves that Isaac has no idea of what is about to happen:

And Abraham took the wood of the burnt offering, and laid it on Isaac his son; and he took in his hand the fire and knife, and the two of them walked together. And Isaac said to his father Abraham, "Father," and he said, "Here I am, my son." And he said, "Here is the fire and the

wood, **but where is the lamb for the burnt offering?**" Abraham said,
"God will provide Himself the lamb for the burnt offering, my son."
And the two of them walked together.   —Gen. 22:6–8

Isaac's question about the sacrificial lamb makes it clear that, at this point, he
himself does not know who the *real* intended victim is. If so, then Isaac was
truly no more than an unwilling participant caught up in events beyond his
control. The same conclusion is reinforced by another detail in the narrative:
at the moment of the sacrifice, the Bible reports that Abraham "bound his son
Isaac and laid him upon the altar" (Gen. 22:9). If Isaac were a willing participant, what need was there to tie him up? And this understanding of Isaac's role
could only be reinforced by what the angel says to Abraham at the end of the
story (Gen. 22:16–18): it is because *you*, Abraham, "have done this and not
withheld your son, your only son" that God will bless *you*. There is no
mention of anything Isaac did because, apparently, he did nothing worth
mentioning. What virtue can be imputed to Isaac in this whole affair?

Isaac Was a Willing Victim

Unless . . . Given the necessity of finding *something* praiseworthy concerning
Isaac in the story, an interpreter might still come up with an indication, no
matter how slight, that Isaac had consented to be sacrificed. And slight indication there was. After all, the text makes no mention of Isaac resisting or trying
to flee. It simply says: "When they came to the place of which God had told
him, Abraham built an altar there, and laid the wood in order, and bound
Isaac his son, and laid him on the altar upon the wood" (Gen. 22:9). Is not this
silence eloquent? After all, Abraham is an old man—well over a hundred, his
age at Isaac's birth (Gen. 21:5). We do not know how old Isaac is, but he is
certainly old enough to ask the question that he asks about the sacrificial lamb,
and old enough to carry the wood and the fire. Conceivably, then, such a boy
or young man could not have been tied up by his aged father if he himself had
struggled or attempted to flee. Thus, if Abraham was indeed able to go ahead
as planned and offer Isaac as a sacrifice, could it have been in any way other
than with Isaac's active cooperation?

A number of sources go out of their way to suggest that Isaac was indeed
a willing participant. Such a view is implied in a passage seen earlier:

Remember what he [God] did with Abraham, and **how he tested Isaac**
. . . For He has not tested us with fire, as He did them, to search their
hearts.   —Jth. 8:26–27

If Isaac was tested by God, it certainly must have been in this incident, for it is the only testlike episode in his whole life. And if it was a test, was it not (as this passage suggests) also specifically a test of faith, a determination of Isaac's willingness to give up his very life should God demand it? So other interpreters as well suggested that Isaac in the episode was the prototype of a religious martyr:

> Eleazar, though being consumed by fire, remained unmoved in his reason . . . and by reason like that of **Isaac**, he rendered the many-headed rack ineffective. —4 Macc. 7:12–14

> Remember . . . the father by whose hand Isaac would have submitted to being slain for the sake of religion. —4 Macc. 13:12 (also 16:20)

> And as he [Abraham] was setting out, he said to his son, "Behold now, my son, I am offering you as a burnt offering and I am returning you into the hands of Him who gave you to me." But the son said to the father, "Hear me, father. If [ordinarily] a lamb of the flocks is accepted as a sacrifice to the Lord with a sweet savor, and if such flocks have been set aside for slaughter [in order to atone] for human iniquity, while man, on the contrary, has been designated to inherit this world—why should you be saying to me now, 'Come and inherit eternal life and time without measure'? Why if not that I was indeed born in this world *in order to* be offered as a sacrifice to Him who made me? Indeed, this [sacrifice] will be [the mark of] my blessedness over other men—for no such thing will ever be [again]—and in me the generations will be proclaimed and through me nations will understand how God made a human soul worthy for sacrifice."
> —Pseudo-Philo, *Biblical Antiquities* 32:2–3

> [Abraham tells Isaac that he is to sacrifice himself:] Isaac, however, since he was descended from such a father, could be no less noble of spirit [than Abraham], and received these words with delight. He said that he never would have been worthy of being born in the first place were he not now to carry out the decision of God and his father and submit himself to the will of both. —Josephus, *Jewish Antiquities* 1:232

> Why was our father Abraham blessed? Was it not because he acted righteously and truthfully through faith? Isaac, knowing full well what was to happen, was willingly led forth to be sacrificed.
> —1 *Clement* 31:2–4

Together in Mind

Beyond such an argument based on common sense and the age of the partici-pants, there was another detail in the biblical text itself that might have indicated that Isaac was a willing participant. For at no time does the biblical account actually say *when* Abraham informed Isaac that he was to be sac-rificed; as the moment approached, Abraham—apparently in silence—simply "built an altar there, and laid the wood in order, and bound Isaac his son, and laid him on the altar upon the wood" (Gen. 22:9). But certainly at some point he must have told Isaac what was going to happen. And, on closer inspection, the biblical passage cited above seems to contain a clue as to when Isaac was told:

> And Abraham took the wood of the burnt offering, and laid it on Isaac his son; and he took in his hand the fire and knife, **and the two of them walked together**. And Isaac said to his father Abraham, "Father," and he said, "Here I am, my son." And he said, "Here is the fire and the wood, but where is the lamb for the burnt offering?" Abraham said, "God will provide himself the lamb for the burnt offering, my son." **And the two of them walked together.** —Gen. 22:6–8

That the phrase "and the two of them walked together" is repeated just two verses after it was first uttered must have struck interpreters as suspicious: why should the Bible repeat itself? And such suspicion could only be rein-forced by the particular placement of the repeated phrase. It comes right after Abraham has told Isaac that God Himself will provide the sacrifice; *we* know that Abraham secretly means by this Isaac himself. But could it not be that Isaac at that moment also understood that this was what Abraham meant? Then "and the two of them walked together" could mean something like: both of them went along with the plan, both knew exactly what they were about to do.

> Going at the same pace—no less with regard to their thinking than with their bodies—down the straight path whose end is holiness, they came to the designated place.[6] —Philo, *Abraham* 172

> [Abraham says to Isaac:] The Lord will provide a lamb for himself for the burnt offering, my son—and if not, you will be the lamb for the

---

6. Philo's "at the same pace" seems immediately predicated on the Septuagint translation of the Hebrew *yaḥdaw*, which it understands as "at the same time" (*hama*). Cf. his *Migration of Abraham* 166.

burnt offering. And the two of them walked together with firm intention.   — *Targum Neophyti* and *Fragment Targum* (Paris Ms.) Gen. 22:8

And the two of them walked together—the one to slaughter, the other
to be slaughtered.   — *Genesis Rabba* 56:4

Offering Foreshadowed Crucifixion

Of all the Hebrew Bible's narratives that were read *typologically*—that is, as
prefiguring the events of the New Testament—perhaps none was so evocative
as the story of Abraham's offering up of Isaac, which was understood by
Christians from early times as a foreshadowing of the crucifixion:

> If God is for us, then who is against us? He who **did not spare** His own
> son but gave him up for us all, will He not also give us all things along
> with him?[7]   —Rom. 8:31–32

> [Jesus was the fulfillment of] that which was foreshadowed in Isaac,
> who was offered upon the altar.   — *Letter of Barnabas* 7:3

> Since indeed Abraham, having followed, in keeping with his faith, the
> commandment of God's word, did with a ready mind give up his only
> begotten and beloved son,[8] for a sacrifice unto God, that God again
> might be well pleased to offer unto Abraham's whole seed His only
> begotten and dearly beloved son to be a sacrifice for our redemption.
>   —Irenaeus, *Against the Heresies* 4:5, 4

Soon enough, other correspondences between the two narratives were
explored:

> And on this account Isaac carried the wood on which he was to be
> offered up to the place of sacrifice, just as the Lord Himself carried His
> own cross.

> Finally, since Isaac himself was not killed—for his father had been
> forbidden to kill him—who was that ram which was offered instead,
> and by whose foreshadowing blood the sacrifice was accomplished?
> For when Abraham had caught sight of him, he was caught by the

7. Here the phrase "did not spare" seems to be a deliberate evocation of the same phrase in Gen.
22:12 and 16.

8. "Only begotten" and "beloved" seem to correspond to Gen 22:1, "Take now your son, your
only one, whom you *love*." In the Septuagint, the Hebrew *yĕḥîdĕkā*, "only one," is understood as
yĕdîdĕkā, "beloved." See also John 3:16.

horns in a thicket. Who then did he represent but Jesus, who, before He was offered up, had been crowned with thorns?

—Augustine, *City of God* 16, 32

❖ ❖ ❖

In short: Abraham's life was marked by many divinely instigated tests (ten in all). Abraham trusted in God and passed each one. Even God's covenant with Abraham in Genesis 15 was a test, since Abraham was given a frightening view of all of future history and other secret things. God initiated Abraham's greatest test, the offering up of Isaac, in order to demonstrate Abraham's faith to Satan or others who doubted Abraham. In this test, Isaac was a knowing and willing participant, for he, no less than his father, put his trust in God. Christian interpreters saw in this episode a foreshadowing of the crucifixion.

10
Lot and Lot's Wife
(GENESIS 18–19)

Lot and his two daughters: they meant well.
(Note pillarized wife and destroyed city in background.)

Lot and Lot's Wife

(GENESIS 18–19)

❖   ❖   ❖

When Abraham first left his homeland of Ur, he was accompanied by his nephew Lot. Later, Lot continued with him to Canaan, but once established there, they separated: Lot took the fertile land of the Jordan valley, settling in Sodom, while Abraham stayed in the territory to the west (Gen. 13:8–12).

Despite this separation, Abraham continued to look after his nephew. When Lot was taken prisoner in the war that broke out between the city-states of the Jordan valley and their eastern overlords (Genesis 14), Abraham went into battle to free him. Later, when God announced to Abraham that He was going to destroy the cities of Sodom and Gomorrah because of their "wickedness" (Gen. 18:16–33), Abraham intervened to try to save them—presumably on Lot's account. Lot was indeed saved, but the whole region was scourged; when Lot's wife looked backward, she became a pillar of salt. Later, in their place of refuge, Lot's daughters conspired to get their father drunk so that they might have relations with him. From the resulting pregnancies were born the ancestors of two nations, Ammon and Moab.

I T W A S H A R D for interpreters to know what to make of Lot. Was he good or bad? On the one hand, he was Abraham's nephew, and like Abraham, he had willingly left Ur and its presumed evils—this certainly made him sound good. Moreover, when Abraham pleaded with God to spare Sodom, he did so on the grounds that destroying the city might mean killing the righteous along with the wicked. Presumably, Lot was among these "righteous"—and, in fact, God then did send angels specifically to get Lot and his family out of Sodom before its destruction. So here too was an indication that Lot was good.

On the other hand, some of Lot's deeds were questionable at best. Given a choice of where to live in Canaan, he had moved right into Sodom. The Bible narrates the event in these terms:

> So Lot chose for himself all the Jordan valley, and Lot journeyed to the east; thus they separated from each other. Abram dwelt in the land of Canaan, while Lot dwelt among the cities of the valley and **moved his tent up to Sodom.** Now the men of Sodom were evil and very sinful against God.   — Gen. 13:11–13

181

If the text observes (quite needlessly, at this point in the story) that the men of Sodom were evil sinners, then why did Lot move in with them? Certainly he could have pitched his tent elsewhere in the valley. Perhaps, after all, he was not much better than the wicked men of Sodom, whom, at one point later on, he addresses as "my brothers" (Gen. 19:7). And although Lot *is* saved from Sodom before its destruction, his subsequent doings are hardly exemplary. He ends up having relations with his two daughters, who get him drunk for the occasion, and the two sons born from these shameful unions end up being the ancestors of the Ammonites and Moabites, the only two peoples whom God specifically excluded from the "assembly of the Lord" (Deut. 23:3). None of this, needless to say, reflects very well on Lot.

Lot the Righteous

It is not surprising that, given these conflicting signals in the Bible itself, ancient interpreters disagreed on how Lot was to be viewed. Some sources describe him as altogether righteous and good:

> Wisdom rescued a **righteous** man when the ungodly were perishing; he escaped the fire that descended on the Five Cities. Evidence of their wickedness still remains: a continually smoking wasteland, plants bearing fruit that does not ripen, and a pillar of salt standing as a monument to an unbelieving soul. For because they passed wisdom by, they not only were prevented from recognizing the good, but also left for mankind a reminder of their folly, so that their faults would not be able to pass unseen.
>
> —Wisd. 10:6–8

> [You are] the one who kindled the fearful fire against the five cities of Sodom, and turned a fruitful land into salt because of those living in it, and snatched away **pious** Lot from the burning.
>
> —Hellenistic Synagogal Prayer, *Apostolic Constitutions* 8.12: 22

> "He who walks with wise men becomes wise . . ." [Prov. 13:20]. This refers to Lot, who accompanied our father Abraham and learned from his good deeds and ways.
>
> —*Pirqei deR. Eliezer* 25

> Lot was a wholly righteous man, but since he did not study [Torah], Abraham did not wish to be his neighbor and said to him, "Depart now from me" [Gen. 13:9].
>
> —*Alphabet of Ben Sira* 268

This tradition of "Lot the Righteous" is likewise found in early Christian sources. Some Christians saw in Lot yet another biblical figure who, while uncircumcised and not part of Israel, was nonetheless blessed:

By turning the cities of Sodom and Gomorrah to ashes, He [God] condemned them to extinction and made them an example to those who were to be ungodly; and . . . He rescued the righteous Lot, greatly distressed by the licentiousness of the wicked (for by what that righteous man saw and heard as he lived among them, he was vexed in his righteous soul day after day with their lawless deeds). —2 Pet. 2:6–8

Because of his hospitality and piety, Lot was saved from Sodom.
—1 Clement 11:1

Lot was saved out of Sodom without circumcision, when those very angels and the Lord led him forth.
—Justin Martyr, Dialogue with Trypho 19:4

[Paul recalls:] When these had passed on I saw another with a beautiful face and I asked, "Who is this, sir?" . . . And he said to me, "This is Lot who was found righteous in Sodom." —Apocalypse of Paul 27

In Sodom and Gomorrah, Lot was righteous.
— (Armenian) Story of Noah (in Stone, Armenian Apocrypha, 93)

Lot also appears in the Qur'an as a righteous figure:

And behold, Lot also was one of those who had been [divinely] sent, and We saved him and his household, every one, except for an old woman [Lot's wife] who stayed behind. —Qur'an 37:132–134

Lot the Wicked

A great many other interpreters nonetheless found Lot to be a less than positive figure. If he was saved in the destruction of Sodom, perhaps (as Gen. 19:29 seemed to imply) it was only because of Abraham's earlier supplications, or because of Abraham's own moral stature:

And in like manner, God will execute judgment on the places where they have done according to the uncleanness of the Sodomites, just as the judgment of Sodom. But Lot we [the angels] saved; for God **remembered Abraham**, and sent him out of the midst of the overthrow.
And he [Lot] and his daughters committed sin upon the earth, such as had not been on the earth since the days of Adam till his time; for the man lay with his daughters. —Jubilees 16:6–8

For Lot was saved not for his own sake so much as for the sake of the wise man, Abraham, for the latter had offered prayers for him.

— Philo, *Questions and Answers in Genesis* 4:54

If he was able to escape Sodom, as Scripture indicates, he owed this more to Abraham's merits than his own. — Origen, *Homilies on Genesis* 5:3

And when the Lord was destroying the cities of the plain, the Lord remembered **Abraham's** merit and He sent forth Lot from the midst of the destruction. — *Targum Pseudo-Jonathan* Gen. 19:29

When the angels overthrew Sodom and saved him [Lot] because of **Abraham's** merit, they said to him "Escape to the mountain lest you perish" [Gen. 19:17], [meaning that] by the merit of that great mountain Abraham you have escaped; now go to him.

— *Pesiqta Rabbati, Bayyom ha-shemini* 3

As mentioned earlier, the fact that Lot *chose* to live in Sodom certainly seemed suspicious. But even his earlier decision to separate from Abraham—caused, the Bible says, by strife between their own shepherds (Gen. 13:7)—did not reflect well on Lot:

[Abraham recounts:] After that day, Lot departed from me because of the deeds of our shepherds. And he departed and settled in the valley of Jordan, taking all his riches with him; and I myself added much to his possessions. As for him, he grazed his flocks and came to Sodom. At Sodom, he bought for himself a house and lived in it. And I lived on the mountain of Bethel. And I was **disturbed** that my nephew Lot had parted from me. — *Genesis Apocryphon* 21:5–7

[Lot] was an unsteady and indecisive person, turning this way and that, sometimes fawning on him [Abraham] with loving embrace, sometimes rebellious and refractory through the instability of his character. — Philo, *Abraham* 212 (also *Questions and Answers in Genesis* 4:47)

It is written, "And there was strife between Abraham's shepherds and Lot's" [Gen. 13:7]. And why did they strive with each other? When a man [that is, Abraham] is righteous, then the members of his household are likewise righteous . . . but when a man is wicked [like Lot], then the members of his household are likewise wicked.

[Later,] God said to them [Lot's shepherds]: I said to Abraham that I would give this land to his sons—to *his* sons and not to that wicked man [Lot] as you suppose. — *Pesiqta Rabbati, Bayyom ha-shemini* 3

When he [Lot] separated from Abraham, Scripture says, "And Lot chose for himself all the Jordan valley" [Gen. 13:11]—that is, Sodom. For Lot saw that the people of Sodom were plunged in wantonness and he chose Sodom **so that he might do as they did**.

Similarly, Lot [later] says to the men of Sodom, "Behold, I have two daughters . . ." Normally, a man will sacrifice himself for his daughters or his wife: either he kills or is killed [on their behalf]. But Lot was ready to turn over his daughters to them for iniquity! Said God to him: Well then, you can keep them for yourself, and eventually little school-children will laugh about you when they read, "And Lot's two daughters became pregnant from their father" [Gen. 19:36].

— *Midrash Tanḥuma, Vayyera* 12

Sodomites' Sexual Sins

If early interpreters were thus somewhat divided about Lot, they were equally perplexed about the city of Sodom. God destroyed it because of the terrible things that were being done there—but what exactly were those things? Strangely, the Genesis narrative does not say. The men of Sodom are said to be "evil and very sinful" (Gen. 13:13), and at one point God observes that the Sodomites' "sin is very grave" (Gen. 18:20), but that is all we are told.

To some interpreters Sodom's sin seemed clear enough: homosexual practices. After all, when the angels sent by God arrived at Lot's house, "the men of Sodom, both young and old, every one of them" (Gen. 19:4) came to surround the house and demanded to have sexual relations with them. Was this not clear proof that the unnamed sin of the Sodomites consisted of just such practices (later known, as a result, by the word "sodomy")?

In addition to specifically homosexual practices, some interpreters attributed to the Sodomites other, heterosexual sins, specifically, adultery and fornication. The reason is a certain verse in the book of Jeremiah:

They [Jerusalemite prophets] **commit adultery** and deal falsely and encourage evildoers, so that no one repents—they are all **like Sodom** to me.

— Jer. 23:14

If God equated adulterers in Jerusalem to the people of Sodom, then it followed that the latter were no less guilty of adultery than of homosexual acts. As a result, Sodom came to be known generally as a place of sexual profligacy:

And in this month the Lord executed his judgments on Sodom, and Gomorrah, and Zeboim, and all the region of the Jordan, and He burned them with fire and brimstone, and destroyed them until this day, even as I have declared to you all their works, that they are wicked and exceedingly sinful, and that they defile themselves and commit fornication in the flesh, and work uncleanness on the earth. And in like manner, God will execute judgment on the places where they have done according to the uncleanness of the Sodomites, just as the judgment of Sodom.

[Later on,] he [Abraham] told them [his descendants] about the punishment of the giants and the punishment of Sodom—how they were condemned because of their wickedness; because of the sexual impurity, uncleanness, and corruption among themselves they died in sexual impurity.

— *Jubilees* 16:5–6, 20:5

You make married women impure, you lie with whores and adulteresses, you marry heathen women, and your sexual relations will be like Sodom and Gomorrah.

— *Testament of Levi* 14:6

My children, recognize in the skies, in the earth, and in the sea, and in all created things, the Lord who made all things, so that you do not become as Sodom, which changed the order of nature.

— *Testament of Naphtali* 3:4

You shall commit fornication with the fornication of Sodom, and shall perish, all save a few, and shall renew wanton deeds with women.

— *Testament of Benjamin* 9:1

And made them an example to those who were to be ungodly; and . . . He rescued the righteous Lot, greatly distressed by the licentiousness of the wicked.

— 2 Pet. 2:6–7

. . . just as Sodom and Gomorrah and the surrounding cities, which likewise acted immorally and indulged in unnatural lust, serving as an example by undergoing a punishment of eternal fire.

— Jude 7

The whole region of that irreligious city was destroyed, where lewdness between males had become as habitual as other deeds that the law declares permissible.

— Augustine, *City of God* 16.30

The Proud and the Stingy

Interestingly, however, there was another tradition that held that the Sodomites' sin actually had nothing to do with homosexual acts or adultery or fornication. Instead, their fault was pride or stinginess, an unwillingness to help the unfortunate of this world.

The origin of this other tradition is not hard to find. It comes from a passage in the book of Ezekiel, where the prophet compares the people's sins to those famous sins of the (now defunct) people of Sodom:

> Behold, this was the guilt of your sister Sodom: she and her daughters had **pride, surfeit of food, and prosperous ease, but did not aid the poor and needy.** They were **haughty**, and did abominable things before Me; therefore I removed them when I saw it. — Ezek. 16:49–50

According to this list, it was primarily the Sodomites' pride and their failure to aid the poor amidst their own prosperity that caused God to smite them. (The "abominable things" may also refer to Sodom's licentiousness, but this is not certain.)

As a result, a great many interpreters read the story of Lot quite differently. He had settled in a city of haughty, wealthy, but inhospitable and tight-fisted people. In such circumstances, Lot was, if anything, a *victim* of the Sodomites, since, as a newcomer and a stranger, he was likely to suffer from their lack of hospitality.

> He did not spare the neighbors of Lot, whose **arrogance** made them hateful.
> — Sir. 16:8

> You [O God] burned with fire and brimstone the **arrogant** Sodomites, who were unseen in their vices, and you made them an example to posterity. — 3 Macc. 2:5

> Others [the Sodomites] had refused to **receive strangers** when they came to them. — Wisd. 19:14

> Now, about this time the Sodomites, overweeningly **proud** of their numbers and the extent of their **wealth**, showed themselves insolent to men and impious to the Divinity, insomuch that they no more remembered the benefits that they had received from Him, hated **foreigners** and avoided any contact with others. Indignant at this conduct, God accordingly resolved to chastise them for their **arrogance**, and not only to uproot their city, but to blast their land so

completely that it should yield neither plant nor fruit whatsoever from
that time forward.　　　　　—Josephus, *Jewish Antiquities* 1:194–195

[Jesus tells his disciples:] And if anyone does not receive you [that is,
fails to be hospitable] . . . truly I say to you it shall be more tolerable on
the day of judgment for the land of Sodom and Gomorrah than for
that town.　　　　　　　　　　　　　　　　—Matt. 10:14–15

Someone who says, "What is mine is mine and what is yours is yours"
[that is, who is unwilling to be generous] . . . this is the disposition
[characteristic] of Sodom.　　　　　　　　　　　　—m. *Abot* 5:10

R. Yehudah said: They announced in Sodom that anyone who gave
bread to the poor, the sojourner or the destitute would be burned.
Now, Pelotit was Lot's daughter and she was married to one of the
leaders of Sodom. She saw a poor man afflicted in the public square
and she was sorely grieved for him. What did she do? Every day, when
she went to draw water, she would take some food from her house and
put it in her pitcher, and so would feed the poor man. The people of
Sodom wondered: how is this poor man managing to live? When they
found out, they took [the woman] to be burned.

　　　　　　　　　　　　　　　　　　—*Pirqei deR. Eliezer* 25

But what were the Sodomites *really* guilty of, fornication or arrogance and
stinginess in the midst of their prosperity? Perhaps it was all of these.

The region of the Sodomites . . . was laden with innumerable injus-
tices, especially those arising from **gluttony** and **lust** . . . The cause of
this excess in licentiousness among the inhabitants was the unfailing
abundance of their wealth, for, provided with deep soil and ample
water, this region every year enjoyed a harvest of all manner of crops
. . . They threw off from their necks the law of nature by indulging in
strong drink, rich food, and forbidden forms of intercourse.

　　　　　　　　　　　　　　　　—Philo, *Abraham* 134–135

Indeed, the fact that the Bible seemed to contain an unnecessary duplication
in its description of the Sodomites—they are said to be both "wicked" and
"sinful" (Gen. 13:13)—might in itself be a subtle hint that two entirely different
and unrelated sorts of sins were involved:

Now the men of Sodom were wicked with their wealth, and they were
sinful with their bodies before the Lord, exceedingly.

　　　　　　　　　　　　　　　　—*Targum Onqelos* Gen. 13:13

And the people of Sodom were wicked toward one another and sinful
with sexual sins and bloodshed and idolatry before the Lord, exceedingly.   — *Targum Neophyti* Gen. 13:13

Abraham's Hospitality

Being stingy and unhospitable, especially to strangers, was no small matter.
From ancient times, this had been considered a particularly grave fault. Indeed, the Sodomites' stinginess (if that was in fact their crime) stood in sharp
contrast to Abraham's behavior. For he was celebrated among early interpreters for his generosity, especially to strangers.

This tradition derives mainly from the description of Abraham's generosity when he encounters God's angels on their way to destroy Sodom. The
incident begins as follows:

> And God appeared to him [Abraham] at the oaks of Mamre, while he
> was sitting at the door of his tent in the heat of the day. And he lifted
> up his eyes and saw three men standing near him; and when he saw he
> **ran** from the door of the tent to meet them, and he **bowed down** to
> the ground. He said: "My lords, if I have found favor with you, please
> do not depart from your servant. Let a little water be taken to wash
> your feet, and take your rest under the tree, while I fetch some bread
> so that you may sate yourselves, after which you may continue on—
> since, after all, you *have* stopped by your servant's place. They an-
> swered: "Do indeed as you have said." So Abraham **hastened** to Sarah
> in the tent, and said, "**Hurry**! Knead three measures of fine flour and
> make cakes!" Then Abraham **ran** to the herd and took a calf, tender
> and goodly, and gave it to his servant-boy, who **hastened** to slaughter
> it. Next he took butter and milk, and the calf that had been slaugh-
> tered, and he served it to them. Then he stood near them under a tree
> while they ate.   —Gen. 18:1–8

The whole lesson of this lengthy passage (and why was such a detailed
description necessary if it were *not* in order to teach some lesson?) seemed to
be that hospitality and generosity to strangers are a great virtue. Thus, seeing
the three strangers (who later turn out to be angels and no mere mortals, Gen.
19:1), Abraham immediately offers them every courtesy. He *runs* to meet them
and with exceeding humility begs them to take a meal; the passage then
stresses how he and his household *hurry* lest these guests be kept waiting one
extra moment.

For interpreters, all this was an indication that Abraham was a man of extraordinary generosity, in particular with regard to strangers:

> That [Abraham] had a multitude of servants is clear . . . [Yet] he himself becomes as an attendant and a servant [to the visiting angels] **in order to show his hospitality.**
>
> — Philo, *Questions and Answers in Genesis* 4:10 (also *Abraham* 107–114)

> All the years of his life he [Abraham] lived in quietness, gentleness, and righteousness, and the righteous man was very **hospitable.** For he pitched his tent at the crossroads of the oak of Mamre[1] and welcomed everyone—rich and poor, kings and rulers, the crippled and the helpless, friends and strangers, neighbors and passersby—[all] on equal terms did the pious, entirely holy, righteous, and hospitable Abraham welcome. — *Testament of Abraham* (A) 1:1–2

> O my sons, be **generous to strangers** and you will be given exactly what was given to the great Abraham, the father of fathers, and to our father Isaac, his son. — *Testament of Jacob* 7:22

> And remember always to welcome strangers, for by doing this, some people have entertained angels without knowing it. — Heb. 13:2

> Abraham . . . used to go out and look all around and when he would find travelers he would invite them into his house. To someone who was not used to eating wheat bread he would [nonetheless] give him wheat bread, to someone who was not used to eating meat he would give meat, and to someone who was not accustomed to drink wine he would nonetheless give wine. Moreover, he went and built for himself a large mansion on the road and would leave food and drink there so that anyone who came by would enter and eat and drink and bless God, and that gave him [Abraham] great satisfaction.
>
> — *Abot deR. Natan* (A) 7

Lot Learned from Abraham

Given this tradition, it seemed likely that Lot had learned from his uncle the lesson of hospitality. For, like Abraham, Lot welcomed the angels and pre-

---

1. Since the Bible specifically mentions that Abraham was at the "oaks of Mamre," this interpretive tradition understands that detail as likewise implying something about Abraham's generosity. For he could have pitched his tent anywhere. If he decided to do so at what was apparently a well-known spot in (or just outside) Hebron (see Gen. 23:17, 19, etc.), he must have done so because he *wanted* to welcome strangers.

vailed upon them to accept his hospitality (Gen. 19:1–3). And if Lot and his family were subsequently spared—the only residents of stingy Sodom not killed in the destruction—was this not further indication that Lot, unlike his neighbors, was indeed generous?

> But the angels came to the city of the Sodomites and Lot invited them to be his guests, for he was very kindly to strangers and had learned the lesson of Abraham's generosity.
> —Josephus, *Jewish Antiquities* 1:200

> Because of his **hospitality** and piety, Lot was saved from Sodom.
> —*1 Clement* 11:1

> "He who walks with wise men becomes wise . . ." [Prov. 13:20]. This refers to Lot, who accompanied our father Abraham and learned from his good deeds and ways.
> —*Pirqei deR. Eliezer* 25

Lot's Wife Sinned

As Lot and his family fled Sodom, Lot's wife disobeyed the order of the angels not to look back (Gen. 19:17), "and she turned into a pillar of salt" (Gen. 19:26). Interpreters found it difficult to understand what was so bad about Lot's wife turning around. The Bible did not say, so some felt free to search out their own explanations. All interpreters agreed that her deed must somehow have been *sinful.* Perhaps she turned around more than once, displaying thereby a flagrant disregard for divine commandments; perhaps her gesture testified to her own indecision or lack of faith; or perhaps she was motivated by too great an attachment to her way of life in Sodom or to the sinful relatives she had left behind:

> But Lot's wife, who during the flight was continually turning round towards the city, overly curious about it, notwithstanding God's prohibition of such action, was changed into a pillar of salt.
> —Josephus, *Jewish Antiquities* 1:203

> And since Lot's wife was a descendant of the people of Sodom, she looked back to see what ultimately would happen to her father's house. And she remains a pillar of salt until the time of the resurrection of the dead.
> —*Targum Neophyti* Gen. 19:26

> Remember Lot's wife: Whoever seeks to gain his life will lose it, but whoever loses his life will preserve it.
> —Luke 17:32–33

Lot was saved from Sodom, when the entire region was judged by fire and brimstone. In this way the Master clearly demonstrated that He does not forsake those who hope in him, but destines to punishment and torment those who turn aside. Of this his wife was destined to be a sign, for after leaving with him she changed her mind and no longer agreed, and as a result she became a pillar of salt to this day, that it might be known to all that those who are of two minds and those who **question the power of God** fall under judgment and become a warning to all generations.

— *1 Clement* 11:1–2

[She] serves as a solemn and sacred warning that no one who starts out on the path of salvation should ever yearn for the things that he has left behind.

— Augustine, *City of God* 10.8

A Visible Reminder

But there was another way of understanding the punishment of Lot's wife, one that was connected to a still larger question in the story of Sodom and Gomorrah.

The inhabitants of this region had sinned; they should have been punished, by all means. But was that a reason for God to blight the landscape forever, turning what once was a flourishing and rich valley into a smoldering wasteland? The biblical narrative offered no explanation, but it was not hard for interpreters to come up with one. If the land itself had been destroyed forever, was this not so that the area would stand as a visible token, a vivid reminder for later generations of what can befall those who defy God's word?

[Sodom and environs] were turned into a smoking waste as a testimony to their wickedness; with plants that bear fruit before they ripen, and a pillar of salt standing there as a memorial of an unbelieving soul. For having passed Wisdom by, they were not only distracted from a knowledge of the good, but also left behind for the world a monument of their folly, so that they were unable to go undetected in their failure.

— Wisd. 10:7–8

And to this day it goes on burning . . . a monument of the disastrous event . . . providing proof of the sentence decreed by the divine judgment.

— Philo, *Abraham* 141

By turning the cities of Sodom and Gomorrah to ashes, He [God] condemned them to extinction and made them an example to those who were to be ungodly.

— 2 Pet. 2:6

Sodom and Gomorrah and the surrounding cities . . . serve as an
example by undergoing a punishment of eternal fire.   —Jude 7

You [O God] burned with fire and brimstone the arrogant Sodomites,
who were unseen in their vices, and You made them an example to
posterity.   —3 Macc. 2:5

In similar fashion, if Lot's wife had been turned into a *pillar of salt,* was it not
so that this pillar might also serve as a visible reminder?

[Lot's wife] was changed to a pillar of salt: I have seen this pillar, which
remains to this day.   —Josephus, *Jewish Antiquities* 203

Of this his wife was destined to be a sign, for after leaving with him she
changed her mind and no longer agreed, and as a result she became a
pillar of salt to this day.   —1 *Clement* 11:1–2

For what is to be learned from the fact that those who were rescued by
the angels were then forbidden to look back—if not that a soul ought
not to return to its old life after it has been freed from it through grace?
. . . Hence, Lot's wife remained [fixed] where she looked back, and she
was turned into salt in order to supply men of faith with a grain of
wisdom, serving as an example of that of which they are to beware.
                                —Augustine, *City of God* 26:30

Lot's Daughters Meant Well

Lot's incestuous union with his daughters seemed to provide obvious grounds
for condemning him:

And [Lot] and his daughters committed sin upon the earth, such as
had not been on the earth since the days of Adam till his time; for the
man lay with his daughters. And behold, it was commanded and
engraved concerning all his seed, on the heavenly tablets, to remove
them and root them out, and to execute judgment upon them like the
judgment of Sodom, and to leave no seed of the man on earth on the
day of condemnation.   —*Jubilees* 16:8–9

It is interesting, however, that some interpreters seized upon a detail in the
biblical text to defend the daughters' actions. For when the daughters resolve
to do this deed, it is because the older says to the younger, "Our father is old,
and there is not a man on earth to come to us after the manner of all the earth"
(Gen. 19:31). Now, in context, this seems to mean merely that Lot's daughters,

dwelling alone in an isolated mountain cave with their father (Gen. 19:30), had no one ("not a man on earth") to turn to for a mate. But perhaps the expression "not a man on earth" meant more:

> These virgins, because of their ignorance of external matters and because they saw those cities burned up together with all their inhabitants, supposed that the whole human race [had been destroyed at the same time], and that no one remained anywhere except the three of them.　　　　　— Philo, *Questions and Answers in Genesis* 4:56

> His maiden daughters, in the belief that the whole of humanity had perished, had intercourse with their father, taking care to elude detection; they acted thus to prevent the extinction of the race.
> 　　　　　　　　　　　　　　　　　　— Josephus, *Jewish Antiquities* 1:205

> In keeping with their simplicity and innocence, these daughters imagined that all humanity had perished, just as the Sodomites had, and that the anger of God had descended upon the whole earth.
> 　　　　　　　　　　　　　　　　— Irenaeus, *Against the Heresies* 4.31.2

> They saw the fire, they saw the burning sulphur, they saw the destruction of everything, and . . . they saw as well that their own mother had not been saved. Thus they imagined that there was taking place something similar to what had happened in the time of Noah, and that they had been left with their father alone to insure the continuity of the human race.　　— Origen, *Homilies on Genesis* 5:4 (also *Contra Celsum* 4.45)

> They believed that the entire world had been destroyed, as in the generation of the flood.　　　　　　　　　　— *Genesis Rabba* 51:8

> Since they [Lot's daughters] thought that a sea of fire had destroyed the whole world, just as water had in the time of Noah, the older said to the younger, "Our father is old, and there is not a man on earth to come in to us after the manner of all the earth. Come let us make our father drink wine" [Gen. 19:31–32].
> 　　　　　　　　　　　　　— Ephraem, *Commentary on Genesis* 19:31

> However, the justification that is offered for the daughters, namely, that they thought that the entire human race had been killed and for that reason lay with their father, still does not exculpate the father.
> 　　　　　　　　　　　　　　　— Jerome, *Questions in Genesis* 19:30

❖   ❖   ❖

In short: Many interpreters held Lot to have been a righteous and good man, whose generosity—in stark contrast to the stinginess of the Sodomites—was at least one reason for his having been rescued from the doomed city. If so, this virtue had no doubt been taught to Lot by his uncle Abraham, whose hospitality to strangers was unparalleled. Despite Lot's apparent virtues, other interpreters believed him to have been wicked and saw his settling in sinful Sodom as hardly accidental. Whether Sodom's sin was stinginess or sexual license, such interpreters judged Lot to have been scarcely better than his neighbors. As for Lot's wife, she was turned into a pillar of salt as a lesson to humanity. His daughters, however, could hardly be blamed for their sin: they believed that all of humanity had perished in the destruction of Sodom, and so were merely seeking to perpetuate the human race.

II
Jacob and Esau

(GENESIS 25–28)

The ladder was a message.

Jacob and Esau

(GENESIS 25–28)

❖　　❖　　❖

Abraham's son Isaac eventually married; his wife was named Rebekah. After some time Rebekah became pregnant with twins, but "the children struggled together in her innards." Seeking divine counsel, she learned that the two infants in her womb were to found two great and rival nations. At the time of their birth, Esau emerged first from the womb, then Jacob, his "younger" (if only by a few minutes) brother. Esau was to become the ancestor of the Edomites, and Jacob the ancestor of the people of Israel.

As they grew, the boys proved to be rather different from each other: Esau was an outdoorsman and a hunter, while Jacob stayed at home. Esau was his father's favorite, Jacob his mother's. Jacob was also apparently the cleverer of the two, for as a youth, he twice got the better of his brother. Once, when Esau was very hungry, Jacob got him to sell his precious birthright for a mere bowl of lentil stew. On another occasion (with the help of his mother), Jacob fooled their father into granting to him the blessing that Isaac had intended to give to Esau. Esau's anger over both incidents was such that Jacob had to flee to Aram, to the house of his uncle Laban. On the way he had a remarkable dream, in which he beheld a great ladder rising into the heavens.

JACOB is the immediate ancestor of the people of Israel. He is, in this sense, the embodiment of the people as a whole, the national hero. Yet in reading this first part of his story, early interpreters could not but be a little disturbed by Jacob's behavior, particularly with regard to his brother, Esau. Esau seems to be a bit of a fall guy in the Bible, and no match for his clever younger brother. Getting Esau to sell his birthright, worth a considerable amount of money,[1] for a bowl of lentils certainly seemed to make Jacob out to be something of sharpster, and the way in which he later tricked their father into blessing him instead of Esau could only confirm that impression.

Needless to say, such behavior scarcely seemed appropriate for the founder of God's people, Israel. Nor, for that matter, did it square with the Jacob we see elsewhere, a man devoted to God and heedless of material possessions, who spontaneously promises to tithe all his wealth to God (Gen. 28:22) and

---

1. According to the law stated in Deut. 21:7, the firstborn brother is to receive a double share of his father's estate; this is his "birthright."

even in time of great distress can only say to Him, "I am not worthy of all You have granted me" (Gen. 32:10). Given this "other" Jacob, interpreters naturally tried to find evidence of Jacob's goodness wherever they could, and to prove that whatever the evil that happened to Esau, it was entirely justified.

Such evidence was not too hard to come by. Early on in their story, the Bible itself contrasts the two brothers in these terms:

> And the two boys grew up. Esau became a man knowledgeable about hunting, a man of the field, but Jacob **was a simple man, dwelling in tents**. Isaac loved Esau, because he ate of the hunt; but Rebekah loved Jacob.
> — Gen. 25:27–28

This contrast—Esau the outdoorsman versus Jacob the homebody—is introduced here, it seems, to provide background for the later story of Isaac's blessing, in which Jacob is able to fool his father precisely because he is at home while Esau is off hunting. But ancient interpreters did not consider these words mere background. Instead, they saw a fundamental statement about the differences in the two brothers' characters.

Jacob Was Not Just "Simple"

Jacob was "a simple man, dwelling in tents"—this in itself seemed to counter the notion that Jacob was a clever trickster. But "simple" in Hebrew (*tām*) can also mean "pure," "innocent," or even "perfect"—and these traits, more than mere "simplicity," would help defend Jacob against the charge of having unfairly taken advantage of his brother. How could someone whom the Bible itself defines as innocent or perfect be anything but utterly virtuous?

> [Rebekah recalls to Isaac when they are both old:] You blessed your **perfect** and true son Jacob because he has **virtue only and no evil**. From the time he has come back from Haran until today he has not denied us anything but always brings us everything in its season. He is sincerely happy when we accept [anything] from him, and he blesses us . . ." Isaac said to her: "I know [this] as well, and I see the actions of Jacob who is with us, that he honors us with his whole heart."
> — *Jubilees* 35:12–13

> And the two boys grew up, and Esau became a man knowledgeable in hunting, a man [who was] lord of the fields, and Jacob was a man **perfect** in good work, dwelling in schoolhouses.
> — *Targum Neophyti* Gen. 25:27

Lest Jacob's stratagem [in getting the blessing that was intended for Esau] be thought of as fraudulent trickery—and lest [therefore] this [incident's] highly significant hidden meaning not be pursued—earlier Scripture had stated that "Esau was a man knowing how to hunt, a man of the fields, but Jacob was a simple man, staying at home." Some have interpreted this [word "simple"] as "without guile." But whether it means "without guile," or "simple," or rather "without pretense," what kind of guile could in any case be involved in the obtaining of a blessing by someone who is "without guile"?

—Augustine, *City of God* 16.37

Jacob the Scholar

And, come to think of it, what did the Bible mean by describing Jacob as "dwelling in tents"? Interpreters were struck by the plural *tents* here—does a person need more than one tent to dwell in? If the word appears in the plural, it must have been intended as a subtle hint that, in addition to staying in his own tent, Jacob also regularly spent time, "dwelt," in another tent. And what sort of tent might that be, if not that of a schoolteacher who could instruct the boy in reading and writing? Perhaps, indeed, the other tent was a full-blown schoolhouse of Jewish learning. (Such apparent anachronisms were, curiously, not a problem for ancient interpreters.)

And . . . Rebekah bore to Isaac two sons, Jacob and Esau, and Jacob was a smooth and upright man, and Esau was fierce, a man of the field, and hairy;[2] and Jacob dwelt in tents. And the youths grew, and Jacob **learned to write**; but Esau did not learn, for he was a man of the field, and a hunter, and he learned war, and all his deeds were fierce. And Abraham loved Jacob,[3] but Isaac loved Esau.   —*Jubilees* 19:13–15

2. The detail of Esau being "hairy" comes from Gen. 25:24, when Esau is said to come out of the womb "all his body like a hairy mantle"; the word "hairy" (*sa'ir*) is meant to suggest Mt. Se'ir, his future homeland. But to interpreters the idea of a "hairy" Esau went well with their picture of Esau the crude, animal-like hunter. Thus Philo: "The ruddy body and hairy hide are a sign of a savage man who rages furiously in the manner of a wild beast" (*Questions and Answers on Genesis* 4:160).

3. Note that the biblical text had said that Isaac loved Esau, but *Rebekah* loved Jacob (Gen. 25:28). Apparently the author of *Jubilees* was bothered by the idea of Jacob being a "momma's boy" and so substituted Abraham for Rebekah, also putting this new clause *ahead of* the one about Isaac loving Esau. In this way not only does Abraham become Jacob's patron (and Abraham doubtless was, in the eyes of most interpreters, even more worthy than Isaac), but it also appears that Isaac's love for Esau was sort of a "consolation prize," since Jacob was already loved by the worthy Abraham.

And the two boys grew up, and Esau was a skilled hunter, a man who went out to the fields, and Jacob was a perfect man who frequented the schoolhouse.
— *Targum Onqelos* Gen. 25:27

And Jacob was a man perfect in good work, dwelling in schoolhouses.
— *Targum Neophyti* Gen. 25:27

. . . the righteous Jacob, who observed the entire Torah, as it is said, "And Jacob was a perfect man, dwelling in tents."[4]
— *Sifrei Deuteronomy* 336

Esau the Wicked

Esau, as noted, is something of a fall guy in Genesis, a big, athletic, not-too-discerning young man. But if Jacob was made out to be altogether virtuous and studious, Esau's image was likewise modified by early interpreters—if anything, in even more radical fashion. He became utterly wicked, a crafty, bloodthirsty embodiment of evil.

Part of the motive for this change is to be found in the later history of Israel, as reflected in the Bible itself. After all, Esau was the ancestor of the Edomites, Israel's close neighbor and sometimes fierce enemy. Later biblical texts frequently heaped scorn on the Edomites,[5] and sometimes this scorn was couched in terms that reflected back on the founder of that nation.

For the violence done to your brother Jacob, shame shall cover you [Esau], and you shall be cut off forever.
— Obad. 1:10

"I have loved you," says the Lord. But you [Israel] say, "How have you loved us?"

"Is not Esau Jacob's brother?" says the Lord. "Yet **I have loved Jacob, but I have hated Esau**; I have laid waste his hill country and left his heritage to jackals of the desert."
— Mal. 1:2–3

In context, both Obadiah and Malachi seem to be talking about the history of the two peoples, Israel and Edom. But reading these verses, interpreters could not help seeing in them as well a characterization of the two original brothers.

4. The fact that Jacob "dwelt in tents," that is, frequented the schoolhouse, was what allowed him to "observe the entire Torah," since the Torah was the normal schoolhouse curriculum.

5. Negative references to the Edomites are not hard to find in the Bible, especially in the later books. Israel's neighboring country is frequently condemned, notably in the brief book of Obadiah, as well as in such passages as Isaiah 34, Jer. 49:7–22, Ezek. 25:12–14, 35:1–15, Psalm 137, and Lam. 4:21–22.

And if God "hated" Esau, the original Esau, then it must have been because he personally was evil:

> There were born two sons, Jacob and Esau. And God loved Jacob, but He hated Esau because of his deeds.
> — Pseudo-Philo, *Biblical Antiquities* 32:5

> And You set apart Jacob for Yourself, but Esau You hated; and Jacob became a great multitude. — *4 Ezra* 3:16

> When Rebekah had conceived children by one man, our forefather Isaac, though they were not yet born and had done nothing either good or bad, in order that God's purpose of election might continue, not because of works but because of his call, she was told, "The elder will serve the younger." As it is written, "Jacob I loved, but Esau I hated." — Rom. 9:10–13

Another indication of Esau's wickedness was the later history of one of his descendants in particular. The Amalekites were one of the tribes that made up the Edomites; their founder, Amalek, was, according to Gen. 36:12, Esau's grandson. The tribe of Amalek had particularly bad associations with later Israelites: the Amalekites attacked Israel at Rephidim (Exod. 17:8–15), and God later commanded the Israelites to "blot out the remembrance of Amalek from under heaven" (Deut. 25:29)—the only nation in the world so condemned. As the ancestor of the Amalekites, then, Esau became, so to speak, retroactively more wicked. Although he himself might seem to be a harmless fall guy in the biblical text, interpreters could not think of Esau without also thinking of the Amalekites and attributing to Esau all the cruelty and baseness of this tribe.

Nor did the chain of descendants stop with Amalek. Centuries later, King Saul of Israel was punished by God for sparing the life of Agag, then king of the Amalekites. But is not mercy one of God's celebrated traits? If, therefore, Saul was *punished* for sparing Agag's life, here was further proof that the Amalekites were in a class by themselves, a people utterly hated by God; and Esau, Agag's remote ancestor, tended once again to be tarred with the same brush. Finally, among Agag's descendants was the evil plotter of the book of Esther, the wicked Haman (Est. 3:1). Haman was the all-time villain of Jewish history, the man who sought "to destroy, to slay, and to annihilate all Jews, young and old, women and children, in one day" (Est. 3:13). If Haman too ultimately descended from Esau, then this certainly clinched the case against Jacob's twin. However benign the person of Esau might appear on the outside, interpreters could have little doubt that he was consummately wicked on the inside.

Good and Evil in Utero

Thus, interpreters sought to read between the lines of the Genesis narrative to find evidence of Esau's fundamentally evil character. One potentially telling detail was the fact that Jacob and Esau were said to struggle in their mother's womb before they were even born. In context, this struggling simply seems to foreshadow the future contentious relations between their descendants, the nations of Israel and Edom. But interpreters saw this struggle in utero as indicating something else, that the two boys were of themselves of fundamentally opposite natures, good and evil:

> Rebekah . . . had conceived the two warring natures of good and evil, and considering the two of them carefully—as wisdom might dictate—she perceived them to be jumping about [inside her], the first skirmishes of the war that was to go on between these contenders.
>
> —Philo, *Cain and Abel* 4

> When she passed by houses of idol-worship, Esau would squirm about, trying to get out, as it says, "The wicked turn astray [*zoru*][6] from the womb" (Ps. 58:4); when she would pass synagogues or study-houses, Jacob would squirm to get out, as it says, "Before I formed you in the womb, I knew you" (Jer. 1:5). — *Genesis Rabba* 63:6

Esau the Warrior

The Bible's description of Esau as a skillful hunter (Gen. 25:27) likewise seemed to offer a clue as to his true nature. Just as the description of Jacob as "simple" and "dwelling in tents" in this verse came to be taken as an indication of Jacob's virtue and scholarliness, so were the words "knowledgeable about hunting, a man of the field" interpreted to Esau's disadvantage. After all, a skillful hunter is (to put it bluntly) someone who is good at killing. Perhaps Esau in fact *enjoyed* killing; if so, then he might not have been particularly bothered even by taking of a human life:

> And the boys grew up, and Esau became a hunter, hunting birds and animals, a man who went out into the fields to kill living things—and

6. This word is apparently being associated specifically with the practice of idolatry, called in Hebrew "foreign [*zarah*] worship." The biblical phrase cited next with regard to Jacob, "Before I formed you in the womb, I knew you" (Jer. 1:5), could likewise be interpreted as: "Before I formed you in the womb, I *caused you to know*." If so, it might imply that God initiates his chosen servants like Jeremiah (and, perhaps as well, Jacob) into the true religion even before they are born.

it was he who killed Nimrod and his son Enoch. But Jacob was a man perfect in his deeds, studying in the academy of Eber, expounding the teachings given by God. — *Targum Pseudo-Jonathan* Gen. 25:27

It was only a small step from the hunter of animals to the killer of men—and, in fact, elsewhere in the Bible another passage made such a step even easier for interpreters. The passage comes later on in the story of the two brothers, when Jacob manages to end up with the blessing intended for Esau. After he learns what has happened, Esau is crushed and asks his father, "Do you not have a single blessing left for me, my father? Bless me as well, father!" (Gen. 27:38). Isaac obliges as best he can:

> From the fatness of the earth shall your dwelling be, and from the dew of heaven on high. And **by your sword shall you live**, and you shall serve your brother; but when you break loose, you shall cast his yoke from your neck. — Gen. 27:39–40

In context, "by your sword you shall live" probably means "You will always have to have your sword at the ready," you will always be defending yourself. These words in any case certainly do not mean "you will be a great warrior," since the next clause goes on to imply that Esau will still be subservient to Jacob. And yet "you will be a great warrior" is precisely how early interpreters came to understand these words. "Esau the Hunter" and "Esau the Warrior" fit well together, and it was not long before these two biblical passages combined to create an Esau who delighted in bloodshed and excelled at warfare.

> And the youths grew, and Jacob learned to write; but Esau did not learn, for he was a man of the field, and a hunter, and he learned war, and all his deeds were fierce. — *Jubilees* 19:14

> What is the meaning of the words, "By your sword you shall live"? Most naturally has [the text] shown that the life of the foolish man [exemplified by Esau] is warfare without peace or friendship . . . For he [rejoices] in strife and avarice, thinking it the part of zeal to do wrong and thereby to overreach [someone else]. — Philo, *Questions in Genesis* 4:235

> God revealed Himself to the descendants of the wicked Esau and said to them, "Will you accept the Torah?" They said to Him: "What is written in it?" He said: "You shall not murder" [Exod. 20:13]. They said to [God]: "But that is the inheritance that our father left to us, 'By your sword shall you live' [Gen. 27:40]." — *Mekhilta deR. Ishmael, Baḥodesh*

Esau Means Rome

From the first century B.C.E. on, the great war-maker in the life of Israel was the Roman empire, which gained political power over the Jewish homeland and later crushed two doughty attempts on the Jews' part to win their independence (68–70 C.E. and 133–135 C.E.). The Romans enforced their rule through military might and the ruthless suppression and punishment of all sources of possible resistance.

It was natural that the Jews, in seeking to understand their present predicament under Roman rule, should look to the Bible for clues—and for hope. To many, the "true" identity of the Romans was not hard to find: their love of war, their swaggering cruelty, and their living "by the sword" all suggested that they were the spiritual descendants of Esau. Indeed, there must have been something comforting in thinking of the Romans as the present-day equivalent of biblical Esau, for just as God had helped Jacob to triumph over his physically larger and stronger brother, so He might help the Jews to throw off the Roman yoke:

> [An angel tells Jacob:] "The Most High will raise up emperors from the descendants of your brother Esau [that is, Rome], and they will receive all the power of the races of the earth who have caused harm to your seed. And they [that is, your "seed"] will be delivered into his [Esau's, that is, Rome's] hands and he will ill-treat them. And he will begin to hold them by force and rule over them, and they will not be able to oppose him, until the day when his decree will go out against them to worship idols and sacrifice to the dead."
>
> — *Ladder of Jacob* 5:8–11

> [Isaac's words in Gen. 27:22] "The voice is the voice of Jacob, but the hands are the hands of Esau" [really refer to the people of Israel and Rome,] for Jacob rules only through his voice, but Esau [Rome] rules only through his hands.   — *Genesis Rabba* 65:19

Perhaps indeed the fact that Jacob seized his brother's heel at the time of their birth indicated that the age of the Romans' ascendancy would be followed by that of the Jews:

> [The angel tells Ezra:] "Jacob's hand held Esau's heel from the beginning, for Esau [that is, the ascendancy of Rome] is the end of this age, and Jacob [the ascendancy of Israel] is the beginning of the age that

follows. For the end of a man is his heel, and the beginning of a man is his hand; between the heel and the hand seek for nothing else, Ezra."

— *4 Ezra* 6:8–10

"And his hand seized Esau's heel" [Gen. 25:26]—there is no kingdom in this world after Esau's kingdom except Israel's alone.

— *Midrash ha-Gadol* Gen. 25:26

Esau the Deceiver

Not only was Esau turned into someone bloodthirsty and cruel, but, in certain sources, he was also viewed as something of a deceiver. This idea came as well to be connected with the description of Esau as a hunter:

Concerning Esau, the hairy one, **wily** in wickedness, [Scripture] says: "Esau was skilled in hunting, a man of the country" [Gen. 25:27]. For wickedness, which goes hunting after the passions, is by nature unable to inhabit the city of virtue. — Philo, *Allegorical Interpretations* 3:2

"Esau became a man knowledgeable about hunting, a man of the field . . ." (Gen. 25:28): Said R. Abbahu [commenting on the apparently unnecessary phrase "man of the field"—for what hunter is not a man of the field?]: he used to hunt both in the field and in the house.

— *Genesis Rabba* 63:10

Esau Didn't Care

In the same attempt to blame Esau wherever possible, ancient readers sought to reinterpret the story of Esau's sale of his birthright. Jacob's success in getting his older brother to sell him this valuable item for a pittance was not understood as implying any ill of Jacob. On the contrary! Jacob was seen as trying to relieve Esau of riches that would otherwise cause him to sin:

The literal meaning [of this story] shows the greed of the younger [brother] in wishing to deprive his elder brother of his rights. But the virtuous man [Jacob] is not greedy . . . [He] understands that a continuous and unlimited abundance of possessions will provide the wicked man [Esau] with the occasion for, and the cause of, sin . . . He considers it most necessary to remove [Esau] from evil . . . for the improvement of character. And this does no harm, but is a great benefit to him. — Philo, *Questions in Genesis* 4:172

In any case, the fact that Esau *agreed* to sell his birthright for almost nothing—and that, afterward, he was said to have "despised" it (Gen. 25:34)—was taken as an indication that this whole episode in the Bible had been intended to illustrate Esau's fundamentally impious nature:

> . . . that no one be immoral and irreligious like Esau, who sold his birthright for a single meal.   —Heb. 12:16

> Scripture thus shows that Jacob did not sell his birthright because of hunger, since it says that after he ate, "Esau got up and left and [still] despised his birthright." He did not sell it because of hunger, therefore, but because he indeed considered it to be worthless and sold it for nothing.   —Ephraem, *Commentary on Genesis* 23:2

Jacob Told the Truth

In short, ancient interpreters exploited every possibility in the Genesis narrative to make Jacob into a model of virtue and Esau into the opposite. But the champions of Jacob still had some explaining to do. For there remained the incident in which Jacob tricked his father into giving him his blessing. How could a moral person do such a thing? It was bad enough that he took advantage of the old man's blindness and misled him by donning hairy animal skins to simulate his brother's hirsute arms. But still worse, Jacob actually lied to his father:

> So he went in to his father and said, "Father?" and he said, "Here I am. Who are you, my son?" And Jacob said to his father, "**I am Esau**, your firstborn . . ." Then Jacob went near to Isaac his father, who felt him and said, "The voice is the voice of Jacob, but the hands are the hands of Esau." And he did not recognize him, because his hands were hairy like his brother Esau's hands, so he blessed him. He said, "Are you really my son Esau?" He answered, "**I am.**"   —Gen. 27:18–24

Americans raised on the story of George Washington and the cherry tree have but to consider passages such as this one to realize what a poor example Jacob might seem to offer growing young minds. No wonder, then, that in retelling these events, ancient interpreters sought to create a somewhat different emphasis in Jacob's words:

> He [Jacob] went in to his father and said, "**I am your son.** I have done as you told me; come and sit down and eat of what I have caught, father, so that you may bless me." . . . And Jacob went close to his

father Isaac, and he [Isaac] felt him and said, "The voice is Jacob's but the hands are the hands of Esau," and he did not recognize him, because there was an ordering from heaven to turn his mind astray . . . And he said, "Are you my son Esau?" and he said, "**I am your son.**"

— *Jubilees* 26:13–19

Here, Jacob tells no lie: he twice asserts what is only the truth, that he is indeed Isaac's son. But how could such a distortion square with what the Bible itself says?

It should be remembered that the biblical text was originally transmitted without punctuation or capital letters, so that where a sentence begins or ends was often a matter of opinion. Exploiting this situation (along with the frequent omission of the verb "to be" in biblical Hebrew), an interpreter might maintain that the opening exchange between Jacob and his father—namely, "Who are you, my son?" "I am Esau, your firstborn"—could just as easily be read as follows: "Who are you? My son?" "I am. [But] Esau is your firstborn." It seems that the author of *Jubilees* had something like this in mind. This same approach is likewise witnessed later on:

"And Jacob said, 'I am Esau your firstborn' [Gen. 27:19]": He stopped in the middle; he said, "I am," but "Esau is your firstborn."

— *Midrash Leqaḥ Tob* 27:19

"I am . . ." Jacob saw in a prophetic vision that his descendants were to stand at Mount Sinai and receive the Ten Commandments, which begin with the words "I am" (Exod. 20:2). [Having mentioned this] he added: "But Esau is your firstborn." — *Midrash Aggadah* 27:19

God Wanted Jacob to Be Blessed

Whatever Jacob might or might not have said (or where in his sentence he might have paused), interpreters were in any case struck by one obvious fact: Jacob does actually succeed in having his father really believe that he is Esau. But how could such a thing have happened? Could a father, even a blind and aged father, manage to confuse two such different sons? And would he likely be taken in by such a shabby trick as the substitution of an animal hide for a hairy human forearm? No one, no matter how old or blind, could fall for such a ruse! Unless . . . unless, reasoned interpreters, it had been God's plan all along that Jacob be blessed by Isaac—in which case, it was God who had guided Jacob's and Isaac's actions. (This hypothesis seemed only to be confirmed by subsequent events, since Isaac did not subsequently withdraw his blessing, and the sacred line did end up being passed down through Jacob, not Esau.)

> And to Isaac as well did God give a son [that is, Jacob], for the sake of Abraham his father.
> He gave him [Jacob] the covenant of the former ones [Abraham and Isaac], and **a blessing rested on the head of Israel;**
> and **He confirmed him in the blessing**, and He gave him his inheritance.[7]
>
> —Sir. 44:22–23

Indeed, to make the deception work, God might have temporarily weakened Isaac's powers of perception and so prevented him from seeing through the sham.

> And he [Isaac] did not recognize him, because there was an ordering from heaven to turn his mind astray. —Jubilees 26:17–18

> Because of a [divine] dispensation the prophet [Isaac] failed in sight, and afterward was again established and became keen of sight. But the dispensation was a blessing, that not a wicked man but one deserving of blessings might obtain it. —Philo, *Questions in Genesis* 4:196

> And it came to pass that when Isaac was old and his eyes were too weak to see, and the holy spirit departed from him[8] so that Jacob would receive the blessings . . . —*Fragment Targum* Gen. 27:1

> Isaac could not change his blessings . . . because he knew that the word of God had been fulfilled, just as it had been told to Rebekah [in Gen. 25:23]. —Ephraem, *Commentary on Genesis* 25:2

If indeed it had been God's will all along to have Jacob gain his father's blessing, then Jacob's conduct in the whole affair was far more justifiable: he was simply doing what was necessary to carry out the divine plan.

---

7. One Hebrew manuscript reads "confirmed him in the birthright," suggesting that Jacob's acquired status as firstborn, purchased from Esau for some porridge, was confirmed by subsequent events. See Exod. 4:22.

8. The point is apparently that the words "to see" in the Bible's "and his eyes were too weak to see" are not necessary: weak eyes are, by definition, eyes that do not see well. For that reason, "see" is taken in the sense of (divinely granted) understanding, supporting the idea that it was not only Isaac's vision that God took away, but also (at least temporarily) his powers of discernment.

The Ladder Was a Message

Having gotten a blessing that his father had intended for Esau, Jacob was now in some danger, for he had aroused Esau's hatred (Gen. 27:41). Rebekah resolved to send Jacob to stay for a while with her brother Laban in Haran, to give Esau time to cool off. Jacob set out on his journey, but at nightfall he stopped to rest:

> And he came to the place and decided to spend the night there, for the sun was setting. And he took from among the stones in that spot in order to put under his head, and he lay down in that place. And he dreamt that there was a ladder set upon the earth whose top reached to heaven, and the angels of God were going up and down upon it.
>
> And the Lord stood above it and said, "I am the Lord, the God of your father Abraham and the God of Isaac. The land upon which you are lying I will give to you and your descendants. And your descendants shall be like the dust of the earth, and you shall extend outward to the west and to the east, to the north and to the south, and all the families of the land shall be blessed through you and through your descendants. For I shall indeed be with you and I shall watch over you wherever you go, and I shall return you to this land; I will not leave you until I have done what I have told you."
>
> And Jacob awoke from his sleep and said, "The Lord is indeed present in this place, and I did not know it." And he was afraid, and he said, "How fearful is this place. Surely this is the house of God and the very gate of heaven." —Gen. 28:11–17

This vision of Jacob's was particularly puzzling to early interpreters. To begin with, why a *dream* at all—why did not God simply speak to Jacob, as He had to Abraham? Moreover, what was this dream intended to communicate? If the point had been merely to tell Jacob that "the land upon which you are lying I will give to you and your descendants," there certainly would have been no need for a ladder with angels going up and down. What is more, something about this dream obviously frightened Jacob, since the text says, "And he was *afraid,* and he said, 'How *fearful* is this place.'" But what could be so frightening about a ladder with angels on it?

Pondering these questions, interpreters came to the conclusion that the ladder itself was some sort of symbolic message about the future, Jacob's own or that of his descendants:

> Perhaps as well [Jacob] caught a glimpse of his own [future] life in this visionary ladder . . . The affairs of men are by their very nature com-

parable to a ladder because of their irregular course. For a single day (as someone well put it) can carry the person set on high downward and lift someone else upward, for it is the nature of none of us to remain in the same circumstances, but rather to undergo all manner of changes . . . So the path of human affairs goes up and down, subjected to unstable and shifting happenstance.

—Philo, *On Dreams* 1:150, 153–156

Jacob then went to Laban his uncle. He found a place and, laying his head on a stone, he slept there, for the sun had gone down. He had a dream. And behold, a ladder was fixed on the earth, whose top reached to heaven. And the top of the ladder was the face of a man, carved out of fire. There were twelve steps leading to the top of the ladder, and on each step to the top there were human faces, on the right and on the left, twenty-four faces including their chests. And the face in the middle was higher than all that I saw, the one of fire, including the shoulders and arms, exceedingly terrifying, more than those twenty-four faces.

[Later, an angel explains the dream to Jacob:] "You have seen a ladder with twelve steps, each step having two human faces which kept changing their appearance. The ladder is this age, and twelve steps are the periods of this age, and the twenty-four faces are the kings of the lawless nations of this age. Under these kings the children of your children and the generations of your sons will be tested; they [the kings] will rise up because of the wickedness of your offspring. And they [the foreign kings] will make this place empty by four ascents because of the sins of your offspring. And upon the property of your forefathers a palace will be built, a temple in the name of your God and your fathers' [God], but in anger against your children it will be made deserted, until the fourth descent of this age."

—*Ladder of Jacob* 1:1–6, 5:1–9

"And he dreamt that a ladder was set on the ground and its top reached to the heavens and the angels of God were going up and down on it . . ." (Gen. 28:12): Said R. Samuel b. Naḥman: Is it possible that these were the ministering angels [whose job it is to serve before God in Heaven]? Were they not instead the guardian angels of the nations of the world [that would rule Israel in the future]?[9] He [God] showed

---

9. This notion of angelic guardians of different kingdoms is reflected in the book of Daniel (Dan. 10:13, 20, etc.).

him [Jacob] Babylon's angel climbing up seventy rungs and going down again. Then he showed him Media's angel going up and down fifty-two, and then Greece's going up and down one hundred and eighty. Then Rome's went up and up, and he [Jacob] did not know how many [rungs it would ascend]. Jacob took fright at this and said: Oh Lord, do you mean that this one has no descent? God said to him: Even if you see him reach the very heavens, I will still cause him to go down, as it is written, "Though you soar aloft like the eagle, though your nest is set among the stars, from there I will bring you down, says the Lord" [Obad. 1:4].
— *Leviticus Rabba* 29:2

Angels Wanted to See Him

But there was another explanation of the same passage. Some interpreters theorized that, whatever it was that Jacob had dreamed, the contents of his dream were not what was being set forth in the Bible. On the contrary, the sudden appearance of the ladder with the angels *actually took place* while Jacob slept on the ground below. But why should a ladder and a group of angels suddenly materialize? The Bible had said that the angels were "going up and down *upon it* [the ladder]," but these same words in Hebrew could be translated as "going up and down *upon him*," that is, upon Jacob, for Jacob's sake. Some early interpreters therefore understood that, while Jacob slept, a band of angels had descended to earth on a great ladder in order to catch a glimpse of this extraordinary individual and then ascended back to heaven:

And he [Jacob] dreamt . . . and the angels who had accompanied him from his father's house went up to announce to the angels on high: "Come and see the righteous man [Jacob] whose likeness is set upon the divine throne, the one whom you have wanted to see." Then the holy angels of God "went up and down to gaze **upon him**."
— *Targum Neophyti, Fragment Targum* (ms. P), Gen. 28:12

Jesus answered him, "Because I said to you, I saw you under the fig tree, do you believe? You shall see greater things than these." And he said to him, "Truly, truly, I say to you, you will see heaven opened, and the angels of God ascending and descending **upon** the Son of man."
— John 1:50–51

❖   ❖   ❖

In short: Jacob and Esau were not what they might at first seem. Esau was actually a wicked deceiver and the cruel ancestor of many of Israel's enemies, from Amalek to the Roman empire. Jacob, by contrast, was a thoroughly righteous and studious young man. Although Isaac had intended to give his blessing to Esau, it was God who caused him to bless Jacob instead, and, despite appearances, Jacob never actually lied to his father. Indeed, so great was Jacob's piety that, when he spent the night at Bethel, the angels of heaven flocked down to earth via the ladder in order to see the countenance of this great man.

12
Jacob and the Angel

(GENESIS 29–32)

Leah brought to Jacob's bed: perhaps a bit too much to drink?

Jacob and the Angel

(GENESIS 29–32)

❖   ❖   ❖

Jacob continued his journey until he reached the house of his uncle Laban, where he was warmly welcomed. Laban had two daughters, Leah and Rachel, and it was not long before Jacob had fallen in love with Rachel, the younger. Laban agreed to give Rachel to Jacob as a wife in exchange for seven years' labor. However, on the night of the wedding, Laban tricked Jacob by substituting Leah. After Jacob discovered the fraud, Laban said that in his country it is considered improper to marry off a younger daughter before the firstborn. He agreed to give Rachel to Jacob as a second wife—in exchange for another seven years' service.

Jacob ultimately had twelve sons by his two wives, Leah and Rachel, and their maidservants, Bilhah and Zilpah. These twelve sons were the ancestors of the twelve tribes of Israel. He also had a daughter, Dinah. Jacob prospered in Laban's house, in part because of a stratagem that allowed him to gain a good part of Laban's flocks in keeping with the terms of an agreement that the two had negotiated. Jacob was now a rich man. But he also sensed the growing resentment of Laban and his family. At length, God commanded Jacob to leave with his wives and children and livestock and head back to his homeland.

Years had passed since his feud with his brother, Esau, and Jacob hoped that the matter had been forgotten. However, as he neared the land where Esau had settled, Jacob received word that his brother was approaching with a small army. Frightened, he sent Esau a lavish gift of livestock in the hope of appeasing him. That night, having sent his family to the other side of the Jabbok ford, Jacob was left alone, and "a man wrestled with him until daybreak." The "man," apparently an angel, blessed Jacob and changed his name to Israel.

T HE REPUTATION of Jacob's uncle Laban among ancient interpreters was quite in keeping with the biblical text. He was held to be a cheat and a scoundrel, the man who switched brides on Jacob's wedding night, then robbed Jacob of his rightful wages (Gen. 31:7, 41–42). Even after Jacob had worked for him for twenty years, Laban nevertheless exclaimed, "The daughters are my daughters, the children are my children, the flocks are my flocks, and all that you see is mine" (Gen. 31:43). He was a selfish, sly, and wicked man.

Jacob Knew Right Away

Of all Laban's machinations, however, the one that bothered interpreters the most was the very first, the switched brides. How could he have succeeded in fooling Jacob on his wedding night? After all, Jacob had waited seven years for Rachel to be his wife—surely he must have known that the woman in his chamber that night was not Rachel, but Leah. What is worse, the Bible seemed to say that Jacob did not discover the fraud until the next morning:

> But in the evening he [Laban] took his daughter Leah and brought her to Jacob; and he went in to her . . . And **in the morning**, behold it was Leah; and Jacob said to Laban, "What is this you have done to me?"
>
> —Gen. 29:23–25

One possible explanation was that Jacob indeed discovered the fraud almost at once but, under the circumstances, waited until later to complain to Laban:

> Laban prepared a banquet, took his older daughter Leah, and gave [her] to Jacob as a wife. But Jacob was not aware [of this], because Jacob thought she was Rachel. He went in to her, and, to his surprise, she was Leah. Jacob was angry at Laban and said to him, "Why have you acted this way?"
>
> —Jubilees 28:3–4

Similarly, if Jacob discovered the deception right away, the fact that he said nothing until the next morning might indicate that he was not entirely opposed to the substitution:

> [Laban] agreed to and promised the marriage of his youngest daughter to him. However, he did not at all aim that this should be, but, rather, contrived some trick. He sent Leah, who was her older sister, to the man for his bed. In any case, it **did not remain hidden** from him; rather he understood the mischievousness and received the other maiden. He was mated with both, who were his kinfolk.
>
> —Theodotus (cited in Eusebius, *Preparatio Evangelica* 9.22.3)

> He had indeed come [to Laban's house] in order to marry only one woman; but when another was put in her place, he did not send away the one that he had unintentionally had intercourse with that night, lest he seem to hold her in derision—and [in any case,] when, for reasons of propagating offspring, there was no law prohibiting the taking of several wives, he took as well the one [Rachel] to whom he had originally pledged to be married.   —Augustine, *City of God* 16.36

Deluded in the Dark

Other interpreters, however, believed that Jacob was indeed fooled until the next morning. Perhaps he was deceived by the darkness, as well as by a bit of overindulgence in the wedding festivities:

> Laban accepted this proposal and, when the time expired, prepared to celebrate the wedding festivities. When it was night, however, he [Laban] sent into Jacob's bedroom (who was quite unaware) the other daughter, who was older than Rachel and unattractive in appearance. Jacob [had been deluded] by wine and the dark.
>
> — Josephus, *Jewish Antiquities* 1:300–301

> In the evening they [the revelers] came to escort them [the wedding couple] in and they put out the candles. He [Jacob] said to them: "What's this?" They said to him, "Do you think that we are immodest, as you people are?"
> — *Midrash ha-Gadol* 29:23

Additional Trickery Required

However, granting that Jacob had been deluded by the darkness did not account for the actions of the two sisters, Rachel and Leah. Why did not Rachel, Jacob's beloved, object to the substitution? To pull off the switch, some additional trickery must have been required:

> Rachel said [to Leah, long after the incident:] "I was prepared for marriage to him [Jacob] first, and it was for my sake that he served our father for fourteen years . . . You are not his [true] wife, it was only by trickery that you were taken to him in my place. My father tricked me and replaced me that night, not permitting Jacob to see me. If I had been there this would not have happened."
> — *Testament of Issachar* 1:10–13

What is more, Leah herself must have actively helped Jacob to be fooled:

> All that night he kept calling her "Rachel" and she kept answering him "Yes?" "But the next morning, behold, it was Leah" [Gen. 29:25]. He said to her, "Liar and daughter-of-a-liar!" She answered: "Can there be a schoolmaster without any pupils? Was it not just this way that your father called out to you 'Esau' and you answered him [see Gen. 27:24]? So when you called me I likewise answered you."
> — *Genesis Rabba* 70:19

In other words, given Jacob's earlier deception of his own father in a similar fashion, he really did not have much right to reproach Leah now.

Weak, Bleary Eyes

Whether or not Jacob was actually deluded, interpreters were equally curious about why Laban had gone to the trouble of switching his two daughters in the first place. Most did not take Laban's own explanation (that the younger daughter was not be married off before the older) as truthful. Instead, they reasoned, Laban had been motivated by a crucial difference in his two daughters' appearances. For when they are first described, they are presented in these terms:

> Now Laban had two daughters: the name of the older was Leah, and the name of the younger was Rachel. Now Leah's **eyes were soft**, but Rachel was comely of form and of appearance. And Jacob loved Rachel.
>
> —Gen. 29:16–18

The significance of the word "soft" seemed to hold the key to understanding this whole incident. For if Leah's eyes were soft and (as the text goes on to add) Jacob preferred Rachel, then perhaps having "soft eyes" was some sort of defect, one that would make Laban have to resort to trickery in order to find Leah a husband. Thus, some interpreters concluded that she indeed had something wrong with her eyes:

> And Leah's eyes were weak.
>
> —Septuagint Gen. 29:17

> For Jacob loved Rachel more than Leah; for Leah's eyes were weak, though her figure was very lovely; but Rachel's eyes were beautiful, her figure was lovely, and she was very pretty.
>
> —Jubilees 28:5

> [At first, it had been decided that] Leah was in fact to be married to Esau, and Rachel to Jacob. But Leah used to stand at the crossroads and ask what Esau was like, and they would say to her: He is an evil man, a murderer, one who robs travelers, and "red and like a hairy mantle all over" [Gen. 25:25], a wicked man who has done all things abominable to God. When she heard these things she wept and said: My sister Rachel and I have come from the same womb, yet Rachel is to be married to the righteous Jacob, while I am to be married to the wicked Esau! And so she wept and afflicted herself until her eyes became soft.
>
> —Midrash Tanḥuma, Vayyeṣe 4

And Leah was bleary-eyed with weeping, for she had prayed God not
to be given to the evil Esau [as a bride]; but Rachel was pleasant in
form and beautiful in appearance.

— *Targum Pseudo-Jonathan* Gen. 29:17

[Leah] had overheard people talking at the crossroads. They had said:
Rebekah has two sons and Leah has two daughters; the older is to go
to the older, and the younger to the younger. Then she stayed at the
crossroads and kept asking: What is the older one like? [They answered:] He is a wicked man, one who robs people. And what is the
younger like? "A simple man, dwelling in tents" [Gen. 25:27]. And so
she wept until her eyelashes fell out.　　　— b. *Baba Batra* 123a

Her [Leah's] eyes were hateful, but [Rachel] was altogether radiant.

— *Cave of Treasures* (W) 31:27

"Nice Eyes, But . . ."

Another approach was possible, however. A number of interpreters saw the
reference to Leah's soft eyes as, in fact, a compliment. In context, however, this
would seem to imply that, *apart from* her soft eyes, Leah was not nearly as
attractive as her sister:

And Leah's eyes were pleasant, but Rachel was beautiful in form and
pleasant in appearance.　　　　— *Targum Onqelos* Gen. 29:17

When it was night, however, he [Laban] sent into Jacob's bedroom
(who was quite unaware) the other daughter, who was older than
Rachel and unattractive in appearance.

— Josephus, *Jewish Antiquities* 1:301

Laban carried out this trickery [in part] because of Leah's unattrac-
tiveness, for during the seven years of Rachel's betrothal, no one had
come to marry her [Leah].　　— Ephraem, *Commentary on Genesis* 27:2

The one woman attracted her husband's favor by her beauty, while the
other seemed to be rejected because of lacking it.

— John Chrysostom, *Homilies* 56

Somewhat similarly:

And Leah's eyes were **lifted upward** in prayer as she asked to be given
to the righteous Jacob as a wife, but Rachel was pleasing in her traits
and beautiful in her appearance.　　— *Targum Neophyti* Gen. 29:17

God Multiplied Jacob's Flocks

Those who are taken advantage of sometimes come out the winner nonetheless. Because of Laban's trickery, Jacob was eventually blessed with a very large family: he ended up with two wives and the two handmaidens they brought with them, and together they bore him twelve sons, the ancestors of the twelve tribes of Israel. Inadvertently, then, Laban had helped to carry out God's plans for Jacob. Ancient interpreters, in stressing Laban's duplicity in the whole affair, sought not only to show that the designs of the wicked come to nought, but also to bring out Jacob's good qualities by contrast. Throughout, they felt, Jacob had tried to deal fairly and honestly even with this slippery relative.

Indeed, if Jacob later ended up with the better part of Laban's flocks, it was not—as the biblical account itself suggests—because of Jacob's clever manipulation of certain streaked wooden rods (Gen. 31:37–43). These rods were either quite irrelevant or else an instrument of divine intervention: in either case, Jacob got the greater share because God, or an angel, had so arranged it:

> They agreed among themselves that he [Laban] would give him his wages; all the lambs and kids which were born a dark gray color or dark mixed with white were to be his [Jacob's] wages. [But] all the dark-colored sheep kept giving birth to [offspring] with variously colored spots of every kind and various shades of dark gray. The[se] sheep would in turn give birth to [lambs] which looked like them. All those with spots belonged to Jacob and those without spots to Laban, [so] Jacob's possessions grew very large.[1] —*Jubilees* 28:27–29

> R. Ḥunia [of Hauran] said: the ministering angels would take [animals] from Laban's flocks and put them into Jacob's flocks.
>
> —*Genesis Rabba* 73:10

> The good man [Jacob] did this not of his own devising, but because divine grace inspired his mind [to do so]. For, you see, it was not done on the basis of any human reasoning, since it was quite extraordinary and beyond the grasp of logic. —John Chrysostom, *Homilies* 57

> You might ask how it was that Jacob could do this, setting the peeled rods at the troughs so that they [the flocks] would breed in front of the rods, since this would appear to be stealing. The answer is that this was

1. Note that there is no mention here of the stripped rods; the pattern of births alone gave Jacob so many flocks.

not, Heaven forbid, anything like stealing, for the angel had already spoken to him [as Jacob later says, Gen. 31:11–12]. What Jacob did he did on the angel's instructions. — *Midrash Leqaḥ Tob* Gen. 30:39

Rachel Was Not a Crook

But what of Jacob's wife Rachel? There was one strange action of Rachel's that threatened the good reputation of this ancestress of Israel and made her look, alas, like a true daughter of Laban. For once Jacob and his wives had resolved to leave Laban's house and to return to Canaan,

> Jacob arose, and set his sons and his wives on camels; and he drove all his cattle, all the possessions which he had acquired, the cattle which he had acquired in Paddan-aram, to go to the land of Canaan to his father Isaac. While Laban had gone to shear his flocks, **Rachel stole her father's household gods** . . . [After Laban caught up with them:] Now Rachel had taken the household gods and put them in the camel's saddle, and sat upon them. Laban felt all about the tent, but did not find them. And she said to her father, "Let not my lord be angry that I cannot rise before you, for the way of women is upon me." So he searched, but did not find the household gods.   — Gen. 31:17–19, 34–35

The Bible's frank statement, "Rachel stole her father's household gods," certainly must have bothered a number of early interpreters. It was, of course, possible to soften the language a bit:

> And Laban went out to shear his flocks and Rachel **took** her father's idols.   — *Targum Onqelos* Gen. 31:19 (also 31:32)

Still, softening the language did not make Rachel's action much more palatable. Why did she take what did not belong to her? And why, later on, did she lie to her father to prevent him from discovering the gods in her saddlebags?

Most interpreters tried to find some good motive for her action—or at least to deny what one might otherwise think from reading the Bible alone, that Rachel actually thought that these household gods were worth owning, perhaps even worth worshipping:

> Rachel, having taken along the images of the gods which it was the custom of her fathers to worship, fled along with her sister and their children and the handmaidens and their sons and their possessions . . . Rachel did indeed bring the images of the gods; she had been taught by Jacob to disdain such idol worship, but, [she thought,] if they [that

is, she and the rest of Jacob's family] were chased down and overtaken by her father, they might have recourse to them [the idols] in order to obtain a pardon. —Josephus, *Jewish Antiquities* 1:310–311

"And Rachel stole the household gods . . ." (Gen. 31:19). Her purpose in this was on God's behalf; for she said: "Now we are going our way. Can we leave this old man in the midst of his idolatry?" That is why Scripture found it necessary to say, "And Rachel stole . . ."[2]

— *Genesis Rabba* 74:5

Happy was Rachel, who concealed the false idols of the Gentiles and declared that their images were full of uncleanness. And let no one believe that she had betrayed the respect and devotion due her father because she sat while he stood . . . When the cause of religion was at stake, faith had a just claim upon the judgment seat, while unbelief, like a defendant, deserved to stand.

— Ambrose, *Jacob and the Happy Life* 5.25

Since she wished to free even her father of idolatry, she took them [the household gods] away.   — Theodoret, *Questions in Genesis*, Gen. 31:19

Why did she steal them? So that they would not tell Laban that Jacob was leaving along with his wives and children and flocks. But can household gods really speak? Yes, as it is written, "The household gods speak falsehood" [Zech. 10:2].   — *Midrash Tanḥuma, Wayyeṣe'* 12

When [Laban] saw all that Jacob had, he said: "All these things belong to me. Since you have taken all of them, why have you also stolen my gods, the household gods before which I used to bow down?" [compare Gen. 31:30]. It was indeed for that reason that Rachel had stolen them, lest they [the gods] tell Laban that Jacob had fled, as well as in order to remove them from her father's house.   — *Pirqei deR. Eliezer* 36

Jacob Struggled with an Angel

Jacob thus fled his father-in-law's house and headed back to his own land, Canaan. At the Jabbok ford, having sent his wife and children to the other side, he encountered a mysterious "man" with whom he struggled all night and who eventually gave Jacob his other name, Israel. Now this seems to be a,

2. The point is that, had this really been a reprehensible act, Scripture would simply not have mentioned it, since it has no particular importance in the story. If it is nevertheless mentioned, it must be because the action somehow reflected well on Rachel or contained some moral lesson.

perhaps *the*, crucial incident in Jacob's life, and interpreters were anxious to understand it fully. Who was this "man," and what did the struggle with him mean?

To most interpreters, it seemed obvious that the man in question was actually an angel. To begin with, that is what the prophet Hosea had said in a passage alluding to the same incident:

> In the womb he [Jacob] seized his brother by the heel, and in his manhood he struggled with God. He struggled with an **angel** and overcame; he wept and he pleaded with him.
>
> —Hos. 12:4–5 (some texts, 3–4)

While this passage itself is not entirely clear (who does the word "he" refer to in "he wept and he pleaded with him"?), it seems indisputable that the words "He struggled with an angel and overcame" refer to the mysterious episode. Thus, the "man" was in fact an angel. And, on reflection, such a conclusion could only have seemed obvious to interpreters. After all, there are a number of other beings first described as men in the Bible who turn out to be angels.[3] What is more, Jacob's opponent ended up blessing him and giving him a new name—just as God had earlier blessed and given a new name to both Abram/Abraham and Sarai/Sarah (Gen. 17:5–6, 15–16). This was another good reason to suppose that Jacob's opponent was a messenger sent by God, that is, an angel. Finally, the whole mysterious nature of the combat—the fact that it takes place late at night and with a strange, unidentified adversary who apparently must depart before sunrise—further suggested some kind of supernatural confrontation.

But identifying the man as an angel posed problems of its own. What was one to make of the new name that the man/angel gave to Jacob?

> And he said to him, "What is your name?" And he said, "Jacob." Then he said, "Your name shall no more be called Jacob, but Israel, for you have **struggled with God and with men**, and you have prevailed.
>
> —Gen. 32:27–28

If Jacob's opponent was an angel, then why should the text say "you have struggled *with God?*" Struggling with an angel is not the same as struggling with God. Likewise, if it was an angel, Jacob's new name should really have been "struggled-with-angel," not "struggled-with-God" (that is, Isra-el).

---

3. The three "men" who visit Abraham in Gen. 18:2 were generally reckoned to be angels; similarly, Daniel is addressed by a quasi-divine "man" in Dan. 12:7. The angel who appears to Manoah is likewise described as a "man" (Jud. 13:10, 11), and Manoah is in fact unaware that he is an angel (Jud. 13:16).

One solution was obvious: "God" here might be just a short way of saying "*angel of* God."

> He said, "Your name shall no more be called Jacob, but Israel, for you have made yourself great **with angels of God** and with men and you have overcome them."
>
> — *Targum Neophyti* Gen. 32:29 (also *Targum Pseudo-Jonathan,* Peshitta)

> He further ordered him to be called Israel. In the Hebrew tongue, this signifies the **adversary of an angel of God.**
>
> — Josephus, *Jewish Antiquities* 1:333

Similarly, "God" in Gen. 32:29 might be understood more generally as "heavenly being" or "heavenly power" (both of which would certainly include angels as well):

> I should like, I said, to learn from you gentlemen what is the force of the name Israel. And as they were silent, I continued: I will say what I know . . . The name Israel means this: a man overcoming power. For *Isra* is "a man overcoming," and *el* is "power."
>
> — Justin Martyr, *Dialogue with Trypho* 125:1–3

> You have grappled with **beings from above** and overcome them, with beings from below and overcome them. "Beings from above" refers to the angel . . . "Beings from below" refers to Esau and his princes.[4]
>
> — *Genesis Rabba* 78:3

Mighty with God's Help

But such was hardly the only way of understanding the meaning of Jacob's new name. The "with" in "struggled with" is somewhat ambiguous, in Hebrew as well as English. It could mean that Jacob had fought "in the company of" or even "with the help of" God. And even the Hebrew for "struggle"—an extremely rare word—might be understood differently: it could also mean something like "was strong" or "was a ruler."

As a result, many interpreters concluded that Jacob's new name had nothing to do with struggling with (in the sense of "against") God or even an

---

4. "Chiefs" (or "princes") is the word used of Esau's descendants in the genealogies of Gen. 37:15–19, 29–30, and 40–43. Thus, our text apparently sees the angel's words, "you have struggled with . . . *men* and prevailed," as a prediction of future events, foretelling not Jacob's personal victory over his brother, Esau, but the victory of Jacob's children, the people of Israel, over Esau's "chiefs," the various Edomite rulers.

angel of God. It meant that Jacob had been strong *with the help of* God or had been *exalted with* (that is, into the company of) God:

> And he said to him, "Your name shall no more be called Jacob, but Israel shall be your name.[5] For you have **been strong with God**, and you shall be powerful with men." — Septuagint Gen. 32:29

> She [Divine Wisdom] protected him [Jacob] from his enemies, and kept him safe from those who lay in wait for him; in his arduous contest she **helped him** to victory, so that he might learn that **godliness is more powerful** than anything. — Wisd. 10:12

> He said, "Your name shall no more be called Jacob, but Israel, for you are great before God and with men, and you have overcome." — *Targum Onqelos* Gen. 32:29

> . . . for you have made yourself great with angels of God and with men and you have overcome them.
> — *Targum Neophyti* Gen. 32:29 (also *Pseudo-Jonathan, Samaritan Targum*)

> . . . for you have been strong with an angel. — Peshitta Gen. 32:29

> For you have ruled with God. — Aquila Gen. 32:29

> Now we understand the passage in this way, that to wrestle *with* Jacob does not mean to wrestle *against* Jacob, but that the angel, who was present in order to save him, and who after learning of the progress he had made gave him the additional name of Israel, **wrestled together with him**, that is, was on his side in the contest and helped him in the struggle. For undoubtedly it was some other against whom Jacob was fighting and against whom his struggle was being waged.
> — Origen, *On First Principles* 3.2.5

Israel Means Seeing God

There was yet another explanation of Jacob's new name that likewise eliminated the implication that Jacob had in any sense struggled with (that is, "against") God. This explanation saw in "Israel" three separate Hebrew words, *'iš rā'â ēl*, "man who saw God" (or perhaps *yašur 'ēl*, "[he] sees God"). Such an understanding of the name would fit exceedingly well in context, since this

---

5. The wording here is slightly different from the traditional Hebrew text cited above. Note the wording of Gen. 35:10 in the traditional Hebrew text, "No longer shall your name be called Jacob, but Israel *shall be your name.*" Cf. Gen. 17:5.

whole episode occurs in a place called Peniel, which means "face of God." The Bible goes on to make a point of explaining this name just after Jacob has gotten his blessing:

> So Jacob called the name of the place Peniel, saying, "For I have seen God face to face, and yet my life has been preserved."   —Gen. 32:30

Similarly:

> And Jacob called the name of that place "Appearance of God."
>
> —Septuagint Gen. 32:31

Now, if the name "Israel" means "man who saw God," then the whole story takes on a somewhat different coloring: Jacob struggled with a "man" who was actually an angel (that is, in this view, an earthly manifestation of God), after which the angel blessed him by changing his name to man-who-saw-God, and Jacob further commemorated the same incident by calling the place "Face [or "Appearance"] of God." What was important, then, was not the conflict itself, but the fact that, in the course of it, Jacob had actually seen God's face:

> For seeing is the lot of the freeborn and firstborn Israel, which [name], translated, is "[the one] seeing God."
>
> —Philo, On Flight and Finding 208 (also On Dreams 172, etc.)

> Therefore, celebrating the resurrection festival on the Lord's day, we rejoice over the one who indeed conquered death, having brought to light life and immortality. For by him you brought the gentiles to yourself, for a treasured people, the true Israel, the friend of God, who sees God.   —Apostolic Constitutions 7.36.1

> In place of "Israel," read "[each] man saw God" ('iš rā'â 'ēl), for all his deeds were straight before Him.
>
> —Seder Eliahu Rabba 25 (some versions, 27)

> Israel means "a man seeing God," while others say it is a "man who will see God."
>
> —Hippolytus of Rome (c. 170–c. 236 C.E.), Pentateuch Fragment 16, on Gen. 49:7

> It is this people alone which is said to "see God," for the name Israel when translated has this meaning.   —Origen, On First Principles 4.3.12

> Israel means "seeing God," in the sense of the knowing and contemplative faculty in man.   —Eusebius, Praeparatio Evangelica 11.6.31

He gave Jacob the new name Israel, which means, "one who sees God."

— John Chrysostom, *Homilies* 58, on Genesis 2–3

However, he [Jacob] then asked for a blessing from that same angel whom he had just overcome. The granting of this [new] name was thus the blessing [mentioned]. For Israel means "one seeing God," which in the end will be the reward of all the saints.

— Augustine, *City of God* 16:39

Thereafter He created a congregation of angels . . . and a firstborn called Israel, which is "the man that sees God."

— *On the Origin of the World* (Nag Hammadi) 105:20–25

Understanding the meaning of Israel in this fashion was an interpretation with far-reaching consequences. For if, in its underlying level of meaning, Israel meant "man seeing God" or (as Philo said) "the mind that contemplates God and the world," then the Bible became not merely the saga of a particular people that had lived in a particular place and time, but the timeless, placeless account of all who seek to "see" God. Early Christians in particular were drawn to this notion. If "Israel" was not so much a proper name as a spiritual state, then one need not have been born a Jew to be a part of it. Indeed, the very identity of Israel could change; the "true Israel" (as one excerpt above says explicitly) became for some Christians not the Jewish people but the new church.

❖ ❖ ❖

In short: Laban was a cheat and a scoundrel. He substituted his less-than-perfect daughter Leah for Rachel not for the reason he gave, but in order to marry her off. Jacob may have discovered the ruse right away but said nothing to Laban until later. Despite Laban's trickery, Jacob dealt fairly with him; that he ended up with a good part of Laban's flocks was the result not of human trickery but of divine intervention. Even Rachel, when she took her father's household gods, did so with the best of intentions. Jacob's wrestling opponent at the Jabbok was an angel. The new name that Jacob received from him, Israel, therefore referred to struggling not with God, but with an angel; it also seemed to mean that Jacob had been exalted with, or helped by, God, and described Jacob as the "man who saw God."

13
Dinah
(GENESIS 34)

Shechem and Hamor ask for Dinah: God ordered their destruction.

Dinah

(GENESIS 34)

❖   ❖   ❖

Once back in Canaan, Jacob and his wives and children stayed for a time near the city of Shechem. On one occasion, Jacob's daughter Dinah went into Shechem. While she was there, the son of Hamor, Shechem's ruler, saw Dinah, "and he seized her and lay with her and violated her." Afterward, Hamor's son—whose name was the same as that of the city, Shechem—wished to keep Dinah as his wife, and he asked his father to approach Jacob to arrange for the marriage.

When Jacob's sons learned of this proposal, they were outraged. However, rather than simply refuse, "they answered Shechem and his father Hamor with guile" (Gen. 34:13). Such a marriage, they said, would be possible only if the bridegroom and all the men of Shechem were circumcised, as they themselves were. Hamor agreed, and all the males of the city underwent circumcision. Three days later, with the men of the city now in pain because of the operation, Jacob's sons Simeon and Levi entered the city and attacked it, killing Hamor and Shechem and all the other males. Jacob protested to his sons, saying that this deed might invite retaliation from other Canaanites, but Simeon and Levi answered, "Shall our sister be treated as a harlot?"

T HE STORY of Dinah is a single, isolated episode, without obvious connection to the rest of Genesis. Dinah herself does not reappear; the Bible does not say if she became pregnant after being raped, nor if she ever married anyone else; essentially, she disappears. As for the consequences of the revenge on Shechem, there were none: the threat of reprisal from the Canaanites (mentioned by Jacob at the end of the story) never materialized. In this sense, the story seems wholly unrelated to the broader historical saga in which it is located, and this only compounded the mystery of its overall meaning for ancient interpreters. Why had it been included in Scripture? To many, it seemed that the story must contain some kind of moral lesson, but if so, the overall message was unclear. The events themselves are narrated with what can only be described as studied neutrality. There is no indication whether Simeon and Levi are to be regarded as heroes or foolish hotheads, nor, for that matter, is there even any clear condemnation of Shechem himself.

God is nowhere mentioned, and at the end of the story we have no idea if this act of revenge was met with divine approval or disapproval.

Uncontrolled Anger

Another biblical text, however, seemed to interpreters to shed light on the true significance of this incident. For, while the story of Dinah is not explicitly mentioned elsewhere in the Hebrew Bible, interpreters from earliest times found an allusion to it at the end of the book of Genesis, when the aged Jacob blesses each of his sons in turn. When he comes to Simeon and Levi, he says:

> Simeon and Levi are brothers, weapons of violence are their stock-in-trade. Into their company let me not come, in their assembly let me not rejoice. For in their anger, they killed a man; and when in a good mood, they maimed an ox! Cursed be their anger, so fierce, and their wrath—how unyielding! I will divide them up in Jacob and scatter them in Israel.
>   —Gen. 49:5–7

Jacob's mention of Simeon and Levi jointly killing "a man" in their anger seemed to be an unambiguous reference to the revenge on Shechem (specifically, to Gen. 34:25–26). And the reference to Jacob's clear disapproval of what these two brothers did seemed to tip the scales against them. After all, Jacob was a righteous man. If, years after the incident, he still blamed his two sons for their deed, was this not the Bible's way of telling us that they had indeed acted reprehensibly?

> Why else did Jacob, our most wise father, censure Simeon and Levi for their irrational slaughter of the entire tribe of the Shechemites, saying, "Cursed be their anger." For if reason could not control anger, he [Jacob] would not have spoken thus.   —4 Macc. 2:19–20

For some, then, the story of the rape of Dinah contained a moral lesson about the control of anger. However heinous Shechem's crime, Simeon and Levi went much too far in their revenge, perpetrating a slaughter that this author could only call "irrational."

Shechem Deserved Death

Surprisingly, however, most interpreters seem to have concluded just the opposite: what Simeon and Levi did was altogether appropriate, even honorable. There were good reasons to think so. To begin with, the tribe descended from Levi was later singled out for a special honor: the Levites became the priestly tribe, the one from which Aaron and all subsequent priests were said to descend (as well as the tribe of Aaron's brother Moses, greatest of the prophets). If Levi were being condemned for his hot temper in the story of Dinah as well as in Jacob's reference to him in Gen. 49:6, why was not the priesthood given to some other tribe? What is more, Shechem's crime *was* heinous. It just did not seem reasonable that the point of this whole story was the overreaction of Simeon and Levi. Certainly the chief villain was Shechem himself. And so, despite Jacob's words in Gen. 49:5–7, most early interpreters were naturally inclined to view Simeon and Levi's action as basically praise-worthy.

Another obvious factor that pushed interpreters to take Simeon and Levi's side was the fact that they were, after all, Jacob's sons, Israelites, while Hamor and Shechem were foreigners. It was a clear case of us-against-them, and even if the story itself is presented in rather neutral terms, interpreters quite naturally supposed that its point was to condemn the "them" and praise the "us." What is more, Shechem was a northern city, situated in Samaria, and, as the (eventually separate) inhabitants of that region came to be viewed with disapproval by many Jews,[1] any biblical story involving their city and their ancestors would almost inevitably be affected. Many interpreters thus concluded that the point of the story of Dinah was the wickedness and depravity of Shechem and the heroism of Simeon and Levi.

But if that was so, a fundamental problem nonetheless remained: were the brothers right to *kill* Shechem? After all, the crime of rape, however hateful, is not normally punishable by death. Indeed, elsewhere in the Bible, the penalty prescribed by God is clearly far less severe:

> If a man meets a virgin who is not betrothed, and seizes and lies with her, and they are found, then the man who lay with her shall give to the father of the young woman fifty pieces of silver, and she shall be his wife as a result of his having violated her; he may not divorce her all his days. —Deut. 22:28–29

The case described in this law seems strikingly similar to that of Shechem and Dinah. For in both, a man rapes a young woman who is neither married nor engaged. In fact, the two texts use nearly identical terms to describe the crime—"seize," "lie with," "violate." Yet the law in Deuteronomy says that the

---

1. Samaritans and Jews doubtless experienced some tensions and strife even in earlier periods, but many biblical scholars now believe that a final rift between the two groups did not occur until late in the second century B.C.E. After that time, Jewish interpreters would certainly tend to regard Samaritans as outsiders or enemies, and, at times, to project such feelings onto their interpretation of biblical texts. See also Chapter 8.

man in such a case should be treated rather leniently. He is simply required to pay a fine and to marry the young woman himself,[2] and he must remain married to her "all his days." Familiar with this law, interpreters could not help wondering why Shechem had been condemned to death.[3] After all, he wanted to marry Dinah, just as the law prescribed; he even wanted to pay her father an extravagant amount of money (Gen. 34:12), doubtless far in excess of the fifty pieces of silver required by the law. Why then did not Jacob and his sons accept the offer?

Foreigners Are Different

One possible answer was obvious: Shechem was a foreigner. The only difference between him and the perpetrator in Deuteronomy is that he was "the son of Hamor the Hivite" (Gen. 34:2), that is, a Canaanite, a foreigner living in the land that God had given to Jacob and his descendants. Perhaps that was why Scripture, after mentioning Shechem's crime, went on to describe it as a "disgrace *in Israel*" (Gen. 34:8)—as if the national honor itself had been violated—and to stress repeatedly that Shechem had in fact "defiled" Dinah (Gen. 34:5, 13, 27).

And so, it is not surprising to find that interpreters highlighted Shechem's foreignness in retelling the story:

> Then Judith . . . cried out to the Lord with a loud voice, and said: "O Lord God of my ancestor Simeon, to whom You gave a sword to take revenge on the **strangers** . . ."
> —Jth. 9:2

> And you, Moses, command the children of Israel and warn them not to give any of their daughters to the **foreigners** and not to marry any **foreign women,** because that is abominable before the Lord. For this reason I have written for you in the words of the Torah everything that the Shechemites did to Dinah . . . Israel will not be free from unclean-

---

2. This is to occur only if the marriage is acceptable to the woman and her family (as later interpreters make plain) and not in violation of other laws. Note that, for later interpreters, this law of rape likewise applied to cases that we would describe as "statutory rape" and seduction.

3. One might argue, of course, that the Torah had not yet been given to Israel, and that this law of leniency was thus not known to Jacob and his sons. But there are many instances in which early interpreters state or imply that Israel's ancestors acted in accordance with laws of the Torah even before they were given. Besides, why should God have allowed Simeon and Levi to act as they did if what they did was wrong? He ought to have punished *them,* or at the very least the biblical account ought to have condemned their action. That such was not the case—indeed, that Levi was later rewarded with the priesthood forever—certainly implied that God approved of their action and that, as a result, *there was some crucial difference* between Shechem and the rapist described in Deuteronomy. See below.

ness while it has a one of the **foreign women** or if anyone has given one of his daughters to any **foreign man**.   — *Jubilees* 30:11–14

[Simeon and Levi later justify their deed:] "It would not be proper for them to say in their congregations and schools, 'uncircumcised [that is, non-Israelite] men defiled virgins, and idol-worshipers [defiled] the daughter of Jacob.'"   — *Targum Neophyti* Gen. 34:31

When Shechem . . . being now enamored of her, asked his father to take the girl for his wife. Hamor, agreeing, went to Jacob to request that Dinah now be legally joined to his son Shechem. Jacob, having no way to gainsay because of the standing of the person asking, still thought it unlawful to marry his daughter to a **foreigner**, and asked permission to hold a council on the subject of his request.
            — Josephus, *Jewish Antiquities* 1:337–338

Intermarriage Is Forbidden

For such interpreters, it was not just that foreigners were somehow not nice, or not deserving of mercy. Rather, the matter turned on the whole issue of intermarriage between Jews and other peoples. A great many biblical texts suggested that marriages between the people of Israel and the other peoples living in Canaan were disapproved of by God, indeed, strictly forbidden:

You shall not make marriages with them, giving your daughters to their sons or taking their daughters for your sons . . . For you are a people holy to the Lord your God; the Lord your God has chosen you to be a people for his own possession, out of all the peoples that are on the face of the earth.   — Deut. 7:3–6

Later biblical books make it clear that, at a certain point after the Jews' return from exile in Babylon, marriages between Jews and non-Jews became a major concern. The book of Ezra thus relates how Ezra discovered with grief that some of his fellow Jews had taken foreign wives—he mentions by name, in addition to Canaanite women, "Hittites, Perizzites, Jebusites, Ammonites, Moabites, Egyptians, and Amorites" (Ezra 9:1)[4]—and goes on to report a solemn undertaking (covenant) that was made with regard to such marriages:

[Shecaniah confesses to Ezra:] "We have broken faith with our God and have married non-Jewish women from the peoples of the land, but even now there is hope for Israel in spite of this. Therefore, let us

---

4. "Amorite" should probably be emended to "Edomite" on the basis of a parallel passage in 1 Esd. 8:69.

make a covenant with our God to divorce these women along with their children, according to the counsel of my lord and of those who tremble at the commandment of our God. Let it be done in accordance with the Torah. Arise, for it is your task, and we are with you; be strong and do it." Then Ezra arose and made the leading priests and Levites and all Israel take an oath that they would do as had been said. And they took the oath.   —Ezra 10:2–5

The book of Ezra then goes on to list individually all those who had taken foreign wives and who were required to divorce them. Nor did the matter of intermarriage slip into obscurity after this episode. Many postbiblical writings likewise stressed that marriages between Jews and non-Jews are a grave sin.

Against such a background, the biblical story of Dinah—and, in particular, the violent reaction of Simeon and Levi—took on a new dimension. Surely a foreign prince who had not only raped Jacob's daughter, but had then subsequently tried to *marry* her, was an arch villain, as much (or more so!) for his marriage proposal as for his original crime. For this reason some interpreters further specified that the marriage proposed by Shechem was actually prohibited:

> If there is a man in Israel who wishes to give his daughter or his sister to any foreigner, he is to die. He is to be stoned because he has done something sinful and shameful within Israel.   —Jubilees 30:7

> Jacob, having no way to gainsay [the proposed marriage] because of the standing of the person asking, still thought it **unlawful** to marry his daughter to a foreigner, and asked permission to hold a council on the subject of his request.[5]   —Josephus, *Jewish Antiquities* 1:337–338

A Wise Answer

But if it was forbidden for Dinah to be given in marriage to a foreigner, then why didn't Jacob and his sons simply say so? Instead, they tricked all the men of Shechem into undergoing circumcision and then, with the town's defenders thereby incapacitated, Simeon and Levi entered the town and killed them all at swordpoint. Not only was this an apparent case of collective punishment, but the brothers had clearly lied to achieve their ends. The Bible does not hide from the facts:

---

5. Note that in this passage Josephus does not even clearly define Shechem's crime as rape; he "stole her away and lay with her." The whole reason for Jacob's reluctance is the fact that marriage to a foreigner would be "unlawful."

The sons of Jacob answered Shechem and his father Hamor **deceitfully**, because he had defiled their sister Dinah. They said to them, "We cannot do this thing, to give our sister to one who is uncircumcised, for that would be a disgrace to us." —Gen. 34:13–14

Some interpreters, however, rose to the defense of the brothers even in this matter. True, the Bible says "deceitfully." But if intermarriage between Jews and non-Jews was forbidden, then what the brothers were saying—at least the part cited above—was hardly deceitful; it was the plain truth. Perhaps, then, "deceitfully" really meant something more like "cleverly" or even "wisely":

They [Dinah's brothers] spoke **deceitfully** with them and dealt **cleverly** with them . . . For this reason I have written for you in the words of the Torah everything that the Shechemites did to Dinah, and [specifically] how the sons of Jacob spoke, saying, "We will not give our daughter to a man who is uncircumcised because that would be a disgrace for us." For it *is* a disgrace for Israel, for those who give and those who take any of the foreign women, for this is unclean and abominable to Israel. — *Jubilees* 30:3, 12–13

And Jacob's sons answered Shechem and his father Hamor with **wisdom** and spoke, because he had defiled Dinah their sister.
— *Targum Onqelos* Gen. 34:13

And Jacob's sons answered Shechem and his father Hamor in the greatness of their **wisdom** and spoke, because he had defiled Dinah their sister.[6] — *Targum Neophyti* Gen. 34:13

"The sons of Jacob answered Shechem [and his father Hamor deceitfully]": R. Samuel b. Naḥman said: Can anyone believe that this was a fraudulent [response], when the Holy Spirit [itself, that is, the divine author of the second half of this verse] said, "for he had [indeed] defiled their sister Dinah"?[7] — *Genesis Rabba* 80:8

The Whole City Was Guilty

Thus, in the view of many interpreters, the brothers were quite right to have killed Shechem for his crime, and even their earlier statement about being

6. Isaac's words to Esau in Gen. 27:35, "Your brother came *in guile*," underwent a similar transformation to "wisdom" in the targums and elsewhere.

7. In other words, the very fact that the second half of this verse—undoubtedly expressing the sentiments of the Bible's inspiring spirit—apparently seeks to justify the brothers' words indicates that they were not being deceitful.

unable to permit their sister to marry an uncircumcised man was, in itself, no deception but simply a statement of fact.

Still, the brothers did more than execute the rapist; they also killed his father, Hamor, and all the men of the town. What was *their* crime? At first glance, this seemed like an egregious case of collective punishment, slaughtering a whole city for a crime committed by one of its citizens. The issue apparently troubled ancient interpreters. Most concluded, however, that if the entire city had been punished, it must in some fundamental way have shared in Shechem's guilt. And here, on close examination, the Bible itself offered ancient interpreters some confirmation. Although elsewhere it is quite specific about Shechem acting alone, in one verse toward the end of the story, the Bible seems to include others in the crime against Dinah:

> And the sons of Jacob came upon the slain and plundered the city, because **they** [the Shechemites] had violated their sister. —Gen. 34:27

The use of the plural in this verse suggested to interpreters that the city as a whole was in some sense guilty of the crime; all its men had played a role. A number of interpreters specifically picked up on this detail:

> [The continuation of Judith's prayer, cited above:] "O Lord God of my ancestor Simeon, to whom You gave a sword to take revenge on the strangers [plural] who had loosed the adornment of a virgin to defile her, and uncovered her thigh to put her to shame, and polluted her womb to disgrace her; for You said, 'It shall not be so'—and **they** did so. Therefore You gave up their rulers to be slain, and their bed, which was ashamed of the deceit **they** had practiced, to be stained with blood, and You struck down slaves along with princes, and princes on their thrones; and You gave their wives for a prey and their daughters to captivity, and all their booty to be divided among your beloved sons, who were zealous for You, and abhorred the pollution of their blood, and called on You for help—O God, my God, hear me also, a widow . . ." —Jth. 9:2–4

> Jacob and his sons were angry at the men of Shechem because **they** defiled Dinah, their sister. So they spoke deceptively with them and acted in a crafty manner toward them and tricked them. Simeon and Levi entered Shechem unexpectedly and carried out punishment on all the Shechemites: they killed every man whom they found there and did not leave a single one alive. They killed them all painfully because **they** had dishonored their sister Dinah. —*Jubilees* 30:3–4

It is proper that they should say in the congregations of Israel and in their schoolhouses, "The uncircumcised were killed on account of a virgin, and idol-worshipers [were killed] because **they** defiled Dinah, the daughter of Jacob."
— *Targum Neophyti* Gen. 34:31

City with a Criminal Past

Other early retellings seem to suggest that the Shechemites were punished not specifically for their complicity in the rape of Dinah, but because it was only the latest incident in a series of crimes stretching back for generations. They and the other Canaanite tribes had always mistreated strangers and taken advantage of the defenseless—perhaps, indeed, that was why it was proper that they all be destroyed:

God smote the inhabitants of Shechem, for they did not honor whoever came to them, whether evil or noble. Nor did they determine rights or laws throughout the city. Rather, deadly works were their care.
— Theodotus, Fragment 7 (cited from Alexander Polyhistor in Eusebius, *Praeparatio Evangelica* 9.22.9)

[Levi recalls:] But I saw that God's verdict upon Shechem was "Guilty"; for they had sought to do the same thing to Sarah and Rebekah as they had [now] done to Dinah our sister, but the Lord had stopped them. And in the same way they had persecuted Abraham our father when he was a stranger, and they had acted against him to suppress his flocks when they were big with young; and they had mistreated Ieblae, his homeborn slave. And in this way they treated all strangers, taking their wives by force and banishing them. But the anger of the Lord against them had reached its term. So I said to my father: Do not be angry, lord, because through you the Lord will reduce the Canaanites to nothing, and he will give their land to you and your seed after you.
— *Testament of Levi* 6:8–7:1

God Said No

Some of the above passages specify that Simeon and Levi were merely instruments of divine justice, that it was God Himself who had decreed the death of the Shechemites, not for purposes of revenge, but as a punishment. Yet, as was observed earlier, the story itself is actually narrated with studied neutrality. There is no indication that God even approved of the violence, never mind that He ordered it. Whence this idea?

Interpreters bent on finding some opening, however slight, in the narrative's neutrality eventually turned their attention to that moment in the story when Jacob's sons first hear of the rape:

> The sons of Jacob came in from the field when they heard of it; and the men were indignant and very angry, because he [Shechem] had committed a disgrace in Israel by lying with Jacob's daughter, and **such a thing ought not to be done.**
> —Gen. 34:7

Why does the biblical narrative add this last phrase? In context, it seems to be what literary critics call "implied direct speech." That is, the text, in reporting the brothers' reaction, presents what they said to one another—"Shechem has committed a disgrace in Israel by lying with Dinah; such a thing ought not to be done!"—without going to the trouble of saying "this is what they said," instead simply stating their thoughts as if from the narrative's own point of view.

Viewed from a certain angle, however, these same words can take on (or be purposely given) a different meaning. For if the Bible adds, "and such a thing ought not to be done," might one not conclude that these are *God's own words?* After all, they are not specifically attributed to the brothers; could they not be in the nature of an "editorial comment" outside the narrative itself? There may even be a hint of such an interpretation in the Septuagint translation of this same verse. The Hebrew phrase (which might be rendered still more literally "and it ought not to be done thus") comes out in the Greek:

> . . . and the men were sorely grieved and very distressed, because he [Shechem] had committed a disgrace in Israel by lying with Jacob's daughter; and it **shall not be** thus.
> —Septuagint Gen. 34:7

The wording "and it *shall not be* thus" might suggest, a touch more in the Greek than in the Hebrew, some sort of editorial comment about future policy, or indeed about the subsequent events, rather than merely the implied direct speech of the brothers.

In any case, other authors clearly presented the idea that Gen. 34:7 contains God's own statement about the Shechem affair—"let it not be done thus."

> You [God] gave a sword to take revenge on the strangers who had loosed the adornment of a virgin to defile her, and uncovered her thigh to put her to shame, and polluted her womb to disgrace her; for **You** said, "It shall not be so"—and they did so.
> —Jth. 9:2

> [The angel of *Jubilees* says:] And **let it not be done thus** henceforth again that a daughter of Israel shall be defiled.
> —*Jubilees* 30:5

God Ordered Their Destruction

It followed that these words in the narrative were actually a divine verdict of execution: having said "let it not be done thus," God then ordered the destruction of the townsfolk or, in the extreme formulation, actually killed them Himself:

> **God smote** the inhabitants of Shechem, for they did not honor whoever came to them, whether evil or noble.
>
> — Theodotus, Fragment 7 (cited from Alexander Polyhistor in Eusebius, *Praeparatio Evangelica* 9.22.9)

> For the verdict was ordered **in heaven** against them, that they might annihilate with a sword all of the men of Shechem because they committed a disgrace in Israel. And the Lord handed them over to Jacob's sons, so that they might exterminate them with the sword and carry out the punishment [decreed] against them. — *Jubilees* 30:5–6

> But I saw that **God's verdict** upon Shechem was "Guilty" . . . So I said to my father: Do not be angry, lord, because through you the Lord will reduce the Canaanites to nothing. — *Testament of Levi* 6:8–7:1

> And Simeon and Levi drew their swords from their sheaths and said, "Behold, have you seen these swords? With these two swords **the Lord God** punished the insult of the Shechemites [by] which they insulted the sons of Israel, because of our sister Dinah whom Shechem the son of Hamor had defiled." — *Joseph and Aseneth* 23:14

Dinah Married Job

The later life of Dinah is passed over in silence. We catch not the slightest glimpse of her in Jacob's household during the long story of Joseph, and while her name is mentioned once more, in passing, in a list of Jacob's descendants (Gen. 46:15), she apparently did not join her father and brothers in going down to Egypt. What became of her?

A number of early sources suggest that Dinah became the wife of Job, the central figure of the biblical book bearing his name. For although that book mentions the fact that Job had a wife, it does not say what her name was. This was just the sort of blank that early interpreters were anxious to fill, especially when they could do so by "borrowing" a name or a character from somewhere else. Now while the book of Job does not say *when* Job lived, Gen. 36:33 mentions a certain "Jobab" among the descendants of Jacob's brother, Esau. If "Jobab" was another form of the name

Job,[8] then Job might have been around—and looking for a wife—at precisely the time when Dinah was returned from Shechem to her father's house.

> [Job says:] I am from the sons of Esau, the brother of Jacob, of whom is your mother Dinah, from whom I begot you. My former wife had died with the other ten children in a bitter death.
>
> — *Testament of Job* 1:5–6

> And they [Simeon and Levi] took their sister Dinah and went away from there. And afterward Job took her as a wife and fathered from her fourteen sons and six daughters, that is, seven sons and three daughters before he was struck down with suffering, and afterward seven sons and three daughters when he was healed.
>
> —Pseudo-Philo, *Biblical Antiquities* 8:7–8

> And Dinah his wife said to him . . .   — *Job Targum*, translating Job 2:9

> R. Abba b. Kahana said: Dinah was the wife of Job.
>
> — *Genesis Rabba* 57:4

> It is said that Job lived in the time of Jacob and that he married Dinah, Jacob's daughter. For it says in Job [that he said to his wife] "You are speaking the way one of the foolish women [*nebalot*] might speak . . ." [Job 2:10], and it says in [regard to Dinah] "For he has committed a disgrace [*nebalah*] in Israel."
>
> —j. *Baba Bathra* 15:2

❖   ❖   ❖

In short: Shechem's crime was particularly heinous because, as a foreigner, he was not to marry a daughter of Jacob's; any such union was a defilement. His offer to marry Dinah and to have his kinsmen intermarry with Jacob's family thus only compounded his offense. Simeon and Levi did well to kill not only him and his father, but the other men of Shechem as well, for they had cooperated in Shechem's crime or had a history of evil behavior. Indeed, Jacob's sons were merely instruments of divine punishment, for God Himself had sentenced the Shechemites to die for their crimes. As for Dinah, she eventually married Job, a descendant of Jacob's brother, Esau.

8. Such an identification is found specifically in a note at the end of the Septuagint version of the book of Job. There it says that Job "was previously named Jobab . . . He himself was the son of Zerah, of the sons of Esau . . . These were the kings who ruled in Edom, which place he himself also governed. First, Balak, the son of Zippor, and the name of his city was Dennaba; and after Balak, Jobab, who is called Job" (Septuagint Job 52:17). A similar tradition is found in a passage of Eusebius' *Praeparatio Evangelica* (9.25:1–4) attributed, via Alexander Polyhistor, to a certain "Aristeas."

14

Joseph's Ups and Downs

(GENESIS 37 AND 39–41)

Joseph falsely accused: a collective accusation.

Joseph's Ups and Downs

(GENESIS 37 AND 39–41)

❖   ❖   ❖

Of all his children, Jacob loved Joseph the most, for he was the "son of his old age"; Jacob gave him a specially decorated outer garment. The other brothers hated the young Joseph and eventually conspired to kill him. At the last minute, however, they relented and instead sold him as a slave to a passing caravan. When they returned home, they told Jacob that Joseph had been killed by a wild animal. Meanwhile, Joseph was brought down to Egypt and sold to Potiphar, a high official of the court. He soon rose to the top of Potiphar's staff. But when Joseph refused to be seduced by Potiphar's wife, she accused him of attacking her, and Joseph was put in jail.

In prison along with Joseph were Pharaoh's chief butler and baker. One night, the two had similar dreams, and each asked Joseph to interpret his. Joseph interpreted the dreams correctly and, in keeping with his words, the chief butler was soon restored to his former post, while the baker was executed.

Sometime later, Pharaoh too had a dream, and the chief butler recommended Joseph to interpret it. Joseph was whisked out of jail and brought to the royal court. After hearing the dream, he explained to Pharaoh that it foretold a period of plenty in Egypt, to be followed by a famine. To help prepare for the lean years ahead, Pharaoh put Joseph in charge of storing up and distributing grain to the whole country. Joseph thus became ruler over all of Egypt, second only to Pharaoh himself. Soon enough, the brothers who had betrayed him would come bowing down before him to ask for grain.

THE STORY of Joseph is the longest single narrative in Genesis. Through it all, what stands out is Joseph's abiding trust in God, for although he is unjustly treated on more than one occasion, he does not lose hope or give in to bitterness. As it happens, he not only ends up ruling over all of Egypt, but, in subsequent chapters, manages to use his high office to teach his brothers a lesson in proper conduct. At the end of his long adventure, he is at last happily reunited with his brothers and his father, Jacob.

Unlike many other biblical stories we have seen, Joseph's had little that seemed to *demand* explanation or interpretation. Interpreters instead devoted their energies to retelling his story in such a way as to highlight Joseph's many virtues, as well as to look deeply into its various little details.

One such detail was the matter of his brothers' hatred for Joseph. After all, the Bible says elsewhere that "you shall not hate your brother in your heart" (Lev. 19:17). Why then did Joseph's brothers—the ancestors of God's chosen people and presumably, therefore, outstanding individuals—hate him so much? Certainly one reason for their hatred according to the biblical narrative was the fact that Joseph was their father's favorite son, as witnessed by the expensive garment that Jacob had given him.

It's a Wise Child

Why should Jacob have favored Joseph over all his other sons? The Bible explains that Joseph was the "son of his [Jacob's] old age" (Gen. 37:3), but this hardly seemed like an adequate reason to ancient interpreters. After all, Benjamin, Joseph's younger brother, was even more of a "son of old age" to Jacob. Since he, no less than Joseph, was a son of Jacob's beloved wife Rachel, there really was no reason for Jacob to favor Joseph over Benjamin. If anything, Benjamin should have been loved more than any of the other brothers.

Considering the situation, interpreters concluded that the Bible must have meant something else by the phrase "son of his old age." If Joseph was not *younger* than all the brothers, perhaps he surpassed them in some other way. Now, in the Bible "old age" is frequently associated with wisdom: "old man" is practically a synonym in biblical Hebrew for "sage" or "wise man" (see, for example, Ezek. 7:26, 26:9, Ps. 105:22, Lam. 5:14, Job. 32:9, Ruth 4:9). Perhaps, then, in saying that Joseph was a "son of his old age," the Bible really meant he was a "son of his wisdom"—that is, Joseph was an exceptionally intelligent child:

> Because he [Joseph] excelled all the other sons of Jacob in wisdom and understanding, his brothers plotted against him.
>
> —Artapanus (cited in Eusebius, *Praeparatio Evangelica* 9.23.1)

> Thus his father, observing in him a noble mind greater than the usual, marvelled at him and admired him, and he loved him more than his other sons. —Philo, *On Joseph* 4

> When Jacob had begotten Joseph by Rachel, he loved him more than the other sons, both because of the beauty of his body and the virtue of his mind, for he excelled in intelligence.
>
> —Josephus, *Jewish Antiquities* 2:9

> And Israel [Jacob] loved Joseph more than his other sons, for he was a wise son to him. —*Targum Onqelos* Gen. 37:3

Eating from the Flocks

Another apparent reason the brothers hated Joseph was that he brought back an "evil report" about them to their father (Gen. 37:2). This report particularly intrigued interpreters. What exactly had Joseph said about his brothers? The Bible itself offered a clue or two:

> These are the generations of Jacob: Joseph was seventeen years old when he was shepherding the flock with his brothers; he was a youth with the sons of Bilhah and the sons of Zilpah, his father's wives. And Joseph brought back an evil report about them to his father.
>
> — Gen. 37:2

The verse seems straightforward enough, but on closer examination it may be seen to contain a minor contradiction. First it says that Joseph was shepherding "with his brothers"—presumably, all of them—and then it adds that he was "with the sons of Bilhah and the sons of Zilpah, his father's wives." The conclusion of interpreters seems to have been that Joseph was indeed shepherding with all of them, but that the sons of Bilhah and Zilpah had been singled out for special attention by the text because Joseph's evil report concerned them in particular. And what were the sons of Bilhah and Zilpah doing that was wrong? Again, from the context it appeared to interpreters that Joseph must have reported something concerning their conduct as shepherds:

> [Joseph's brother Gad recalls:] And Joseph said to his father, the sons of Zilpah and Bilhah are killing the best animals and eating them against the advice of Judah and Reuben. He saw that I had set free a lamb from the mouth of a bear, which I then killed, but that I had killed the lamb when I was saddened to see that it was too weak to live; and we had eaten it.   — *Testament of Gad* 1:6–7

> "And Joseph brought an evil report . . ." [Gen. 37:2]. Said R. Meir: [Joseph said:] Your sons are guilty of eating limbs taken from a living animal.   — *Genesis Rabba* 84:7

Thus, according to this interpretation, Joseph had seen his brothers eating the animals that were put in their charge. Rightly or wrongly, he had reported this back to his father, thus incurring his brothers' hatred.[1]

---

1. The passage from the *Testament of Gad* in fact suggests that it was all a mistake: the lamb in question had been so badly mauled by a bear that it was too weak to live anyway.

Resembled Jacob in All Things

However, this same biblical verse also seemed to provide other reasons for the brothers' hatred:

> These are the generations of **Jacob: Joseph** was seventeen years old when he was shepherding the flock with his brothers.   — Gen. 37:2

The phrase "These are the generations of Jacob" would, one might expect, normally be followed by a list of Jacob's sons, beginning with the oldest (that is how other such "These are the generations of . . ." work in the Bible). But here there is no list at all. Instead, only one son is mentioned, Joseph. Interpreters thus understood that Scripture was trying to imply by this wording that Joseph was Jacob's son *par excellence*, that, of all his sons, Joseph was the one who was most like Jacob himself:

> [Joseph recalls at the end of his life:] And [God] preserved me to old age in strength and in beauty, for I was like Jacob **in all things**.
> — *Testament of Joseph* 18:4

> "These are the generations of Jacob: Joseph . . ." [Gen. 37:2]: So it appears that Joseph resembled his father **in all things**, and all that happened to Jacob similarly happened to Joseph.
> — *Midrash Tanḥuma, Wayyesheb* 1

If so, here was another reason for the other brothers to be resentful.

Deeds of Youthful Foolishness

Finally, the same biblical verse states that Joseph was seventeen years old, but then adds that he was a "youth." This word (*na'ar*) is usually used for boys younger than seventeen—in fact, it is even what Scripture calls the three-month-old Moses (Exod. 2:6). And why, in any case, should the text say that Joseph was a "youth" after it had already told us his exact age? Interpreters therefore concluded that "youth" was intended here to refer to Joseph's behavior rather than merely his age:

> For when he is keeping the flock with his illegitimate brothers [the sons of Bilhah and Zilpah], he is spoken of as young . . . The "young" disposition, then, is one that cannot as yet play the part of shepherd with its true-born brothers.   — Philo, *On Sobriety* 12–14

He was seventeen years old, yet [the text] says he was a "youth"? But this means he did deeds of youthful foolishness: he bedaubed his eyes and smoothed back his hair and raised his heel.　　*— Genesis Rabba 84:7*

Joseph's immature behavior while shepherding with his brothers, alluded to in Scripture's use of the single word "youth," thus provided yet another good reason for his brothers' hatred.

For the Price of Shoes

Whatever the precise cause, Joseph's brothers did indeed hate him, and that is why they sold him as a slave to caravanners bound for Egypt. One minor detail is left hanging in this part of the story. The Bible says that Joseph's brothers "sold him to the Ishmaelites for twenty pieces of silver" (Gen. 37:28),[2] but it does not say what the brothers did with the money. A number of texts, however, contain the somewhat strange assertion that they then spent the money on shoes:

[Zebulon recalls the incident:] In his [Joseph's] price I had no share, my children. But Simeon and Gad and six others of our brothers took the price of Joseph and bought sandals for themselves and their wives and their children.　　*— Testament of Zebulon 3:1–2*

And they sold Joseph to Arabs for twenty pieces of silver and they bought shoes with them.　　*— Targum Pseudo-Jonathan Gen. 37:28*

And each of them took two pieces of silver to buy shoes for their feet.　　*— Pirqei deR. Eliezer 38*

The source of this tradition originally had nothing to do with the story of Joseph. Once, in ancient times, the prophet Amos had rebuked the people of Israel in these terms:

Thus says the Lord: For three transgressions of Israel, and for four, I will not revoke [the punishment]: for their selling a righteous man for silver, and a needy one for a pair of shoes.　　*— Amos 2:6*

In these words Amos meant to indict Israel for its lack of pity (for the passage continues: ". . . they that trample the head of the poor into the dust of the earth, and turn aside the way of the afflicted . . .") as well as for its overall

---

2. In the Septuagint the text says "twenty pieces of *gold*"; that was probably closer to the price of a slave at the time this translation was made.

sinfulness.[3] But in time, this general condemnation came to be understood as a specific reference to the story of Joseph. For Joseph certainly was a "righteous man"—righteousness was his outstanding characteristic—and the traditional Hebrew text does say that he was sold "for silver." Who could Amos have been talking about if not him? As a result, the second part of the verse, "and a needy one for shoes," was likewise understood to apply to Joseph, leading to the idea that Joseph's brothers had indeed bought shoes with the money realized on the sale of their brother.

Joseph's Great Virtue

Sold as a slave, Joseph ended up in the house of Potiphar. What took place next—the attempt of Potiphar's wife to seduce Joseph, his steadfast refusal of her advances and, finally, her false accusation against him—was really only one small part of Joseph's tumultuous story. But, for various reasons, the encounter of Joseph and Potiphar's wife eventually came to be seen by ancient interpreters as *the* central episode of his life. His ability to resist temptation came to be seen as Joseph's great virtue, and many suggested that Joseph's rise to power came as a reward for this virtue:

> Remember the deeds of the fathers, which they did in their generations; and receive great honor and an everlasting name. Was not Abraham found faithful when tested, and it was reckoned to him as righteousness? Joseph in the time of his distress kept a commandment [that is, the prohibition against adultery], and became lord of Egypt.
>
> —1 Macc. 2:51–53

> It is for this reason, certainly, that the temperate Joseph is praised, because by mental effort he overcame sexual desire. For when he was young and in his prime, by his reason he nullified the frenzy of his passions. Not only is reason proved to rule over the frenzied urge of sexual desire, but also over every desire.　　—4 Macc. 2:2–4

> You, O Lord, did not neglect Joseph, but gave him to rule over Egypt— a reward of the **self-control** that You enable.
>
> —Hellenistic Synagogal Prayer, *Apostolic Constitutions* 8.12:24

R. Yudan said in the name of R. Benjamin b. Levi: [Joseph] was rewarded in kind. Thus, his mouth, which had abstained from sinning

---

3. Amos 8:6 also makes it clear that reference to "selling the righteous" for silver or shoes does not refer specifically to Joseph, since in this verse personified Israel confesses to "buying the poor for silver and the needy for a pair of shoes."

[with Potiphar's wife, was rewarded by Pharaoh's words], "You shall be over my house, and *by your mouth* shall all my people be ordered" [Gen. 41:40]; similarly, his neck, which had abstained from sin [in the same incident], was rewarded: "Then Pharaoh . . . put a golden chain around his *neck*" [Gen. 41:42] . . . his body, which likewise abstained from sin, he [Pharaoh] "arrayed in garments of fine linen" [Gen. 41:42]. — *Genesis Rabba* 90:3

The centrality for interpreters of the incident with Potiphar's wife may be seen even in this apparently well-rounded summary of Joseph's life:

When a righteous man [Joseph] was sold, Wisdom did not desert him, but delivered him from sin. She [Wisdom] descended with him into the dungeon, and when he was in prison she did not leave him, until she brought him the scepter of a kingdom and authority over his masters. Those who accused him she showed to be false, and she gave him everlasting honor. — Wisd. 10:13–14

Although Potiphar's wife is not mentioned directly, this brief overview never-theless contains two separate allusions to the seduction story: Wisdom "deliv-ered [Joseph] from sin," that is, from the clutches of his master's wife, and later "those who accused him [namely, of having tried to attack Potiphar's wife] she [Wisdom] showed to be false."

A Very Handsome Man

If early interpreters were fond of celebrating Joseph's virtue in resisting the sin of adultery, they were no doubt also puzzled by one aspect of the story: Why did Potiphar's wife try to seduce her own servant? After all, he was far below her station. Would not a woman bent on adultery turn to one of her social equals, rather than to a mere household slave? But they saw an answer to this question in the Bible itself:

So [Potiphar] left all that he had in Joseph's charge, and he [Potiphar] had no concern save for the bread that he ate. Now Joseph was **comely of form and comely of appearance**. And it came to pass, after these things, that his master's wife cast her eyes upon Joseph, and said, "Lie with me." — Gen. 39:6–7

The fact that Scripture went out of its way to assert that Joseph was hand-some—indeed, that it used such an emphatic turn of phrase as "comely of form and comely of appearance"—and that, right after this assertion, it went on to recount his mistress's adulterous proposal, both seemed intended to explain why Potiphar's wife had acted as she did. She found herself irresistibly attracted to the handsome Joseph. As a result, early interpreters placed great stress on Joseph's unique handsomeness:

> She [Potiphar's wife] was driven mad by the youth's handsomeness.
>
> —Philo, *On Joseph* 40

> [Joseph recounts:] And He [God] gave me beauty as a flower, beyond the beautiful ones of Israel.   —*Testament of Joseph* 18:4

> Therefore Joseph was comely in appearance and beautiful to look upon, because no wickedness dwelt in him—for the face makes manifest the troubles of the spirit.   —*Testament of Simeon* 5:1

> When Jacob had begotten Joseph by Rachel, he loved him more than the other sons, both because of the beauty of his body and the virtue of his mind.[4]   —Josephus, *Jewish Antiquities* 2:9

Girls Climbing the Walls

The idea that Joseph was uniquely handsome did not derive solely from the Bible's describing him as "comely of form and comely of appearance," however. Another verse in the Bible contributed greatly to Joseph's reputation for being attractive to women, at least according to some interpreters. The crucial verse is found in that series of blessings with which Jacob blesses his sons before his death. When he turns to Joseph, Jacob says:

> Joseph is a fruitful bough, a fruitful bough upon a spring; the vines climb upon a wall.   —Gen. 49:22

Now, the Hebrew of this text is extremely difficult, and the above translation (which appears in many modern Bibles) is merely one way of trying to understand its words. But the phrase it translates as "fruitful bough" literally means only "son of fruitfulness" or "son who has been fruitful." How, then, did translators get the idea that this meant, specifically, a fruitful plant or "bough"? Noticing that this "son of fruitfulness" was said to be "upon a spring" or fountain, they concluded that the fruitful thing being referred to had to be *some sort of plant* whose fruitfulness (the verse seemed to be saying)

---

4. Note that these last two quoted passages are apparently trying to explain why Scripture had said both "comely of form" and "comely of appearance." Josephus and the *Testament of Simeon* both seem to understand this apparent repetition as reflecting two different *kinds* of beauty, physical and spiritual.

came from its having been planted next to a source of water.[5] And once this was decided, the last part of the verse—which more literally says, "the daughters climbed the wall"—was interpreted as a further reference to this same plant, its daughter-*vines*. Hence, "the vines climb a wall." Actually, the roots (so to speak) of this interpretation are quite old:

> My son who will grow great,[6] Joseph, my son who will be blessed **like a vine standing on a spring of water**; two tribes will come forth from his sons [and] they will each receive a portion and inheritance.
> — *Targum Onqelos* Gen. 49:22

Here, not only is the same plant image present, but the daughter-vines are given additional meaning: they represent, specifically, the tribes of Joseph's two sons, Ephraim and Manasseh, each of whom acquired an equal share with Joseph's brothers in Jacob's inheritance.

But there was another way of reading this verse. In this other reading, Jacob calls Joseph a "son of fruitfulness" or "son who has been fruitful" because he is, quite literally, his *son,* and one who has been, and will continue to be, fruitful and great. If so, then there is no reference to a plant here at all,[7] and thus no necessity for the "daughters" to be daughter-vines. They might be simply daughters, ordinary young women. But then, why should these daughters have been mentioned here, what was their connection with Joseph? The verse says, "the daughters climb the wall." Interpreters therefore surmised that the "daughters" or young women in question were climbing a wall or some other high structure in order to *catch sight of Joseph*, the man described in Gen. 39:6 as "comely of form and comely of appearance."

> My son who has grown great, Joseph, my son who has grown great and mighty . . . the daughters of the kings and satraps looked at you [from] upon the windows and listened to you from the lattices.
> — *Targum Neophyti* Gen. 49:22

> And when [the Egyptian sages] praised you [Joseph], the daughters of the rulers [of Egypt] would walk along the walls . . . so that you might look at them. — *Targum Pseudo-Jonathan* Gen. 49:22

5. This idea was reinforced by such biblical verses as Jer. 17:8 and Ps. 1:3, where the righteous man is compared to a tree planted next to a stream.

6. The phrase "son who has been fruitful" is transformed here into a prediction of the future, "my son who will be fruitful," hence, "who will grow great."

7. It so happens that the word for "spring," *'ayin*, can also mean "eye." Interpreters who rejected the plant approach therefore took the verse to be referring to a fruitful son who was "appealing to the eye," "overcoming the [evil] eye," and so forth.

> A growing son, Joseph, a growing son and handsome of mien; the girls ran about upon the wall. — (Vulgate) Gen. 49:22

Elsewhere Jerome, translator of the Vulgate, explained this passage's meaning:

> And the sense of this section is: O Joseph, you who are thus called because the Lord added you to me, or because you are to be the greatest among your brothers . . . O Joseph, I say, you who are so handsome that the whole throng of Egyptian girls looked down from the walls and towers and windows.
> — Jerome, *Hebrew Questions in Genesis* 49:22

The same tradition may stand behind a scene in a considerably earlier text:

> Joseph said to [Potiphar:] "Who is this woman who is standing on the **upper floor** by the window? Let her leave this house," because Joseph was afraid, saying, "This one must not molest me too." For all the wives and **daughters** of the noblemen and satraps of the whole land of Egypt . . . when they saw Joseph, suffered badly because of his beauty.
> — *Joseph and Aseneth* 7:3–4

Cast Down Their Jewelry

Indeed, one version of this interpretation—building further on the word "climb" (ṣaʿadah) which resembles a Hebrew word for jewelry (eṣʿadah)—has the daughters cast their precious jewels and gold in front of Joseph so that he might take notice of them:

> For all the wives and daughters of the noblemen and satraps of the whole land of Egypt . . . when they saw Joseph, suffered badly because of his beauty. But Joseph despised them; and the messengers whom they sent to him with gold and silver and valuable presents Joseph sent back with threats and insults. — *Joseph and Aseneth* 7:4

> The daughters of the kings and satraps looked upon you from the windows . . . and cast down before you their bracelets, rings, and necklaces, ornaments and all kinds of gold, hoping that you might lift your eyes and look at one of them. — *Targum Neophyti* Gen. 49:22

> The daughters of the rulers [of Egypt] would walk along the walls and cast down in front of you bracelets and golden ornaments so that you might look at them. — *Targum Pseudo-Jonathan* Gen. 49:22

Moreover, Joseph rode in a chariot and crossed the whole territory of Egypt, and the Egyptian girls would climb up on the wall and cast down upon him golden rings that he might perchance look upon their beauty.
— *Pirqei deR. Eliezer* 39

Thus, the biblical evidence for Joseph's good looks became stronger and stronger. Not only does the Bible refer to him with the emphatic "comely of form and comely of appearance," but ancient interpreters saw in Jacob's blessing of Joseph a further allusion to Joseph's appearance: the young ladies of Egypt were so smitten by him that they cast their valuable jewelry at his feet, just in the hope of stealing a glance. No wonder Potiphar's wife could not restrain her passion!

Joseph Was Not Tempted

According to most ancient interpreters, Joseph reacted to such attentions as a model of chastity and virtue: never once was he even tempted to submit to the advances of Potiphar's wife. Indeed, in retelling the story, they delighted in exaggerating his resistance:

And she pleaded with him for one **year** and a second, but he refused to listen to her. She embraced him and held on to him in the house in order to compel him to lie with her, and closed the doors of the house and held on to him; but he left his garment in her hands and **broke the door** and ran away from her to the outside. — *Jubilees* 39:8–9

[Joseph recalls:] How often did the Egyptian woman threaten me with death! How often did she give me over to punishment, and then call me back and threaten me, and when I was unwilling to lie with her, she said to me: You will be my master, and [master] of everything that is in my house, if you will give yourself to me.

[Even after I was imprisoned,] often she sent to me in saying: Consent to fulfill my desire and I will release you from the bonds and deliver you from the darkness. And **not even in thought** did I ever incline to her . . . When I was in her house, she used to bare her arms and breasts and legs, that I might go with her, and she was very beautiful, splendidly adorned in order to beguile me. But the Lord guarded me from her attempts. — *Testament of Joseph* 3:1–3, 9:1–2, 5

Remembered Jacob's Teachings

At the same time, interpreters wondered what it was that had allowed Joseph to remain unswayed by his master's wife, especially in the face of such pressures as described above. What enabled Joseph to resist? The Bible itself seemed to contain one clue:

> But he [Joseph] refused and said to his master's wife: "Lo, having me my master has no concern about anything in the house, and he has put everything that he has in my charge; there is no one greater than me in the house, nor has he kept back anything from me except yourself, in that you are his wife. How then could I do this great wickedness and **sin against God**?"
> —Gen. 39:8–9

Joseph refused to cooperate because it would have been a *sin*. But how could he have known such a thing? Pagan societies might also outlaw adultery, but they certainly would not define it as a "sin against God" (the latter meaning, to ancient interpreters, the one supreme God worshiped by Israel). Thus, Joseph's own words here implied that someone—presumably, his own father, Jacob—had taught him that adultery was a sin against God. Faced with temptation, Joseph must therefore have remembered his father's teachings:

> And his master's wife lifted up her eyes and saw Joseph, and she loved him, and pleaded with him to lie with her. But he did not surrender himself, and he remembered the Lord and what his father Jacob used to read to him from the words of Abraham, that no man is to commit adultery with a woman who has a husband; that there is a death penalty which has been ordained for him in heaven before the most high Lord. And Joseph remembered what he had said and refused to lie with her.
> —Jubilees 39:5–7

> But I remembered the words of my father, and going into my chamber, I wept and prayed to the Lord.
> —Testament of Joseph 3:1–3

> Joseph said, "I will not sin before the Lord God of my father Israel nor in the face of my father Jacob." And the face of his father Jacob, Joseph always kept before his eyes, and he **remembered his father's commandments**.
> —Joseph and Aseneth 7:4–5

> Joseph overcame his impulses because of the strong teaching that he had received from Jacob.
> —Targum Pseudo-Jonathan Gen. 49:24

Saw Jacob's Face

Other interpreters suggested that it was not only the memory of Jacob's teachings, but a strategically timed vision of Jacob's face, that allowed Joseph to stand up in the face of temptation:

> And the **face of his father Jacob** Joseph always kept before his eyes, and he remembered his father's commandments.
>
> —Joseph and Aseneth 7:4–5

> R. Huna said in the name of R. Matna: He saw the image of his father and his desire departed. —*Genesis Rabba* 87:8

> "And she seized him by the garment . . ." [Gen. 39:12]: At that moment, the image of his father entered and appeared to him in a vision.
>
> —b. *Soṭah* 36b

This motif actually has its origin in another part of Jacob's blessing of Joseph at the end of Genesis. Modern translators generally render the difficult Hebrew of this verse as follows:

> Yet his [Joseph's] bow remained unmoved, his arms were made agile, by the hands of the Mighty One of Jacob, by the name of the **Shepherd, the Rock of Israel.** —Gen. 49:24

Ancient interpreters, understanding this verse as a reference to Joseph's resistance to temptation, explained that that resistance came about because Joseph saw[8] the rock (that is, the stone figure or image) of Israel (another name for Jacob). At least the first part of this interpretation appears explicitly in another ancient translation:

> Yet his [Joseph's] bow remained unmoved, his arms were made hasty by his master Jacob; thence there **appeared** the rock of Israel.
>
> —*Samaritan Targum* (M) Gen. 49:24

A Collective Accusation

After Joseph fled from her clutches, leaving his garment behind, Potiphar's wife resolved to turn her frustrated seduction into an accusation of attempted rape:

8. This verb is obtained by pronouncing the word *rō'eh* in Gen. 49:24 ("shepherd") as *rā'āh,* "saw."

And when she saw that he had left his garment in her hand and fled and got out of the house, she called to the people of her household and said to them, "See! A Hebrew man has been brought to us to 'sport' with us—he came into me to lie with me, and I cried out with a loud voice. When he heard that I lifted up my voice and cried, he left his garment with me and fled." —Gen. 39:13–15

Interpreters were struck by one detail in this false accusation. Potiphar's wife suddenly switches to the plural at one point: "A Hebrew man has been brought to *us* to 'sport' with *us*." The "royal we," as we have seen, is rather rare in biblical Hebrew. Why was she suddenly speaking of "us"?

Ancient interpreters concluded that the plurals were no rhetorical flourish. What Potiphar's wife was actually doing was trying to get the people of her household—particularly the female servants and other women—to join her in accusing Joseph. In the biblical narrative she is Joseph's sole accuser, but interpreters concluded from the "we's" that she must have persuaded others to support her story:

Those who accused him [Joseph] she [Wisdom] showed to be false and gave him everlasting honor. —Wisd. 10:14

[Potiphar's wife later tells her husband:] "You have brought to us," she said, "a Hebrew boy as a house-servant, who not only led you astray when you casually and without inquiry set him over your household, but now has had the audacity to dishonor my body. For, not satisfied to have availed himself merely of the **women among his fellow slaves**, he has become utterly lustful and lascivious and has sought to lay his hands upon me, the mistress of the house, as well." —Philo, *On Joseph* 51

"She called to the people of her household . . ." [Gen. 39:14]: She put the righteous one in the mouths of all of them. —*Midrash ha-Gadol* Gen. 39:14

She cried out in a loud voice and her servants assembled in order to be witnesses for her, [attesting] not to what she had [actually] wanted to do, but to what she wished to claim. —Ephraem, *Commentary on Genesis* 35:1

On that particular day, they all went to their idolatrous rites, but she made herself out to be sick. When her [female] friends came back, they went to visit her. They said to her: What is wrong that your face is thus? She told them the entire episode. They said to her: You have no remedy but to tell your husband thus and so, so that he will shut him [Joseph] up in prison. She said to them: I beg of you—each of you say that he also sought the same from you. And so they did.

— *Midrash Abkir* in *Yalqut Shimoni* Gen. 39:14

Pharaoh's Servants Applauded

Clamped into prison because of his mistress's false accusation, Joseph did not lose hope, and soon enough, his rescue came. Having successfully interpreted the dreams of his cellmates, Pharaoh's chief butler and baker, he eventually came to the attention of Pharaoh himself. Joseph's interpretation of Pharaoh's dream then led to his rapid ascent:

This proposal [concerning the coming famine and how to head it off] seemed good to Pharaoh and to all his servants. And Pharaoh said to his servants, "Can we find such a man as this, in whom is the spirit of God?" So Pharaoh said to Joseph, "Since God has shown you all this, there is none so wise and discerning as you are; you shall be over my house and all my people shall order themselves as you command; only as regards the throne will I be greater than you."   —Gen. 41:37–40

Thus, in a matter of a few hours, Joseph rose from the status of prisoner to second-in-command of all of Egypt!

Interpreters noticed, however, that Pharaoh's advisers never answered his question—"Can we find such a man as this, in whom is the spirit of God?" On the one hand, the text says that Joseph's interpretation and proposal "seemed good" to them, so perhaps they were happy at Joseph's rise to power.

All of the pharaoh's princes, all of his servants, and all who were doing the king's work loved him because he conducted himself in a just way.

— *Jubilees* 40:8

The king, having heard both his interpretation of the dreams, so exactly and skilfully divining the truth, and his advice to all appearance most profitable in its foresight for the uncertainties of the future, bade his companions come closer to him so that Joseph might not hear, and said: "Sirs, shall we find another man such as this, who has in him the spirit of God?" When they with one accord praised and applauded his words . . .   — Philo, *On Joseph* 116, 119

Joseph Had Been Scorned

On the other hand, professional jealousy being as common in ancient times as in modern ones, some interpreters assumed that Pharaoh's question had gone unanswered because his advisers could not bring themselves to praise Joseph. After all, had he not been introduced to Pharaoh a few minutes earlier with the disdainful description "a boy, a Hebrew, a slave" (Gen. 41:12)? Perhaps this description captured what most Egyptians thought of Joseph:

> [Aseneth answers her father's proposal that she marry Joseph:] Why does my lord and father speak words such as these, to hand me over, like a captive, to a man [who is] an **alien**, and a **fugitive**, and was **sold** [as a slave]?
>
> *— Joseph and Aseneth 4:9–11*

> Said R. Samuel b. Naḥmani: Cursed are the wicked, for [even when they wish to], they cannot perform a good deed properly. [Thus, the chief butler said:] a youth, that is, a fool; a Hebrew, that is, someone different [from us]; and a slave, for it had been established by Pharaoh in the royal writings that a slave could not become king.
>
> *— Genesis Rabba 89:7*

In short: Joseph was his father's favorite because he was exceptionally intelligent, as well as because he resembled Jacob in all things. His brothers hated him because of their father's favoritism, and because Joseph had reported on their activities while shepherding their flocks. After they sold Joseph as a slave, they used the money to buy shoes. Joseph's greatest act, and the key to his later success, was his resistance to temptation while a slave in Potiphar's house. He was never tempted by Potiphar's wife, because the memory of his father's teachings, and/or a sudden vision of his father's face, saved him from error. In Pharaoh's court, his wisdom was so dazzling that all approved him for high office—although his apparently lowly origins may nonetheless have caused resentment.

15

Jacob's Sons
in Egypt

(GENESIS 42–50)

Jacob blessed his sons and Joseph's at the end of his life.

Jacob's Sons
in Egypt

(GENESIS 42–50)

❖   ❖   ❖

Famine now descended on Egypt, just as Joseph had predicted, and it was not long before Joseph's brothers went down to Egypt in search of grain. When they came before the Egyptian official in charge of grain distribution— Joseph himself—they did not recognize him. He recognized them, however, and accusing them of being spies, threw them into jail. After three days, Joseph set them free, on the condition that they return with their youngest brother, Benjamin, who had not accompanied them to Egypt. Joseph also kept Simeon as a prisoner, to make sure that they would indeed return.

After some time (for Jacob was reluctant to let his youngest son leave), the brothers did return with Benjamin, and Joseph invited them to his house to a feast, while still keeping his identity secret. Afterward, he gave them fresh sacks of grain and sent them on their way. However, Joseph had instructed his steward to hide his silver goblet in Benjamin's sack, and once the brothers had left, he sent his steward in pursuit in order to accuse them of having stolen the goblet. When the goblet was indeed found in Benjamin's sack, Benjamin was seized as the thief. The brothers returned to Joseph, and Judah intervened, offering to be imprisoned himself in Benjamin's place.

Now Joseph could no longer restrain himself; he burst into tears and said, "I am Joseph." He assured his stupefied brothers that he bore them no resentment and told them to go to Canaan and return with their father, Jacob, so that they might all live in Egypt together. This they did, and Jacob and his sons and grandchildren settled in the land of Goshen. Before his death, Jacob blessed Joseph's two sons, Ephraim and Manasseh. Then he blessed his own sons, each in turn, and asked that, after he died, they make sure to return him for burial in Canaan. They did as he asked. Some time later, just before his own death, Joseph was to make a similar request: "When God remembers you and brings you up out of this land . . . you shall carry up my bones from here."

AFTER REVEALING his true identity to his brothers, Joseph was quick to reassure them of his good will, even though they had sold him as a slave and caused him so much hardship. "Do not be distressed or angry that you sold me here," he said, "for it was God who sent me before you, for sustenance . . . It is not you who sent me here, but God" (Gen. 45:5, 8). Thus, once again, Joseph showed himself to be a model of virtue. His behavior was likewise in keeping the most literal interpretation of God's commandment elsewhere, "You shall not hate your brother in your heart . . . You shall not take vengeance or bear a grudge against the sons of your own people" (Lev. 19:19–20).

A Good Reason for Concealing

But, given these facts, interpreters could not help wondering why Joseph had nevertheless put his brothers through the imprisonment, worry, and suspense that he did. If he did not bear any grudge, why did not Joseph identify himself to them as soon as they came down to Egypt to buy grain?

Interpreters generally believed that Joseph must have had a good reason for concealing his identity. Perhaps the very fact that Joseph's brothers did *not* recognize him struck him as extraordinary—as if it was indeed God's will that he keep his identity secret from them. If so, he only acted in accord with this divine hint, disguising with great effort his warm feelings toward his brothers and (as Scripture says, Gen. 42:7) acting like a stranger toward them when in fact he felt otherwise:

> He [Joseph], seeing those who had sold him, immediately recognized them all, though none of them recognized him. It was not **God's will** to reveal the truth as yet, for cogent reasons which were best at the time kept secret . . . [Joseph] forcibly dominated his feelings and, keeping them under the management of his soul, with a carefully considered purpose, he **pretended** . . . to be hostile and annoyed.
>
> —Philo, *On Joseph* 165

Similarly:

> If, however, it was because of his [Joseph's] greatness and rank and harsh manner of speaking [to them] that they [the brothers] did not recognize him, this was done by God in order that he remain hidden from them until all his dreams had come to pass through the very ones who had sold him so that they [the dreams] would turn out to be false.
>
> —Ephraem, *Commentary on Genesis* 37:7

Another possibility was that Joseph wished to have news of his family but was not sure that he could trust his brothers enough to question them directly:

It was in order to discover news of his father and what had become of him after his own departure that he so acted; he moreover desired to learn the fate of his brother Benjamin, for he feared that, by such a ruse as they had practiced on himself, they might have rid the family of him also. — Josephus, *Jewish Antiquities* 2:99

Joseph Tested His Brothers

Or perhaps it was that Joseph himself was bent on *testing* his brothers, manipulating events so as to see if they would once again be guilty of standing idly by as their younger brother (Benjamin, this time) was unjustly taken from them. If so, the brothers eventually passed Joseph's scrutiny:

And Joseph devised a plan whereby he might learn their thoughts as to whether thoughts of peace prevailed among them.

And Joseph saw that they were all in accord with one another in goodness, and he could not restrain himself, and he told them that he was Joseph. — *Jubilees* 42:25, 43:14

All this and what had gone before was intended to test what feeling they showed under [Joseph's] very eyes toward his own mother's son [Benjamin] . . . This was the reason why he accused them of spying, and questioned them about their family in order to know whether that brother was alive and had not been the victim of a plot . . . This again was why, after inviting them to the hospitality of his table, he entertained his mother's son on a richer scale than the rest, but meanwhile observed each of them to judge from their looks whether they still kept some secret envy . . . Finally . . . he [decided to] pretend that the cup had been stolen and to charge the theft to the youngest, for this would be the clearest way of testing the real feeling of each, and their attachment to the brother thus falsely accused. — Philo, *On Joseph* 232–235

This he did to test his brothers and see whether they would assist Benjamin when he was arrested for theft and in apparent danger, or would abandon him, assured of their own innocence, and return to their father. — Josephus, *Jewish Antiquities* 2:125

Joseph Disdained Revenge

Whatever Joseph's precise motive in keeping his identity a secret, one thing was clear from the Bible: Joseph did not harm his brothers, though he certainly had the power to do so. For interpreters, this was a highly significant point, and one that some did not hesitate to expand upon or embroider:

> Promoted to so high a command, invested with the first office after the king, looked up to by east and west, flushed with the vigor of his prime and the greatness of his power, with the opportunity of revenge in his hands, he might have shown vindictiveness; he did not do so.
>
> [Later, Joseph's brothers] recalled how he saw them straightaway on their first trip [to Egypt], when he certainly could have put them to death or, at the very least, refused to provide them with food against the famine, so, far from taking vengeance, he treated them as worthy of his favor, and indeed, he gave them food for nothing [by later ordering that their money be returned to them].[1]
>
> —Philo, *On Joseph* 165–166, 249

> [Benjamin recalls:] Joseph also urged our father to pray for his brothers, that the Lord would not hold them accountable for their sin which they so wickedly committed against him.   — *Testament of Benjamin* 3:6

> [Simeon says:] And when we went down to Egypt, and he bound me as a spy, I knew that I was suffering justly, and I grieved not. Now Joseph was a good man, and had the Spirit of God within him; being compassionate and full of pity, he bore no malice against men, but loved me just as the rest of his brothers.   — *Testament of Simeon* 4:3–4

> And when we went down to Egypt, Joseph bore no malice against us.
>
> — *Testament of Zebulon* 8:5

> And Joseph recognized his brothers, but was not known by them. And he did not deal vengefully with them, and he sent and summoned his father from the land of Canaan; and he went down to him.[2]
>
> —Pseudo-Philo, *Book of Biblical Antiquities* 8:10

It is clear that, to all these interpreters, Joseph's initial accusation and imprisonment of his brothers as spies, as well as all the subsequent psychological manipulations and machinations, could not have been caused by any linger-

---

1. In the story this detail seems to be part of Joseph's psychological manipulations, but here it is attributed to his generosity toward his brothers.

2. Note that Joseph "did not deal vengefully with them" is all that this author has to say about Joseph's back-and-forth dealings with his brothers. For Pseudo-Philo, the disdaining of revenge was the whole point.

ing resentment on Joseph's part for what his brothers had done to him. He was, on the contrary, utterly forgiving.

Reuben Lost His Inheritance

After Joseph made himself known to his brothers, the whole family was reunited in Egypt and settled there in the rich land of Goshen. But before Jacob died, he made a strange declaration to his son Joseph:

> And now, your two sons, who were born to you in the land of Egypt before I came to you in Egypt, are mine: Ephraim and Manasseh shall be mine, as Reuben and Simeon are. And the offspring born to you afterward shall be yours; they shall inherit from the share of their brothers [Ephraim and Manasseh]. —Gen. 48:5–6

Apparently, what Jacob does here is officially "adopt" Joseph's two sons, Ephraim and Manasseh, for purposes of inheritance. Thus, instead of the two of them later *dividing* what would have been Joseph's fair share of the inheritance, each of them is to get a whole share on his own, just as Reuben, Simeon, and the other brothers will. And so it indeed turned out. When the Israelites returned to their homeland after the exodus, there was not one tribe called "Joseph," but two separate tribes, Ephraim and Manasseh, each with its own (large and fertile) territory.

In effect, then, Joseph ended up acquiring a *double share* of the inheritance for his children. Now this was apparently not an unusual phenomenon in ancient Israel. As a matter of course, the firstborn was given a double share of his father's estate. There was only one trouble. Joseph was not the firstborn, Reuben was. In fact, Jacob's giving him a double share of the inheritance seemed to stand in flagrant contradiction to a law later given to Israel:

> If a man has two wives, and one of them is favored over the other; and if they have both borne him children, the favorite wife and the non-favorite, but the firstborn son belongs to the non-favorite; then on the day when he assigns his possessions as an inheritance to his sons, he may not give preference to the son of the favorite wife over the son of the non-favorite wife, the [real] firstborn. But he shall acknowledge the firstborn, the son of the non-favorite wife, by giving him a double portion of all that he has, for he is indeed the firstborn, and the right of the firstborn belongs to him. —Deut. 21:15–17

This actually sounds strikingly like the case of Jacob and his two wives, Leah and Rachel. For it was clear from the beginning that Rachel was Jacob's favorite; *she* was the one he wanted to marry, and he only ended up with Leah because of Laban's trickery. But Leah had the first child, Reuben. And, as the firstborn, Reuben should have gotten a double portion as his inheritance. Yet it seemed that, by "adopting" Ephraim and Manasseh, Jacob was in fact giving a double portion not to Reuben but to Joseph, Rachel's son. Is it possible that Jacob was going counter to the way of the Torah?

Interpreters certainly would have been troubled by such a thought, were it not for a cryptic passage that suggested otherwise. It comes, once again, in the series of blessings that Jacob gives to each of his sons at the end of Genesis, just before he dies.[3] When he turns to bless Reuben, Jacob says:

> Reuben, you are my firstborn, my might and the beginning of my strength, preeminent in pride and preeminent in power. Unstable as water, you shall not have preeminence, because you went up to your father's bed; then you defiled it, you went up to my couch.
>
> —Gen. 49:3–4

In Hebrew, these words are more difficult than the translation printed above might suggest. (In fact, *all* translations of this passage are partly guesswork, for scholars today are still puzzled by how the words are to be fitted together.) But the phrases "you went up to your father's bed . . . you went up to my couch" seem, at any rate, fairly clear. They apparently allude to an earlier episode in Reuben's life, in which he is said to have had relations with his father's own concubine, Bilhah. Perhaps it was because this incident was so shameful that it had all but been passed over in silence in the earlier Genesis narrative. For it is related there in a single verse, Gen. 35:22 ("While Israel dwelt in that land, Reuben went and lay with Bilhah, his father's concubine; and Israel heard of it").

In any case, years later, when Jacob gives his final blessing to Reuben, he is apparently still thinking of this incident. And what he seems to say is that *because* "you went up to your father's bed," you will not be getting from me what you otherwise might, "you shall not have preeminence." In other words, because you, Reuben, sinned with Bilhah, you will not be getting the double portion that normally goes to the firstborn. Instead (as Jacob's "adoption" of Ephraim and Manasseh in Gen. 48:5–6 suggests), that double portion has been allocated to Joseph.

None of this is stated openly in Jacob's blessing of Reuben. However, this

3. We have already examined two of these, the joint blessing of Simeon and Levi and that of Joseph (see above, Chapters 13 and 14).

interpretation of those ambiguous words is actually found in another passage within the Hebrew Bible. It comes in a section far removed from our story, in a parenthetical remark at the beginning of the book of Chronicles:

> The sons of Reuben, the firstborn of Israel (for he *was* the firstborn; but because he defiled his **father's couch,** his birthright was given to the sons of Joseph the son of Israel, so that he is not enrolled in the genealogy according to that birthright) . . .   —1 Chron. 5:1

Here, quite unambiguously, Reuben is said to have lost his birthright because he "defiled his father's couch." (In fact, this very phrase is quoted from Jacob's blessing, where Jacob says "you *defiled* it, you went up to *my couch*" [Gen. 49:4].)

This same interpretation of Jacob's blessing of Reuben is found, not surprisingly, among the Bible's ancient interpreters. It not only accounted for a somewhat ambiguous biblical text (Gen. 49:3–4), but also explained why Jacob had actually done nothing wrong in "adopting" Ephraim and Manasseh (Gen. 48:5–6) so as to give Joseph a double portion in the inheritance.

> And Israel [Jacob] blessed his sons before he died. And he told them everything that would happen to them in the land of Egypt and he informed them [about] what would happen to them in the last days. And he blessed them and he gave to Joseph a **double portion** in the land. And he slept with his fathers.   —*Jubilees* 45:14–15

> Reuben, you are my firstborn, my strength and the beginning of my sorrow . . . The birthright was yours, and kingship and the high priesthood were destined for you. But because you sinned, Reuben my son, the birthright was given to my son Joseph, and the kingship to Judah, and the high priesthood to Levi's tribe.
>   —*Targum Neophyti* Gen. 49:3

A similar interpretation may appear in this fragmentary text:

> "Reuben, you are my firstborn, the beginning of my strength, preeminent in pride and preeminent in power. You have been wanton as water—you shall not have preeminence. You went up to your father's bed, then you defiled it; he ascended his couch" [≅ Gen. 49:3–4]. The interpretation is that he reproached him because he slept with Bilhah his concubine and he said "You are my firstborn" [. . .] Reuben was the beginning of his order.   —(4Q252) *Genesis Pesher* 4:3–7

But interpreters still could not help wondering what exactly had happened between Reuben and Bilhah. As we have just seen, this episode is recounted in a single verse, Gen. 35:22—as if the whole matter was too awful to mention.[4] How could one of Jacob's sons, the ancestor of the whole tribe of Reuben, have committed such a reprehensible deed? And how could Bilhah, ancestress of two tribes, have cooperated? Seeking the answer to these questions, interpreters found some help in the very words of Jacob's blessing, cited above.

Bilhah Bathing

A number of ancient sources suggest that there were extenuating circumstances in Reuben's crime. He had not simply approached Bilhah with an indecent proposal. Instead, the whole sorry business came about because he had caught sight of her while she was bathing:

> And Reuben saw Bilhah, Rachel's maid, the concubine of his father, bathing in water in a private place, and he loved [desired] her.
>
> *— Jubilees 33:2*

> [Reuben recalls:] Had I not seen Bilhah bathing in a covered place, I would not have fallen into this great iniquity. For my mind taking in the thought of the woman's nakedness would not allow me to sleep until I had done the abominable thing. *— Testament of Reuben 3:11*

The same tradition may be echoed elsewhere:

> Our rabbis said: You [Reuben] sinned **with water,** let one who is drawn from water [that is, Moses] come and bring you back, as it is said, "Let Reuben live and not die" [Deut. 33:6]. *— Genesis Rabba 98:4*

These accounts all reflect a common tradition suggesting that Reuben saw Bilhah bathing. In that sense, then, Reuben's sin was a little like that of David and Bathsheba, which likewise began with David seeing Bathsheba bathing (2 Sam. 11:2). This hardly exonerated Reuben, but the implied comparison might have made his crime seem somewhat less monstrous.

While this interpretation was certainly designed to apologize for Reuben's deed, it is worth pointing out that it is based (however tenuously) on the words of Jacob's blessing:

> Reuben, you are my firstborn, my might and the beginning of my strength, preeminent in pride and preeminent in power. **Unstable as**

---

4. Presumably for similar reasons of modesty, the Mishnah (*Megillah* 4:10) prescribes that this verse not be translated in the synagogue.

water, you shall not have preeminence, because you went up to your father's bed; then you defiled it, you went up to my couch.

—Gen. 49:3–4

The word "unstable" in the above, standard, translation is itself somewhat free, an attempt to make sense of a difficult phrase. The Hebrew word in question more properly means "immoral" or "wanton"—and so it was understood by ancient interpreters. But how can something be as wanton as water— water *isn't* wanton! In the absence of a clear answer, some interpreters apparently combined the reference to "water" with the somewhat similar account of David's sin with Bathsheba in order to suggest that, if Reuben is being compared *to* water (and in a way that did not make much sense), perhaps it was because water itself had something to do with Reuben's crime: Like Bathsheba, Bilhah had been *in water,* bathing, and it was seeing her in her bath that incited Reuben to do what he did. (Indeed, the relatively rare word "wanton" [*pahaz*] may have further brought to mind the Hebrew root *hazah,* "behold, see," and suggested that Reuben had beheld something or someone in water— Bilhah bathing—and had consequently been drawn to sin.)

Bilhah Was Asleep

As for Bilhah, it was significant that Jacob's words make no mention of her. They simply say that Reuben *alone* "went up" to Jacob's bed.

Unstable as water, you [Reuben] shall not have preeminence, because you [singular] went up to your father's bed; then you defiled it, you went up to my couch. —Gen. 49:4

If Reuben alone went up to Jacob's bed, then it must have been that Bilhah was *already in the bed* when Reuben "went up." (Further, if it was *Jacob's* bed, then Jacob must have been away at the time.) Thus, there was no reason not to conclude that Bilhah had in all innocence gone to bed alone that night, indeed, that she was asleep at the time and, hence, a wholly innocent victim.

And he [Reuben] hid himself at night, and he entered the house of Bilhah [at night] and he found her sleeping alone on a bed in her house. And he lay with her, and she awoke and saw, and behold Reuben was lying with her in the bed, and she uncovered the border of her covering and seized him,[5] and cried out when she discovered that

5. It may be that the text here has been confused in the process of transmission; it would make more sense if it said that *he* (Reuben) "uncovered the border of her covering and seized *her,* and *she* cried out when she discovered that it was Reuben."

it was Reuben. And she was ashamed because of him, and released her hand from him, and he fled. —*Jubilees* 33:3–5

[Reuben recalls:] For while our father Jacob had gone to Isaac his father . . . Bilhah became drunk and was asleep uncovered in her chamber. Having then gone in and seen her nakedness, I did the impiety, and leaving her sleeping, I departed.

—*Testament of Reuben* 3:11–15

"You went up to your father's bed"—This indicates that he went in to Bilhah when she was asleep. For this reason she was not cursed [by Jacob] along with him. —Ephraem, *Commentary on Genesis* 42.2

In sum, both participants could point to extenuating circumstances in this sin. Reuben had been led on by the sight of Bilhah in her bath, and Bilhah herself was fast asleep when he had approached to commit his sin.

Jacob Foretold the Future

Jacob blessed each of his children at his bedside. The "blessing" of Reuben (really more of a reprimand than a blessing), as we have just seen, was understood to fill in some of the gaps in the story of Reuben's sin with Bilhah, as well as to explain why the double portion of the firstborn was taken away from Reuben and given to Joseph. Reuben's was thus a highly significant blessing, as were those parts of the blessings of Simeon and Levi and Joseph examined in earlier chapters. But the blessing that was probably the most significant of all for early interpreters was that of Judah. Once again, the words are cryptic, the translation far from certain:

> Judah are you, your brothers shall praise you; your hand shall be on the neck of your enemies, your father's sons shall bow down to you.
> Judah is a lion's whelp; from the prey, my son, you have gone up. He stooped down, he lay as a lion, and as a lioness—who dare rouse him?
> The scepter shall not depart from Judah, nor the ruler's staff from between his feet, until he comes to Shiloh [or "until Shiloh comes"], and to him shall be the obedience of peoples.
> Binding his foal to the vine and his ass's colt to the choice vine, he washes his garments in wine, and his vesture in the blood of grapes; his eyes shall be red with wine, and his teeth white with milk. —Gen. 49:9–12

This passage had great significance for interpreters in part because of the overall framework of Jacob's blessings. As already noted, some of the blessings seemed to talk about past events: Reuben's sin with Bilhah, Joseph's dazzling appearance and his resistance of temptation, Simeon and Levi's attack on the city of Shechem. Yet when Jacob sets out to utter these blessings, he does not say, "Let me tell each of you what I think of you on the basis of your past deeds." Instead he says:

> Gather yourselves together, that I may tell you what shall befall you in
> days to come.   —Gen. 49:1

In other words, however much the blessings make reference to the past, they are essentially predictions of the future—the future of both the individual sons and of the tribes that will spring from them. And this was how interpreters generally viewed them:

> And Israel [Jacob] blessed his sons before he died. And he told them everything that would happen to them in the land of Egypt and he informed them [about] what would happen to them in the last days.[6]
>   —Jubilees 45:14

> After passing seventeen years in Egypt, Jacob fell sick and died. His sons were present at his end, and he offered prayers that they might attain happiness and foretold to them in prophetic words how each of their descendants was destined to find a home in Canaan, as in fact long after came to pass.   —Josephus, Jewish Antiquities 2:194

In short, the blessings contained *predictions,* prophecies. For this reason, the part of Judah's blessing that begins "The scepter shall not depart from Judah. . ." could not but attract attention. In context, of course, these lines clearly refer to the future: in time to come, Jacob is saying, the royal dynasty to be established in Israel will come from Judah's offspring and it "shall not depart." And so it was: King David, who established that dynasty centuries after Jacob's death, was indeed from the tribe of Judah. What Jacob seemed to be predicting, then, was not only that a descendant of Judah—David himself—would end up being king, but also that no one from another tribe would ever take over the kingship, "The scepter shall not depart from Judah."

---

6. The author thus sees a two-tiered set of predictions in Jacob's blessings: some parts have to do with the immediate future ("everything that would happen to them in the land of Egypt"), other parts with the remote future, the "last days." The same dual scheme may also underlie Josephus' words (in the next quotation): Jacob prays for his sons' immediate happiness, but he also prophesies concerning their descendants in Canaan.

Kingship Will Not Depart Forever

But, of course, the scepter *did* depart from Judah. Centuries later, the Jewish homeland was conquered by the Babylonians in 587 B.C.E. The king, scion of the Davidic dynasty, was led away in chains, and never again did a descendant of David sit on the royal throne. Instead, the people of Israel went on to suffer a long period of outside domination by one foreign ruler after the next. As time went on, people yearned more and more for the restoration of the Davidic kingship and the military and political power that went with it.

It was at this point that the words of Jacob's blessing of Judah became particularly significant. For, had Jacob been wrong in saying that "the scepter shall not depart from Judah"? *Perhaps not,* perhaps the meaning of these words was not that someone from Judah would always rule Israel (and, that, as a consequence, Israel would never be ruled by foreigners), but that, on the contrary, no matter how much Israel was dominated by foreign rule, it would eventually regain the rule over its own house, that is, "the scepter shall not depart from Judah *forever.*"

Such an interpretation now seemed virtually required by the words of the next line, "until he comes to Shiloh [or "until Shiloh comes"], and to him shall be the obedience of peoples." For whatever the *other* words meant, the "until" seemed to imply that, sometime in the future, something was going to happen to affect the state of affairs in the previous line. Certainly Jacob did not mean to say that the scepter would not depart *until* such-and-such occurred at Shiloh. First of all, nothing had happened at Shiloh (a city in Israel) or anywhere nearby at the time when the people of Israel lost their "scepter" and independence to the Babylonians. And, second, why should Jacob bless his son Judah by telling him that his tribe would rule *until* such-and-such a time? For these reasons, interpreters understood Jacob to be saying that the scepter would not depart *forever* from Judah, that it would remain, as it were, in storage, until some later point. These words were thus taken as a prediction of the *restoration* of kingship to Judah.

> The ruler shall not depart from the house of Judah, nor the scribe from his children's children **forever.** — *Targum Onqelos* Gen. 49:10

The word "forever" here does not correspond to any word in the Hebrew original of this verse. Instead, it represents a conscious attempt by this translator to make sense of an ancient prophecy. Jacob could not have meant that kingship simply would not depart from Judah, not even once, since that had not turned out to be true. The real meaning must therefore have been that it would not depart forever, that sometime it would be restored. Similarly:

[Judah says:] The Lord will bring upon them factions, and there will be continuous wars in Israel, and my rule shall be ended by a foreign people, **until** the salvation of Israel comes, **until** the God of righteousness appears, so that Jacob may enjoy peace, along with all the nations. He will guard the power of my kingdom forever. For with an oath the Lord swore to me that my kingship will not depart from my seed all the days, **forever.**   — *Testament of Judah* 22:1–3

Here, the author makes explicit that Jacob did *not* mean by "The scepter shall not depart" that Judah would always rule. On the contrary, says Judah, "my rule shall be ended by a foreign people." Foreigners will indeed conquer and rule over us. What, then, did "The scepter shall not depart" mean? It meant that "my kingship will not depart from my posterity *all the days, forever.*"

Another King Will Come

In reading Jacob's blessing of Judah in this fashion, interpreters were not only trying to bring their hopes and dreams to bear on a somewhat ambiguous biblical passage. They were also, consciously or otherwise, reading that passage in the light of other parts of the Bible—God's own words to prophets like Isaiah and Jeremiah assuring them that Israel's fortunes would indeed someday be restored as before. For it was the great message of these and other prophets that a time was coming, and not far off, when divine justice would once again reign supreme, and afflicted, storm-tossed Israel would return to her former greatness.

A number of such prophetic passages seemed to speak of an individual who would bring about or inaugurate this return. Presumably, this individual would be a king in the Davidic line, "a sprout from the stock of Jesse [David's father]" (Isa. 11:1), who would once again bring justice and righteousness to his people.[7] This figure came, in time, to be referred to by the Hebrew word *māšîăḥ* ("anointed one"), originally a somewhat elegant synonym for "king." It entered English as the word "messiah."

Did Jacob's blessing refer to such an individual? Not necessarily. But in saying "The scepter shall not depart" he was certainly alluding to the king's power—and it was only a short step from the king's power to the king or ruler himself. It is thus noteworthy that, from the time of the Septuagint on,

---

7. Numerous other passages from the Hebrew Bible suggest that Israel's savior would come from the house of David and, hence, the tribe of Judah. See also: Jer. 23:5, 30:9, 33:15, 17, 22; Ezek. 34:23–24; 37:24–25; Hos. 3:5; Amos 9:11; Mic. 5:1; Zech. 3:8; 6:11–12.

"scepter" in this verse was sometimes translated or understood as "ruler" (the person) or "king."

> A **ruler** shall not be absent from Judah, nor a **leader** from his loins.
> —Septuagint Gen. 49:10

> A **ruler** will not depart from the tribe of Judah so long as Israel has dominion, and he who sits on David's throne [will not be c]ut off.[8]
> —(4Q252) *Pesher on Genesis* 5:1–2

> The **ruler** shall not depart from the house of Judah, nor the scribe from his children's children forever. — *Targum Onqelos* Gen. 49:10

To these interpreters it seemed that Jacob was prophesying not simply about Israel's return to glory but about a particular individual who would preside over this restoration. "Scepter," as a matter of fact, soon came to be understood as a divine codeword for this messiah, the one who would restore Israel's fortunes. Part of the reason is that another passage, one that also seems to predict the coming of such a king, likewise uses the term "scepter": "A star will proceed from Jacob, and a *scepter* shall rise from Israel" (Num. 24:17).[9] Surely this was no coincidence. If both this verse and Jacob's blessing refer to this future individual as a scepter, it must be that "scepter" is the messiah's official title or nickname.

> Then shall the Scepter of my kingdom shine forth, and from your [that is, Judah's descendants'] root shall arise a stem; and from it shall grow a rod of righteousness to the Gentiles, to judge and to save all that call on the Lord. — *Testament of Judah* 24:5–6

Until a New King Comes

In line with this same tendency, interpreters were inclined to see in the phrase "Until he comes to Shiloh" a further hint about the coming of the expected ruler. The word "until" seemed to imply that this phrase referred to the *time* when the new ruler would arrive.

But what did the city of Shiloh have to do with all this? There was no obvious connection between this old site of a temple (1 Sam. 1:3 and elsewhere) and the future restoration of kingship. Fortunately, the vagaries of the

---

8. This text represents a double translation, Hebrew *šēbeṭ* being represented in the words "ruler" *and* "tribe." The latter part of this sentence is based on Jer. 33:17.

9. This passage is discussed more fully below; see Chapter 24.

Hebrew writing system, and the rules of Hebrew grammar, allowed for other interpretations.

> A ruler shall not be absent from Judah, nor a leader from his loins, until there come the things stored away **for him**; and he is the expectation of the nations. —Septuagint Gen. 49:10

> The ruler shall not depart from the house of Judah, nor the scribe from his children's children forever; until the messiah comes, **to whom** belongs the kingdom, and to him shall the peoples be obedient.
> — *Targum Onqelos* Gen. 49:10

> . . . until there comes the one **to whom** it [in some versions, "the kingdom"] belongs. —Peshitta Gen. 49:10

> Kings shall not cease from the house of Judah, nor yet scribes teaching the law from the sons of his sons, until the time that the anointed king comes, **to whom** belongs the kingdom.
> — *Targum Neophyti* Gen. 49:10

The name "Shiloh" does not appear here at all. Instead, these translators apparently understood the same Hebrew letters as "what is his" or "what belongs to him" (*šellô*)—hence, also, "the things stored away *for him*." Perhaps they were influenced by a similar verse elsewhere in the Bible:

> And you, O unhallowed wicked one, prince of Israel, whose day has come, the time of your final punishment—Thus says the Lord God: Remove the turban, and take off the crown; this shall not be this [that is, "this shall not remain as it is"] . . . A ruin, ruin, ruin I will make it; even this shall not be, until there comes the one **to whom belongs** ['*ašer-lô*, literally, "whose is"] the right, and I shall give it.
> —Ezek. 21:30–33 (some texts, 25–27)

A Ruler of the World

Lastly, interpreters saw in Jacob's words to Judah a hint that this king or leader, once he did arrive, would be no mere local potentate; his arrival would be heralded worldwide. Consider the last clause of the Genesis verse:

> The scepter shall not depart from Judah, nor the ruler's staff from between his feet, until he comes to Shiloh [or "until Shiloh comes"], and to him shall be the obedience of **peoples**. —Gen. 49:10

The mention of "peoples" certainly suggested to interpreters some connection between the promised king and the other nations of the world. However, what exactly that connection would be was far from clear, at least judging by this verse; the word translated as "obedience" here (in Hebrew, *yiqqĕhat*) is rather rare and must have puzzled more than one ancient interpreter.

The Septuagint translators apparently associated it with the root meaning "to expect" or "wait for" (*qwh*). This yielded, approximately: "to [or "for"] him is the expectation of the peoples," or, somewhat more elegantly, "he is the expectation of the nations."

> A ruler shall not be absent from Judah, nor a leader from his loins, until there come the things stored away for him; and he is the expectation of the nations. —Septuagint Gen. 49:10

But this rare word does actually occur in one other place in the Bible, where it seems to have a meaning somewhat different from "expectation":

> The eye that mocks a father and scorns the *yiqqĕhat* of a mother will be plucked out by river ravens and devoured by vultures.
> —Prov. 30:17

The apparent sense of this proverb is that someone who mocks and scorns his parents will die unburied.[10] While the precise sense of the word *yiqqĕhat* is not absolutely clear here either, it seems likely that it refers to something that is normally given or owed to a mother—obedience, respect, and so forth. (This is, in any case, a common theme in Proverbs—see Prov. 1:8, 6:20, 20:20, 23:22, and so on.) If so, then the same word in Jacob's blessing must mean not that nations are "waiting for" or "expecting" him, but that once he arrives, the nations of the world will look to him as children look to their parents—obediently, respectfully, perhaps even fearfully:

> [Isaac blesses Judah:] "Be a prince—you and one of your sons [presumably: in every generation]—for Jacob's sons. May your name and the name of your sons be one that goes and travels around in the **entire earth** and the regions. Then the **nations** will be frightened before you; all the nations will be disturbed; all peoples will be disturbed."[11]
> —*Jubilees* 31:18

10. That is, since he has failed to honor his parents, his children will not honor him, even failing to perform the duty of burial, the most basic filial obligation.

11. It is not certain that the author of *Jubilees* is consciously referring to Gen. 49:10 here—after all, the speaker is Isaac, not Jacob. But Jacob's blessings do not appear in *Jubilees* in any case, and it seems clear that here, as in Gen. 49:10, the subject is the grant of kingship to the tribe of Judah. On

The ruler shall not depart from the house of Judah, nor the scribe from his children's children forever; until the messiah comes, to whom belongs the kingdom, and to him shall the peoples be **obedient.**

— *Targum Onqelos* Gen. 49:10

Kings shall not cease from the house of Judah, nor yet scribes teaching the law from the sons of his sons, until the time that the messiah king comes, to whom belongs the kingdom, and to him shall all the kingdoms be **subservient.** — *Targum Neophyti* Gen. 49:10–11

This last translation in particular reflects belief (supported by other biblical passages, to be sure) in a messiah who will *rule the world.* This notion came to be known to those outside Israel as well:

But what more than all else incited them [the Jews] to war was an ambiguous oracle, likewise found in their Sacred Scriptures, to the effect that at that time one from their country would become ruler of the **world.** This they understood to mean someone of their own race, and many of their wise men went astray in their interpretation of it. The oracle, however, in reality signified the sovereignty of Vespasian, who was proclaimed emperor on Jewish soil.

— Josephus, *Jewish Wars* 6:312–313 (also 3:399–403)

An old and long-standing belief had spread throughout the orient to the effect that it was fated at that time for the rulers of Judaea to hold sway over **all things.** This prediction—which later events showed to have referred to the Roman emperor—the Jews attributed to themselves, and rebelled.

— Suetonius, *Vespasian* 4:5 (see also Tacitus, *History* 5.13)

If the "peoples" in Gen. 49:10 suggested a worldwide ruler, the verse that follows, with its evocation of wine growing and abundant vineyards, was eventually interpreted in keeping with the same idea. For it was not a far jump from the "blood of the grape"—an elegant kenning for wine in Gen. 49:11—to blood pure and simple (cf. Isa. 63:1–6).

How pleasing is the messiah king who is destined to rise from the house of Judah, who girds his loins and goes out to do battle against his enemies and kills kings and rulers, reddening the mountains with

---

balance, therefore, it certainly seems plausible that the mention of the nations' "fright" (the same term in Hebrew means "respect") may indeed be a reflection of the word *yiqqĕhat* in Gen. 49:10 and Prov. 30:17.

the **blood** of their slain and whitening the valleys with the fat of their men. His clothes are wallowed in **blood**, like one who presses grapes.

— Targum Neophyti Gen. 49:10–11

At the same time, worldwide conquest might lead to worldwide peace, the same peace spoken of so frequently by Israel's prophets and visionaries. Perhaps this was another reason for the mention of other "peoples" in Gen. 49:10.

> [Judah says:] The Lord will bring upon them factions, and there will be continuous wars in Israel, and my rule shall be ended by a foreign people, until the salvation of Israel comes, until the God of righteousness appears, so that Jacob may enjoy peace, along with all the **nations.**
>
> *— Testament of Judah* 22:1–2

Why Did Joseph Put It Off?

After Jacob finished blessing his sons, he died, and—in keeping with his wishes (Gen. 47:29–30)—his last remains were transported to Canaan for burial. When Joseph died some years later, he made a similar, but not identical, request:

> And Joseph said to his brothers, "I am about to die; but God will remember you, and bring you up out of this land to the land which he swore to Abraham, to Isaac, and to Jacob." Then Joseph caused the sons of Israel to swear, saying "God will remember you, and you shall carry up my bones from here." *—Gen. 50:24–25*

This request struck ancient interpreters as rather strange. For why indeed did not Joseph ask that his bones be taken up to Canaan right away, as Jacob had requested? Why wait until the time when "God will remember you"? Several answers were proposed:

> And he [Joseph] put them [his brothers] on oath regarding his bones, for he knew that the Egyptians would not take him and bury him in the land of Canaan. For Makamaron, king of Canaan, while living in the land of Assyria, fought in the valley with the king of Egypt . . . and the gate of Egypt was shut, and no one went out of Egypt and no one went in. And Joseph died . . . and they buried him in the land of Egypt.
>
> *— Jubilees* 46:6–8

The bones of Joseph the Egyptians kept in the treasure-houses of the palace, since their wizards told them that at the departure of Joseph's bones there would be darkness and gloom in the whole land and a great plague on the Egyptians, so that even with a lamp no one could recognize his brother.   — *Testament of Simeon* 8:1–3

Joseph was the one who buried his father—and there was none among the brothers greater than him [Joseph] . . . Who then was there greater than Joseph [who might in turn bury him, and so maintain the principle of "buried by someone greater"]? . . . It was Moses who was found worthy [to take care] of Joseph's bones [and for this reason Joseph had to wait for final burial until the time of the Exodus].

— m. *Soṭah* 1:9

According to *Jubilees*, a war had caused the Egyptian border with Canaan to be sealed, so that Joseph's bones could not be transported immediately. Knowing this, Joseph therefore asks his brothers to make sure that he would eventually be buried there. According to the *Testament of Simeon*, the Egyptians were planning to hide Joseph's bones in order to prevent the Exodus and the accompanying plagues, which had been predicted by Pharaoh's "wizards." It is for that reason (for Joseph has been forewarned, or else has foreseen these events himself) that he makes his strange request. According to the Mishnah, Joseph knew that his bones would have to wait until the time of Moses for him to have been buried by someone even greater than himself.

But how did Joseph know that there *would* eventually be an exodus? For he asserts, as if it were a fact known to him, that one day "God will remember you, and bring you up out of this land" (Gen. 50:24). Interpreters concluded that Joseph, like other ancestors of Israel, must have been blessed with prophetic gifts:

By faith Joseph, at the end of his life, made mention of the exodus of the Israelites and gave directions concerning his bones.   — Heb. 11:22

Joseph's statement to his brothers that "God will remember you" indicated to interpreters that the events that were to follow—the enslavement of the Hebrews and their subsequent redemption—were known to Joseph at the moment of his death. Believing that the redemption would indeed come about, he requested "by faith" that his bones be transported at that time.

❖   ❖   ❖

In short: Joseph never sought revenge against his brothers for what they had done to him. Instead, his accusations against them and his manipulations of them were designed to test them or to teach them. Because of his virtue,

Joseph was granted the double portion normally given to the firstborn. Reuben had lost this privilege as a result of his sin with Bilhah, which, however, was not as reprehensible an act as it might have appeared: there had been mitigating circumstances, and Bilhah herself was in any case quite innocent. Jacob's blessings, given to his sons before his death, foretold the future of the people of Israel; in particular, his blessing of Judah predicted a restoration of Israel's fortunes by a future king. Jacob's request to be buried in Canaan was honored immediately after his death. Joseph, however, requested that his remains be brought to Canaan only at the time of the Exodus.

16

Growing Up
in Pharaoh's Court

(EXODUS 1–4)

Pharaoh's wise men predicted a future savior.

Growing Up in Pharaoh's Court

(EXODUS 1–4)

❖   ❖   ❖

Jacob's descendants thus settled down in Egypt. But the Egyptians soon forgot Joseph and all that he had done for them, and they made the Israelites into slaves. Pharaoh, the Egyptian king, even decreed that all newborn Israelite boys were to be thrown into the River Nile. One Israelite mother obeyed this decree, but in such a way as to save her child: she put him into the Nile inside a little box. The baby floated up near Pharaoh's daughter, who was bathing in the river, and she decided to save his life and adopt him as her own. She named him Moses, "drawn up [from the water]."

When Moses was grown, he became aware of his people's suffering and tried to help them. One day, he saw an Egyptian beating a Hebrew man, and Moses killed the Egyptian. But word of this deed soon spread, and Moses fled to Midian to escape punishment. There he married Zipporah, daughter of Jethro, the priest of Midian.

While Moses was in Midian, God spoke to him from a burning bush and told him to return to Egypt in order to free the Israelites and lead them out of Egypt. Moses did not feel qualified for this mission, being "heavy of speech and heavy of tongue," but he reluctantly agreed and headed back to Egypt.

THE BOOK of Exodus introduces us to Moses, the greatest of the prophets and the man who led the people of Israel out of slavery in Egypt and to the land given to them by God. Naturally, ancient readers of the Bible were interested in every detail touching on the life of this central figure, including his early years.

A Plan to Finish Them Off

The story of Moses begins with a brief description of how the Israelites came to be slaves in Egypt:

> And there arose a new king over Egypt, who did not know of Joseph. He said to his people, "Behold, the people of Israel are greater and mightier than we are. Let us deal wisely with them, lest they increase further, and it shall be that when war breaks out, they will join with

our enemies and fight against us, and then will depart from the land."
They therefore set taskmasters over them in order to oppress them
with their burdens, and they built store cities for Pharaoh, Pithom and
Raamses. —Exod. 1:8–11

A number of things in this passage attracted the attention of interpreters, but
perhaps none so much as the phrase used by the Egyptian king "Let us deal
wisely with them." For the word "wisely" brought to mind the fact (attested in
the story of Joseph) that Pharaoh, the Egyptian king, was constantly surrounded by his own circle of wise men and advisers (Gen. 41:8). To whom,
then, could he have been speaking here if not to these same wise men? Indeed,
in saying "Let us deal *wisely* with them," the king seemed not only to be
appealing to these sage advisers for help, but urging them to come up with
some particularly wise plan for dealing with Israel.

So it was that ancient interpreters came to view Pharaoh's various decrees
against the people of Israel as part of some clever plan drawn up by these
advisers. But what was clever about it? Pharaoh's original complaint was that
the Israelites were growing too numerous ("Behold, the people of Israel are
greater and mightier than we are," Exod. 1:9). Interpreters therefore came to
the conclusion that the hard labor decreed by Pharaoh was not really for the
purpose of building cities or the like, but was actually designed to diminish
the Israelite population, perhaps discouraging them from having further
children:

And with the rearing of pyramid after pyramid they **exhausted our
race**, which was thus apprenticed to all manner of crafts and became
inured to toil . . . The Egyptians wished to **finish off** the Israelites with
hard labor. —Josephus, *Jewish Antiquities* 2:203–204

"And He saw our oppression" (Deut. 26:7) . . . this refers to marital
separation, as it is written, "[And God remembered his covenant with
Abraham, with Isaac, and with Jacob] and God saw the Israelites, and
God knew" (Exod. 2:24–25).[1]
—*Passover Haggadah* (cf. *Midrash ha-Gadol* on Deut. 26:7
[*Midrash Tanna'im* 56:7])

1. God's covenant with Abraham, Isaac, and Jacob included the promise of numerous descendants (Gen. 15:5, 17:16, 21:12, 35:11). If later, when the Israelites were in Egypt, the Bible says that God
remembered this covenant and then "saw" the Israelites and "knew" (without saying *what* God
knew), one might conclude by this juxtaposition that God (1) remembered his promise of numerous
descendants, (2) saw how the Israelites had ceased multiplying in Egypt, and (3) knew therefore that
the Israelites were willingly abstaining from marital relations.

"And they embittered their lives with hard labor, with mortar and bricks, and with *all the work in the field*" (Exod. 1:14): Were they working in the fields? Was it not in the city [for the text had just said that "they built store *cities* for Pharaoh," Exod. 1:11]? But the Egyptians had decreed that the Israelite men should sleep out in the fields while the women slept in the cities, in order to prevent them from multiplying further. — *Midrash Abkir* (cited in *Yalqut Shimoni* 163)

Why Only the Boys?

But if the hard labor had been decreed in order to stop the Israelites from increasing, why then did Pharaoh further order that all the Israelites' newborn boys be killed? Interestingly, many interpreters concluded that this new decree was *not* issued because (as the Bible itself seems to indicate, Exod. 1:12) the first strategy had not succeeded. After all, Pharaoh was in a position to make his plans succeed. Moreover, if his purpose in issuing a new decree had been to stop the growth of the Israelite population, it certainly would have made more sense for him to order that newborn *girls* be killed, since, if the boys were now killed and there were, as a consequence, fewer available husbands, this would not necessarily mean fewer Israelite births.[2] Thus, interpreters concluded that the new decree about killing the boys must have had a somewhat different purpose.

> He ordered that the females who were born be allowed to multiply— since woman is, by her natural weakness, unfit for warfare—but that the males be destroyed, so that these would not increase in the various cities. For a mighty abundance of men can be a military outpost [for an invader] which will be hard to capture or get rid of.
> — Philo, *Life of Moses* 1:8

> And the Egyptians answered their king, saying, "Let us kill their males, and we will keep their females so that we may give them to our slaves as wives. And whoever is born from them will be a slave and will serve us." — Pseudo-Philo, *Biblical Antiquities* 9:1

> He ordered all the females born to the Hebrews to be [allowed to be] brought up, since women are unfit for warfare, whereas the males were to be destroyed. — Clement of Alexandria, *Miscellanies* 1.23.2

2. This is because, in biblical times, one man could have several wives. In a polygamous marriage, each wife may theoretically end up having as many children as she would have had if she had a husband all to herself.

What need had Pharaoh to allow the females to stay alive? This is what they said: "We will kill the males and keep the females for wives for ourselves," for the Egyptians were plunged in wantonness.

— *Exodus Rabba* 1:18

A Future Savior

As for Pharaoh's subsequent decree to cast the newborn boys into the Nile (Exod. 1:22), interpreters reasoned that this order must have had yet another, quite separate rationale. Again, it seemed unlikely that the midwives' flimsy pretext (that the Hebrew women gave birth before the midwife could arrive, Exod. 1:19) ought to have deterred Pharaoh from his original plan. Instead, interpreters fixed on the fact that, immediately after telling of Pharaoh's order to cast the boys into the Nile, the Bible goes on to narrate the tale of Moses' birth. If Pharaoh's wise men were indeed so wise, perhaps they had foreseen Moses' birth and told the king that the Israelites' savior—a boy—was indeed about to be born:

> One of the priestly scribes (who were able to foretell the future with extreme accuracy) then announced to the king that there would be born at that time to the Israelites one who, after he was grown up, would bring low the rule of the Egyptians while exalting the Hebrews, and would surpass all in virtue and gain glory never to be forgotten. The king, in keeping with this sage's advice, therefore ordered that any male offspring of the Israelites should be cast into the river and exterminated. — Josephus, *Jewish Antiquities* 2:205–206

> He [Pharaoh] was panicked . . . by those [royal counselors] who, based on the number of years elapsed, declared that the Hebrews were about to be liberated. — Ephraem, *Commentary on Exodus* 1:2

> The wizards said to Pharaoh, "A boy is destined to be born, and he will lead Israel out of Egypt." He [Pharaoh] considered the matter and said: "Cast all the male children into the Nile, and he [this future savior] will be cast in with them." — *Pirqei deR. Eliezer* 48

Jannes and Jambres

Thus, both Pharaoh's initial decision to make the Israelites slaves and his later decrees about killing the newborn boys were more than they might first appear. They were actually attempts by Pharaoh to stave off disaster—to diminish the Israelite population as a whole, and then to kill off the Israelites' future savior at birth. Such were the harsh measures prescribed by Pharaoh's close advisers.

Who were these advisers? They reappear later in the book of Exodus, when Moses, now grown, goes to Pharaoh to gain the Israelites' freedom and matches wits with the men of Pharaoh's court. Once again, however, the text fails to give their names and simply refers to them throughout as Pharaoh's "wise men" or "wizards." Nevertheless, a number of ancient texts do supply names for at least two of these sages, Jannes and Jambres. ("Jannes" seems to be a form of the Hebrew name *Yoḥanan*, "John"; "Jambres" [or "Mamre"] is of uncertain origin):

> In days gone by, Moses and Aaron arose by the hand of the Prince of Lights [that is, the Good Spirit], but Belial [Satan] in his cunning raised up **Yoḥana** [Jannes] **and his brother** when Israel was saved for the first time.　　　　　　　　　　　　　　　— *Damascus Document* 5:17–19

> But understand this, that in the last days there will come times of stress. For men will be lovers of self, lovers of money . . . lovers of pleasure rather than lovers of God, holding the form of religion but denying the power of it . . . As **Jannes and Jambres** opposed Moses, so these men also oppose the truth, men of corrupt mind and counterfeit faith.　　　　　　　　　　　　　　　　　　　　— 2 Tim. 3:1–8

> Then Pharaoh fell asleep, and he saw in his dream, and behold [a great balance, and] all of the land of Egypt was in one scale and a young kid in the other, and the scale with the kid in it outweighed the other scale. Whereupon he sent for the wizards of Egypt and he told them his dream. Then Jannes and Jambres, the chief wizards, spoke up and said to Pharaoh: A son is to be born to the people of Israel, and through him they will bring the land of Egypt to ruin. Therefore, Pharaoh, the king of Egypt, followed their advice and said to the Jewish midwives . . . [Exod. 1:16].　　　　　　　— *Targum Pseudo-Jonathan* Exod. 1:15–16

> [Nicodemus tells Pontius Pilate:] "For Moses also, when he was sent by God into Egypt, did many signs which God commanded him to do before Pharaoh, king of Egypt. And there were there servants of Pharaoh, Jannes and Jambres, and they also did signs not a few which Moses did, and the Egyptians held them as gods, Jannes and Jambres. And since the signs which they did were not from God, they perished as well as those who believed in them."
> 　　　　　　　　　　　　— *Gospel of Nicodemus (Acts of Pilate)* 5:1

Said **Joḥana and Mamra** to Moses, "Are you bringing straw to Ḥafarayim?"[3]
—b. Menaḥot 85a

Now, it is noteworthy that in the biblical account, the unnamed counselors or
wizards of Pharaoh do more than merely give advice. They duplicate Moses'
feat of turning his staff into a snake (Exod. 7:11), and match his skill in turning
the Nile to blood (Exod. 7:22) and summoning the frogs (Exod. 8:7). Even if
they were ultimately outdone by Moses (Exod. 8:18, 9:11), their exploits certainly suggested that these were extraordinary magicians. Soon their abilities
became proverbial:

> [A demon tells king Solomon:] I, King Solomon, am called Abezethi-
> bou . . . I was present at the time when Moses appeared before Phar-
> aoh, king of Egypt, hardening his heart. I am the one whom Jannes
> and Jambres, those who opposed Moses in Egypt, called to their aid. I
> am the adversary of Moses in [performing] wonders and signs.
>
> <div align="right">— <i>Testament of Solomon</i> 25:2–4</div>

> And in the presence [of the ki]ng, he [Jannes] opposed Moses and his
> brother Aaron by doing everything t[hey had done].
>
> <div align="right">— Fragment from putative <i>Jannes and Jambres</i></div>

> There is another magical group, deriving from Moses, Jannes, Lotapes,
> and the Jews, but many thousands of years after Zoroaster.
>
> <div align="right">— Pliny the Elder (d. 79 c.e.), <i>Historia Naturalis</i> 30.2.11</div>

> Next are Jannes and Jambres, Egyptian sacred scribes, men judged to
> be inferior to none in magic, when the Jews were expelled from Egypt.
> They were chosen by the people of Egypt to stand up to Musaeus
> [here, Moses], the leader of the Jews, and a man most powerful in
> prayer to God.   <div align="right">—Numenius (second century c.e.), <i>On the Good</i></div>

> If you find one trivial reason that might have led me to woo Pudentilla
> for the sake of some personal advantage, if you can prove that I have
> made the very slightest profit out of it, I am ready to become Carmen-
> das, Damigeron, that Moses whom you know about, Johannes [Jan-
> nes], Apollobex, Dardanus himself, or any other magician of note
> since the time of Zoroaster and Ostanes.   <div align="right">—Apuleius, <i>Apology</i> ch. 90</div>

---

3. When Moses first performed miracles in Egypt, the Egyptian wizards thought he was, like
them, a mere magician, of which there was no short supply in Egypt. They therefore asked him, "Are
you bringing straw to Ḥafarayim?"—that is, are you bringing coals to Newcastle, supplying Egypt
with what it already has in abundance?

Balaam, Job, and Jethro

A later tradition identified Pharaoh's counselors not as Jannes and Jambres, but as three prominent figures known from elsewhere in the Bible, Balaam, Job, and Jethro. (All three were deemed to have lived in the time of Moses, and all three were non-Israelite sages; for both these reasons, it seemed at least possible that *they* might have been the unnamed wise men of Pharaoh in the book of Exodus.) Of the three, Balaam was judged to have been the one who was truly wicked—in part, no doubt, because of the role he later played during Israel's wanderings in the wilderness (see Chapter 24).

> There were three who counseled [Pharaoh], Balaam, Job, and Jethro. Balaam, who actually counseled [Pharaoh to kill the newborns], was later killed; Job, who was silent, was therefore condemned to suffering [as described in the book of Job]; Jethro, who fled, [was rewarded].
> —b. *Soṭah* 11a

It is interesting, however, that the tradition that identified Balaam as one of Pharaoh's counselors sometimes came to be connected as well with that of Jannes and Jambres. These two were thought to be Balaam's sons or servants:

> And after they [Moses and Aaron] left, Pharaoh sent and called to Balaam the magician and **Jannes and Jambaris** [*sic*] his sons the sorcerers.   — *Chronicles of Moses* (cited in *Yalqut Shimoni* 173)

> And God was angry that he [Balaam] was going to curse them [the Israelites] and the angel of God stood in the road to oppose him, and he [Balaam] was riding on his ass, and his two servants, Jannes and Jamris [*sic*] were with him.   — *Targum Pseudo-Jonathan* Num. 22:22

Death by Water

Instructed by his advisers, Pharaoh first ordered that the newborn Hebrew boys be killed by the midwives at the time of birth, but later issued a new decree to the people as a whole: all newborn boys were to be cast into the Nile. In considering this new order, interpreters wondered why the Bible mentioned the *means* by which the newborn boys should be killed, "cast into the Nile." Some could not but see in this detail a hint of that great principle of divine justice, "measure for measure." For just as Pharaoh now sought to kill off the Israelites with water, so were the Egyptians later punished when Pharaoh's own troops were killed with water at the Red Sea (Exod. 14:28):

Just as the men of Egypt cast their [the Israelites'] sons into the river, so He took revenge on one million, and one thousand strong and ardent men perished on account of one infant whom they threw into the midst of the river.
— *Jubilees* 48:14

When they [the Egyptians] had resolved to kill the infants of your holy ones (although one child [Moses] who had been [thus] exposed was saved), You took from them as punishment a host of their own children, and destroyed them all at once with a mighty flood. — *Wisd.* 18:5

[God speaks to Moses' parents through a prophetic dream:] "Behold, he who will be born from you will be cast forth into the water; likewise, through him the water will be dried up [at the Red Sea]."
— Pseudo-Philo, *Biblical Antiquities* 9:10

By the same measure by which they [the Egyptians] measured out, so was it measured out to them. They said, "Cast every newborn boy into the Nile" [Exod. 1:22], so You measured out to them by the same measure, as it says, "Pharaoh's chariotry and army He cast into the sea" [Exod. 15:4].
— *Mekhilta deR. Ishmael, Shirta* 4 (end)

This idea—that Pharaoh's decree about casting the newborns into the Nile resulted in the Egyptians being punished with water—later came to be combined with the traditions about Pharaoh's wise men. In this new version of the story, it is Pharaoh's counselors who come up with the idea of drowning the newborns in the Nile, but they do so for a rather unusual reason. Their extraordinary sagely powers had led them to consult the greatest source of wisdom of all, the Bible—even before it had been given to mankind!—and, pondering its words, they had come to the conclusion that water was indeed the best means of finishing off the Israelites:

"Come, let us deal wisely . . ." [Pharaoh's counselors replied:] To what shall we sentence the Israelites? If we sentence them [to die] by fire, [we risk divine reprisal], for it is written [in the Bible], "For behold, the Lord shall come with fire" [Isa. 66:15] and "For with fire the Lord passes judgment" [Isa. 66:16]. If we sentence them [to die] by the sword, it likewise says, "and by his sword [He will punish] all flesh" [Isa. 66:16]. Let us therefore sentence them [to die] by water, for God has already sworn that he will nevermore bring a flood into the world, as it is said, "For this is like the waters of Noah to Me: as I swore that the waters of Noah should no more go over the earth . . ." [Isa. 54:9].
What they did not understand was that, while God would never-

more bring a flood over the whole world, upon a single nation he might indeed bring a flood [as he brought the Red Sea down upon the Egyptian soldiery, Exod. 14:28]. What is more, He did not bring it down upon them, but they rushed willingly into the waters, as it says, "And the Egyptians fled into it" [Exod. 14:27]. Hence R. El'azar said: Why is it written, "by the very thing by which they mistreated them . . ." [Exod. 18:11]? They got cooked in their own stewpot.[4]

—b. Soṭa 11a

Schooled in Every Wisdom

Cast into the Nile, Moses ended up being saved by Pharaoh's daughter, who raised him as her own. The Bible says nothing, however, of the education that Moses received in Pharaoh's court. Such a great leader, ancient readers assumed, certainly must have received a proper schooling. But why, then, did the text not mention Moses' education?

To make matters worse, when God later tells Moses to go to Pharaoh in order to argue his people's cause, Moses replies, "Oh my Lord, I am not a man of words . . . but I am *heavy of speech and heavy of tongue*" (Exod. 4:10). Eloquence, in the ancient world, was thought to be largely the result of schooling—and it was one of the most important things a person could possess. Was Moses thus saying that his education had been incomplete, and that this all-important trait was somehow lacking in him? This would have constituted a serious flaw in the eyes of ancient readers (just as, say, most modern political candidates would be at a decided disadvantage if the record showed that they had dropped out of high school). And in any case, the idea that Moses had *not* received a thorough education was certainly contradicted by the eloquent words he spoke throughout the Bible—and in particular by the book of Deuteronomy, which is, almost from beginning to end, one long, highly eloquent speech uttered by Moses just before his death. For all such reasons, then, ancient interpreters were quick to supply what the book of Exodus had omitted, some account of Moses' schooling:

> [Moses says:]
> Throughout my boyhood years the princess did,

---

4. That is, they had tried to kill the Jews with water, now they themselves were drowned in the Red Sea. The comparison may be strengthened by a pun, for the Hebrew for "mistreated" here (*zādû*) sounds like the same verb used of Jacob when he cooked [*wayyazzed*] the stew he later sold to Esau (Gen. 25:29).

for princely rearing and instruction apt,
provide all things, as though I were her own.
                        —Ezekiel the Tragedian, *Exagōgē* 36–38

Arithmetic, geometry, the lore of meter, rhythm, and harmony, and
the whole subject of music . . . were imparted to him by learned
Egyptians. These further instructed him in the philosophy conveyed in
symbols . . . He had Greeks to teach him the rest of the regular school
course, and the inhabitants of the neighboring countries for Assyrian
literature and the Chaldean science of the heavenly bodies.
                        —Philo, *Life of Moses* 1:23

Pharaoh's daughter adopted him and brought him up as her own son,
and Moses was educated in all the wisdom of Egypt, and he was
powerful in his words and actions.   —Acts 7:21–22

Or perhaps his education was homegrown after all:

[The angel tells Moses:] Afterwards, when you had grown up, you
were brought to the daughter of Pharaoh and you became her son. But
Amram, your [Israelite] father, taught you writing. And after you
completed three weeks [of years, that is, twenty-one years], he brought
you into the royal court.   —*Jubilees* 47:9

When Moses had finished the years of his education, he was taken into
Pharaoh's house.   —Ephraem, *Commentary on Exodus* 2:4

Moses' Speech Defect

If Moses was indeed thoroughly educated, however, it was still necessary to
explain his later words to God, "Oh my Lord, I am not a man of words . . . but
I am heavy of speech and heavy of tongue" (Exod. 4:10). How could someone
schooled in every branch of wisdom, including eloquence, be "heavy of
speech"? It occurred to interpreters that Moses might have been referring here
not to any lacuna in his education, but to an actual speech defect, some
physical deformity of his mouth or tongue that prevented him from speaking
in the usual fashion.[5] There may be a hint of this in one early Greek recounting
of the story of Moses:

---

5. Moses elsewhere describes himself as "uncircumcised of lip" (Exod. 6:12), and this unusual
expression might likewise indicate some physical deformity.

I am not by nature eloquent;
my tongue with difficulty speaks, I stammer,
so that I cannot speak before the king.
— Ezekiel the Tragedian, *Exagōgē* 113–115

He [Moses] pleased his parents by his beauty, but grieved them by his
speech impediment. — Ephraem, *Commentary on Exodus* 2:4

Some interpreters not only maintained that Moses was indeed the victim of a
physical deformity that impeded his speech, but even suggested how he might
have acquired that deformity. Their explanation connected Moses' speech
problems to the tradition (seen above) of Pharaoh's wise men and their
warnings about a boy that might grow up and save Israel:[6]

At one time she [Pharaoh's daughter] brought Moses to her father and
showed him and told him that, having considered the royal succession,
and if God did not will her to have a child of her own, then were this
boy, of such godly appearance and nobility of mind, and whom she
had miraculously received through the grace of the river, brought up
as her own, he might "eventually be made the successor to your own
kingship." Saying these things, she gave the child into her father's
hands, and he took him and, as he embraced him, put his crown on the
child's head as an act of affection toward his daughter. But Moses took
it off and threw it to the ground and, as might befit a young child,
stepped on it with his foot. Now this appeared to hold an evil omen for
the kingdom. Seeing this, the sacred scribe who had foretold how his
[Moses'] birth would bring low the Egyptian empire, rushed headlong
to kill him, and, crying out dreadfully, said: "This, O King, this is the
child whom God had indicated must be killed for us to be out of
danger! He bears witness to the prediction through this act of treading
on your sovereignty and trampling your crown . . ." But Thermouthis
[Pharaoh's daughter] snatched him away, and the king, having been so
predisposed by God (whose care for Moses saved him), shrank back
from killing him. — Josephus, *Jewish Antiquities* 2:232–236

And [after Moses was adopted by Pharaoh's daughter], Pharaoh took
him and embraced him, but he [Moses] took Pharaoh's crown from
off his head and put it on his own head . . . And Pharaoh's counselors

6. The following passages all bear witness to a single tradition. The earliest of them, from
Josephus, shows no awareness of what was clearly the story's original rationale—to explain how
Moses became "heavy of speech and heavy of tongue"—since Josephus makes no mention of the
burning coal or test found in the other versions.

were disturbed: . . . some said to kill him, and some said to burn him. Now Jethro [one of Pharaoh's counselors] was seated among them. He said to them: This child has no sense yet, as you can verify if you bring before him on a platter a piece of gold and a burning coal. If he puts his hand out for the burning coal, then he has no sense and he ought not to be condemned to death; but if he puts his hand forth to the gold, then he does have sense and you should kill him. At once they brought before him a piece of gold and a burning coal, and Moses put forth his hand to take the gold. But the angel Gabriel came and pushed his hand aside and his hand seized the coal and he put it to his mouth with the coal still in it and his tongue was injured, and from this he became "heavy of speech and heavy of tongue" (Exod. 4:10).[7]

— *Exodus Rabba* 1:26

And they brought before the child a charger with burning coals, and a charger with gold red like the fire, saying "If he catches at the gold, it is evident that he took hold of the king's beard purposely, but if he catches at the fire, he did it innocently in his ignorance. And Moses stretched out his hand unto the fire, and sparks stuck on the child's finger, and he cried out, and carried his finger quickly to his mouth, and held it to his tongue, and his tongue was burned; wherefore Moses, the savior of Israel, came to be of slow tongue and stammering in the house of Pharaoh.

— Armenian Apocrypha, *History of Moses* (Issaverdens, pp. 113–114)

Jealous of Moses

Growing up in Pharaoh's court, the young Moses must have become a prominent figure in Egyptian society. Indeed, according to one tradition, his talents and high standing caused others—even the king himself—to be jealous of Moses. It was to escape the king's jealousy, and not because Moses had killed an Egyptian beating a Hebrew, that Moses fled:

When [the Egyptian king] saw the fame of Moses, he was jealous of him and tried to kill him on some pretext . . . But when Aaron, the brother of Moses, found out about the plot, he advised his brother to flee to Arabia.

— Artapanus (cited in Eusebius, *Praeparatio Evangelica* 9.27.7, 17)

7. It seems that this explanation may have been inspired by another biblical passage, that of the call of the prophet Isaiah. For when Isaiah is sanctified for prophecy, an angel touches him on the lips with a burning coal (Isa. 6:6–7).

These [Egyptians] . . . counseled the king to kill him [Moses]. He had in fact arrived on his own at the same course of action, out of envy for Moses' abilities in warfare and of [fear of] his own [concomitant] loss of standing, and so, urged on by these holy sages, he now was prepared to try and kill Moses. He, however, found out about the plot before-hand, and secretly fled. — Josephus, *Jewish Antiquities* 2:254–255

Zipporah the Ethiopian

Moses fled to Midian. No sooner did he arrive there than he acted to save the daughters of Jethro, the priest of Midian, as they watered their flocks at the well.[8] Invited to Jethro's dwelling, Moses soon married one of the daughters, Zipporah, and settled down at his father-in-law's house. Interestingly, later on, the Bible speaks of Moses' having married an *Ethiopian* woman:

> Miriam and Aaron spoke out against Moses, because of the Cushite [Ethiopian] woman whom he had married, for he had indeed married a Cushite woman. — Num. 12:1

In context, it might seem that this was a different wife. Yet, since the text nowhere else mentions this other wife, some interpreters naturally concluded that Zipporah was, in fact, the "Ethiopian" in question.

> [Zipporah introduces herself to Moses:]
> This land, O stranger, all bears Libya's name,
> but tribes of sundry races dwell throughout;
> the **dark-skinned Aethiops.** Yet there is one
> who ruler, prince, and sole commander, he
> rules all this state and judges mortal men;
> a priest, the father of myself and these.
> — Ezekiel the Tragedian, *Exagōgē* 60–65

Moses fled into Midian and there he married Zipporah the daughter of Jethro, who was, as may be surmised from the names of those born from Keturah, of the stock of Abraham, for he [Jethro] was a descendant of Jokshan, who was born to Abraham by Keturah. And from Jokshan was born Dedan, and from Dedan, Reuel, and from Reuel,

---

8. According to the tradition described earlier, Jethro was an adviser in Pharaoh's court. But, of course, the biblical text says that he was the "priest of Midian" who became Moses' father-in-law (Exod. 3:1). How, then, did Jethro get from Pharaoh's court to Midian? As briefly glimpsed above (excerpt from b. *Soṭa* 11a and *Exodus Rabba* 1:9), he was said to have fled Egypt after Pharaoh's wicked decree to kill Israel's newborn boys.

Jethro and Hobab, and from Jethro, Zipporah, whom Moses married
. . . Now, it says that Abraham had sent his sons **to the east** to dwell
there.[9] And it is for this reason that Aaron and Miriam said at Haz-
eroth that Moses had married an Ethiopian woman.

—Demetrius the Chronographer (cited in Eusebius,
Praeparatio Evangelica 9.29.1, 3)

Miriam and Aaron spoke against Moses with regard to the Ethiopian
wife that he had taken—but was not this Ethiopian woman Moses'
own wife Zipporah? For just as an Ethiopian woman's skin is distinct
from that of others, so was Moses' wife Zipporah [distinguished,]
lovely in appearance and beautiful of form, and distinguished in good
deed from all the women of that generation.

—*Targum Neophyti* Num. 12:1

Miraculously Burning Bush

Now established in Midian, the son-in-law of a prominent citizen, Moses
might indeed have lived out his life in peace and prosperity. But one day, God
summoned Moses to return to Egypt to free the Israelites.

The way in which God first called Moses aroused the curiosity of many
interpreters. For, according to the biblical account, Moses saw a wondrous
sight: "And behold! a bush was burning, but the bush was not consumed"
(Exod. 3:2). But, when one thinks about it, what is so wondrous about such a
spectacle? Surely the Creator of the universe could have chosen something
much more dramatic and impressive than a simple thornbush that somehow
keeps on burning! It is not surprising that some early writers, in retelling the
story, therefore felt obliged to change the Bible's description to make it appear
a little more miraculous:

Moses prayed to God that the people might be delivered from their
sufferings. While he was thus supplicating, fire suddenly appeared **up
out of the ground** (he [Artapanus] says), and it burned, **although**

---

9. Gen. 25:6. Demetrius' point is that Zipporah was actually a distant relative of Moses, since
they both descended from Abraham. He derives this idea from Gen. 25:2–3, which says that Abraham
was the father of Jokshan, and Jokshan was the father of Dedan. One old form of Gen. 25:3, reflected
in the Septuagint version, then adds that Dedan was the father of Reuel. Since, according to Exod. 2:18,
Zipporah's father (or, according to Demetrius, grandfather) was called Reuel, it would seem that
Zipporah in fact descended from Abraham. If so, Demetrius argues, then she was not really an
"Ethiopian," but was so called in Num. 12:1 because she was among those descendants of Abraham
that had settled in "the east," a region that included Ethiopia.

there was no firewood nor other wooden substance in that place. Moses was frightened by what happened and he fled. But a divine voice told him to make war against Egypt and to save the Jews and lead them to their ancient homeland.

—Artapanus (cited in Eusebius, *Praeparatio Evangelica* 9.27.21)

One line of interpretation stressed that not only was the bush not consumed by the fire, but its green leaves and fruit were in fact unchanged despite the blaze:

[Moses says:]
Aha! What token this from yonder bush,
some sign beyond belief to mortal men?
A bush that sudden burns, with raging flame,
and yet its shoots remain all green and fresh.

—Ezekiel the Tragedian, *Exagōgē* 90–93

Here it was that he witnessed an amazing prodigy: a fire was ablaze on a bramble-bush, yet had left its **vesture of green and its bloom intact,** nor had one of its **fruit-laden branches** been consumed, although the flame was great and exceeding fierce.

—Josephus, *Jewish Antiquities* 2.266

. . . [the bush was] **green** and not consumed.

— *Targum Neophyti* (marginal note) Exod. 3:2

Moses saw a great miracle, for he saw the bush and it was **blossoming** and shooting up in the midst of the fire.   — *Midrash ha-Gadol* Exod. 3:2

The reason for this particular embellishment is not hard to find. In describing the burning bush, the traditional Hebrew text had referred to the "burning fire" in a somewhat unusual phrase (*labbat 'ēš*) whose first word sounded a bit like the word for "blossom" (*liblēb*). Interpreters apparently took this as a subtle hint that the bush was in fact blossoming despite the fire.[10]

The Medium Was the Message

Others, however, saw in the miracle of the burning bush another purpose. The bush was *in itself* a message. God had chosen to speak to Moses out of a

10. Moreover, the traditional Hebrew text contains an irregular spelling of this phrase (*labbat 'ēš* instead of *lahăbat 'ēš*), one that even more directly suggested the connection with "blossom" (*liblēb*).

burning thornbush because the bush itself would symbolically tell Moses something about Israel's endurance of Egyptian oppression:

> There was a bush, a thorny, puny sort of plant, which, without anyone setting it on fire, suddenly started burning and, although spouting flames from its roots to the tips of its branches, as if it were a mighty fountain, it nonetheless remained unharmed. So it did not burn up, indeed, it appeared rather invulnerable; and it did not serve as fuel for the fire, but seemed to use the fire as *its* fuel. Toward the very center of the flames was a form of extraordinary beauty, which was like nothing seen with the eye, a likeness of divine appearance whose light flashed forth more brightly than the fire, and which one might suppose to have been an image of the One Who Is [God]. But let it rather be called an angel [that is, a herald], for, with a silence more eloquent than any sound, it heralded by means of a sublime vision things that were to happen later on. For the bush was a symbol of those who suffer the flames of injustice, just as the fire symbolized those responsible for it; but that which burned did not burn up, and those who suffered injustice were not to be destroyed by their oppressors.
>
> — Philo, *Life of Moses* 1:65–67

> And why was God revealed to him [Moses] in this way? Because he [Moses] was having his doubts and wondered if the Egyptians might not succeed in destroying Israel. Therefore, God showed him a burning fire, yet it [the bush] was not consumed. He said to him: just as this bush is burning in the fire but is not consumed, so the Egyptians will be unable to destroy Israel.
>
> — *Exodus Rabba* 2:5

"I Am the One Who Is . . ."

From the midst of the burning bush, God commissioned Moses to return to Egypt and free the people of Israel. But Moses protested that he was unfit for the job and, among the reasons for his hesitation, he mentioned the fact that he would be unable even to tell the Israelites the name of the God who had appeared to him, since he himself did not know His name (Exod. 3:14). God's answer, "I am who I am," might at first sound like a polite but firm "Mind your own business." But that could not be God's real intention, since in the very next verse, He does in fact tell him His name. What, then, could "I am who I am" possibly mean?

The word "I-am" in Hebrew sounds somewhat like the proper name of God that appears in the next verse. That name is written in Hebrew with the letters YHWH.[11] Like the word "I-am," this name of God seemed to be derived from the Hebrew root meaning "to be" or "cause to be." Thus, in saying "I am who I am," God might not have been putting Moses off, but revealing to him something about His very nature. So it appeared to the ancient Greek translators of the Bible:

> And God said to Moses, "I am the One who is ["the being One"]." And He said, "Thus shall you say to the children of Israel, 'The One who is' has sent me to you."
> — Septuagint Exod. 3:14

This translation—which clearly seeks to deviate from the biblical text, since there are more literal ways of saying "I am who I am" in Greek—understands God to have been telling Moses something about His nature, "I am the One who is." This translation was of great significance to Greek-speaking Jews, since it resonated with elements of the Greek philosophical tradition; "the One who is" became a way of referring to God.

> All men who were ignorant of God were thus foolish by nature: they could not perceive the **One who is** from the good things that are visible.
> — Wisd. 13:1

> And in this way You spoke to Moses, your faithful and holy servant, in the vision at the bush: I am the One Who Is, this is for Me an eternal name, and a remembrance to generations of generations.
> — Hellenistic Synagogal Prayer, *Apostolic Constitutions* 7.33.6

> I am the **One who is,** but you consider in your heart.
> I am robed with heaven, draped around with sea,
> the earth is the support of my feet, around my body is poured
> the air, the entire chorus of stars revolves around me.
> — *Sibylline Oracles* 1:137–140

> Grace to you and peace from **Him who is** and who was and who is to come.
> — Rev. 1:4

11. Because of its great sanctity, this name ceased to be pronounced by Jews, who systematically substituted for it the Hebrew word for "my Lord" ['ădônay]. Substituting "my Lord" for this name is an old tradition witnessed in many ancient texts, including the Septuagint, which regularly uses the word *Kurios* ("Lord") in its place. Most modern Bibles likewise substitute the word "Lord," writing it in small capitals (Lord) to make clear that the word is a substitute for this proper name of God. Since it has four consonants in Hebrew, the name is sometimes referred to as the Tetragrammaton, from the Greek for "four-letter [name]."

In particular, Philo of Alexandria regularly referred to God in his writings as "the One who is," and on several occasions he set out his own under-standing(s) of God's words to Moses in this passage:

> It follows that no name can legitimately be assigned to the One who truly exists. For, to the prophet [Moses], curious as to what he should answer those who inquire about His name, He said, "I am the One who is," which means that it is my nature to *be*, not to be called.
>
> —Philo, *On the Change of Names* 11

> This is why Moses will say of Him, as best he may in human speech, "I am the One who is," since those who come after Him do not exist in the sense of [true] being, but are merely by reason of appearances said to exist. —Philo, *The Worse Attacks the Better* 160

> [God said:] "I am the One who is" to [express the idea] that, although there are not in God *things* that a man can seize upon, he may still apprehend His existence. —Philo, *On Dreams* 231

"I Am the Eternal . . ."

At the same time, the Hebrew words for "I am who I am" can also be understood as "I will be as I am [now]," or "I will be who I will be," or even "I will cause to be [those] whom I will cause to be." To other interpreters, therefore, this pronouncement seemed to be a statement about God's eternity, or a promise:

> And the Lord said to Moses, "I am who I am," and He said, "Thus shall you say to the Israelites: He who spoke and created the world in the beginning, and who is later [in the time to come] to say *Be* and they shall be—He is the one who sent me to you."
>
> — *Targum Neophyti* Exod. 3:14

> R. Isaac said: God said to Moses: "Say to them: 'I am the One who was, I am the One right now, and I am the One who will be in the time to come. That is why the word "I-am" appears here three times.'"
>
> — *Exodus Rabba* 3:7

Perhaps in this sense:

> I am the Alpha and the Omega, says the Lord God, who is and who was and who is to come, the Almighty. —Rev. 1:8

Somewhat differently:

God said to Moses: "Moses, say to the Israelites that my name is 'I will be who I will be.' And what does 'I will be who I will be' mean? Just as you are [that is, act] with Me, so will I be [act] with you . . . If they [Israel] open [their hands to the poor] and give, so will I open [my hand] to them, 'The Lord will open his treasure-house to you . . .' (Deut. 28:12)." —Midrash Wehizhir, *Mishpatim* (Leipzig ed. p. 85)

An Angel in the Hotel

In the ensuing exchange, God commissioned Moses to return to Egypt and free the Israelites. After much discussion, Moses agreed to accept the mission and set out on the return journey. No sooner had he departed, however, than Moses had an encounter that nearly cost him his life:

> And it happened that, at an inn along the way, the Lord met him [Moses] and sought to kill him. But Zipporah took a flint and cut off her son's foreskin, and touched it to his feet and said, "You are a bridegroom of blood to me," and He left him alone. Thus, it was then that she said "bridegroom of blood" for circumcision.
>
> —Exod. 4:24–26

These verses seemed completely mysterious. Why, having commissioned Moses to return to Egypt, should God then decide to kill him? And why should Zipporah's circumcising her son and her mention of a "bridegroom of blood" have apparently led to God's leaving "him" (Moses?) alone? Even today, most biblical commentators seem baffled by this brief passage.[12]

In grappling with it, ancient interpreters first came to the understandable conclusion that it could not actually have been God who sought to kill Moses. For, not only did that seem quite unlikely in the larger context, but it would have hardly been appropriate for God to "seek to kill" anyone—if He *sought* to kill someone, then that someone would be killed! Moreover, the text does not say "God sought to kill him" (though this is clearly what is implied); it only says "[he] sought to kill him." But if not God, then who?

> It happened that, on the way, in the inn, an **angel of the Lord** met him and sought to kill him. —Septuagint Exod. 4:24

---

12. Its point may in fact be to explain the existence of the expression (apparently well known in biblical times) "bridegroom of blood." The story would seem to be explaining that this phrase does *not* imply that circumcision should or may be performed on a man just before his marriage (as opposed to at infancy), but that "bridegroom of blood" originated at the time when Moses, the "bridegroom" of Zipporah, was saved thanks to being *bloodied* by the circumcision of their son. If so, then "bridegroom of blood" notwithstanding, infancy is the only proper time for circumcision, as the Bible elsewhere maintains (Gen. 17:12).

[A friendly angel later relates:] And you [Moses] know . . . what **Prince Mastema** [a wicked angel] desired to do with you when you returned to Egypt, on the way, when you met him at the shelter. Did he not desire to kill you with all of his might and save the Egyptians from your hand, because he saw that you were sent to execute judgment and vengeance upon the Egyptians? But I delivered you from his hand.

—Jubilees 48:2–4

And it happened that, at an inn along the way, an **angel of the Lord** met him and sought to kill him. — *Targum Onkelos* Exod. 4:24

And Zipporah took a flint and cut the son's foreskin and brought it near the feet of **the Destroyer.** — *Targum Neophyti* 4:25

[Zipporah said after the incident:] "How strong is this blood of circumcision, that it rescued this bridegroom from the **Angel of Death.**" — *Fragment Targum* (P) Exod. 4:26

Circumcision Delayed Is Circumcision Denied

Thus, it was an angel that tried to kill Moses. But why? The biblical text relates that Zipporah managed to save Moses by circumcising her son. This seemed to suggest that circumcision—or, rather, the absence of it—had something to do with the angel's attack on Moses in the first place. For, since God's covenant with Abraham called for all boys to be circumcised eight days after their birth (Gen. 17:12), it seemed only logical that the reason for the attack on Moses at the inn was that Moses had somehow been negligent with regard to this important duty and had failed to circumcise his son within the prescribed time limit. To delay circumcision even for a brief time was to deny its crucial importance.

Great indeed is [the commandment of] circumcision, for there was not the slightest delay concerning it granted [even] to the righteous Moses.
—m. *Nedarim* 3:11

And so, when, along the way, he [Moses] sought to take care of their lodgings[13] and as a consequence neglected the matter of circumcising

---

13. Why would the Bible mention that this incident took place "at the inn" unless it was to hint that the inn had something to do with the reason for the attack? Hence, this interpreter reasons, Moses, in taking care of finding an inn, neglected something more important. Note further that the Hebrew word for "inn" (*malōn*) sounds like the verb for "circumcise" (*mūl*), perhaps suggesting a relationship between the two in the story.

his son Eliezer, "... the Lord met him [Moses] and sought to kill him"
[Exod. 4:24].   — *Exodus Rabba* 5:8

A Prenuptial Agreement

But was Moses really the sort to neglect God's requirements? Given the fact
that his father-in-law was a "priest of Midian," some interpreters were more
inclined to place the blame elsewhere:

> At the time that Moses had said to Jethro, "Give me Zipporah your
> daughter as a wife," Jethro said to him, "Accept this one condition that
> I will tell you and I will give her to you as a wife." He said: "What is it?"
> Jethro said to him: "The son that is born to you first will be given over
> to idolatry [and, hence, not circumcised], those [born] thereafter can
> be given to the worship of [your] God." He accepted this condition ...
> For that reason did the angel seek to kill Moses at the inn, whereupon
> "Zipporah took a flint and cut the foreskin of her son."
> — *Mekhilta deR. Ishmael, Jethro, Amalek*

> And Zipporah took a flint and cut off the foreskin of her son, and
> brought it near the feet of the destroyer and said, "The bridegroom
> [Moses] wanted to circumcise, but **his father-in-law did not allow
> him** to; and now may the blood of this circumcision atone, so that it
> might rescue the bridegroom from the hands of the Angel of Death."
> — *Fragment Targum* (V) Exod. 5:25

Perhaps it was Zipporah who made this stipulation:

> He married Zipporah who bore him two sons: one he circumcised, but
> the other she did not let him circumcise. For she took pride in her
> father and brothers [who were uncircumcised], and although she had
> agreed to be Moses' wife, she did not wish to adopt his religion ... She
> thus allowed one to continue on the circumcision of Abraham, while
> forbidding the other [to be circumcised], through whom her father's
> tradition of the foreskin would be preserved.
> — Ephraem, *Commentary on Exodus* 2:8

Thus Zipporah or her father, Jethro, the Midianite priest, was responsible for
Moses' failing to circumcise his son—and because of it, Moses nearly perished
on his way back to Egypt.

❖   ❖   ❖

In short: Pharaoh consulted his wise men about getting rid of the Israelites, and it was these sages—particularly Jannes and Jambres—who suggested two strategies, one aimed at reducing the Israelite population and the other at killing off Israel's future redeemer. Nevertheless, that redeemer (Moses) was not killed, but grew up in Pharaoh's court, where he was educated in all the ways of wisdom. Once grown, he had to flee to Midian; there he married an "Ethiopian," Jethro's daughter Zipporah. God appeared to Moses in the burning bush, a symbol of the Israelites' future victory over Egypt, and told Moses to return to Egypt. He also revealed to him the secret significance of His name. Moses set out for Egypt, but on the way, an angel tried to kill him for having failed to circumcise his son. Zipporah's swift action saved Moses' life.

17

The Exodus from Egypt

(EXODUS 5–12)

The tenth plague, death of the firstborn:
divine punishment of the Egyptians.

The Exodus from Egypt

(EXODUS 5–12)

❖   ❖   ❖

Back in Egypt, Moses and his brother Aaron now asked Pharaoh to free the Israelites, but he refused and even increased their burdens. As instructed by God, Moses and Aaron then performed a miracle before Pharaoh and his magicians: Aaron's staff turned into a snake, and when the magicians duplicated this feat, Aaron's staff swallowed up theirs. Still, Pharaoh refused to free the people, so God brought down a series of plagues on Egypt: the Nile turned to blood; frogs covered the land; gnats or lice afflicted the people, and their houses were filled with swarming hordes; a plague struck the Egyptian cattle and flocks; boils appeared on the skin of man and beast; hail destroyed much of the Egyptian crop, then locusts ate up the rest; a thick darkness covered the land of Egypt for three days. Despite all these, Pharaoh remained obdurate, for God had "hardened his heart." At last, Moses announced a tenth and final plague from God: every Egyptian firstborn in the land would be killed, after which the Israelites would be allowed to go. He further instructed the people to put lambs' blood on their doorposts and lintels as a sign, and to commemorate their going out of Egypt with a special feast each year. The Israelites requested valuables from the Egyptians, so that they might leave the country with riches.

A Godlike Man

When God sent Moses to meet with Pharaoh, he again objected that he was not a man of words and thus ill-suited for the job. God's reply struck interpreters as particularly significant:

> And the Lord said to Moses, "See, I make you a God to Pharaoh, and
> Aaron your brother shall be your prophet."   —Exod. 7:1

The apparent meaning of these words is: "It does not matter if you are not a man of words; Aaron will speak on your behalf, just as a prophet speaks on behalf of God." Still, that is not exactly what the text says: God actually tells Moses that He is making him a *God* to Pharaoh. This turn of phrase seemed particularly striking in view of the fact that God had said something similar the last time Moses had claimed that he could not speak to Pharaoh: "He

[Aaron] shall be a mouth for you, you shall be to him *as God*" (Exod. 4:16). Surely the fact that Moses had twice been compared to God was no coincidence.

> Beloved of God and men was Moses (may his mention bring good),
> And **He honored him as God**, and kept him strong in the heavens.[1]
>
> —Sir. 45:1–2

Some even concluded, on the basis of this verse (and certain others), that there was indeed something Godlike about Moses, that he was like no other human being on earth:

> [Moses has a prophetic dream:]
> On Sinai's peak I saw what seemed a throne
> so great in size it touched the clouds of heaven.
> Upon it sat a "man"[2] of noble mien,
> becrowned, and with a scepter in one hand,
> while with the other He did beckon me.
> I made approach and stood before the throne.
> He handed o'er the scepter and He bade
> me mount the throne, and gave to me the crown;
> then He himself withdrew from off the throne.
> I gazed upon the whole earth round about:
> things under it and high above the skies.
>
> —Ezekiel the Tragedian, *Exagōgē* 68–78

> I propose to write the life-history of Moses . . . the greatest and most perfect man . . . And did not he [Moses] enjoy an even greater partnership with the Father and Creator of all things, having been found worthy of [being called by] the same form of address? For he was named God and king of the entire nation.[3]
>
> —Philo, *Life of Moses* 1:1, 158

> And He made him as God over the mighty ones, and as a cause of reeling to Pharaoh.   —(4Q374) *Apocryphon of Moses* A

---

1. Ben Sira apparently connects God's calling Moses a "God to Pharaoh" with the tradition of Moses' ascent to heaven at Mt. Sinai (see Chapter 20, "Celestial Sinai"), for he immediately adds, "and kept him strong in the heavens." In other words, his "Godlikeness" was confirmed by his heavenly ascent.

2. The Greek word *phōs* here means "man," but the clear suggestion is that the occupant of this heavenly throne is God.

3. That Moses was also proclaimed "king" is derived from Deut. 33:5, "Then he became king in Jeshurun," on which see Chapter 25.

And so that law-giving [of the Torah], being believed to come from God, has caused this man to be ranked **higher than his own [human] nature**. — Josephus, *Jewish Antiquities* 3:320

He said, "Moses, Moses." He revealed to him that he was to wear **divinity** and prophecy . . . He said [to Moses]: I am the God of your fathers. **Take divinity from Me**, and with it make your prophecy strong. — *Tibat Marqa* 4b, 5b

The idea that Moses was Godlike may seem strange nowadays. Why should interpreters have gone out of their way to find evidence of it in the Bible? Certainly one motivating factor was the very prominence of the Torah (Pentateuch), which Moses delivered to Israel: it was not just *a* prophetic book, but *the* book, the central revelation given to humankind. That made Moses different—not only from ordinary human beings, but even from the other prophets and chosen servants of God. The Bible itself said as much, noting specifically that none of the other prophets could compare to Moses (Num. 12:6–8, Deut. 34:10). Did not all this, as well as some of the specific events that occurred when Moses climbed to the top of Mt. Sinai (see Chapter 20, "Heavenly Moses"), suggest that he was, or became, superhuman, halfway between God and humanity? Of special importance, in this latter context, was the fact that God there told Moses to "come up the mountain to Me" (Exod. 24:12):

The peace of the Lord be on Moses, the man who arrived at a level to which no other man attained . . . And when God said to him, "Come up the mountain to Me" [Exod. 24:12] and he went up to Him and the cloud covered him for six days [Exod. 24:16]; his body became holy and yet holier, and he went up from the domain of humanity to the domain of the angels . . . A holy prophet that went up from the level of men to the level of God. — *Tibat Marqa*, "And Moses Died" 265b, 91b

Perhaps in reaction to this tendency, other interpreters were at pains to insist that, in calling Moses a "God to Pharaoh," God really meant not that Moses was a divine being but only that he was Pharaoh's superior. Indeed, perhaps God was simply paying Moses a compliment:

Behold I have appointed you Pharaoh's **master**, and Aaron your brother will be your **interpreter**. — *Targum Onqelos* Exod. 7:1

What is the meaning of [the assertion] "The Lord of Hosts, He is the king of glory" [Ps. 24]? It means that [as the one who rules over all glory] He can assign part of his glory to those that fear Him. Thus, He is called "God," yet He called Moses "God," as it says, "Behold, I have made you a God to Pharaoh." — *Midrash Tanḥuma, Beha'alotekha 9*

God said to Moses: Wicked Pharaoh has made himself into a god, as it is said, "[Pharaoh declares:] The Nile is mine, I made [it] myself" [Ezek. 29:3], therefore, let him see you and say that you are indeed a god [by comparison, that is, when you bring the plagues on Egypt]. — *Exodus Rabba 8:1*

No Mere Magician's Trick

In any case, God dispatched Moses to Pharaoh's court where, as instructed, he and Aaron performed the miracle with Aaron's staff to show Pharaoh the power of God. Yet interpreters were puzzled by a number of details in the narrative. Why did Moses and Aaron have to resort to what looked like a magician's trick—indeed, why bother "proving" God's power in the first place? Moreover, did not the fact that Pharaoh's magicians managed to duplicate the feat, turning *their* staffs into snakes, seem to imply some basic similarity between God's power and that of pagan deities? This was hardly the sort of lesson the Bible would wish to impart. Finally, was having Aaron's staff-snake swallow those of Pharaoh's magicians really a sufficiently miraculous demonstration of God's superiority?

That such issues concerned ancient interpreters is evident from some of the additions that they introduced in retelling these same events:

> [God and Moses speak as in Exod. 4:2:]
> "Say, what is this you hold within your hand?"
> "A staff, the **chastener of beasts and men**."[4]
> "Now cast it on the ground and move away;
> a fearful serpent you in awe shall see."
> "See, there I cast it down—be gracious, Lord!
> **How dreadful, huge!** Be merciful to me!"
> — *Ezekiel the Tragedian, Exagōgē 120–125*

---

4. The fact that Moses and Aaron used a staff might, after such a description, seem less reminiscent of a magician using a wand; here, it appears only appropriate that a staff be used, since God's purpose is indeed to "chasten beasts and men" through this initial demonstration and the subsequent plagues that the rod summons down on the Egyptians.

The **king said** to perform some sign for him. Moses threw down the staff which he was holding and made it a snake. When **all were terrified**, he seized its tail, picked it up, and made it a staff again.

—Artapanus (cited in Eusebius, *Praeparatio Evangelica* 9.27.27)

(Note that, according to Artapanus, the demonstration comes at Pharaoh's request, rather than, as in the Bible, at the initiative of Moses and Aaron.[5] Still more striking, there is not even any mention here of Pharaoh's wizards duplicating Moses and Aaron's feat, nor does Aaron's snake swallow anything. Sometime later, however, the text notes that, after Moses turned the Nile to blood, "they [the wizards] then, through some superstitious tricks and charms, *made a serpent* and changed the color of the river.")

When all the potentates had been gathered at the palace, Moses' brother took his staff and, gesturing with it so that all could see, cast it down on the ground. At once the staff turned into a snake, and those standing around were aghast. Retreating in fear, they started to flee. However, all the so-called wise men and magicians that were present said to them, "What are you so astonished at? We are not exactly unpracticed in these matters—indeed, we can use our skill to do exactly the same things." With that, each of them cast down the staff that he was holding, and a group of snakes began wriggling around the first one. That snake, however, lifted himself above the others, thrust out his breast, opened his mouth wide, and then, drawing in his breath, scooped up all those around him as fish are scooped up in a net, and drew them to himself. After he had swallowed them, he resumed his original nature and turned back into a staff.

—Philo, *Life of Moses* 1:91–93

They [Pharaoh's wizards] threw their staffs down, and they became snakes. But Moses, undaunted, said: "O King, I hardly disdain Egyptian wisdom, but I should say that the deeds that I do are superior to their magic and their skill in the same way that God's deeds are superior to ordinary human ones. And I shall now demonstrate that my deeds were not [done by] witchcraft or misleading true perception, but that they were miracles done through the providence and power of God." Saying these things, he cast his staff to the earth, command-

---

5. It is true that, while Pharaoh makes no such request in the biblical narrative (Exod. 7:10), that he *would* do so may be implied in God's words (Exod. 7:9). Note further that in the Bible, but not in Artapanus, it is Aaron's staff.

ing it to turn into a serpent. It obeyed and, surrounding the staffs of the Egyptians, which **looked as if** they were snakes, devoured them until they were all gobbled up.   —Josephus, *Jewish Antiquities* 2:285–287

Pharaoh Didn't Realize

God could have freed the Israelites in any manner He chose. He could have instantaneously transported them back to their ancestral homeland, or struck Pharaoh dead as soon as he refused to let them go, or brought about their freedom in some other, immediate fashion. Instead, He took the slow route. Moses repeatedly demanded that Pharaoh free the people, and Pharaoh repeatedly refused, thus bringing down a series of plagues on himself and the Egyptian people. All this was part of the divine plan, the Bible says, for God had purposely "hardened Pharaoh's heart" and *made* him stubborn, causing him to refuse Moses.

Interpreters could not but wonder why God had chosen this course. True, the Bible mentions a number of reasons for God's "hardening Pharaoh's heart." The purpose was to make the Exodus itself a miraculous event, with "signs and wonders" (Exod. 7:3, 10:1); to show to the Egyptians, who worshiped idols, God's exclusive power (Exod. 7:5, 9:16; see also 3 Macc. 2:6); to make God's name great throughout the world (Exod. 9:16, Neh. 9:10); and to ensure that the Israelites might tell of the Exodus for generations to come (Exod. 10:2). Still, it hardly seemed fair for God to have "hardened Pharaoh's heart" and then to punish him and his people as a result.

Struggling with this problem, some concluded that hardening Pharaoh's heart did not actually mean causing him to be stubborn and "hard-hearted." Instead, it meant that God had caused Pharaoh to be (or, rather, remain)[6] undiscerning, preventing him from seeing the obvious, namely, that he was powerless against his real opponent, who was not Moses or the people of Israel, but their God, the one true God. There was good reason to understand the biblical expression "to make [a person's] heart hard [or "heavy"]" as meaning "to make undiscerning."[7] Such an understanding would also accord well with what Pharaoh himself says in Exod. 5:2, "Who is the Lord, that I should heed His voice?" and it would fit as well with what Moses tells Pharaoh later on:

---

6. Pharaoh's hardness of heart may have been his natural disposition in any case, so that God's action only reinforced this natural trait; see Exod. 3:19, 1 Sam. 6:6.

7. See in this sense Isa. 6:10.

As soon as I have gone out of the city, I will stretch out my hands to the Lord; the thunder will cease, and there will be no more hail, so that you may know that the earth is the Lord's. But as for you and your servants, I know that **you do not yet fear the Lord.** — Exod. 9:29–30

It is only much later, at the Red Sea, that the Egyptians at last seem to have understood that "the Lord is fighting for them [the Israelites] against the Egyptians" (Exod. 14:25).

In other words, God had not exactly compelled Pharaoh to refuse, but had only kept Pharaoh and his servants in a state of ignorance, not knowing that God rules the universe or believing that his actions passed unobserved:

> The Lord hardened Pharaoh's heart, **so that he did not know that**
>   **his deeds were revealed to God.**
> His [God's] mercies are shown to all creatures, but His light and
>   His darkness He apportioned to humanity.[8]
>
> — Sir. 16:15–16

> To escape from Your hand is impossible;[9] for the ungodly [Egyptians],
> **who refused to recognize You**, were scourged by the strength of Your
> arm. — Wisd. 16:15–16

> But God **hardened their** [the Egyptians'] **minds** and they did not
> perceive that they were entering the sea.
> — Pseudo-Philo, *Biblical Antiquities* 10:6

> What then? Israel failed to obtain what it sought. The elect obtained it,
> but the rest were **hardened**, as it is written, "God gave them a spirit of
> stupor, eyes that should not see and ears that should not hear, down to
> this very day" [based on Isa. 29:10 and Deut. 29:4]. And David said,
> "Let their table become a snare and a trap, a pitfall and a retribution
> for them; let their eyes be darkened so that they cannot see, and bend
> their backs forever" [Ps. 69:22–23]. — Rom. 11:7–10

> But their [that is, the Israelites'] minds were hardened; for to this day,
> when they read the old covenant, that same veil remains unlifted.
> — 2 Cor. 3:14

8. This verse is somewhat obscure, and it may in any case be a later addition to the original text. The sense seems to be that God shows his mercy [that is, is merciful] to all beings [cf. Ps. 145:9–10], but He does not necessarily reveal His role to all—for example, He "hardened" Pharaoh's heart and kept the Egyptians in darkest ignorance. See also below.

9. Cf. Deut. 33:39, Tobit 13:2.

Divine Punishment of the Egyptians

There was another possibility, however: God hardened Pharaoh's heart and caused him to remain adamant in order to bring down upon him and the Egyptians a series of plagues—plagues that were sent as a punishment for the Egyptians' enslavement and mistreatment of the Israelites for so many years. In other words, the ten plagues did not result from Pharaoh's "hardness of heart" itself; on the contrary, that "hardness of heart" was simply the means for having the Egyptians continue to hold out until they had been fully punished for their earlier crimes:

> And everything happened according to your word, ten great and cruel judgments came upon the land of Egypt, **so that you might execute vengeance upon it** for Israel. And the Lord did everything on account of Israel and according to his covenant which he made with Abraham, that He would take vengeance upon them just as they had made them serve by force. —*Jubilees* 48:7–8 (cf. 18)

> Ten **punishments** afflicted the country—a perfect number for the **chastisement** of those who had sinned to perfection.
> —Philo, *Life of Moses* 96

> You, O Lord, did not ignore the Hebrews when they were being worn down by hard labor under the Egyptians, but, in keeping with the promises to the fathers, You saved them, having **punished** the Egyptians . . . You exacted **vengeance** on the Egyptians with ten plagues.
> —Hellenistic Synagogal Prayer, *Apostolic Constitutions* 8.12.24–26

Now, it is noteworthy that two of the above passages specifically connect this idea of punishing the Egyptians with the promise to Abraham or "promises to the fathers." For, in fact, the idea of the ten plagues as punishment is actually based on the precise wording of God's warning to Abraham about the enslavement of his descendants:

> The Lord said to Abram, "Know of a surety that your descendants will be sojourners in a land that is not theirs, and will be slaves there, and they will be oppressed for four hundred years. But **I will bring judgment** on the nation which they serve, and afterward they shall come out with great possessions." —Gen. 15:13–14

The words "I will bring judgment" suggested to interpreters that the ten plagues were more than God's means of freeing the Israelites, or of showing his glory—they were a way of *punishing* the Egyptians. (To "judge" in Hebrew is not merely to determine the accused person's guilt or innocence, but also to condemn to a certain punishment or even, simply, to punish.) This verse in Genesis (see also Exod. 6:6, 7:4, and so on) thus allowed interpreters to view the whole narrative of the ten plagues in a way that better accorded with their idea of God's justice. So, similarly:

> "For I have hardened his heart and the heart of his people" [Exod. 10:1]—this teaches that he prevented them from repenting so as to exact payment from them.   — *Midrash ha-Gadol* Exod. 10:1

All this notwithstanding, the fact that God had "hardened Pharaoh's heart" and then gone on to punish him and the other Egyptians still seemed problematical. Or was it simply an example of the supremacy of the divine will?

> Is there injustice on God's part? By no means! For He says to Moses, "I will have mercy on whom I have mercy, and I will have compassion on whom I have compassion" [Exod. 33:19]. So it depends not on man's will or exertion, but upon God's mercy. For the Scripture says to Pharaoh, "I have raised you up for the very purpose of showing my power in you, so that my name may be proclaimed in all the earth" [Exod. 9:16]. So then He has mercy upon whomever He wills, and He hardens the heart of whomever He wills.   — Rom. 9:14–18

Deservedly Punished by Water

As to the plagues themselves, was there not something to be learned from their very nature? For, surely, the fact that God had chosen to afflict the Egyptians by doing such things as turning the waters of the Nile to blood must have had some special, hidden significance. Some interpreters, as we have glimpsed briefly (Chapter 16, "Death by Water"), believed that the principle of "measure for measure" generally determined God's choice of punishment, and they did not have trouble finding this principle at work in the various plagues:

> [God afflicted the Nile, creating] an ever-flowing source of streaming water befouled with blood **as a reproach for the decree to kill the infants.**   — Wisd. 11:6–7

Another possibility was that water had been struck first in the plagues because it—or, more specifically, the Nile—had a special place of honor among the Egyptians:

Since the Egyptians accord special honor to water—for they believe it to have been the first element in the creation of the universe—He saw fit to summon the water to be punished first, as a lesson to those who believed it worthy of veneration.   — Philo, *Life of Moses* 1:98

Why did He bring the plague of [turning the Nile to] blood upon them first? Because Pharaoh and the Egyptians worshiped the Nile. God said to Moses: Go and strike their very gods in front of them.

                                            — *Midrash Tanḥuma* (ed. Buber), *Waera* 14

God said to Moses: By the very thing about which he [Pharaoh] boasts—[that is, the Nile] as it is said, "Oh Pharaoh, king of Egypt, great monster that lies in the midst of its streams and says, 'My Nile is mine, I made [it] myself!' [Ezek. 29:3]"—by that very thing shall the afflictions start.   — *Yalqut Shimoni* 182

A Dark Dungeon for Egypt

The plague of darkness, which made the Egyptians into prisoners in their own houses for three days (Exod. 10:23), likewise seemed a perfect punishment for those who had turned the Israelites into prisoners and forced laborers:

For those men [the Egyptians] deserved to be deprived of light and imprisoned in darkness, those who had kept your sons imprisoned, through whom the unextinguishable light of the Torah was later to be given to the world.   — Wisd. 18:4

They [the Egyptians] had planned to keep them [the Israelites] in prison, God brought upon them the [plague of] darkness, as it says, "And one man could not see his fellow, and no one could leave his place for three days" [Exod. 10:23].   — *Midrash Tanḥuma* (ed. Buber) 22a

Metaphorical Darkness

Apart from its role in making the Egyptians themselves prisoners, the darkness that struck the land of Egypt seemed to some to represent the whole Egyptian captivity itself. It was perhaps in thinking of this plague in particular—as well as the association of imprisonment with the dark dungeon—that the Psalmist had described the entire Exodus as a *going forth from darkness:*

> Their hearts were bowed down with hard labor, they fell down,
>   with no one to help.
> Then they cried to the Lord in their trouble, and He delivered
>   them from their distress.
> He took them **out of darkness and deep shadows**, and snapped
>   their chains.
>   — Ps. 107:12-14

Little wonder, then, that ancient interpreters should employ the same imagery in their descriptions of, or allusions to, the Exodus:[10]

> But you are a chosen race, a royal priesthood, a holy nation, God's own people, that you may declare the wonderful deeds of Him who called you out of darkness into his marvelous light.   — 1 Pet. 2:9

> Therefore we shall acknowledge and praise and sing and glorify and exalt . . . the One who performed for our ancestors—and for us—all these miracles: He took us out of slavery into freedom, and from suffering to joy, from mourning to celebration, and from darkness to great light.[11]   — m. Pesaḥim 10:5

Justifiable Death for the Firstborn

The final plague, which brought death to the Egyptians' firstborn children and even to the firstborn of their cattle, was the most severe of all. Perhaps such a deadly plague was necessary for Pharaoh finally to realize the error of his ways:

> [God says:] Pharaoh won't be moved by what I say
> until his firstborn child lies as a corpse;
> then, moved with fear, he'll send the people forth.
>   — Ezekiel the Tragedian, *Exagōgē* 147–150

Still, the very nature of this plague raised great questions for interpreters. Even if it was necessary to kill Pharaoh's firstborn, was it likewise required to kill the firstborn of all the other Egyptians, and even harmless beasts? True, some saw once more, in this plague, the principle of "measure for measure":

10. This theme may also be present in the verse in Ben Sira that, in one version, reads: "The Lord hardened Pharaoh's heart, so that he did not know that his deeds were revealed to God. His [God's] mercies are shown to all creatures, but his *light and his darkness* he apportioned to humanity" (Sir. 16:15–16).

11. Cf. Isa. 9:1: "The people that walked in darkness saw *a great light,* and light broke forth on those who dwelt in a land of deep shadow."

When they [the Egyptians] had resolved to kill the infants of your holy ones (although one child [Moses] who had been [thus] exposed was saved) You took from them as punishment a host of their own children.
—Wisd. 18:5

But other interpreters were apparently bothered by what happened to the Egyptians, and they sought to put the best face possible on this divine decree:

After this there came the tenth and final judgment surpassing all the previous ones: [it was] not the killing of *all* the Egyptians—for God had not intended that the whole country be turned to a wasteland, only that it be admonished—nor even that of the majority of men and women of all ages. These others He permitted to live, and death was decreed only for the firstborn, starting with the eldest of the king's own sons and ending with that of the lowly grinder-woman.
—Philo, *Life of Moses* 1:134

". . . from the firstborn of Pharaoh who sat on the throne to the firstborn of the prisoner confined to the dungeon . . ." [Exod. 12:29]. Had the prisoners done anything wrong [to be so punished]? But it was [the fact] that they had rejoiced at Israel's troubles and had said, "We do not mind being prisoners, so long as Israel is suffering . . ." . . . But then why does the verse continue, ". . . and all the firstborn cattle" [Exod. 12:29]—even if these others [that is, the prisoners] had sinned, what did the cattle do? But it was [the fact] that cattle were worshiped by the Egyptians [as witnessed by Exod. 8:26]. [They were killed] so that the Egyptians should not therefore say, "Our [object of] worship is stronger, for it withstood the decrees of God."
—*Midrash Wehizhir, Bo* p. 5

Egyptians Gave Willingly

After the last plague had befallen Egypt, Pharaoh finally relented and the Israelites were free to go. They did not, however, depart empty-handed. From the beginning, God had intended that the Israelites leave with some of the Egyptians' own prize possessions. He had said as much to Abraham:

The Lord said to Abram, ". . . I will bring judgment on the nation which they serve, and afterward they shall come out with **great possessions.**"
—Gen. 15:13–14

Surely these "great possessions" were not their own, for the Israelites were miserable slaves. Where would these riches come from? God had explained to Moses from the burning bush on Mt. Horeb:

> And I will give this people favor in the sight of the Egyptians, so that when you go, you shall not go empty-handed, but each woman shall ask of her neighbor, and of the woman who dwells in her house, jewelry of silver and gold, and clothing, and you shall put them on your sons and on your daughters; thus you shall **despoil** the Egyptians.
> —Exod. 3:21–22

There was something extremely troubling in this whole matter. To begin with, the verb translated as "ask" above is also the normal word for "borrow"—and borrowing, in context, seemed the more likely meaning. After all, would the Egyptian women give away their valuable silver and gold or clothing (which, in those days, was also a thing of great value) to the Israelites just because they had "asked" for them? It seemed, therefore, more likely that the Israelite women were to borrow these possessions. And was it not in that sense (since the possessions were never to be returned) that they were said to "despoil" the Egyptians?

God repeated these instructions to Moses just before the last plague:

> Speak now in the hearing of the people, that they ask, every man of his neighbor and every woman of her neighbor, jewelry of silver and gold.
> —Exod. 11:2

The timing of this reminder certainly seemed designed to fit a possible deception, for the items were to be requested *before* the last plague, that is, before it was clear that the Israelites were leaving for good. Moreover, the phrase "speak *in the hearing of* the people" literally means "in the ears of." Did this not suggest some sort of secret communication?

> Speak therefore **secretly** in the ears of the people.
> —Septuagint Exod. 11:2

Perhaps most condemning, though, is the Bible's description of the event after it had taken place:

> The people of Israel had also done as Moses told them, for they had asked of the Egyptians jewelry of silver and of gold, and clothing, and

the Lord had given the people favor in the sight of the Egyptians, so they had **lent** to them. And they despoiled the Egyptians.

—Exod. 12:35–36

Here, the Hebrew (and the Greek of the Septuagint, for that matter) seem to leave little doubt that the Egyptians had merely *lent* their valuables to their neighbors. And so, the whole thing sounded highly questionable to interpreters, as if the Israelites indeed despoiled the Egyptians, and on God's instructions!

In considering these matters, many were no doubt troubled. There was, however, one small Scriptural warrant for viewing things in a more positive fashion. For the book of Psalms, in describing the same events, had said:

> Then He led forth Israel with silver and gold, and not one of His
> tribes gave way.
> Egypt was **glad** when they left, for fear of them had fallen upon it.

—Ps. 105:37–38

If Egypt was glad when they left, then it could not have been the case that the Israelites had tricked the Egyptians into lending them their silver and gold, otherwise the Egyptians would have been quite distressed and angry when they found out the Israelites were going (or at least, certainly, not "glad"). Here, then, was proof, albeit somewhat slender, from the Bible itself that no fraud had occurred.

But then why had the Egyptians willingly parted with their valuables? Perhaps it was, as the Psalmist suggested, because the Egyptians wished to speed them on their way at any cost, or perhaps it was, as the mention of "neighbors" in Exod. 3:21 and 11:2 might suggest, because of some personal tie between individual Egyptians and Israelites. Indeed, it might have been a combination of both:

> They honored the Hebrews with gifts; some [did so] so that they [the Hebrews] might depart more quickly, others because of the neighborly relations that they had had with them.

—Josephus, *Jewish Antiquities* 2:314

Fair Wages at Last

To other interpreters, however, another logic suggested itself: the Egyptians' gold and silver was not so much a gift as a repayment, compensation for the years of hard toil the Israelites had given Egypt without wages. After all, in the passage cited above, God had told Abraham,

But I will bring judgment on the nation which they serve, and afterward they shall come out with great possessions.   — Gen. 15:14

Did not this juxtaposition suggest that the "great possessions" were also part
of God's "bringing judgment" on the Egyptians—that, as it were, the Egyptians had been sentenced by God to lose their gold and silver in compensation? Thus, if the text said the Israelites had "asked" for these valuables, then
this request had been granted for the simple reason that the Egyptians knew
full well that the money was owed to the Israelites in any case:

> But ere you go I'll grant the people favor;
> one woman from another shall receive
> fine vessels, jewels of silver and of gold
> and clothing, things which one may carry off,[12]
> so as to **compensate them for their deeds.**
>   — Ezekiel the Tragedian, *Exagōgē* 162–166

They asked the Egyptians for vessels and garments, vessels of silver,
and vessels of gold, and vessels of bronze,[13] in order to despoil the
Egyptians in return for the bondage in which they had forced them to
serve.   — *Jubilees* 48:18

She [Wisdom] entered the soul of a servant of the Lord [Moses], and
withstood dread kings with signs and wonders. She gave to holy men
the **reward for their labors** ... Therefore the righteous plundered the
ungodly.   — Wisd. 10:16–17, 20

For they took with them great spoils ... not out of any love of lucre,
nor, as their accusers would have it, out of covetousness for the property of others (whence could one get such an idea?). But, first of all,
they were thus simply receiving the wages owed to them for their
service all that time; and, secondly, they were taking some revenge [on
the Egyptians] for having been made into slaves—and in a lesser

---

12. This specification that the items were portable seems designed not to tell us anything about
the nature of the gifts per se, but to supply another "proof" that the Israelites had not defrauded the
Egyptians. For the Egyptians certainly knew that such valuables are easily walked off with; if they
nonetheless gave them to the Israelites, it must have been in the knowledge that this was a true gift,
and not a loan.

13. These "vessels of bronze" are nowhere mentioned in the biblical passages cited. They are
apparently added here because, after the Israelites embark on their desert wanderings, they are
instructed to build a tabernacle, many of whose parts are made of bronze (see Chapter 21). The
Israelites presumably brought with them from Egypt that bronze, along with the silver and gold and
other fine things mentioned in connection with the tabernacle.

degree and not as would be fair, for who can compare mere monetary loss to the loss of one's freedom, when, for his freedom, any thinking man is prepared to sacrifice not merely his personal property, but life itself?
— Philo, *Life of Moses* 141

The Egyptians [once lodged a complaint against the Jews centuries after the Exodus and] said: It is written in the Torah, "Let every woman ask of her neighbor jewelry of silver and gold . . ." [Exod. 11:2]. Now give us back what is ours! Gebiha replied: For four hundred and thirty years Israel was enslaved in your midst, six hundred thousand people [in all]: give each of them two hundred *zuz* per year, which totals eight million six hundred thousand *mina*, and then we will return to you what is yours!
— *Megillat Ta'anit* (ms. Oxford; cf. Lichtenstein, p. 330)

But why had Scripture so emphasized these treasures taken by the Israelites on their way out of Egypt? Certainly, the fact that the Israelites were later to use silver and gold and other precious things in the building of the tabernacle (see Chapter 21) demanded explanation: these valuables, it seemed, had come from the Egyptian booty. But to those of an allegorical bent, this fact seemed in itself to contain a lesson about the relationship of ordinary, secular learning—corresponding to the Egyptians' goods—to the sacred learning found in Scripture. For secular learning was

as poor as the store of gold and silver and clothing that the people of Israel brought with them out of Egypt in comparison with the riches they afterward attained in Jerusalem and reached their height in the reign of King Solomon.
— Augustine, *De Doctrina Christiana* 2.42.63

All such readings notwithstanding, some interpreters nevertheless took the text at face-value: not only did they conclude that the Israelites had indeed "borrowed" the Egyptians' goods, they even imagined the sort of excuse the Israelites might have come up with to make such a borrowing plausible:

And the Lord said to Moses: Let not one of you go out empty-handed, but let a woman go to a neighbor-woman and request apparel, saying, Give [this] to me so that I may adorn myself before my God, and I will bring it back to you. And let the men do likewise[14] and take with them all the beauty of Egypt.
— *Historical Paleya* (Popov p. 74)

14. The mention of the men brings Exod. 3:22, which speaks of women asking their (female) neighbors, in line with Exod. 11:2, which specifically includes men.

The Symbolic Passover Laws

After Moses announced the tenth and last plague, he gave Israel its first collective commandments, namely, the various requirements connected with the observance of the first Passover (Exod. 12:1–28). Since, from this point on, the Pentateuch regularly contains all sorts of laws and instructions about various matters in daily life, this first speech was seen by interpreters as a particularly significant event.

To some, it was noteworthy that the Passover sacrifice was to be performed by everyone (Exod. 12:3)—not just the priests or members of one tribe, but all of Israel together:

> For . . . the devout children of good folk brought sacrifices and **with one accord** established the divine law, so that the holy people **shared all the same things**, both blessings and dangers.   —Wisd. 18:9

> In this month, about the fourteenth day, when the moon is becoming full, is held the commemoration of the crossing, a public festival called in Hebrew *Pascha* . . . on which the **whole nation** acts as priest, each individual bringing what he offers on his own behalf and dealing with it with his own hands . . . On this occasion the whole nation performs the sacred rites and acts as priest.
> —Philo, *Moses* 2:224 (also *Special Laws* 2:145)

The other details of the procedure outlined struck readers as strange: the sacrifical lamb of each household was to be killed in the evening, then a bunch of hyssop was to be dipped into its blood and touched to the lintel and two doorposts (Exod. 12:7, 22). No bone of the sacrificial animal was to be broken (Exod. 12:46), and its meat was to be eaten with unleavened bread, that is, flat bread specially prepared without any yeast (Exod. 12:8, 15). All this was to be eaten with "your loins girded and your sandals on your feet" (Exod. 12:11). Certainly requirements such as these contained some hidden message:

> They shall roast it in fire without breaking any of its bones within it because no bone of the children of Israel will be broken. Therefore the Lord commanded the children of Israel to observe the Passover on its appointed day. And it is not fitting to break any bone from it because it is the day of the feast and it is the day of the command.
> —*Jubilees* 49:13–14

"They baked their dough which they brought out of Egypt into unleavened cakes" [Exod. 12:39], that is, they kneaded the savage, un-

tamed passion with the aid of reason that softened it as though it were food.
　　　　　　　　　　　　　　　　　　　—Philo, *Cain and Abel* 62

That which is leavened and fermented rises, while that which is unleavened is low. Each of these is a symbol of types of soul, one being haughty and swollen with arrogance, the other being unchangeable and prudent, choosing the middle way rather than extremes because of a desire and zeal for equality.
　　　　　　　　　　　—Philo, *Questions and Answers in Exodus* 1.15

That is why we have been commanded to "eat the unleavened bread with bitter herbs" [Exod. 12:8]—not as a relish, but because the mass of men . . . think that the unlearning of passion is a [source of] bitterness, though to a mind that welcomes effort it is really a joy and a feast.　　　　　　　　　　　　—Philo, *Preliminary Studies* 162

Why does He command to place some of the blood upon the doorposts and upon the lintel of every house? . . . Since our soul is threefold, the heart is compared to the lintel, desire to the house, and reason to the two doorposts.　　　—Philo, *Questions and Answers in Exodus* 1.13

"And you shall take a bunch of hyssop . . ." [Exod. 12:22]: For they [the Israelites] had made themselves as lowly as the hyssop [see 1 Kings 4:33 (other texts, 5:13)] in repenting of their sins . . . "and daub it upon the lintel" [Exod. 12:22. This represents] Abraham . . . for just as the lintel is high up, so was he the greatest of the patriarchs; ". . . and on the two doorposts . . ." [Exod. 12:22. that is,] through the merit of Isaac and Jacob. All this teaches us that it was by virtue of these [ancestors] that they [the Israelites] left Egypt.　　　　　　　—*Exodus Rabba* 1:36

The (Paschal) Lamb of Christianity

A central idea of early Christianity was that the crucifixion itself was comparable to a sacrificial offering—the ultimate sacrifice, after which none would be necessary. Since the crucifixion took place at the time of the Passover holiday (Mark 14:12 and elsewhere), a special correspondence between the laws regarding the Passover sacrifice and the events recounted in the Gospels was assumed:

But when they [the Roman soldiers] came to Jesus and saw that he was already dead, they did not break his legs . . . For these things took place that the Scripture might be fulfilled, "Not a bone of him [the Passover lamb] shall be broken."

—John 19:33–36 (see also 1:29, Rev. 5:6–12, 6:1, etc.)

For Christ, our paschal lamb, has been sacrificed. Let us therefore celebrate the festival, not with the old leaven, the leaven of malice and evil, but with the unleavened bread of sincerity and truth.

—1 Cor. 5:7–8

Gird up the loins of your thinking, be sober, and set your hope fully upon the grace that is coming to you at the revelation of Jesus Christ . . . You know that you were ransomed from the futile ways inherited from your fathers, not with perishable things such as silver and gold, but with the precious blood of Christ, like that of a **lamb without blemish or spot**.   —1 Pet. 1:13, 18–19

❖   ❖   ❖

In short: Moses was not merely God's chosen servant—he was made Godlike himself and surpassed all other human beings. The wonders that he and Aaron performed before Pharaoh were no mere feats of ordinary magic but truly supernatural events. Yet God "hardened Pharaoh's heart," preventing him from understanding the nature of his opponent, so that the Egyptians might be appropriately punished for all the evil that they had done to Israel. That punishment came in the form of ten plagues, which were designed to requite the Egyptians "measure for measure," fitting their punishments to their own sins or that which they had sought to do to the Israelites. Before the Israelites left, the Egyptians willingly gave them their gold and silver—for this was less than what was owed to the people of Israel for so many years of involuntary servitude. The laws of Passover contained symbolic messages about the true meaning of the narrative.

18

The Red Sea

(EXODUS 13:1–15:21)

Egyptians drowned at the Red Sea: light and dark together.

The Red Sea

(EXODUS 13:1–15:21)

❖ ❖ ❖

After the tenth plague had befallen Egypt, Pharaoh at last relented and the Israelites started on their way out of the land of Egypt. As they journeyed, God led them with a pillar of cloud, which went before them during the day, and a pillar of fire at night to light their way. Soon after they had left, however, Pharaoh regretted his decision, and he dispatched his crack charioteers to pursue them. These came within sight when the Israelites were camped near the Red Sea.

When they saw the Egyptians approaching, the Israelites panicked, but Moses stretched his hand out over the Red Sea and the waters divided, forming a dry path on which the Israelites could cross to the other side. Pharaoh's charioteers tried to follow, but their chariots became bogged down in the mud. Then Moses stretched his hand over the sea once again, and the water returned to its prior condition, drowning Pharaoh's army. Safe on the other side, the Israelites sang a song of praise.

THE ISRAELITES did not just set out on their journey from Egypt on their own. Instead, they were guided on their way by supernatural means, the alternating presence of a pillar of fire and a pillar of cloud:

> And the Lord went before them by day in a pillar of cloud to lead them along the way, and by night in a pillar of fire to give them light, to travel by day and by night. He did not remove the pillar of cloud by day, nor the pillar of fire by night, from before the people.　— Exod. 13:21–22

The pillar of fire certainly made sense, since fire could provide light for the journey at night, and a whole pillar of it would be easily seen. But why a pillar of *cloud* during the day? This seemed a strange choice of materials.

Pillar of Luminous Cloud

Some ancient interpreters concluded that the daytime pillar, no less than the nighttime one, served to light up the Israelites' path.[1] In other words, the pillar

---

1. Because the Bible was transmitted without punctuation, one might conclude from Exod. 21:22 (cited above) that *both* pillars served "to give them light."

333

of cloud—whatever the role of its "cloudiness"—provided a brilliant source of light:

> Therefore you provided a flaming pillar of fire as a guide for their unknown journey, and a **harmless sun** for their glorious wandering. For those men [the Egyptians] deserved to be deprived of light and imprisoned in darkness, those who had kept your sons imprisoned, through whom the imperishable light of the law was to be given to the world.
> — Wisd. 18:3–4

> Take note, most noble Moses, of this place
> which we have found near yonder airy glen . . .
> From thence a lustrous light **now** flashes forth,
> [which is,] by night, a sign, like to a fiery pillar.
> — Ezekiel the Tragedian, *Exagōgē* 243–247

> A cloud whose shape was like a tall pillar proceeded before the throng, **shining like the sun** during the day, and like fire at night, so that they would not go astray in their travels but would follow in the footsteps of an unerring guide.
> — Philo, *On Moses* 1:166

Similarly:

> "He did not remove the pillar of cloud by day" [Exod. 13:22]—[in the sense that] the light of the sun did not overcome it; "nor the pillar of fire by night" [Exod. 13:22]—[in the sense that] the light of the moon did not overcome it.
> — *Midrash ha-Gadol* Exod. 13:22

Alternately, it was possible to interpret the light of the pillar(s) as a figure of God's mercy:

> Pharaoh, the former ruler of this Egypt, with his multitude of chariots, high and mighty in his lawless insolence and boastful tongue, you destroyed in the depths of the sea with his proud host, Father, causing the light of your mercy to shine upon the people of Israel.
> — 3 Macc. 6:4

Protective Covering

But if the pillar of cloud was a source of light, then why "cloud" at all? Could not the same pillar of fire have traveled before the Israelites both day and night? The presence of two kinds of pillars suggested that this pillar of cloud had a further function—and indeed, the book of Psalms seemed to say as much:

He spread a cloud for **covering**, and fire to give light by night.

> —Ps. 105:39

Another verse in the psalms likewise suggested that, quite apart from the Exodus, it was in general God's nature to provide illumination and shelter at the same time:

For the Lord God is a sun and a shield.

> —Ps. 84:11

Moreover, the prophet Isaiah, in foreseeing a similar twofold manifestation of God over Mt. Zion, had also specified that a divine cloud would be provided for protection:

And God will create over the whole site of Mount Zion and her assemblies a cloud by day and smoke and the brilliance of burning fire by night ... It will be for a **shade** by day from the heat, and for a refuge and a **shelter** from the storm and rain.   —Isa. 4:5–6

Fortified by such evidence, numerous interpreters thus asserted that the purpose of the pillar of cloud was also to provide shade and protection from the blazing desert heat:

She [Wisdom] gave to holy men the reward for their labors; she guided them along a marvelous way, and became shelter to them by day, and a starry flame through the night.   —Wisd. 10:17

You comforted them with a pillar of fire at night, for light, and a pillar of cloud by day, for shade.

> — Hellenistic Synagogal Prayer, *Apostolic Constitutions* 8.12.26

And for you water sprang forth from a rock, and a cloud was following for shade from the heat and protection from the frost, yielding tidings of the fashion and promise of another new heaven.

> — Justin Martyr, *Dialogue with Trypho* 131:6

He gave them a pillar of fire by night for light and guidance, and a cloud by day for a covering.   — *Didascalia Apostolorum* ch. 23

An Angel in the Cloud

There was, however, another matter that seems to have influenced early ideas about the nature of this pillar of cloud. For in several places the Bible suggests that the Israelites were in fact led out of Egypt by an angel:

Then the angel of God who went before the host of Israel moved and went behind them.

— Exod. 14:19

[God tells the Israelites:] Behold, I am sending an angel before you, to guard you on the journey and to bring you to the place which I have prepared. Give heed to him and hearken to his voice, do not rebel against him, for he will not pardon your transgression, for my name is in him.

— Exod. 23:20–21

[Moses later tells the Edomites:] The Egyptians dealt harshly with us, and with our fathers; and when we cried to the Lord, He heard our voice, and sent an angel and brought us out of Egypt.

— Num. 20:15–16

Who was this angel? The Bible does not say, nor does it ever actually represent the angel in the act of doing what the two above passages suggest, namely, leading the Israelites on their journey. But there was one verse that strongly implied that such an angel was indeed present during the crucial events at the Red Sea, *hidden* inside the pillar of cloud:

And the angel of God who was going before the Israelite camp moved and went behind them, and the pillar of cloud moved from in front of them and stood behind them.

— Exod. 14:19

The angel moved and the pillar of cloud moved. Was it not thus obvious that the angel was inside the cloud?

And perhaps, concealed within the [pillar of] cloud, one of the deputies of the great King, an unseen angel, went as a pathfinder, whom physical eyes were not permitted to behold.

— Philo, *On Moses* 1:166

Perhaps this angel was to be identified with divine Wisdom:

[Wisdom speaks:]
I went forth from the mouth of the Most High, and like a mist
  I covered the earth;
I dwell in highest heaven, and my throne is in a pillar of cloud.

— Sir. 24:3–4

She [Wisdom] . . . guided them along a marvelous way, and became shelter to them by day, and a starry flame through the night.

— Wisd. 10:17

This idea of the pillar concealing an angel or divine Wisdom may have played an additional role in ancient interpretation. For, yet another biblical description of the pillars of cloud and fire appears, this time in the book of Nehemiah:

[Ezra prays:] But You in Your great mercy did not abandon them in the desert. The pillar of cloud did not depart from above them during the day to indicate the path for them, nor did the pillar of fire at night, to light for them the path on which they should proceed. And Your **good spirit** You provided to instruct them.　　　　　—Neh. 9:19–20

What was this additional source of instruction, the "good spirit" that God provided? Since (as with the "angel" just examined), this "good spirit" is not actually represented as taking part in the Exodus itself, an interpreter might naturally conclude that it was likewise hidden (indeed, perhaps it was to be identified with the mysterious angel sent by God, since the word "spirit" was often taken to mean "angel"). And since, in the above passage, the verse preceding this mention of the "good spirit" speaks of the two pillars, it likewise must have seemed reasonable to conclude that, in one or both of these two pillars, God had also provided his good spirit—or divine Wisdom—to instruct the people.

There may be a hint of such an understanding in the New Testament:

I want you to know, brothers, that our fathers were all under the cloud, and all passed through the sea, and all were baptized into Moses **in the cloud** and in the sea, and all ate the same spiritual food and all drank the same spiritual drink.　　　　　—1 Cor. 10:1–4

This text seems to suggest that "immersion" in the cloud, no less than immersion in water, was a kind of baptism or initiation—perhaps a sort of *spiritual* baptism, since no actual water was required (see also Acts 11:15 and [1QS] *Community Rule* col. 4:20–21). If so, then the cloud was no ordinary cloud, but a spiritual, purifying mass.

Final Payment

The Israelites continued their march out of Egypt. But then the Egyptians, who had at first asked them to leave Egypt (Exod.12:31–33), suddenly decided to pursue them and bring them back. Why? Surely the Egyptians should have realized they would only bring more trouble on themselves. The Bible says that God "hardened Pharaoh's heart" and led him to this decision (Exod. 14:4). Some interpreters suggested that God did this so that the Egyptians might finally pay off their full debt for having enslaved and ill-treated the Israelites:

And it [the hardening of Pharaoh's heart] was conceived of by the Lord our God so that He might smite the Egyptians and throw them into the midst of the sea.　　　　　—Jubilees 48:17

> For the fate they deserved drew them on to this end, and made them forget what happened, in order that they might fill up the punishment which their torments still lacked. —Wisd. 19:4–5

In particular, by drowning the Egyptian army at the Red Sea, God was punishing them for having ordered the Israelite babies drowned in the Nile. (See Chapter 16, "Death By Water.")

Get Back Our Goods!

Other interpreters noticed that the words that came just before the pursuit, "What have *we* done to free Israel from serving *us?*" (Exod. 14:5) were in the plural. Was this not a hint that Pharaoh was no longer the only one whose heart was hardened?

> Pharaoh and his army and all the rulers of Egypt, the chariots and their riders, were plunged into the Red Sea and perished, for no other reason than that **their** foolish hearts were hardened after the signs and wonders had been accomplished in the land of Egypt by Moses, the servant of God. —1 Clement 51:5

What could have caused the Egyptian people to urge a pursuit of the Israelites? The answer seemed obvious: they must have had second thoughts about the silver and gold they had given the Israelites before their departure:

> They came to Pharaoh and said, "What is it that we have done in sending forth Israel? Arise, ready your chariots and we will all give chase with you until we return them to our service. After all, they were our slaves and our fathers' slaves before us. Why did we ever let them leave Egypt? Perhaps we can even get back the things that they borrowed from us, leaving us with nothing." —*Tibat Marqa* 54a

> [The people said:] "We have freed the Hebrews after they have taken our riches and our clothes. It would be better to die than that the Hebrews put the Egyptian kingdom to shame." —Ephraem, *Commentary on Exodus* 14:1

Rebellion at the Sea

When the Israelites turned and suddenly saw the Egyptians closing on them, they found themselves trapped between the Red Sea and the arriving army. Panicked, they cried out to Moses, "Was it because there were no graves in

Egypt that you took us into the wilderness to die?" (Exod. 14:11). Moses, however, reassured them, and the Red Sea split in two, creating a path of dry, land for the Israelites to walk on.

Psalm 106 contains a brief retelling of these events of the Exodus, but with one puzzling addition:

> Our fathers in Egypt did not understand your miracles, they did not recall your many mercies, and they **rebelled at the sea, at the Red Sea.**
> — Ps. 106:7

The highlighted words seemed particularly difficult: what "rebellion" is meant here? (Furthermore, why the repetitive "at the sea, at the Red Sea" in the traditional Hebrew text?)[2]

Out of this verse developed a tradition that elaborated the Israelites' brief complaint to Moses in Exod. 14:11–12 into a full-scale revolt. According to this tradition, it is not only (as the Bible says there) that the Israelites, seeing the approaching Egyptians, complained to Moses; in addition, forgetting God's previous miracles, they now rebelled at the Red Sea:

> And now they forgot all those miracles done by God [an allusion to Ps. 106:7] in order to free them, and they turned against Moses, so much so that in their faithlessness they wished to stone the prophet[3] even as he urged them on and promised them that they would be saved, and they resolved to surrender to the Egyptians.
> — Josephus, *Jewish Antiquities* 2:327

But a close reading of Moses' precise words to the rebels in Exod. 14:13–14 reveals that even they were not of one mind:

> And the Israelites formed four groups at the time they were standing at the Red Sea; one said, "Let us fall into the sea"; another said, "Let us return to Egypt"; another said, "Let us make battle formations against them," and another said, "Let us cry out in their direction and confuse them." To the group that said "Let us fall into the sea" Moses said, "Do not fear, **stand up** [that is, don't fall] and see the salvation of the Lord that He will do for you today" [Exod. 14:13]. To the group that said "Let us return to Egypt" Moses said, ". . . For, in the manner in which you

---

2. Some ancient (e.g., the Vulgate) and modern translators read not ʿal yām, "at the sea," but ʿelyôn, "the Most High." The Septuagint translators read ʿolîm, "going up." The traditional Hebrew text's version might suggest that they rebelled *concerning* the sea.

3. The idea of "stoning" Moses comes from a later verse, Exod. 17:4, as well as Ps. 68:28.

see the Egyptians today [that is, as their slaves], do not ever again see them **in slavery** anymore" [≅ Exod. 14:13]. To the group that said, "Let us make battle formations against them," Moses said, "... The Lord is the one who will fight for you" [Exod. 14:14]. And to the group that said "Let us cry out in their direction and confuse them" Moses said, "Be silent" [Exod. 14:14, so that later, in Exod. 15:1, you may] "give glory and praise and exalt God."

— *Targum Neophyti* Exod. 14:13–14

Some thought that the most miserable death would be a welcome blessing, while others, believing it to be better to perish by the elements of nature than to become a laughing-stock to their enemies, planned to throw themselves into the sea and, loaded with some heavy substances, sat waiting by the shore so that when they saw the foe near at hand they might leap down and easily sink into the depths.

— Philo, *Moses* 2:249

Then, in considering the fearful situation of the moment, the sons of Israel were split in their opinions according to three strategies. For the tribes of Reuben, Issachar, Zebulun, and Simeon said: "Come, let us cast ourselves into the sea. For it is better for us to die in the water than to be killed by our enemies." But the tribes of Gad, Asher, Dan, and Naphtali said: "No, but let us go back with them . . ." But the tribes of Levi, Judah, Joseph, and Benjamin said: "No, but let us take up our weapons and fight them . . ." And when Moses [cried out], God rebuked the sea [Ps. 106:9] and the sea was dried up.

— Pseudo-Philo, *Book of Biblical Antiquities* 10:3–5

At the [Red] Sea they were divided into three groups and each group spoke its peace, and the great prophet Moses replied to each. The first group said: "Let us return and let us serve them [as slaves,] for it is better for us [to do thus] than to die in the desert" [≅ Exod. 14:12]. To them the great prophet Moses said: "You shall not see them ever again" [Exod. 14:13]. The second group said: "Let us flee from the Egyptians into the midst of the desert." To them the great prophet Moses said: "Stand up and see the salvation of the Lord that He will do for you today" [Exod. 14:13]. The third group said: "Let us go and fight with the Egyptians." To them the great prophet Moses said: ". . .The Lord is the one who will fight for you—and you be silent" [Exod. 14:14].

— *Tibat Marqa* 217a

More than One Miracle

God split the Red Sea in two—here, surely, was a miracle. And yet, interpreters were inclined to suppose that more than one miracle had occurred. To begin with, another account of the Exodus in the book of Psalms seemed to say that all of nature was thrown into turmoil in the event:

> You redeemed Your people with Your mighty arm, the children of
>   Jacob and Joseph.
> The waters saw You, O God, the waters saw You and trembled, the
>   very depths shook.
> The clouds poured out water and the heavens thundered, Your
>   lightning-darts flashed about.
> The crash of Your thunder was in the whirlwind, lightning lit up
>   the land, the earth trembled and shook.
> You made Your path through the sea, Your way through the watery
>   depths, though Your traces were not seen.
> You led your people like a flock, by the hand of Moses and Aaron.
>   —Ps. 77:15–20

Interpreters were spurred by such passages to view the crossing of the sea itself as fraught with the supernatural. Indeed, more than once the Bible implied that several different miracles were involved:

> . . . And the **signs** [miracles] and deeds that He did within Egypt, to
> Pharaoh the Egyptian king and to all the land, and which He did **to the**
> **army of Egypt,** its horses and chariotry, over whom He caused the
> waters of the Red Sea to flood as they pursued you, and the Lord
> destroyed them to this very day.   —Deut. 11:3–4

Read in a certain way, this text might be held to suggest that God's signs (in the plural) were actually done in two places, "within Egypt" and again at the Red Sea. Similarly:

> And You saw our fathers' oppression in Egypt, and You heard their cry
> at the Red Sea. **Then you performed signs and wonders** against
> Pharaoh and all his servants and all the people of the land, for you
> knew that they had ill-treated them; and so You made for yourself a
> name, as it is to this day. And You split the sea before them, and they
> crossed on dry land amidst the sea.   —Neh. 9:9–11

If one takes seriously the sequence of actions presented here, it seems that God performed "signs and wonders" for Israel *after* having heard their cry at the

Red Sea. If so, these signs and wonders—again in the plural—were performed in addition to the signs and wonders that constituted the ten plagues. Still more explicitly:

> [Later, the Israelites] forgot God their savior, who had done
>   marvelous things in Egypt,
> wonders in the land of Ham, **miracles** [in the plural] **at the Red Sea.**
>
> —Ps. 106:21–22

It may thus be no accident that some interpreters referred to a plurality of miracles at the Red Sea.

> Those protected by Your hand passed through [the Red Sea] as one nation, after gazing on marvelous wonders.   —Wisd. 19:8

More explicitly:

> Ten miracles were done for our ancestors in Egypt, and ten more on the Sea.
>
> —m. Abot 5:4

> R. Yose ha-Gelili said: How can we deduce that the Egyptians not only suffered ten plagues in Egypt, but fifty plagues at the Red Sea? With regard to [the plagues in] Egypt, what does the text say? "And the wizards said to Pharaoh, 'It is the finger of God!'" At the Red Sea, however, what does the text say? "And God saw the mighty hand which the Lord had used against the Egyptians . . ." [Exod. 14:31]. If, by the "finger of God" they had suffered ten plagues, one might conclude that at the Red Sea [where the "hand of God" appeared] they were stricken with fifty plagues!   —Passover Haggadah

A Grassy Plain

One particular miracle seemed to be implied by the prophet Isaiah in regard to the crossing of the Red Sea.

> [God] led them [the Israelites] through the depths, like a horse in the desert they did not stumble, **like cattle going down into the valley.**
>
> —Isa. 63:13–14

Read in a certain way, these lines suggested to interpreters that the Red Sea had been made not only passable, but dry as a desert—or perhaps even turned into a grassy valley:

For [at the Red Sea] the whole creation in its nature was fashioned anew, complying with your commandments, so that your children might be kept unharmed. The cloud was seen overshadowing the camp, and dry land emerging where water had stood before, an unhindered way out of the Red Sea, and a **grassy plain** out of the raging waves.

—Wisd. 19:6

And the Israelites went on dry land through the water, and there came forth perfumed springs of water and fruit trees and greenery and fine morsels.

— *Targum Pseudo-Jonathan* Exod. 15:19

Miraculous Timing

Despite such evidence of the miraculous, some people nevertheless were inclined to see the miracle as one of timing rather than a reversal of the natural order:

Now the Memphites say that Moses was familiar with the countryside and watched for the ebb tide, and he conveyed the multitude across through the dry sea. But the Heliopolitans say that the king rushed down on them with a great force, together with the consecrated animals, since the Jews had acquired and were carrying off the property of the Egyptians. But a divine voice came to Moses to strike the sea with his rod and divide it. When Moses heard, he touched the water with the rod and thus the flowing water separated and the host went through a dry path.

— Artapanus (cited in Eusebius, *Praeparatio Evangelica* 9.27.35–37)

After the sun had set, there arose a particularly stormy southwind which caused the sea to retreat. While it was normally subject to the ebb-tide, now it was thrust back more than usual against the shore and sank as into a chasm or a whirlpool . . . At God's command Moses struck the sea with his staff, and it was split and divided in two.

—Philo, *Moses* 1:176–177

Each of these things I have recounted just as they are told in Sacred Scripture. And let no one wonder at the astonishing nature of this thing, that a road to safety was found through the sea itself—whether [this happened] by God's will or simply through happenstance—for an ancient people innocent of any wrongdoing. For indeed, it was but a short while ago that the Pamphilian Sea moved backwards for those who were accompanying Alexander, king of Macedonia, thus offering them a path through itself when no other way out existed, and so to overcome, as was God's will, the Persian empire. All those who have written down Alexander's doings are in agreement on this. However, each may decide on his own concerning such matters.

—Josephus, *Jewish Antiquities* 2:347–248

If Looks Could Kill . . .

In the crucial sequence of actions that preceded the Egyptians' downfall, there was one additional strangeness to be accounted for:

And there was the cloud and **the darkness, and it lit up the night** . . . The Egyptians pursued, and followed them [the Israelites] into the midst of the sea, all Pharaoh's horses, his chariots, and his horsemen. And at the morning watch, the Lord looked out over the Egyptian camp in [or "with"] the **pillar of fire and cloud,** and discomfited[4] the Egyptian camp. —Exod. 14:20, 23–24

Here was something indeed strange: a single pillar apparently made of fire and cloud simultaneously, and in it, or with it, God *looked* out over the Egyptians. Interpreters concluded that by "looking" God actually afflicted the Egyptians, and afflicted them by means of this twofold cloud:

He [Artapanus] says that when the Egyptians went in with them and pursued, fire shone out from in front of them and the sea again flooded the path. All the Egyptians were destroyed by both the fire and the flood. —Artapanus (cited in Eusebius, *Praeparatio Evangelica* 9.27.35–37)

The cloud was watching over them from behind, and in its midst was a divine sort of image, flashing forth with the brightness of fire.

—Philo, *Life of Moses* 2:254

And He cast upon them naphtha and fire and hailstones.

— *Targum Neophyti* Exod. 14:24

And God, looking out over the camp of the Egyptians through the columns of fire and cloud, **killed** their armies. — (Vulgate) Exod. 14:24

The cloud turned the sea to mud, and the pillar of fire **made it boil** like pitch, so that the horses' hooves became detached . . . And they con-

---

4. Like "discomfited," the Hebrew word it translates (*hāmam*) was not a particularly common one, and its meaning may not have been clear to all interpreters. Indeed, it may have sounded somewhat like a more common term meaning "heat."

founded *(wayyahom)*: This word means a plague, as it says "And He will throw them into great confusion, until they are destroyed" [Deut. 7:23].
— *Mekhilta deR. Shimon bar Yoḥai* 14:24

Light and Dark Together

Other interpreters noted that, just before this mention of God looking out on the Egyptians, the text says that the pillar "went in-between the Egyptian camp and the Israelite camp, and there was the *cloud and the darkness and it lit up the night*" (Exod. 14:20 in the traditional Hebrew text). They therefore concluded that the "fire" part of the twofold cloud had been for the purpose of illuminating the Israelite side, and the "cloud" part for darkening the Egyptians':

A night of gloom and darkness overwhelmed them [the Egyptians].
— Josephus, *Jewish Antiquities* 2:344

And there was the cloud, and it darkened the Egyptians, but for Israel it was light the whole night.
— *Targum Onqelos* Exod. 14:20

The cloud was [half] darkness and half light. The darkness darkened the Egyptians, and the light [was] for Israel.
— *Targum Neophyti* Exod. 14:20

The cloud was half light and half darkness: the light shined upon Israel and the darkness cast darkness on the Egyptians.
— *Fragment Targum* (P) Exod. 14:20

Ups and Downs of the Egyptians

The waters of the Red Sea swept over the pursuing Egyptians, killing them to a man. The grateful hymn the Israelites sang after being saved (the "Song of the Sea") retells these same events—but with some interesting changes. For example, the song says that Egyptians "plunged to the depths like a stone" (Exod. 15:5) and "sank like lead in the mighty waters" (Exod. 15:10). Then what did the narrative mean by saying that the Israelites, after they reached safety on the opposite side, "saw the Egyptians dead *on the seashore*" (Exod. 14:30)? Where were the Egyptians—on the beach or at the bottom of the sea? Interpreters reasoned that the Egyptians must have first sunk to the bottom and later risen to the surface—either to prove to the Israelites that the Egyptian army was indeed destroyed, or perhaps to provide the Israelites with the Egyptian armor and weapons for the future:

She brought them over the Red Sea, and led them through deep waters; but she drowned their enemies, and **spat them up** from the depth of the sea. Therefore the righteous **plundered** the ungodly.

—Wisd. 10:18–20

[Moses predicts:] I see [God's help] preparing for the fight and casting a noose around the necks of the enemy. It drags them down through the sea; they **sink like lead** into its depths. At present, you see them still alive, but I have a vision of them dead, and today, you too **will see their corpses**.   —Philo, *Moses* 2:252

[After the drowning of the Egyptians in the Red Sea,] the sea and the land argued between themselves: the sea said to the land, "Take your children" [since they *were* land-dwellers and, in that sense, your "children"]. The land said to the sea, "Take your dead bodies" [that is, you are the one responsible for their death, *you* take them]. The sea did not want to take them and the land did not want to take them.

— *Targum Neophyti* Exod. 15:12

Red Sea as Baptism

Early Christians found in the Old Testament foreshadowings of the New, as well as of later Christian doctrines and practices. The crossing of the Red Sea (like the flood in the narrative of Noah) was seen as a foreshadowing of the Christian sacrament of baptism:

I want you to know, brothers, that our fathers were all under the cloud, and all passed through the sea, and all were baptized into Moses in the cloud and **in the sea.**   —1 Cor. 10:1–2

And so, when the people, having been set free from Egypt and the power of the Egyptian king, escaped when it passed through water, that same king and all his forces were likewise killed by water. Could there be a more obvious prefiguring of the sacrament of baptism?

—Tertullian, *On Baptism* 10

The whole story of the exodus [is] a prefiguring [*tupos*] of the salvation acquired through baptism.

—Didymus the Blind, *On the Trinity* 2:14 (PG 39.697 A)

[Referring to 1 Cor. 10:1–4:] You may thus see how much Paul's way of reading differs from mere literalism. What the Jews consider to have

been a crossing of the Red Sea, Paul calls baptism; what they believe to
have been a cloud, he calls the Holy Spirit.

— Origen, *Homilies on Exodus* 5:1

How Did They Know the Words?

In introducing the "Song of the Sea," the Bible says, "Then sang Moses and the
Israelites." But since the song is all about the events that had just taken place,
it was obviously a brand new composition. Interpreters therefore wondered
exactly how Moses and the Israelites could spontaneously all sing the same
song. Perhaps, somehow, they just managed to do so:

They sang hymns, O Lord, to your holy name, and praised **with one
accord** your defending hand. — Wisd. 10:20

When the Israelites came up from the Red Sea, they sought to praise
God, and the holy spirit came over them and they praised Him.[5]

— Tosefta *Soṭah* 6:2

To some, however, the song itself seemed to imply otherwise. Its first
words were not (in the traditional Hebrew text) "*We* shall sing" but "*I* shall
sing." As a matter of fact, the previous verse puts the verb "sing" in the
singular, as if it really meant, "Then Moses sang this song, and along with him,
the other Israelites." Both these points seemed to indicate that Moses sang
first, and that the Israelites somehow joined in:

All the [Israelites] were persuaded by Moses to sing with hearts in
accord[6] the same song . . . The prophet [Moses] . . . no longer able to
contain his delight, led off the song, and those who heard him joined
together in two choirs to sing with him the story of these same deeds.

— Philo, *Moses* 2:257

They [the Israelites] passed the whole night in hymns and rejoicing,
and **Moses himself composed** a song of praise to God in thanks for
His kindness, and it was written in hexameters.

— Josephus, *Jewish Antiquities* 2:346

5. Although in its present context these words are used to support the antiphonal recitation of
the song, the phrase "the holy spirit came over them" may first have been used to maintain that Moses
and the Israelites were all simultaneously inspired to sing the song.

6. The phrase "with hearts in accord" may be designed to explain why Exod. 15:1 refers to Moses
and the Israelites singing as one.

"Moses and the Israelites" means that Moses sang the song on behalf of all the Israelites.
— *Mekhilta Shirtah* 1

Rabbi Akiba explained: "Then sang Moses and the Israelites this song to the Lord, and they said, *saying* . . ." This [word "saying"] teaches that the Israelites would repeat each and every thing that Moses said, as those who recite the Hallel. Rabbi Nehemiah said: As those who recite the Shema, and not as those who recite the Hallel.[7]
—m. *Soṭah* 5:4

Moses the prophet sang the song in sections, and when he would finish one section, he would be silent, and all the elders would answer with the words, "Sing to the Lord, for He has triumphed gloriously, horse and his rider has He cast into the sea," and all of Israel would say, "My strength and my song, and He is become my salvation" until "the Lord is a hero in war, the Lord is His name."
— *Tibat Marqa* 72b, 104a

Moses sang and all the people sang back after him.
—Ephraem, *Commentary on Exodus* 15:1

Other versions of the text did not present this contradiction between everyone singing and the words "*I shall sing*":

Let us sing to the Lord, for He is greatly glorified.
—Septuagint, *Targums* Exod. 15:1

Sing [plural] to the Lord.
— *Samaritan Pentateuch* Exod. 15:1

Seeing God at the Sea

There were some indications that the events at the Red Sea were more than a miraculous event in history; the Israelites themselves seem to have caught a glimpse of God's very being, as it were. After all, the Bible says that, at the time of the events, Israel "*saw* the mighty hand" with which God had defeated the Egyptians (Exod. 14:31). Was this just a manner of speaking, or did they really *see?* Later on, Moses recalls:

And the Lord brought us out of Egypt with a mighty hand and an outstretched arm, with great fear, and with signs and wonders.
—(traditional Hebrew text of) Deut. 26:8

7. The precise distinction presented here is in dispute. Cf. Tosefta *Soṭah* 6:2–3; *Mekhilta Shirta* 1; j. Talmud *Soṭah* 5:6; b. *Soṭah* 30b, b. *Sukkah* 38a–39a.

But the word for "fear" might be identified with the root meaning "see":

And the Lord Himself brought us out of Egypt, with His great strength, and His mighty hand, and His high arm, and with **great visions**, and with signs and wonders.
— Septuagint Deut. 26:8 (cf. Deut. 4:34)

. . . with a great sight . . .
— *Targums Onqelos, Peshitta, Pseudo-Jonathan* Deut. 26:8

. . . with great sights . . .
— *Targum Neophyti* Deut. 26:8

. . . with fearsome visions . . .[8]
— (Vulgate) Deut. 26:8

"With great fear" [Deut. 26:8]: this refers to the revealing of God's very being [*Shekhinah*].
— *Passover Haggadah*

Many interpreters thus concluded that the Israelites actually saw God at the Red Sea. Indeed, this same idea seemed also to be reflected in the song itself. For here the Israelites said, "This is my God and I will glorify Him, the God of my father and I will exalt Him" (Exod. 15:2). Did not the word "this" also imply that the Israelites, when they uttered it, were actually seeing God before them, so vividly present that they could say "this"?

R. Eli'ezer said: [from the word "this" we know] that the lowliest servant-girl at the Red Sea perceived what the prophets Isaiah and Ezekiel had not.
— *Mekhilta deR. Ishmael, Shirtah* 3

Infants Sang Too

But if so, here was a problem. Granted, the Israelites might actually have seen God at the Red Sea and therefore said, "This is my God." But how could they tell, by looking at Him, that *this* was also "the God of my father" as the rest of Exod. 15:2 maintains? Certainly there was nothing about His appearance to indicate that He was also the God of Israel's ancestors.

To this question ancient interpreters apparently developed an ingenious answer: the words of the song, "This is my God and I will glorify Him, the God of my father and I will exalt Him," were actually sung by two different groups of singers: first the fathers in Israel sang "This is my God . . ."; then their children, down to the littlest newborn, sang in reply "The God of my father . . ."

8. This is apparently an attempt to harmonize the two traditions surrounding this word, "fear" and "vision."

They sang hymns, O Lord, to your holy name, and praised with one accord your defending hand; because wisdom opened the mouth of the dumb, and made the **tongues of babes** speak clearly.

—Wisd. 10:20–21

Said R. Yose the Galilean: when Israel came up from the Sea and saw that their enemies were now corpses stretched out on the shore, they all praised God. Even the newborn on his mother's knees and the suckling at his mother's breast, when they saw the presence of God the newborn lifted his neck and the suckling removed his mouth from his mother's breast, and all sang forth and said, "This is my God and I will praise Him [my father's God and I will exalt him]."

—Tosefta Soṭah 6:4

Miriam's Separate Song

Exod. 15:20–21 reports that Aaron's sister Miriam sang a song along with all the women at the Red Sea. Much speculation surrounded this song. The only words cited from it, "Sing to the Lord, for He has acted gloriously, horse and rider has He cast into the sea," match almost perfectly the first line of the men's song. Did Miriam thus simply form a women's chorus to sing along with the men, yet separately? Such modest behavior seemed altogether praiseworthy, and a number of authors specifically mentioned it:

They set up two choirs, one of men and one of women, on the beach, and sang hymns of thanksgiving to God. Over these two choirs Moses and his sister presided and led the hymns.   —Philo, *Moses* 1:180

The people were divided into two groups on that day, so that they might sing the wondrous hymn to Him who split the sea and drowned their oppressors on that day. Moses led the men in singing and Miriam the women.   —Ephraem, *Commentary on Exodus* 15:3

Or was that one choir?

This wonderful sight and experience, an act transcending word and thought and hope, so filled with ecstasy both men and women that, forming a single choir, they sang hymns of thanksgiving to God their Savior, the men led by the prophet Moses and the women by the prophetess Miriam.   —Philo, *The Contemplative Life* 87

At the same time, some ancient interpreters supposed that the Israelite women must have sung their own song, with different words, at the Red Sea.

One text found among the Dead Sea Scrolls apparently contained the words of such a song attributed to Miriam. Unfortunately, only a fragment of it has survived:

> You have put to shame . . .
> For You are clothed [?] in majesty . . .
> Great are You, savior are You . . .
> The enemy's hope has perished, and he is forgotten . . .
> They have been lost in the mighty water, the enemy . . .
> Praise to the heights . . . You gave . . .
> Who does gloriously.
> — (4Q364) Reworked Pentateuch fragment 6, col. 2

A New Song

The rescue of the people of Israel from exile and foreign domination in Egypt gave hope to later generations. Perhaps later misfortunes would likewise be reversed, and just as the Israelites sang the "Song of the Sea," they would someday sing a new song:

> Therefore, behold, I will allure her, and lead her back into the wilderness, and speak tenderly to her . . . And there she shall sing as in the days of her youth, as at the time when she came out of the land of Egypt.
> — Hos. 3:14–15

> Was it not You who dried up the sea, the waters of the great deep, who made the depths of the sea into a path for the redeemed to pass over? [So, similarly] those who have been ransomed by the Lord shall return, and come to Zion with singing.
> — Isa. 51:10–11

In later times, too, this new song figured in visions of the future—or perhaps it was simply the "Song of the Sea" to be sung in new circumstances:

> The four living creatures and the twenty-four elders fell down before the Lamb, each holding a harp, and with golden bowls full of incense, which are the prayers of the saints, they sang a new song.
> — Rev. 5:8–9

> And I saw what appeared to be a sea of glass mingled with fire, and those who had conquered the beast and its image and the number of its name, standing beside the sea of glass with harps of God in their hands. And they sing the **song of Moses**, the servant of God, and the

song of the Lamb, saying "Great and wonderful are your deeds, O Lord God the almighty. Just and true are your ways, O King of the ages."

—Rev. 15:2–3

Perhaps also:

And he [an archangel] was telling me [Enoch] all the deeds of the Lord, the earth and the sea, and all the elements and the courses and the life . . . and the Hebrew language, every kind of language of the **new song of the armed troops,** and everything that it is appropriate to learn.

—2 Enoch (A) 23:1–2

Eventually there developed a traditional enumeration of songs that had marked important moments in Israel's past history—and one song, a "new" one, that would be sung at the final redemption:

The tenth song [to be sung in Israel's history] is one for the time to come, as it is said, "Sing to the Lord a new song, let his praise reach to the ends of the earth" [Isa. 42:10], as elsewhere it says, "Sing to the Lord a new song, let His praise be in the multitude of the pious" [Ps. 149:1].

—Mekhilta deR. Ishmael, Shirta 1

❖   ❖   ❖

In short: On their way out of Egypt the Israelites were led during the day by a pillar of cloud that both gleamed brightly and yet sheltered them from the sun; inside it was an angel, or perhaps divine wisdom. The Egyptians as a group had resolved to pursue the Israelites to recover their possessions. Seeing them approach, the Israelites panicked and sought to rebel against Moses. They formed different groups, each with its own plan of action, but Moses soon put down their rebellion. Then the Red Sea split in two and the Israelites crossed to the other side. This crossing was accompanied by further miracles, and God finished off the Egyptian troops not merely by drowning them but by burning them with flashing fire. The Egyptians sank to the bottom of the sea, but later floated up to the shore. Seeing this, the Israelites broke into song, either singing simultaneously with Moses or repeating each verse after him. The words of their song attested that the Israelites actually caught sight of God at that moment. In similar fashion, a "new song," like the "Song of the Sea," will mark the coming of future redemption.

19

Into the Wilderness

(EXODUS 15:22–18:27)

The symbolic hands of Moses: was he praying?

Into the Wilderness

(EXODUS 15:22–18:27)

❖   ❖   ❖

The Israelites' rejoicing at the Red Sea was short-lived. No sooner had they escaped the Egyptian army than new troubles began: now there was not enough fresh water to drink or food to eat. Once again, God intervened. At Marah, Moses was able to make the bitter waters drinkable by means of a tree that God had shown him. Later, as the Israelites were making their way to Sinai, God provided an edible substance called "manna" which the people could collect from the wilderness floor.

When they reached Rephidim, the Israelites were attacked by a desert-dwelling tribe, the Amalekites. In the ensuing battle, the Israelites triumphed, curiously, because Moses held his hands in the air while he watched the battle. Afterwards, Moses' father-in-law, Jethro, paid a brief visit to the Israelites in the wilderness.

Water, Water...

The fact that, as soon as the Egyptians had been drowned, God miraculously intervened to provide the Israelites with drinking water (Exod. 15:22–25) seemed to confirm that the different appearances of water in the Exodus story were no coincidence:

> For by those very things through which their enemies were punished, they [the Israelites] benefited in [time of] need. Instead of an ever-flowing source of streaming water befouled with blood as a reproach for the decree to kill the infants [an allusion to the waters of the Nile, which were turned to blood (Exod. 7:20)], You gave the Israelites an abundant source of water when it was not expected.   — Wisd. 11:5–7

> God's way of healing is not man's way. In human healing, that which is used for hurting is not used for healing—one strikes with a knife and heals with a bandage. Not so with God: The very means by which He strikes He also heals.   — *Mekhilta Wayhi* 5

A Symbolic Tree

Apart from this general principle of correspondence, however, some of the details connected with God's providing water for the Israelites called out for explanation.

At Marah, for example, Moses made the bitter water drinkable by casting into its midst a certain divinely indicated tree (or some piece of wood taken from it). The Bible then says:

> There He gave them [Israel] law and statute and there He tested them. And He said to them, "If you are careful to obey the Lord your God, and do what is right in His eyes, and heed His commandments and keep all His statutes, then I will put none of the diseases upon you which I put upon the Egyptians, for I am the Lord, your healer."
>
> —Exod. 15:25–26

Why did Moses have to use a special tree to make the water drinkable? And what could the words just cited, about heeding divine commandments and statutes, possibly have to do with this tree or the bitter waters? To more than one interpreter it seemed as if the tree in the story must have really been some kind of symbol:

> [God] showed him [Moses] the **tree of life** from which He cut [a piece] and he received it cast it into Marah, and the waters of Marah became drinkable. —Pseudo-Philo, *Biblical Antiquities* 11:15

> And Moses prayed to God and He showed him a "tree" and . . . took from it a **teaching of the Torah** and cast it into the waters and the waters became drinkable; [and so] there He gave [Israel] laws and statutes and there [Israel] tested Him." — *Targum Neophyti* Exod. 15:25

> Similarly, water was healed of its bitterness and changed into fresh, drinkable water by the staff[1] of Moses. This wood was the Messiah, transforming by himself waters which were previously bitter and poison into those most salutary **waters of baptism**.
>
> —Tertullian, *On Baptism* 9

The ancient interpreters [*dôrĕšê rĕšûmôt*] said: He showed him [Moses] words of divine teaching [Torah] which Scripture compares

---

1. The Hebrew word used in Exod. 15:25 can mean either "tree" or "wood." The Septuagint translators used the word *xulon*, which means almost exclusively the latter. Many interpreters who knew the Bible only in Greek or Latin therefore assumed that the "wood" in question was none other than Moses' staff, identified typologically with the cross.

to wood, as it is said "[The Torah] is a tree of life for those who cling to it . . ." [Prov. 3:10].   — *Mekhilta Wayyassa' 1*

The Water Was Divine Wisdom

Beyond this, however, another connection seemed possible. After all, divine teachings were themselves sometimes compared to water, and the search for God's presence or instruction likened to a kind of thirst:

[God says:] Oh, all you who thirst, come to the waters . . . incline your ear, and come to Me.   — Isa. 55:1, 3

They have abandoned Me, the spring of flowing waters.   — Jer. 2:13

For with You is the fountain of life.   — Ps. 36:9

The fountain of wisdom is a flowing stream.   — Prov. 18:4

In keeping with such passages, some interpreters came to think of water in general—and, in particular, the water that the Israelites thirsted for in the desert—as symbolizing divine wisdom or the Torah:

. . . until God send forth the flowing waters of His supernal wisdom and so provide drink of unfailing healthfulness to the wandering soul.
                            — Philo, *Allegorical Interpretations* 2:86

The fountain of divine wisdom runs sometimes with a gentler and more quiet stream, at other times more swiftly and with a fuller and stronger current.   — Philo, *The Worse Attacks the Better* 117

. . . to distort, by [giving] false teachings to your people, the Torah which you have taught me in my heart, and so to deprive the thirsty of the drink of **knowledge** [cf. Isa. 32:6].   — (1QH) *Thanksgiving Hymns* 4:11

The well [dug in the desert, Num. 21:16–18] is the Torah.
                                          — *Damascus Document* 6:3

The ancient interpreters [*dôrĕšê rĕšûmôt*] said "And they did not find water . . ." refers to divine teachings, which are compared to water [in Isa. 55:1]. And since they [the Israelites] were [by this interpretation] separated from "water" for three days and thereupon rebelled, for this reason did the prophets and sages make it a rule that the Torah is to be read publicly on the Sabbath [Saturday], on Monday, and on Thursday

[so that Israel would never again be deprived of "water" three days in a row].
— *Mekhilta Wayyassaʾ* 1

And they went for three days in the desert in idleness from the divine commandments.
— *Targum Pseudo-Jonathan* Exod. 15:22

The Food of Angels

But God gave the people more than water (symbolic or otherwise). During their desert wanderings, Israel was fed by God with the special food called "manna," which first appeared as the people journeyed from Elim to Sinai (Exod. 16:1–4). It was hard for interpreters to tell exactly what this manna was. On the one hand, it was sometimes described as "bread" (though the Hebrew word can also simply mean "food"):

I will rain bread from heaven.
— Exod. 16:4

They asked, and He brought them quails, and He gave them bread from heaven in abundance.
— Ps. 105:40

Yet surely "bread *from heaven*" was different from ordinary bread. Perhaps it was "from heaven" not just in the sense that it came down from the sky, but because it was truly heavenly food not normally intended for mortals:

But those who honor the true eternal God
inherit life, dwelling in the luxuriant garden
of Paradise for the time of eternity,
feasting on sweet bread from starry heaven.
— Fragment 3 from *Sibylline Oracles* (cited in Theophylus, *To Autolycus* 2:46–49)

Perhaps, more precisely, it was the bread eaten by the inhabitants of heaven, the angels. Indeed, another verse from Scripture seemed to say as much:

Yet He commanded the skies above, and opened the door of Heaven; and he rained down upon them manna to eat, and gave them the grain of heaven.
Man ate the **bread of the mighty**, he sent them food in abundance.
— Ps. 78:23–25

He rained down upon them manna to eat, and gave them the bread
of heaven.
Man ate the bread of **angels.**

—Septuagint Ps. 78 (77):24–25

You fed your people the food of angels and funished them bread from
heaven.   —Wisd. 16:20

[Moses says to the Israelites:] Know that you have eaten the bread of
angels for forty years.   —Pseudo-Philo, *Biblical Antiquities* 19:5

I pitied your groanings and gave you manna for food; you ate the
bread of angels.   —4 *Ezra* 1:19

"The bread of the mighty" [in Ps. 78:25 means that] they ate the bread
that the ministering angels eat, according to R. Aqiba.   —b. *Yoma* 75b

Heavenly Grain

There was good reason to believe that manna actually took the form of little
grains or particles. After all, it *rained* down from heaven, presumably in drops
or flakelike pieces, and a number of other biblical verses seemed to support
this hypothesis:

And when the dew had risen, there was on the surface of the wilderness something thin and scratchy, thin as frost on the ground.

—Exod. 16:14

Now the manna was like coriander seed, and its appearance like that
of bdellium. The people went about and gathered it, and ground it in
mills or beat it in mortars, and boiled it in pots, and made cakes of it.

—Num. 11:7–8

Therefore, a number of interpreters understood that the manna falling to
earth must have resembled some form of precipitation. The mention of
manna's whiteness, its comparison to frost, and the fact that it seemed to melt,
all suggested to some that manna was like snow. Others, however, believed it
was more like rain, or dew, or none of these.

God rained for them meal like millet, very similar in color to snow.
—Artapanus (cited in Eusebius, *Praeparatio Evangelica* 9.27.37)

A strange, extraordinary rain, not water, nor hail, nor snow, nor ice,
such as are produced by changes in the clouds at the winter solstice,

but of grains exceedingly small and white, which, poured down in a continuous flow, lay in heaps in front of the tents.   —Philo, *Moses* 1:200

For, while Moses raised his hands in prayer, a **dew** descended and, as this congealed about his hands, Moses, surmising that this too was a nutriment come to them from God, tasted it and was delighted; and, whereas the multitude in their ignorance took this for **snow** and attributed the phenomenon to the season of the year, he instructed them that this heaven-descending dew was not as they supposed but was sent for their salvation and sustenance.

—Josephus, *Jewish Antiquities* 3:26–28

The ministering angels ground up the manna and it would then fall upon the Israelites and they would eat it.

—*Midrash Tanḥuma, Beshallaḥ* 22

Adapted to Any Taste

As for its taste, here too, the biblical evidence was mixed:

Now the house of Israel called its name manna; it was like coriander seed, white, and the taste of it was like wafers made with honey.

—Exod. 16:31

The taste of it was like the taste of oil-extract.   —Num. 11:8

Understandably, some interpreters came to the conclusion that the Bible was describing not so much the taste of manna itself as the people's reaction to it; its taste thus must have changed depending on who was eating it:

[The manna was] ready to eat without toil, providing every enjoyment and suitable for every taste. For this sustenance of Yours demonstrated your sweetness toward your children; complying with the wishes of the one who was eating it, it adapted itself to suit each person's desires.

—Wisd. 16:20–21

They said to him [Moses]: This manna that God has given us, we can taste in it the taste of bread, the taste of meat, the taste of fish, the taste of locusts, the taste of all the delicacies in the world.

—*Mekhilta deR. Ishmael, Amaleq* 1

R. Joshua said: Anyone who wanted something baked, it would come baked for him, and anyone who wanted it boiled, it would be boiled for him. R. El'azar ha-Moda'i said: Anyone who wanted to eat something baked would taste in it [the manna] all the baked goods of the world, and anyone who wanted to eat something boiled would taste in it all the boiled dishes in the world. —*Mekhilta deR. Ishmael, Shirtah* 4

And the fact that it says that it [manna] was "like coriander and its taste was as honey" [Exod. 16:31] is intended to show that the manna was pleasing to any taste. —Ephraem, *Commentary on Exodus* 16:3

Spiritual Sustenance

But the Bible did not answer unequivocally even the most basic question about this substance—was it good to eat or wasn't it? "Bread of angels" sounded pretty good, as did "wafers made with honey." Similarly:

You did not withhold your manna from their mouths . . . For forty years you sustained them in the wilderness and they did not lack a thing [see also Deut. 2:7]. —Neh. 9:20–21

On the other hand, the Israelites seem to have gotten tired of manna; they say "Our throats are dry and there is nothing to eat, the only thing that we see is manna" (Num. 11:5), and again, "There is no bread and there is no water, and our throats are tired of this *low-grade food*" (Num. 21:5). Recalling these times, Moses says:

[God] fed you in the wilderness with manna, which your fathers did not know, in order to humble you and test you. —Deut. 8:16

Then it would seem that the manna really wasn't very tasty after all. How could these contradictions be resolved? Perhaps the most satisfactory explanation was that manna was really some kind of spiritual sustenance and not a food at all:

He calls it manna, that is, the divine word [*logos*], oldest of beings [cf. Prov. 8:22]. —Philo, *Worse Attack the Better* 118

The food of the soul is not earthly but heavenly, as we shall find abundantly demonstrated in Scripture. "Behold, I rain upon you bread out of heaven . . ." [Exod. 16:4]—you see that the soul is fed not with things of earth, which are perishable, but with such **words** as God shall have poured like rain out of that supernal and pure region of life to which the prophet has given the title of "heaven."

—Philo, *Allegorical Interpretations* 3:162

Let all those who are perfect of path praise Him.
Let them open their mouths [in thanksgiving] for God's kindnesses
    with the lyre of salvation.
Let them seek out His **manna**.

—(4Q511) *Songs of the Sage*[b]

All were baptized into Moses in the cloud and in the sea, and all ate the
same **spiritual** food and all drank the same spiritual drink.

—1 Cor. 10:2–4

So they said to him, "Then what sign do you do, that we may see, and
believe in you. What work do you perform? Our fathers ate the manna
in the wilderness, as it is written, 'He gave them bread from heaven to
eat.'" Jesus then said to them: "Truly, truly, I say to you, it was not
Moses who gave you the bread from heaven; my Father gives you the
true bread from heaven. For the bread of God is that which comes
down from heaven, and gives life to the world."

—John 6:30–33 (also 6:41–49)

[God said at the Exodus:] If I bring Israel to the[ir] land right away,
every man will be taking possession of his field and vineyard and they
will neglect the Torah. Therefore I will send them around the desert
for forty years so that they will eat manna and drink the water of the
well and thus the **Torah** will be incorporated into their bodies.

—*Mekhilta deR. Ishmael, Wayhi* 1

The Traveling Rock

The Israelites continued their journey into the wilderness and eventually
came to a place called Rephidim. Once again, there was no water to drink, and
the people fell to complaining. God then ordered Moses to strike a certain
rock so that water would gush out of it for the people to drink. The Bible notes
that Moses "called the place Massah and Meribah" ("testing" and "contention"
in Hebrew).

The Israelites moved on. But what happened to the gushing rock? Ancient
interpreters found some indication that the rock did not stay at Rephidim, for,
some time later, in a different place—Kadesh—a similar thing happened:
water was miraculously produced when Moses struck a rock with his staff
(Num. 20:7–12). The text then adds, "These were the waters of Meribah"
(Num. 20:13). If *these* were the "waters of Meribah," then they must somehow
have moved from Rephidim to Kadesh. And that is just what interpreters

concluded. They deduced that the gushing rock had traveled with the Israelites from Rephidim to Kadesh, indeed, that it went on to accompany them during all their subsequent wanderings—a traveling water supply.

> Now He led His people out into the wilderness; for forty years He rained down for them bread from Heaven, and brought quail to them from the sea and brought forth a well of water to **follow** them.
>
> And it [the water] followed them in the wilderness forty years and went up to the mountains with them and went down into the plains.
> —Pseudo-Philo, *Book of Biblical Antiquities* 10:7, 11:15

> I want you to know, brethren, that our fathers were all under the cloud, and all passed through the sea, and . . . all drank the same spiritual drink. For they drank from the supernatural Rock which **followed** them. —1 Cor. 10:1–4

> And so the well that was with Israel in the desert was like a rock the size of a large container, gushing upwards as if from a narrow-neck flask, **going** up **with them** to the mountains and going down with them to the valleys. —Tosefta *Sukkah* 3:11

Such a conclusion could only be reinforced by the observation that, although the Israelites were in the desert for forty years, from the time of that first incident at Rephidim, shortly after they left Egypt, until near the end of their travels at the end of the book of Numbers, there is no mention of the people lacking water to drink. Here, then, was another indication that water had been miraculously supplied to them for all those years—by this same traveling fountain.

Miriam's Well

Interpreters noticed something else: this second mention of the Israelites not having water to drink takes place right after the death of Miriam, Moses' sister (Num. 20:1). They therefore concluded that the death of Miriam was in fact the cause of the Israelites' not having water. Perhaps the gushing rock that had followed them all those years had done so only because of Miriam, so that after she died, the rock no longer supplied them with water. (And indeed, there is some indication that, after Miriam's death, the Israelites were now suddenly *plagued* with a water shortage—this shortage is mentioned not only in Num. 20:2 but again at Num. 20:19 and 21:5.) Hence it appeared that the gushing rock (or "moveable well") should be chalked up to the virtue of Miriam. It came to be known as the Well of Miriam.

> And these are the three things that God gave to his people on account of three persons; that is, the well of the water of Marah for Miriam and the pillar of cloud for Aaron and the manna for Moses. And when these came to their end [i.e., died], these three things were taken away from them.   —Pseudo-Philo, *Biblical Antiquities* 20:8

> And the king of Arad heard . . . that Miriam the prophetess had died, thanks to whose merit the well had sprung up, and that the well was hidden away.   —*Targum Neophyti* Num. 21:1

> And there was no water there for the people of the assembly, because Miriam the prophetess had died and the well had been hidden away.
>   —*Fragment Targum* Num. 20:1

> There arose three great leaders for Israel, and these are they: Moses, and Aaron, and Miriam. And three great gifts were given by them to Israel, namely, the well and the pillar of cloud and the manna. When Miriam died, the well departed, but it returned to them because of the merit of Moses and Aaron.   —*Seder Olam* 10 (see also 9)

> When Miriam died, the well departed.   —*Mekhilta Wayyassa'* 5 (end)

Amalek Destroyed at the End-Time

While the Israelites were camped at Rephidim, the tribe of Amalek came and attacked them. The Amalekites must have been particularly blameworthy, since, of all of the Israelites' enemies, they were the only ones whose name God promised to "blot out from under heaven" (Exod. 17:14). Indeed, long after the attack at Rephidim, Israel itself was commanded to destroy the Amalekites—"Blot out the name of Amalek! Do not forget!" (Deut. 25:19).

What made the Amalekites so evil? As we have seen (Chapter 11, "Esau the Wicked"), they were descended from Esau, who was himself thought by interpreters to be a wicked schemer. But what is more, God's commandment to destroy the Amalekites was not fulfilled in Moses' time and, as a result, they continued to cause Israel trouble during much of later history. It was the Amalekite king Agag who caused King Saul's downfall (1 Samuel 15), and Agag's descendant Haman (Est. 3:1) later hatched a plan to destroy all the Jews of his own day.

Reflecting on the evil Amalekites, interpreters found one verse that seemed to explain much of what was to happen. In telling the story of the soothsayer Balaam, the Bible reported:

> Then he [Balaam] saw Amalek, and took up his discourse, and said, "Amalek was the first of nations, but his **end** will be destroyed."
> —Num. 24:20

The word "end" here probably means "descendants." (The Septuagint had translated it "seed.") But for some interpreters, "end" suggested the "end of days," the time when God would bring present-day reality to a close and reestablish the divine order. They therefore saw in Balaam's words a prediction that God's commandment to destroy Amalek would only finally be fulfilled in the "end of days"—indeed, that Amalek's ultimate destruction had a lot to do with setting the world aright:

> Then the seed of Canaan will perish, and there will not be a remnant to Amalek . . . Then the whole earth will rest from trouble, and all of it under heaven from war.   — *Testament of Simeon* 6:3–4

> Then he [Balaam] saw the Amalekite, and he took up his prophetic parable and he said: The first of the nations to take up arms against Israel was of the house of Amalek, and in the **final end of days** they will take up arms against them once again; but they will eventually be destroyed, and their destruction shall be forever.
> — *Fragment Targum* Num. 24:20

> For the son of God shall destroy by the roots the whole house of Amalek in the end of days.   — *Letter of Barnabas* 12:9

Because of all this, Amalek was sometimes understood not only as evil, but as a representation of the devil.

The Symbolic Hands of Moses

The actual defeat of the Amalekites at Rephidim was accomplished in an extraordinary fashion. Whenever Moses lifted his hands in the air, the Israelites seemed to prevail—almost as if his hands had some magical property about them. Needless to say, such an idea was utterly abhorrent to most ancient interpreters. If Israel won the battle, they reasoned, it was not because of any magic, but because God so willed. They therefore felt there must have been some other explanation for the role of Moses' hands in the story:

But when they were about to engage in the fight, his hands were affected in a most marvelous way. They became alternately very light and very heavy, and whenever they were in the former condition and rose aloft, [Israel] was strong and distinguished itself by its valor, but whenever his hands were weighed down, the enemy prevailed. Thus, by **symbols**, God showed that earth and the lowest regions of the universe were the portion assigned to the one party, and the ethereal, the holiest region, to the other; and that, just as Heaven holds kingship in the universe is superior to earth, so this nation [Israel] would be victorious over its opponents in war.
— Philo, *Moses* 1:217

But did Moses' hands actually make Israel win, and was it they that crushed Amalek? Rather [this text means that] when Moses lifted his hands toward Heaven, Israel would look upon him and put their trust in Him who ordered Moses to do so; then God would perform miracles and wonders for them.

— *Mekhilta deR. Ishmael, Amaleq* 1 (see also m. *Rosh ha-Shanah* 3:5)

And it happened that, whenever Moses would raise his hands in prayer, the Israelites would prevail and be victorious, but when he would withhold his hands from prayer, the Amalekites prevailed.

— *Targum Neophyti* Exod. 17:11

The Christian Battle with Amalek

Later, for Christians, the symbolism of Moses' hands changed somewhat (though the idea that they were symbolic remained). Outstretched, they became a symbol of the crucifixion. What is more, Joshua, since his name in the Greek Bible was identical with that of Jesus, became an important figure in the overall story: it was he who enabled the defeat of Amalek, now identified with the devil.

The Spirit, speaking to the heart of Moses, [tells him] to make a representation of the cross and of him who was to suffer upon it . . . So Moses placed one shield upon the other in the midst of the fight, and standing there, raised above them all, kept stretching out his hands, and so Israel again began to be victorious; then, whenever he let them drop they began to perish. Why? So that they might know that they cannot be saved if they do not hope in him.   — *Letter of Barnabas* 12:2–3

When the people waged war with Amalek, and the son of Nave [Nun], by the name of Jesus [the Greek form of Joshua] led the fight, Moses himself prayed to God stretching out both hands, and Hur with Aaron supported them the whole day, so that they might not hang down when he became weary. For if he gave up any part of this sign, which was an imitation of the cross, the people were beaten, as is recorded in the writings of Moses; but if he remained in this form, Amalek was proportionally defeated, and he who prevailed did so by the cross.

— Justin Martyr, *Dialogue with Trypho* 110

While Joshua was fighting Amalek, Moses was praying, seated, his hands extended, because wherever the Lord fought against the devil [that is, Amalek], the form of the cross was necessary—the cross by which Jesus was to win the victory.   — Tertullian, *Against Marcion* 3:18

Moses prefigured him [Christ], stretching out his holy arms, conquering Amalek by faith so that the people might know that he is elect and precious with God his father.

— *Sibylline Oracles* 8:251–253

Jethro the Polytheist

After their victory over Amalek, the Israelites were visited briefly by Jethro, Moses' father-in-law. Jethro was a somewhat puzzling figure for interpreters. On the one hand, he is described as a "priest of Midian" (Exod. 3:1, 18:1), and this certainly meant that he worshiped other gods. On the other hand, no sooner did he arrive to visit Moses than he said: "Blessed be the Lord who has delivered you out of the hand of the Egyptians and out of the hand of Pharaoh. Now I know that *the Lord is greater than all gods*" (Exod. 18:10–11). These words certainly seemed to suggest that Jethro repudiated other gods, or at least believed that the Lord was greater than them.

Faced with this somewhat mixed picture, interpreters characteristically adopted one extreme or the other. Some saw Jethro as a totally negative figure and suggested that even these intended words of praise for the God of Israel were mere hypocrisy:

For when he wants to draw attention to his own piety and says, "Now I know that the Lord is greater than all gods," he instead convicts himself of impiety for those who know how to judge such matters. They will say to him, "Blasphemer! . . . You stand nonetheless proven guilty of dissembling when you compare two incomparables and say that you know that the greatness of the One Who Is is 'beyond' all gods. For if you truly knew what IS, you would not have thought that any other god has any power of his own."

—Philo, *On Drunkenness* 3:341

Similarly:

They said: There was not any form of idol-worship that Jethro had not tried out in the whole world, [otherwise he could not have said that God is greater] "than **all** the gods."   —*Mekhilta deR. Ishmael, Amaleq* 1

Jethro the Good

Others, however, saw in Jethro a positive figure, and one whose religious orientation was not different from that of Moses:

[Jethro says to Moses:]
God gave you this sign for good.
Would that I might live to see these things transpire.

—Ezekiel the Tragedian, *Exagōgē* 83–84

In support of the positive view of Jethro was his statement about the Lord being "greater than all the gods"—indeed, perhaps that statement could be interpreted as an out-and-out rejection of other gods:

Now I know that the Lord is great, and there is none beside Him.

—*Targum Onqelos* Exod. 18:11

In addition, Jethro had proposed to Moses a better way for administering justice, a suggestion that Moses adopted (Exod. 18:13–26). This certainly implied that Jethro was a good man. What is still more, in the course of making this suggestion, Jethro had said to Moses, "God be with you!" (Exod. 18:19)—again implying that he believed in the same God as Moses.

But if so, how could this God-fearing man have been a "priest of Midian"? Perhaps the title really didn't mean "priest":

And Jethro, the priest of Midian . . .   —Exod. 18:1

And Jethro, the priest of Midian . . .   —Septuagint Exod. 18:1

And Jethro, the **ruler** of Midian . . .

—*Targums Onqelos, Neophyti, Pseudo-Jonathan* Exod. 18:1

Alternately, it may have been that Jethro had indeed once worshiped other gods and served as "priest of Midian," but at some point had seen the folly of his ways and converted to the true religion. Perhaps this was what he meant by "Now I know that the Lord is greater" (Exod. 18:11). Indeed, the reason for his visit to Moses may have been his desire to convert:

> Jethro was a priest of idolatry but he saw that it was worthless and so rejected it and and planned to repent [i.e., convert] even before Moses came.
> — *Exodus Rabba* 1:32

> And he said to Moses, "I, Jethro, your father-in-law, am coming to you in order to be converted."
> — *Targum Pseudo-Jonathan* Exod. 18:6

> [Jethro's] name was [also] Ḥobab [Num. 10:29] because he loved [*ḥibbeb*] the Torah, and amongst all the **converts** there was none who loved the Torah as Jethro did.
> — *Sifrei Numbers* 78

❖   ❖   ❖

In short: At Marah, God slaked the Israelites' thirst for divine learning or Torah, represented by water. The "tree" with which this was accomplished was likewise the Torah, which is called the "tree of life." As for manna, it was indeed the "bread of angels," a food whose taste changed to suit the desires of whoever ate it, since it was in any case a wholly spiritual food. Throughout their wanderings, the Israelites were followed by a rock that gushed water; this was the Well of Miriam, so called because it was given to Israel on account of Miriam's merits.

The Amalekites who attacked the Israelites at Rephidim were the embodiment of evil itself; they will only be destroyed in the end of days. Moses won the battle against them by raising his hands toward heaven, a wholly symbolic gesture. As for Jethro, Moses' father-in-law, he was a good man who had come to reject the worship of other gods: he now believed only in God.

20
At Mt. Sinai
(EXODUS 19–24)

*(top) Moses ascends to heaven on a smoky mountain to receive the Torah,
with Joshua in background; later (bottom) he instructs the people.*

At Mt. Sinai

(EXODUS 19–24)

❖   ❖   ❖

The Israelites were now camped in the wilderness of Sinai, at the "mountain of God." Moses climbed up the mountain and God told him that Israel would become His "special people" if they agreed to obey Him and keep His covenant. The people agreed and purified themselves in preparation for what was to follow. On the third day, amid thunder and lightning, God came down in fire upon the mountain and spoke the Ten Commandments (the Decalogue).

In addition to the Decalogue, God gave the Israelites numerous other laws at Mt. Sinai. Some of these had to do with relations between one person and another, others with relations between human beings and God. The people accepted all these requirements enthusiastically. Moses entered the cloud where God was and stayed on the mountain forty days and forty nights.

AT MT. SINAI, God made His great covenant (an agreement or compact) with Israel, by which they became His special people. For ancient interpreters, this was a most—perhaps *the* most—significant event in the whole Hebrew Bible. Not only did it establish a unique relationship between one people and the Lord of all, but the laws and commandments that God gave to Israel became a central preoccupation for Jews ever afterward. They tried to arrange every detail of their lives to accord with these divine laws, and the laws themselves were studied down to their tiniest particulars.

Heaven on Earth

But what exactly happened on the day in question? The events themselves appeared elusive. On the one hand, it seemed that God had, as it were, gone down to meet Moses on top of the mountain: the Bible says specifically "And the Lord went down upon the mountain" (Exod. 19:20) and elsewhere reports that God "called to him [Moses] from the mountain" (Exod. 19:3). On the other hand, God later says, "You have seen for yourselves that I have talked with you *from heaven*" (Exod. 20:21), and still later Moses recalls, "*Out of heaven* He caused you to hear His voice" (Deut. 4:36). So where was God really? The book of Nehemiah summed up the paradox:

You went down upon Mount Sinai, and You spoke with them from the heavens.

—Neh. 9:13

There was, however, another biblical passage that likewise seemed to refer to the events at Mt. Sinai, and here interpreters found a possible solution to the problem:

He **bowed down the heavens** and came down; thick darkness was under His feet . . .
The Lord also **thundered in the heavens,** and the Most High made his voice heard, hailstones and coals of fire.

—Ps. 18:9, 13

Taken at face value, this passage suggests that God brought part of heaven with Him, "bowing" or bending it down to the mountain. If so, then this might explain how He could simultaneously be on Mt. Sinai and yet "thunder in the heavens." A number of ancient interpreters therefore specifically alluded to this "bending down" of heaven when they retold the events at Sinai:

You **bent down** the heavens and shook the earth, and moved the world, and made the depths to tremble, and troubled the times. And your glory passed through the four gates of fire and earthquake and wind and ice, to give the law to the descendants of Jacob, and your commandments to the posterity of Israel. — 4 Ezra 3:18–19

And I brought them to the foot of Mt. Sinai, and I **bowed** the heavens and came down and congealed the flame of fire and stopped up the channels of the abyss and impeded the course of the stars and muffled the sounds of thunder and quenched the fullness of the wind and rebuked the many clouds and stayed their movements and interrupted the storm of the heavenly hosts so as not to break my covenant. For all things were set in motion when I came down, and everything was brought to life when I arrived. — Pseudo-Philo, *Biblical Antiquities* 23:10

R. Akiba said: One verse says, "For I have spoken to you from the heavens" [Exod. 20:21] while another says "And the Lord descended upon the mountain" [Exod. 19:20]. This teaches that God must have bent the highest parts of heaven down to [touch] the top of the mountain and then spoken with them there—from the heavens! And so it is written "And he bent the heavens and went down, and there was darkness under His feet" [Ps. 18:10].

— *Mekhilta deR. Ishmael, Baḥodesh* 9

Celestial Sinai

Another possibility existed, however: instead of heaven coming down to the mountain, the mountain might have ascended into heaven.

> Beloved of God and men was Moses (may his mention bring good),
> And He honored him as God, and kept him strong in the **heavens**.[1]
> — Sir. 45:1

> The Torah is not in heaven, that one should say, "Who will **go** up to heaven for us like the prophet Moses and take it down for us and teach us its laws so that we could do them."
> — *Targum Neophyti* (marginal gloss) Deut. 30:12

> "And they [the Israelites] stood at the foot of the mountain . . ." [Exod. 19:17]. This teaches that the mountain was actually uprooted from its place, and then they came close and stood underneath it, as it is said, "They came close and stood at the foot of [literally, "underneath"] the mountain" [Deut. 4:11].
> — *Mekhilta deR. Ishmael, Baḥodesh* 3

> Mt. Sinai was uprooted from its place and the heavens opened and the top of the mountain went into the heavens and the darkness covered the mountain.
> — *Pirqei deR. Eliezer* 41

Heavenly Moses

If the mountain actually ascended into heaven, and Moses with it, then surely Moses was transformed in the process: one cannot ascend into heaven and remain an ordinary human being. Indeed, Scripture seemed to imply as much when it had God say, "Come up *to Me* on the mountain" (Exod. 24:12). Did not Moses' ascent into heaven mean that he himself became, as it were, divine?[2]

> What is the meaning of the words, "Come up to Me to the mountain and be there . . ." [Exod. 24:12]? This signifies that a holy soul is made divine by ascending not to the air or to the ether or to heaven [which

---

1. God "kept him strong" in the sense that Moses did not eat or drink for forty days (Exod. 24:18), but the point is that Ben Sira says that this happened "in the heavens" whereas the Bible merely says that Moses was "on the mountain." (The Greek text of Sirach reads "kept him strong *in the fears*," but this appears to be an error in the transmission of the Hebrew original.)

2. See also Chapter 17, "A Godlike Man."

is] higher than all, but to [a region] above the heavens. And beyond the world there is no place but God.

— Philo, *Questions and Answers in Exodus* 2:40

At the time when God said to him "Come up to me on the mountain . . ." and he went up to Him, then the "cloud covered him for six days" [Exod. 24:16] his body was made holy and yet holier still, and he ascended from the level of human beings to the level of the angels.

— *Tibat Marqa* 265b

". . . Moses, the man of God" [Deut. 36:1] [This phrase can be also be read "Moses, a man, God"]: a man when he [first] ascended on high, God when he [later] descended below.

— *Pesiqta deR. Kahana, Zot ha-berakhah* 1

God Spoke All Ten

On the morning of the third day, amid thunder and lightning, God spoke the words of the Decalogue to all the people. Or did He? Ancient interpreters noticed an interesting thing: in the Ten Commandments, God starts speaking in the first person, "I am the Lord your God . . . You shall have no other gods before Me . . . I am a jealous God," and so forth. But then, after the first two commandments, the text suddenly switches to the third person:

> You shall not take the name of the Lord your God in vain; for the **Lord** will not hold him guiltless who takes **His** name in vain.   — Exod. 20:7

From here on, all references to God are in the third person, as if someone else were talking *about* God rather than God Himself talking directly to the Israelites. But was this the case—and if so, why?

A number of ancient interpreters seem to go out of their way to say that (despite such evidence) God in fact spoke *all* the words of the Decalogue Himself:

> The ten "words" or "oracles"—in truth, laws or statutes—were **delivered by** the father of all when the nation, men and women alike, were assembled together.

> The Ten Commandments which **God Himself** uttered in a manner befitting His holiness.   — Philo, *The Decalogue* 32, 175

> You gave to them a law, ten oracles uttered by Your voice and engraved by Your hand.   — Hellenistic Synagogal Prayer, *Apostolic Constitutions* 7.33.4

And then the Lord spoke **to His people** all these words, saying . . .
— Pseudo-Philo, *Biblical Antiquities* 11:6

And all heard a voice which reached the ears of all from on high, in such a way that not one of those ten words escaped them . . . The people, having thus heard from the very mouth of God that of which Moses had told them, rejoicing in these commandments dispersed from the assembly.   — Josephus, *Jewish Antiquities* 3:90, 93

And they said to Moses: "You be the one to speak with us so that we can hear . . ." This teaches that they did not have the strength to receive [directly] more than the Ten Commandments, as it says [*after* the Decalogue is given, Deut. 5:6–18], "If we continue to hear the voice of the Lord we shall die" [Deut. 5:22].   — *Mekhilta deR. Ishmael, Baḥodesh* 9

God Spoke Only Two

Such assertions notwithstanding, there was good reason to suppose that, in fact, God had not spoken the entire Decalogue directly to Israel. After all, in retelling these events, Moses said:

> The Lord spoke with you face to face at the mountain, out of the midst of the fire, while I stood between the Lord and you at that time to **declare to you** the word of the Lord; for you were afraid because of the fire, and you did not go up into the mountain. He said, "I am the Lord your God . . ."   — Deut. 5:4–6

This passage clearly presents Moses as restating to the Israelites what God Himself had said. Indeed, one might conclude from this that the Israelites actually heard nothing directly from God. But somewhat later on, Moses states that, on the day in question, the Israelites had said: "Let me *hear no more the voice* of the Lord my God, or see this great fire any more, lest I die" (Deut. 18:16). The implication is that the Israelites did indeed hear the divine voice directly—at least for a little while. Putting this conclusion together with the observed switch from the first-person singular to the third person within the Decalogue, an interpreter might conclude that God had spoken to the Israelites directly at first and then, at their insistence, had stopped:

> Rabbi Joshua said: The Israelites heard only two commandments directly from God: "I am the Lord your God . . ." and "There shall be no other gods beside Me . . ."
> — *Song of Songs Rabba* 1:2, *Pesiqta Rabbati Ten Commandments* 2

The Ten Were All

The Decalogue obviously occupies a special position in the Bible. These "ten words" are listed as a unit (Exod. 20:1–17), and afterward the narrative resumes, having highlighted, so it seems, these ten commandments in particular. Elsewhere the Bible speaks of God having given Moses two "tables of stone" on which laws are written (Exod. 24:12, 31:18, 32:15–16, 34:1–4). One might think that *all* the laws of the Pentateuch were written on these two tables, but the Bible specifies that they contained specifically the "ten words":

> He was there with the Lord forty days and forty nights; he neither ate bread nor drank water. And he wrote upon the tables the words of the covenant, the ten words.   —Exod. 34:28

> [Moses recalls:] And He declared to you his covenant, which he commanded you to perform, the ten words; and He wrote them upon two tables of stone.
>
> And He wrote on the tables, as at the first writing, the ten words which the Lord had spoken to you on the mountain.   —Deut. 4:13, 10:4

But the very specialness with which these ten commandments are treated was a problem—and a major one at that. After all, the Pentateuch certainly contained far more commandments than these ten: numerous other statutes and rules and laws were likewise given by God to Israel, at Mt. Sinai as well as afterward (613 in all, according to a later tradition). What was so special about these ten that they in particular should have been written on the two tables?

Some people apparently claimed that *only* these commandments truly came from God. This view is attributed in rabbinic literature to the "sectarians" or "heretics" (*mînîm*); specifically, it was evoked to explain why the public reading of the Decalogue, which at one point figured prominently in the liturgy of the Jerusalem Temple, came to be discontinued in later liturgical practice:

> [Before this change came about:] The one in charge [of the priestly course in the Jerusalem Temple] would say to them [the priests]: Make the benediction (and then they did); read the Ten Commandments; recite the *Shema‘* [Deut. 6:4–9].   —m. *Tamid* 5:1

R. Matna and R. Samuel b. Naḥman both said: The Ten Commandments ought by right [still] to be read [publicly] every day. Why are they not so read? Because of the contention of the heretics [to the effect] that these ten **alone** were given to Moses on Mt. Sinai.

—j. *Berahot* 1:8

The same idea—that the totality of God's laws consisted of the "ten words" written on the two tables—may be hinted at elsewhere as well:

But when he [Moses] came,
leading this people, which God led from Egypt
to the mountain, Sinai, God also gave forth
the Law from heaven, having written all just ordinances on two tables
and enjoining them to perform it.

— *Sibylline Oracles* 3:254–258

No doubt this notion was connected to the idea (seen above) that God had spoken the Decalogue *directly* to the Israelites. For, if these ten commandments had been singled out in this way—and further singled out by being written down as a group on the two tables—then these facts alone highlighted the specialness of the Decalogue and deserved particular mention:

You gave them a law, ten oracles uttered by Your voice, and engraved by Your hand.　—Hellenistic Synagogal Prayer, *Apostolic Constitutions* 7.36.4

If they were not the *only* laws given by God, why had He so singled them out?

The Decalogue Epitomizes

Some interpreters reasoned that, if God had indeed given Israel many other laws besides the Decalogue, then perhaps the Decalogue had been specially singled out because it constituted some kind of a summary or *epitome* of these other laws as well. After all, a body of more than six hundred rules and regulations—governing all sorts of matters both sacred and profane—might not be the sort of thing an ordinary person could memorize and keep constantly in mind. At a relatively early point, therefore, interpreters theorized that the Decalogue had been given because it in itself constituted not only ten particular commandments, but a list of ten general categories of laws, a précis from which all the other laws might be derived:

Those [laws] which were uttered by Him personally and by Him alone [that is, the Decalogue] were [at the same time] laws and **general legal categories**, while those which were uttered through the prophet [Moses] were all [merely] the former.　—Philo, *The Decalogue* 19

That the Decalogue was some sort of epitome or précis may also underlie the following:

> And a ruler asked him: "Good Teacher, what shall I do to inherit eternal life?" And Jesus said to him, ". . . **You know the commandments**: Do not commit adultery, Do not kill, Do not steal, Do not bear false witness, Honor your father and mother . . ."
>
> —Luke 18:19–20 (cf. Matt. 19:16–19, Mark 10:17–19)

> And God said to Moses, "Climb up the mountain to My presence and stay there and I will give you the stone tables on which are intimated the rest of the words of the Torah and the six hundred and thirteen commandments which I have written down to instruct them."[3]
>
> — *Targum Pseudo-Jonathan* Gen. 24:12

Even without claiming that the Decalogue was an exact summary or set of general headings of divine law, some interpreters seemed to see in it the essence of Torah:

> On the verse "In the path of righteousness I [Wisdom, that is, the Torah] walk, in the midst of paths of statute[s]" [Prov. 8:20] R. Ḥuna said: [This is comparable] to the bodyguards of a noblewoman who, when she passes through a [crowded] street, take out their swords and weapons both in front of her and in back. So is it with the Torah, there are regulations in front of her and in back of her. In front of her, as it says, "there He gave them law and statute" [Exod. 15:25], and in back of her, as it says, "These are the laws which you shall place before them . . ." [Exod. 21:1].[4]
>
> — *Midrash ha-Gadol Mishpaṭim* 21:1 (see also *Pesiqta deR. Kahana* 12:8)

Five and Five

As noted in passing, the Bible repeatedly states that the Decalogue was written down on two stone tables:

---

3. Since Exod. 24:12 itself says, "and I will give you the stone tables *and* the Torah *and* the commandments which I have written to instruct them," it might seem to follow that the "Torah and commandments" mentioned are being given *in addition* to the stone tables and what is actually written on them; hence they are "intimated" there, perhaps because they are suggested by the words of the Decalogue itself.

4. From this excerpt it would follow that the Torah consists only of that which is between the two passages cited, namely, the Decalogue.

[Moses recalls:] And He declared to you his covenant, which he commanded you to perform, the ten words; and He wrote them upon two tables of stone.   —Deut. 4:13

Why should there have been two? Surely the whole Decalogue could have fit on a single table if that were desired. (Indeed, archaeologists have discovered numerous tablets of clay and other materials from the ancient Near East; on a single one of these, many more words than those of the Decalogue are usually fitted.)

Ancient interpreters reasoned that if the Ten Commandments were written on two stone tables instead of one, the purpose must have been to highlight a fundamental division within the Decalogue itself: it seemed to break down into two groups of five. This was most evident in the second group of five, which consisted exclusively of "Thou shalt nots." Looking closer, interpreters further noticed that these prohibitions all concerned relations among human beings, while the first five, by contrast, seemed to deal largely with matters between man and God. The distinction was not absolutely clear-cut—honoring one's father and mother was on the "man and God" side—but perhaps some explanation even for that could be found (see below). After all, the Bible itself mentions repeatedly that these commandments were written on *two* tables; it seemed reasonable to suppose that the division into two groups was fundamental.

We find that He divided the ten into two sets of five which He engraved on two tables, and the first five obtained the first place, while the other was awarded the second . . . One set of enactments begins with God the father and maker of all, and ends with parents, who copy His nature by begetting particular persons. The other set contains all the prohibitions, namely, adultery, murder, theft, false witness, [and] covetousness.   —Philo, *The Decalogue* 50–51

Another striking difference between the first and second fives was that, while the name of God is evoked frequently in the former, it appears nowhere in the latter. Perhaps this, too, was no coincidence:

[The Roman emperor Hadrian said to R. Joshua b. Ḥannaniah:] "Come and travel with me to [my] provinces." Everywhere that he brought him he saw his [the emperor's] portrait had been put up. He said: "What is that?" He answered, "My portrait." Finally he [the emperor] took him to an outhouse. He said to him, "Your Majesty, I can see that you are the ruler of this whole province, and that your portrait is put up everywhere, but in this place it is not put up." He said to him: "Are you supposed to be the sage of the Jews? Would it be an honor for a king to have his portrait put up in such a lowly place as this, in such a filthy and despised place?" He answered: "So [with regard to the last five commandments,] would it be to God's glory to have His name connected with murderers and adulterers and thieves?"

— *Pesiqta Rabbati* 21

Which Ten Commandments?

That God gave Israel ten commandments or "words" is quite clear (Exod. 34:28, Deut. 4:13, 10:4). But how they were to be divided up is far from clear: the Bible does not actually assign them numbers indicating where each begins and ends—neither when they were first given to Moses (Exodus 20) nor when Moses later repeated them (Deuteronomy 5). As a result, different systems developed for numbering the commandments.[5]

Some interpreters saw the first-person statement about God in Exod. 20:2 ("I am the Lord your God, who brought you out of the land of Egypt, out of the house of bondage") as the first commandment—a commandment to recognize the existence of God and His role in history. The second commandment would then be the prohibition of worshiping any other god, having "other gods before [or "beside"] Me" (Exod. 20:3); the prohibition of making graven images (Exod. 20:4) that follows next was, according to this system, considered to be a continuation of the same idea, hence, part and parcel of the second commandment:[6]

> The **first** commandment that went forth from the mouth of God was . . . "My people, children of Israel, I am the Lord your God, who redeemed and brought you redeemed out of the Egyptian servitude . . ." The **second** commandment that went forth from the mouth of God was . . . "My people, children of Israel, you shall have no other God beside Me." — *Targum Neophyti* Exod. 20:2–3

Another system of numbering the commandments kept the words of Exod. 20:2 ("I am the Lord your God, who brought you out of the land of Egypt, out of the house of bondage") as a kind of prologue or annex to what follows, the prohibition of having other gods. Considered in this fashion, the first commandment thus became the requirement to believe in and worship

---

5. What is more, even the verse numbers differ in different editions of the Bible.
6. This system of numbering is the one adopted by rabbinic Judaism.

one God alone. The prohibition of making graven images (Exod. 20:4) was then considered to be a separate commandment, the second:

> The first set of five [commandments] is concerned with: [1] the ruler-ship of a single One, by which [rulership] the world is governed; [2] statues and idols and, in general, images made by human hands . . .
>
> — Philo, *The Decalogue* 51

> The first word [commandment] teaches us that God is one and that He only must be worshiped. The second commands us to make no image of any living creature for adoration.
>
> — Josephus, *Jewish Antiquities* 3:91

Nor did the possible variations end there. Some interpreters saw the two parts of Exod. 20:17 (20:14 in some Bibles)—"You shall not covet your neighbor's house; you shall not covet your neighbor's wife"—as two separate command-ments, while others saw only one. What is more surprising, even the order of the commandments was not invariable. The traditional Hebrew text first prohibits murder (Exod. 20:13), then adultery (Exod. 20:14), then stealing (Exod. 20:15), and this order is found as well in the Samaritan Pentateuch and other ancient witnesses. The Septuagint tradition preserves a different order, nay two![7] In Exodus, these prohibitions are first adultery, then stealing, and then murder, while at the repetition of the Decalogue in Deuteronomy 5, the order is adultery, murder, stealing. This last ordering also appears promi-nently in other sources:

> You shall not commit adultery, you shall not murder . . .
>
> — *Nash Papyrus* (Hebrew manuscript, second century B.C.E.)

> The other set of five contains all the prohibitions: adultery, murder, stealing, false witness, covetousness.   — Philo, *The Decalogue* 51

> You shall not commit adultery, for your enemies [the Egyptians] did not commit adultery with you, but you went out "with hand held high" [Exod. 14:8]; You shall not murder, in that your enemies gained power over you in order to kill you, yet you saw their death. You shall not be a false witness against your fellow.[8]
>
> — Pseudo-Philo, *Biblical Antiquities* 11:10–13

7. In some manuscripts; others follow the traditional Hebrew text.

8. In this source, the prohibition of stealing is inexplicably omitted.

The commandments, "You shall not commit adultery, You shall not kill, You shall not steal, You shall not covet . . ."

—Rom. 13:9 (see also James 2:11)

And Jesus said to him, ". . . You know the commandments: Do not commit adultery, Do not kill, Do not steal, Do not bear false witness, Honor your father and mother . . ."

—Luke 18:19–20 (contrast: Matt. 19:16–19, Mark 10:17–19)

These confusions were only augmented by two allusions to the Decalogue found elsewhere in the Hebrew Bible, verses that presented two more variations on the order of these commandments:

There is no faithfulness or kindness or obedience to God in the land, [but only] swearing and lying, **murder and stealing and adultery** . . .

—Hos. 4:1–2

Behold, you trust in deceptive words to no avail. Will you **steal, murder, commit adultery, swear falsely** . . . ? —Jer. 7:8–9

The last order is reflected in at least one later retelling:

[God says:] "I said to them to honor father and mother, and they promised they would do it. And I ordered them not to steal, and they agreed. And I told them not to commit murder, and they held it as agreed that they would not do it. And I commanded them not to commit adultery, and they did not reject this."

—Pseudo-Philo, *Biblical Antiquities* 44:6

It was one thing to receive commandments from God, quite another to carry them out. For, carrying them out inevitably required getting into the little details of things, specifics not necessarily mentioned in the general law. This was especially true of the Decalogue, whose blanket prohibitions seemed to call out for further explanation. When it said, for example, "You shall not murder" (in some translations, "kill"), was the Decalogue referring only to fellow human beings, or might the prohibition also extend to animals? With regard to human beings, did the Bible mean that taking another human life was forbidden under *any* circumstances? What about killing someone who is trying to kill you? And did this same prohibition apply to warfare? Capital punishment?

Such questions had to be answered—there could hardly not have been a time in which at least some people had to confront them in their daily lives. One way to try to answer them was to look elsewhere in the Bible: perhaps something could be found in other chapters that went beyond the general prohibition "You shall not murder." In this case, in fact, further information was not lacking. Since, for example, God had specifically told Noah, "Every moving thing that lives shall be food for you; as I gave you green plants, I give you everything" (Gen. 9:3), it seemed that killing animals for food—or for sacrifices to God, for that matter—was clearly permitted. (True, the Bible went on to forbid eating certain kinds of animals because of their "uncleanness"— see Leviticus 11—but this only supported the overall idea that killing animals for food was itself permitted.) Similarly, warfare (Deuteronomy 20) and capital punishment (Gen. 9:6, Exod. 21:12–17, and frequently thereafter) seemed clearly to be countenanced by the Bible.

But often, the information found elsewhere in the Bible seemed inconclusive. Take, for example, the Decalogue's commandment concerning the Sabbath:

> Remember the Sabbath day to keep it holy. Six days shall you labor and do all your work; but the seventh day is a sabbath to the Lord your God; in it you shall not do any work, you, or your son or your daughter, your manservant or your maidservant, or your cattle or the sojourner who is within your gates.   —Exod. 20:8–10

Here, a host of questions arose. What did "you shall not do any work" mean? Certainly one could not perform one's usual profession on the Sabbath—a farmer could not farm, a roofer could not fix roofs. But could one do work that was not one's usual profession—could a roofer putter around his garden on the Sabbath, planting and weeding and harvesting? Could a farmer climb up on his roof to fix a leak? And if *all* work was forbidden, did that also include things like cooking or cleaning? Presumably, such tasks might be the regular profession of "your manservant or your maidservant." If this is what they normally did for you, since *they* were forbidden to work as well, did that mean that no cooking or cleaning whatsoever was to be done? Or were you allowed to cook and clean but not they? As for not working with one's cattle, did this mean that it was forbidden to milk the cows on the Sabbath? Would that not bring them pain instead of rest?

Elsewhere the Bible also discusses the law of the Sabbath, but these further provisions do not necessarily answer the above questions. For example, Exod. 34:21 states: "Six days shall you work, but on the seventh day you shall rest; in *plowing time* and in *harvest time* you shall rest." Was the mention of these agricultural seasons intended merely to stress that, no matter how pressing the need for intensive labor might be, the Sabbath was to be strictly observed? Or was their mention intended to tell us something about what *kinds* of work were forbidden (and, by implication, what other kinds of work were permitted)? Jer. 17:21–22 further says that even carrying burdens on the Sabbath is forbidden: "Let them not take out a burden from their houses on the Sabbath."[9] But what was a "burden"—a sack of grain? A book? Moreover, this verse seemed to imply that going out of one's house *without* a burden certainly was permitted. Yet Exod. 16:29 says, "Let no man go out of his place on the seventh day." Which was correct? The book of Isaiah further says that God will reward Israel

> . . . if you turn back your foot from the sabbath, from doing your pleasure on My holy day, and call the sabbath a delight and the holy [day] of the Lord honorable; if you honor it, not going your own ways, or seeking your own pleasure, or **speaking a word** . . .   —Isa. 58:13

Here was further information, but hardly clarification. On the contrary, such passages only raised more questions: What did "doing your pleasure on My holy day" include? Did the mention of not "speaking a word" mean that one had to pass the entire day in silence?

One might suppose that all such questions ought to be resolved by each person separately, as a matter of individual conscience. But such an answer was not acceptable in ancient Israel. To begin with, the Bible itself requires that the Sabbath law be enforced, prescribing the death penalty for anyone who works on the Sabbath (Exod. 35:2). How could the courts decide who had violated this law unless what was forbidden was spelled out in all its particulars? Indeed, how could ordinary people know what might subject them to the death penalty and what not? Moreover, quite apart from the question of punishment, how could a person's own conscience reach a decision about the proper way to keep the Sabbath if what the Bible had to say on the subject seemed at times contradictory or even incomprehensible? Finally, conscience or not, ought there not to be some agreed standard of observance? If all people were free to determine the law for themselves, could the law truly be said to exist?

For all these reasons, the Sabbath laws, indeed, *all* biblical laws were the object of particular interpretive scrutiny. From a very early period, no doubt, a body of authoritative interpretations accompanied the various legal prescriptions given by God to Israel, and these are reflected here and there in the Bible itself as well as in contemporaneous and subsequent Jewish and Christian writings. The ten laws of the Decalogue alone gave rise to an impressive body of interpretation.

---

9. See also Neh. 13:15–16.

No Talk of Weekday Matters

About the Sabbath itself, the Decalogue's curt "Remember the Sabbath day to keep it holy" was subject to a host of applications and elaborations. Not all of these could even be called "interpretations." Further practices and traditions—in the form of numerous specific do's and don'ts—soon characterized the Jewish observance of this special day of celebration and devotion to God, and some of these had no apparent connection to what the Bible said about the Sabbath:

> The *halakhot* [established practices] of the Sabbath are like mountains hanging by a hair—there is little that is written [in the Bible] but numerous *halakhot*. —m. Ḥagigah 1:8

But many Sabbath practices did indeed come from Scripture—or, rather, from the interpretation of Scripture. Thus, as quoted above, the book of Isaiah suggested that God would reward the people of Israel if, on the Sabbath day, they would take care to "honor it [the Sabbath], not going your own ways, or seeking your own pleasure, or *speaking a word*" (Isa. 58:13). If this last phrase did not refer to refraining utterly from speaking, then what did it mean?

Interpreters came to the conclusion that the forbidden "word" in question referred to speaking about things *connected with working*. In other words, when God forbade "work" on the Sabbath, He forbade not only doing the work itself, but even planning it, talking about it, or arranging it on the Sabbath:

> The man who does any work on it [the Sabbath] is to die. Any man who desecrates this day; who lies with a woman; who **says anything about work on it**—that he is to set out on a trip on it, or about any selling or buying—or who on it draws water which he had not prepared for himself on the sixth day; or who lifts any load to bring it outside his tent or his house is to die. —*Jubilees* 50:8

> And on the sabbath day, let no one speak a vain or empty word, nor press his fellow about any debt, nor let him judge concerning wealth or profit. Let him not speak concerning matters of craft or work **to be done the next morning**. —*Damascus Document* 10:17–18

> A man may not hire workers on the sabbath [to work the next day], nor even instruct his fellow to hire workers for him. —m. *Shabbat* 23:3

Guard the Sabbath Borders

When does the Sabbath begin? At dawn? On the preceding midnight? Even earlier? The Bible does not provide a clear answer. But this was obviously an important question: if people were to do no work on the Sabbath, they had to know at what hour of the day this prohibition came into effect each week.

There is good evidence that, even within biblical times, the normal Jewish practice was to start the Sabbath not on Saturday morning, but at or near sunset on Friday. (This is still the Jewish practice today.)

> [Nehemiah recalls:] Then I remonstrated with the nobles of Judah and said to them, "What is this evil thing that you are doing, profaning the sabbath day? . . ." And so, **when it began to be dark** at the gates of Jerusalem before the sabbath, I ordered that the doors should be shut and gave orders that they not be opened until after the sabbath.
>
> —Neh. 13:17–19

In the light of this passage, then, work was to be stopped before the beginning of the Sabbath in the evening. But how much before? A number of texts suggest that the time to stop working came some time before the arrival of the Sabbath—perhaps even in the middle of Friday afternoon—lest some circumstance arise that might compel people to violate the deadline.

> After pursuing them for some distance, they were obliged to return because the hour was late. For it was the **day before the sabbath,** and for that reason they did not continue their pursuit.   —2 Macc. 8:25–26

> Caesar Augustus, Pontifex Maximus with tribunician power, decrees as follows: . . .The Jews may follow their own customs in accordance with the law of their fathers . . . that they need not give bond [to appear in court] on the sabbath or on the day of preparation for it after the ninth hour [of the day, roughly, 3:00 P.M.].
>
> —Josephus, *Jewish Antiquities* 16:162–163

But if Jews ceased work as early as the middle of Friday afternoon, was this not one of those practices that really had no Scriptural justification, one of those "mountains suspended by a hair"? Some ancient interpreters thought otherwise. For they noticed that, when the Decalogue is repeated in Deuteronomy 5, the wording of the Sabbath law is slightly different: among other things, instead of saying "*Remember* the sabbath day" as in Exod. 20:8, there the text says to "keep" or "guard" it (Deut. 5:12). Perhaps this was not an innocent variation; perhaps the word "keep" or "guard" had been used in the repetition to introduce a new idea, that the Sabbath's holiness had to be *safeguarded* by having people cease work well before the Sabbath's entry:

> No one shall do work on Friday from the time when the sphere of the sun is distant from the gate [by] its [the sun's] full size, for this is why it is said, "**Guard** the Sabbath day to sanctify it" [Deut. 5:12].
>
> — *Damascus Document* 10:14–17

Other interpreters explained the practice somewhat differently:

> Shammai the elder said: "Remember" it [the Sabbath] from the time before it has entered, and "guard" it from that time forward.
>
> — *Mekhilta deR. Shimon b. Yoḥai* p. 148

> "Remember" and "guard"—*remember* before [the Sabbath starts] and *guard* it after [the Sabbath is over]. From this it was deduced that one is to add [time] from the profane [that is, from the rest of the week] to the sacred [that is, the Sabbath]. — *Mekhilta deR. Ishmael, Yitro* 7

Do Not Go Out Too Far

Exod. 16:29 says, "Let no man go out of his place on the seventh day." This commandment comes in the midst of the account of the manna that God gave to the Israelites during their desert wanderings: a person was not to "go out of his place" on the Sabbath in search of manna, and—in order to compensate— a double portion of manna would be distributed to the people of Israel on the sixth day.

Theoretically, then, this commandment not to leave one's "place" might well be understood to have applied only during the time of the wilderness wanderings, and to have been given specifically with regard to manna. However, that is not how ancient interpreters saw it: this law applied to *them* as well. But then, what did it mean not to leave one's "place"? Most ancient interpreters felt that "place" must not be limited to one's own actual house or grounds—that would be too narrow a construction. Instead, the sense of the restriction must be not to travel too far from one's home, for example, not to set out on a journey.

> Any man who does work; who goes on a **trip;** who works farmland, whether at his home or in any other place . . . a man who does any of these things on the sabbath is to die. — *Jubilees* 50:12

> We are not permitted to travel either on the sabbath or on a festival.
>
> — Josephus, *Jewish Antiquities* 13:252 (also 14:227)

At some point, however, a further question arose: what constitutes going on a trip? Certainly if one moved about within one's own town or village, that was not traveling; but could one, for example, go beyond the walls of a city? Here Scripture offered some help, for, in describing the establishment of cities for the Levites, the Bible said:

> The pasture lands of the cities which you shall give to the Levites shall reach from the wall of the city outward a thousand cubits all around. And you shall measure, outside the city, for the east side two thousand cubits, and for the south side two thousand cubits, and for the west side two thousand cubits, and for the north side two thousand cubits, the city being in the middle; this shall belong to them as pasture land for their cities.
> —Num. 35:4–5

This passage seemed definitely to establish that the territory belonging to a city extended even beyond its walls. How far was not exactly clear: the passage first speaks of a thousand cubits (between a quarter and a third of a mile) and then of two thousand. But one or the other must have been the permitted distance beyond the city walls.

> [On the Sabbath] let no one walk about outside his city more than a thousand cubits.   —Damascus Document 10:21 (see also 11:5–6)

> Then they returned to Jerusalem from the mount called Olivet, which is near Jerusalem, a sabbath day's journey away.[10]   —Acts 1:12

> There was a great courtyard in Jerusalem called Beit Ya'zeq, and that was where witnesses [testifying about the new month] would go ... At first [the practice was that] they would not budge from there the whole day [if it was the Sabbath; later] Rabban Gamli'el the Elder decreed that they could travel up to **two thousand cubits** in any direction. And not only these [witnesses], but likewise a midwife on her way to assist in childbirth, or someone on his way to save a person from a fire, or from an enemy soldier, or from [drowning in] a river, or from a cave-in—all these are like townsmen of the city, and they may [therefore travel] **two thousand cubits** in any direction.
> —m. Rosh ha-Shanah 2:5

On that same day R. Akiba interpreted: "And you shall measure, outside the city, for the east side two thousand cubits" [Num. 35:5]

10. The actual distance involved here is apparently a little more than half a mile, that is, two thousand cubits.

while earlier it says "from the wall of the city outward a thousand cubits all around" [Num. 35:5]. One cannot say [that it means] a thousand cubits, since it [also] says two thousand, and one cannot say [that it means] two thousand, since it already said one thousand. How can these be reconciled? A thousand cubits of open land, and two thousand is the sabbath limit.   —m. Soṭah 5:3

Do Not Take Vain Oaths

Quite apart from the commandment about the Sabbath, there were other laws in the Decalogue that, on close inspection, likewise seemed puzzling. Take, for example, the prohibition that comes just before the Sabbath commandment:

> You shall not take the name of the Lord your God in vain; for the Lord will not acquit anyone who takes His name in vain.   —Exod. 20:7

What, in concrete terms, is being forbidden here? Mentioning God's name needlessly? Under *any* circumstances? From an early point, this commandment was explained as referring specifically to the taking of oaths using God's name. Many interpreters understood it as a prohibition of taking such oaths when they were not necessary:

> Do not accustom your mouth to **oaths,** and do not habitually utter
>   the name of the Holy One;
> for as a servant who is continually under scrutiny will not lack
>   bruises, so also the man who always swears and utters the name
>   will **not be cleansed** from sin.[11]
>   —Sir. 23:9–10

> The [Decalogue] forbids us to take God's name in vain: the good man's word, it means, should itself be an **oath**—firm, unswerving, utterly free from falsehood, securely planted on truth. And if indeed circumstances should require us to swear, then the oath should be made by father and mother . . . for parents are likenesses and copies of the divine power.   —Philo, *Special Laws* 2:2

11. The overall sense of this puzzling verse seems to rest on the comparison between the "servant who is continually under scrutiny" and the person who needlessly swears oaths by the name of God. Just as the former is, by the nature of his situation, bound to be punished sooner or later, so does the one who swears needlessly put himself in harm's way: ultimately he too will have (divinely inflicted) bruises, for the Lord will not "cleanse him" from the sin of a vain oath. The word "cleanse" here alludes to the end of Exod. 20:7, which more literally says that the Lord will not cleanse anyone who takes His name in vain.

The first word [commandment] teaches us that God is one and that He only must be worshiped. The second commands us to make no image of any living creature for adoration, the third not to swear by God on any frivolous matter. — Josephus, *Jewish Antiquities* 3:91

Elsewhere the taking of needless oaths is likewise condemned, though without specific allusion to the Decalogue:

[Whoe]ver attests to a thing by the divine name for any [. . . shall be punished]. — (1QS) *Community Rule* 6:27

If someone sins against you, speak to him peacefully . . . and if he confesses and repents, forgive him. But if he denies, do not dispute with him, **lest he take an oath** and you thereby sin doubly.

— *Testament of Gad* 6:3–4

Again, you have heard that it was said to the men of old, "You shall not swear falsely, but shall perform to the Lord what you have sworn." But I say to you, Do not swear at all, either by heaven, for it is the throne of God, or by the earth, for it is His footstool [Isa. 66:1], or by Jerusalem, for it is the city of the great King [Ps. 48:2] . . . Let what you say be simply "Yes" or "No"; anything more than this comes from the evil one. — Matt. 5:33–37

But above all, brethren, do not swear, either by heaven or by earth or with any other oath, but let your yes be yes and your no be no, that you may not fall under condemnation. — James 5:12

For I am swearing to you, my children—but look! I am not swearing by any oath at all, neither by heaven nor by earth nor by any other creature which the Lord created. — 2 *Enoch* (J) 49:1

It says [in Scripture]: "And if you swear, 'As the Lord lives' in truth, in justice, and in uprightness . . ." [Jer. 4:2]. God said to Israel: Do not think that it is permissible for you to swear by My name, even if it is a true oath; you may not swear by My name unless you have all these traits [that is, truth, justice, and uprightness], as it is [also] written, "Fear God and serve Him and cling to Him and by His name shall you swear" [Deut. 10:20].[12] — *Midrash Tanḥuma, Mattot* 1

12. This last verse is similarly being interpreted to mean that only if you fear God and serve Him and cling to Him may you swear by His name.

No False Oaths

If some interpreters understood Exod. 20:7 as referring to vain oaths, others apparently associated this commandment specifically with taking a *false* oath:

> You shall not swear by the name of the Lord your God in vain, for the Lord will not find innocent anyone who swears by His name **falsely.**
>
> — *Targum Onqelos* Exod. 20:7

> My people, my people, house of Israel: You shall not swear in vain by the name of the Lord your God, and you shall not take an **oath** by My name **and lie**, for I, the Lord your great God call [people] to account, and I will call to account anyone who lies by my name.
>
> — *Fragment Targum* (P) Exod. 20:7

> "You shall not take the name of the Lord in vain . . .": Do not hasten to take a **false** oath and let not an oath be habitual in your mouth, for great is the punishment thereof.   — *Midrash of the Ten Commandments* 3

This interpretation might seem strange, since the commandment itself says nothing about falsehood and only refers to taking God's name in vain. But the word "vain" in Hebrew is sometimes synonymous with "false," especially with regard to speech.[13] Indeed, the connection of these two terms is particularly evident elsewhere in the Decalogue, in the prohibition regarding testimony against one's neighbor. For in fact this commandment appears in two different forms in the traditional Hebrew text:

> You shall not bear witness **falsely** against your neighbor.
>
> — Exod. 20:16

> You shall not bear witness **in vain** against your neighbor.
>
> — Deut. 5:20

The apparent interchangeability of the words "falsely" and "in vain" in these two versions of the same law may have convinced ancient interpreters that, in Exod. 20:7 as well, "in vain" means "falsely."

Honor Your Heavenly and Earthly Fathers

Why should the Decalogue have said, "Honor your father and your mother"? Murder, adultery, theft, false witness, even coveting another's property—prohibitions such as these were, arguably, necessary if society was to function at

---

13. See Exod. 23:1; Ps. 12:3, 24:4, 41:7, 144:8; Prov. 30:8; Ezek. 12:24, 13:6, 21:34, etc.

all. As for the laws that began the Decalogue—recognizing God as the only God and outlawing idolatry, not taking God's name in vain, and keeping the Sabbath—these seemed fundamental matters for Israel in particular, the people whom God had chosen as His own. But between these two groups of laws came the strange provision about honoring parents. Surely *this* was not a fundamental requirement for a well-ordered society. Parents did not need to be honored, however nice a thing it might be; indeed, perhaps some parents did not deserve to be honored. And if the intention behind this commandment was simply to make sure that children take care of their parents in their old age, when they might no longer be able to provide for themselves, then let the law state that!

Faced with these questions, ancient interpreters sought to understand this commandment with reference to its position within the laws of the Decalogue. Surely it was no accident that it came where it did; perhaps its very existence was to be explained by the similarity between honoring parents and honoring God. (This would also serve to maintain the five-and-five division discussed above.)

> They [the Jews] honor only the Immortal who always rules, and then their parents.
>
> — *Sibylline Oracles* 3:593–594

> After giving the commandment concerning the seventh day, he gives a fifth commandment concerning the honoring of parents, putting it on the borderline between the two sets of five. For it is the last of the first set, in which laws of the sacred are given, and yet it is connected as well to the second set, which deals with the duties of man to man. I believe the reason to be this: the very nature of parenthood places it on the borderline between the immortal and the mortal, the mortal because they [that is, parents] belong to [the class of] men and other animals through the perishability of the body; the immortal because the act of generation assimilates them to God, the parent of all.
>
> — Philo, *Decalogue* 106–107 (also *Who Is Heir* 171–172; *Special Laws* 2:225)

> Honor God foremost, and afterward your parents.
>
> — Pseudo-Phocylides, *Sentences* 8

> The Torah ranks the honoring of parents second only to that of God . . . It requires respect to be paid by the young to all their elders because God is the most ancient of all.   — Josephus, *Against Apion* 2:206

It says "Honor your father and mother," while elsewhere it says
"Honor the Lord with your wealth" [Prov. 3:9]. Honoring one's father
[and mother] is thus equated with honoring God.

— *Mekhilta deR. Shimon b. Yoḥai* p. 152

Perhaps influenced by the same motif:

Whoever fears the Lord will honor his father and will serve his parents
as masters.

— Sir. 3:7 (from Greek and Old Latin texts)

. . .] Honor Him as a father [. . .

— (4Q415) *Sapiential Work A* fragment 2, col. 2

I had said to them to love father and mother, yet they did not honor
Me, their creator. — Pseudo-Philo, *Biblical Antiquities* 44:7

A Mishap to the Baby

Beyond the Decalogue lay further laws and commandments, indeed, nearly
the whole of the next three chapters (Exodus 21–23) consists of additional legal
instructions given by God to Moses on Mt. Sinai (nor do God's laws end
there!). Many of these additional laws concern ordinary features of daily life;
some have to do with legal disputes between human beings, cases involving
negligence and damages and the like; others belong to the sphere of criminal
law; and yet others are in the domain of cultic law—sacrifices, sacred festivals,
and other matters having to do with the service of God.

Interpreters investigated each of these laws with great care. It could hardly
have been otherwise, since God had demanded their proper and complete
observance. But, as with the laws of the Decalogue, even the simplest prescrip-
tion can sometimes create ambiguities. And some of the laws that come after
the Decalogue are anything but simple. Take, for example, the following:

When men strive together and hurt a pregnant woman so that her
offspring come out, and there is no mishap, he [the one who struck
her] shall be punished in accordance with what her husband shall
impose upon him, and it will be given over to adjudication. But if there
is a mishap, then you shall give a life for a life [literally, "a soul for a
soul"]—an eye for an eye, a tooth for a tooth, a hand for a hand, a foot
for a foot, a burn for a burn, a wound for a wound, a bruise for a
bruise. — Exod. 21:22–25

This law comes in the midst of a series of statutes concerned with liability for personal injury. This particular case involves a pregnant woman, apparently an innocent bystander at a fight, who is struck by one of the fighters in such a way that she miscarries.[14] The above translation is an attempt to duplicate some of the difficulties of the law as it appears in the traditional Hebrew text. And difficulties there certainly are. What, for example, does the text mean by saying "and there is no mishap" when the case itself describes a mishap? Apparently, the mishap mentioned refers to something other than, still more severe than, a miscarriage. Or is it the case that the "mishap" applies to *some* kinds of miscarriages but not all? Then there is the apparent contradiction in the penalty described when there is no "mishap": on the one hand, the guilty party seems to have to pay whatever the husband demands (he "shall be punished in accordance with what her husband shall impose upon him"), while on the other hand the matter "will be given over to adjudication"—so that perhaps he *won't* be punished in accordance with the husband's demands at all, but will be subject to the judges' decision. And beyond this question is that of the general principle that follows, "An eye for an eye." How does this principle relate to the previous case? And how is such a general principle to be enforced in other cases?

These difficulties are apparent even in ancient attempts to translate or restate this law:

> If two men are fighting, and a pregnant woman is struck in her belly, and her child comes out **not fully formed**, he shall pay a fine. As the woman's husband shall impose, he shall pay it with a valuation. But if it is fully formed, he shall give a soul for a soul. An eye for an eye, a tooth for a tooth, a hand for a hand, a foot for a foot, a burning for a burning, a wound for a wound, a stripe for a stripe.
>
> —Septuagint Exod. 21:22–25

The Septuagint's interpretation (for it has apparently deviated from direct translation here) holds that the "mishap" in question is the death of a baby at a relatively advanced state of development, that is, one that was "fully formed" in the womb. If the accident happens *before* the baby is fully formed, then the guilty party is merely fined; but if the baby is fully formed, then the man who struck her is liable to the death penalty. Among other things, this interpretation seems to imply that the unformed fetus is not yet a "soul" for whom the principle of "a soul for a soul" may be implied.

---

14. The Hebrew expression seems to refer to miscarriage, although it might arguably refer to the provoking of spontaneous labor.

If a man comes to blows with a pregnant woman and strikes her on the belly and she miscarries, then, if the result of the miscarriage is unshaped and undeveloped, he must be fined both for the outrage and for obstructing the artist Nature in her creative work of bringing into life the fairest of living creatures, man. But if the offspring is already shaped and all the limbs have their proper qualities and places in the system, he must die, for that which answers to this description is a human being, which he has destroyed in the workshop of Nature, who had decided [only] that the hour was not yet right for bringing it [the baby] out into the light, like a statue lying in a studio requiring nothing more than to be carried outside and released from confinement. — Philo, *Special Laws* 3:108–109

Here Philo basically follows the Septuagint: the "mishap" occurs in the case when a fully formed human being has been killed. Indeed, Philo's image of the completed statue implies, still more clearly than the Septuagint, that the baby in question was just about to be born. Philo also adds a more explicit version of the Septuagint's rather obscure phrase, "he shall pay it with a valuation." For Philo, this phrase apparently refers to two separate payments (or assessments), one for the act itself against the pregnant woman ("the outrage") and the second for the damage done in destroying a fetus before its time. Finally, it is to be noted that here Philo distorts somewhat the initial situation: there is no mention of the men fighting and, hence, no hint (as there certainly might be in the Bible) that the damage was accidental.[15]

A Mishap to the Mother

Jerome translated the same passage in markedly different fashion:

If men were fighting and someone struck a pregnant woman and she miscarried but she herself lived, he will be subject to a fine, as much as the woman's husband shall request and as the judges decree. If, however, her death shall follow, let him pay a soul for a soul, an eye for an eye, a tooth for a tooth, a hand for a hand, a foot for a foot, a burning for a burning, a wound for a wound, a bruise for a bruise.
— (Vulgate) Exod. 21:22–25

According to Jerome's understanding, the "mishap" in question has nothing to do with the fetus's stage of development, but relates to the life of the

15. Philo treats the same law elsewhere, *Preliminary Studies* 137, where, however, he more accurately reflects the situation described in the biblical text.

mother. If the mother's life is unharmed, then the offender simply pays a fine—otherwise, it is a "soul for a soul." Not surprisingly, the Vulgate here is in consonance with rabbinic interpreters:

> "And there is no mishap . . ." that is, to the woman.
>
> —*Mekhilta deR. Ishmael, Neziqin* 8

As for the fine itself, Jerome accurately duplicates, without deciding, the ambiguity of the traditional Hebrew text: "as much as the woman's husband shall request and as the judges decree" does not really say who, in the end, will determine the amount of the fine.

The same line of interpretation is attested earlier, in rabbinic texts as well as in Josephus' restatement. Note, however, what the latter adds:

> He who kicks [!] a pregnant woman, if the woman miscarries, he shall be fined **by the judges** for having, by the destruction of the fruit of her womb, diminished the population, and a sum is also to be given by him to the woman's husband. If she should **die** by the blow, then he likewise shall die, the law deeming it fit that a soul be paid for a soul . . .
>
> One who maims someone will suffer the same, being deprived of that which he deprived the other, unless the one who was maimed is willing to accept money [instead]. For the law permits the victim to establish damages for the incident, unless he wishes to be particularly severe.
>
> —Josephus, *Jewish Antiquities* 4:278–280

Here again, as in the *Mekhilta deR. Ishmael* and the Vulgate, it is the life of the mother, and not the state of the fetus, that defines whether a "mishap" has occurred. At the same time, there are a number of common points with Philo's interpretation. Like Philo, Josephus deletes the "men fighting" and presents the case as a direct and apparently intentional injury to the mother; and as Philo states, if there is no "mishap," then *two* fines are to be paid. Indeed, Josephus offers his own rationale for the two fines: one is paid for the damage to society as a whole, since the offender "by the destruction of the fruit of her womb, diminished the population," while the second is paid to the family of the injured party.

Somewhat different is the interpretation of this fine offered in an early rabbinic source:

> "In accordance with what her husband shall impose upon him"—I might think this means as much as he [the husband] should want [to

impose]; that is why the text says "and it will be given over to adjudication"—this means that he shall pay only what the judges say.

— *Mekhilta deR. Ishmael, Neziqin* 8

Money for an Eye

Josephus also offers a striking interpretation of the famous biblical injunction "an eye for an eye." This law, calling for the offender to suffer as a penalty the same offense that he himself has inflicted, is paralleled in many other legal codes outside the Bible, where it is sometimes referred to as the "law of the talion" (*lex* or *ius talionis*). Some biblical interpreters stoutly defended the principle:

> Our law exhorts us to equality when it ordains that the penalties inflicted on offenders should correspond to their actions, that their property should suffer if the wrongdoing affected their neighbor's property, and their bodies if the offence was a bodily injury, the penalty being determined according to the limb, part, or sense affected, while if his malice extended to taking another's life, his own life should be the forfeit. To tolerate a system in which the crime and punishment do not correspond, have no common ground, and belong to different categories, is to subvert rather than uphold legality.
>
> — Philo, *Special Laws* 3:182

> The Boethusians[16] had a book of decrees that said: "An eye for an eye, a tooth for a tooth" [means that] if someone knocked out his fellow's tooth, he should knock out his tooth [in return], if he blinded his fellow's eye, he should blind *his* eye, [so that] both of them are the same. — *Megillat Ta'anit* [ms. Oxford, compare Lichtenstein p. 331]

Josephus, however, seems to know of another interpretation, according to which "an eye for an eye" does not necessarily always mean that. Instead, at least in cases of injury (rather than death), he asserts that "the law permits the victim to establish damages for the incident."[17]

The same principle was stated still more strongly elsewhere:

16. A certain Jewish group in late antiquity is usually referred to by this name in rabbinic texts. However, in some of the most reliable manuscripts this name is written as two words, *bêt sîn;* it has been proposed that the name be understood not as "Boethusians" but as "the house [or "academy"] of the [Es]senes."

17. How indeed could the law of "an eye for an eye" work in the case of the man who struck a pregnant woman and caused her to miscarry? Josephus' statement that "the law permits the victim to

Does not Scripture say an eye for an eye? Why not take this literally to mean the [offender's] eye [is to recompense the victim's]? Let this not even enter your mind! . . . R. Dosthai b. Yehudah said: An eye for an eye means monetary compensation. But could not actual retaliation be meant? What then would you say if the eye of one was big and the eye of the other was little—how in such a case will an [actual] eye for an eye [be just]? . . . R. Simeon b. Yoḥai said: . . . What can you say in the case of a blind man who put out the eye of someone, or of a maimed person [without arms] who caused someone else's hand to be cut off, or of a lame person [without legs] who caused someone else's leg to be broken? How can I uphold the principle of an eye for an eye in such cases?

—b. *Baba Qamma* 83b–84a

Traditions of the Elders

Jewish observance of the laws in the Torah was sometimes at odds with what appeared to be required by the biblical text itself. Sometimes a particular practice seemed to be a very stringent interpretation (or expansion) of what the Bible demanded (for example, ceasing all work on Friday afternoon). At other times actual practice looked more lenient (accepting payment in lieu of "an eye for an eye"). Most of the time, the Bible's prescriptions were made more *specific* in everyday practice; general strictures were understood as applying in this case but not that case, in this fashion but not that. Moreover, there were all manner of things not mentioned in the Bible at all about which, nevertheless, religious regulations and strictures existed.

In short, accepted practices in the observance of religious law—what people actually did in their daily lives—seemed to depend on far more than what was written in the Decalogue or any other legislation in the Bible. Rabbinic Judaism, we have seen, was candid about these "mountains suspended by a hair" not being explicitly rooted in the biblical text. Indeed, some such practices were, from the same standpoint, not even "suspended by a hair" but frankly "floating in the air" (m. *Ḥagigah* 1:8).

A question then naturally arose: by whose authority were these other practices and stipulations established? The practices themselves were frequently spoken of as the "traditions of the elders," and this in itself gave them a certain authority. If they had been handed down by the *elders* (or "fathers")

---

establish damages for the incident" implies that he understands the words of Exod. 21:23, "he will be subject to a fine, as much as the woman's husband shall request," as extending to other cases of injury or "maiming."

since ancient times, was not this fact alone sufficient to guarantee their validity?

> But I will tell the story[18] of Moses as I have learned it, both from the sacred books, those wonderful monuments of his wisdom which he has left behind him, and from some of the **elders of the nation**, for I have always interwoven **what I was told** with what I read.
>
> — Philo, *Moses* 1:4

> Besides these [laws] there is a host of other things which belong to **unwritten customs and institutions** or are contained in the laws themselves.[19]
> — Philo, *Hypothetica* 7:6

> Why has Israel been given over to the Gentiles as a reproach? Why has the people whom You have loved been given over to godless tribes, and the **law of our fathers** made of no effect, and the **written arrangements** [*dispositiones*] no longer existent?[20]
> — 4 Ezra 4:23

> For you have heard of my former life in Judaism, how I persecuted the church of God violently and tried to destroy it; and I had advanced in Judaism beyond many of my own age among my people, so extremely zealous was I for **the traditions of my fathers**.
> — Gal. 1:13–14 (also Philem. 3:5–6)

> Now when the Pharisees gathered together to him [Jesus], with some of the scribes, who had come from Jerusalem, they saw that some of his disciples ate with hands defiled, that is, unwashed. For the Pharisees, and all the Jews, do not eat unless they wash their hands, observing the **tradition of the elders**; and when they come from the market place, they do not eat unless they purify themselves; and there are many other traditions which they observe, the washing of cups and pots and vessels of bronze.
> — Mark 7:4–5 (also Matt. 15:1–20)

18. Here Philo may mean not only the story of Moses' life, but the explanation of the laws he promulgated, since it is particularly in the latter area that he seems most to depend on the traditions of the "elders of the nation."

19. Philo likewise says elsewhere that Jews are trained by "the sacred laws *and the unwritten customs* to acknowledge one God who is the Father and Maker of the world" (*Embassy to Gaius* 115); the indicated phrase similarly suggests that Philo conceives of authoritative teaching as falling into two categories, that which is written in Scripture and that which has been transmitted in unwritten form. This conception is quite distinct from the concept of "unwritten law" in Philo, which is hardly to be equated with the "oral Torah" of later rabbinic literature. See also *Special Laws* 4:149–150.

20. The expression "law of our fathers" here (also in 2 Macc. 6:1, 7:37) appears in conjunction with the "written arrangements" and it may be that this juxtaposition is intended to include both Scripture and the "traditions of the elders" that accompanied the biblical text.

The Pharisees had passed on to the people certain ordinances handed down by the fathers and not written in the laws of Moses, for which reason they are rejected by the sect of the Sadducees, who hold that only those ordinances should be considered valid which were written down, and those which had been handed down by the fathers need not be observed. —Josephus, *Jewish Antiquities* 13:297 (see also 13:408, 17:41)

[Baruch writes to his exiled brethren:] "And give this letter and the traditions of the Torah to your children after you, as also your fathers handed down to you." —*2 Baruch* 84:9

Moses Was Given More than the Torah

But the authority of orally transmitted traditions—even traditions that had been handed down by the elders from ages past—was nonetheless open to question. If such teachings were not written down in one of the sacred books, who could guarantee that they *had* to be observed? Indeed, if they were so important, why didn't they appear in the Bible itself? A famous edict of Justinian I, emperor of the Eastern Roman empire between 527 and 565 C.E., later forbade the teachings handed down by the elders precisely on the grounds that they have no divine authority:

But that which is called by them [the Jews] *deuterosis* [apparently, Mishnah] we forbid completely, because it is **not included among the sacred books and has not been transmitted to us by the prophets** . . . they add unwritten prattle derived from the outside and devised to corrupt ordinary men. —Justinian, *Novella* 146 (553 C.E.)

Long before this time, however, another answer to the question of the authority of such teachings had been put forward. *These nonbiblical teachings also stemmed from Moses.* After all, it hardly seemed reasonable that, at the time of the great revelation at Mt. Sinai, God would give Moses a law forbidding work on the Sabbath without also telling him what the word "work" does or does not include and at what time of day one has to stop working. If such things were not actually spelled out in the Bible itself, Moses must nonetheless have asked about them; presumably, the answers that he received must have been passed on to the people in some form other than the Pentateuch.

Oral Teachings from Moses

Some interpreters thus asserted that the chain of teachings referred to above as the "traditions of the elders" had begun with Moses himself. He had indeed learned specific rules and applications beyond what was included in the Pentateuch, and these further teachings he had passed on to the Israelites orally. Ever after, such oral teachings had been transmitted from generation to generation. (This idea of authoritative, orally transmitted teachings was characteristic of the school that was to become rabbinic Judaism.) Since, according to this line of thought, these oral teachings had originally come from God through Moses, they of course had authority equal to what was written in the Pentateuch. Some rabbinic texts even speak of *two* Torahs, the oral and the written, both going back to the Sinai revelation:

And Aaron said to them: "Be patient, For Moses will come [down from Mt. Sinai], and he will bring judgment near to us and will illuminate the law for us and will **explain from his own mouth** the law of God and set up rules for our race."
— Pseudo-Philo, *Biblical Antiquities* 12:2

The people, having thus heard from God Himself that of which Moses had told them, rejoicing in these commandments, dispersed from the assembly. But later on, they continually went to his tent, to ask him also to provide laws from God. And he both established laws and, in after times, **indicated how they should act in all circumstances.**
— Josephus, *Jewish Antiquities* 3:93–94

Moses received the Torah at Mt. Sinai and passed it on [orally] to Joshua and Joshua to the elders and the elders to the prophets and the prophets passed it on to the men of the Great Assembly.
— m. *Abot* 1:1 (see also m. *Pe'ah* 2:6, *'Eduyyot* 8:7, *Yadayim* 4:3)

It happened that some stood before Shammai and said to him, "Rabbi, how many *torahs* do you have?" He said, "Two, one that is written and one that is oral."
— *Abot deR. Natan* (A) 15

"These are the statutes and the ordinances and the laws [literally, *torahs*, in the plural] which the Lord made between Him and the people of Israel on Mount Sinai by Moses" [Lev. 26:46] . . . [The phrase] *and the laws* indicates that two *torahs* were given to Israel, one in writing and one orally.
— *Sifra Behuqqotai* 8

Said R. Shimon b. Resh Laqish: "And I will give you the tables of stone, the Torah and the commandments, which I have written to teach them" [Exod. 24:12]: the *tables* refers to the ten commandments, the *Torah* to the Pentateuch [as a whole], the *commandments* to the Mishnah; *which I have written*—these are the prophets and the writings

[that is, the rest of Scripture, and] *to teach them*—this is the Talmud. All of these were given to Moses at Mt. Sinai.
—b. *Berakhot* 5a

In an elaboration of this idea, even teachings clearly ascribed not to Moses, but to later figures—biblical prophets or even postbiblical sages and interpreters—were sometimes asserted to have been part of the same great revelation at Mt. Sinai:

> That which the prophets were later to prophesy in every subsequent age, they received here at Mount Sinai. For thus did Moses report to Israel [Deut. 29:13–14] "Not with you alone do I make this covenant . . . but with those who are standing here among us today, and with those who are not here among us today." Now [the last clause] is not worded as "not *standing* among us today," but only "not among us today," for these are the souls that were yet to be created, who have no substance, and of whom "standing" could not be said. For though they did not exist at the time, every one of these received his portion . . . And [so,] not only did all the prophets receive their prophecies from Sinai, **but also the sages** who were to arise in every generation—each one of them received his [teaching] from Sinai, as it is written, "These words the Lord spoke to all your assembly on the mountain amid the fire, the cloud, and the darkness, with great voice, and He will not add" [Deut. 5:19].[21]
> —Midrash Tanḥuma, Yitro 11

A Hidden Torah

At the same time, the provisions of these orally transmitted teachings were, where possible, asserted to be interpretations of things actually found in the written text rather than totally independent of it. This idea, present in rabbinic writings, is found as well in the writings of the Qumran community, which speak of "hidden things" and "revealed things" in the Torah, the former apparently esoteric interpretations of the "revealed" text. These interpretations were hidden in the sense that they were not immediately obvious but had to be searched out and understood between the lines:

> They [that is, those "evil men who walk in the path of wickedness"] are not counted among [the members of] His covenant, since they do not search out or interpret his statutes in order to learn the **hidden things** [that is, hidden interpretations]; because [of their ignorance of these things] they have gone astray and incurred guilt. And [furthermore,]

---

21. These last words are interpreted to mean that God added nothing in later times to what had been imparted at Sinai. Note that others translate the verse: "And He did not cease."

with regard to the **revealed things**, they have acted high-handedly [that is, they have intentionally violated the laws whose interpretation is well known]. — (1QS) *Community Rule* 5:10–11

What is more, these laws were hidden in the sense that they were to be kept secret from those outside the community; members were thus urged to separate themselves from

> the Men of the Pit, and to keep hidden the [secret] counsel of the Torah from among the men of perversion; but to reproach [only] those who choose the Way with true knowledge and right judgment, each according to his spirit and what is proper for the time, to guide them in knowledge and so to introduce them to wonderful and true secrets within members of the community.
> — (1QS) *Community Rule* 9:16–18

Moses' Secret Book

There existed, however, another explanation for practices and laws not specifically contained in the Pentateuch. Like the "oral-tradition" explanation, this one likewise went back to Mt. Sinai: Moses had indeed received far more information there than what he had written in the Pentateuch. However, these further teachings were not passed on orally but written down *in another book,* one that was to remain secret for a time.[22] Indeed, such a secret book might have contained all manner of other divine revelations, not only applications of divine law (which included such vital issues as the proper calendar by which to calculate feasts and holidays, or the particulars of cultic purity or uncleanness), but revelations concerning the past or future history of Israel:

> Moses remained on the mountain for 40 days and 40 nights while the Lord showed him what [was] beforehand as well as what was to come. He related to him the divisions of all the times, both of the Torah and of the "testimony." He said to him: . . . "Now you write this entire message which I am telling you today . . . then this **testimony** will serve as evidence."[23]
> — *Jubilees* 1:4–8

22. This claim was not created merely to solve the problem mentioned, namely, that of justifying legal practices not found in the Bible itself. In general, the claim that this or that biblical figure had written a secret book was very common in Second Temple times: it was a way for later authors to attribute to a biblical figure their own ideas about various subjects—the natural world, biblical history, the end of days. Such pseudepigrapha (falsely ascribed works) make up much of the surviving literature of the period.

23. The "*Torah* and the testimony" is a phrase that occurs in Isa. 8:20. The author of *Jubilees* liked it because it suited well his own purpose: he took "Torah" to be a reference to the written text of the

[God says to Moses:] "Let them not become unclean in these things which I am commanding you upon this mountain."[24]

— *Temple Scroll* 51:6–7

Then He [God] said to me [Ezra], "I revealed myself in a bush and spoke to Moses, when my people were in bondage in Egypt; and I sent him and I led my people out of Egypt and I led him up to Mt. Sinai. And I kept him with me many days. And I told him many wondrous things, and showed him the secrets of the times and declared to him the end of the times. Then I commanded him, saying, "These words you shall publish openly, and these you shall keep secret."

— *4 Ezra* 14:3–6 (also 14:37–47)

Other passages refer to esoteric teachings that were transmitted to Moses without, however, specifying that they had been written down in a book:

The Heavens which are under the throne of Mighty One were severely shaken when He [God] took Moses with him [on Mt. Sinai]. For He showed him many warnings together with the ways of the Law and the end of time, as also . . . the likeness of Zion with its measurements, which was to be made after the likeness of the present sanctuary. He also showed him [other things].   — *2 Baruch* 59:4–5

The narrative and life of Adam and Eve, the first-made, revealed by God to Moses his servant when he received the tables of the law of the covenant from the hand of the Lord, after he had been taught by the archangel Michael.   — *Apocalypse of Moses* 1:1

A Book before Moses

Indeed, the secret book need not necessarily have been revealed to Moses (or to Moses alone); some other ancient worthy might likewise serve as the conduit for authoritative legal (and other) teachings:

[Enoch says:] And now, my son Methuselah, all these things I recount to you and write down for you . . . Blessed are all the righteous, blessed

---

Pentateuch, and used "testimony" (he actually understood this word more in the sense of "solemn warning") to refer to his own book. *Jubilees* was presented as the solemn warning that God's angel had delivered to Moses on Mt. Sinai, a warning about, among other things, the dire consequences of failing to observe the proper calendar ("the divisions of all the times").

24. That is to say, all the words of this text, the *Temple Scroll*, were likewise asserted to have been dictated to Moses at the time of the Sinai revelation.

are all those who walk in the way of righteousness and do not sin like
the sinners in the numbering all their days in which the sun journeys
in heaven . . . for men go wrong in respect of them and do not know
them exactly . . . The year is completed in three hundred and sixty-
four days.   — 1 Enoch 82:1–6

[Abraham instructs Isaac:] Eat its [the sacrifice's] meat during that day
and on the next day; but the sun is not to set on it on the next day until
it is eaten . . . because this is the way I found [it] written in the books
of my ancestors, in the words of Enoch and the words of Noah.
                                                              — Jubilees 21:10

[Jacob's son Levi recalls:] For thus my [fore]father Abraham commanded me, for thus he found in the writings of the book of Noah
concerning the blood.   — Aramaic Levi Document 57

Children of the Chosen

In the biblical narrative, the laws given to Moses on Mt. Sinai are presented as
part of an agreement or covenant: if the Israelites agree to obey these laws,
then they will be God's special people. The Israelites accept this offer, saying,
"All that the Lord has spoken we will do and we will be obedient" (Exod. 24:7).

Yet ancient interpreters could not help wondering why God had chosen
Israel to receive this divine offer. After all, these same laws, and this same
agreement, could have been proposed to other peoples, indeed, to all of
humanity. Why did the Lord of All make this offer to one particular people—
and a rather small people at that?

Elsewhere, the Bible indicates that God's special relationship with Israel
did not come about simply because, on the day in question, they accepted the
laws at Sinai. Instead, the Israelites' special status went back at least to the time
of their ancestors, Abraham, Isaac, and Jacob. Indeed, it was only because
these ancestors had, by their devotion to God, pleased Him in days of yore that
God continued to care for their offspring:

[Moses tells the Israelites:] The Lord took delight in your ancestors
and loved them; [hence it was that] He chose their descendants after
them, you yourselves, from all other peoples, as it is to this day.
                                                              — Deut. 10:15

Some interpreters therefore felt that this distinguished ancestry was what
caused God to make Israel His special people (and, presumably, therefore to

offer them the covenant at Mt. Sinai): Israel had been set apart, as it were, long before Mt. Sinai.

[Ezra prays:] "You made with him [Abraham] an everlasting covenant, and promised him that You would never forsake his descendants, and You gave him Isaac, and to Isaac You gave Jacob and Esau. And You set Jacob apart for Yourself, but Esau You did reject; and Jacob became a great multitude."

—4 Ezra 3:15–16

Singled Out from the Start

In another place, the Bible suggested that Israel had been singled out as God's future possession even earlier, at the time when humanity was first being divided up into different nations and peoples:

When the Most High was apportioning out nations, at the time that
    He separated humanity [into different peoples],
He established the boundaries of peoples according to the number
    of the sons of God.[25]
But God's own portion is His people, Jacob his allotted heritage.

—Deut. 32:8–9

This seemed to mean that God had decided to take personal charge over Israel, whereas the fortunes of other peoples were given over to heavenly subordinates, angels (the "sons of God") or other powers:

He [God] chose Israel to be His people. He made them holy and gathered them apart from all mankind. For there are many nations and many peoples, and all belong to Him. He made spirits [that is, angels] rule over all in order to lead them astray from following Him. But over Israel He made no angel or spirit rule because He alone is their ruler.

—Jubilees 15:30–32

For every nation He appointed an angel, but Israel is the Lord's
    own portion.

—Sir. 17:17

[At the time of the tower of Babel] God called out to the seventy angels that surround his throne of glory and said to them: "Come and let us confuse their speech." And whence do we know that God called out to them? It is said "Come let us go down" [Gen. 11:7]; it does not say "Let

---

25. The traditional Hebrew text reads, "sons of Israel."

Me go down" but "Let *us* . . ." And whence do we know that He cast lots among them [the angels]? It says "When the Most High was apportioning [that is, allotting] nations . . ." [Deut. 32:8], and His lot fell upon Abraham and his household, as it says "But God's own portion is His people, Jacob his allotted heritage." — *Pirqei deR. Eliezer* 24

Indeed, according to another text, Israel was singled out even earlier, at the time of the creation of the world:

[At the conclusion of the creation:] He [God] said to us [angels]: "I will now separate off a people for Myself from among My nations. They too will keep the sabbath. I will make the people holy to Me, and I will bless them, just as I [blessed and] made holy the sabbath day. I will make them holy to Me [and] in this way I will bless them: they will become My people and I will be their God. I have chosen [for this role] the sons of Jacob among all of those whom I have seen. I have recorded them as my firstborn son and have made them holy to Me throughout the ages of eternity. — *Jubilees* 2:19–20

Although the time of the occurrence is not specified, it seems that God may likewise have already decided at the time of the creation of the world that Wisdom (that is, the Torah and its laws) was to dwell with this small people:

[Wisdom speaks:] Then the Creator of all things gave me a com-
    mandment, and the one who created me [Wisdom] assigned a
    place for my tent.
And He said, "Make your dwelling in Jacob, and in Israel receive
    your inheritance."
From eternity, in the beginning, He created me, and for eternity I
    shall not cease to exist.
In the holy tabernacle I ministered before Him, and so I was
    established in Zion.
— Sir. 24:8–10

Other Nations Knew Anyway

Perhaps, then, the special relationship implied by the Sinai covenant was based on an earlier decision or commitment of God's: Israel became God's "own possession" because of its meritorious ancestors or some even earlier feature of history. Still, was this a reason for God to promulgate His laws among only one people? Quite apart from their role in the covenant with

Israel, were not these laws a potentially valuable thing for *all* nations to know? Would not all derive benefit from a divinely crafted set of statutes?

To this question ancient interpreters gave different answers. On the one hand, the idea that all of humanity had received some set of laws after the flood (see Gen. 9:1–7) seemed to resolve at least part of the difficulty: the statutes given to Israel at Mt. Sinai were perhaps more detailed, but all human beings had in any case been given a basic legal code long before. Philo in more than one place suggested a basic identity between God's laws and nature itself, so that any virtuous individual would end up doing what God's laws required even without being specifically acquainted with them. That explained why, for example, Israel's illustrious ancestors could have behaved in conformity with the laws long before Mt. Sinai:

> The first generations, before any at all of the particular statutes was set in writing, followed the unwritten law with perfect ease, so that one might properly say that the enacted laws are nothing else than memorials of the life of the ancients, preserving for a later generation their actual words and deeds. For they were not scholars or pupils of others, nor did they learn under teachers what was right to say or do; they listened to no voice or instruction but their own; they gladly accepted conformity with **nature**, holding that nature itself was, as indeed it is, the most venerable of statutes, and thus their whole life was one of happy obedience to law.
> — Philo, *Abraham* 4–5

Similarly:

> When Gentiles, who do not have the law [that is, the Torah], do **by nature** what the law requires, they are a law by themselves, even though they do not have the law. They show that what the law requires is written on their hearts, while their conscience also bears witness [warns them] and their conflicting thoughts accuse or perhaps excuse them.
> — Rom. 2:14–15

Other Nations at Fault

On the other hand, a number of ancient sources implied that if the other nations of the world did not possess and observe the laws of the Bible, it must be their own fault. Perhaps they had been too proud to accept these laws as their own, or simply had not bothered to learn them:

For each of the inhabitants of the earth knew when he acted un-
righteously, and they did not know My law because of their pride.

— *2 Baruch* 48:40

[God says to Moses at Mt. Sinai:] "For I have given an everlasting Law
into your hands, and by it I will judge **the whole world**. For this will
be a warning. For if men say, 'We did not know You, that is why we did
not serve You,' I will nonetheless make a claim upon them, because
they have not learned My law." — Pseudo-Philo, *Biblical Antiquities* 11:2

The same idea may be present in *4 Ezra*, although it is not clear whether this
text is speaking of all of humanity or whether "those who came into the
world"[26] might refer specifically to Israel:

Let many perish who are now living, rather than that the law of God
which is set before them be disregarded. For God strictly commanded
those who came into the world, when they came, what they should do
to live and what they should observe to avoid punishment. Nevertheless they were not obedient, and they spoke against Him; they devised
for themselves vain plans. — *4 Ezra* 7:20–22

A similar theme in rabbinic literature suggests, more radically, that the
covenant offered to Israel at Mt. Sinai had indeed been offered to the other
nations of the world, but that these had turned it down:

The nations of the world were asked to accept the Torah, and this [was
done] so as not to give them grounds for saying [to God], "If we had
been offered [the Torah] then of course we would have accepted it
upon ourselves." So they *were* offered it and did not accept it upon
themselves, for it says [with reference to the Sinai revelation], "The
Lord came from Sinai and [earlier had] dawned from [Mt.] Seir
[home of the Edomites] upon them, He shone forth from Mt. Paran
[home of the Ishmaelites, Gen. 21:21], He proceeded from ten thousand holy ones, with **the fire of law** in His right hand to them. Yea, He
favored peoples . . ." [traditional Hebrew text of Deut. 33:1–3]. [This
indicated that] He revealed Himself to the descendants of the wicked
Esau [that is, the Edomites] and said to them, "Will you accept the
Torah upon yourselves?" They said: "What is written in it?" He said to
them: "You shall not murder." They said to Him, "But this is the
inheritance that our ancestor [Esau] bequeathed to us, as it is said 'And
by your sword shall you live' [Gen. 27:40]." He then appeared to the

---

26. The same phrase apparently refers to all of humanity in m. *Rosh ha-Shanah* 1:2.

Ammonites and Moabites and said to them, "Will you accept the Torah upon yourselves?" They said: "What is written in it?" He said to them: "You shall not commit adultery." They said to Him: "But we are all of us [the product of] adultery, as it is written 'And Lot's two daughters became pregnant from their father' [Gen. 19:36]—so how can we accept it?" He revealed Himself to the Ishmaelites and said to them: "Will you accept the Torah upon yourselves?" They said: "What is written in it?" He said to them: "You shall not steal." They said to Him: "But this is the blessing by which our ancestor was blessed, 'And he will be a wild ass of a man, his hand against all . . .' [Gen. 16:12], and it [likewise] is written 'For I have been stolen from the land of the Hebrews' [Gen. 40:15, implying that the Ishmaelites stole Joseph and sold him subsequently]" But when [at length] He came to the people of Israel, "the fire of law from His right hand [was given] to them" [Deut. 33:2]. They exclaimed with one voice: "Everything God has spoken we will do and obey" [Exod. 24:7].

— *Mekhilta deR. Ishmael, Baḥodesh 5*

One Christian answer to the same question held that the divine laws were a temporary measure designed for Israel, a "custodian"[27] into whose care this people had been placed for a time:

Why then the law [Torah]? It was added because of transgressions, till the offspring should come to whom the promise had been made . . . Now before faith came, we were confined under the law, kept under restraint until faith should be revealed. So that the law was our custodian until Christ came, so that we might be justified by faith. But now that faith has come, we are no longer under a custodian.

— Gal. 3:19–25

Remember This Blood

When Moses wished, finally, to seal Israel's acceptance of God's laws and covenant, he did so in a rather strange way:

And Moses took half of the blood [of the sacrifices offered at Mt. Sinai] and put it in basins, and half of the blood he threw against the altar . . . And Moses took the blood [in the basins] and threw it on the people and said, "Behold the blood of the covenant which the Lord has made with you in accordance with these words."   — Exod. 24:6–8

27. In Greek, *paidagōgos,* a child's tutor or supervisor.

This gesture of sprinkling the blood *on the people* had no ready correspondent in later Temple practice and certainly must have seemed strange to interpreters. Some suggested that the phrase "on the people" in this passage really meant "on account of the people," for the people's sake:

> And Moses took the blood [in the basins] and threw it **on the altar** to atone for the people. — *Targum Onqelos* Exod. 24:8

> "And Moses took the blood and threw it upon the people"—on the altar in the name of the people. — *Midrash Tanna'im* p. 57

The book of *Jubilees* offers a rather clever rationale for this gesture. The author begins by explaining the biblical holiday known as Feast of Weeks (or Pentecost).[28] This holiday is first explicitly mentioned by Moses at Mt. Sinai (Exod. 34:22), but (as is his wont with biblical holidays) the author of *Jubilees* claims that this day was actually set aside long before Moses proclaimed it a holiday at Mt. Sinai: it was observed by Noah after the flood, at the time when God forbade the eating of an animal's blood with its flesh (Gen. 9:4). For the author of *Jubilees*, this was a central prohibition, and this book therefore specifies something that does not appear in the biblical text itself:

> And Noah and his sons **swore an oath** that they would not eat any blood which was in any flesh. And he made a covenant before the Lord God forever in all generations of the earth in that month.
> — *Jubilees* 6:10

The reason for this oath is that the expression "Feast of Weeks" in Hebrew could also be translated "Feast of Oaths." For the author of *Jubilees,* that is why this holiday was first established, to commemorate the oath of Noah and his sons never to eat any blood.

> Therefore it is ordained and written in the heavenly tablets that they should observe the Feast of Weeks [or Oaths] in this month, once per year, in order to renew the covenant in all respects, year by year . . . And from the day of the death of Noah, his sons corrupted it [the feast] until the days of Abraham, and they ate blood. But Abraham alone kept it. And Isaac and Jacob and his sons kept it until your days, [Moses,] but in your days the children of Israel forgot it until you renewed it for them on this mountain [Sinai]. — *Jubilees* 6:17–19

28. See Exod. 34:22, Lev. 23:15–21; in Hebrew the name of this holiday is written *šb'wt*, which means both "weeks" and "oaths." The latter is quite irrelevant to the name of the holiday, but the author of *Jubilees* found a connection.

What is the connection between all this and the blood Moses sprinkled on the people at Mt. Sinai? According to *Jubilees*, the Sinai revelation took place precisely at the time of the Feast of Weeks (*Jubilees* 1:1). For that reason, Moses took the occasion to "renew" the covenant originally made between God and Noah, and to reinaugurate that covenant's stipulation not to eat any blood. Therefore, the Bible's description of Moses sprinkling blood onto the people took on a new significance. It was a not-too-subtle reminder of the prohibition that, for *Jubilees*, stood at the heart of the covenant: "Do not eat any blood!"

❖   ❖   ❖

In short: God "bowed down" the heavens onto Mt. Sinai and was thus simultaneously in the heavens and on the mountain. Nevertheless, in ascending "up to God" Moses was changed and became, as it were, divine himself. When God uttered the Decalogue He may have uttered all ten commandments, or perhaps only two; the Decalogue in any case was something of an epitome of all the laws to be given to Israel and so had been specially transmitted. Among its provisions was the commandment to keep the Sabbath, with many provisions not specifically stated as such in the Bible; a prohibition of using God's name in the taking of false or vain oaths; and a commandment to honor one's parents because of their likeness to the divine Creator. In addition to the Decalogue, many other laws were given, such as the famous principle "an eye for an eye," which really meant "payment of the value of an eye for an eye."

Moses was also given further information on Mt. Sinai, both about the application of biblical laws to daily life and about the future of the people of Israel. He passed this information on to the people but did not include it in the Pentateuch itself. God gave these laws to Israel as part of His special covenant with them, a covenant that was offered to them because of things that had happened centuries earlier. Nevertheless, the other nations of the earth would be held accountable for not having heeded these laws or having turned down God's covenant themselves.

21
The Golden Calf
(EXODUS 25–34)

Moses grew horns.

The Golden Calf

(EXODUS 25–34)

❖   ❖   ❖

Standing on Mt. Sinai, Moses was instructed by God for forty days and forty nights. God told him to build a special tent, or "tabernacle," which would serve as a divine sanctuary in the midst of the Israelite camp. God described the details of the tabernacle's dimensions and construction, as well as everything concerning the priests who were to serve in it, in great detail.

When God had finished, He gave Moses the two stone tables of law to take down the mountain. But the people of Israel had gone astray. During Moses' absence, they had commissioned his brother, Aaron, to make a great golden image of a calf, and they had worshiped it and brought offerings. Seeing this, God now wished to destroy the people, but Moses prayed at once for their forgiveness, and God relented.

When he reached the Israelite camp and saw for himself what had happened, Moses threw the stone tables from his hands and broke them at the foot of the mountain. Later, he sought God's assurance that He would still be with the people, and asked to see God's glory. Moses then prepared two new stone tables and went back up the mountain; he stayed there for another forty days and nights, and came down again with the inscribed stone tables. At last he assembled the people and they together built the tabernacle as God had planned.

THE BUILDING of the tabernacle, a movable sanctuary that the Israelites could take with them during their wanderings, was a subject of great interest. After all, God had said: "Let them build Me a sanctuary, and I will dwell in their midst" (Exod. 25:9). The tabernacle, in other words, was to be nothing less than God's home on earth.

Its construction was not, however, simply ordered in such general terms. Every spar and plank and beam that was to go into the structure was detailed in God's lengthy instructions. In fact, when God commanded Moses concerning the building of the tabernacle, Moses was not simply *told* what its dimensions were to be and what materials were to be used. Apparently, he was actually shown a model or plan of the future tabernacle:

> [God says to Moses:] "According to all that **I am showing you**—the pattern [*tabnît*] of the tabernacle and the pattern of all its accoutre-

ments—so you shall make it . . . And see that you make them according to their pattern, which is being **shown** to you on the mountain.

And you shall erect the tabernacle according to the plan for it which has been **shown** to you on the mountain." —Exod. 25:9, 40; 26:30

Ancient interpreters found this a remarkable idea—one that sounded even more remarkable in the Septuagint, where the (somewhat ambiguous) word translated above as "pattern" came out rather less ambiguously as "model" or "prototype." It seemed, in other words, as if God had shown Moses some actual thing after which the tabernacle was to be shaped.

A Celestial Sanctuary

But what could that thing have been? It was unlikely that God had brought down to Mt. Sinai a miniature scale-model of the future tabernacle. However, long-established tradition held that somewhere in heaven—to which, according to one understanding, Moses had ascended on Mt. Sinai—was a great, celestial sanctuary. This idea, as already mentioned, had ancient roots. The prophet Isaiah had seen in a vision God "sitting upon a throne high and lifted up" (Isa. 6:1), and this may indeed refer to God's throne in the heavenly sanctuary. The very stars in the sky, according to this same ancient conceit, are actually part of an angelic choir or cadre of heavenly priests who serve God in the celestial sanctuary.

Later writers sometimes bear witness to these same ideas:

[Enoch reports on his vision:] And in everything, it [the heavenly sanctuary] so excelled in glory and splendor and size that I am unable to describe to you its glory and its size. And its floor [was] fire, and above [were] lightning and the path of the stars, and its roof also [was] a burning fire. And I looked and I saw in it a high throne, and its appearance [was] like ice and its surroundings like the shining sun.

—1 Enoch 14:16–18

[Isaac says to Levi:] "May He make you and your descendants [alone] out of all humanity approach Him to serve in His temple [on earth] like the angels of the presence and the holy ones [in heaven]."

—Jubilees 31:14

[Levi says:] And the angel opened to me the gates of heaven, and I saw the holy temple and the Most High upon a throne of glory.

—Testament of Levi 5:1–2

And those men lifted me up from there, and they carried me up to the seventh heaven. And I saw there an exceptionally great light, and all the fiery armies of the archangels, and the incorporeal forces and the . . . cherubim and the seraphim and the many-eyed thrones . . . And then they went to their places in joy and merriment and in immeasurable light, singing songs with soft and gentle voices, while presenting the liturgy to Him gloriously.

— *2 Enoch* (J) 20:1–4

We [Christians] have such a high priest, one who is seated at the right hand of the throne of the Majesty in heaven, a minister in the sanctuary and the true tent which is set up not by man but by the Lord.

— Heb. 8:1–2

After this I looked and lo, in heaven an open door! . . . At once I was in the Spirit, and lo, a throne stood in heaven, with One seated on the throne . . . And round the throne, on each side of the throne, are four living creatures, full of eyes in front and behind . . . And the four living creatures, each of them with six wings, are full of eyes all round and within, and day and night they never cease to sing, "Holy, holy, holy, is the Lord Almighty, who was and is and is to come" [based on Isa. 6:3].

— Rev. 4:1–2, 6, 8 (also 21:10–27, the heavenly Jerusalem)

What was the nature of this heavenly sanctuary? Most ancient readers assumed that it was a fixed structure, a temple. But some sources referred to it as a "tabernacle," as if it were a holy tent that God had created in the skies:[1]

> [Wisdom says:] Of old, from the beginning, God created me, and
>   for eternity I shall not cease.
> In the holy tabernacle[2] I ministered before Him, and so I was
>   established in Zion.
>
> — Sir. 24:9–10

And the tabernacle of highest loftiness, the glory of His kingdom,
    the shrine . . .

— (4Q 403) *Songs of the Sabbath Sacrifice* 1.2.10

---

1. Some support for this idea may be found in Isa. 40:22, "It is He who sits above the circle of the earth, and its inhabitants are like grasshoppers; it is He who stretches out the heavens like a curtain, and stretches them out like a tent to dwell in."

2. This reference is somewhat ambiguous: it may refer to the earthly tabernacle carried by the Israelites in the wilderness, or it may refer to a heavenly one in which Wisdom served.

. . . a minister in the sanctuary and the **true tent** which is set up not by man but by the Lord.
— Heb. 8:1–2

Copied from Heaven

Whether the heavenly sanctuary was a temple or a tent, ancient interpreters asserted in any case that the earthly tabernacle built by Moses, or the temple built by Solomon, was nothing but a copy of this heavenly structure:

[Solomon says:] You commanded me to build a temple on your holy mountain, and an altar in the city of your abode, a copy of the sacred tabernacle which you prepared from the very first. — Wisd. 9:8

[The true temple] is not this building that is in your midst now; it is that which will be revealed, with Me, that was already prepared from the moment I decided to create paradise. I showed it . . . to Moses on Mount Sinai when I showed him the likeness of the tabernacle and all its vessels. — 2 Baruch 4:3, 5

They [the priests in Jerusalem] serve as a copy and shadow of the heavenly sanctuary; for when Moses was about to erect the tabernacle, he was instructed by God, saying, "See that you make everything according to the pattern which was shown to you on the mountain" [Exod. 25:40]. — Heb. 8:5 (also 9:24)

Rabbinic tradition likewise saw a correspondence between the two sanctuaries:

Said R. Phinehas: The sanctuary on earth is located precisely in correspondence to the heavenly sanctuary, as it is said, "You have made an abode to dwell in, O Lord, the sanctuary of the Lord that Your hands have established" [Exod. 15:17]. "Abode" [makon] here [should be understood as] "situated in correspondence to" [mekuwwan keneged] your dwelling place. — j. Berakot 4:5

[Jacob said:] "This is the house of God, and this the gate of heaven" [Gen. 28:17] . . . R. Simeon b. Yoḥai said: The heavenly sanctuary [referred to here by Jacob as "the gate of heaven"] is eighteen miles above the earthly one, since [the numerical value of the words] "and this" is eighteen. — Genesis Rabba 69:7

A Likeness of the Universe

The details of the tabernacle given to Moses on Mt. Sinai thus corresponded to those of the heavenly sanctuary. No wonder, then, that God had described the making of the tabernacle in such detail; in building it, the Israelites were, in a sense, recreating what was heavenly on earth.

But what about the other things connected with the tabernacle? God's instructions included detailed specifications for the clothes that the priests should wear. Much later, after the Temple in Jerusalem had been built, the priestly clothing was held to be one of the most striking things to be seen there. Indeed, eyewitnesses were so moved by the sight of the priests' garments that they went to great lengths to describe them:

> The Holy One exalted like Himself [that is, in holiness] Aaron of the
>   tribe of Levi, and He made [this] an everlasting law [that is, that
>   the priesthood should belong to his descendants].
> He placed splendor upon him, so that he might serve Him in glory.
> He girded him with mighty apparel, and clothed him with bells.
> He crowned him wholly in honor, and honored him in glory and
>   strength, with breeches, robes and cloak.
> Then he encircled him with bells, with pomegranates round about,
>   to make melody as he walked,
> to make their ringing heard in the temple, as a [continuous] token
>   of the sons of his people.
> With a holy garment, of gold and blue and purple, the work of an
>   embroiderer;
> with the breastpiece of judgment, the ephod and the belt; with
>   twisted scarlet, the work of a craftsman;
> with precious stones on the breastpiece, engraved as signet in their
>   settings,
> every stone a glorious one, as a reminder, in engraved letters, of the
>   number of Israel's tribes;
> with a gold crown, cloak, and turban, and a diadem enscribed like a
>   signet with "Holiness,"
> Glorious splendor and stunning appearance, a delight to the eyes,
>   the height of beauty.
> Before his time there never were such things.
>
> — Sir. 45:6–13

How glorious was he [the high priest] looking forth from the tent,
and when he went forth from the place of curtain.
Like a brilliant star shining from amidst the clouds, like the full
moon at festival-time;
Like a dazzling sun in the kingly Temple, or the rainbow's colors
seen with the clouds;
Like a budding flower on a bough in springtime, or a lily sprung up
along watercourses,
Like a northern flower in the summer heat, or the glowing coal of
the incense offering;
Like a blossoming olive tree, vigorous, and whose branches abound
in fruit—
[Such was the high priest] when he donned his glorious vestments
and put on his garments of splendor.

—Sir. 50:5–11

It was an occasion of great amazement to us when we saw Eleazar
engaged in his ministry, and all the glorious vestments, including the
wearing of the garment with precious stones upon it in which he is
vested . . . Their [the priests'] appearance makes one awestruck and
dumbfounded. A man would think he had come out of this world into
another. I emphatically assert that every man who comes near the
spectacle of what I have described will experience astonishment and
amazement beyond words, his very being transformed by the hal-
lowed arrangement on every single detail.   —*Letter of Aristeas* 96, 99

Why were these garments so striking? To some observers it seemed that the
priests' clothing, no less than the tabernacle itself, had a significance far
greater than might first appear. They were a representation or likeness of the
universe itself:

On his [Aaron's] full-length robe [that is, the ephod] there was a
representation of the entire cosmos, and glories of the fathers upon his
four rows of carved stones, and Your splendor on the diadem upon his
head.   —Wisd. 18:24

The high priest is bidden to put on a similar dress when he enters the
inner shrine to offer incense . . . and also to wear another, the forma-
tion of which is very complicated. In this it would seem to be a likeness
and copy of the universe.   —Philo, *Special Laws* 1:84 (also *Moses* 2:117)

If one reflects on the construction of the tabernacle and looks at the vestments of the priest and the vessels which we use for the sacred ministry, he will discover that . . . every one of these objects is intended to recall and represent the universe.   —Josephus, *Jewish Antiquities* 3:180

Aaron Tried to Stop Them

Having received his final instructions about building the tabernacle and making the priestly garments, Moses was ready to go back down the mountain—when God reported to him the astounding news: the people had "gone astray" in his absence and made for themselves a golden calf to worship. Unbelievable as this might appear, still more incredible was the fact that the Bible attributes to Aaron, Moses' own brother, a central role in the incident:

> The people saw that Moses was taking a long time to come down from the mountain, and they complained to Aaron and said to him: "Come, make gods for us that will go before us; for this Moses fellow who brought us out of Egypt—we do not know what has become of him." And Aaron said to them, "Take off the rings of gold which are in the ears of your wives, your sons, and your daughters, and bring them to me." So all the people took off the rings of gold which were in their ears, and brought them to Aaron. And he took [them] from their hands and shaped [them] with a carver and made [them] into a molten calf. And they said: "These are your gods, O Israel, who brought you out of the land of Egypt."   —Exod. 32:2–4

These verses make it seem as if Aaron had quite willingly supplied the people with an idol to worship—in fact, he even seems to have taken the initiative after hearing the people's complaint. But why? Had not Moses left Aaron (along with Hur) in charge of things during his absence (Exod. 24:14)? He hardly ought to have gone along with a rebellion against the very man who had left him in charge. Moreover, God was later to appoint Aaron and his descendants as His special servants, priests for all eternity. It seemed to interpreters most unlikely that God should select someone who had willingly encouraged the people to idolatry. For all such reasons, interpreters theorized that Aaron had not taken the initiative in the golden calf incident, nor even simply submitted to the people's request. He must have done something first to try to stop them, and if the Bible did not say so specifically, perhaps it was simply because his opposition proved ineffective:

And while he was on the mountain, the mind of the people became corrupt, and they gathered together against Aaron, saying, "Make gods for us whom we may serve, in the same way as the other nations have, because that Moses through whom wonders were done before our eyes has been taken away from us." And Aaron said to them: "Be calm. For Moses will come, and he will bring judgment near to us and will explain the law to us and will set forth from his own mouth the law of God and establish rules for our people." And though he was speaking, they did not pay attention to him.

— Pseudo-Philo, *Biblical Antiquities* 12:2

[Aaron said:] "Behold, did he not go up the mountain in your own sight? Were you not there when he went into the cloud? Go up the mountain yourselves, then, and if if you do not find him and Joshua still there, then do whatever it pleases you to do. But if you have manna, and if you have quail, and the pillar [of cloud] and the clouds [of glory], how could he not be there? For everything that you have, you have because of him." — Ephraem, *Commentary on Exodus* 32:1

Aaron Feared for His Life

A detail in the biblical text, however, suggested to interpreters another reason for Aaron's apparent encouragement of idolatry:

And he took [them] from their hands and shaped [them] with a carver and made [them] into a molten calf. And they said: "These are your gods, O Israel, who brought you out of the land of Egypt." **And Aaron saw**; and he built an altar before it; and Aaron made a proclamation and said, "Tomorrow shall be a feast to the Lord." — Exod. 32:4–5

What did Aaron see? It must have been something rather frightening, since it was apparently this *seeing* that led him to take the next and fateful step of building an altar in front of the calf so that it could be worshiped.

By an interesting coincidence, the same Hebrew letters translated as "saw" could be read as if they spelled "was afraid." Some interpreters therefore concluded that Aaron had not so much *seen*—after all, the text should really have said that he *heard* the people proclaiming "These are your gods . . ."—as *taken fright,* and it was this sudden fear that had impelled him to do what he did. Perhaps he had been afraid from the start that the rabble, being numerous and powerful, might harm him if he did not make them an idol and an altar with which to worship it.

But Aaron, **fearful** because the people were very strong, said to them, "Bring us the earrings of your wives." . . . And they put them into the fire, and they were fashioned into a shape, and out came a molten calf.

— Pseudo-Philo, *Biblical Antiquities* 12:3

And Aaron was afraid and and built an altar in front of them.

— Peshitta, *Samaritan Targum of Pentateuch* (ms. J) Exod. 32:5

Hur Murdered by the Rabble

Along with this understanding of the Hebrew verb as "feared" was another, which held that Aaron had indeed *seen* something. However, what he saw was not spelled out in the biblical text. (As noted, "These are your gods . . ." was something that Aaron heard, not saw). Interpreters therefore felt free to deduce on their own what it was that he saw. Indeed, combining the sense of "feared" and "saw," some specified that he saw something that caused him to take fright:

And Aaron **saw** Hur [slaughtered] before it and **was afraid**; and he built an altar in front of it.

— *Targum Neophyti* (with marginal note), *Fragment Targum* Exod. 32:5

But when he thus argued with them, Aaron saw that they wished to stone him as they had [done to] Hur. For it was to Hur that Moses, when he climbed up the mountain, had ordered the elders to bring their disputes [see Exod. 24:14]; yet when Moses went down again, there is no [further] mention of him [in the Bible], and for this reason it is said that he was killed in the rebellion which broke out against Aaron over the making of the calf, because he had rebuked them [for idolatry]. Lest, therefore, they now kill Aaron himself and so become guilty of this crime, or lest they make for themselves many calves, and not just one; or lest they go back to Egypt (even if they should not actually enter it), he cunningly ordered that they bring the earrings of their wives, [hoping that] it might come about that these [women] would stop their husbands from making the calf so as to keep their earrings untouched.

— Ephraem, *Commentary on Exodus* 32:2

When the people of Israel started to do that deed [of the golden calf], they first went to Hur and said to him, "Come, make a god for us," since he did not do as they said they went and killed him . . . Afterward they went to Aaron and said to him, "Come, make us a god." When

Aaron heard he **took fright,** as it is said "And Aaron **was afraid** and he built an altar in front of it."

— Leviticus Rabba 10:3

The Letters Flew Off

Seeing the people bowing down to an idol was too much: Moses took the stone tables that God had given him and threw them to the ground. No doubt he was right to be angry. Still, it disturbed many that his anger should express itself in the destruction of the two stone tables. After all, these had been given to Moses by God and were "written by the finger of God" (Exod. 31:18). There could hardly be a more sacred object in the whole world.

Some interpreters supposed that Moses could not have allowed himself to destroy the divine writing. And there was the thinnest of justifications for such a conclusion. For, in retelling these same events later on, Moses says:

> "I seized the two tables and cast them from off my two hands and broke them **before your eyes.**"
> —Deut. 9:17

The expression "before your eyes" must have seemed a bit unusual here. After all, if the meaning of this phrase was simply that everyone had seen Moses break the tables, well, so what? Why should Moses apparently stress that relatively trivial circumstance in retelling the story? If, therefore, Moses said that everything had happened "before your eyes," was this not an indication that what had happened was something altogether remarkable, something that the human eye would not normally get to see? Perhaps bolstered by this consideration, some interpreters concluded that a miracle must have accompanied this act: the letters first flew off the stone tables, leaving them empty— for it was only under such circumstances that Moses would have allowed himself to break the tables in the first place:

> And Moses hurried down and saw the calf. And he looked at the tables and saw that the **writing was gone,** and he hurried to break them.
> —Pseudo-Philo, Biblical Antiquities 12:5

> He [Moses] looked at them [the tables] and saw that the writing had flown off of them. He said: How can I give Israel tables that are worthless? I will instead take them and break them, as it is said, "I took the two tables and cast them from my two hands and broke them in your sight" [Deut. 9:17].
> —Abot deR. Natan (A) 2

> And he [Moses] threw the tables from his hand and broke them on the side of the mountain, but the holy writing that was on them flew off

and ascended to the heavenly ether, where it cried out: Woe to the people who have heard at Sinai from God's own mouth [the command-ment], "You shall not make for yourselves an image or a statue or any picture," and yet within forty days they made for themselves a molten calf which has no real substance. — *Targum Pseudo-Jonathan* Exod. 32:19

Tables Became Too Heavy

Reading the same biblical verse, it seemed to other interpreters that Moses might have been having trouble holding on to the two tables:

> "I seized the two tables and cast them from off my two hands and broke them before your eyes."   —Deut. 9:17

Why did Moses say he seized the tables—wasn't he holding them already? The word "seized" therefore implied that Moses had struggled with them: they had started to slip from his hands and he seized them, trying to hold on, but they got away from him and he ended up casting them "from off my two hands" (another phrase that implied more falling than being thrown down on pur-pose) and shattering them into pieces. If so, then there was really nothing blameworthy in his breaking the tables: it was all an accident.

But why should the tables suddenly be too heavy? Had not Moses carried them all the way down the mountain? Putting this observation about the word "seized" together with the tradition of the flying writing, interpreters con-cluded that the letters had helped to support the tables, actually making them lighter in Moses' hand. Once they flew off, the tables suddenly became much heavier.

> And his hands were opened, and he became like a woman bearing her firstborn who, when she is in labor, her hands are upon her chest and she has no strength to help herself bring forth.
> —Pseudo-Philo, *Biblical Antiquities* 12:5

> The tables weighed forty *seah* each, but the writing buoyed them up [and allowed Moses to carry them]. When the writing flew off, they [suddenly] became too heavy for Moses' hands and they fell and were broken.   —j. *Ta'anit* 4:5

Divine Traits of Character

When Moses climbed back up Mt. Sinai to be given the second set of inscribed tables, God once again came down in the cloud. But this time the subject was not the laws which the Israelites were to observe but, instead, God's own nature:

> The Lord passed before him and He said: "The Lord,[3] the Lord, a God merciful and compassionate, slow to anger, and abounding in steadfast love and faithfulness, keeping steadfast love for thousands, forgiving iniquity and transgression and sin, but who will by no means clear [guilt], visiting the iniquity of the fathers upon the children and the children's children, to the third and the fourth generation."
>
> —Exod. 34:6–7

This revelation was altogether extraordinary: nowhere else had God's traits of character, as it were, been set forth as such. It was as if, in response to an earlier request of Moses—"I pray You, show me Your glory" (Exod. 33:18)—God now revealed to His prophet something of His very nature.

From earliest times this self-revelation was deemed to have the highest importance. Moses himself alludes to it somewhat later in the Pentateuch:

> [Moses says:] "And now, I pray you, let the power of the Lord be great, as You promised, saying, 'The Lord is slow to anger and abounding in steadfast love, forgiving iniquity and transgression, but He will by no means clear [the guilty], visiting the iniquity of the fathers upon children, upon the third and upon the fourth generation.' Pardon the iniquity of this people, I pray You, according to the greatness of your steadfast love."
>
> —Num. 14:17–19

What is more, in numerous later biblical verses, this same revelation of God's nature and characteristics is repeated or alluded to, and in the same order. It seems that, from a very early period, the qualities of divine mercy and compassion mentioned in this verse, along with God's assertion of his faithfulness to Israel and willingness to forgive sins, became central items in the Israelites' thinking about God, ideas that were returned to again and again. Here are but some of the more obvious references:

> Return to God, for He is compassionate and merciful, slow to anger and abounding in steadfast love, and relenting from [inflicting] evil.
>
> —Joel 2:13

3. It is not clear from the traditional Hebrew text if this first "the Lord" should be part of the quotation or be the subject of the previous verb. If the latter is the case, then the text should be translated: "The Lord passed before him and the Lord said: 'The Lord, a God merciful and compassionate . . .'" If the former understanding is adopted, then it is furthermore unclear who speaks the words that follow, whether God (that is, "and He said . . .") or Moses (in which case, "and he said . . ."). Some Septuagint texts have only one "the Lord."

I know that You are compassionate and merciful, slow to anger and abounding in steadfast love, and relenting from [inflicting] evil.

—Jon. 4:2

Who is like You, O God, forgiving sin and passing over transgression for the remnant of his people, not holding on to anger forever, for He takes delight in steadfast love. He will once again be merciful and overcome our faults and cast all our sins to the depths of the sea. May You give faithfulness to Jacob and steadfast love to Abraham, as You once swore to our ancestors of old.   —Mic. 7:18–20

And You, O lord, merciful and compassionate God, slow to anger and abounding in steadfast love and faithfulness.

—Ps. 86:15

He made known His ways to Moses, His acts to the people of Israel:
Merciful and compassionate is the Lord, slow to anger and
    abounding in steadfast love.
He will not chide forever, nor keep His anger for all times.
He does not deal with us as befits our sins, and has not requited us
    in keeping with our transgressions.

—Ps. 103:7–10

He has left a remembrance of His miracles, compassionate and
    merciful is the Lord.

—Ps. 111:4

Light shines for the righteous amidst darkness, [God is] merciful
    and compassionate and good.

—Ps. 112:4

Compassionate and righteous is the Lord, and our God is merciful.

—Ps. 116:5

Compassionate and merciful is the Lord, slow to anger and
    abounding in steadfast love.

—Ps. 145:8

But You are a God ready to forgive, compassionate and merciful, slow to anger and abounding in steadfast love, and You did not forsake them.   —Neh. 9:17 (also 9:31)

For compassionate and merciful is the Lord your God; He will not turn His face from you if you return to Him. —2 Chron. 30:9

It is not surprising, therefore, that these same traits continued to be recited or evoked by later writers. They had become a famous catalog of divine traits:

Consider the ancient generations and see: who ever trusted in the Lord and was put to shame?
Or who ever persevered in the fear of the Lord and was forsaken?
Or who ever called upon him and was overlooked?
For the Lord is compassionate and merciful, He forgives sins and saves in time of affliction.

—Sir. 2:10–11

[And You purify] Your servant from all his sins [through your great m]ercies. [As You a]nnounced through Moses [that You would forgive iniquity] and transgression and sin atoning fo[r guilt] and faithlessness. —(1QH) *Thanksgiving Hymns* 29, col. 17:12–13

And You, my God, are [a merciful and compassionate God] slow to anger, bountiful in favor, foundation of tr[uth].

—(4Q511) *Songs of a Sage^b*

[Ezra says:] "I know, O Lord, that the Most High [**God**] is now called **merciful**, because He has mercy on those who have not yet come into the world; and **compassionate**, because He is compassionate to those who turn in repentance to his Torah; and **patient** ["slow to anger"], because He shows patience toward those who have sinned, since they are His own works; and bountiful, because He would rather give than take away; and **abounding in compassion** ["abounding in steadfast love"], because He makes His compassions abound more and more to those now living and to those who are gone, and to those yet to come, for if He did not make his compassions abound, the world with those who inhabit it would not have life; and giver, because if He did not give out of His goodness, so that those who have committed iniquities might be absolved of them, not **one ten-thousandth** of mankind could live ["keeping steadfast love for thousands"]; and judge, because if He did not pardon those who were created by His word and blot out the multitude of their sins, there would be left only very few of the innumerable multitude." —4 Ezra 7:132–140

For He is **merciful** whom you honor, and **compassionate** in whom you hope, and **true** [or "faithful"] so that He will do good to you and not evil. — *2 Baruch* 77:7

[Moses prays:] May Your **mercy** be made strong with Your people, and Your **compassion** with Your inheritance, Lord, and may Your **long-sufferingness** toward the people of Your choice [be] in Your place, for You have delighted in them above all [others].

— Pseudo-Philo, *Biblical Antiquities* 19:8

Steadfast Love for Thousands of Generations

If this catalog of traits was deemed of central importance, it nevertheless contained some points in need of further clarification. For example, what did it mean to say that God kept "steadfast love for thousands"? In context, it seemed that "thousands" meant *thousands of generations*. After all, the text continues:

> . . . keeping steadfast love for thousands, forgiving iniquity and transgression and sin, but who will by no means clear [guilt], visiting the iniquity of the fathers **upon the children and the children's children, to the third and the fourth** [generations]. — Exod. 34:7

The idea seems to be that God maintains His loving protection for thousands of generations even for those who sin, since it is His nature to forgive "iniquity and transgression and sin." However, this is no blank check, since He also punishes sin, indeed, visits the iniquity of sinful fathers upon the children, grandchildren, and even on to the fourth generation (although the text literally says, "to the 'thirds' and 'fourths'").

That generations were meant seemed to be confirmed by a similar passage in the Decalogue:

> For I, the Lord your God, am a zealous God, visiting the sin of the fathers on the sons, on the "thirds" and on the "fourths" of those who hate Me, but acting with steadfast love toward the thousands, for those who love Me and keep My commandments. — Exod. 20:5–6

Here again the Bible seems to be talking about generations, with the "thirds" and "fourths" following the second generation, that is, the "sons." Not surprisingly, then, ancient interpreters explicitly referred this passage's various numbers to generations:

. . . requiting the sins of the fathers upon the children, to the third and the fourth **generation** for those who hate Me, and granting mercy to the thousands for those who love Me and keep my statutes.

—Septuagint Exod. 20:5–6

. . . to the third and the fourth **generation** . . . mercy to a thousand **generations.** —*Targums Onqelos, Neophyti,* etc., Exod. 20:5

For I am the Lord your God, a zealous God, and visiting the sins of the sleeping [the dead] sinners upon the[ir] living sons if they walk in the paths of their parents, up until the third and fourth **generation,** but showing mercy **for a thousand generations** to those who love Me and keep my commandments. —Pseudo-Philo, *Biblical Antiquities* 11:6

That a thousand generations was also meant in Exod. 34:7 seemed to be confirmed by yet another verse in the Pentateuch:

And you shall know that the Lord your God is God, the faithful God who keeps his covenant and his steadfast love for a thousand generations for those who are faithful to Him and keep his commandments.

—Deut. 7:9

Following the lead of such texts, many later interpreters specified that "thousands" in Exod. 34:7 meant thousands of generations:

Keeping goodness for thousands of generations, forgiving transgressions and rebellion . . . —*Targum Onqelos* Exod. 34:7

But such an understanding, unless modified, ran into difficulties. For, after all, if God kept his steadfast love "for thousands of generations," then how could He likewise visit the sins of fathers on their children, grandchildren, and so forth? The two actions seemed to contradict each other. Perhaps "keeping steadfast love" (since "keeping"—or "saving up"—steadfast love seemed a strange word to use here) really implied a combination or balance of opposites:

Keeping [strict] justice and acting mercifully for thousands . . .

—Septuagint Exod. 34:7

Do not say "I have sinned, but nothing can befall me, for the Lord
is slow to anger."
Do not depend on forgiveness [so that you] add one sin to another.
Do not say, "The Lord is merciful, and He will erase all my sins," nor
say "His mercies are many, so my many sins He will forgive."
For with Him are **both mercy and anger.**

—Sir. 5:4–6

Along the same lines, it might be that, while the interests of strict justice were
suspended, they were not utterly forgotten:

Keeping steadfast love and goodness for thousands of generations,
forgiving and remitting sins and passing over rebellions and atoning
for transgressions and acquitting; but He will not acquit **on the great
day of judgment,** recalling the sins of wicked fathers upon rebellious
sons and grandsons, until the third and fourth generation.

— *Targum Neophyti* Exod. 34:7

No Pardon for the Wicked

Indeed, it could be that in speaking here simultaneously of "steadfast love for
thousands" along with punishments visited upon the third and fourth generations, the Bible was intentionally distinguishing between two classes of sinners. That is, the "thousands" mentioned by God were the "good" sinners,
people who, although they sinned, were sorry and sought to repent; such
people did indeed gain God's forgiveness. After all, such a distinction was
virtually stated in the passages cited earlier, which spoke of God

visiting the sin of the fathers on the sons, on the "thirds" and on the
"fourths" of those who **hate Me,** but acting with steadfast love toward
the thousands, for those who **love Me** and keep My commandments.

—Exod. 20:5–6

And you shall know that the Lord your God is God, the faithful God
who keeps his covenant and his steadfast love for a thousand generations for those who are **faithful** to Him and keep his commandments.

—Deut. 7:9

So too, in regard to Exod. 34:6–7, it seemed that God's mercy "for the thousands" was intended for the "good" sinners. The truly wicked did not repent;
it was of them that God had said that He visits the "iniquity of the fathers
upon the children and the children's children":

Keeping goodness for thousands of generations, forgiving transgressions and rebellion and pardoning sins for those who **return to His Torah**; but to those who do not return, He does not pardon, visiting the sins of the fathers on rebellious children, and on their children's children to the third and fourth generations.

— *Targum Onqelos* Exod. 34:7

There may be a hint of such an understanding as well in the continuation of the passage from Ben Sira cited earlier:

For with Him is both mercy and anger, and His wrath will rest
 upon the **wicked.**
So do not delay in returning to Him [that is, **repenting**], and do not
 dawdle from day to day; for His wrath will come forth in a flash,
 and you will perish on a day of punishment.

— Sir. 5:6–7

It is noteworthy that the phrase "for a thousand generations" (in Deut. 7:9) was also interpreted as a promise to keep alive those whom God loves for a thousand generations:

. . . is a guarantee for them to keep them alive for a thousand generations, as it is written, "who keeps his covenant and his steadfast love for a thousand generations" [Deut. 7:9].   — *Damascus Document* 19:1–2

Thousands of Sins Forgiven

Another solution to the same problem was to understand "thousands" in this passage as referring to *thousands of sins*. In that case, the sentence in Exod. 34:6–7 ought perhaps to be redivided as follows: "The Lord, the Lord, a God merciful and compassionate, slow to anger, and abounding in steadfast love and faithfulness; keeping steadfast love; for [or "by"] thousands forgiving iniquity and transgression and sin . . ." The assertion that God forgives "for" or "by" thousands would then appear to mean that God does not count up or reckon each and every sin, but forgives them by the thousands, without strict accounting:

O **merciful** and **compassionate**, forgive us our **iniquities** and **unrighteousness**, and **transgressions**, and shortcomings. **Reckon not every sin** of your servants and handmaidens, but cleanse us with the cleansing of your truth.   — *1 Clement* 60:1–2

And after these things you will remember the Lord and repent and He will bring you back, because He is **merciful** and **compassionate, not**

reckoning evil to the sons of men, since they are flesh and the spirits of deceit deceive them in all their actions.   — *Testament of Zebulon* 9:7

The same interpretation may also underlie this:

For You are the Lord Most High [God], of great compassion, slow to anger, and very merciful, and repent over the evils of men. You, O Lord, according to your great goodness have promised repentance and forgiveness to those who have sinned against You, and in the multitude of your mercies you have appointed repentence for sinners that they may be saved . . . For the sins I have committed are more in number than the sand of the sea; **my transgressions are multiplied**, O Lord, they are multiplied.   — Pr. of Man. 7–9

Moses' Face Beamed Light

When Moses came down the mountain for the second time, his face was somehow changed because of his having spoken with God (Exod. 34:29). Most modern translations suggest that his face "beamed" or "shone." However, the precise meaning of the Hebrew word is far from clear, and even today, scholars are divided as to what its true significance might be. Some have suggested that rather than beaming, Moses' face had become rough or disfigured as a result of his prolonged exposure to God's presence. Whatever the case, when the people saw him they were at first afraid to come near. Moses therefore put on a veil and wore it over his face whenever he spoke to the people, and took it off again when he went in before God.

But what really happened to Moses' face? Many ancient interpreters were apparently influenced by the fact that the word "skin" in Hebrew sounds very much like the word for "light"; this similarity, along with other factors, to be sure, led them to suggest that Moses' face actually "beamed" in the sense of giving forth light:

Now, when Moses went down from the mountain—and the two tables were in Moses' hands—as he was going down from the mountain Moses did not know that the appearance of the skin of his face had **become glorious** when He had been speaking with him.
      — Septuagint Exod. 34:29

Then, after the said forty days had passed, he went down and his appearance was far more beautiful than when he had gone up, so that those who saw him were filled with awe and amazement; their eyes could not continue to stand the dazzling brightness that flashed from him like the brilliance of the sun.   — Philo, *Moses* 2:70

And Moses came down. And when he had been bathed with invisible light, he went down to the place where the light of the sun and the moon are; and the light of his face surpassed the splendor of the sun and the moon, and he did not even know this. And when he came down to the sons of Israel, they saw him but did not recognize him.

—Pseudo-Philo, *Biblical Antiquities* 12:1

Moses did not know how great was the glorious splendor of his face.

— *Targum Onqelos* Exod. 34:29

Moses did not know that the glorious splendor of his face was shining.

— *Targum Neophyti* Exod. 34:29

The Israelites could not look at Moses' face because of its brightness.

—2 Cor. 3:7

It may be that this same motif was in the back of Ben Sira's mind when he wrote:

> Anyone who acts fairly will be rewarded, and every man will find his due.
> The Lord hardened Pharaoh's heart, so that he did not know that his deeds were revealed to God.
> His mercies are apparent to all creatures, and His **light** and His praise he shared with man.
>
> —Sir. 16:14–16

This last verse is somewhat obscure, and it and the preceding one may in any case be later additions to the original text. It seems, however, that in juxtaposing to the mention of Pharaoh's hard-heartedness with the assertion that God's merciful deeds are (normally) apparent to all, the author had in mind the miracles of the Exodus, which indeed would have been apparent even to Pharaoh, had not God "hardened his heart." If Ben Sira then added immediately that God "shared His light and His praise" with mankind, he probably meant specifically with a single man, Moses, whose face shone (Exod. 34:29) and who was called a "God to Pharaoh" (Exod. 7:1).

Moses Grew Horns

Most ancient translators and interpreters thus understood Moses' face to have beamed with light. However, one significant exception is Jerome's translation of the verse in question:

> When Moses went down from Mount Sinai, he was holding the two
> tables of the testimony, and he did not know that **his face was horned**
> as a result of his speaking with God. — (Vulgate) Exod. 34:29

This translation was apparently based on the apparent connection of the word
"beam" with "horn" in Hebrew: not only did this make good philological
sense, but horns elsewhere were sometimes an ornament in headgear and a
sign of distinction. The implications of Jerome's translation were not witnessed at once, but starting in the late Middle Ages, Western sculptors and
painters frequently represented Moses as having horns.

❖   ❖   ❖

*In short: The tabernacle built by the Israelites was modeled on God's sanctu-
ary in heaven, and the priests' clothing similarly bore the likeness of the
universe. Although Aaron participated in the sin of the Golden Calf, he was
an unwilling participant: he was afraid for his own life, having seen the
rabble murder Hur. Moses cast down the stone tables but did not destroy the
divine writing on them, since the letters had already flown off. Indeed, their
flight may have caused the tables suddenly to grow heavier and thus to fall
from Moses' hands. Later, when Moses sought divine reassurance after the
people's sin, God told him that He keeps His steadfast love for thousands of
generations of repentant sinners, while visiting the iniquity of the fathers
upon their descendants in the case of those who were unrepentant. When
Moses descended once again from the mountain, his face beamed light or,
possibly, sprouted horns.*

22

Worship in the Wilderness

(LEVITICUS 1–NUMBERS 10)

(Horned) Moses teaches the meaning of the laws:
gentle birds for gentle people.

Worship in the Wilderness

(LEVITICUS 1–NUMBERS 10)

❖   ❖   ❖

With the building of the tabernacle complete, God revealed to Moses further laws connected with worship: the different sorts of animal sacrifices and other offerings that could be made, and the proper procedure to be followed by priests. Then Moses' brother, Aaron, along with Aaron's sons, underwent consecration as priests. However, two of Aaron's sons—Nadab and Abihu— soon went astray: they brought an "unholy fire" before God and were burned to death.

God instructed Moses in many other matters connected to holiness: purity and impurity, the time and requirements of various festivals, and miscellaneous laws governing relations among neighbors and between man and God. To mark the dedication of the tabernacle's altar, each of the chiefs of Israel's twelve tribes brought an offering before God.

T HE LAWS about sacrifices that begin the book of Leviticus were a necessary preliminary to inaugurating regular worship in the tabernacle. Once this information was imparted, Israel could begin to offer up the different sorts of sacrifices—burnt offerings, grain offerings, sin offerings, and so forth—that were to be the focus of worship not only during the forty years of desert wanderings, but for centuries and centuries afterward. Yet no sooner were the sacrifices explained and the priests—Aaron and his sons—consecrated and put to the task of making the first offerings, than there occurred the strange death of Aaron's sons Nadab and Abihu, burned by a fire from God.

An Error in Priestly Procedure

What was the sin of Nadab and Abihu? The Bible says that they had brought an "unholy" or "foreign" fire before God. What exactly was wrong with this offering is not specified, nor did God's words cited immediately afterward—"I will be sanctified among those who are close to Me, and before all the people I will be glorified" (Lev. 10:3)—seem to clarify matters much. However, to many interpreters it appeared that the two brothers certainly must have been guilty of violating proper priestly procedure (since the text did say that they

441

had brought their offering "in such a way as He had not commanded them" [Lev. 10:1]):

> The two elder [sons of Aaron], Nadab and Abihu, did not bring [the kind of] incense as Moses had ordered, but the sort that they had used previously. They were burnt to death.
>
> —Josephus, *Jewish Antiquities* 3:209

> And Moses said, "This is what the Lord said to me at Sinai: When they come before Me, I will sanctify the tabernacle, so that if they are not careful in the sacrificial service, I will burn them with My own scorching fire, [and this is established] so that I may be glorified in the sight of all the people."   —*Targum Pseudo-Jonathan* Lev. 10:2–3

The fact that the incident is immediately followed by a divine commandment, issued to Aaron and his remaining sons, not to drink wine or strong drink when they enter the tent of meeting "lest you die" (Lev. 10:9) implied to others that Nadab and Abihu must have been drunk at the time they entered the tabernacle:

> R. Ishmael explained: Aaron's sons died because they entered [the tabernacle] drunk with wine.   —*Leviticus Rabba* 12:1

A Holy Death

All this notwithstanding, some interpreters claimed that *no* sin had been committed, and that Nadab and Abihu's death was actually a form of exaltation. After all, God's words in Lev. 10:3 (cited above) seemed to refer to Nadab and Abihu as "those who are close to Me" (in the Septuagint, "who draw near to Me"), and this sounded like a virtue, not a fault. What is more, the two were said to have died "before the Lord" (Lev. 10:2); did not this phrase seem to imply that they had not actually died in the tabernacle, but had ascended to heaven and died there? If so, then their being "burnt" was really a necessary preliminary to their ascending into heaven like the smoke or vapor of a fire:

> [Nadab and Abihu] were not seized by a wild beast, but were taken up by a rush of fire unquenchable, by an undying splendor, since in sincerity they cast aside sloth and delay and consecrated their zeal, hot and fiery, flesh-consuming and swiftly moving, to piety. [This fire] was "foreign" [Lev. 10:1] to earthly existence, since it belonged to the realm of God . . . Wafted by a favorable breeze and carried to the heights of heaven, they there passed away, like a wholly burnt offering [from the tabernacle] into celestial splendor.   —Philo, *On Dreams* 2:67

It is thus that the priests Nadab and Abihu die in order that they might live, receiving an incorruptible life in exchange for mortal existence, and being transferred from the [domain of the] created to the uncreated. As an allusion to [this] immortality it is said in regard to them that they died "before the Lord" [Lev. 10:2], which means they [really] came to life, since a dead body may not come into God's presence. And [hence it says] "This is what the Lord has said, 'I will be sanctified in those who draw near to me'" [Septuagint Lev. 10:3].

—Philo, *On Flight and Finding* 59

[On Mt. Sinai] God had said to Moses, "Moses, sometime in the future I will be made present to the people of Israel and will be sanctified *by them* in this house [the tabernacle], as it is said, 'There I will be made present to the people of Israel, and it [the tabernacle] will be sanctified with my glory [alternate reading, 'with my being honored']' [Exod. 29:43]." This divine statement was made to Moses on Mt. Sinai, but he himself did not understand it until the incident [of Nadab and Abihu] occurred. [When, just before that incident, God was made present to the people (Lev. 9:24),] Moses said to God: "Master of the Universe, who is there more beloved [to You] than me and my brother Aaron? [Are we not the ones] by whom this house will [now] be sanctified?" After Aaron's two sons entered to sacrifice and came out burnt, Moses [now understood and] said to Aaron, "Aaron my brother, your sons died for the sake of sanctifying God's name. That is what He meant by 'I will be made holy by those who are near [and dear] to me [that is, Nadab and Abihu] and [then, as a result] before all the people I will be honored' [Lev. 10:3]." — *Leviticus Rabba* 12:2

Such an interpretation was only strengthened by the Bible's description of Aaron as "silent" (Lev. 10:3) after Moses explained to him the significance of what had happened, and its instruction that Aaron and his remaining sons not mourn (Lev. 10:6). Did not all this further indicate that Nadab and Abihu had died a holy death?

[Some people] are mourned as though they are dead, even though they are still alive, since the life that they live is worthy of lamentation and mourning . . . On the other hand, Moses does not allow Nadab [and Abihu], those holy principles, to be mourned.

—Philo, *On Dreams* 2:66–67

When Aaron heard [Moses' explanation] and understood that his sons were beloved [to God], he fell silent [and did not mourn their death] and was rewarded for his silence, which is why it says specifically "and Aaron was silent" [Lev. 10:3].   — *Leviticus Rabba* 12:2

Coats Not Burned

One related detail in the incident attracted interpreters' attention. After the burning, Moses ordered that the bodies of Aaron's two sons be removed:

> And Moses called Mishael and Elzaphan, the sons of Uzziel, Aaron's uncle, and said to them, "Draw near, carry your brethren from before the sanctuary out of the camp." So they drew near, and carried them **in their coats** out of the camp, as Moses had said.   — Lev. 10:4–5

Whose coats were used to remove the bodies? It hardly seemed likely that Mishael and Elzaphan would have used their own coats—after all, everyone knew that the wearing of priestly coats was an essential in the sanctuary (Exod. 28:40–43). Interpreters thus concluded that "their" coats meant Nadab's and Abihu's. But if these two brothers had been burned, how could their coats have survived? Here, then, was another indication that the "burning" did not mean that they were physically burned:

> Therefore, they did not lift them up in their own coats, but in those of Nadab and Abihu, who had been devoured by fire and taken up on high.   — Philo, *Allegorical Interpretations* 2:57–58

Other interpreters seem to preserve a reminiscence of the same interpretation:

> They were burned to death: the fire shot forth onto them and started to burn their chests and faces, and no one could put it out.[1]
>   — Josephus, *Jewish Antiquities* 3:209

> And a flame of fire came forth from before the Lord with anger, and divided itself into four strands, and they entered their nostrils and burned their souls, but their bodies were not destroyed.
>   — *Targum Pseudo-Jonathan* Lev. 10:2–3

> "And the fire consumed them . . ." [Lev. 10:3]: their souls were burned but not their garments, as it says "And they [their brothers] came near and lifted them up in their coats" [Lev. 10:5]—the garments of those being carried.   — *Sifra, Shemini* 34

---

1. By this wording Josephus apparently wishes to imply that the divine fire killed them almost instantly, perhaps by its fumes, after having only *started* to burn "their chests and faces." That would explain how their coats survived while they did not.

Control of Appetites

The account of the death of Nadab and Abihu is followed by additional laws, those concerned with matters of purity and impurity. Such laws were related to the general topic of sacrifices and the priestly service, since impurity (a state transmitted by touching, or being in proximity to, certain substances) made a person unfit for contact with the sanctuary and its service. Various requirements were established for people to be cleansed after becoming impure.

In presenting the overall topic of impurity, the Bible begins with a list of "impure" animals, fish, and birds, which may not be eaten, and sets out as well the permissible species (Leviticus 11; see also Deut. 14:3–20). For example, an animal that "parts the hoof and is cloven footed and chews the cud" (Lev. 11:3) is permitted for food. This means that beef and lamb, for example, can be eaten, but pork or ham cannot (since pigs do not chew the cud). Many ancient interpreters were puzzled by these requirements. If God created all animals, and if certainly many of the forbidden animals nonetheless made for a meal every bit as tasty and healthful as the permitted ones, then why were only some animals declared "pure" and permitted as food?

To some it seemed that the laws of pure food must serve a higher, moral purpose. Their aim was to teach mastery over one's bodily desires and appetites:

> All the animals of land, sea, or air which have the finest and fattest meat, thus titillating and exciting pleasure, he [Moses] sternly forbade them to eat, knowing that they set a trap for the most slavish of the senses, taste, and produce gluttony, an evil very dangerous both to soul and body . . . Now among the different kinds of land animals there is none whose flesh is so delicious as the pig's, as all who eat it agree.
>
> —Philo, *Special Laws* 4:100–101

> When we are attracted to forbidden foods, how do we come to reject the pleasures to be gained from them? Is it not because reason has the power to control appetites? . . . Accordingly, when we crave seafood or fowl or the meat of four-legged beasts or any sort of food that is forbidden to us under the Law, it is through the mastery of reason that we abstain. —4 Macc. 1:33–34 (also 4:16–27)

Similarly:

> Said R. El'azar b. 'Azariah: Whence do we know that a person should not say, "I have no desire to eat the meat of a pig" . . . ? On the contrary, [he should say:] "I do indeed so desire, but what can I do? My heavenly

Father has so ordered me." This is the meaning of "I have separated you from [other] peoples, that you should be mine" [Lev. 20:26].

— *Yalqut Shimoni 626*

Ruminating with One's Mind

Still, such an explanation did not account for the particulars of the forbidden animals. Why, in particular, had the Bible stressed cloven hoofs and chewing the cud (ruminating) as requirements? To some it seemed that this specification was designed to teach that "rumination" in the mental sense—chewing things over in one's mind—was a crucial virtue:

Everything pertaining to conduct permitted us toward these creatures and towards beasts has been set out symbolically . . . For example, all cloven-footed creatures and ruminants quite clearly express, to those who perceive it, the phenomenon of memory. Rumination is nothing but the recalling of life and constitution, life being usually constituted by nourishment. 						— *Letter of Aristeas* 150, 153–154

He [Moses] adds a general method for proving and testing the ten kinds [of clean animals] based on two criteria, the parted hoof and the chewing of the cud. Now both of these are symbols . . . For just as a cud-chewing animal after biting through the food keeps it at rest in the gullet, again after a bit draws it up and chews it and then passes it on to the belly, so the student, after receiving from the teacher through his ears the principles and lore of wisdom, prolongs the process of learning, since he cannot at once comprehend and grasp them securely, until, by using memory to call up each thing that he has heard . . . he stamps a firm impression of them on his soul.

— Philo, *Special Laws* 4:106–107

Again, Moses said: "Eat any animal that is cloven-hooved and chews its cud . . ." [cf. Lev. 11:3]. What, then, does he mean? Be joined to people who fear the Lord, with people who mull over in their hearts the special meaning of the teaching that they have received, be with those who speak of, and observe, the Lord's ordinances, with those who know that meditation is a joyful task and who ruminate on the word of the Lord. 				— *Letter of Barnabas* 10:11

Gentle Birds for Gentle People

As for permitted and forbidden fowl, interpreters noticed that the latter category prominently included birds of prey and birds that feed on dead bodies, while the former featured grain-fed, domesticated birds. Surely here too was a symbolic message:

> Do not take the contemptible view that Moses enacted this legislation because of an excessive preoccupation with mice and weasels or such creatures. The fact is that everything has been solemnly set in order for unblemished investigation and amendment of life for the sake of righteousness. The birds which we use are all domesticated and of exceptional cleanliness, their food consisting of wheat and pulse—such birds as pigeons, turtledoves, locusts, partridges, and in addition, geese and others of the same kind. As to the birds which are forbidden, you will find the wild and carnivorous kinds, as well as others which dominate by their own strength and who find their food at the expense of the forementioned domesticated birds, which is an injustice . . . By calling them pure, he [Moses] has thereby indicated that it is the solemn binding duty of those for whom the legislation has been established to **practice righteousness** and not lord it over anyone by relying on their own strength, nor to deprive a person of anything, but to govern their lives righteously in the manner of those gentle creatures among the birds who feed on plants that grow in the ground and who do not exercise a domination leading to the destruction of their fellow creatures. — *Letter of Aristeas* 144–147

> It might perhaps be considered only fair that all wild animals that feed on human flesh should [be ruled edible and so] suffer from humans what humans suffer from them. But Moses enjoined that we abstain from enjoying such animals, even though they do make for an appetizing and delectable meal. But he was considering what is suitable to a **gentle-mannered soul** . . . Of [the birds] he disqualified a vast number of species, in fact all those that prey on other birds or on men, creatures which are carnivorous and venomous and in general use their strength to attack others. But doves, pigeons, turtledoves, and the tribes of cranes, geese and the like he reckons as belonging to the tame and gentle class, and gives to any who wish full liberty to make use of them as food. — Philo, *Special Laws* 4:103, 117

"You shall not eat the eagle, nor the hawk, nor the kite, nor the crow" [Lev. 11:13–16]. You shall not, he [Moses] is saying, be joined or make yourself similar to those men who do not know how to provide food for themselves through toil and sweat, but in their wickedness plunder things that belong to others and lie in wait—[acting all the while] as if they were walking around quite innocently—looking around for someone to plunder in their greed, in quite the same way that these birds [mentioned above] do not provide food for themselves but sit around idly, looking for some way to eat the flesh of others.

— *Letter of Barnabas* 10:4

Day of Repentance

In the midst of the other laws concerned with purity and holiness comes the Bible's description of a special day, the Day of Atonement, in which the people of Israel are cleansed of their sins and forgiven (Leviticus 16). The description of its rites is long and detailed, but certainly the most striking thing about it was its effect. Each year the people of Israel would be cleansed from their accumulated sins:

> [God said to Moses:] And it shall be a statute to you [Israelites] forever that in the seventh month, on the tenth day of the month, you shall afflict yourselves [with fasting] and shall do no work, either the native or the stranger who sojourns among you. For on this day shall atonement be made for you to cleanse you from all your sins; before the Lord you shall become clean. —Lev. 16:29–30

The idea that the most grievous sins could be, as it were, washed away simply by following the procedure of sacrifice and fasting prescribed for the Day of Atonement certainly sounded good—in fact, too good. Surely, interpreters reasoned, the intention was not to suggest that the Temple ceremony on its own could effect forgiveness: the sinner must have had to do something more than merely fast for a day. After all, the prophet Isaiah had railed against just such a mechanical notion of the efficacy of fasting:

> Behold, in the day of your fast you pursue your own affairs and oppress all your workers. Behold, you fast only to quarrel and to fight and to hit with the wicked fist. Fasting like yours this day will not make your voice to be heard on high . . . Is not this the fast that I choose: to loose the bonds of wickedness, to undo the thongs of the yoke, to let the oppressed go free, and to break every yoke? Is it not to share your

bread with the hungry, and bring the homeless poor into your house; when you see him unclothed, to cover him, and not to hide yourself from your own flesh? —Isa. 58:3–7

Elsewhere, as well, Scripture made clear that sincere repentance—from the heart—was required by God:

Let us lift up our hearts, not [merely] our hands to God in heaven; we have transgressed and rebelled, and You have not forgiven us.
— (variant reading of) Lam. 3:41

And so, interpreters in general came to the conclusion that something more than mere fasting and sacrifices was required on the Day of Atonement (although, strikingly, the Bible itself had not so specified). Surely one could not simply sin in the expectation that one's sins would be forgiven and then turn around and sin again. At the very least, one had to seek to abandon one's sinful ways for good:

And about the Israelites it has been written and ordained [that, on the Day of Atonement] if they **repent** in righteousness, He will forgive all their transgressions and pardon all their sins. —*Jubilees* 5:17

[On the Day of Atonement,] those who now have been purified by **conversion to a better way of life** will have washed away their old lawlessness through a **new adherence to law**. —Philo, *Special Laws* 1:188

One who touches a dead body, bathes [in order to remove his impurity], and then touches it again, what good will his washing have done him?
Such is a person who fasts for his sins and then goes and does them again.
—Sir. 34:25–26

So long as a person holds a source of impurity in his hand, then even if he washes in the [waters of] Siloam or in all the waters of Creation, he can never be purified. But if he casts the impurity from his hand, a bath of [the minimum measure] is sufficient to [purify] him. So [similarly] does it say, "He who confesses and abandons [his sin] will gain mercy" [Prov. 28:13]. —Tosefta *Ta'aniyot* 1:8

One who says, "I will sin and then I will repent, I will sin and I will repent," it will not be given to such a person to repent. [If he says,]

"I will sin and the Day of Atonement will atone [for me]," the Day of
Atonement will not atone.

— m. *Yoma* 8:9

What may be the Jewish substratum of a later Christian text likewise stresses
that fasting is only effective if one is pure and prays with a pure heart:

Remember that from the time when He created the heavens, the Lord
created the fast, for a benefit to men on account of the passions and
desires which fight against you, so that evil will not inflame you. "But
it is a pure fast that I have created," said the Lord . . . Let the pure one
fast, but whenever the one who fasts is not pure, he has angered the
Lord and also the angels. And he has grieved his soul, gathering up
wrath for himself for the day of wrath. But a pure fast is what I created,
[to be observed] with a pure heart and pure hands. It releases sin, it
heals diseases, it casts out demons, it is effective up to the throne of
God for an ointment and for a release from sin by means of a pure
prayer.

— *Apocalypse of Elijah* 1:15–22

The Day of Partial Atonement

If one did, however, sincerely repent of one's misdeeds, could *all* sins be
atoned for? The Bible did indeed say "all your sins" in various formulations
(Lev. 16:16, 21–22, 30, 34). Some interpreters took this "all" as inclusive:

[On the Day of Atonement] men from morning to evening use their
time in the offering of humble prayers by which they might appease
God and ask for remission of their sins, **both intentional and unintentional,** hoping for a good outcome not by dint of themselves, but
by the gracious nature of the One who prefers forgiveness to punishment.

— Philo, *Special Laws* 2:196

Others, however, doubted that the Day of Atonement could be, in this sense,
a blank check. Quite apart from the matter of repentance, perhaps the atonement spoken of here applied only to certain kinds of sins—for example, those
committed by mistake—but not others:

And about the Israelites it has been written and ordained [that, on the
Day of Atonement] if they repent in righteousness, He will forgive all
their transgressions and pardon all their sins. [But what does this "all"
mean?] It is written and ordained that He will have mercy on all who
repent of all their **errors** once a year.

— *Jubilees* 5:17

The righteous constantly searches his house to remove his unintentional sins. He atones for [sins of] ignorance by fasting and humbling his soul, and the Lord will cleanse every devout person and his house.

— *Psalms of Solomon* 3:7–8

But into the second, [inner, area] only the high priest goes, and he but once a year [that is, on the Day of Atonement], and not without taking blood which he offers for himself and for **the errors** of the people.

— Heb. 9:7 (also 5:2)

Or perhaps only sins committed against God were atoned for by the day alone:

The Day of Atonement may atone for sins of a man toward God, but for sins committed against one's fellow, the Day of Atonement will not atone until the person himself seeks to assuage his fellow.

— m. *Yoma* 8:9 (cf. m. *Shebu'ot* 1:6)

Hatred Means Hypocrisy

In addition to sacrificial worship, the food laws and other matters of purity and impurity, and the regulations of the Day of Atonement and other holidays, Leviticus also focuses on a number of issues connected with everyday morality. At first glance these might seem clear enough:

You shall do no injustice in judging: you shall not be partial to the poor nor defer to the rich, but in righteousness shall you judge your neighbor. You shall not go about as a tale-bearer among your people, and you shall not stand idly by the blood of your neighbor: I am the Lord. You shall not hate your brother in your heart; you shall surely reproach your fellow, and you shall bear no sin because of him. You shall not take vengeance or bear a grudge against your countrymen, and you shall love your neighbor as yourself: I am the Lord.   — Lev. 19:15–18

And yet, laws such as these were, when one stopped to consider them, just as puzzling as the laws of pure and impure foods. For if they were indeed laws—divine commandments, and not just good advice—how could anyone be expected to obey them fully? How, in particular, could such a common thing as gossip or slander ("tale-bearing") be outlawed completely? How could the Bible forbid hatred or the bearing of a grudge—emotions that are perfectly natural in certain circumstances, and perhaps even laudable in some? Most puzzling of all, how could the Bible *command* us to love, to "love your neighbor as yourself"? Were there not at least some neighbors whom it was impossible to love (and who, in any case, did not seem to merit such love)?

With regard to the prohibition of hating one's brother "in your heart," interpreters saw this last phrase as a crucial qualification. Hatred in the heart, they reasoned, meant hatred that was unexpressed, that remained hidden inside. There was good reason to think this. After all, the book of Proverbs more than once suggested that hatred of this sort leads to hypocrisy and lying:

> He who hates **dissembles with his lips**, harboring treachery inside
> himself;
> Though he make his voice kindly, do not trust him, for there are
> seven abhorrences **in his heart**.
>
> — Prov. 26:24–25

> He who **conceals** hatred has lying lips, and he who utters slander
> is a fool.
>
> — Prov. 10:18

If hatred "in the heart" meant concealed hatred, then it seemed that the Bible was outlawing not hating per se, but hiding that hatred under a veil of hypocrisy and lying:

> [Gad confesses:] And now, my children, each of you love his brother
> and remove hatred **from your hearts**, and love one another in deed
> and word and thought. For in my father's presence I would **speak
> peaceably** to Joseph, but when I went out from him, the spirit of
> hatred darkened my mind and aroused my soul to kill him.
>
> — *Testament of Gad* 6:1–2

Reproach Prevents Hatred

If one is thus forbidden to hide hatred "in the heart," what is the alternative? Many interpreters found an answer in the words just following the prohibition of hidden hatred seen above in Lev. 19:17: "You shall surely reproach your fellow, and you shall bear no sin because of him." In other words, instead of hating in secret, one ought to tell the offending party openly of one's grievance, reproach him and so avoid committing any sin on his account.

> Reproach a friend **before getting angry,** and give place to the
> Torah of the Most High.
>
> — Sir. 19:17

If anyone sins against you, speak to him peacefully, having banished the poison of hatred, and do not maintain treachery in your soul.
— *Testament of Gad* 6:3

You shall not hate any man, but some you shall reproach, others you shall pray for, and others you shall love more than your own life.[2]
— *Didache* 2:7

Reproach Gently to Prevent Sin

It is not clear to what the phrase "and you shall bear no sin because of him" in Lev. 19:17 refers: the sin in question might be something done by the offended party if he does not reproach his fellow—hating him in his heart, or, as Ben Sira suggests above, "getting angry." Other interpreters, however, believed that the sin being referred to was some further sin that might be occasioned by the act of reproaching: too sharp a reproach might lead the other party to take a false oath in protesting his innocence, or to curse with the divine name. In any case, many therefore stressed that the act of reproaching was to be done in the gentlest manner, lest it in itself become the cause of further sin:

Reproach each other in tru[th] and humility and in loving considera-tion to a man. Let one not speak to hi[m] in anger or contentiousness or stub[bornly or in a] mean spirit, and let him not hate him in [. . .] his heart, but on that very day let him reproach him and not bear sin because of him. — (1QS) *Community Rule* 5:24–6:1

And if he confesses and repents, forgive him. But if he denies, do not dispute with him, **lest he swear** and you thereby sin doubly.
— *Testament of Gad* 6:4

"You shall not hate your brother in your heart; you shall surely re-proach your fellow . . ." Might you understand this to mean that you should reproach him even to the point of embarrassment? Scripture says, "You shall bear no sin because of him."
— *Sifra* ("*Mekhilta de'arayot*") ad Lev. 19:17

There may be a reminiscence of this same interpretation in the following:

2. That is, hatred is to be avoided in some cases by reproaching the offender; in others by praying on the offender's behalf (perhaps because he is incapable of accepting reproach, so "you shall bear no sin because of him," Lev. 9:17—see below); and in yet other cases by loving the offender "more than your own life," an allusion to Lev. 9:18, "You shall love your neighbor *as yourself.*"

Do not grumble, brethren, against one another, that you may not be judged . . . But above all, my brothers, do not swear . . . that you may not fall under condemnation.   —James 5:9–12

Reproach before Charging

A wholly different interpretation, however, likewise existed, this one based on an attempt to understand the law of reproach in its overall context in the Bible. For the paragraph of laws cited above starts with the words "You shall do no injustice *in judging:* you shall not be partial to the poor nor defer to the rich, but in righteousness shall you judge your neighbor" (Lev. 19:15). Was it not possible that the commandment to reproach one's fellow (along with the others in this passage) was connected specifically to the world of courts and lawsuits? If so, then perhaps "reproach your fellow" meant, originally, "don't rush to take him to court." In other words, one ought to try to settle disputes on one's own; only someone who hates his fellow in his heart will use the occasion of an infraction to haul him before the judges:

> If a brother stumbles, it [hatred] wants to report it forthwith to everyone, and is eager for him to be brought to trial for it and punished and put to death.   — *Testament of Gad* 4:3

Soon enough, this line of interpretation led to the inclusion of "reproach" as a necessary preliminary to bringing official charges against someone. The offender had to be reproached—in fact, in the presence of witnesses—before he could be officially charged with a crime:

> Moreover, let a man not bring against his fellow a matter before the "Many" [a quasi-judicial body] which had no reproach before witnesses.   — (1QS) *Community Rule* 6:1

> Any man from the members of the covenant [of the Qumran sect] who brings against his fellow a charge which has had no reproach before witnesses, but brings it out of anger, or tells it to his Elders in order to shame him, he is guilty of taking revenge and holding a grudge . . . His sin is upon him insofar as he did not carry out the commandment of God who said to him, "You shall surely reproach your fellow and shall bear no sin because of him."
> — *Damascus Document* 9:3–8

If your brother sins against you, go and tell him his fault, between you and him alone. If he listens to you, you have gained a brother. But if he does not listen, take one or two others along with you, so that every word may be confirmed by the evidence of two or three witnesses.

—Matt. 18:15–16

But someone [in the church] who is hard and froward and overreaching and blasphemous [and] a hypocrite . . . the Enemy [Satan] is at work in him. Reproach him, therefore, and rebuke him and upbraid him, and put him forth for correction; and afterwards, as we have already said, receive him back, so that he may not utterly perish. For when such people are corrected and reproached, you will not have many lawsuits. — *Didascalia Apostolorum* ch.11

Love As You Would Be Loved

Thus, the Bible was understood not to outlaw hatred per se, but hidden hatred, and to indicate that the way to prevent such hidden hatred was through open reproach (if only in the judicial sense). But what then of the law found in the very next verse, "You shall love your neighbor as yourself" (Lev. 19:18)? Did not this commandment go well beyond outlawing hatred, hidden or otherwise, and enjoin people to act lovingly toward one another under any circumstances?

The answer depended, of course, on how the words were understood. They might mean, to be sure: You shall love your neighbor *in the same way that you love yourself.*

And among yourselves, my sons, be loving of your brothers as a man **loves himself**, with each man seeking for his brother what is good for him, and acting together on the earth, and loving each other as themselves. — *Jubilees* 36:4

Or even:

You shall not hate any man, but some you shall reproach, others you shall pray for, and others you shall love more than your own life.

— *Didache* 2:7

You shall love your neighbor even above your own soul [life].

— *Letter of Barnabas* 19:5

But this was hardly the only possible sense for ancient interpreters, perhaps not even the most likely. After all, loving one's neighbor every bit as much as one loves oneself—expending as much time and effort and worldly goods on him as on oneself, indeed, in time of danger not giving one's own life precedence over that of one's neighbor—seems like a tall order indeed, virtually an inhuman one. So perhaps the commandment was intended in some other sense, something like: You shall love your neighbor as you yourself *would be loved,* that is, treat your neighbor with love in the same way that you yourself would want to be treated:

> The way of life is this: First, you shall love the Lord your Maker, and secondly, your neighbor as yourself. And whatever you do not want to be done to you, you shall not do to anyone else.[3] — *Didache* 3:1–2

> Do not take revenge and and do not hold onto hatred, and love your neighbor; for what is hateful to you yourself, do not do to him; I am the Lord. — *Targum Pseudo-Jonathan* Lev. 19:18

Love Only Your Neighbor

But there was a far more restrictive way of understanding this same verse. "Your neighbor" might not necessarily mean all human beings. This Hebrew word actually means something more like "your friend," and while it can simply mean "your fellow," it is basically used in this section of Leviticus interchangeably with "your brother" and "your kinsman." Thus, there were certainly grounds to claim that not all people are, in this sense, one's "neighbor." It was, in any case, a good question:

> And behold, a lawyer stood up to put him to the test, saying, "Teacher, what shall I do to inherit eternal life?" He said to him, "What is written in the Torah? Have you read it?" And he answered, "You shall love the Lord your God with all your heart, and with all your soul, and with all your mind; and your neighbor as yourself." And he said to him, "You have answered right; do this, and you will live." But he, desiring to justify himself,[4] said to Jesus, "And who is my neighbor?"
>
> —Luke 10:25–29

3. This last sentence thus seems, as in the next example as well, to be a kind of gloss, an explanation of what loving your neighbor "as yourself" entails. It may have been a standard gloss, adduced here somewhat in contradiction to the understanding that underlies *Didache* 2:7 (cited earlier). According to this understanding, the phrase "as yourself" is to be taken as a kind of shorthand: You shall love your neighbor *as you yourself would like to be loved,* that is, what is hateful to you do not do to him.

4. That is, to justify a rather limited sense of who is to be included under the term "neighbor." Jesus' answer, the famous parable of the Good Samaritan, suggests another answer: even the despised Samaritans native to the land north of Judea were to be included under that rubric.

This same question was no doubt posed by others as well, part of a lively debate about just how far, and to whom, the commandment to love one's "neighbor" extends.

This debate focused not only on the ambiguities of the word "neighbor," but as well on the fact that one could read the specific sequence of words in Lev. 19:18 as constituting a single phrase, "your-neighbor-as-yourself." If so, then perhaps the Bible was not at all saying that one ought to love *any* neighbor—however defined—as oneself, but rather that one had a duty to act lovingly only toward those neighbors who were "like yourself," who belonged to the same group or community or the like.

Such an interpretation seems to underlie numerous passages among the Dead Sea Scrolls, which sharply distinguish between members of that particular community—to whom were applied the various commandments of Leviticus 19 seen above—and all others. With others, there was no obligation to "love" in keeping with Lev. 19:18, or even not to "hate in your heart," à la Lev. 19:17 (nor, therefore, to reproach, as specified in the same verse). Indeed, if "neighbor," "brother," and "kinsman" in all these verses referred only to members of one's own group, then perhaps it was, on the contrary, a duty to hate outsiders:

> [Community members are ordered] not to reproach or enter into disputes with the Men of the Pit and to keep hidden the [secret] counsel of the Torah from among the men of perversion; but to reproach [only] those who choose the Way with true knowledge and right judgment [that is, fellow members of the community] . . . These are the indications of the path for the wise one in these times, both as to his loving and his hating: eternal hatred for the Men of the Pit, in the spirit of hiding. —(1QS) *Community Rule* 9:16–17, 21

The idea that the commandments to reproach and love apply only to "friends" may also be echoed elsewhere:

> [The Torah] holds sway over relations **among friends**, [so that one] reproaches them for having acted badly. —4 Macc. 2:13

Indeed, it seems that such an interpretation as this of Lev. 19:17–18 underlies Jesus' words in the Sermon on the Mount:

> You have heard that it was said, "You shall love your neighbor **and hate your enemy. . .**" —Matt. 5:43

The Whole Torah

Understood in this fashion, "You shall not hate your *brother* . . . You shall love your *neighbor* as yourself" paradoxically became a summons to hate all those who were not in the category of "brother" or "neighbor"! Still, while such an interpretation did exist, many other interpreters understood this commandment in a broader way. Indeed, from an early period (as we have already glimpsed), Lev. 19:18 seems to have been exalted as a central principle and the epitome of all the Torah's laws concerning relations between human beings (just as the other "You shall love," Deut. 6:4, epitomized all laws concerning relations between man and God):

> And he [Abraham] commanded them [his descendants] that they should guard the way of the Lord so that they might do righteousness and each one might **love his neighbor** and that it should be thus among all men, so that each one might proceed to act justly and rightly toward them upon the earth.   —*Jubilees* 20:2

> [Isaac says to his sons Jacob and Esau:] And I am commanding this, my sons, that you might perform righteousness and uprightness upon the earth, so that the Lord will bring that which the Lord said that He would do for Abraham and for his seed. And among yourselves, my sons, be **loving of your brothers** as a man loves himself, with each man seeking for his brother what is good for him, and acting together on the earth, and loving each other as themselves . . . And now I will make you swear by the great oath . . . that you will fear Him and worship Him, and that each one will love his brother with compassion and righteousness, and that neither will desire evil for his brother from now and forever all the days of your lives.   —*Jubilees* 36:3–4, 7–8

> Throughout all your life love the Lord and one another with a true heart.   — *Testament of Dan* 5:3

> Keep the Law of God, my children; achieve integrity; live without malice, not tinkering with God's commandments or your neighbor's affairs. Love the **Lord and your neighbor**.

> With every man in pain I joined in lament, and with a poor man I shared my bread, I did not eat alone. I did not move any boundary-mark. I did deeds of piety and truth all my days. I loved the Lord with

all my might; in the same fashion, I also loved every man as my own children.   — *Testament of Issachar* 7:5–6 (see also *Testament of Joseph* 11:1, *Testament of Zebulon* 5:1)

But among the vast number of particular truths and principles studied, two, one might almost say, stand out higher than all the rest, that of [relating] to God through piety and holiness, and that of [relating] to fellow men through a love of mankind and of righteousness.

— Philo, *Special Laws* 2:63

The way of life is this: First, you shall love the Lord your Maker, and secondly, your neighbor as yourself. And whatever you do not want to be done to you, you shall not do to anyone else.   — *Didache* 3:1–2

And one of them, a lawyer, asked him a question, to test him. "Teacher, which is the great commandment in the law?" And he said to him, "You shall love the Lord with all your heart, and with all your soul, and with all your mind. This is the great and first commandment. And a second is like it, You shall love your neighbor as yourself. On these two commandments depend all the law and the prophets."

— Matt. 22:35–40

The commandments . . . are summed up in this one sentence, "You shall love your neighbor as yourself."   — Rom. 13:9

For the whole law is fulfilled in one word, "You shall love your neighbor as yourself."   — Gal. 5:14

If you really fulfill the **royal** law, according to the Scripture "You shall love your neighbor as yourself," you do well.   — James 2:8

"And you shall love your neighbor as yourself"—R. Akiba said: This is the great general principle in the Torah.   — *Sifra Qedoshim* 4

❖   ❖   ❖

In short: Nadab and Abihu may not have sinned at all but died a holy death and ascended to heaven. The divine fire burned them internally, so that their clothes and flesh were unhurt. Among the laws given to Israel after this incident, the laws governing pure food were intended to teach self-control and to impart moral guidance. The Day of Atonement service required sincere repentance in order to be effective, and even so not all sins were thereby atoned for. The sin of concealed hatred and its attendant hypocrisy was to be avoided by the practice of open reproach, which, however, might also serve as a required preliminary to judicial remedy. "You shall love your neighbor as yourself" did not necessarily apply to all human beings; nevertheless, it was seen as a great general principle and the epitome of the Torah's commandments concerning relations among human beings.

23

Trouble along
the Way

(NUMBERS 11–17)

The spies return: whose bad idea?

Trouble along the Way

(NUMBERS 11–17)

❖   ❖   ❖

As they traveled from Egypt to their future homeland in Canaan, the Israel-
ites bemoaned their state, and some of the rabble in their midst cried out for
meat, saying that they were tired of the manna that God had supplied them.
In response, God sent them an abundance of quails from the sea, but before
these could be eaten, a great plague struck the people because of their craving.
Still they did not stop their complaints, turning them now against their
leader Moses. Moses' own sister and brother, Miriam and Aaron, spoke out
against him because of his Cushite wife and moreover challenged his author-
ity. God defended Moses and turned Miriam's skin "white as snow" as a
punishment. Moses prayed for her and she recovered.

Next, Moses sent out spies to scout out the land of Canaan, which Israel was
to conquer. When they returned, they reported that the land itself was
fruitful, "flowing with milk and honey," but that its inhabitants were fear-
some giants, too strong to be conquered. Only two of the twelve spies, Caleb
and Joshua, dissented, urging the people to take heart and trust in God. But
the people did not listen and again railed against their leaders, Moses and
Aaron. In response, God decreed that the entire adult population of Israel
would, because of their complaining, be condemned to die in the wilderness
before entering the land: only the young (everyone under twenty) and the
two dissenting spies, Joshua and Caleb, would live to enter the land.

No sooner had that incident passed than another rebellion occurred: a
group led by Korah, Dathan, and Abiram challenged Moses' authority,
saying that he had exalted himself over everyone. In the ensuing confronta-
tion, the earth opened up and swallowed the rebels. Subsequently a plague
destroyed another group who had complained, and more than fourteen
thousand people were killed. Finally, to show that Aaron's selection for the
priesthood had been divinely sanctioned, a miracle occurred: from among
twelve staffs, representing the twelve tribes, Aaron's alone budded overnight
and bore fruit.

Quails Weren't for Grousing

The quails that God sent down for the complaining rabble seemed like a
well-deserved punishment. After all, He had miraculously supplied them with

manna in the desert, but instead of appreciating this munificence, these people actually dared to belittle it (Num. 11:6). No wonder God spoke of the quails as of a threat:

> Therefore the Lord will give you meat, and you shall eat. You shall not eat one day, or two days, or five days, or ten days, or twenty days, but a whole month, until it comes out of your nostrils and becomes loathsome to you, because you have rejected the Lord who is among you.
>
> —Num. 11:18–20

In fact, what happened was still worse: no sooner had the people picked up the quails and started to eat them than God's anger turned against them in a great plague that struck "while the meat was yet between their teeth" (Num. 11:33). The quails thus seemed to be part of this divine punishment for unbelief, and the fact that the site was called Kibroth-hattaavah (roughly, "Gourmets' Graveyard") only seemed to confirm that the quails and the plague came together to teach the Israelites to control their appetites.

Yet some interpreters were inclined to think otherwise. To begin with, it seemed a little strange that God should at the same time give the complainers what they asked for and also punish them for asking. If their request for meat was unjustified, then why had He bothered to send the quails at all? And there was another good reason to doubt that the quails were part of any divine punishment. For this was not the first time that quails had been mentioned in connection with the Israelites' wanderings. Earlier, just after the crossing of the Red Sea, the Bible had briefly alluded to the provision of quails along with the manna.

> And the Lord said to Moses, "I have heard the murmurings of the people of Israel; say to them, 'At twilight you shall eat flesh, and in the morning you shall be filled with bread; then you shall know that I am the Lord your God.'" In the evening **quails** came up and covered the camp; and in the morning dew lay round about the camp [and with it, the manna]. —Exod. 16:11–13

Elsewhere as well, the quails were presented alongside the manna as twin manifestations of God's goodness:

> They asked, and he brought quails, and gave them bread from heaven in abundance.
>
> —Ps. 105:40

These passages essentially place the quails in the same miraculous category as manna. And indeed, was not quail a strangely dainty delicacy to be provided to desert wanderers? For all these reasons, God's sending of the quails seemed quite wondrous and beneficent. What is more, the quails mentioned in Numbers 11 were, for many interpreters, identical with, or at least a continuation of, the quails mentioned in Exod. 16:13. Since the quails in the Exodus passage were clearly a good thing, there was little reason to doubt that in the Numbers passage as well they were simply one more example of God's extraordinary kindness to His people.

As a result, interpreters sought to separate sharply God's provision of the quails in Numbers 11 from the subsequent plague that struck the Israelites (or to pass over the latter in silence). The plague was a punishment for complaining, but the quails were not part of that punishment:

> You exhibited **kindness** to your people and prepared for the satisfaction of their fierce craving **an exotic delicacy** of quail food; so that . . . your people, only briefly made to want, might partake of an exotic dish.
> —Wisd. 16:2–3

> [The Israelites] were supplied with the means of luxurious living, since God was pleased to provide to them abundantly, and more than abundantly, in the wilderness all the foods which are found in a rich and well-inhabited country. For in the evenings a continuous cloud of quails appeared from the sea and overshadowed the whole camp, flying close to the land, so as to be an easy prey. —Philo, *Moses* 1:209

> "God and I," [Moses] said, "even though vilified by you, will never cease our efforts on your behalf . . ." As he was speaking, the camp became filled with quails on every side, and they gathered round them and collected them. However God, not long **afterward**, chastised the Hebrews for their abusive insolence toward Him.
> —Josephus, *Jewish Antiquities* 3:298–299

> **As a reward** for the calf that Abraham had fed to the ministering angels, God gave Israel quail on two occasions.
> —*Seder Eliahu Rabba* p. 60

A Wife Related to Prophecy

The next instance of Israel's complaining started off strangely: Miriam and Aaron "spoke against Moses because of the Cushite [Ethiopian] woman whom he had married" (Num. 12:1). As discussed in Chapter 16 ("Zipporah the Ethiopian"), the identity of this Ethiopian woman posed a problem, since the only wife of Moses mentioned until now was Zipporah, who was a

Midianite, not an Ethiopian. Beyond that problem, however, was that of the relevance of this Ethiopian wife to the rest of Miriam and Aaron's accusation—which had nothing to do with his wife or wives and concerned instead Moses' authority as a prophet:

> And they [Miriam and Aaron] said: "Has the Lord indeed spoken only through Moses? Has He not spoken through us also?"　　—Num. 12:2

Faced with this problem, interpreters sought some hidden connection between the subject of prophecy and Miriam and Aaron's mention of this other "wife":

> It was God Himself who married the Ethiopian woman to Moses; she stands for unchangeable resolve, intense and fixed . . . Just as in the eye the part that sees is black, so the soul's **power of vision** is called a woman of Ethiopia.　　—Philo, *Allegorical Interpretation* 2:67

In other words, in speaking against this Ethiopian wife, what Aaron and Miriam were really denouncing was Moses' extraordinary status as a visionary. Alternately, perhaps they had mentioned Moses' wife because he had separated from her[1] in order to devote himself exclusively to prophecy:

> "And they said, 'Is it only with Moses that the Lord has spoken?'" (Num. 12:2): Did He not also speak with the patriarchs? Yet *they* did not separate themselves from [the commandment of] being fruitful and multiplying. And did He not also speak with us? Yet we have not separated ourselves from [the commandment of] being fruitful and multiplying.　　—*Sifrei Numbers* 99

Trusted Servant Par Excellence

To this question of Miriam and Aaron—"Has the Lord indeed spoken only through Moses? Has He not also spoken through us?" (Num. 12:2)—God offered a striking response. Moses was indeed different from all others:

---

1. That such a separation had taken place is suggested by the precise wording of the verse: "Miriam and Aaron spoke against Moses because of the Ethiopian woman whom he had married, *for he had married an Ethiopian*" (Num. 12:1). The emphasized words seem to have been written lest the fact of Moses' marriage to this woman otherwise be unknown; might this not be because the woman in question had subsequently been divorced or had separated from Moses, so that there was no current evidence of this marriage? Moreover, if the woman in question was indeed Zipporah, then there was a further indication that she and Moses had separated, namely, "Now Jethro, Moses' father in law, had taken Zipporah, Moses' wife, *after he had sent her away*" (Exod. 18:2).

"If there is a prophet among you, I make Myself known to him in a vision, I speak with him in a dream. Not so with My servant Moses: he is the one **trusted in My whole house**; with him I speak mouth to mouth, clearly, and not in dark speech, and he beholds the form of the Lord. Why then were you not afraid to speak against My servant Moses?"
— Num. 12:6–8

The idea that Moses was, like a trusted servant of a king, allowed in any room of the divine palace, caught the imagination of ancient interpreters, who therefore emphasized trustworthiness as one of Moses' outstanding virtues. Indeed, "trusted in the house" sometimes became a shorthand reference for Moses' exalted status:

In faithfulness and humility,[2] He singled him [Moses] out from all others.
— Sir. 45:4

[Moses was] that sacred spirit, worthy of the Lord, manifold and incomprehensible, master of words, **faithful** in all, the divine prophet of the whole earth, the perfect teacher in the world.
— *Testament of Moses* 11:16

Only God Himself, and the one who is God's friend [that is, Abraham] is [called] faithful, just as Moses is [also] said to have been found "faithful in all His house" [Num. 12:17].
— Philo, *Allegorical Interpretation* 3:204

And in this way You spoke to Moses, your faithful and holy servant, in the vision at the bush: I am the One Who Is, this is for Me an eternal name, and a remembrance to generations of generations.
— Hellenistic Synagogal Prayer, *Apostolic Constitutions* 7.33.6

Now Moses was trusted in all of God's house as a servant, to testify to the things that were to be spoken later, but Christ was trusted *over* God's house as son.
— Heb. 3:5–6

Moses rejoiced in his allotted portion, for "trusted servant" is what You called him.
— Fragment of ancient *qerobah* incorporated in synagogue prayer

2. "Faithfulness" in Hebrew is from the same root as "trusted" and is thus an apparent allusion to Num. 12:7; Moses' extraordinary humility was mentioned in the same episode, Num. 12:3.

Since the Greek *pistos* can mean both trustworthy and trust*ing*, having faith, those who knew the Bible in Greek sometimes highlighted *faith* as one of Moses' virtues:

> Moses is attested to be foremost [in faith] since he is "faith-ful in all My house."   —Philo, *Allegorical Interpretation* 3:228

> He [Jesus] was faithful to Him who appointed him, just as Moses also was faithful [trusted] in God's house.   —Heb. 3:2

Whose Bad Idea?

When, following this incident, Moses sent out spies to scout the land, the result was catastrophe: because the spies came back with dire reports of the Canaanites' strength and size, the people lost heart, and God sentenced them to wander in the wilderness for forty years. Apparently, then, sending out the spies was not a particularly good idea.

But whose idea was it? The incident is introduced with these words:

> Then the Lord said to Moses, "Send out for yourself men to spy out the land of Canaan which I am giving to the people of Israel; send one man from each tribe."   —Num. 13:1–2

Here it seems clear that God commanded Moses to send out the spies; the initiative was certainly not Moses'. Later on, however, Moses characterized the events in somewhat different fashion:

> [Moses recalls:] Then all of you [Israelites] came near me and said, "Let us send men before us, that they may explore the land for us, and bring us word again of the way by which we must go up and the cities into which we shall come." **The thing seemed good to me**, and I took twelve men of you, one man for each tribe, and they turned and went up.   —Deut. 1:22–24

Here the decision to send the spies is made by Moses at the people's urging; God has no role in the decision.

So which was it? Some interpreters decided that the latter was most likely the case, for surely an omniscient God would not have ordered that the spies be sent only to become angry later at the reaction to their ill report:[3]

3. There is some support for this position in the text of Num. 13:2 itself, which reads "Send out *for yourself* men to spy out," perhaps implying that, in so saying, God was acceding to some request of Moses, or at least stating that the purpose of the mission was *for* Moses but not for God.

After this battle he [Moses] came to the conclusion that . . . he ought to inspect the land in which the nation proposed to settle . . . He chose twelve men, corresponding to the number of tribes.
— Philo, *Moses* 1:220–221

[Moses tells the Israelites:] "Let us prepare for the task [of conquering Canaan]. For they [the Canaanites] will not give us their land without a fight, but will be deprived of it [only] with great struggle. So let us send out spies who can look over the land's riches and the strength of its [people's] forces." — Josephus, *Jewish Antiquities* 3:301–302

It was taught: Resh Laqish said: "[It says] Send *for yourself*" [Num. 13:2]—that is, in accordance with your own decision." — b. *Soṭah* 34b

Still, the wording of Num. 13:1 is quite clear on one point: God did tell Moses to send the men. Perhaps, then, what Moses meant in Deut. 1:22–24 was that he had approved the sending of spies in keeping with God's command:

And Moses sent twelve men as spies to spy out the land, for so it had been commanded him. — Pseudo-Philo, *Biblical Antiquities* 15:1

"And I said to you . . ." [Deut. 1:21]: He said to them: I am not telling you this on my own authority, but it is on God's authority that I am saying this to you . . . "The thing seemed good to me . . ." [Deut. 1:23] to me it seemed good, but not to God. — *Sifrei Deuteronomy* 19–21

Solemnly Warned

After hearing the spies' discouraging report, the people began to bemoan their fate and even proposed to return to Egypt (Num. 14:4). Joshua and Caleb tried to calm them and warned them not to rebel against God, but they would not listen. At length God told Moses that He intended to strike them down with pestilence (Num. 14:12). It was only after Moses pleaded on the people's behalf that this death sentence was rescinded.

To some it must have seemed that God's reaction was unwarranted. After all, the spies' report *was* discouraging: could the people really be blamed for panicking? And even if their conduct was not proper, was it worthy of punishment by death? Considering such matters, interpreters no doubt turned to the warning issued to the people by Caleb and Joshua, "Do not rebel against the Lord" (Num. 14:9). To anyone schooled in the ways of divine justice, these words not only indicated the gravity of the crime involved, but further showed that the people had subsequently acted willfully, proceeding with their rebellion even after having been solemnly warned:[4]

> So was it also with the six hundred thousand strong, who all
>   perished for their willful wrongdoing [*zedon libbam*].
> If so, then one who is stiff-necked, will it surely be astonishing if
>   he is not punished.
>
> —Sir. 16:10–11

> Joshua, because he fulfilled the commandment, became a judge in Israel. Caleb, because he [officially] warned the assembly [apparently *heʿid bāʿedāh*] received an inheritance in the land.[5]   —1 Macc. 2:55–56

> It was not with the lightness of men that God had been brought to this wrath against them, but He had deliberately passed sentence upon them.   —Josephus, *Jewish Antiquities* 3:315

Perhaps the same was implied elsewhere:

> [. . .] to them at Kadesh: "Arise, take possession of [. . .]"[6] their spirit and they did not heed their creator, the commandments of their teacher; they spoke rebelliously in their tents [Ps. 106:25, see also Deut. 1:27] and the wrath of God was kindled against their company.
>
> —*Damascus Document* 3:7–9

Tassels Set Off Revolt

Between the account of the spies' return and the next ill turn in Israel's fortunes, the revolt of Korah and his allies, came Moses' promulgation of the law of tassels. On God's instruction, Moses announced that the Israelites were to make tassels on the corners of their garments; upon each corner tassel was to be a special blue thread "so that you shall remember and do all My commandments" (Num. 16:37–41). Immediately after this announcement, the Bible begins its account of Korah's revolt.

4. That a rebellion did take place is also implied by Deut. 9:23–24, Ps. 106:25.

5. It is all the more striking that this "warning" is the reason given here for Caleb's reward, since everywhere else the reason is that Caleb "wholly followed" (*mille' 'aḥar-*) God: Num. 14:24, 32:13; Deut. 1:36; Josh. 14:9, 14.

6. In both bracketed sections, the medieval copyist has apparently omitted something from the original text. The latter probably read something like: "And God said to them at Kadesh, 'Arise, take possession of the land which I have given you' [Deut. 9:23]. But they rebelled against His [!] spirit [see Ps. 106:33] and they did not heed."

Interpreters therefore could not help concluding that the promulgation of this law had something to do with Korah's revolt:

> In that time He commanded that man [Moses] about the tassels. And then Korah and two hundred men with him rebelled and said, "Why is an unbearable law imposed upon us?"
>
> — Pseudo-Philo, *Biblical Antiquities* 16:1

> What did Korah do [after hearing the law of tassels]? He went and made some garments that were completely dyed blue. Then he went to Moses and said: Moses our teacher, is a garment that is already completely blue nonetheless obliged to have the [blue corner] tassel? He said: It is . . . Whereupon Korah said: the Torah is not of divine origin, and Moses is not a prophet and Aaron is not the high priest.
>
> — j. *Sanhedrin* 10:1

Moses Accused of Favoritism

In the biblical narrative, Korah complains to Moses and Aaron: "You have gone too far! For all the congregations are holy, every one of them, and the Lord is among them; why then do you exalt yourselves above the assembly of the Lord?" (Num. 16:3). It is not clear from this exactly what Korah's complaint was, but later Moses rebuked him and his followers:

> Is it too small a thing for you that the God of Israel has separated you from the congregation of Israel . . . to do service in the tabernacle of the Lord [as Levites]? Would you now seek the priesthood also?
>
> — Num. 16:9–10

Apparently, then, Korah's complaint was that he was only a Levite (charged with lesser duties in the sanctuary) and not a full-fledged priest (compare Num. 16:40). But if so, what had he meant by accusing Aaron *and Moses* of "exalting yourselves above the assembly of the Lord"? Moses' descendants had not been given the hereditary priesthood—it was awarded to Aaron and his sons. The same question was posed more sharply by a brief recapitulation of the events in the book of Psalms:

> And they became jealous of Moses in the camp, and of Aaron, the Lord's holy one.
>
> — Ps. 106:16

Why were the would-be priests jealous of *Moses?*

Considering these matters, some interpreters concluded that Korah, in desiring the priesthood, ended up accusing Moses of favoritism, indeed, nepotism. Moses, he said, had chosen his own brother, Aaron, for the hereditary priesthood not on the basis of any divine dictate, but out of a corrupt desire to appoint his close relatives to this high position:[7]

> Then, conspiring with each other, and collecting in great numbers, [Korah and his followers] raised an outcry against the prophet [Moses], declaring that he had bestowed the priesthood on his brother and nephews because of their relation to him, and given a false account of their being chosen, which had not really been done under divine direction.
> — Philo, *Moses* 2:278

> [Korah said that] in defiance of the laws he [Moses] had given the priesthood to his brother Aaron, not by the common decree of the people but by his own vote.
> — Josephus, *Jewish Antiquities* 4:15

> Whereupon Korah said: . . . Moses is not a prophet and Aaron is not the high priest.
> — j. *Sanhedrin* 10:1

> [Moses told Korah:] "This quarrel that you are stirring up is not with me but with God."[8]
> — *Midrash Tanḥuma, Qorah* 6

Moses Was Polite

The charge of favoritism would no doubt make any leader angry, and Moses was no exception (Num. 16:15). How much more remarkable, then, that he did not seek at once to rally his forces against Korah for personal revenge, or even speak harshly to Korah and his allies. Instead, he addressed them politely and stressed their special status as Levites (Num. 16:8–10). Was not all this included in Scripture to impart a lesson, namely, the virtues of controlling one's anger?

> When Moses was angry at Dathan and Abiram, he did nothing against them in anger, but controlled his anger with reason.   — 4 Macc. 2:17

> At first very seriously, but without loss of temper, which was indeed alien to his nature, he [Moses] endeavored with words of admonition to bring them to a better mind and to refrain from transgressing the appointed limits or revolting against the sacred and hallowed institutions.
> — Philo, *Rewards and Punishments* 77

7. This motif is an elaboration of Moses' own words in Num. 16:28: "Hereby shall you know that the Lord has sent me to do all these works, and that it has *not been of my own accord*." In so saying Moses seems to be combating an unstated accusation that he acted on his own authority in some matter and not on God's.

8. That is, the fact that Aaron is a priest and you are not is not my decision, but God's.

"And Moses said to Korah: 'Please listen, you Levites . . .'" [Num. 16:8]:
It is said that Moses sought to have Korah change his mind and so
spoke to him politely and appeasingly . . . All these things Moses said
to appease Korah, yet you do not find Korah saying anything back to
him. For he [Korah] was clever in his wickedness. He said: If I answer
him, I know that, since he is a great sage he will overwhelm me with
his words and overcome me and I will end up making peace with him
against my will.   — Midrash Tanḥuma, Qoraḥ 6

Korah's Symbolic Death

In response to Korah's challenge to his authority, Moses had warned that the
rebels would not "die the common death of all men"; they would be punished
in some supernatural fashion so that "you shall know that the Lord has sent
me [Moses] to do these things." (Num. 16:28). And so it was:

And as he [Korah] finished speaking all these words, the ground under
them split asunder, and the earth opened its mouth and swallowed
them up with their households and all the men that belonged to Korah
and all their goods. And all Israel that were round about them fled at
their cry; for they said, "Lest the earth swallow us up!" And fire came
forth from the Lord, and consumed the two hundred and fifty men
offering the incense.   — Num. 17:31–35

Granted, Korah was guilty and deserved punishment, perhaps indeed death in
some supernatural fashion. But to be swallowed up by the earth was certainly
an unprecedented way to die. Perhaps the very fact that the earth was involved
had some special significance:

This too we should not fail to note, that the work of punishing the
impious was shared by earth and heaven, the fundamental parts of the
universe. For they had set the roots of their wickedness on earth, but
let it grow so high that it rose up to the sky. Therefore each of the two
elements supplied its punishment: the earth burst forth and parted
asunder to drag down and swallow those who had then become a
burden to it, while heaven poured down the strangest of rainstorms, a
great stream of fire to blast them in its flames.[9]
                                              — Philo, Moses 2:285–286

9. Technically, the "fire" that came down from heaven did not punish Korah and his followers,
but targeted those Israelites who reproached Moses following Korah's death (Num. 16:35).

And God was angry and said: I commanded the earth, and it gave me Adam; and to him two sons were born at first, and the older rose up and killed the younger, and then the earth quickly swallowed his blood. But I drove Cain out and cursed the earth and spoke to the parched land, saying, "You will swallow up blood no more." But now the thoughts of men are very corrupt; behold, I command the earth, and it will swallow up body and soul together, and their dwelling place will be in darkness and the place of destruction, and they will not die but melt away until I remember the world and renew the earth.

—Pseudo-Philo, *Biblical Antiquities* 16:2–3

A Truly Dangerous Figure

For others, Korah's supernatural death seemed to indicate that the danger posed by him was greater than might first appear. After all, in the biblical story, Korah is simply a dissatisfied Levite who craves higher status and rallies to his support two hundred and fifty men. This was hardly a major revolt! But in reflecting on the Korah episode, interpreters came to the conclusion that far more must have been involved; the very nature of Korah's supernatural death, as well as the fact that the Bible had taken the trouble to recount the whole episode in detail, seemed to argue that Korah was a truly dangerous figure whose rebellion had almost led to destruction:

Thus it was that a sedition, for which we know of no parallel whether among Greeks or barbarians, broke out among them: this sedition brought them all into peril of destruction.

—Josephus, *Jewish Antiquities* 4:12

Woe to them [ungodly men]! For they walk in the way of Cain and abandon themselves for the sake of gain to Balaam's error, and perish in Korah's rebellion.

—Jude 11

For the adherents of Korah, Dathan and Abiram were made a monument and example of the destruction of schismatics; and everyone who imitates them shall perish even as they did.

—*Didascalia Apostolorum* ch. 23

Aaron's Symbolic Staff

Following Korah's rebellion, another incident demonstrated the legitimacy of the Aaronide priesthood. Numbers 17 recounts the story of Aaron's staff, which, alone among twelve staffs representing Israel's twelve tribes, miracu-lously budded and bore fruit overnight. In context, this miracle confirmed God's choice of Aaron and his sons. But interpreters noticed a difference between what God had said would happen—"And the staff of the man whom I choose *shall sprout*" (Num. 17:5)—and what actually did happen:

> And the next day Moses went into the tent of the testimony and behold, the staff of Aaron for the house of Levi had sprouted and put forth buds and produced blossoms, and it bore ripe almonds.
>
> —Num. 17:8

Having the staff bud as predicted certainly would have sufficed to confirm Aaron's choice for the priesthood. Why had God taken the additional step of having the staff bear fruit—and almonds at that?

Perhaps the actual outcome—that the staff would bear almonds—had been known to Moses all along. He simply had not told the Israelites in advance in order to avoid further dissension:

> And Moses took the staffs out, and the staff of Aaron was found not only to have budded, but also to be bearing fruit. What do you think, my beloved—that Moses did not know beforehand that this was going to happen? Of course he knew, but he acted in this way so that there should be no disorder in Israel.
>
> —1 Clement 43:5–6

To other interpreters, however, it seemed that the detail of the staff bearing almonds must contain some further teaching:

> Now, the fruits [which grew on Aaron's staff] were nuts, which in nature are the opposite of other fruits, for in most cases—the grape, the olive, the apple—there is a difference between the seed and the edible part, [and moreover] the edible part is on the outside and the seed is enclosed within. But with a nut, the seed and the edible part are identical, and [they are] inside, shielded and guarded . . . In this way, it [the nut] symbolizes perfect virtue.
>
> —Philo, *Moses* 2:180–181

> And the staff of Aaron sprouted and flowered and yielded seed of almonds. Now that which happened then was like what Israel [Jacob] did when he was in Mesopotamia with Laban the Syrian when he took almond rods and put them at the cisterns of water; and the flocks came to drink and were divided among the peeled rods, and they brought forth white and specked and many-colored kids. So [in the case of Aaron's budding staff,] the assembly of the people was like the

flock of sheep. And as the flocks brought forth according to the almond staff, so the priesthood was established through almond staffs.

—Pseudo-Philo, *Biblical Antiquities* 17:2–4

For Christians, the budding rod of the Old Testament came to be identified with the cross in the New Testament:

> There will again be one exceptional man from the sky
> who stretched out his hands on the **fruit-bearing wood** . . .
> divinely born, wealthy, sole-desired flower,
> good light, **holy shoot, beloved plant.**
>
> —*Sibylline Oracles* 5:256–258, 261–262

❖   ❖   ❖

In short: The quails sent by God to the Israelites were altogether good, part of God's beneficence to His people. As for Miriam and Aaron's complaints about Moses' Ethiopian wife, they really concerned his prophesying. God may not actually have ordered Moses to send out the spies, but His desire to kill the people after their cowardly reaction was based on the solemn warning that had been previously delivered to them. Korah used the law of the tassels as a means for fomenting revolt against Moses, whom he accused of favoritism in naming Aaron to the priesthood. Moses reacted without anger to Korah's accusations, but Korah's supernatural death testified to the gravity of his crimes. The almonds with which Aaron's rod budded contained a hidden lesson about God's ways.

24

The Bronze Serpent, Balaam, and Phinehas

God puts His word in Balaam's mouth.

The Bronze Serpent, Balaam, and Phinehas

(NUMBERS 21–32)

❖ ❖ ❖

When the people continued their complaining, God afflicted them further, this time with fiery serpents; many Israelites died. Moses prayed to God on the people's behalf, and God instructed him to fashion a serpent and place it on a pole, so that anyone who was bitten might look at the serpent and live. Moses then made a serpent out of bronze and this protected the people. Later, as they continued their travels, the Israelites came to Beer ("Well"), so called because of the well that was dug there and the song sung by the Israelites on that occasion.

When the Israelites arrived at the plains of Moab, the Moabite king, Balak, sent a delegation to the east to invite Balaam, a man specially endowed with the powers of cursing and blessing, to curse the Israelites and so stop their advance. Balaam set out on his donkey for the journey, but on the way the donkey suddenly balked, refusing to advance. When Balaam whipped her, the donkey began to speak, protesting the beating. An angel then appeared and told Balaam that his donkey had stopped because she had seen him (the angel), whereas Balaam had not. Chastened, Balaam resumed his journey.

Once in Moab, Balaam sought to oblige Balak but found himself unable to curse Israel—indeed, instead of cursing, he ended up blessing Israel, predicting in different oracles this people's glorious future. Balak dismissed Balaam in anger.

Afterward, the Israelites sinned with the Moabite daughters, sacrificing to their gods and yoking themselves to Baal Peor. Then one of the Israelites brought a Midianite woman to his brothers in the very presence of Moses and Aaron. When he saw this, Phinehas ran the couple through with his spear, thereby averting a plague from Israel. God rewarded Phinehas' zeal with a covenant of perpetual priesthood.

THE BRONZE SERPENT fashioned by Moses profoundly troubled ancient interpreters. After all, a man-made object that had the power to cure snakebites if one simply looked at it—did this not smack more of magic than proper belief? What was worse, this same bronze serpent was later said to have become an object of idolatry in itself:

And he [Hezekiah] did what was right in the eyes of the Lord, according to all that David his father [ancestor] had done. He removed the
high places, and broke the pillars, and cut down the Asherah. And he
broke in pieces the bronze serpent that Moses had made, for until
those days the people in Israel had burned incense to it.

—2 Kings 18:3–4

All of this made interpreters wonder why God had told Moses to make the
bronze serpent in the first place. If He had wanted to heal the people, surely
He could have done so directly.

Looking Didn't Cure

One thing, however, struck interpreters in the episode: God had ordered
Moses not just to make the bronze serpent, but to "put it on a pole" (Num.
21:8). Why this additional specification? The word used for "pole" here (*nēs*)
was sometimes used elsewhere in the Hebrew Bible for "sign," including the
miraculous sense of "signs and wonders." Interestingly, the same was true of
the word used by the Septuagint translators, *sēmeion*, which could also mean
"sign" or even "omen," and the Aramaic *'āt* (used by *Targum Onqelos*). Thus,
God's instruction to put the serpent "on a pole" might be understood, in the
Hebrew Bible itself and in various translations, as meaning that the serpent
was to be used as, or turned into, a symbol or signal of some sort, rather than
directly curing the people:

> Even when fierce and furious snakes attacked the people and the bites
> of writhing serpents were spreading death, Your anger did not con-
> tinue to the bitter end; their short trouble was sent to them as a lesson,
> and they were given a **sign** of salvation to remind them of the require-
> ments of Your law. For any man who turned toward it was saved, not
> by the thing he looked upon, but by You, the savior of all. In this way
> You convinced our enemies that You are the deliverer from every evil.
> — Wisd. 16:5–8

> Now did this serpent actually kill people or heal people? Rather it
> means that when Moses did so, the Israelites looked at him [or "it"]
> and put their trust in Him who ordered Moses so to do; then God
> would send them healing.   — *Mekhilta deR. Ishmael, Amaleq* 1

Alternately, it might be that the whole point of putting the serpent "on a
pole" was to get the Israelites to look upward; this would remind them of the
true source of their healing:

"Make for yourself a fiery serpent and put it on a pole, and anyone who is bitten will see it and live" [Num. 21:8]. And was the [bronze] serpent capable of killing or bringing back to life? Rather, whenever Israel looked upward and subjugated their wills to that of their heavenly Father, they would be healed. —m. *Rosh ha-Shanah* 3:5

And Moses made a bronze serpent and put it on an **elevated** [or "hanging"] place, and it happened that when a snake would bite a man, he would look upon the bronze serpent and direct his thoughts toward God and live. — *Targum Pseudo-Jonathan* Num. 21:9

Similarly:

Everyone, then, "whom a serpent shall have bitten, when he looks on it shall live" [Num. 21:9]. This is quite true. For if the mind, when bitten by pleasure, the serpent of Eve, succeeds in beholding the beauty of self-mastery, [that is,] the serpent of Moses, and through **beholding this, behold God Himself**, he shall live; only let him look and mark well. — Philo, *Allegorical Interpretation* 2:81

Serpent Was Like Moses' Hands

If indeed the purpose of this magic-like act of making a bronze serpent was really only to draw the Israelites' attention to God, then it was not very different from Moses' upraised hands during the battle at Rephidim (see Chapter 19). Some interpreters therefore specifically associated the two episodes:

"And whenever Moses would lift up his hands, Israel would triumph . . ." [Exod. 17:11]. But were Moses' hands capable of making war or undermining war? Rather this is to tell you that whenever Israel looked upward and subjugated their wills to that of their heavenly Father, they would triumph; but if they did not, they would fall. A **similar** instance: "Make for yourself a fiery serpent and put it on a pole, and anyone who is bitten will see it and live" [Num. 21:8]. And was the [bronze] serpent capable of killing or bringing back to life? Rather, whenever Israel looked upward and subjugated their wills to that of their heavenly Father, they would be healed. —m. *Rosh ha-Shanah* 3:5

And he says again to Moses—when Israel was being warred upon by strangers [Exodus 17]— . . . the Spirit, speaking to the heart of Moses, [tells him] to make a representation of the cross and of him who was to suffer upon it . . . So Moses placed one shield upon the other in the midst of the fight, and standing there, raised above them all, kept stretching out his hands, and so Israel again began to be victorious . . . [Later,] Moses made **another representation** of Jesus . . . for the Lord made every serpent to bite them, and they were perishing . . . Moses therefore made a graven serpent. —*Letter of Barnabas* 12:2, 5–6

Shall then the serpent be thought to have saved the people at that time, which, as I have already said, God crushed at the first, and will slay with the great sword, as Isaiah cries aloud [Isa. 27:1]? And shall we accept such things so unintelligently . . . and not as symbols? And shall we not find a reference to the image of the crucified Jesus in the sign ["pole" in Num. 21:8], [just as] Moses, by stretching out his hands together with him who was surnamed by the name of Jesus [Joshua], caused your people to gain the day [at Rephidim]?
—Justin Martyr, *Dialogue with Trypho* 112:2

Balaam the Wicked

Balaam was another somewhat ambiguous figure (like Lot or Esau) whose portrayal troubled ancient interpreters. On the one hand, he seemed unarguably *good*. He was a true prophet of God, a man who "knows the knowledge of the Most High" (Num. 24:16) and whose effectiveness at blessing and cursing (Num. 22:6) could hardly have existed without God's help. In the Bible, Balaam steadfastly refused to say anything not authorized by God, repeatedly scorning the pleadings of royalty and the promises of certain gain that stood behind them. What is more, Balaam's words were unequivocally favorable to Israel, and he even predicted the coming of their long-awaited messiah (see below). How could such a figure be thought of as anything but good?

On the other hand, the whole episode of Balaam's balking, talking donkey did not show him in a good light. It was as if Scripture wished to say that any dumb animal would make a better prophet than Balaam. What is more, the fact that Balaam *did* end up journeying to Moab did not speak well of him; why did he bother going if it was not to reap the material rewards promised by Balak's envoys? Moreover, there was good reason to believe that—despite his fulsome oracles—Balaam was indeed an enemy of Israel, one who eventually sought to harm them in some way other than cursing (see below).

Perhaps an objective evaluation of this conflicting evidence would nevertheless find that Balaam's positive characteristics outweighed his negative ones. Yet ancient interpreters by and large chose the opposite path: Balaam became "Balaam the Wicked," the prophet for hire who was only interested in his own material gain and self-aggrandizement:

> With his soothsayer's mock wisdom, he defaced the stamp of heaven-sent prophecy.　　　　　　　　　　— Philo, *On the Change of Names* 203

> [Balaam] was a sophist, an empty conglomeration of incompatible and discordant notions. It was his desire to do harm to the goodly by laying curses upon him, but he could not, for God turned his curses into a blessing in order that he might convict the unrighteous one of his villainy and at the same time make good His own life of virtue.
> 　　　　　　　　　　— Philo, *Worse Attacks the Better* 71

> Woe to them [ungodly men]! For they walk in the way of Cain and abandon themselves for the sake of gain to Balaam's error, and perish in Korah's rebellion.　　　　　　　　　　— Jude 11

> And the donkey said to Balaam: Where are you going, wicked Balaam? O foolish one! If you are unable to curse me, an unclean beast who will die in this world and will not enter the world to come, how much less are you capable of cursing the sons of Abraham, Isaac and Jacob, for whose future merit the word was created and whose merit attaches to them?　　　　　　　　　　— *Targum Neophyti* Num. 22:30

> Anyone who possesses these three things is of the followers of our father Abraham, but he who possesses three others is of the followers of the wicked Balaam . . . [About the latter it is written:] "And you, O God, will bring them down to destruction, men of bloodshed and falsehood will not live out half their allotted time—but I shall trust in you" [Ps. 55:23].　　　　　　　　　　— m. *Abot* 5:19

What caused most ancient interpreters to overlook Balaam's "good side" so completely? Among other factors, perhaps it was the treatment accorded Balaam elsewhere in Scripture that proved decisive. For his story is mentioned later on as well:

> [Moses explains God's law]: "No Ammonite or Moabite may enter the assembly of the Lord . . . because they hired against you Balaam the son of Beor from Pethor of Mesopotamia, to curse you. Nevertheless the Lord your God would not hearken to Balaam but the Lord your God turned the curse into a blessing for you, because the Lord your God loves you."　　　　　　　　　　— Deut. 23:3–5

[God tells Israel:] "Then Balak the son of Zippor, king of Moab, rose and fought against Israel, and he sent and invited Balaam the son of Beor to curse you, but I would not listen to Balaam; therefore he blessed you; so I delivered you out of his hand." —Josh. 24:9–10

These subsequent mentions of Balaam state outright what the Numbers narrative somehow does not, that Balaam actually *tried* to curse Israel, but that God "would not listen" or even changed Balaam's intended message, "turned the curse into a blessing." (In the Numbers account, on the contrary, Balaam consistently says from the outset that he will only speak what God orders.) Read in the light of these subsequent passages, the Numbers narrative took on a more sinister air. Somewhat sinister, too, was the Balaam mentioned by a later prophet:

O my people, remember what Balak king of Moab devised, and what Balaam the son of Beor answered him, and what happened from Shittim to Gilgal, that you may know the saving acts of the Lord.

—Mic. 6:5

Although this text only hints, its evocation of God's "saving acts" after mentioning Balak and Balaam certainly seems to suggest that God had saved Israel from something these two men had devised (again, see below).

Finally, there was the matter of Balaam's death. It is mentioned twice in Scripture:

They [the Israelites] slew the kings of Midian with the rest of their slain, Evi, Rekem, Zur, Hur, and Rea, the five kings of Midian; and they also slew Balaam the son of Beor with the sword. —Num. 31:8

Balaam also, the son of Beor, the soothsayer, the people of Israel killed with the sword among the rest of their slain. —Josh. 13:22

If Balaam was such a benefactor of Israel, why did they kill him? Indeed, why would his killing be mentioned so prominently, featured alongside that of five enemy kings as if it were an achievement of comparable importance, and then be mentioned again in the book of Joshua—why unless Balaam was indeed a wicked and dangerous enemy of Israel? Swayed by such considerations as these, most interpreters therefore presented the whole of Balaam's history in a negative light, so that even relatively innocent details took on a new coloring.

God Knew Who They Were

To convince Balaam, the famous soothsayer, to travel to Moab and curse Israel, the Moabite king Balak sent a delegation to Balaam's home. Balaam

received the men and told them to spend the night so that he might consult
with God:

> And God came to Balaam and said, "**Who are these men** with you?"
> And Balaam said to God, "Balak the son of Zippor, king of Moab, has
> sent to me, saying, 'Behold a people has come out of Egypt . . . come
> now, curse them for me.'"   —Num. 22:9–11

God's question disturbed ancient interpreters: did He not know who the
envoys were? There was nothing in Balaam's response to indicate that *he*
understood the question as anything more than a request for information.
And yet, interpreters reasoned, perhaps that was the whole point. Perhaps
God's question was a test of Balaam's character:

> And God said to him by night: "Who are these men who have come to
> you?" [Num. 22:9]. And Balaam said, "For what purpose, Lord, do you
> **test** the human race? They cannot pass, for You knew what things were
> to happen in the world even before You founded it. And now, en-
> lighten your servant if it be right that I set out with them."
>   —Pseudo-Philo, *Biblical Antiquities* 18:4

> God **tested** three and found them all [deficient, namely, Cain,
> Hezekiah, and Balaam]: When Balak sent for the wicked Balaam God
> said to him, "Who are these people with you?" Balaam should have
> said: "Master of the universe! Everything is revealed to You and there
> is not one thing that is hidden from You, yet you are asking *me?*"
> Instead, he said to Him: "Balak the son of Zippor has sent to me . . ."
> Said God: Since that is how you answer Me [although I obviously
> know the situation!], "You shall not curse the people" [Num. 22:12].
> Said God: "O most wicked one! It is written about Israel that 'Whoever
> touches you is like one who touches the apple of His [God's] eye'
> [Zech. 2:8], yet you nevertheless are headed off to touch them and
> curse them, therefore let [your] eye fall out," as [Balaam is later
> described as] "the oracle of Balaam . . . whose eye is closed" [Num.
> 24:3].   —*Numbers Rabba* 20:6

A Prophet for Hire

Balaam at first refused to go to Moab and curse Israel, but he changed his
mind after Balak sent a new delegation, "more numerous and honored than
the first" (Num. 22:15). Obviously, Scripture was seeking to make some point
in narrating Balaam's turnaround. Perhaps this second delegation caused him
to reconsider because its higher status appealed to Balaam's vanity. Or perhaps

it was the message the delegation brought from Balak, "I will surely do you great honor," which might be understood as a somewhat polite way of saying, "I will pay you a lot of money." In either case, Balaam's willingness to receive this second delegation, and his ultimate decision to go back with them to Moab, did not speak well of his character. Although no actual sums are mentioned by the text, interpreters concluded that a great deal of money must have been involved. Was Balaam thus not an arrogant, greedy individual?

> The envoys then returned to the king without success, but others, selected from more highly reputed courtiers, were at once appointed for the same purpose who brought **more money** and promised **more abundant** gifts. Enticed by these present and prospective offers and impressed by the high rank of those who were inviting him, [Balaam] gave way, again dishonestly alleging a divine command.
>
> — Philo, *Moses* 1:267–268

> Balak wished to persuade the Almighty through gifts and to buy [His] decree through money [given to Balaam].
>
> — Pseudo-Philo, *Biblical Antiquities* 18:11

> Balak fumed and accused him [Balaam] of transgressing the agreement whereby, in exchange for **liberal gifts**, he had obtained his services.
>
> — Josephus, *Jewish Antiquities* 118

> Forsaking the right way they have gone astray; they have followed the way of Balaam, the son of Beor, **who loved gain** from wrongdoing but was rebuked for his own transgression: a dumb ass spoke with human voice and restrained the prophet's madness.
>
> — 2 Pet. 2:15–16

> Woe to them [ungodly men]! For they . . . abandon themselves **for the sake of gain** to Balaam's error.
>
> — Jude 11

> Anyone who possesses these three things is of the followers of our father Abraham, but he who possesses three others is of the followers of the wicked Balaam. A good eye, a humble spirit, and a modest appetite—such belong to the followers of our father Abraham. An evil eye,[1] **a haughty spirit, and a large appetite**—these belong to the followers of the wicked Balaam.
>
> — m. *Abot* 5:19

> [Commenting on the above part of the Mishnah:] "A haughty spirit"—whence do we know that this is characteristic of Balaam? From his saying "For the Lord refuses to allow me to go with you"

---

1. Presumably a reference to his mean-spiritedness.

[Num. 22:13]—[what he meant was:] "Do you really think you are the sort of people I would go with?! Shall I not [wait and] go with others of higher station?" For in the end what does the text say?—"And once more Balak sent officials, but more numerous and of higher station than those" [Num. 22:15]. And whence do we know that Balaam had a large appetite? From his saying, "Even if Balak were to give me a whole house full of silver and gold, I could not transgress the word of the Lord my God in the slightest detail" [that is, he would not have mentioned silver and gold if that were not what was really on his mind].
— Abot deR. Nathan (B) ch. 45

At first he was a holy man and a prophet of God, but afterward, through disobedience **and the desire for lucre**, when he tried to curse Israel, he was called by the Holy Writ a "soothsayer" [Josh. 13:22].
— Jerome, Questions in Genesis 22:22

Balaam Foresaw the Messiah

Although he went to Moab with base motives, Balaam did indeed end up blessing instead of cursing Israel, foretelling a glowing future for this emerging nation. And his predictions proved true: Israel did become a great nation, at least for a time—although subsequent conquerors eventually deprived it of much of its territory and freedom.

As we have already seen (Chapter 15, "Another King Will Come"), Jews in these later times were animated by the hope that they might once again live as in their heyday; they dreamt of a day when an anointed leader (Hebrew *māšiaḥ*, Greek transliteration *messiah*) would arise to restore their fortunes. In considering Balaam's oracles, some interpreters felt that, at one point, the eastern soothsayer had alluded as well to such far distant events as these. Peering far into the future, Balaam had glimpsed the rise of just this future leader:

> I see it [or "him"], but not now; I behold it [or "him"], but not
> close:
> a star shall proceed from Jacob, and a scepter shall rise from Israel,
> and he shall crush the outskirts of Moab, and break down all the
> sons of Sheth,
> and Edom shall be dispossessed, and Seir's enemies shall inherit her,
> yea, Israel shall triumph.
> And he shall rule from Jacob, and destroy the city's survivor[s].
— Num. 24:17–19

Here indeed seemed to be a reference to some great leader in Israel's future. To begin with, Balaam's description of what he saw as in the *distant* future was significant for ancient interpreters. He was not talking about anything that was going to happen in his own day, such as Israel's conquest and settlement of the land, especially since he seemed to have referred to these in his previous oracles, apparently even alluding there to the establishment of kingship in Israel (Num. 24:7). What was "distant," therefore, must be well beyond such events. If so, then what Balaam was describing was a period of Israelite dominion such as had not been known since the highpoint of David's military might, a time when all of Israel's enemies would fall before it and foreign nations would be ruled "from Jacob." Since these things had not happened *yet,* interpreters reasonably concluded that the person being spoken of had yet to come.

What is more, Balaam had prefaced these words by telling Balak that he would now set forth "what this people shall do to yours *in the end of days*" (Num. 24:14). This last phrase sometimes means only "in time to come" in the Bible, but it later acquired the meaning of "in the time of the end," that is, the great moment in the future when life as we know it will come to an end. Was it not obvious, therefore, that Balaam was talking about *the* future king or leader, the same one spoken of elsewhere in the Bible, who would at last set Israel's fortunes aright in the end-time?

Such a hypothesis could only seem to be confirmed by the curious similarity of Balaam's oracle to what Jacob had said earlier about the future king. For, in blessing his son Judah at the end of his life, Jacob had said:

> The **scepter** shall not depart from Judah, nor the ruler's staff from between his feet, until he comes to Shiloh [or "until Shiloh comes"], and to him shall be the obedience of peoples. —Gen. 49:10

As noted earlier (Chapter 15), the "scepter" spoken of in these lines was taken by some interpreters as a reference to the future leader. Both prophecies were said to regard "the end of days" (Gen. 49:1, Num. 24:14). If so, then the fact that Balaam also spoke of a scepter arising from Israel could hardly be coincidental. Balaam and Jacob must have been talking about the same man. Indeed, that the scepter was a *man* and not merely a symbol of kingship seems to have been stressed by ancient translators:

> A star shall rise out of Jacob, and a **man** shall spring out of Israel.
> —Septuagint Num. 24:17

> When a king arises from Jacob and an anointed one [*měsîḥa'*] is installed . . .
> —*Targum Onkelos* Num. 24:17

A king is destined to arise from the house of Jacob and a savior and ruler from the house of Israel. — *Targum Neophyti* Num. 24:17

A star shines forth from Jacob and a leader from Israel.
— Peshitta Num. 24:17

A Ruler of the World

There was a further striking congruence between Jacob's blessing and Balaam's oracle. Jacob said about the future leader, "and to him shall be the obedience of peoples," while Balaam asserted that, after subduing Israel's enemies, "he shall rule from Jacob." Taken together, these comments seem to imply that the future leader would rule not only Israel itself but the mass of humanity:

> Then the Lord will raise up a new priest, to whom all the words of the Lord will be revealed; and he will execute a **true judgment upon the earth** in the course of time. And **his star will arise** in heaven, as a king, lighting up the light of knowledge as by the sun of the day.[2]
> — *Testament of Levi* 18:3

> I see it, but it is not now, I observe it, but it is not near: when a king arises from Jacob and an anointed one [*měšîḥaʾ*] is installed, then he will kill the chiefs of Moab and will **rule over all mankind**.
> — *Targum Onkelos* Num. 24:17

At Qumran as well, Balaam's words were understood as a prediction of a coming war and subsequent domination by Israel (though without specific mention of a future leader):

> It is not our strength or might that triumphs, but Your strength and the force of Your great power, as You announced to us of old, saying "**a star shall march from Jacob**, a scepter shall rise from Israel, and he shall crush the outskirts of Moab, and break down all the sons of Sheth. And he shall rule from Jacob, and destroy the city's survivor. And the enemy shall be dispossessed, and Israel shall triumph." And by Your anointed ones, those who behold things to come, You have announced to us the times of the wars of [that is, "to be waged by"]

---

2. It is not clear if this passage represents the work of a Christian editor of the *Testaments* (who clearly added Christian references elsewhere) or if it is part of an earlier, Jewish document that referred to the figure of the Levitical Messiah known in the *Testaments* and other Second Temple texts. The latter seems to me more likely, however.

Your hands, to fight against our enemies, striking down the legions of Belial, the seven "nothing" nations, by means of the downtrodden people redeemed by You. ―(4QM) *War Scroll* 11:5–9

There was another verse connecting Balaam's oracles with this theme of a future, universal ruler. Somewhat earlier in the same chapter, Balaam said about Israel:

How fair are your tents, O Jacob, your encampments, O Israel! . . . Water shall flow from his [Israel's] buckets, and his seed shall be in many waters, his king shall be higher than **Agag**, and his kingdom shall be exalted. ―Num. 24:5, 7

Agag was the Amalakite king who lived in the time of King Saul (1 Samuel 15), Israel's first king, and the "exalted" kingdom of the next clause might arguably be David's. But perhaps not; perhaps the kingdom mentioned here was likewise well in the future, a kingdom "exalted" because it would be more powerful than Israel had ever been thus far.

Interestingly, the Septuagint text presented these verses in a strikingly different, and more openly imperial, version:

There shall **go forth a man** from his [Israel's] seed and he shall **rule many nations**; and his kingdom **shall be exalted above Gog,** and his kingdom shall be magnified. ―Septuagint Num. 24:7

The phrases "there shall go forth a man . . . and he shall rule many nations" certainly sounded to interpreters like the prediction of a future, universal ruler. What is more, the mention of Gog (here in place of the similar-sounding Agag above),[3] the mythic enemy to be defeated "in the end of days" (Ezek. 38:16), further suggested that the future ruler would preside over a great military victory, one that would bring about a kingdom of unprecedented greatness:

For "there shall come forth a man," says the oracle, and leading his army into war he will subdue great and populous nations.
―Philo, *Rewards and Punishments* 95

Similarly:

The king will be mighty who is exalted over his sons and he will rule over mighty peoples and will be stronger than Agag his king.
―*Targum Onqelos* Num. 24:7

3. "Gog" also appears in the *Samaritan Pentateuch* version of this verse.

Their king shall arise from among them, and their savior will be from them; he shall gather their exiles from the lands of their enemies, and his sons shall rule over great nations. He will be stronger than Saul [who] spa[red] Agag, the Amalekites' king, and the messianic king's kingdom will be exalted. — *Targum Neophyti* Num. 24:7

The Star Is the Messiah

And so, it was a great and universal leader that Balaam had seen rising in the distant future. This future figure seemed to be called two different names in Balaam's prophecy, the "star" of Jacob and Israel's "scepter" (the latter being the same word used of this king in Gen. 49:10). "Star" thus took its place, alongside "scepter," as a way of referring to the future leader of Israel, whose light would fill the heavens:

And his **star** will arise in heaven, as a king, lighting up the light of knowledge as by the sun of the day. He will **shine** as the sun on the earth and will remove all darkness from under heaven, and there will be peace on earth. — *Testament of Levi* 18:3

He [the eschatological priest] will atone for the members of his generation, and he will be sent to his countrymen. His word will be like the word of heaven, and his teaching conforms to the will of God. His eternal sun will **shine**, and his light will blaze in all the corners of the earth. Then darkness will disappear from the earth, and shadows from the dry land. — (4Q541) *Aaronic Text A* fragment 9

R. Aqiba interpreted, "A star shall proceed from Jacob" as "[Simon bar] Kosiba has come forth out of Jacob."[4] When R. Aqiba saw bar Kosiba he said, "This is the anointed king [that is, the messiah]." — j. *Ta'anit* 4:8 (68d)

I Jesus have sent my angel to you with this testimony for the churches. I am the root and the offspring of David, the bright morning **star**. — Rev. 22:16

Moses himself made it known beforehand that there was to arise a star, as it were, from the seed of Abraham when he said thusly: "A star shall arise from Jacob and a leader from Israel." — Justin Martyr, *Dialogue with Trypho* 106:4 (also 126:1)

4. For this reason Simon bar Kosiba, leader of the Jewish revolt against the Romans in 133–135 C.E., came to be called bar Kokhba, "son of the star."

For God has established you [the "Chief of the Congregation" who is to come in the future] as the **scepter**. — (1QSb) *Scroll of Blessings* 5:27

[Judah predicts:] Then shall the **Scepter** of my kingdom shine forth, and from your [that is, Judah's descendants'] root shall arise a stem; and from it shall grow a rod of righteousness to the Gentiles, to judge and to save all that call on the Lord.

— *Testament of Judah*, 24:5–6; Origen, *Contra Celsum* 1:59

The Star Will Precede the Scepter

However, there was another way of understanding the words of Num. 24:17: "star" and "scepter" might not be synonymous at all. This same verse could be understood as saying that *when* a star proceeds from Jacob, *then* the scepter shall arise from Israel. If so, then the star and the scepter are hardly identical: the star precedes the scepter and perhaps even heralds his arrival. One text from Qumran clearly suggests that the star in question was indeed a known figure, the community's own "interpreter of the Torah." This leader's proceeding "from Jacob" was thus an event that had already taken place, an actual journey that this man had undertaken from the territory of Jacob to the land of Damascus; as for the scepter prophesied by Balaam, he had yet to arrive:

[Commenting on the verses "You shall bear the booth (*sukkat* instead of *Sikkuth*) of your king and the precise determination (*kiwwun* instead of *Kiyyun*) of your images (and) the **star** of your God, whom you established for yourselves; and I will send you into exile beyond **Damascus** . . ." (Amos 5:26–27):] The "star" is the Interpreter of the Torah **who entered Damascus**, in keeping with what is written, "A star shall proceed from [the land of] Jacob and a scepter arises from Israel" [Num. 24:17]. The "scepter" is the leader of the whole congregation, and when he arises he will "break down all the sons of Seth"—that is, those who escaped in the first period of visitation [punishment].

— *Damascus Document* 7:18–21

According to this reading, the star and the scepter are quite different figures: the star has, at the time of this text's writing, already arrived, while the scepter is still to come.

Alternately, the star referred to by Balaam might be a real star in the sky, one whose appearance precedes and announces the arrival of the scepter:

Then the Lord will raise up a new priest, to whom all the words of the Lord will be revealed; and he will execute a true judgment upon the earth in the course of time. And **his star will arise in heaven, as a king**, lighting up the light of knowledge as by the sun of the day.

— *Testament of Levi* 18:3

Perhaps in this sense as well:

[Judah predicts:] And after these things a star will rise for you from Jacob in peace, and a man will arise from my seed like the sun of righteousness. — *Testament of Judah* 24:1

Now when Jesus was born in Bethlehem of Judea in the days of Herod the king, behold, wise men from the East came to Jerusalem, saying, "Where is he who has been born king of the Jews? For we have **seen his star** in the East and have come to worship him." —Matt. 2:1–2

Moses himself made it known beforehand that there was to arise a **star, as it were, from the seed of Abraham** when he said thusly: "A star shall arise from Jacob and a leader from Israel." And another verse says: "Behold a man; the East [or "a Branch"][5] is his name." Accordingly, when a star arose in the sky at the time of his birth, as is recorded in the account of the apostles, the magi of Arabia, taking cognizance of the sign, went to worship him.[6]

— Justin Martyr, *Dialogue with Trypho* 106:4

Balaam Counseled Seduction

Immediately after the Balaam episode, catastrophe occurred:

While Israel dwelt in Shittim the people began to play the harlot with the daughters of Moab; they invited the people to the sacrifices of their gods, and the people ate and bowed down to their gods. So Israel yoked itself to Baal of Peor, and the anger of the Lord was kindled against Israel. — Num. 25:1–3

Given the fact that this incident of harlotry and idolatry occurred right after Balaam's departure, interpreters could not help thinking Balaam might have

5. The Greek noun *anatolē*—derived from the same root as "rise" used in the Septuagint version of Num. 23:17, "A star shall *rise* in Jacob"—is frequently used to mean "the East, Orient" (that is, the place where the sun *rises*). In the Septuagint, however, it also translates the Hebrew word *ṣemāḥ*, "bud," "branch."

6. Note that here Justin apparently seeks to reconcile the two distinct interpretations that we have been tracing, namely that "star" refers to a person and that the "star" is a real star whose appearance heralds that of the Messiah.

had something to do with it. Such suspicions could only be strengthened by what Moses said sometime later, when the Israelites spared the women and children in their attack against Midian:

> Moses said to them: "Have you let all the women live? Behold, these women were to Israel **in the matter of Balaam** [or "as Balaam said"], to act treacherously against the Lord in the matter of Peor, and so the plague came among the congregation of the Lord. —Num. 31:16

The precise meaning of Moses' words was not entirely clear, but it certainly sounded as if Balaam, although he was said to have already gone home (Num. 24:25), was nonetheless involved. Perhaps before leaving he had *counseled* Balak to use the women to lead Israel astray:

> Moses said to them: "Have you let all the women live? For they were to the Israelites in keeping with the word of Balaam **to turn astray**, to show contempt for the word of the Lord with regard to Peor, and a plague came upon the congregation of the Lord."
>
> —Septuagint Num. 31:16

> They were a **stumbling-block** to the Israelites at the advice of Balaam, to falsify in the name of the Lord in the matter of the idol of Peor.
>
> — *Targum Neophyti* Num. 31:6

An ancient prophet's reference to Balaam, mentioned earlier, reinforced this interpretation:

> O my people, remember what Balak king of Moab devised, and what Balaam the son of Beor answered him, and what happened **from Shittim to Gilgal,** that you may know the saving acts of the Lord.
>
> —Mic. 6:5

Since the same place-name, Shittim, was mentioned at the start of the Baal Peor incident (Num. 25:1), it seemed to interpreters that Micah was referring specifically to that incident. If so, Micah was saying that Balaam did indeed "answer" something to Balak that resulted in the sin of Baal Peor.

> Taking him by the right hand, he [Balaam] counseled him [Balak] in strict privacy as to the means by which, as far as might be, he should defend himself against the army of the enemy [Israel] . . . His advice was this. Knowing that the one way in which the Hebrews could be overthrown was disobedience, he set himself to lead them, through wantonness and licentiousness to sacrilege, [that is,] through a great sin to a still greater one, and put before them the bait of pleasure. "You

have in your countrymen, king," he said, "women of outstanding beauty, and there is nothing to which a man more easily falls captive than a woman's beauty . . . But you must instruct them not to allow their wooers to enjoy their charms at once . . . One of those [women] should say, with a saucy air: 'You must not be permitted to enjoy my favors until you have left the ways of your fathers and become a convert to honoring what I honor. That your conversion is sincere will be clearly proved to me if you are willing to take part in the libations and sacrifices which we offer to idols of stone and wood and other images.'"   — Philo, *Moses* 1:294–298

Then Balaam said to him: "Come, let us plan what you should do to them. Pick out the beautiful women who are among us and in Midian, and stand them naked and adorned with gold and precious stones before them. And it shall be, when they see them and lie with them, they will sin against their Lord and fall into your hands; for otherwise you cannot fight against them . . ." And afterward, the people were seduced after the daughters of Moab. For Balak did everything that Balaam had shown him.   — Pseudo-Philo, *Biblical Antiquities* 18:13–14

[Balaam told Balak:] "If you yearn for some short-lived victory over them, you may achieve it as follows: Take from among your daughters the most beautiful and those most capable of overcoming, by means of their beauty, the chastity of those who behold them, and dress them in splendor to add to their beauty, and send them to the area of these [Israelites'] camp, and order them to have relations with their young men when they ask it."   — Josephus, *Jewish Antiquities* 4:129

But I have a few things against you: You have some there who hold the teaching of Balaam, who taught Balak to put a stumbling block before the sons of Israel, that they might eat food sacrificed to idols and practice immorality.   — Rev. 2:14

"They called to the people and offered sacrifices to their gods" [Num. 25:2] for they followed Balaam's advice . . . and set up tents and put prostitutes in them with all their finery . . . Whenever a Jew would pass by in the market place . . . a girl would come out in her adornments and her perfume and seduce him by saying, "Why is it that we love you and yet you hate us—here, take this piece of merchandise for free—after all, we are both descended from a single ancestor, Terah, the father of Abraham. Wouldn't you like to eat from our sacrificial offerings?"
                                        — *Midrash Tanḥuma, Balaq* 18

A Leader among Priests

For his part in punishing the offending couple, who had publicly flouted God's rule, Phinehas was given a special reward:

> And the Lord said to Moses, "Phinehas the son of Eleazar, son of Aaron the priest, has turned back my wrath from the people of Israel, in that he was jealous [some translations, "zealous"] with my jealousy ["zeal"] among them, so that I did not consume the people of Israel in my jealousy ["zeal"]. Therefore, say: 'Behold, I give to him my covenant of peace; and it shall be to him, and to his descendants after him, the covenant of perpetual priesthood, because he was jealous ["zealous"] for his God and made atonement for the people of Israel.'"
>
> —Num. 25:10–13

This certainly sounded like a fine reward, but interpreters were puzzled by one thing. Phinehas was the son of Eleazar, grandson of Aaron, hence already in line for the hereditary priesthood. What then could it mean for God to give him "the covenant of perpetual priesthood . . . to him, and to his descendants after him"? Perpetual priesthood was already his by birth! Indeed, the recent episode of Korah's rebellion, and the subsequent budding of Aaron's rod, had highlighted the fact that the priesthood was to be the exclusive property of the "descendants of Aaron" (Num. 16:40), including, of course, Phinehas. Was God thus giving a gift that already belonged to the recipient?

One possibility was that Phinehas was being singled out even among the priests. Perhaps what God was giving Phinehas as a reward for his zeal was the promise of a leadership role forever:

> And likewise Phinehas the son of Eleazar was [third?] in glory
> in his being zealous for the God of all, and he stood with Him in the breach:
> his heart spurred him to action, and he made atonement for the Israelites.
> Therefore for him as well He established a law, a covenant of peace
>   to **uphold the sanctuary;**
> that the **high priesthood should be for him and his descendants forever.**
>   —Sir. (Hebrew, ms. B) 45:24

> Phinehas the son of Eleazar is the third in glory, for he was zealous in the fear of the Lord;
> and he stood fast when the people turned away, in the ready goodness of his soul, and made atonement for Israel.

Therefore a covenant of peace was established for him, **that he
should be a leader of the sanctuary and of the people,**
that he and his descendants should have the **greatness of** [perhaps
"within"] **the priesthood forever.**

—Sir. (Greek) 45:23–24

Phinehas the Immortal

But there was another possibility. Perhaps by "covenant of eternal priesthood"
what Scripture meant was that Phinehas *himself* was to be a priest forever—
that he would never die. Support for this idea was found in an allusion to this
episode in the book of Psalms:

Then they attached themselves to the Baal of Peor, and ate sacrifices
offered to the dead;
they provoked the Lord to anger with their doings, and a plague
broke out among them.
Then Phinehas stood up and interposed, and the plague was stayed;
and it was **reckoned to him as righteousness from generation to
generation forever.**

—Ps. 106:28–31

The phrase "reckoned to him as righteousness" had appeared with regard to
Abraham in Gen. 15:6, where it seemed to mean that Abraham's faith had
caused God to "find in his favor" (as in a trial), or at least that his faith would
be remembered as a point in Abraham's favor. That seemed likewise to be the
sense here in regard to Phinehas' zeal. But how could God keep on extending
this act of reckoning Phinehas' zeal as righteousness "from generation to
generation *forever*"? With a little imagination, the text might seem to imply
that with each successive generation, Phinehas' zeal would argue in his favor
and prevent him from dying. In other words, the meaning of this "covenant of
eternal priesthood" was that Phinehas himself would always be a priest, "from
generation to generation forever."

The Bible did offer some substantiation for this theory. For, long after the
incident and long after everyone else, including Joshua, had died, Phinehas is
nonetheless mentioned:

[At the end of the period of the Judges,] the people of Israel inquired
of the Lord (for the ark of the covenant of God was there in those days,
and Phinehas the son of Eleazar, son of Aaron, **ministered before it in
those days**), saying . . .

—Judg. 20:28

According to this text, Phinehas was still alive, functioning as a priest, at the time of the war against the Benjaminites in the book of Judges. If so, then perhaps he was destined for immortality—for at this point he was already endowed with extraordinary longevity.

Equally extraordinary, the Hebrew Bible contains no account of his death.[7] Certainly such an outstanding and revered leader would have been mourned by Israel; why was nothing said of his death and burial, when that of his contemporaries Aaron, Miriam, and Joshua had all been narrated? On the other hand, after the above mention in Judg. 20:28, Phinehas is not heard of again. Putting these two facts together, some interpreters concluded that Phinehas was indeed immortal. At some point after his last appearance in the Bible, he must have ascended into heaven, very much like Enoch and Elijah. In other words, his covenant of an "eternal priesthood" meant that he personally would continue to live forever:

> And in that time [at the end of the period of the Judges,] Phinehas laid himself down to die, and the Lord said to him, "Behold, you have passed the 120 years that have been established for every man. And now, rise up and go from here and dwell in Danaben on the mountain and dwell there many years . . . And afterward you will be lifted up into the place where those who were before you were lifted up, and **you will be there** until I remember the world.
>
> —Pseudo-Philo, *Biblical Antiquities* 48:1–2

> ". . . because he was jealous ["zealous"] for his God and made atonement for the people of Israel . . ." [Num. 25:13]. "Atoning" [*lkpr*] is not written here, but [*wykpr,* which can also mean] "and he will atone" for the people of Israel. For until this very time he has **not departed**, but still lives and makes atonement until the resurrection of the dead.
>
> — *Sifrei Numbers* 131

> ". . . behold I am giving him [Phinehas] My covenant of peace"—that **he is still alive.** — *Numbers Rabba* 21:3

> [God tells Moses:] "Swear to him with an oath in My name: Behold I am decreeing for him My covenant of peace. And I will make him the envoy of the covenant **and he shall live forever** to proclaim the news of redemption at the end of days."
>
> — *Targum Pseudo-Jonathan* Num. 25:12–13

7. Note that the Septuagint does contain a report of Phinehas' death in Josh. 24:33.

Phinehas Is Elijah

If the death of Phinehas was not mentioned, neither is the birth of Elijah, the great northern prophet who lived after the breakup of the United Monarchy. Phinehas and Elijah had a number of points in common, most prominently the fact that both were described, in very similar language, as being "jealous" (or "zealous") for the Lord (1 Kings 19:10, 14). It occurred to more than one interpreter that this might not be coincidental. After all, Elijah was also apparently immortal, having ascended into heaven alive (2 Kings 2:11). Moreover, Elijah's immortality was difficult to justify: he was not described (as Enoch had been) as one who "walked with God" and was extraordinarily righteous; and if he was a prophet, well, so were many others whose lives had nonetheless come to an end. How better to explain Elijah's zeal *and* immortality than to say that he was actually Phinehas in disguise? God had indeed granted Phinehas immortality because of his zealous good deed, a "covenant of eternal priesthood," and Phinehas had actually spent a nice stretch of his immortality on earth, living for many more years than one would expect from a normal human being. If, thereafter, his death is not reported in the Bible, it is because he never died. But the Bible said nothing about his ascending into heaven either. What must have happened, therefore, was that God simply ordered him to be hidden for a time on earth, until he suddenly reappeared as Elijah (1 Kings 17:1), under which guise he continued his mission on earth until his final ascent.

> And in that time Phinehas laid himself down to die, and the Lord said to him, ". . . Now, rise up and go from here and dwell in Danaben on the mountain and dwell there many years, And I will command my eagle, and he will nourish you there [this is what happens to Elijah, 1 Kings 17:4], and you will not come down to mankind until the time arrives and you will be tested in that time; and you will shut up the heaven then, and by your mouth it will be opened up [true of Elijah, not Phinehas: 1 Kings 17:1]. And afterward you will be lifted up into the place where those who were before you were lifted up [2 Kings 2:11], and you will be there until I remember the world. Then I will make you all come, and you will taste what is death." And Phinehas went up and did all that the Lord commanded him.
> — Pseudo-Philo, *Biblical Antiquities* 48:1–2

> He [Kohat] lived until he saw Phinehas, **that is, Elijah the high priest,** who is to be sent to the exile of Israel in the end of days.
> — *Targum Pseudo-Jonathan* Exod. 6:18

God said to him, "What are you doing here, Elijah?" [1 Kings 19:9] And he said, "I have been very zealous . . ." [1 Kings 19:10]. God said to him: "You are always being zealous! You were zealous at Shittim about forbidden sexual unions, as it says, 'Phinehas the son of Eleazar, [son of Aaron the priest, has turned back my wrath from the people of Israel],' and here you are being zealous again."   — *Pirqei deR. Eliezer 29*

❖   ❖   ❖

In short: God instructed Moses to make the bronze serpent not so that it would heal the Israelites, but as a symbol or a means to turn their thoughts to God. Although he may have seemed good at first, Balaam was a truly wicked individual, moved only by greed and vanity. He sought to harm the Israelites by cursing them, but God turned his curses to blessings. These blessings were true oracles, and in one or two in particular, Balaam foretold the coming of the Messiah. Frustrated in his attempt to curse Israel, Balaam counseled Balak to use beautiful women to lead Israel astray, and this led to the sin of Baal Peor. Phinehas, who acted zealously on God's behalf in that episode, was rewarded with eternal life; he is perhaps to be identified with Elijah.

25

The Life of Torah

(DEUTERONOMY 1–34)

Moses' last vision: did he argue with the angel?

The Life of Torah

(DEUTERONOMY 1–34)

❖　　❖　　❖

After forty years of wandering in the wilderness, the Israelites arrived at last in the plains of Moab and camped along the Jordan River prior to entering the land of Canaan. There Moses addressed them at length, discussing the lessons of all that had happened to them as well as reviewing many of the divine laws and statutes that had been given to them. He exhorted the people to obey faithfully all of these laws and to lead their lives in keeping with them, detailing the divine blessings that belong to all who adhere to God's ways and warning of the dire consequences of disobedience.

Moses himself, however, was not to enter the land with the people: God had instructed him to die in that place and to transfer leadership of the people to his servant Joshua. Thus, having taken leave of the people with a prophetic song and final blessing of the tribes, Moses died in Moab and was buried on the far side of the Jordan.

MUCH OF THE BOOK of Deuteronomy appears to go over matters discussed earlier, not only Israel's earlier history but many of the laws revealed to Moses in previous books. Yet there is also a good deal that is new. The laws reviewed in Deuteronomy are sometimes presented in somewhat different form, so that even such basics as the Decalogue (presented again in Deut. 5:6–18) contain new elements, from which interpreters sought to derive additional teachings (see, for example, Chapter 20, "Guard the Sabbath Borders"). Quite apart from such reviewed material, however, Deuteronomy has much that is altogether new. In particular, the Bible stresses here as nowhere before the importance of remaining faithful to the one true God and keeping His Torah.

The Great Teaching

Perhaps the most striking statement of this duty occurs toward the beginning of Moses' long address to the people:

> [Moses said:] "Hear, O Israel: the Lord is our God, the Lord alone. And you shall love the Lord your God with all your heart and with all your soul and with all your might."　　　　—Deut. 6:4–5

These verses came to be considered something like the "great teaching" of the Pentateuch. After all, by the time of the ancient interpreters, the Israelite doctrine of monotheism—that there is only one God in the universe—had long distinguished Israel from other peoples. It had come to be viewed as the hallmark of the Jewish religion, mentioned by any who spoke of, or in the name of, Israel's faith:

> There is an ancient saying about Him:
> "He is one"—self-completing, and all things completed by Him,
> In them He Himself circulates. But no one has seen Him
> With the souls that mortals have, He is seen by the mind.
> —Aristobulus, Fragment 4 (cited in Eusebius,
> *Praeparatio Evangelica* 13.12.5)

> There is one God, sole ruler, ineffable, who lives in heaven,
> self-begotten, invisible, who Himself sees all things . . .
> He Himself, eternal, revealed Himself
> as existing in the present, and previously, and in the future.
> For who, being mortal, could see God with eyes?
> —*Sibylline Oracles* 3:11–12, 15–17 (also Fragment One 7–11, 15–18)

True enough, the Bible's own laws envisaged the possibility that some people might *not* believe that there is only one God, and strict punishment was prescribed for renegade Israelites, either individual family members (Deut. 13:6) or whole cities (Deut. 13:15), who supported the worship of other, foreign gods. Eventually, however, the people of Israel came to be so identified with the belief in a single God that, to some, these laws seemed quite unnecessary:

> [Judith tells the elders of her city about the Jews:] "For never in our generation nor in these present days has there been any **tribe** or **family** of people or **city of ours** which worshiped gods made by [human] hands, as was done in days gone by (for that was why our fathers were handed over to the sword, and to be plundered, so that they suffered a great catastrophe before our enemies). But we know no other God but Him."
> —Jth. 8:18–20

In keeping with Israel's identification as *the* people of monotheism, the phrase in Deut. 6:4 translated above as "the Lord alone" (or, equally valid, "the Lord is one") was taken by many as a flat-out assertion that only one God exists, comparable to other assertions in the same book (see Deut. 4:35, 39). This affirmation, along with the commandment that followed it—namely, that this one single Deity in the universe is to be loved "with all your heart and with all your soul and with all your might"—thus seemed to sum up all that the Pentateuch had to say about God. Indeed, along with another commandment that also began "And you shall love" (that is, the commandment to love one's neighbor as oneself, Lev. 19:18), this law in Deuteronomy was often held up as the epitome of all of divine teaching:

> Throughout all your life love the Lord and one another with a true heart.　　　　　　　　　　　　　　　　　　　　　— *Testament of Dan* 5:3

> Keep the Law of God, my children; achieve integrity; live without malice, not tinkering with God's commandments or your neighbor's affairs. Love the Lord and your neighbor.
> — *Testament of Issachar* 5:1–2 (see also 7:6; *Testament of Joseph* 11:1;
> *Testament of Zebulon* 5:1)

> One of them, a lawyer, asked him [Jesus] a question to test him: "Teacher, what is the **great commandment** in the law?" And he said to him, "You shall love the Lord your God with all your heart, and with all your soul, and with all your mind" [Deut. 6:5]. This is the great and first commandment. And a second is like it, You shall love your neighbor as yourself [Lev. 19:18]. On these two commandments depend all the law and the prophets."　　　　　　　　　　　— Matt. 22:35–40

> The way of life is this: First, you shall love the Lord your Maker, and secondly, your neighbor as yourself. And whatever you do not want to be done to you, you shall not do to anyone else.　　　— *Didache* 3:1–2

> Be humble in heart, hate bitter power,
> and, above all, love your neighbor as yourself,
> and love God from the soul and serve him.
> — *Sibylline Oracles* 8:480–482 (ca. 175 C.E.)

These Words Twice a Day

One reason why this commandment in Deuteronomy to love God came to be so significant had to do with the verses that immediately followed it:

> [Moses said:] "Hear, O Israel: the Lord is our God, the Lord alone. And you shall love the Lord your God with all your heart and with all your soul and with all your might. And let **these words** which I command you today be upon your heart. And you shall teach them to your children, speaking of them when you stay in your house or travel on

the road, and when you lie down and when you rise up. And you shall bind them as a sign upon your hand, and they shall be a frontlet between your eyes. And you shall write them on the doorposts of your house and on your gates."

— Deut. 6:4–9

In context, "these words" might refer to everything that Moses had said and was about to say "today," that is, the day of his final address to the Israelites— in other words, virtually the whole book of Deuteronomy. But if so, was it reasonable to expect the Israelites to keep an entire biblical book "upon your heart," indeed, to speak of it continually and write it on their doorposts and gates? On reflection, it seemed more likely to interpreters that "these words" must refer specifically to the words that Moses had just uttered, namely, "the Lord is our God, the Lord alone" and "you shall love the Lord your God with all your heart." *These* were the words that the people of Israel were to keep continuously in mind, to teach their children, and to write on their doorposts and gates. The very fact that Moses had singled out these words in particular was a clear indication of their overriding importance.

So it was that Deut. 6:4–5 (and soon enough, the whole paragraph of Deut. 6:4–9) came to occupy a special place in Judaism. Known as the Shema (from its opening word, *Šěmaʿ,* "Hear"), it was indeed learned by heart as well as copied and enclosed in special boxes affixed to doorposts (*mězuzôt*) or put into little cases (*těfillîn,* "phylacteries") worn upon head and heart as a form of piety. Moreover, since the passage said "these words" were to be spoken of "when you lie down and when you rise up," Jews made a practice of doing just that, reciting them every morning and evening.

Furthermore, in our clothes he has given us a distinguishing mark as a reminder [see Num. 15:37–41], and similarly **on our gates and doors** he has commanded us to set up the **words** so as to be a reminder of God. He also strictly commands that the sign shall be **worn on our hands,** clearly indicating that it is our duty to fulfill every activity with justice, having in mind our own condition, and above all the fear of God. **He also commands that "on going to bed and rising" men should meditate on the ordinances of God.**

— *Letter of Aristeas* 158–160

With the entrance of day and of night, I shall enter into the covenant of God, and with the going out of evening and of morning, I shall speak His laws.

— (1QS) *Community Rule* 10:10

[In the Jerusalem Temple the priests] would read aloud the Ten Commandments and [the paragraphs beginning] *Šěmaʿ* [Deut. 6:4–9], "And it shall come to pass if you hearken . . ." [Deut. 11:13–21], "And the

Lord said . . ." (Num. 15:37–41), and they would bless the people with three blessings.[1]   —m. *Tamid* 5:1

Here then is the code of those laws of ours which touch our political constitution . . . Two times each day, **at dawn and when it is time to go to sleep**, let all acknowledge to God the gifts that He has bestowed upon them through their deliverance from the land of Egypt; the offering of thanks being by its nature praiseworthy, and something that is done both in response to past favors and so as to invite future ones. And let them likewise **inscribe on their doors** the great things that God has worked on their behalf . . . and **bear written texts of these things on their head and arms,** so that God's beneficence toward them may be seen on all sides.   — Josephus, *Jewish Antiquities* 4:212–213

The School of Shammai maintain: at night everyone must [actually] lie down in order to recite the Shema, and in the morning must [actually] stand up [in order to recite it], since it says "And you shall speak of them . . . when you lie down and when you rise up" (Deut. 6:7). But the School of Hillel say: Let everyone recite it in his own way [in whatever position he wishes], as it says [in that very same verse that you should speak of them] "As you travel on the road" [Deut. 6:7].[2] If so, then why does the text say "when you lie down and when you rise up"? [Only in order to indicate the time of day when the Shema is to be recited, both morning and night, that is,] *at the time* when people go to bed and *at the time* when people rise up.   — m. *Berakhot* 1:3

A Particular Prophet

Beyond this basic teaching, Deuteronomy contains other new material as well. For example, in his final instructions to Israel, Moses at one point returned to a subject evoked earlier (Exod. 22:18, Lev. 19:31, 20:6, 27), the outlawing of

---

1. Deut. 11:13–21 apparently came to be connected with the Shema because of its strikingly similar wording, in particular its call to "love the Lord your God . . . with your whole heart and whole soul" (Deut. 11:13) as well as its commandments to put "these words upon your hearts and souls, and bind them upon your hands . . . speaking of them when you stay in your house or travel on the road, when you lie down and when you get up" (Deut. 11:18–19). If it was a commandment to recite Deut. 6:4–9 daily, it could hardly be less of a requirement to recite Deut. 11:13–21. As for the law of tassels (Num. 15:37–41), it was apparently first connected with the recitation of these passages because of its stated purpose, "so that you will be reminded to perform all My commandments" (Num. 15:40).

2. This phrase is understood as meaning, "as you proceed *in your way,*" that is, whatever way you wish.

practices of witchcraft, divination, and the like. This time, however, he connected this ban with the subject of prophecy:

> When you come into the land which the Lord your God is giving to you, you shall not learn to do the abominable practices of those nations. There shall not be found among you anyone who burns his son or his daughter as an offering, anyone who practices divination, a soothsayer, or an augurer, or a sorcerer, or a charmer, or a medium, or a wizard, or a necromancer . . . For these nations, which you are about to dispossess, give heed to soothsayers and to diviners; but as for you, the Lord your God has not allowed you so to do. **The Lord your God will raise up for you a prophet like me** from among you, from your brethren; he is the one whom you shall heed. Just as you requested of the Lord your God at Horeb on the day of the assembly, when you said, "Let me not hear again the voice of the Lord my God, or see this great fire any more, lest I die." And the Lord said to me, "They have rightly said all that they have spoken. I will raise up for them **a prophet like you** from among their brethren, and I will put my words in his mouth, and he shall speak to them all that I command him." —Deut. 18:9–18

This passage apparently explains why it is that Israel will not need such soothsayers as the Canaanites had; instead, God will raise up prophets who, as His direct representatives, will communicate God's wishes and plans to the people. But tangentially, this passage also addresses another issue, namely, why God will ever afterward speak to Israel through prophets rather than by addressing each and every Israelite directly. The text here explains that, on the day when all of Israel stood at Mt. Sinai, the people protested that they were afraid to hear the divine voice directly (see Exod. 20:18–19, Deut. 5:24–25, as well as Chapter 20, "God Spoke Only Two") and requested that Moses alone hear it. Ever afterward, this passage asserts, it will thus be God's practice to appoint prophets "like you [Moses]" to exercise this same function.

And yet, could there ever really be another prophet like Moses? Elsewhere the Bible gives a negative answer:

> And **there did not arise since in Israel a prophet like Moses**, whom the Lord knew face to face, none like him for all the signs and wonders which the Lord sent him to do in the land of Egypt, to Pharaoh and to all his servants and to all his land, and all the great and terrible deeds which Moses did in the sight of all Israel. —Deut. 34:10–12

What then could God mean by speaking of another prophet "like you"? It occurred to some interpreters that the Bible here might not be speaking at all about those biblical prophets who followed Moses in subsequent centuries. Great as they were, they were not equal to Moses, to whom God spoke "mouth to mouth" (Num. 12:8). Perhaps, instead, the text was talking about *a particular prophet* in the future, one who would indeed be Moses' equal (or perhaps Moses himself resurrected) and whose arrival would usher in a new age. After all, Deut. 18:9–18 had spoken of *a* prophet in the singular—"He is the one whom you shall heed . . . I will put my words in his mouth, and he shall speak to them all that I command him." Might this not mean that, sometime long in the future, a specific prophet would arise, one who would truly be "like" Moses? It was far from clear whether such a future prophet was to be identified with Israel's Messiah or whether he would accompany him or herald his arrival:[3]

And they shall be governed by the instructions in which the members of the community were instructed at the start, until the **coming of the prophet** and of the anointed ones [messiahs] of Aaron and Israel.
—(1QS) *Community Rule* 9:10–11

. . . until the Most High send His salvation in the ministration of the unique **prophet**. 		— *Testament of Benjamin* 9:2

[Peter said:] "And now, brethren, I know that you acted in ignorance, as did also your rulers. But what God foretold by the mouth of all the prophets, that his messiah should suffer, he thus fulfilled . . . Moses said, 'The Lord God will raise up for you a prophet from your brethren as he raised me up. You shall listen to him in whatever he tells you. And it shall be that every soul that does not listen to that prophet shall be destroyed from the people.' And all the prophets who have spoken, from Samuel and those who came afterwards, also proclaimed these days." 		— Acts 3:17–24 (also 7:37)

And this is the testimony of John, when the Jews sent priests and levites from Jerusalem to ask him, "Who are you?" He confessed, he did not deny, but confessed, "I am not the messiah." And they asked him, "What then? Are you Elijah?" He said, "I am not." "**Are you the prophet?**" and he answered, "No." . . . They asked him, "Then why are you baptizing, if you are neither the messiah, nor Elijah, nor **the prophet?**" 		— John 1:19–25

3. The latter idea was connected with the return of the prophet Elijah predicted in Mal. 4:5; cf. Sir. 48:10.

When the people heard [Jesus'] words, some of the people said, "This is really the prophet." Others said, "This is the messiah."

—John 7:40–41 (also 6:14, 7:52, 9:17)

[The date of the Exodus from Egypt] is a night of guarding and it is arranged in advance for the redemption . . . when the world will reach the period of being redeemed, and the iron bars will be broken, and the generations of the wicked will be destroyed, and **Moses** will come up from the wilderness and the anointed king [Messiah] will come forth from Rome [or "from on high"].

— *Targum Neophyti* Exod. 12:42 (also *Fragment Targum* [ms. V] Exod. 12:42)

"Every valley will be raised up" [Isa. 40:4]: [God said: In the time of the redemption] I will raise up Moses, the man who was buried in the valley, as it says, "And he was buried in the valley" [Deut. 34:6] . . . And the Messiah will come to redeem them and God will say to him: I swear that my sons will not be redeemed until Moses their teacher comes.

— *Aggadat Bereshit* 67 (p. 133)

All this notwithstanding, some Jews specifically rejected the idea that a second Moses, or the first, was yet to come:

"It is not in heaven": Moses said to them [the Israelites]: [I say this] lest you say that **another Moses is going to arise** and he will give us another Torah from the heavens—therefore as of now I am telling you that it [such a Torah] is not in heaven, that nothing of it remains in heaven.

— *Deuteronomy Rabba* 8:6

Do Not Displace Old Practices

Among the subjects treated for the first time in Moses' final address was that of the boundary markers that divide one person's land from another's:

In the inheritance [that is, the inherited land] which you will hold in the land that the Lord your God gives you to possess, you shall not displace your neighbor's boundary-mark which the men of old have set.

—Deut. 19:14

The law certainly seemed straightforward enough: old boundary-marks were not to be shifted. Still, it seemed strange that such a law should have to be stated at all. On the one hand, it could hardly have been intended to forbid adding on to one's own property, since that certainly was permitted (within the constraints of other biblical provisions). And if, on the other hand, the

Bible here meant to forbid the actual alteration or erasure of established property lines—well, certainly such a thing would fall under other, previously announced provisions, especially those connected to the return to one's ancestral property in the Jubilee year (Lev. 25:13, 28) as well as the general prohibition of theft.

If it was strange that moving boundary-marks should be prohibited once in Deuteronomy, it was still stranger to see this matter appear there a second time:

> Cursed be he who displaces his neighbor's boundary-mark—and let
> all the people say "Amen."   —Deut. 27:17

This verse comes amidst a list of things that are specially condemned;[4] the list was to be recited publicly after the Israelites entered the land given to them by God. But what was so important about displacing a boundary-mark that it should appear on this list?

Thus, there was some reason to suspect that this biblical law meant more than might appear at first. Indeed, was not displacing a boundary-mark mentioned elsewhere in the Bible in terms that seemed to suggest that this was a symbolic act standing for much more than changing physical boundaries?

> The princes of Judah have become like those who displace the boundary-mark; upon them I will pour out my wrath like water.
>   —Hos. 5:10

> Do not speak in the hearing of a fool, for he will not esteem the
>   wisdom of your utterances.
> Do not displace an ancient boundary-mark nor enter into the fields
>   of orphans,
> for their Redeemer is strong, He will take up their cause against you.
> Apply your mind to instruction and your ear to words of knowledge.
> Do not withold discipline from a child.
>   —Prov. 23:9–13

In the second passage cited, the prohibition of displacing a boundary-mark comes in a series of general maxims about life (rather than in a law code); did this context not prove that the injunction as well was really some kind of general advice, that the "boundary-mark" actually stood for a whole class of things that should not be disturbed? Indeed, the joining of this prohibition

---

4. The same is true of the list of wicked activities in Job 24:2–4: "displacing landmarks" is the first thing mentioned.

with that of entering the fields of (defenseless) orphans suggested that the real subject might be what these two actions had in common: both were examples of disrespect for limits established in the past, limits that could be breached only because those who established them were no longer alive. Seen in this light, displacing any such boundary-mark was indeed a heinous act of disrespect and exploitation. No wonder that Hosea, in the first passage, compared Judah's behavior in time of political crisis to that of such boundary-switchers.

Swayed by these considerations, some ancient interpreters thus came to the conclusion that the prohibition of Deut. 19:14 (and Deut. 27:17) actually referred to displacing long-established practices. Such an interpretation was only fortified by a closer examination of the law's wording. After all, if the purpose were merely to forbid the shifting of boundary stones, it would have been enough to say, "You shall not displace your neighbor's boundary-mark." If the text went on to add "which the men of old have set," was this not a further clue that the point was not the moving of actual stones, but the upsetting of *anything* established long ago? The point was clinched by one final appearance of the phrase:

> Do not displace the boundary-mark of old **set by your fathers**.
>
> — Prov. 22:28

Once again, the phrase "set by your fathers" puts the emphasis on the longstanding nature of that which was being overturned—indeed, "your fathers," even more than "men of old" (Deut. 19:14), seemed designed to evoke respect and honor. And so it was: "displacing a boundary-stone" became a prohibition of upsetting anything that had been established long ago:

> Another commandment of general value is "You shall not displace your neighbor's boundary-marks which your forerunners have set up" [Deut. 19:14]. Now this law, we may consider, applies not merely to allotments and boundaries of land in order to eliminate covetousness, but also to the safeguarding of ancient customs. For customs are unwritten laws, the decisions approved by men of old, not inscribed on monuments nor on leaves of paper which the moth destroys, but on the souls of those who are partners in the same citizenship.
>
> — Philo, *Special Laws* 4:149

> For, if you delight in [Ada, symbol of delight in worthless materialism], you will desire to twist everything and turn it around, shifting the boundaries that are fixed for things by nature. Moses, full of indignation at such people, pronounces a curse on them saying,

"Cursed is he that shifts his neighbor's boundaries" [Deut. 27:17]. By "neighbor" or "nearby" is meant that which is good.

— Philo, *The Posterity and Exile of Cain* 84

When the man of scoffing arose, who poured out for Israel from the waters of falsehood and caused them to go astray in a trackless wilderness . . . to turn from the paths of righteousness and to uproot the boundary-mark which the men of old have set.

— *Damascus Document* 1:14–16

And in the time of the land's destruction there arose the "displacers of boundary-marks" and they caused Israel to go astray . . . for they urged disobedience to the commandments given by God through the hand of Moses.   — *Damascus Document* 5:20–21 (also 19:13–16)

Let it not be permitted to displace boundary-marks, whether of your own land or of the land of others with whom you are at peace; beware of uprooting, as it were, a stone laid firm by God's decree for eternity. For out of this come wars, seditions, even from that desire of the covetous to overstep their boundaries. In truth, those who displace a boundary **are not far from transgressing the [other] laws as well.**

— Josephus, *Jewish Antiquities* 4:225

"Do not displace the boundary-mark of old set by your fathers" [Prov. 22:28]: Rabbi Simeon b. Yohai said: If you see a custom of your forefathers observed, do not reject it.   — *Midrash on Proverbs* 22

. . . those who fall into evil deeds, and who abandon the **eternal boundaries** and the path of the heavenly church.

— Origen, *Commentary on Matthew* 27:39–43

Necessary Paperwork

Does the Bible permit a man to divorce his wife? It certainly seemed so to some interpreters. Divorce, metaphorical and actual, is mentioned in numerous biblical texts (Ezek. 44:22, Hos. 2:4, Ezra 10:3, and so on), and the "divorced woman" is spoken of as an accepted fact in various laws promulgated in the Torah (Lev. 21:7, 14, 22:13; Num. 30:10; Deut. 22:19, 29). However, the Bible never spells out exactly *how* divorce should be accomplished. It comes closest in a rather complicated law dealing with another matter, remarriage:

When a man takes a woman and makes her his wife, and it turns out that she does not find favor in his eyes because he has found an indecency of something about her, and he writes for her a **bill of divorce** and puts it into her hand and releases [divorces] her from his house, so that she departs from his house; if she then goes and becomes another man's, and the latter man [also] rejects her and writes a **bill of divorce** for her and puts it into her hand and releases her from his house—or if this latter man who had taken her to wife should [subsequently] die—her first husband, who had divorced her, cannot now take her back again as his wife after she has been defiled, for that is an abomination before the Lord. —Deut. 24:1–4

Quite apart from the matter of remarriage, which is its overt subject, this law seems to teach something "between the lines" on the subject of divorce. To begin with, the passage apparently holds that divorce is indeed an acceptable practice under certain circumstances. What is more, it seems to make mention of the actual procedure for divorce, since it says (not once but twice) that the husband is required to prepare some sort of document, a "bill of divorce," and to give it to his wife, indeed, to "put it into her hand." The same bill of divorce is mentioned elsewhere in the Bible as well:

Thus says the Lord: "Where is your mother's bill of divorce, if I have released [divorced] her?" —Isa. 50:1

[God said to Jeremiah about Israel:] "And I released her and I gave her the bill of her divorce, yet her faithless sister Judah did not fear, but went and played the harlot as well." —Jer. 3:8

What was the purpose of such a document? As put into practice in later times, the bill of divorce both certified that the divorced woman was officially available for remarriage and, as well, secured her property rights as part of the first marriage's dissolution.

The first day of Marḥeŝwan, in the sixth year, at Maṣadah. I, Joseph son of Naqsan of [. . .]h, resident of Maṣadah, this day divorce and separate of my own free will from you, Miriam, daughter of Jonathan of Hanablata, resident of Maṣadah, who have previously been my wife, so that you now may freely go out and be the wife of any other Jewish man whom you may wish. May this be to you as a bill of divorce and a certificate of separation.

—P. Murabbaʿat 19 (bill of divorce discovered at Murabbaʿat in Judah, apparently written in 71 C.E.)

The essential content of the bill of divorce [is]: "You are hereby permitted to [be married to] any man." R. Judah said: "May this be to you from me a bill of divorce and a writ of separation and a certificate of severance, [permitting you] to go and be married to any man whom you will."   —m. Giṭṭin 9:3

No Divorce—Except for Indecency

Another thing emerged from a close reading of the law of remarriage. The text seemed as well to suggest the *circumstances* under which a husband was allowed to divorce his wife. It says specifically that he can do so if "it turns out that she does not find favor in his eyes because he has found an indecency of something about her." This certainly sounded to interpreters as if the Bible was defining the acceptable grounds for divorce.

Unfortunately, this definition clarified very little. What is "an indecency of something"? Elsewhere in the Bible, the word "indecency" (or "nakedness") frequently refers to prohibited sexual relations. A person's (or the land's— Gen. 42:9) "indecency" ought normally to be covered up; to uncover it was therefore to gain intimate knowledge of it. This being the case, some interpreters understood Deut. 24:1–4 to be stipulating that divorce could occur only when a husband had found his wife to have committed some (sexual) "indecency." Such an interpretation had the advantage of seeming to rule out frivolous divorces or divorces initiated because of mere lust. After all, elsewhere in the Bible divorce is strongly criticized as an institution—certainly it was not to be initiated lightly:

You ask, Why does He not [accept your offerings]? Because the Lord was a [marriage] witness between you and the wife of your youth whom you have now betrayed, though she is your companion and your wife by covenant . . . So take heed, and let no one betray the wife of his youth. For [I] **hate divorcing**, says the Lord.   —Mal. 2:14–16

If, in Deut. 24:1–4, the Bible specifically mentions "an indecency of something" as the grounds for a divorce, does this not imply that sexual indecency is the only proper ground for a divorce? The normal expectation would therefore be that a couple would remain married for life. Indeed, if the Bible elsewhere orders even the king not to "multiply wives" (Deut. 17:17), does it not follow that ordinary people are certainly expected to remain in lifelong, monogamous marriages?

And let him [the king] not marry a woman from all the daughters of the nations, but let him acquire a wife only from his father's clan, from his father's kin. And let him not take another woman in addition to her,[5] for she **alone** shall be with him **all the days of her life; but if she dies** he may marry another woman from his father's clan and kin.[6]

— *Temple Scroll* 57:15–19

They have been snared in two matters: in fornication, by marrying two women while both were still alive, whereas the principle of creation is "male and female created He them" [Gen. 1:27], and those who went into the ark "entered the ark two by two" [Gen. 7:9], and about the prince it is written "Let him not have many wives [that is, more than one]" [Deut. 17:17].[7]   — *Damascus Document* 4:20–5:2

When his mother Mary had been betrothed to Joseph, before they came together she was found to be with child of the Holy Spirit, and her husband Joseph, being a just man and unwilling to put her to shame, resolved to divorce her quietly.   — Matt. 1:18–19

"It was also said, 'Whoever divorces his wife, let him give her a certificate of divorce' [≅ Deut. 24:1]. But I say to you that everyone who divorces his wife, except on the ground of unchastity, makes her an adulteress; and whoever marries a divorced woman commits adultery."   — Matt. 5:31–32 (also 19:3–9, Mark 10:2–12)

To the married I give charge, not I but the Lord, that the wife should not separate from her husband (but if she does, let her remain single or else be reconciled to her husband)—and that the husband should not divorce his wife.   — 1 Cor. 7:10–11

The School of Shammai said: Let not a man divorce his wife unless he found in her some matter of indecency [immorality] as it is said, "because he has found an **indecency** of something about her" [Deut. 24:1].   — m. *Giṭṭin* 9:10

---

5. That is, the law of Deut. 17:17 forbidding the king to "multiply wives" is interpreted as meaning having a multiplicity of wives, more than one.

6. This passage not only outlaws polygamy for the king, but seems to imply, in the words highlighted, that divorce followed by remarriage is likewise not countenanced: death is the only circumstance in which remarriage can occur.

7. Here the overt prohibition is that of polygamy; however, the wording "while both were still alive" suggests—in keeping with the previously cited passage—that death is normally the only circumstance that would allow a man to marry two women even sequentially.

Any Old Reason Is Valid

And yet there was something troubling about such an interpretation. To begin with, the Bible elsewhere stipulates that if a married woman is found to have had relations with another man, "both of them shall die" (Deut. 22:22); what need was there for a divorce under such circumstances? Moreover, the case of a wife merely suspected of unfaithfulness is likewise dealt with quite separately in the Bible (Num. 5:11–31), without any mention of divorce proceedings. It was difficult, therefore, to suppose that an act of proven or even suspected unfaithfulness was the only possible reason for divorce. What is more, the biblical laws governing the case of the slandering groom (Deut. 22:13–19) and that of a rapist or seducer of an unmarried woman (Deut. 22:28–29) both stipulate that the man in question "may not divorce her [the victim] all his life." It would seem strange for such a stipulation to have been made if divorce were in any case permitted only after infidelity: were these laws an invitation to the former victims of slander or rape subsequently to commit adultery with impunity? On the contrary, such a stipulation would only seem to make sense if, under normal circumstances, divorce was indeed something a husband might well consider if he were merely dissatisfied with his spouse. Finally, if unfaithfulness were the only valid reason for divorce, then the Bible's wording in Deut. 24:1–4 seems rather strange: why should it say, "if it turns out that she *does not find favor in his eyes* because he has found some indecency about her"? Certainly adultery is no trifle, not a matter of "finding favor" or not—it is a crime that is strictly prohibited! "Finding favor" seemed to suggest that lesser matters might be involved.[8]

In the light of all such considerations, some interpreters understood the Bible to be giving the broadest latitude with regard to divorce, allowing the husband to separate from his wife for almost any good reason:

---

8. What is more, the phrase translated "an indecency of something" ought really to have been worded differently in Hebrew if the intended meaning had been, specifically, adultery. The Bible ought to have said a "matter [or "instance"] of indecency" (*dĕbar 'erwāh*). As it stands, "an indecency of something" (*'erwat dābār*) at least suggests that the "indecency" might be metaphorical, an "indecency" of speech or of behavior rather than, specifically, *the* indecency of forbidden sexual relations. This seems to be the case with Deut. 23:14, the only other biblical occurrence of the phrase "an indecency of something," since here it certainly does not refer to infidelity in particular. Such observations as these stand behind the dispute between the schools of Hillel and Shammai in m. *Giṭṭin* 9:10 (below).

Another commandment is that if a woman, after being divorced from her husband **for any cause whatever**, marries another . . .

— Philo, *Special Laws* 3:30 (restating Deut. 24:1–4)

He who desires to be divorced **for any reason whatsoever** from the wife who is living with him—and with many mortals such may arise—must certify in writing that he will have no further relations with her, since in this way will the woman obtain the right to cohabit with another man. — Josephus, *Jewish Antiquities* 4:253

The School of Shammai said: Let not a man divorce his wife unless he found in her some matter of indecency [immorality] as it is said, "because he has found an **indecency** of something about her" [Deut. 24:1]. But the School of Hillel say: Even if she [merely] spoiled his food, as it says, "because he has found an indecency of **something** about her" [Deut. 24:1]. Rabbi Akiba says: Even if he found another woman prettier than her, as it says, "and it turns out that she does not find favor in his eyes" [Deut. 24:1].[9] — m. *Giṭṭin* 9:10

Don't Muzzle Me

Moses' last address contained a number of divine commandments touching on the treatment of animals. Thus, for example, a stray ox or sheep or donkey had to be returned to its rightful owner (Deut. 22:1–4), a roosting or brooding mother bird had to be spared (Deut. 22:6–7), and so forth. Commandments such as these seemed to bear directly on *human* behavior—on relations with one's neighbor (to whom the stray animal, after all, belonged) or on the quality of mercy in general. But what of a commandment like:

You shall not muzzle an ox when it treads out the grain. — Deut. 25:4

Clearly, it may be unkind to muzzle an ox while surrounding him with a tempting meal; but why should the Torah be concerned with such matters? As a matter of fact, if the ox is otherwise well fed and well cared for, why not muzzle it? Perhaps muzzling under such circumstances may even be wise, and certainly it would not be cruel. Considering these questions, some interpreters concluded that this law was intended for its larger implications—indeed, that it had been promulgated principally to apply to humans:

9. That is, it "turns out that," after seeing the prettier woman, "she does not [any longer] find favor in his eyes."

[Paul writes:] This is my defense to those who would interrogate me: Do we not have the right to our food and drink? . . . Who serves as a soldier at his own expense? Who plants a vineyard without eating any of its fruit? [compare Deut. 20:6] . . . For it is written in the law of Moses, "You shall not muzzle an ox when it is treading out the grain." Is it for oxen that God is concerned? Does He not speak entirely for our sake? . . . If we have sown spiritual good among you, is it too much if we reap your material benefits?   —1 Cor. 9:3–11

Let the elders who rule well be considered worthy of double honor, especially those who labor in preaching and teaching. For Scripture says, "You shall not muzzle an ox when it is treading out the grain," and "The laborer deserves his wages."   —1 Tim. 5:17

The law could cut both ways, however. Perhaps the image of the unmuzzled ox was intended to caution against binging:

For the bishops ought to be nourished from the revenues of the Church, but not to devour them; for it is written, "You shall not muzzle the ox that treads out [the corn]." As then the ox which works unmuzzled in the threshing floor eats, indeed, but does not consume the whole, so you also who work in the threshing floor which is the Church of God, be nourished from the Church.

— *Didascalia Apostolorum* ch. 8

Rabbinic exegetes invoked the same law (albeit in the framework of an *a fortiori* argument) for purposes of a human analogy:

If, in the case of an ox, whose life one is not commanded to preserve, one is nonetheless commanded [by Deut. 25:4] not to muzzle, does it not stand to reason that a human being, whose life one *is* commanded to preserve, ought not to be prevented from eating [in keeping with Deut. 23:25]?   —b. *Baba Meṣi'a* 88b

Small Commandments as Important as Big

Among the laws that Moses transmitted in his final address were some whose importance and centrality were unmistakable, such as the commandments to love God (Deut. 6:5) or to pursue justice (Deut. 16:20). Some interpreters wondered, therefore, if commandments such as these were not inherently more important than others—like some of the animal laws just mentioned, or the prohibition of eating the meat of a buzzard (Deut. 14:13),[10] or the regulation forbidding the retrieval of a forgotten sheaf (Deut. 24:19). Could it be that all these laws were of equal weight in God's eyes?

The answer might seem surprising, but the Bible itself indicates in several places that even the slightest deviation from the divine laws is not to be countenanced:

> You shall not add to the word which I command you, nor take away from it; that you may keep the commandments of the Lord your God which I command you.
>
> —Deut. 4:2

> Lest his [the king's] heart be exalted above his kinsmen's and lest he depart from the commandment[s] to the right or left [that is, in the slightest way] . . .
>
> —Deut. 17:20

> [Joshua charged all of Israel:] Be exceedingly strong to keep and perform all that is written in the book of Moses' Torah without departing from it to the right or the left.
>
> —Josh. 23:6

Taking their clue from such verses, a number of ancient writers went out of their way to assert that the apparently small commandments were just as important as the others. They saw the Torah's laws as a system, each of whose parts (no matter how apparently minor) is crucial to the integrity of the whole:

> To transgress the law in matters either small or great is quite the same [to us], for in either case the law is being treated with disdain.
>
> —4 Macc. 5:20

> [Jesus said:] "For truly I say to you, until heaven and earth pass away, not an iota, not a dot, will pass from the law until all is accomplished. Anyone who relaxes even one of **the least** of these commandments and teaches men so, shall be called least in the kingdom of heaven; but he who does them and teaches them shall be called great in the kingdom of heaven."
>
> —Matt. 5:18–19

> For whoever keeps the whole law but fails in one point has become guilty of all of it.
>
> —James 2:10

> Rabbi said: Be careful with a minor commandment as with a major one, for you do not know what reward is given for keeping one commandment or another.

---

10. This bird, the *rā'āh*, is not mentioned in the similar list of forbidden birds in Lev. 11:13–19.

Ben Azzai said: Run after a minor commandment just as after a major
one.   —m. *Abot* 2:1, 4:2

Torah Refines (Like Fire)

Thinking along these same lines, some interpreters suggested that the ultimate
purpose of the Torah's system of laws did not necessarily lie in the particulars
themselves. Instead, God had set forth the specific requirements in order to
ensure that people would devote themselves wholly, and in the minute details,
to His service. Interpreters thus sometimes described the Torah as exercising
a refining effect on those who hold true to its statutes and, in keeping an image
common in the Psalms and elsewhere, depicted the Torah as a refining fire:

> Do not take the contemptible view that Moses enacted this legislation
> because of an excessive preoccupation with mice or weasels or such-
> like creatures. The fact is that everything has been solemnly set in
> order for unblemished investigation and amendment of life for the
> sake of righteousness . . . No ordinance has been made in Scripture
> without purpose or fancifully, but to the intent that through the **whole
> of our lives** we may also practice justice to all mankind in our acts,
> remembering the all-sovereign God.   — *Letter of Aristeas* 146, 168

> We, O Antiochus, who have been persuaded to govern our lives by the
> divine law, think that there is no more important constraint than for
> us to remain obedient to the law . . . You sneer at our philosophy as if
> those who live by it do so without good reason, but it teaches us
> self-control, so that we rule over all our pleasures and desires, and
> trains us in courage, so that we willingly endure any suffering. It
> educates us in justice, in order that we be equitable in all our dealings,
> and it teaches us religiosity, so that we worship the one true God with
> proper reverence.   — 4 Macc. 5:16–24

> Admirable too, and worthy of God, is the saying that the voice pro-
> ceeded from the fire, for the oracles of God have been refined and
> assayed as gold is by fire [an apparent allusion to Ps. 12:7, 18:30, 119:140,
> or Prov. 30:5]. And it conveys too, symbolically, some such meaning as
> this: since it is the nature of fire both to give light and to burn, those
> who resolve to be obedient to the divine utterances will live forever as
> in unclouded **light** with the laws themselves as stars illuminating their
> souls, while all who are rebellious will continue to be burnt . . . by their
> inward lusts.   — Philo, *The Decalogue* 48

"The oracles of God are refined [as a metal]" [Psalm 18:30] . . . Rab said: the reason the commandments were given was to refine [as a metal] human beings.[11] For, what does it matter to God, [for example,] if an animal is slaughtered [by having its neck cut] at the gullet or at the windpipe, but the purpose [of divine commandments governing such things] is to refine human beings. — *Genesis Rabba* 44:1

The Gift of the Torah

In the biblical narrative, the laws given through Moses are presented as part of an overall agreement, the covenant between God and Israel. At Mt. Sinai, the Israelites had accepted God's offer to be His people on condition of keeping His commandments; they said, "All that the Lord has spoken we will do and we will be obedient" (Exod. 24:7).

Reflecting back on these events at the end of Moses' life, however, the Bible presents the commandments as much more than a divine requirement. It describes them as constituting in themselves a source of great benefit and well-being, indeed, observing the Torah was, according to Moses' last address, to be associated or equated with the people's continued life in the land and all its blessings:

And now, O Israel, give heed to the statutes and the ordinances which I teach you, and do them, **so that you may live.**   —Deut. 4:1

You shall walk in all the way which the Lord your God has commanded you, that you may **live,** and that it may go well with you, and that you may **live long** in the land which you shall possess.

—Deut. 5:30 (some texts, 5:33)

All the commandments which I command you this day you shall be careful to do, that you may **live and multiply.**   —Deut. 8:1

[If you obey the commandments of the Lord your God] which I command you this day, by loving the Lord your God, by walking in his ways, and by keeping his commandments and his statutes and ordinances, then you shall **live and multiply,** and the Lord your God will bless you in the land which you are entering to take possession of it.

—Deut. 30:15–16

11. Ps. 18:30 might also be understood (in keeping with a rare but nonetheless attested active form of the verb in late and postbiblical Hebrew) as meaning that the "oracles of God do refine [as a metal]." Rab's explanation is apparently based on this understanding.

Lay to heart all the words which I enjoin upon you this day, that you may command them to your children, that they may be careful to do all the words of this Torah. For it is no trifle for you, **but it is your very life**, and thereby you shall live long in the land which you are going over the Jordan to possess.   —Deut. 32:46–47

Later generations followed and elaborated this line of thought. They too saw in the laws given by God more than a set of divine requirements. The laws constituted a recipe for well-being, a divinely given guidebook for the right way to live. By giving these laws to Moses on Mt. Sinai, God was in effect bestowing a great gift on Israel, and a source of great pleasure:

> The Torah of the Lord is perfect, it restores one's soul;
> The Lord's statutes are sure and make the simple wise . . .
> They are more to be desired than gold, even much fine gold,
> sweeter also than honey and drippings of the honeycomb.
>   —Ps. 19:7–10

> My soul is consumed with longing for your laws at all times . . .
> Your laws were my songs inside my dwelling-place . . .
> How I love your Torah, I speak of it the whole day long!
>   —Ps. 119:20, 54, 97

Ancient interpreters carried on this same theme. They held that adhering to the Torah was in itself a source of pleasure and that it provided many other benefits to all who kept its commandments.

> If you desire wisdom keep the commandments, and the Lord will
>   bestow her upon you.
>   —Sir. 1:26

> Nothing is better than the fear of the Lord,
>   nothing is sweeter than obeying the commandments.
>   —Sir. 23:27

> Whoever keeps the Torah preserves himself.
>   —[Heb. ms. B] Sir. 35:24 (cf. Prov. 19:6)

My children, be courageous and grow strong in the Torah, for by it you will gain honor.   —1 Macc. 2:64

She [Wisdom] is the book of the commandments of God, and the law that endures forever. All who hold fast to her will **live** [compare Prov.

3:18] and those who forsake her will die. Turn, O Jacob, and take her; walk toward her shining light. Do not give your glory for another, or your advantages to a foreign people. **Happy are we,** O Israel, for we know what is pleasing to God.

—Bar. 4:1–4

Therefore you also, children, be attentive to the commandments of the Lord . . . Keep the law of the Lord and do not be attentive to evil as to good, but concentrate on **what is truly good,** and hold fast to it in all the commandments of the Lord, being well versed in it and finding rest therein.

— *Testament of Asher* 6:1–3

[Baruch prays:] Your law is life, and Your wisdom is the right way.

— *2 Baruch* 38:2

[Moses says:] It is God who **graces you** with these commandments, using me as an interpreter. May they become an object of veneration for you, fight for them more even than for your wives and children. For by following them you will gain a life of happiness, enjoying an earth that is fruitful and a sea that is untroubled, and children begotten in nature's way; and you will be feared by any enemy.

—Josephus, *Jewish Antiquities* 3:87–88

This is the path of Torah: Bread and salt shall you eat, and drink water by measure; you shall sleep upon the ground, and live a life of privation, and in Torah shall be your work. And if you do thus, "You shall be happy, and it will be well with you" (Ps. 128:2)—*Happy* [refers to] this world, and *well* to the world to come.

Greatest is the Torah, for it gives life to those who perform it[s commandments] in this world and in the world to come, as it is said, "It is a tree of life to those who hold on to it, and all who maintain it are blessed" [Prov. 3:18].

—m. *Abot* 6:4, 7

Once the wicked regime [Rome] decreed that Jews be forbidden to study the Torah. Pappus b. Judah subsequently found R. Aqiba nonetheless convening groups in public for the study of Torah. "Aqiba," he said, "are you not afraid of the regime?" He said: "Let me answer you with a comparison: It is like a fox that was walking along the riverbank when he saw some fish moving in groups from place to place. He said to them: 'What are you fleeing from?' They said: 'From the nets that the human beings cast over us.' He said to them: 'Wouldn't you like to climb up onto the dry land so that you and I might live together as your ancestors and mine once did?' They said: 'Are you indeed the one who is alleged to be the cleverest of animals? You are not clever but foolish! For if there is danger in the place where we do live [that is, our natural environment], is it not all the more so in the place where we must die?' So is it with us now: for we sit and study Torah, about which it is said, 'For it is your life and your length of days' (Deut. 30:20); were we to abandon it, we would be in far greater danger."

—b. *Berakhot* 61b

Not in Heaven Anymore

Moses had transmitted to the people the way of life prescribed by the Torah. Now it was up to them to live in accordance with it:

[Moses said:] "For this commandment which I command you this day is not too hard for you, neither is it far off. It is not in heaven, that you should say, 'Who will go up for us to heaven and bring it to us, that we may hear it and do it?' Neither is it beyond the sea, that you should say, 'Who will go over the sea for us, and bring it to us, that we may hear it and do it?' But the word is very near you: it is in your mouth and in your heart, so that you can do it."   —Deut. 30:11–14

The meaning seemed clear enough: I have passed the Torah on to you, now go and do it! Still, if that were the case, interpreters had to wonder why the Bible mentioned going up to heaven or across the sea at all. Perhaps these words were a way of saying that, apart from what is written in the Torah, divine wisdom is quite inaccessible to humanity:

Who has gone up into heaven and taken her [Wisdom], and brought her down from the clouds? Who has gone over the sea and found her, and will buy her for pure gold? No one knows the way to her, or is concerned about the path to her. But He who knows all things knows her, He found her by His understanding . . . This is our God: no other can be compared to him. He found the whole way to knowledge, and gave her to Jacob his servant and to Israel whom He loved. Afterward she appeared on earth and lived among men. She is the book of the commandments of God, and the law that endures forever.

—Bar. 3:29–32, 3:35–4:1

Rather different, however, was another interpretation that held Moses' words to mean that the Torah is *no longer* in heaven; that is, now that it has been given over to human beings, it is up to them to teach it and interpret it with no further recourse to prophetic intermediaries:

The Torah is not in heaven, that one should say, "If only we had someone like the prophet Moses who might go up to heaven and take it down for us and teach us its laws so that we could do them."

— *Targum Neophyti* Deut. 30:12

It is not in Heaven, that one should say, "Who shall ascend to Heaven for us and take it and teach it to us so that we may do it?"; and it is not across the great sea, that one should say, "Who will cross the great sea for us and take it and teach it to us so that we may do it"; but the [divine] word is nearby to you, **in your study houses**—open your mouths in order to read them [the divine commandments], and purify your hearts so that you may do them.

— *Targum Pseudo-Jonathan* Deut. 30:11–14

It is taught elsewhere [in the Mishnah, *Kelim* 10:5]: if someone divided [the oven widthwise] into strips and put sand between each strip, then according to R. Eliezer it [the oven] is ritually pure; according to the [majority of] scholars [that is, his colleagues] it is impure . . . On that day R. Eliezer answered every argument in the world [against his position], but still they [his colleagues] did not accept [it]. [Then] he said to them, "If my ruling is correct, let this carob tree so demonstrate." The carob tree thereupon was uprooted a hundred cubits out of its place (some say four hundred cubits). They answered: "One does not make proof with a carob tree." Then he said to them, "If my ruling is correct, let this watercourse demonstrate it," whereupon the watercourse began to flow backwards. They said: "One does not make proof with a watercourse." He said to them: "If my ruling is correct, let the walls of the study house demonstrate it," whereupon the walls started to fall. But R. Joshua rebuked them [the walls] and said, "When scholars are disputing with each other, by what right can you interfere?" For this reason they did not fall out of respect for R. Joshua, nor did they return to being straight, out of respect for R. Eliezer, and they are still standing in that position. Finally he said to them, "If my ruling is correct, let it be demonstrated from heaven [by God directly]." A heavenly voice went forth and said, "Why should you dispute with R. Eliezer, since his ruling is correct in all instances?" Whereupon R. Joshua stood up and said, "**It is not in heaven.**" Now what does this [expression] "it is not in heaven" mean [in Deut. 30:12]? R. Jeremiah said, "Once the Torah was given at Mt. Sinai, one is not to take a heavenly voice into consideration, since You have written at Mt. Sinai with regard to the Torah, 'to incline after the majority' [Exod. 23:2]."

[Later,] R. Nathan encountered Elijah [temporarily descended from heaven]. He asked him: "What did God do after that happened?" [Elijah] said: "He laughed and said, 'My sons have defeated Me, My sons have defeated Me.'" —b. *Baba Metzia* 59b

It is certainly against the common drift of such passages—that the true teaching and application of biblical laws are now in your midst, just waiting to be observed—that Paul's allusion to the same biblical verse ought to be understood. Paul's (polemical, in that case) claim is that the *presentness* spoken of in Deut. 30:11–14 does not apply to laws at all:

Moses writes that the man who practices the righteousness [religious observance] which is based on the Torah shall live by it. But the righteousness based on faith says, "Do not say in your heart, 'Who will ascend into Heaven?'" (that is, to bring Christ down) or "Who will descend in the abyss?" (that is, to bring Christ up from the dead). But what does it say? "The word is near you, on your lips and near your heart" (that is, the word of faith which we preach). —Rom. 10:6–8

A Choice for Each Person

As Moses' final charge to the Israelites was drawing to a close, he summed up his message in a striking formulation:

See, I have set before you today life and good, death and evil; in that I am commanding you today to love the Lord your God, to walk in His ways, to keep His commandments, laws and statutes, so that you live and multiply;[12] and so that the Lord your God bless you in the land which you are entering to inherit. But if your heart turns aside and you do not listen but are drawn away to worship other gods and serve them, I solemnly warn you today that you shall perish, you shall not live long in the land which you are crossing the Jordan to enter and possess. I call heaven and earth to witness in warning you today: I have set before you life and death, blessing and curse; therefore choose life, so that you and your descendants may live.
—(traditional Hebrew text of) Deut. 30:15–18

12. Another form of the text, represented by the Septuagint, reads: "See, I have set before you today life and good, death and evil; *if you obey the commandments of the Lord your God which I command you this day*, to love the Lord your God, to walk in His ways, to keep His commandments, laws and statutes, then you shall live and multiply."

"Therefore, choose life"—here was a powerful summons. And yet . . . who would *not* choose life? Indeed, given the choice that Moses first delineates, between "life and good, death and evil," one would certainly have to be bent on self-destruction to opt for the latter pair. In what sense could these represent a *real* choice, two real alternatives?

It was not hard to see that by "choose life" Moses meant that Israel should resolve to keep the divine commandments, "to walk in His ways, to keep His commandments, laws and statutes." This would result in "life" in the sense[13] of *the people's continued life for generations* in the promised land, "that you live and *multiply* . . . that you *and your descendants* may live." Choosing "death"— that is, being "drawn away to worship other gods and serve them"—would inevitably result in exile and banishment; in other words, death meant that "you shall not *live long* in the land which you are crossing the Jordan to enter and possess."

Such was the choice presented by Moses. But it was not a big jump to find in his words a still more elemental choice: between, on the one hand, each individual's dedication to the good, that is, living in accordance with God's will, and, on the other hand, the surrender to the evil lurking in every human heart. Put in those terms, the choice was not a collective, national one, but a choice facing each individual in his or her own lifetime. Choosing the good would (quite apart from Israel's continued life in its homeland) allow a person to enjoy the rewards that God normally grants to the righteous in their own individual lives, since God's all-seeing eye monitors the behavior of each human being:

> In the beginning God created man, but He put him in a despoiler's
> hands, He gave him over to his own inclination.
> If you so wish, you may keep the commandment[s], and [keep] faith
> in doing God's will.
> Before you are fire and water—reach out for whichever you wish.
> Before a man are **life and death,** and whichever he chooses will be
> given to him.
> Great is the Lord's wisdom, He has great power and sees all:
> God's eyes behold His creatures and He knows each man's deeds.
>
> —Sir. 15:14–19

> . . .]And He sets [before you . . .
> t[wo] paths, one good [and one bad . . .

13. Attested as well above in the passages cited in "The Gift of Torah."

and He will bless you, but if you go on the [bad] path[. . .
and f[all u]pon you and destroy you[. . .[14]

— (4Q473) *The Two Ways* 2–5

God has given two paths[15] to the sons of men, and two inclinations, and two ways of acting, and two forms of living, two ends. Thus, all things come in pairs, one corresponding to the other: two paths, of good and of evil, in [keeping with] which are the two inclinations within our breasts that choose between them.

— *Testament of Asher* 1:3–5

And therefore we have an oracle of this kind recorded in Deuteronomy. "Behold, I have set before your face life and death, good and evil; choose life." So then in this way He puts before us both truths: first, that men have been made with a knowledge of both good and evil, its opposite; second, that it is their duty to choose the better rather than the worse. — Philo, *The Unchangeableness of God* 50

A Choice of Two Paths

Thus, the choice being presented by Moses was really a choice between two ways of life, two paths. In restating this choice, many sources (as we have just seen in the *Testament of Asher*) therefore speak of two paths (or "ways," in the sense of paths or roads). Although the "path of life" and "path of death" do not appear as such in Deuteronomy, these terms do appear elsewhere:

And to this people shall you say: Thus says the Lord: Behold I put before you the path of life and the path of death. — Jer. 21:8

How natural, then, that Moses' words should be transformed by later writers into a reference to these two paths. (Indeed, the choice between two paths may at one point have been fleshed out into a now-lost standard list of do's and don'ts—based on the Decalogue and other material—that circulated widely under the name "The Two Ways"):

The path of life and the path of mortality have I given to you, and the curses: and you shall choose the path of life.

— *Targum Neophyti* Deut. 30:19

14. All the occurrences of "you" in this passage are in the second-person singular.
15. On the connection of these "two paths" with the choice stated by Moses, see below.

See, I have put before you this day the path of life, which is the good path, and the path of mortality, which is the evil path.

— *Fragment Targum* (V) Deut. 30:15

There are two ways, one of life and one of death, and great is the difference between the two ways. — *Didache* 1:1

There are two ways of teaching and of power, the one of light and the one of darkness, and great is the difference between the two ways. Over the one have been arrayed the light-bearing angels of God, but over the other the angels of Satan.

The way of light is this: if someone desire to go on the way to the appointed place, let him be zealous about what he does . . . [and] not be joined to those who walk on **the way of death.**

— *Letter of Barnabas* 18:1–2, 19:2

[God says:] And I gave him [Adam] his free will and I pointed out to him the two ways, light and darkness. And I said to him, "This is good for you, but that is bad," so that I might come to know whether he has love toward me or abhorrence, and so that it might become plain who among his race loves me. — *2 Enoch* (J) 30:15

I myself proposed two ways, of life and death,
and proposed to the judgment to choose good life.

— *Sibylline Oracles* 8:399–400

And Moses [says], "I have set before your face the way of life and the way of death. Choose the good and walk in it."

— Origen, *First Principles* 3.1.6

"Behold, I have set before your face the way of life and the path of death." — *Apostolic Constitutions* 7.1.1

It is said, "I have set before you life and death, blessing and curse" [Deut. 30:19]. Lest Israel should say, "Since God put before us **two paths**, the path of life and the path of death, let us go along whichever one we prefer," the text went on to say, "And you shall choose life" [Deut. 30:19]. — *Sifrei Deuteronomy* 53

Nice Road at First

If God confronts humanity with such a weighty choice, why is it that many people nevertheless choose wrongly, forsaking God's path for a life of selfishness and self-indulgence? Obviously, such people are deluded by the superficial attractiveness of a life without constraints. To some it occurred that, if the Bible presents the choice in terms of two paths, then each individual stands, as it were, at a fork in the road, looking down two rival routes. If many end up choosing the bad road, is it not because this road is, at first glance at least, more attractive?

> And Abraham saw two roads. The first road was strait and narrow and the other broad and spacious . . . [The angel Michael then explained to Abraham:] "This strait gate is the gate of the righteous, which leads to life, and . . . the broad gate is the gate of the sinners."
> — *Testament of Abraham* (A) 11:2, 10

> Enter by the narrow gate; for the gate is wide and the way is easy that leads to destruction, and those who enter by it are many. For the gate is narrow and the way is hard that leads to life, and those who find it are few. — Matt. 7:13–14

> This is like someone who was sitting at a crossroads and before him were two roads, one whose beginning was smooth but whose end was thistles, and the other whose beginning was thistles but whose end was smooth. So he would inform passers-by and say to them: "Do you see the road whose beginning is smooth? You will go on the smooth part for two or three steps, but eventually it turns into thistles. But do you see the road whose beginning is thistles? You will go in the thistles for two or three steps, but eventually it turns out smooth."
> — *Sifrei Deuteronomy* 53 (continuation of passage cited above)

The Path to the Afterlife

If the Bible, in this passage, sets forth a basic choice confronting each individual—two different paths or ways of living—why does it call the one "life" and the other "death"? After all, all human beings die; all are, in that sense, on the path to death. Yet to some interpreters it seemed clear that the Bible's choice of words was no dramatic hyperbole. It must have meant by "life," life in the world to come. After all, Moses went on to tell the people to "therefore choose life, so that you . . . may live"; why tell people who are already living to do something so that they might live? (In Hebrew, as in English, there are other ways of saying "so that you might continue to live" or "so that you might live long.") What is more, other biblical texts speak of the "road of [or "to"] life" in such a way as to suggest that the "life" in question is the reward after death:

Heeding instruction is the **road to life**, but one who neglects reproof leads astray.

—Prov. 10:17

The wise man's is the **road of life upward**, that he may turn from Sheol [the underworld] beneath.

—Prov. 15:24

Seen in this light, Moses did indeed seem to be referring to life after death. His message was thus that by seeking to keep the commandments of the Torah an individual was indeed "choosing life," choosing to be among those righteous who would be rewarded after their death. Such an interpretation may underlie the targumist's use of the word "mortality" (instead of simply "death") as the opposite of life:

The path of life and the path of **mortality** have I given to you, and the curses: and you shall choose the path of life.

— *Targum Neophyti* Deut. 30:19

See, I have put before you this day the path of life, which is the good path, and the path of **mortality**, which is the evil path.

— *Fragment Targum* (V) Deut. 30:15

In any case, the interpretation of "life" as the reward of the righteous was stated outright elsewhere:

[Ezra asks an angel:] "What good is it to us, if an eternal age has been promised to us, but we have done deeds that bring death . . . For while we lived and committed iniquity we did not consider what we should suffer after death." He answered and said, "This is the meaning of the contest which every man who is born on earth shall wage, that if he is defeated he shall suffer what you have said, but if he is victorious he shall receive what I have said. For this is the way of which Moses, while he was alive, spoke to the people, saying, 'Choose for yourself life, that you may live.'"

— *4 Ezra* 7:119, 126–129

[The angel Michael then explained to Abraham:] "This strait gate is the gate of the righteous, which leads to life, and those who enter through it come into Paradise. And . . . the broad gate is the gate of the sinners, which leads to destruction [Gehenna, hell] and to eternal punishment."

— *Testament of Abraham* (A) 11:2, 10–11

Enter by the narrow gate; for the gate is wide and the way is easy that leads to destruction, and those who enter by it are many. For the gate is narrow and the way is hard, that leads to life, and those who find it are few.
— Matt. 7:13–14

See, I have arrayed before you this day the life of the world to come and the goodness of the garden of Eden, and the death which the wicked will die and the evils of Gehenna.
— *Targum Neophyti* (marginal note) Deut. 30:15

Thus did Moses say to Israel: "Do you see the wicked who are prospering **in this world**? They prosper for two or three days, but eventually they regret it . . . Do you see the righteous who suffer in this world? They suffer for two or three days, but eventually they will rejoice [in the world to come]."
— *Sifrei Deuteronomy* 53 (continuation of passage cited above)

Consider Heaven and Earth

Moses concluded his final address to the Israelites with a song (Deut. 32:1–43) designed to warn them of the perils to come in later times. At the very beginning of this song, however, Moses did not address the Israelites directly. Instead, he spoke to the sky and the earth:

Give ear, O heavens, and I shall speak, and let the earth hear the words of my mouth. May my teaching drop as the rain, my speech distil as the dew, as the gentle rain upon the tender grass, and as the showers upon the herb.
— Deut. 32:1–2

Why should Moses have addressed his words to these impersonal bodies when, by the Bible's own account (Deut. 31:19–21, 28–30), the purpose of this song was to warn Israel? True enough, a later prophet was to begin his prophetic book in a similar manner:

Hear, O heavens, and give ear, O earth, for the Lord has spoken . . .
— Isa. 1:2

But to observe this was only to reinforce the question: why should a prophet talk to heaven and earth rather than Israel? To make matters worse, Moses *did* soon turn his speech to Israel directly and unambiguously: "Do you requite this to the Lord, you foolish and senseless people?" (Deut. 32:6). If he eventually spoke *to* Israel, what sense could there be in addressing heaven and earth at all?

Now, it so happened that the same opening line of Moses' song could be read differently:

Give ear to the heavens as I speak, and **let the earth be heard**[16] [in] the words of my mouth.

Although it is a little forced, reading the opening verse in this fashion would have the effect of indeed making Moses address the Israelites from the very start: he simply began by telling them to give ear to, to heed, the examples of the heaven and the earth. And why heaven and earth? Because they are eternal and unchanging and thus, along with the rain and dew that fall from heaven to earth (evoked in this song's opening as well), are an example of how God's laws are unceasingly obeyed and put into action. All this contrasted sharply with the picture of Israel's inconstancy in Moses' song:

"Give ear, O heavens, and I shall speak . . ." [Deut. 32:1]—God said to Moses: Say to Israel, **Consider** the heavens that I created to serve you. Do you think that they have changed their behavior? Do you think the sun has said, "I will no longer rise in the east and give light to the whole world"? . . . "And let the earth hear the words of my mouth . . ." [Deut. 32:1]—And **consider** the earth that I created to serve you. Do you think that it has changed its behavior? Do you sow seeds in it and it does not flourish? Or do you even sow wheat in it and it gives back barley?
— *Sifrei Deuteronomy* 306

The same interpretation may be reflected in earlier writings:

Contemplate all the events in heaven, how the lights in heaven do not change their courses, how each rises and sets in order, each at its proper time, and they do not transgress their law. **Consider** the earth, and understand from the work which is done upon it, from the beginning to the end, that no work of God changes as it becomes manifest. Consider the summer and the winter, how the whole earth is full of water, and clouds and dew and rain rest upon it . . . And understand in respect of everything and perceive how He who lives forever made all these things for you . . . but you have not persevered, nor observed the law of the Lord, but you have transgressed, and have spoken proud and hard words with your unclean mouth against His majesty. You hard of heart!
— *1 Enoch* 2:1–5:4

Somewhat similarly:

16. Or, "hear [second-person singular] the earth."

Sun and moon and stars do not change their order; so you also, do not change the law of God in the disorder of your doings.

— *Testament of Naphtali* 3:2

Heaven and Earth Were Already Witnesses

But another answer to the same question existed, and this one as well depended on re-pronouncing the opening line of Moses' song in an unexpected way. For these same words could also be parsed as follows:

The heavens **gave ear** while I spoke, and the earth **heard** the words of my mouth.

Read in this fashion, Moses' opening words seemed to refer to some earlier occasion when he had spoken. Interpreters had little difficulty determining what that occasion might have been. It must have been the time when, with the heavens ablaze with lightning and the earth in turmoil before him, Moses had stood at the foot of Mt. Sinai and solemnly transmitted to all of Israel the words of God's covenant. Since heaven and earth were present, they must have heard Israel's acceptance of the commandments, "All that the Lord has spoken we will do" (Exod. 24:7). If so, the fact that the heavens gave ear and the earth heard at that time was being mentioned by Moses now because he wished to remind Israel that, although he himself was about to die, *they* could nevertheless testify against Israel in the future, after the people had abandoned those same commandments:

And he [Moses] spoke to them, saying, "Behold I am going to sleep with my fathers and I am going to my ancestors. And I know that you shall go and abandon the words [that is, the divine commandments] that have been set forth for you by me, and God shall become angry with you and leave you and depart from your land . . . I, however, call heaven and earth to witness against you, **for heaven hear[d] and earth g[a]ve ear,** for God was revealing [at Mt. Sinai] the purpose of the world and He set out for you His supernalities, lighting within you the eternal lamp. And [as a result of their testifying,] you shall remember, O wicked ones, how I spoke to you and you answered, saying: 'All that God has spoken to us we will do and we will obey [Exod. 24:7]. But if however we disobey and go astray, then He shall call a witness against us and he will cut us off.'"   — Pseudo-Philo, *Biblical Antiquities* 19:2–4

[Moses said to Israel:] "The heavens **gave ear** as I spoke" [that is, an alternate understanding of Deut. 32:1], because the Torah was given out of heaven, as it is said, "You have seen that I have spoken with you from heaven" [Exod. 20:22]; "and the earth **heard** the words of my mouth" [Deut. 32:1] because Israel was standing on it at the time, and they said, "All that the Lord has spoken, we will do," **and it was heard** [an alternate understanding of Exod. 24:7]. — *Sifrei Deuteronomy* 306

Moses Did Not Want to Die

At the end of the book of Deuteronomy, God instructed Moses:

> Ascend this mountain of the Abarim, Mount Nebo, which is in the land of Moab, opposite Jericho, and view the land Canaan, which I am giving to the people of Israel as a possession; and die on the mount which you ascend and be gathered to your ancestors.
>
> —Deut. 32:49–50

Moses did as he was told: "So Moses the servant of the Lord died there in the land of Moab according to the word of the Lord" (Deut. 34:5). All this could not but strike readers as an example of obedience and courage in the face of the inevitable. And yet . . . this was not the first time that Moses had been told by God to die. Even before the end of the previous book, the book of Numbers, God is represented as telling Moses to accept his fate:

> The Lord said to Moses, "Go up onto this mountain of Abarim and see the land which I have given to the people of Israel. And when you have seen it, be gathered to your fathers [that is, die] as your brother Aaron was gathered."
>
> —Num. 27:12

Apparently, however, that one notice was not sufficient, for God has to repeat the same thing in Deut. 32:49–50—in fact, on several intervening occasions as well:

> And the Lord said to Moses, "Behold the time has come for you to die."
>
> —Deut. 31:14

> And the Lord said to Moses, "Behold, now you will sleep with your fathers."
>
> —Deut. 31:16

What is more, on at least one occasion Moses appears to have protested God's decree that he die before entering the land of Canaan:

> [Moses recalls:] And I besought the Lord at that time, saying, "O Lord God, you have only begun to show your servant your greatness and your mighty hand . . . Let me go over, I pray, and see the good land

beyond the Jordan, that goodly hill country, and Lebanon." But the Lord was angry with me on your account, and would not listen to me; and the Lord said to me, "Let it suffice you; speak no more to me of this matter. Go up to the top of Pisgah and lift up your eyes westward and northward and southward and eastward, and behold it with your eyes, for you shall not cross over this Jordan."   —Deut. 3:23–27

These, and yet other references, suggested to some interpreters that Moses might not in fact have been so eager to accept the divine decree. Perhaps, on the contrary, God's repeated instructions to Moses to die indicated that Moses was unwilling:

After these things, God spoke to him [Moses] **a third time**, saying, "Behold, you are going off now to sleep with your fathers."[17]
        — Pseudo-Philo, *Biblical Antiquities* 19:6

And so, when . . . the Lord said to him, "Go up into this mountain of Abarim, Mt. Nebo . . ." Moses thought to himself "Perhaps this ascent will be similar to the ascent of Mt. Sinai." Therefore he said, "Let me go and sanctify the people." The Lord said to him: "Not at all! Go up and behold the land which I am giving to Israel as a possession, and die on the mountain which you ascend and be gathered to your ancestors—just as your brother Aaron died on Mt. Hor and was gathered to his fathers." Whereupon Moses opened his mouth in prayer and said: "Master of the world, if you please, let me not be like the person who had an only son that was taken prisoner, and he went and redeemed him at great cost and taught him wisdom and skill and acquired a wife for him and set up a kingly gazebo for him [and so on] and just when the time came for him to celebrate with his son and daughter-in-law [at their wedding] . . . the person in question was suddenly summoned by the king to the law court and was sentenced to death, and they did not even allow him to enjoy his son's celebration. So similarly have I labored for this people . . . and now that the time has come for me to cross the Jordan and inherit the land, I am sentenced to die! Please, allow me to cross the Jordan and enjoy Israel's celebration, and after that I will die."
        — *Targum Pseudo-Jonathan* Deut. 32:49–50

17. This verse essentially parallels Deut. 31:16, save that there the text does not draw attention to the fact that Moses has already previously been told that it is time for him to die. The "third time" seems to be in addition to Deut. 31:14 and Num. 27:12.

"And die upon the mountain which you ascend" [Deut. 32:50]. He said to Him: Master of the world! Why should I die? . . . Is it not better that people [be able to] say, "Here is Moses [still alive], the one who took us out of Egypt and split the sea for us and brought down the manna for us and performed miracles and wonders," rather than their saying "Moses *was* such-and-such" and "Moses *did* thus-and-so"?

— *Sifrei Deuteronomy* 339

A heavenly voice went forth and said to him [Moses], You only have an hour left to live in this world. He said to Him: O Master of the world! Let me [instead] go about like a bird, flying all over the world, gathering food on the earth and drinking water from streams and at night going back to his nest. God said to him: Enough! He said to him: Master of the world! [But You are called] "The rock whose deeds are perfect [for all His ways are just]" [Deut. 32:4]! And he began to weep, and he wept and said: To whom shall I go who can seek mercy on my behalf?

— *Pețirat Moshe* (Jellinek, *Beit ha-Midrasch* 1.125)

The theme of Moses' reluctance to die came to be lovingly elaborated in song and prayer:

Said the Lord from the midst of his Shekhinah [the divine Presence]:
"For what reason are you [Moses] afraid of death?
I have decreed it upon all creatures."
Moses grew faint when he heard this thing,
And at once he went to the great [city of] Hebron.
He cried out and summoned Adam from his grave.
"Tell me why you sinned in the Garden,
[Why] you tasted and ate from the tree of Knowledge.
You have given your sons over to weeping and wailing!
The whole garden was before you, yet you were not satisfied.
Oh why did you rebel against the Lord's commandment?"

— *Targumic Tosefta: Alphabetical Acrostic on the Death of Moses,*
Oxford-Bodleian 2701/9 p. 64b

When, in the hearing of an humble one [Moses], it was said, "Die!"
He replied to the living God, "Must I?
If I can become Joshua's servant, serving him the same way,
Then I can continue living, being my servant's valet . . .
Oh, what a boon was given on the day that I was told:
Ascend the mountain to Me and stay there . . . [Exod. 24:12].

Likewise, what ill befell me on the day I was told
Ascend the mountain of Abarim and die there" [Deut. 32:49–50].
　　　—Yannai, *Liturgical Poem for Deut. 31:14* (M. Zulay, *Piyyuṭei Yannai* 254–255)

The tradition of Moses' reluctance to obey God's decree may be related to another that held (without any apparent scriptural justification) that Moses wept just before his death:

> How extraordinary was this outburst of weeping and wailing of the multitude may be conjectured from what next befell the lawgiver [Moses]. For he, who had ever been persuaded that men should not despond as the end approached, because this fate befell them in accordance with the will of God and by a law of nature, was yet by this conduct of the people reduced to tears.
> 　　　　　　　　　　　　—Josephus, *Jewish Antiquities* 4:322

> He said to them, "Happy are you, O Israel, who is like you? A people saved by the Lord . . ." [Deut. 33:29], and he went and blessed them and then lifted up his voice and wept . . . He departed from them with great weeping and Israel likewise wept and cried out with a great and bitter cry.　　　　　—*Peṭirat Moshe* (Jellinek, *Beit ha-Midrasch* 1.126–127)

> The whole congregation stood before him [Moses, as he ascended Mt. Nebo]. And his eyes sent forth tears like flowing rivers, not for himself, but for the congregation.　　　　　　　　　　—*Tibat Marqa* 258b

Moses Disputed with an Angel

If Moses was indeed reluctant to die, it occurred to some interpreters that there may have actually been a dispute between him and the angel dispatched to bring about his death (or to take charge of his soul after his death). Moses was, after all, no ordinary individual: he had spoken to God "face to face" (Deut. 34:10), and God had even conferred the title of "God" upon him (see Chapter 17, "A Godlike Man"). How could even an angel tell such a person what to do? Elsewhere the Bible spoke of God "rebuking" Satan (Zech. 3:2); would not Moses have similarly rebuked any angel sent to fetch his soul?

> At that time God ordered the angel of death: Go and bring Moses' soul to Me. Off he went and stood before him [Moses] and said to him: Moses, give me your soul. He said to him: You are not even authorized

to stand in the place where I stand, yet you say to me "Give me your soul"? [And thus] he **rebuked** him and he went off shame-faced.

— *Sifrei Deuteronomy* 305

This tradition may be related to another, in which Satan apparently disputed with the angel Michael at the time of Moses' death:

But when the archangel Michael, contending with the devil, disputed about the body of Moses, he [himself, that is, Michael] did not presume to pronounce a reviling judgment upon him, but said, "The Lord rebuke you" [Zech. 3:2].

— Jude 9

A heavenly voice went forth and said to Moses: "How long will you continue to torture yourself? For you only have two hours left! [That is, accept your fate!]" Now Samael, chief of the Satans [or "accusers"], was waiting in anticipation for the time when Moses would die, [so that] perhaps he would receive his soul like that of other people; he was waiting like someone expecting great happiness. When Michael, Israel's angel, saw Samael the wicked angel waiting for Moses' death, he lifted up his voice and wept and Samael the angel was joyful and laughing. Michael said to him: Wicked one! I am weeping and you are laughing?!

— *Peṭirat Moshe* (Jellinek, *Beit ha-Midrasch* 1.125)

Moses' Last Vision

When Moses finally ascended Mt. Nebo to die, the Bible relates that God showed him the land that was to be given to the people of Israel:

And the Lord showed him all the land, Gilead as far as Dan, all Naphtali, the land of Ephraim and Manasseh, all the land of Judah as far as the farthest sea, the Negeb and the Plain, the valley of Jericho the city of palms, as far as Zoar. And the Lord said to him: "This is the land of which I swore to Abraham, to Isaac, and to Jacob." — Deut. 34:1–4

That Moses could see all this from the top of a mountain, even a very high one, seemed most unlikely. It therefore occurred to more than one interpreter that Moses must in fact have ascended into heaven—or at least gotten close enough to peer inside:

Then the Lord showed him the land and all the things that are in it and He said: "This is the land which I am giving to my people." And He showed him the place from which the clouds lift up the water for irrigating the whole land, and the place from which the river receives its watering, and the land of Egypt, and the place of the heaven from which the holy land alone drinks. And He showed him the place from which the manna rained down for the people, and as far as the paths [leading to] paradise. And He showed him the measurements of the sanctuary and and the number of the offerings and the signs by which they would begin to chart the skies. And He said: "These things are prohibited to the human race because they have sinned by them . . . As for you, however, I will receive you from there and I will glorify you along with your ancestors [that is, in heaven], and I will give you rest in your sleep and I will bury you with peace."

—Pseudo-Philo, *Biblical Antiquities* 19:10–12

Given such a heavenly vista, it was certainly possible that Moses was also shown a view of the future, indeed, all of time until its very end:

Do not read "until the farthest sea" [*'ad hayyām hā'aḥărôn*, Deut. 34:3] but "until the last day" [*'ad hayyôm hā'aḥărôn*]. This teaches that He showed him the whole world from the day of creation until the day when the dead will be brought back to life.   — *Sifrei Deuteronomy* 357

[At Mt. Nebo Moses said:] I stand at the level of prophecy and behold the ages [to come] and what will happen in them and what is destined to be.   — *Tibat Marqa* 254b

Buried by God (or the Angels)

When at last Moses' death came to pass, the Bible relates:

So Moses the servant of the Lord died there in the land of Moab, according to the word of the Lord, and he buried him in the valley in the land of Moab opposite Beth Peor, and no man knows his burial-place to this day.   — Deut. 34:5–6

The phrase "he buried him" is really the biblical Hebrew equivalent of "they buried him" or even "he was buried." That is, an impersonal singular active verb is used—like the impersonal plural active in English, "they buried him"—as a way of saying that a certain action was accomplished without specifying who actually accomplished it. Still, if that is the meaning of "he buried him," then how could it be that "no man knows his burial-place to this day"? Certainly whoever did the burying would not willfully conceal Moses' burial place. And so some interpreters concluded that this impersonal verb was not impersonal at all: "he buried him" really meant "He buried him," that is, God Himself had buried Moses' body on the mountain but kept its location hidden from the Israelites:

[God said to Moses:] "As for you, however, I will receive you from there [the earth] and I will glorify you along with your ancestors [that is, in heaven], and I will give you rest in your sleep and I will **bury you with peace.**" . . . And He buried him with His own hands on a high place and in the light of the world.

— Pseudo-Philo, *Biblical Antiquities* 19:12, 16

God Himself was the one who took care of [burying] him, as it is said, "And He buried him in the valley . . ." [Deut. 34:5].   — m. *Soṭah* 1:9

He was buried by the hand of God on Mt. Nebo and "no man knows his burial-place until" the day of Vengeance.   — *Tibat Marqa* 108a

Still, the idea of God performing a human action such as burial no doubt bothered more than one commentator. It was apparently for that reason that some implied or specifically included the angels in Moses' burial:

He was buried with no one present, surely by no mortal hands but by **immortal powers.**   — Philo, *Moses* 2:291

The great prophet Moses went up Mt. Nebo in the sight of six hundred thousand Israelites and **all the angels** were arrayed to receive him . . . And he was buried there by God, as it says, "And he buried him in the valley."   — *Tibat Marqa* 269a

He [God] appeared above him [Moses] with His Memra, and legions of ministering angels were with Him; Michael and Gabriel laid out for him a golden couch . . . Metatron and Yophiel and Uriel and Yephephi-yah, chiefs of wisdom, laid him upon it, and with His Memra he bore him four miles and buried him in the valley just opposite Beth Peor.

— *Targum Pseudo-Jonathan* Deut. 34:6

Buried under a Cloud

If God or the angels buried Moses, that still does not explain why his burial place should be unknown "to this day" (Deut. 34:6). Surely people could see at least the general area on Mt. Nebo where the burial took place. Perhaps, then, the true sense of the place being unknown "to this day" was that God had commanded that the location be kept secret (even though it may have been known at the time). That Mt. Nebo had been declared off-limits, a secret hiding place "to this day," may be suggested elsewhere:

> One finds in the records that Jeremiah the prophet . . . having received an oracle [following the destruction of the Jerusalem Temple], ordered that the tent and the ark should follow with him, and that he went to the mountain where Moses had gone up and had seen the inheritance [that is, the land] of God. And Jeremiah came and found a cave, and he brought there the tent and the ark and the incense altar and he sealed up the entrance. Some of those who followed him came up to mark the way but could not find it. When Jeremiah learned of it, he rebuked them and declared: "**The place shall be unknown** until God gathers his people together again and shows his mercy. And then the Lord will disclose these things, and the glory of the Lord and the cloud will appear."
> — 2 Macc. 2:1, 4–8

If, however, Moses had indeed been buried by God or the angels, perhaps that fact alone was sufficient to explain why his burial place was unknown: the burial itself must have taken place under cover of a great cloud, just as had God's appearance on Mt. Sinai:

> And while he [Moses] said goodbye to Eleazar and Joshua and was still communing with them, a cloud suddenly descended upon him and he disappeared in a ravine. But he has written of himself in the sacred books that he died, for fear lest they should venture to say that by reason of his surpassing virtue he had gone back to the Deity.
> — Josephus, *Jewish Antiquities* 4:326

According to Josephus, Moses wrote the end of the Torah *before* his death, and specifically included an account of his own death lest people say that he never died. But Josephus leaves somewhat open the question of what really happened: a divinely sent cloud covered him and took him away. The same cloud is found elsewhere as well:

> At the time when Moses was about to die a luminous cloud surrounded the place of sepulcher and blinded the eyes of the bystanders. Therefore nobody could see either the dying lawgiver or the place where his body was buried.
> — *Catena* preserved by Fabricius in his *Codex Pseudoepigraphicus Veteris Testamenti* 2.121–122

When he [Moses] got to the top of the mountain, a cloud came down
and lifted him up from the sight of all the congregation of Israel.

— *Tibat Marqa* 269a

Not Buried at All

Yet another possibility existed. Perhaps no one knew where Moses was buried
because his burial at Mt. Nebo was only temporary: his true final resting place
was in heaven.[18]

Some say that Moses never died but is alive and serving on high: for it
says here, "And Moses died *there*. . ." [Deut. 34:5] and it says elsewhere
that "he [Moses] was *there* with the Lord" [Exod. 34:28]. Just as in this
latter case [the word "there" was used when] he was alive and serving
on high, so here as well [this word indicates that] he was alive and
serving on high.   — *Midrash ha-Gadol, Zot habberakhah* 4:5

Somewhat similarly:

And therefore we are told that no man knows his grave. For who has
powers such that he could perceive the passing of a perfect soul to Him
that Is?   — Philo, *The Sacrifices of Abel and Cain* 10

"No one knows his burial place to this day"—this you ought to
understand in the sense of being borne on high rather than that of
burial.   — Ambrose, *On Cain and Abel* 1.2.8

Perhaps, indeed, the remark in Deut. 34:6 about Moses' burial place being
unknown was intended to highlight the fact that the "spiritual" Moses was not
buried at all:

Joshua the son of Nun saw a double Moses being taken away, the one
with the angels, the other deemed worthy of burial in the ravine.

— Clement of Alexandria, *Miscellanies* 6.132.2

It is said that two Moses were seen, one alive in spirit and the other
dead in body.   — Origen, *On Joshua* 2.2

18. This understanding is somewhat akin to the idea mentioned by Josephus above, that some
people might claim that Moses "had gone back to the Deity."

The Supreme Philosopher

"And there never again arose in Israel a prophet like Moses, whom God knew face to face" (Deut. 34:10). This is the Bible's closing tribute to Moses. Yet to some interpreters its very wording seemed to suggest a qualification: there never was another *prophet* like Moses, but there may have been other sorts of figures who *were* like Moses. For, certainly, his achievements extended into areas other than prophecy. Perhaps in these other domains Moses was merely one in a series of illustrious figures, to whom he was indeed comparable. This seemed particularly true in the area of philosophy.

> For our lawgiver Moses proclaims arrangements of nature and preparations for great events by expressing that which he wishes to say in many ways, by using words that refer to other matters (I mean matters relating to outward appearances). Therefore, those who are able to think well marvel at his wisdom and at the divine spirit, in accordance with which he has **also** been proclaimed a prophet.[19]
>
> — Aristobulus, Fragment 2 (cited in Eusebius, *Praeparatio Evangelica* 8.10.3–4)

> This Moses became the teacher of Orpheus. When he reached manhood, he bestowed on humanity many useful contributions, for he invented ships, machines for lifting stones, Egyptian weapons, devices for drawing water and fighting, and **philosophy**.
>
> — Artapanus, Fragment 3 (cited in Eusebius, *Praeparatio Evangelica* 9.27.4)

> As a general he had **few** to equal him, and as a prophet none, insomuch that in all his utterances one seemed to hear the speech of God Himself.   — Josephus, *Jewish Antiquities* 4:329

> "And there never again arose in Israel a prophet like Moses": Among the prophets there never arose [one like him], but among the kings there did, [as it says] "And Koheleth [that is, King Solomon] sought to find pleasing words, rightly written, words of truth" [Eccles. 12:10].
>
> — *Yalqut Shimoni* 966

---

19. "Proclaimed a prophet" may be a reference to, specifically, Deut. 34:10. Beyond this, however, what is noteworthy is this passage's somewhat apologetic stance vis-à-vis the title of prophet. Aristobulus seems to be saying that Moses was first and foremost a great thinker who proclaimed "arrangements of nature" and whose wisdom was widely admired. If such is not apparent at first glance, this is because he often used metaphorical language. Similarly, if he was called a prophet, this was more a reflection of the divine spirit inspiring him than of the overall nature of his message.

In general, it is striking that, while the Bible presents Moses as the greatest of the prophets, ancient interpreters frequently described him in other terms, as we have seen: "lawgiver," "king," "high priest," "sage," "interpreter," and "teacher." Perhaps at least part of this shift came about because—as may be implied by the last passage cited—the office of sage or wise man had come to rival or even overlap with that of prophet in later times.[20]

In keeping with this, Hellenistic writers sometimes presented Moses not only as a great thinker, but as one of the *earliest*, from whom later philosophers therefore must have learned much. (Although this is not an exegetical motif per se—that is, it was not specifically connected to Deut. 34:10 or to any other biblical verse—it certainly affected the way some interpreters approached the whole Pentateuch or assessed the significance of Moses' life and work.)

> Among [Moses' admirers] are the philosophers already mentioned and many others, including poets, who took significant material from him and are admired accordingly.
>
> It is evident that Plato imitated our legislation and that he had investigated thoroughly each of the elements in it . . . So it is very clear that [he] took many things [from it]. For he was very learned, as was Pythagoras, who transferred many of our doctrines and integrated them into his own system of beliefs.
>
> It seems to me that Pythagoras, Socrates, and Plato with great care follow him [Moses] in all respects. They copy him when they say that they hear the voice of God, when they contemplate the arrangement of the universe, so carefully made and so unceasingly held together by God. —Aristobulus, Fragment 2.4, 3.1, and 4.4 (cited in Eusebius *Praeparatio Evangelica* 8.10.4, 13.12.1, 4)

And concerning Moses the same author [Alexander Polyhistor] further adds many things. Of these it is worthwhile to hear the following: "And Eupolemus says that Moses was the **first wise man**, that he first taught the alphabet to the Jews, and the Phoenicians received it from the Jews." —Eupolemus (cited in Eusebius, *Praeparatio Evangelica* 9.26.1)

> In regard to this, Heracleitus, taking law and opinions from Moses like a thief, says, "we live their death, and we die their life," intimating that the life of the body is the death of the soul.
>
> —Philo, *Questions in Genesis* 4.152

20. See Chapter 1.

And therefore it seems that some Greek legislators did well when they copied from the most sacred tables of Moses the proposition that hearing is not accepted as evidence, meaning that what a man has seen is to be judged trustworthy, but what he has heard is not entirely reliable.

— Philo, *Special Laws* 4:61

He [Moses] represented Him as One, uncreated and immutable to all eternity; in beauty surpassing all mortal thought; made known to us by His power, although the nature of His real being passes knowledge. That the wisest of the Greeks learned to adopt these conceptions of God from principles with which Moses supplied them I am not now concerned to urge; but they have borne abundant witness to the excellence of these doctrines, and to their consonance with the nature and majesty of God. In fact, Pythagoras, Anaxagoras, Plato, and the Stoics who succeeded him, and indeed nearly all the philosophers appear to have held similar views concerning the nature of God.

In two points, in particular, Plato **followed the example of our law-giver:** He prescribed the primary duty of the citizens a study of their laws, which they must all learn word for word by heart. Again, he took precautions to prevent foreigners from mixing with them at random, and to keep the state pure and confined to law-abiding citizens.

Our **earliest imitators** were the Greek philosophers, who, though ostensibly observing the laws of their own countries, yet in their conduct and philosophy were Moses' disciples, holding similar views about God and advocating the simple life and friendly communion between man and man.

— Josephus, *Against Apion* 2:168, 257, 281

❖   ❖   ❖

In short: Among the things taught by Moses in his final address was the great teaching of the Shema, which Israel was to recite each morning and evening. Moses also spoke of numerous laws, including the prohibition of displacing old boundary-marks, by which were meant ancient practices. The procedure for divorce was likewise spelled out, along with the proper grounds for undertaking it. The law about not muzzling an ox really referred to human beings. In general, apparently small commandments in the Torah were to be observed as carefully as the great ones, since the Torah had been given as a single whole for the purpose of refining those who observe it and turning their hearts to the service of God. In this sense it was a great gift that God had given Israel, and it was now in Israel's hands to determine its application. Moses thus urged the people to "choose life," by which he meant that each individual should choose the "path of life," which would ultimately lead to rejoicing in the world to come. In his farewell song, Moses reminded the people that heaven and earth had heard their acceptance of the Torah at Mt. Sinai and told them of things to come.

When he was summoned by God to die, Moses pleaded to be allowed to continue living, but at last he ascended Mt. Nebo as God had commanded. From there he entered into heaven, or close to heaven, to contemplate not only all the land but future history as well. After his death, Moses was buried by God Himself or the angels. He was not only the greatest prophet, but the supreme philosopher and teacher, from whom the Jews and, indeed, all peoples had learned the truth about God and human life.

26

Afterword

For the swallows and storks that breed in Italy do not breed
in all lands. Do you not know that those Syrian date palms
that bear fruit in Judea cannot do so in Italy?

Varro, *Res Rusticae* 2.1.27

I HOPE that readers surveying the preceding chapters will be surprised—as
I admit I still am—at the extent to which ancient biblical interpretation has
survived "between the lines," as it were, of books like *Jubilees*, the Wisdom of
Solomon, the *Testaments of the Twelve Patriarchs*, and other writings from the
period covered. These books give eloquent testimony to the central place
accorded to the interpretation of the Bible during this period, as well as to the
resourcefulness and even, occasionally, the brilliance of its interpreters. Many
of the motifs discussed above survived into later Jewish or Christian writings
and went on to accompany and illuminate the biblical text in later centuries;
their importance can hardly be gainsaid. But to me it has seemed at least
equally important to try to identify, and to understand the exegetical thinking
behind, motifs that, for one reason or another, were passed over or misunderstood by later generations—motifs that, no less than their better-known
fellows, attest to the rich store of biblical interpretation in ancient times.

None of this, of course, is to say that this book has exhausted, or even
adequately treated, its subject. However central the Torah (Pentateuch) was to
Jews *and* Christians in antiquity, however much the interpretation of, specifically, its verses and chapters form the bulk of ancient biblical interpretation, the first five books hardly account for the total of the Bible As It Was. A
companion volume of, I am afraid, almost equal bulk could be assembled
from ancient interpretations or elaborations of material found in the rest of
the Hebrew Bible. And even with regard to the Pentateuch, much material has
had to be passed over for reasons of economy. Still, it is my hope that the
foregoing pages do represent at least a good bit of what the average Jew or
Christian in those days knew of the Bible, what the Bible *was* for most people
of the time.

To this hope is joined another: that this book may therefore help scholars
and ordinary readers to have a somewhat different picture of the Bible as a
whole from that generally presented in most high school or university courses

as well as in textbooks, introductions, and biblical commentaries. I should make it clear that I have written this book not to substitute for those others but to supplement them, and this because of my own conviction that the Bible nowadays, whatever else it may be, is more intimately connected to its past history of interpretation than most people as yet concede. I should like, in the following pages, to explain why—via a brief tour of the history of biblical interpretation after the period covered by the present volume.

The approach to Scripture—as well as many of the specific interpretations—documented in the preceding chapters proved to be decisive in the Bible's later history. As I have tried to indicate along the way, a great many of the specific motifs that first appeared in *Jubilees* or the Wisdom of Solomon or Philo were echoed in later Jewish or Christian writings of the second, third, or fourth centuries C.E. These same interpretations were then repeated, sometimes modified or elaborated but rarely abandoned, by commentators, homilists, legists, philosophers, cyclopedists, and others throughout the whole of the Middle Ages and beyond. It was especially in these later writings that the assumptions and results of ancient biblical interpretation achieved a status that might well be called canonical. Retold, cited (and alluded to more often than cited), preached, epitomized, represented physically in synagogue mosaics, church capitals, illuminated manuscripts, or stained glass windows, these interpretations essentially *became* the Bible, their message deemed to be immanent in texts which, only on the sort of pedantic examination that ordinary mortals rarely undertake, turned out not to be saying explicitly what interpreters had always said they said.

Of course, it would be wrong to suggest that biblical interpretation remained basically unchanged from the opening centuries of the common era through the end of the Middle Ages. Quite to the contrary, interpreting the Bible during this period was one of the most vibrant and dynamic fields of human endeavor. Both Jews and Christians developed existing forms and created whole new genres of scriptural exposition, and members of each group heightened the level of sophistication well beyond anything imagined by earlier interpreters. Rabbinic exegesis concentrated in particular on developing new ways of promoting all of Scripture (including, eventually, the Oral Law as well) to a single, wholly integrated, and unitary level of sanctity.[1]

1. I mean by this specifically such genres as the *petiḥta'* and the *yelammedēnu* midrashim, both of which seek to assert (by acting out) the direct relationship of the Hagiographa or the Oral Law to this or that verse from the Pentateuch. This was certainly a rabbinic innovation; see my *In Potiphar's House*, 261–264.

Christian biblical commentary, once it had regulated the doctrinal struggles and squabbles of its early centuries, came to focus on the multifarious *sensus spiritualis*, an approach that soon blossomed into the theoretical exploration (even if practical application was not always feasible) of the four senses of Scripture.[2] Still later, Jewish biblical interpretation had to wrestle with the impact of Islamic civilization. First in the East, then in medieval Spain, Arabic philosophy and grammatical and philological research had their effect on Jewish biblical *commentary* (now the principal interpretive genre). The Jewish Karaites during the same period challenged long-standing rabbinic doctrines and forced the defenders of the Rabbis to reckon with a host of new issues. Then, with the waning of the Middle Ages, Jewish mysticism created its own approach to interpreting Scripture.

Meanwhile, among Christians, the church's own internal development and, in particular, the rise of scholasticism along with the proliferation of monastic orders and the flowering of Christian scholarship within them, produced new needs in regard to Scripture and new ways of fulfilling them. Attempts to systematize Christian beliefs in the West, from their theoretical beginnings in Augustine and Boethius through Thomas Aquinas, had profound impact on the Bible's role within the church and, ultimately, on the daily life of Christians. What is more, the off-and-on encounter with Judaism (and, through it, with some of the same forces with which Judaism itself was then wrestling) was felt in Christian biblical interpretation particularly from the twelfth century onward. This encounter was hardly symmetrical from the standpoint of political power, and the Jews sometimes paid the price for speaking their minds; even when such was not directly the case, Christian reference to the *mendacia Iudaeorum* ("lies of the Jews") or, at the very least, their *fabulae*, is omnipresent in medieval Christian discourse about the Bible almost whenever the Jews are taken into account. And yet, the Jewish-Christian encounter as represented, in the high Middle Ages, at the Abbey of Saint-Victor or, somewhat later, in the *Postillae* of Nicholas of Lyra stand for something better, spots of creative interaction between two faiths that share a common Scripture.

In fact, a bird's-eye survey of these developments reveals so much variety and change that the basic elements of continuity may seem to be lost in the shuffle. They should not be. For all the dynamism of these centuries, much of the heritage of ancient biblical interpretation survived virtually unaltered. Quite apart from the welter of detail that endured from earlier times, it is important to point out that the basic attitude toward Scripture—specifically,

2. DeLubac, *Exégèse Médiévale*, remains the master treatment of this subject.

the four assumptions charted in Chapter 1—remained altogether untouched by the developments briefly surveyed above. The Bible was still, and more than ever, fundamentally cryptic, relevant, and perfect, the inspired word of God. In presenting these assumptions earlier, I stressed that there was nothing obvious or inevitable about them and that they are hardly the assumptions that readers bring to bear when reading *other* texts. That they continued to accompany the reading of Scripture throughout the Middle Ages (indeed, that they have survived, despite the great sea change to be described presently, even to the present day) is tribute enough to the enduring influence of that band of largely anonymous interpreters of Scripture whose writings have been the object of this study.

Yet the end of the Middle Ages and the start of the Renaissance do mark a new chapter in the history of biblical interpretation.[3] Why this should be so is difficult to say, but it is in any case true that this change was merely part of that great shift in human consciousness which was the Renaissance in general. The various specifics to which that shift is traditionally connected—the invention of the printing press, political changes on the Italian peninsula, and so forth—no doubt played a role, but it is difficult to believe that, in the end, factors such as these were decisive in the case of the Bible. Whatever the reasons, the fact of the change is obvious. Within the space of a century or so, biblical interpretation ceased being what it had been for so long previously, a matter of *auctoritas* and the creative elaboration of principles established for all time. Now those principles were themselves open to question—everything was open to question. Had Jerome correctly translated this verse? Had not Augustine contradicted himself here? And ought we not better understand this passage in the light of the biblical king's position at the time, or on the basis of the rules of Hebrew rhetoric, or thanks to this tradition that the Jews have passed along in their books?

Italy was the place where it began, but soon enough the new mentality and new methods of study spread elsewhere on the Continent. The names of the leading lights of this intellectual movement—Egidio Viterbo and Xanctes Pagninus, Conrad Pellican and Sebastian Münster, François Vatable, Jean LeMercier, G. G. Postel, Gilbert Genebrardus, the Scaligers, Francis Junius, Andreas Masius, B. Arias Montano, M. Flacius Illyricus, V. Schindler, and dozens more—are largely forgotten, but their way of thinking and of approaching the biblical text survive in the work of more modern biblical critics. Indeed, no modern scholar, I think, would have difficulty identifying his or her own activity with that of these men. Their interests ranged from the

---

3. I have examined this subject in somewhat greater detail in "The Bible in the University."

minutely philological (where they often had recourse to linguistic comparison, to cognates in "Chaldaic" and occasionally Arabic) to broader issues: the reliability of the Masoretic text, the system of Hebrew poetry, the authorship and unity of various books, the nature of prophecy and divine inspiration. At times they pointed out errors or impossibilities in the text; at times they proposed emendations. They referred to one another by name, and relatively frequently; references to more distant predecessors are far less common. None of this is particularly remarkable until it is juxtaposed to Christian biblical scholarship of just a century or two earlier, whose laconic, crabbed style and flat assertions (usually presented as if already known to the reader, or else bolstered by invocations of the hoariest authorities—even when, indeed, especially when, seeking slightly to modify or reinterpret the received wisdom) and whose (at times deceptively) static quality and utter submission to text and tradition all seem light years away from current notions of scholarly inquiry.

Scripture now became "ancient" and "Oriental." Both of these new perceptions were in a sense a logical extension of the activity with which the Renaissance proper had begun, namely, the learned study of and commentary on texts from ancient Greece and Rome. Following the ideas of these classicists, Renaissance biblicists too showed a concern for producing correct texts through manuscript comparison and emendation, and still more significantly, they took to heart the classicists' new appreciation of the gap between "us" and "the ancients," "our" Latin and "theirs." Israel too was an ancient people, indeed, the most ancient, so that even after all translations had been scrutinized and corrected in accordance with the most advanced information, if there nevertheless remained expressions, sentiments, or ideas that seemed foreign or even repugnant, Renaissance scholars were less likely to attribute the difficulties to the domain of "mysteries" or divine caprice. They no longer automatically believed, with Augustine, that anything that contradicts doctrine or simply does not concern right conduct or questions of faith must therefore be interpreted figuratively (*De Doctrina Christiana* 3.10.14). They were more likely to explain such deviations with reference to some feature native to the language or culture of Israel, for Israel was distant from themselves, distant in both time and space. The ancient and Oriental way of saying things was not necessarily their own way, and so the *Hebraismus*, the *proprietas* of that language, had to be appreciated for what it was. By extension, the ancient and Oriental way of telling a story, preaching a sermon, or even conceiving of things divine, was bound to be different from that of more modern non-Orientals, and this difference alone could account for much that had previously been inscrutable in Scripture.

With all this, the aim of biblical study imperceptibly began to change (again, spurred by the classical model) from learning *from* Scripture to learning *about* Scripture. Bible study increasingly became dependent on the tools of research and a knowledge of the Bible's origins and manner of composition, the historical circumstances in which it was created and transmitted; these subjects themselves became the curriculum. It did not happen all at once, and precisely because "from" and "about" were so easily commingled, even as it did happen this all-important change was not recognized for what it was.

And yet . . . few institutions are so resistant to change as the establishments of religion. One might well ask how so fundamental a shift, even if some of its far-reaching consequences were unperceived at first, could have been allowed to take place by those institutions which had theretofore championed so different a view of the Bible and its proper study. The answer, or at least part of the answer, is that a fundamental alliance had been forged from the very beginning between the new biblical scholarship and the Protestant Reformation.

Biblical scholarship had itself certainly played a role (still, my sense is, somewhat underappreciated) in precipitating the Reformation. For it was not merely a revulsion at the sale of indulgences and the like, but the growing conviction (fostered by the new science) that the Bible might not really mean what the church had been saying it meant all these years, that emboldened the Reformers to throw off the church's authority in all things. This perception, once embodied in diverse critical insights here and there into the biblical text, soon announced its own political potential. Scripture interpreted aright had a power of its own, one that might well topple that of entrenched but merely human authority. Luther's famous words before Emperor Charles V at the Diet of Worms in 1521 are still eloquent in their opposing of these two:

> Unless I be convinced by evidence of Scripture or by plain reason—for I do not accept the authority of the Pope or the councils alone, since it is demonstrated that they have often erred and contradicted themselves—I am bound by the Scriptures I have cited, and my conscience is captive to the Word of God. I cannot and will not recant anything, for it is neither sage nor right to go against conscience. God help. Amen.

Here much is made apparent in few words: the enthronement of Scripture (along with "plain reason") as supreme authority; the pointed opposition of this authority to that of the pope; and finally, the suggestion that the latter's errors and contradictions in, among other things, scriptural interpretation have ultimately invalidated the church's very authority. Almost from the start, the central issue was what Luther elsewhere called the pope's "right of interpreting Sacred Scripture by the sole virtue and majesty of his exalted office and power, against all intelligence and erudition"[4]—the latter two being, of course, the hallmarks of recent biblical scholarship.

If the modern movement of biblical scholarship helped to make the Reformers' stance more than that of mere malcontents or religious opportunists, the Protestant denominations that they founded subsequently provided biblical scholarship with its greatest ongoing sponsor. Surely it is no coincidence that biblical scholarship over the last two centuries in particular has been almost exclusively a Protestant activity, pursued in Germany, England, Scandinavia, and America, and only to a much lesser extent, and with far less impressive results, in the traditionally Catholic parts of Europe. This is of course not to say that the church from the beginning turned its back on the new learning. On the contrary, it is remarkable the extent to which, instead of just sticking to tradition and vehemently invoking the unbroken chain of church authority in all its force, Catholic scholars themselves sometimes argued as learned Hebraists, and their efforts as exegetes in the sixteenth century were sometimes indistinguishable from those of their Protestant contemporaries. A knowledge of Hebrew, to whatever ideology's service it was put, passed in that century from being the sign of a truly erudite scholar to being simply the *sine qua non* for undertaking serious Old Testament work. Indeed, it was in the sixteenth century that Hebrew entered the mainstream of education, and a solid trilingual foundation—in Latin, Greek, and Hebrew— was now at the heart of humanistic studies in the emerging institutions of higher learning in Europe.[5] With the passage of time, however, and the development of biblical scholarship's own internal dynamic, it became more and more of a distinctly Protestant enterprise, and this is obviously related to the institutional factors cited—or has been until the last half-century or so. In our own day biblical scholarship has lost most of its denominational coloring and, in North America at least, has recently moved its intellectual center from the seminary to the university's Department of Religious (or Near Eastern) Studies.

In any case, this whole course of events has dramatically affected the way the Bible is perceived, and taught, in our own day. It is certainly no accident that, as suggested earlier, only "half" of the Bible's story has generally been

4. "Assertio Omnium Articulorum M. Lutheri per Bullam Leonis X, Novissimam Damnatorum" in his *Werke*, 7:96.

5. Goshen-Gottstein, "Humanism and the Flowering of Jewish Studies—From the Christian to the Jewish Renaissance."

found worthy of study in universities, for example. Courses there—elsewhere as well—tend to be devoted exclusively to what, with some justification, might rather be called the "pre-Bible." Students are led backward through the stages of individual biblical books' composition, breaking things down to their putative original components, which can then be studied and explained in terms of the political or social history of the ancient Near East. None of this is particularly harmful, I think, but the fact that this is *all* most students are likely ever to know about the Bible certainly is. How difficult would it be for such courses to be reconfigured so as to complete the picture, moving from the "pre-Bible"—whether the subject be the Pentateuch or Isaiah or the Psalter—to the Bible proper, those same chapters or books as they were known to, *and interpreted by,* Jews and Christians in the formative centuries that are the focus of the present study?

That is, God's covenant with Abraham in Genesis 15 is certainly illuminated by a knowledge of the conventions of covenants and treaties apparent in those that have survived from the ancient Near East; discussions of the historicity of the Exodus, the identity of the pharaoh in question, the participating tribes, and so forth likewise illuminate any treatment of the first half of the book of Exodus. However, for the reasons already outlined, it seems to me a terrible distortion to make these *all,* or even most, of what is said about those chapters. Certainly for most of the Bible's history what was important about Abraham and his covenant with God were precisely those things that such a treatment is likely to omit, namely—"Abraham the Monotheist" and "Abraham Saw a Dire Future," or, with regard to the Exodus, "Divine Punishment of the Egyptians," "Egyptians Gave Willingly," and "The (Paschal) Lamb of God." The point is not a subtle one, and yet, alas, it still needs to be made.

To be sure, the picture has begun to change. In part this change is due to recent developments in the study of the Bible's formative period itself. The discovery of the Dead Sea Scrolls starting in the late 1940s has spurred a new interest in the closing centuries before the common era and the first century of the common era. Historians, archaeologists, linguists, and others have focused on this period as never before. Those scrolls contain not only biblical manuscripts and compositions specific to the community proper, but as well works like *Jubilees* and other biblical Apocrypha and Pseudepigrapha. As a result, these fields too are currently enjoying unprecedented popularity. The study of the New Testament and other aspects of early Christianity have likewise been revitalized by these same events.

Among other things, these developments have helped to break down the barrier assumed to exist between, on the one hand, the Bible itself and, on the other, the postbiblical activity called interpretation. What numerous seminal studies in the last two decades have demonstrated is that biblical interpretation was an ongoing process that began well within the biblical period itself—in fact, rather early within the biblical period. Later writers interpreted earlier texts and elaborated them, modified them, sometimes extended them or simply rewrote them. This process, well in evidence in preexilic material in the Hebrew Bible, then built with growing force following the Babylonian exile until it reached the heights of energy and creativity documented in the very writings surveyed in this volume, some of which, at least, predate the composition of the last parts of the Hebrew Bible. In other words, modern scholarship, for its own reasons, has come to break down utterly the chronological separation between *writing,* seen as belonging to the biblical period, and *interpreting,* previously largely thought to be postbiblical.

With the disappearance of this barrier has come, I think, a new respect for those most ancient interpreters and interpolators and redactors, *verba* that are not *ipsissima,* the theological "spin" put on ancient narratives and oracles by those anonymous figures who sought divine guidance in all the sacred writings that had survived from an earlier day. Their work, though perhaps less ambitious and far-reaching than that of later interpreters, is cut from the same cloth, suggesting a fundamental continuity between the Bible's own writers and compilers and those (only somewhat later) interpreters whose writings have been my subject.

In view especially of this most recent turn in the course of biblical scholarship, it has been, as I say, one of my hopes in compiling this book that ancient biblical interpretation might more commonly be studied side by side with the Bible itself. This may be a naive goal, but I believe not. Indeed, for one final reason now to be mentioned, I think that such study of ancient interpretation alongside that of the Bible itself may indeed find support "from another place" (Esth. 4:14).

I will be revealing no secrets in saying that the fruits of the modern scholarly movement surveyed above have ultimately been somewhat unsettling to traditional religious belief. The central role played by the Bible in Judaism and the various Christian denominations could not but be undermined by scholarship that has sought to demonstrate that books previously thought to be of unitary authorship are in fact the work of different hands and different periods, that narratives previously conceived to impart moral lessons are to be reunderstood as shabby political allegories, and that the revered prophecies of this or that honored figure should rather be explained as *vaticinia ex eventu.* All this, and much more, has been the legacy of the great change in the direction and tenor of biblical scholarship that the Renaissance inaugurated and the Reformation took up and made its own.

My purpose in surveying the history of modern biblical scholarship has hardly been to bemoan its rise, nor yet to indict specifically the Protestant movement for the disquieting effect that this scholarship has had on traditional beliefs. (However much the beginnings of this discipline were allied with the rise of the Protestant denominations, in the end the force that has driven biblical scholarship to its disturbing conclusions has been scarcely different from the force that drove Galileo or Darwin or Einstein to theirs.) But what I intend by raising the matter of modern biblical scholarship's disturbing conclusions is to suggest one final reason for which the material studied on the previous pages ought to be of interest to all readers of the Bible nowadays.

The pioneers of modern biblical scholarship did not, by and large, address themselves to the subject of ancient biblical interpretation, save of course to denounce its conclusions as fanciful and wrong-headed. But this fact alone is sufficient to indicate the extent to which these scholars failed to understand the mission upon which they were embarked. For them, the heritage of ancient biblical interpretation was no more than a source of obscurity, an obstacle to the proper appreciation of what, with a naïveté which from the perspective of the late twentieth century can only be described as touching, some biblical critics liked to refer to as the "real Bible." That Bible was just waiting to be discovered underneath the accumulated misconceptions of centuries of sermonizing and religious posturing. Not all, to be sure, shared in this illusion, but enough did—still driven by the residue of that initial surge of Protestant energy—so that, even with the uncertainty or hesitations of more insightful biblicists, the "pre-Bible" nonetheless became the true one, a grail whose curative powers were sure to work their magic once its precise location could definitively be pinned down.

What is, as I say, naive about this view is its failure to take into account the crucial role played by ancient interpreters in the very emergence of the Bible. It was to them, and not, by and large, to the biblical texts themselves, that we owe each of the four assumptions described in Chapter 1; and it was these assumptions that made the Bible—more than most modern biblicists ever dreamed—*biblical.* Failing to understand this, what the modern critical movement set about doing was returning biblical texts to the state they were in before there was a Bible, which is to say, turning the unitary, seamless, Word of God into the contradictory, seamy, words of different men and schools and periods.

It is difficult not to sympathize with the thinking that led to this impasse.

Was it not in the ear of Moses, Isaiah, or Jeremiah that the divine word had been whispered? These were the true prophets, and anything that was not theirs—the work of anonymous redactors or editors or scribes—ought simply to be done away with as lacking any standing or authority. (And so it was, and still largely is today.) How much less was the standing or authority of those who were not even bearers of the texts, but mere commentators, retellers, interpreters! Certainly their activity could be of no consequence to the real meaning of the Bible—for if it was, then the whole edifice of biblical authority, predicated on the direct whispering of the divine voice in those prophetic ears, threatened to topple in any case.

Given such a mentality, one can scarcely wonder that this scholarly movement, enlisting the considerable talents of European and American savants for more than three centuries, pursued so single-mindedly a goal that would ultimately prove so destructive to the object of their study. For what these scholars generally failed to realize was that the far-reaching consequence of their researches would be the separation of biblical texts from the great, fostering environment of ancient interpretation which had allowed the Bible to emerge in the first place, that is, which had allowed its diverse members to be combined into the great, unitary, sacred corpus that would occupy the central place that Scripture did occupy, and still does, in Judaism and Christianity.

To put it another way, the spindly sapling of texts that began to sprout even before the first millennium B.C.E. was only enabled to grow into the great date palm of Scripture thanks to the nourishing presence of the ancient interpretations, and interpretive *assumptions,* that soon enveloped and strengthened its roots. This vital soil, in itself endowed with all the nutrients of human piety, fortified with the heaven-sent, engendering liqueurs of rain and dew, and, let it be said, no stranger to the benefits of an occasional admixture of natural fertilizing agents—this soil was what allowed the tree to take root and flourish. The mission upon which modern biblical scholarship set out, then, without quite understanding it, was to uproot Scripture from that soil the better to study the whole plant and the plant alone. The result, seen from such a perspective, was altogether predictable, unavoidable even.

"After such knowledge, what forgiveness?" The fate of the Bible in the modern world is certainly not the subject of the anthologist or compiler. I may, however, permit myself the parting observation that, if modern scholarship has been slow in recognizing the central role in the development of the Bible played by its earliest interpreters, this realization has now at last begun to make itself felt within the field of biblical theology proper. With it comes another kind of disquiet, for an awareness of the interpreter's crucial role inevitably leads to a hermeneutic of far less simple-minded appeal than the one that had prevailed for so many centuries. Such difficulty notwithstanding, it seems clear to me that, willy-nilly, the decisive part played by the anonymous biblical interpreters of the centuries just before and after the start of the common era must ultimately be recognized in any new disposition of biblical theology's forces. The activity of ancient biblical interpreters was a—perhaps *the*—striking instance of how interpretation is inevitably a kind of second authorship. It was *their* Bible, and no ragtag collection of ancient Near Eastern texts, that was canonized in the closing centuries of the Second Temple period, and their Bible is, to an extent with which all who love God's word must reckon, ours today.

Abbreviations

Terms and Sources

Bibliography

Illustration Credits

Index

Abbreviations

AB: Analecta Biblica
AJS Review: Association for Jewish Studies Review
ANRW: Aufstieg und Niedergang der römischen Welt
AOT: Apocryphal Old Testament, ed. H. F. D. Sparks (Oxford: Clarendon, 1984)
APAT: Die Apocryphen und Pseudepigraphen des Alten Testaments, ed. E. Kautsch (Tübingen: Mohr, 1900)
APOT: The Apocrypha and Pseudepigrapha of the Old Testament, ed. R. H. Charles (Oxford: Clarendon, 1963)
ASE: Annali di storia dell'esegesi
AusBR: Australian Biblical Review
AUSS: Andrews University Seminar Studies
BASOR: Bulletin of the American Schools of Oriental Research
BI: Bar Ilan (Annual)
BJRL: Bulletin of the John Rylands Library
BO: Bibbia e Oriente
BS: Biblia Sacra
CBQ: Catholic Bible Quarterly
C.N.R.S.: Centre National de Recherches Scientifiques
CRJANT: Compendia Rerum Judaicarum ad Novum Testamentum
CTJ: Calvin Theological Journal
DJD: Discoveries in the Judaean Desert
DSD: Dead Sea Discoveries
EB: Estudios Biblicos
EJL: Early Jewish Literature (SBL series)
ETL: Ephemerides Theologicae Lovienses
EY: Eretz Yisrael
GCS: Die griechischen christlichen Schriftsteller der ersten drei Jahrhunderten
HAR: Hebrew Annual Review
HSL: Hebrew University Studies in Literature
HSM: Harvard Semitic Monographs
HTR: Harvard Theological Review
HUCA: Hebrew Union College Annual
IEJ: Israel Exploration Journal
Int: *Interpretation*
JAOS: Journal of the American Oriental Society
JBL: Journal of Biblical Literature
JEA: Journal of Egyptian Archaeology
JETS: Journal of the Evangelical Theological Society
JJS: Journal of Jewish Studies

JLA: Jewish Law Annual
JNES: Journal of Near Eastern Studies
JQR: Jewish Quarterly Review
JR: Journal of Religion
JSJ: Journal for the Study of Judaism in the Persian, Hellenistic, and Roman Periods
JSNT: Journal for the Study of the New Testament
JSOT: Journal for the Study of the Old Testament
JSOTSS: Journal for the Study of the Old Testament Supplement Series
JSP: Journal for the Study of the Pseudepigrapha
JSQ: Jewish Studies Quarterly
JSS: Journal of Semitic Studies
JThS: Journal of Theological Studies
JTS: Jewish Theological Seminary
KI: Kirche und Israel
LCL: Loeb Classical Library (Harvard University Press)
MC: Miscelanea Comillas
MGWJ: Monatschrift für Geschichte und Wissenschaft des Judentums
NRT: Nouvelle Revue Théologique
NT: Novum Testamentum
NTS: New Testament Studies
OS: Oudtestamentlische Studien
OTP: Old Testament Pseudepigrapha, 2 vols., ed. J. Charlesworth (Garden City, N.Y.: Doubleday, 1983–1985)
PAAJR: Proceedings of the American Academy of Jewish Research
PG: Patrologiae cursus completus: Patrologia Graeca-Latina, ed. J. P. Migne (Paris: Migne, 1857–1866)
PL: Patrologiae cursus completus: Patrologia Latina, ed. J. P. Migne (Paris: Migne, 1857–1866)
QAY: Qobeṣ 'al Yad
RB: Revue Biblique
REJ: Revue des Etudes Juives
RHdR: Revue de l'Histoire des Réligions
RHR: Revue d'Histoire Réligieuse
RiB: Rivista Biblica
RQ: Revue de Qumran
RSR: Revue de Sciences Réligieuses
SBL: Society of Biblical Literature
SC: The Second Century
SCS: Septuagint and Cognate Studies (series of SBL)
SP: Studia Philonica
SPat: Studia Patristica
SR: Studies in Religion
ST: Scripta Theologica
STJD: Studies on the Texts from the Judaean Desert
TAPA: Transactions of the American Philological Association
TB: Tyndale Bulletin
TS: Theological Studies

VC: *Vigiliae Christianae*
VT: *Vetus Testamentum*
VTS: *Vetus Testamentum Supplements*
ZAW: *Zeitschrift für die Alttestamentliche Wissenschaft*
ZNW: *Zeitschrift für die Neutestamentliche Wissenschaft*

Terms and Sources

An asterisk marks terms and sources for which there is a separate entry.

(4Q540–541) Aaronic Text A: One of the *Dead Sea Scrolls, this text was found at *Qumran and originally thought to be an independent composition centering on the biblical figure of Aaron, Moses' brother. More recently, it has been identified as possibly a part of the *Aramaic Levi Document, fragments of which were discovered in the *Cairo Genizah as well as at Qumran, and itself related to the Levi section of the *Testaments of the Twelve Patriarchs. See Puesch, "Fragments d'un apocryphe de Lévi."

Abot deR. Natan: A collection of elaborations and interpretation of biblical texts presented in the form of a commentary on the mishnaic tractate *Abot* (since this tractate is sometimes called in English "[Sayings of] the Fathers," *Abot deR. Natan* is sometimes referred to as *The Fathers according to R. Nathan*). The text is preserved in two versions, A and B, printed side by side in the edition of S. Schechter, *Abot de Rabbi Nathan.* (The two versions have been translated individually into English by J. Goldin and A. Saldarini respectively.) However, a recent study, M. Kister's "Avot de-Rabbi Nathan: Studies in Text, Redaction and Interpretation" (unpublished doctoral dissertation, Hebrew University of Jerusalem, 1993), has shown that version A in fact survives in two principal branches which are quite distinct from each other. Kister's study strongly asserts the need for a new critical edition of the texts. As to dating, Kister concludes that while the "origins" of this text may belong to the end of the tannaitic period (late second century C.E.), the extant versions themselves can hardly be dated earlier than the sixth century C.E. "at the very earliest." All translations mine.

Acts of Andrew: A New Testament apocryphon recounting the bravery of a Christian martyr condemned to death by crucifixion. Translation: James, *The Apocryphal New Testament.*

Acts of the Apostles: A New Testament book continuing the narrative of the gospel of Luke (the two were written by a single author); Acts recounts the story of the Christian movement and its various leaders, including a large section devoted to the life of *Paul. It has been dated to c. 80–85 C.E. Translation: Revised Standard Version, sometimes modified slightly.

Acts of Pilate: see *Gospel of Nicodemus

(4Q370) Admonition on the Flood: This brief *Qumran text was published and translated by Newsom, "An Apocryphon on the Flood Narrative."

(4Q180–181) Ages of Creation: see *Pesher of the Periods

aggadah: see *halakhah

Aggadat Bereshit: A collection of twenty-eight homilies on Genesis and related readings in the prophets and psalms. This text has been dated to the tenth century of the common era. Text: Buber, *Aggadat Bereshit.* All translations mine.

Ahiqar, (Aramaic) Sayings of: This very ancient text (perhaps mid-sixth century B.C.E.) circulated widely in the ancient Near East. It contains no biblical interpretation per se, but has been cited here once or twice because of certain parallels to themes found among ancient interpreters. Translation: Lindenberger in Charlesworth, *OTP* 2:494–507.

al-Asaṭir (Kitāb): A Samaritan apocryphon that recounts and elaborates biblical history, focusing on the figures of Adam, Noah, Abraham, and Moses. The book itself is ascribed to Moses but was actually composed in medieval times; however, it contains many earlier interpretive motifs. Text: Ben-Ḥayyim, "The Book of Asatir." All translations mine.

Alexander Polyhistor: Ancient historian cited by *Eusebius of Caesarea, *Jerome, and other interpreters. He was born c. 105 B.C.E. and wrote his history of the Jews, Samaritans, and other peoples sometime during the latter half of the first century B.C.E. His work in turn sometimes cites earlier sources, Jewish and Samaritan.

allegorical interpretation: A way of explaining Scripture whereby people, places, and events are held to stand for abstract or nonmaterial entities, such as temptation, the soul, and so forth. This form of interpretation, championed by *Philo of Alexandria and his Alexandrian Jewish predecessors and, among Christians, by *Clement of Alexandria and *Origen (and, to a lesser extent, by later figures as well) is to be distinguished from *typological interpretation.

Alphabet of Ben Sira: A composite Jewish text, part of it satirical, written in perhaps the ninth or tenth century C.E.; it contains an account of Ben Sira's conception and subsequent events, followed by a series of proverbs and commentaries. Edition: Yassif, *The Tales of Ben Sira in the Middle Ages,* identified here by page number. (On this edition, see Dan's review in *Qiryat Sefer.*) All translations mine.

Alphabet of R. Aqiba: see *'Otiyot deR. Aqiba

Ambrose of Milan (c. 339–397 C.E.): Bishop of Milan and an influential author, interpreter, and hymnist. Most citations from Ambrose herein are from McHugh, *Saint Ambrose.*

amora'im: see *Rabbis, the

'Amram, Visions of (or *Testament of*): see *Visions of 'Amram

Ancient Synagogal Prayers: see *Hellenistic Synagogal Prayers

Aphrahat (the Persian; also Aphraates): An early representative of Syriac Christianity, Aphrahat flourished in the mid-fourth century C.E. I have cited from this source relatively rarely, the connection of Aphrahat's writings to, specifically, biblical interpretation preserved in rabbinic texts having been amply demonstrated by Ginzberg, *Die Haggada* and *Legends,* as well as in Funk, *Die Haggadische Elemente in den Homilien des Aphraates.* All citations are taken from this last work.

apocalypse (in general): see *Pseudepigrapha

Apocalypse of Abraham: An account of Abraham's recognition of the folly of idol-worship and a subsequent revelation to him of heavenly secrets. (In my opinion this text may have been influenced by the *Ladder of Jacob,* with which it shares a number of common elements.) The text survives only in various Slavic translations; it was rendered into Slavonic either directly from Hebrew or through an intermediary Greek translation. Principal text: the edition and manuscript variants found in Rubinkiewicz, *L'Apocalypse d'Abraham en Vieux Slave;* also consulted: Philonenko-Sayar and Philonenko, *L'Apocalypse d'Abraham,* and the two editions printed in Tikhonravov, *Pamyatniki,* 32–57. All translations mine.

Apocalypse of Adam: A gnostic treatise found in the *Nag Hammadi library in the form of a revelation given to Adam and communicated to his son Seth. The treatise may be among the earliest Nag Hammadi documents, perhaps going back to the first or second century C.E. Translation: MacRae in Charlesworth, *OTP* 1:707–719.

Apocalypse of Elijah: In its present form a Christian treatise on various subjects. The final redaction of the *Apocalypse of Elijah* has been dated to the latter part of the third century C.E. However, its first section, at least, with its reference to "the fast" (that of the Day of Atonement), is evidently of Jewish origin, and the same is true of other sections as well. If these Jewish parts were, like the rest, originally composed in Greek, then Alexandria would seem to be a probable provenance for them and they would then likely not have been written after the first century C.E. Translation: Wintermute in Charlesworth, *OTP* 1:721–753.

Apocalypse of Moses: See, for description, *Life of Adam and Eve.* Translation: Johnson in Charlesworth, *OTP* 2:249–778, sometimes modified on the basis of the text in Bertrand, *La vie grecque d'Adam et Eve.*

Apocalypse of Paul: see *Revelation of Paul*

Apocalypse of Sedrach: A late Greek treatise of composite character; while its final form has been dated to the tenth or eleventh centuries C.E., some scholars have suggested that part of it is based on earlier materials going back to the opening centuries of the common era. Translation: Agourides in Charlesworth, *OTP* 1:605–613.

Apocrypha (Greek: "hidden things," that is, things to be hidden away): A collection of writings, mostly from the end of the biblical period, that were accepted by early Christians as Scripture but that, because they were eventually excluded from the Jewish Bible, came to be regarded by many later Christians as belonging to a special category. They were included in the Bible of Western Christianity, but under the name "Apocrypha"; later, many Protestant churches excluded them in part or in toto from their canon. These books are, along with the *Pseudepigrapha, particularly interesting to biblical scholars, since many of them contain retellings of biblical stories or reflections on particular passages or people in the Bible, and thus can provide us with a snapshot of how parts of the Bible were being interpreted from the third century B.C.E. onward. Among the best known books of the Apocrypha are *Sira[ch], *Wisdom of Solomon, *Judith, *Baruch, the Letter of *Jeremiah, Susanna, 1 and 2 *Maccabees, and Tobit.

(11Q11) Apocryphal Psalms[a]: The remnant of what appears to have been a collection of pseudo-Davidic psalms concluding with a somewhat reworked version of Psalm 91. The

manuscript, found at *Qumran, belongs to the late first century B.C.E.; the date of the psalms' composition is unknown. A theme in the surviving part of the manuscript is the opposition to devils and alien spirits. Text: Puech, "Les deux derniers psaumes davidiques du rituel d'exorcisme." All translations mine.

(4Q464) Apocryphon^b (or An Exposition on the Patriarchs): a *Qumran text whose manuscript dates from the late first century B.C.E. (though the text itself may well have been composed earlier). It is cited here from Stone and Eshel, "An Exposition on the Patriarchs (4Q464)," and Eshel and Stone, "The Holy Tongue at the End of Days."

Apocryphon of John (Secret Book of John): An important gnostic work dealing with the creation and highlighting the role of the (lower) creator-god Ialdabaoth. This treatise, found in the *Nag Hammadi library, may not have been known as such to *Irenaeus, but its main ideas are certainly reflected in his *Against the Heresies* and thus existed before 185 C.E. Translation: Layton, *Gnostic Scriptures*, 23–51; *The Coptic Nag Hammadi Library.*

(4Q374) Apocryphon of Moses A: A very fragmentary *Qumran manuscript from the early Herodian period; it apparently retold or referred to biblical history, specifically the Egyptian exodus. The text seems not to have been composed by members of the Qumran community but to have been brought there from elsewhere. It was published by Newsom, "4Q374: A Discourse on the Exodus/Conquest Tradition." All translations mine.

Apostolic Constitutions: A composition of eight volumes written in the late fourth century C.E. The first six volumes are based in large measure on the *Didascalia Apostolorum; scattered through the seventh and eighth are prayers, some of which appear to be remnants of ancient Jewish synagogal compositions of a considerably earlier period. See *Hellenistic Synagogal Prayers.

Apuleius, Lucius (fl. 155 C.E.): Born in Madauros, Numidia, Apuleius is best known for his bawdy narrative *The Golden Ass;* he mentions Moses and "Johannes" (apparently, Jannes) as prominent magicians in *Apologia*. Translation: Butler, *The Apologia and Florida of Apuleius.*

Aquila, Symmachus, and *Theodotion:* The authors of three post-*Septuagint translations of the Bible into Greek. All three were included in *Origen's *Hexapla* (composed around 230–245), a work that presented for comparison the Hebrew text of the Bible, a transcription of that text into Greek letters, an edition of the Septuagint translation, and these three later Greek versions. Unfortunately, the *Hexapla* itself has been lost, perhaps a victim of its very bulk (it ran to nearly seven thousand pages); all that survives of these three versions are scattered fragments and citations here and there. The date and interrelationship of these three translations is in dispute, but they all seem to belong to the second century C.E. They themselves differ in translation "style," Aquila's being rather literal, Theodotion's and Symmachus' somewhat freer. As revisions of the Septuagint version, they shed light on the later development of interpretive traditions. An edition of most (but not all) surviving fragments was published by Field, *Origenis Hexaplorum quae supersunt.* All translations mine.

Aramaic Levi Document (The *Qumran fragments of this text were for a long while identified by the siglum "1Q and 4QTestLevi ar^a" and so on, though the sigla [1Q21] *Aramaic Levi*, [4Q213] *Aramaic Levi^a*, and [4Q214] *Aramaic Levi^b*, etc., have begun to be used; [4Q540–41] *Aaronic Text A* may also be part of this same text): An Aramaic text, parts of which were first found in the *Cairo Genizah and later at *Qumran. It was at first taken to be the "original" version of which the Greek *Testament of Levi* was thought to be a translation (see *Testaments of the Twelve Patriarchs*); now scholars know the relationship of the two texts to be somewhat more complicated. The oldest Qumran copy has been dated to the second century B.C.E.; if Milik's theory of a priestly "trilogy" is correct (see *Visions of 'Amram*), then this text may be considerably earlier, though probably not as early as Milik himself has suggested (third century B.C.E., "if not towards the end of the fourth"; *Books of Enoch* 24). On the relationship of this text to *Jubilees*, see Kugel, "Levi's Elevation." All translations mine.

Aristeas, Letter of: see *Letter of Aristeas*

Aristobulus: Sometimes described as the first known Hellenistic Jewish philosopher, Aristobulus lived in Ptolemaic Egypt, apparently in the mid-second century B.C.E. He is said to have written extensive, allegorical commentaries on Scripture, though only a few fragments of his writings have survived in citations from later, Christian, writers. Aristobulus argued that Greek wisdom had originally come from Jewish sages. In the cultural encounter between Judaism and Hellenism, he is thus less syncretistic than *Artapanus but somewhat less reactionary than, say, the author of the third Sibylline oracle. With regard to the allegorical interpretation of Scripture, one might see a chain of tradition originating with Aristobulus and extending to the author of the *Letter of Aristeas*, the *Wisdom of Solomon, *Philo of Alexandria, *Clement of Alexandria, to *Origen and later writers. Text and translation consulted: Eusebius, *La Préparation Évangélique*; translation: Collins in Charlesworth, *OTP* 2:831–842.

Armenian Apocrypha (of the Hebrew Bible): A number of exegetical motifs have survived in apocryphal writings preserved in Armenian. In this book I have included citations from two collections of Armenian apocrypha, Issaverdens, *Uncanonical Writings of the Old Testament*, and Stone, *Armenian Apocrypha Relating to the Patriarchs and Prophets*. Translations are by the respective authors of these collections and identified by author and page number.

Artapanus: A Hellenistic author cited by *Alexander Polyhistor and, subsequently, *Eusebius (and reflected as well in *Clement of Alexandria's *Miscellanies*). The three surviving fragments of Artapanus' work—which was apparently entitled *Concerning the Jews*—relate to Abraham, Joseph, and Moses. This treatise may belong to the second century B.C.E., though even this broad dating is only approximate. Its heterodox and syncretistic character led some earlier scholars to suggest that its author was not Jewish, but most studies of Artapanus nowadays seem to reject this notion. Text and translation: Holladay, *Fragments from Hellenistic Jewish Authors*, vol. 1; also Collins in Charlesworth, *OTP* 2:897–903.

Assumption of Moses: A text, which survives in incomplete form and only in Latin, consisting largely of Moses' farewell speech to Joshua just before his death. Scholars have generally dated the original text's composition to the early first century C.E.; it was apparently cited by the author of the New Testament Epistle of Jude, 9. Text: Tromp, *The Assumption of Moses;* all translations mine. Tromp, while agreeing with other scholars that the Latin text is indeed a translation from a Greek version, casts doubt on the contention of most that this Greek text was in turn a rendering of a Semitic (Hebrew or Aramaic) original. On this matter, however, the common wisdom is most likely correct.

Athanasius (c. 296–377): Bishop of Alexandria, theologian, and the author of various treatises. Text and translation: Athanasius of Alexandria, *Contra Gentes.*

Augustine of Hippo (354–430): Highly influential Christian thinker and theologian; there is scarcely a more important figure in the history of Western Christianity. Born in North Africa, Augustine adopted for a time the dualistic faith of Manichaeism before returning to Christianity (his mother's religion); he was baptized in 387. In seeking to combat the heresies of his day, Augustine gradually came to articulate his own understanding of Christian teaching in a number of separate works. In this book I have cited primarily from his magnum opus, *The City of God,* particularly books 14–16; though even this section of the work could hardly be described as merely one of biblical exegesis, the interpretations contained or presumed within it went on to play a highly significant role in subsequent understandings of Scripture in the West. Text and translation: Augustine, *The City of God against the Pagans;* I have, however, retranslated a number of passages myself.

Azariah, Prayer of: see *Prayer of Azariah

b.: Appears in Hebrew or Aramaic names as an abbreviation for *ben* or *bar,* "son of"; also stands for *B(abylonian Talmud), just preceding the name of the tractate, thus b. *Pesaḥim* 34a.

B.C.E.: before the common era (="B.C.").

Babylonian Talmud: A massive compendium of Jewish learning and biblical exegesis redacted in Babylon in the fifth and early sixth centuries C.E. but containing a great deal of earlier material. Organized in the form of a digressive commentary on the *Mishnah, it ends up citing and explaining much of the Hebrew Bible and is thus a valuable collection of rabbinic biblical interpretation. All translations mine.

Barnabas, Letter of (or *Epistle of*): see *Letter of Barnabas

Baruch, book of (or *1 Baruch*): The first of several works attributed to Baruch, Jeremiah's scribe. It was probably composed sometime in the second century B.C.E., though its apparently composite character and ambiguous affiliations make dating quite difficult. Translation: Revised Standard Version of the Bible with Apocrypha, sometimes modified slightly.

2 Baruch (or *Syriac Apocalypse of Baruch*): This book survives in a Syriac version of an apparently Greek text that itself may well be a translation of an originally Hebrew work. It purports to contain Baruch's account of the fall of Jerusalem and subsequent laments, divine revelations of the future, and discussions of divine justice. The text was apparently written in the wake of the Romans' destruction of the Jerusalem Temple and is therefore dated to the late first century C.E. It bears some affinities to *4 Ezra and contains much material of interest to the history of ancient biblical interpretation. Translation: Klijn in Charles, *APOT* 1:615–652. Also consulted: Bogaert, *Apocalypse de Baruch.*

3 Baruch (also *Greek Apocalypse of Baruch*): This book survives in two forms, Slavonic and Greek; these may, but not necessarily do, stem from a text originally composed in a Semitic language. This brief text may have been written in the late first or second century C.E. Translation of both the Slavonic and Greek texts by Gaylord in Charlesworth, *OTP* 1:653–679.

4 Baruch (or *Parale[i]pomena Ieremiou* or *Things Omitted from Jeremiah*): This book briefly recounts the destruction of the Jerusalem Temple and subsequent events. The text was probably originally composed in Hebrew but survives in Greek and other languages. Some elements seem to connect it, or at least one form of the text, to the time of the Bar Kokhba revolt (Kugel, *In Potiphar's House*, 173–213), and it contains a few items of interest to the history of biblical interpretation. Text and translation (occasionally modified): Kraft and Purintun, *Paraleipomena Jeremiou.*

(4Q559) Biblical Chronology: A fragmentary Aramaic text from *Qumran that presents a genealogical chain which apparently stretched from Abraham through (at least) the period of the Judges. Translation mine.

Book of Adam: A book belonging to the "secondary Adam literature": see *Life of Adam and Eve.*

Book of the Bee: A late (thirteenth-century C.E.) retelling of biblical material containing many ancient interpretive expansions, some of these found as well in the *Cave of Treasures.* Syriac and Arabic texts with translation: Budge, *Book of the Bee.*

(1Q23, 4Q203, 530, 531, and 6Q8) Book of Giants: A group of Aramaic texts from *Qumran closely related to *1 Enoch*, but which J. T. Milik has suggested existed as a separate work identified as the *Book of Giants.* The existence of such a work had been known from a passing reference to it in the Gelasian Decree (sixth century C.E.); earlier this century W. B. Henning succeeded in reconstructing part of the book from fragments of a Manichaean version of it preserved in different middle Iranian manuscripts. (See further Henning, "The Book of Giants"; Milik, *Books of Enoch*, 298–339; Reeves, *Jewish Lore in Manichaean Cosmogony.*) Milik recognized that the Qumran Aramaic texts might indeed contain the original *Book of Giants.* The Qumran texts seem to date from as early as the last third of the first century B.C.E., but the time of the book's composition is conceivably still earlier. All translations mine.

C. E.: common era (= "A. D.").

Cairo Genizah: The name conventionally given to a storeroom of old manuscripts located adjacent to a synagogue in Fostat (Old Cairo), Egypt. The existence of valuable literary treasures within this storeroom had been known to Western scholars since at least the eighteenth century, and a few fragments were taken from it before the Genizah came to the attention of Solomon Schechter, a young scholar at Cambridge University, in the late nineteenth century. In 1896 he negotiated the removal of a large quantity of its contents back to England; additional manuscripts were then removed by other scholars and collectors and deposited in various libraries around the world. Among the most sensational finds of the Cairo Genizah were manuscripts of the long-lost original Hebrew text of the book of Ben *Sira, the *Damascus Document, numerous fragments of long-lost versions of the Palestinian *Targums, and previously unknown *piyyuṭim* (liturgical poetry) and other writings of numerous medieval Hebrew authors. The Genizah has also provided valuable material for the overall political, social, and intellectual history of the Jews in the medieval period, as well as insights into specific figures and incidents.

(4Q177) Catena A: A *Qumran text interweaving biblical verses from various psalms and prophetic texts and supplying their interpretation. It has been proposed that this text may be part of (4Q174) *Florilegium. See Steudel, *Der Midrasch zur Eschatologie.*

Cave of Treasures: A collection of ancient traditions surrounding various figures and stories from the Bible, particularly the book of Genesis. (The cave in question is one in which Adam was said to have deposited the myrrh and incense that he took with him on his way out of the Garden of Eden, and which also served as a place of prayer and the burial place of Adam and other patriarchs; see also *Apocalypse of Moses* 29:3–6.) The book is apparently not a unitary document, and while its existence as such can be dated only to the Middle Ages, some scholars have speculated that an early form of the book may have been composed in the third or even second century c.e., it in turn having incorporated exegetical traditions from earlier sources. The book was at one time attributed to *Ephraem Syrus, but its true author is unknown; it was apparently originally composed in Syriac and exists in various forms in Syriac, Arabic, Ethiopic, Coptic, and Georgian. I have drawn on the editions and translations of Bezold, *Die Schatzhöhle,* and Su-Min Ri, *La Caverne des trésors* (this edition distinguishes between the Western [W] and Eastern [E] Syriac traditions), as well as the translation of Budge, *The Book of the Cave of Treasures.*

Chronicles of Moses (Dibrei ha-Yamim shel Mosheh): A late medieval work, which, like the book of Yashar, retells biblical history—adorned with many interpretive traditions—in biblical, rather than later, Hebrew style. Text: Jellinek, *Beit ha-Midrasch,* 2:1–11; Shinan, *Dibrei ha-Yamim shel Mosheh.* All translations mine.

Chronicles of Yeraḥme'el (or Jerahmeel): A late (eleventh- to twelfth-century) retelling of much biblical and later material, incorporating material from far earlier sources, some of them now lost. Translation: Gaster, *The Chronicles of Jerahmeel* (reissued with an excellent bibliographical prolegomenon by Haim Schwarzbaum).

Chrysostom, John (c. 347–407 c.e.): An outstanding preacher (his name means "golden-mouthed" in Greek), John was an important biblical expositor, the author of a series of homilies on Genesis and other biblical books. Chrysostom was educated at Antioch and was an opponent of allegorical exegesis. Text: Homilies in *PG* vol. 53. All translations mine.

1 Clement (First Letter of Clement): An early Christian letter apparently authored by a certain Clement, (third) bishop of Rome. The letter was written in the late first century c.e. and contains some material bearing on the interpretation of figures from the Hebrew Bible. Text and translation consulted: Jaubert, *Clément de Rome, Epitre aux Corinthiens.* All translations mine.

Clement of Alexandria (c. 150–c. 215 C.E.): Christian theologian and interpreter, author of the massive *Miscellanies* (*Stromata* or *Stromateis*) and other works; he was an important conduit for the Alexandrian allegorizing approach to Scripture and was greatly influenced in particular by Philo's methods as well as much of the content of his commentaries. (See further van den Hoek, *Clement of Alexandria and His Use of Philo.*) Text: Stählin, *Clemens Alexandrinus*, vols. 2 and 3 (*GCS* 15 and 17); all translations mine.

Colossians, Letter to the: A New Testament letter attributed to Paul but thought by many scholars to have been written by one of his followers. If the latter is true, it was probably composed not long after the time of Paul's own letters, perhaps between 65 and 70 C.E. The letter attacks Judaizing and other disapproved practices and beliefs. See also *Paul. Translation: Revised Standard Version, with occasional, slight modifications.

(4Q252) Commentary on Genesisᵃ: see *Genesis Pesher*

(1QS; also 4Q255–264; 5Q11) Community Rule (a translation of the Hebrew name *Serekh ha-Yaḥad*; also called the *Manual of Discipline*): A book of community regulations found in various copies at *Qumran, it is among the most important of the *Dead Sea Scrolls. (It differs significantly from another rulebook associated with the Qumran community, the *Damascus Document*; perhaps, as some scholars have suggested, they were intended for different groups within this religious sect.) Written in Hebrew, this text provides much information about the interpretation of biblical laws at Qumran. All translations mine.

(4Q264) Community Ruleᶻ: This brief fragment from *Qumran has been identified as part of a community rule, though not apparently part of the (1QS) *Community Rule* described above. The apparent subject of this fragment is the prohibition of work on the Sabbath. Translation mine.

Concept of Our Great Power: A Christian gnostic apocalypse, one of the texts of the *Nag Hammadi library. Its original composition in Greek has been dated to before the late fourth century C.E. Translation: *Coptic Nag Hammadi Library.*

1 and 2 Corinthians (First and Second Letters to the Corinthians): Two letters found in the New Testament; they are believed to be authentic letters of Paul and articulate much of his theology. The first letter has been dated to around 54 C.E., and the bulk of the second to the following year. See also *Paul. Translation: Revised Standard Version, with occasional, slight modifications.

Damascus Document (or *Covenant of Damascus* or *Damascus Covenant*): A Hebrew text that derives from the same community known to us via the *Dead Sea Scrolls but that—through means not entirely clear—ended up in the hands of at least two medieval scribes, one from the tenth and the other from the twelfth century C.E., who copied the text; their copies were eventually deposited in the storeroom of a Cairo synagogue (see *Cairo Genizah), where they were discovered by Solomon Schechter at the end of the nineteenth century. Schechter published the *Damascus Document* in 1910 under the title *Fragments of a Zadokite Work* and it has since been the object of much scholarly scrutiny. Although Schechter properly identified the text as stemming from a Jewish group living at the end of the biblical period, this identification was contested by other scholars, and in any case the text's full significance could not begin to be understood until the *Qumran documents began to appear some fifty years later, including further fragments of this text (4Q266–273; 5Q12, and 6Q15). The *Damascus Document*—so-called because of its mention of "the land of Damascus" (whether the actual city or some symbolic reference was intended is still debated) as the place of the making of a "new covenant"—contains laws of the community as well as exhortations, warnings, and not a little direct or indirect interpretation of biblical passages. It differs significantly from another rulebook associated with the Qumran community, the *Community Rule;* perhaps, as some scholars have suggested, the fact that the *Damascus Document* speaks of the "camps" and the "assembly of the towns of Israel" indicates that it was intended for people who espoused the same beliefs as the Qumran community but who did not actually live at Qumran. (The rather stricter *Community Rule* might then have been the rulebook of those who actually lived at Qumran.) Such a picture of a sect with many satellite communities scattered in different towns would accord well with *Josephus' description of the *Essenes in his *Jewish War* 2:124–127. Text: Qimron and Broshi, *Damascus Document Reconsidered.* All translations mine.

Day of Atonement 'Abodah (Anonymous): The 'Abodah was a type of poem specially composed for the liturgy of the Day of Atonement (Yom Kippur). The one cited here (Chapter 6) is printed in Goldschmidt, *Maḥzor leyamim nora'im,* "Introduction," p. 19.

Dead Sea Scrolls: This is the name popularly used for a group of manuscripts found in the general area of Khirbet *Qumran, a site along the shores of the Dead Sea, starting in 1947. Justly described as the greatest manuscript find in history, this collection of biblical manuscripts and other writings seems to have belonged to a group of ascetic Jews who retreated to this desert locale perhaps in the second century B.C.E. and who continued to exist there until 68 C.E. The group may be identified with the *Essenes, a religious sect described by *Philo of Alexandria, *Pliny the Elder, and *Josephus; these Essenes may in turn be the same sect as the "Boethusians" known from rabbinic literature.

The Dead Sea Scrolls have provided a wealth of information about the history and development of the biblical text itself, about first-century Judaism and the roots of Christianity, and about biblical interpretation as it existed just before and after the start of the C.E. Some of the Dead Sea Scrolls texts cited in this book include the (1Q20)*Genesis Apocryphon, the (1QS)*Community Rule (Serekh Hayyaḥad), the *Damascus Document, the (11Q)*Temple Scroll, (4Q252) *Genesis Pesher, and (4Q394–399)* Halakhic Letter (or Miqṣat Ma'asê Hattorah). (The numbering system used by scholars to refer to Dead Sea Scrolls and related texts starts with the site at which the text was found. In the case of Qumran documents, "4Q" refers to the fourth cave at Qumran in which texts were discovered, "11Q" to the eleventh, and so forth.)

Demetrius the Chronographer: A Greek-speaking Jewish historian who probably lived in Alexandria, Egypt, sometime near the end of the third century B.C.E.; he is thus arguably the earliest in a series of Jewish historians, poets, and philosophers who wrote in Greek in the closing centuries B.C.E., a list that also includes *Aristobulus, *Eupolemus, *Theodotus, *Artapanus, and others. Demetrius is called the "chronographer" because, in the few surviving fragments of what was apparently his history of biblical times, the dating of events and the reconciling of the ages of different biblical figures play a prominent role. Text and translation: Holladay, *Fragments from Hellenistic Jewish Authors*, 1:51–92; Hanson in Charlesworth, *OTP* 2:843–854.

Deuteronomy Rabba (also *Debarim Rabba*): A collection of independent rabbinic sermons of the *Tanḥuma-Yelammedenu* type tied to various passages in Deuteronomy; see also **Midrash Tanḥuma*. The collection apparently originated in the land of Israel, probably sometime after the mid-fifth century c.e., but its date and history of redaction and transmission remain obscure. Texts used: *Midrash Rabba* (Vilna ed.); Lieberman, *Midrash Debarim Rabba*.

(4Q504) Dibrei hamme'orot: See **Words of the Luminaries*

Didache: "The Teaching [of the Twelve Apostles]" is a Christian manual of probably the mid-second century c.e. The Greek text was first discovered in Constantinople in 1873 and subsequently other copies and versions have been identified. It contains much material apparently inherited from an earlier period; in particular, its doctrine of the two paths (or ways), paralleled in **Letter of Barnabas* 18–21, the **Doctrina Apostolorum*, and still earlier texts, seems to go back to a Jewish tradition that circulated widely in Second Temple times (see Chapter 25). Text and translation consulted: Rorsdorf and Tuilier, *La Doctrine des douze apôtres*. All translations mine.

Didascalia Apostolorum: An early Christian text presented as the teaching of twelve apostles but actually a pseudepigraphon. It contains legal and moral exhortations (including extensive sections on the functions of various church officials, bishops, deacons and deaconesses, as well as "widows"), along with extensive passages of biblical citation and interpretation. It was originally composed in Greek, probably somewhere in Syria or Palestine in the third century c.e. It survives in complete form in Syriac as well as in extensive Latin fragments. Translation: Connolly, *Didascalia Apostolorum*. In addition, fragments of the Greek original are recoverable from the **Apostolic Constitutions*, whose first six volumes are based in large measure on the *Didascalia*. Text: Funk, *Didascalia et Constitutiones Apostolorum*.

Didymus the Blind (c. 313–398 c.e.): Christian theologian and biblical commentator in Alexandria, author of *On the Trinity* and other works. Text: *PG* vol. 39. All translations mine.

Diodorus Siculus (first century b.c.e.): Author of the *Bibliotheca Historica*, a work that includes a number of passages bearing on the Jews and their history (much of its information has been borrowed from still earlier sources). Text and translation: Stern, *Greek and Latin Authors*, 1:169–189.

Doctrina Apostolorum: An early Christian text whose exhortation concerning the two ways (or paths) is reminiscent of those found in the **Didache* and the **Letter of Barnabas*, perhaps all three going back to a common source, an original, standard exhortation on the subject that existed in Judaism (see Chapter 25). Text (in Latin): Schlecht, *Doctrina XII Apostolorum*. All translations mine.

Ecclesiasticus, Book of: see **Sira(ch)*

Elephantine Papyri: A group of Aramaic papyri discovered at the beginning of this century on the island of Elephantine (Yev) in Egypt. Many of them were written during the fifth century b.c.e. by members of a Jewish military colony stationed there and have revealed much about the life, legal practices, religion, and culture of this colony. (In addition to such texts, others, including fragments of the *(Aramaic) Sayings of *Aḥiqar*, were also found.)

1 *Enoch* (*First Book of Enoch*): There circulated in late antiquity a number of works attributed to Enoch, an antediluvian figure mentioned briefly in Gen. 5:21–24. The very fact that this biblical passage apparently asserted that Enoch had been "taken" by God while he was still alive seemed to imply that he continued to exist in heaven—indeed, that he exists there still. From such a vantage point, Enoch could presumably not only observe all that was happening on earth, but was privy to all the secrets of heaven, including the natural order and God's plans for humanity's future.

A number of anonymous writers who wished to discourse on such subjects attributed their writings to Enoch, and eventually a composite Book of Enoch—and then *Books* of Enoch—began to circulate. Our present 1 *Enoch* comprises a number of different works. Most or all were apparently originally written in Aramaic, and parts of these Aramaic texts have turned up among the *Dead Sea Scrolls. The most ancient manuscripts found—drawn from the "Book of Luminaries" (or "Astronomical Book") section (that is, chapters 72–82) of our present 1 *Enoch*, and the "Book of the Watchers" (1 *Enoch* 1–36)—have been dated well back into the third century B.C.E. (However, the composite nature of even these subsections is clear. See: VanderKam, *Enoch and the Growth of an Apocalyptic Tradition*, esp. 110–130; Stone, "Enoch, Aramaic Levi, and Sectarian Origins.") Some have questioned the antiquity of the "Parables [or "Similitudes"] of Enoch" section (chapters 37–71), which is not attested in any of the Dead Sea Scrolls fragments, but their absence there may be due to chance: there is nothing in the contents of this section to justify a late date.

In short, the oldest parts of 1 *Enoch* may well constitute the most ancient Jewish writings to have survived outside the Bible itself. Newer sections were eventually blended in with the old, and the entire Book of Enoch was subsequently translated into Greek and from Greek into ancient Ethiopic (Ge'ez), in which language alone the book survived in its entirety.

Scriptural interpretation was hardly the major concern of 1 *Enoch*. The very figure of Enoch the sage in this book has been shown to have been influenced by Mesopotamian models, and the astronomical learning and other materials presented in this book likewise bespeak the transmission of ancient, eastern lore. Nevertheless, a number of figures and incidents associated with biblical narratives also appear, and in what is said about some of them it is possible to see the outline of some very ancient interpretation, in particular, a grappling with difficulties associated with the story of Noah and the flood. In citing from 1 *Enoch*, I have generally used the text and translation of Knibb, *Ethiopic Book of Enoch*. Because the Ethiopic texts sometimes differ significantly from the Aramaic fragments of 1 *Enoch* found at Qumran, I have also indicated where appropriate the parallel passages in these Aramaic fragments and related material (that is, 4Q201–02, 204–12) and relied upon them for specific points.

2 *Enoch* (*Second Book of Enoch*): This text recounts Enoch's heavenly journey and the things revealed to him, then turns to Enoch's successors, Methuselah and Nir, and ends with the story of Melchizedek. It survives only in Slavonic, in two recensions, both of

which are represented in various manuscripts. The origins of *2 Enoch* are quite mysterious. The Slavonic texts certainly represent a translation from the Greek, which may
indeed have been the original language of composition. As for its date, in view of some
of the biblical interpretations found in this book, which are paralleled in ancient Jewish
sources, it may well be that the earliest kernel of this text goes back (as some have
suggested) to the beginning of the common era; on the other hand, the absence of any
mention of it in Greek or Latin patristic writings is troubling. Text: Vaillant, *Le Livre des
Secrets d'Hénoch*. Translation: Andersen in *OTP* 1:102–221, identified as belonging either
to version J or version A, that is, Library of the Academy of Sciences, Leningrad, mss.
13.3.25 and 45.13.4, respectively.

3 Enoch (Hebrew Apocalypse of Enoch): The name *3 Enoch* was coined by H. Odeberg for
his 1928 edition of this mystical Hebrew treatise; it is known elsewhere as the *Book of
Hekhalot* ("Palaces"), the *Chapters of R. Ishmael,* and other names. The text itself, while
an early landmark in the history of Jewish mysticism, is late within the context of the
present study, belonging perhaps to the fifth or sixth century c.e. Translation: Alexander in Charlesworth, *OTP* 1:223–315.

Ephesians, Letter to the: A New Testament letter attributed to Paul but more likely written
by a disciple of his late in the first century c.e. See also: *Paul. Translation: Revised
Standard Version.

Ephraem (sometimes written Ephrem or Efrem) *Syrus:* Outstanding poet and biblical
commentator of Syriac Christianity. Ephraem was born in or around Nisibis c. 309 c.e.
and eventually moved to Edessa, where he died in 373 c.e. His hymns and exegetical
writings contain numerous parallels to, and developments of, earlier Jewish motifs
attested both in contemporaneous rabbinic writings as well as in the literature of
Second Temple Judaism. For his *Commentary on Genesis and Exodus* I have used the text
of Tonneau, *Sancti Ephraem Syri in Genesim et in Exodum Comentarii.* Too late to be
incorporated systematically (but nonetheless consulted here and there): Matthews and
Amar, *St. Ephrem the Syrian.* For Ephraem's *Hymns* I have used the poetic renderings of
McVey, *Ephrem the Syrian,* modified here and there in consultation with the original
Syriac, and Kronholm, *Motifs from Genesis 1–11 in the Genuine Hymns of Ephrem.*

Essenes: See the description of rival Jewish groups under *Rabbis, the; see also *Damascus
Document.*

Eupolemus (active in mid-second century b.c.e.): A Greek-speaking Jewish historian,
apparently the same "Eupolemus the son of John" referred to in 1 Macc. 8:17 as having
been sent to Rome in 161 b.c.e. as part of a Jewish delegation (see also 2 Macc. 4:11;
Josephus, *Jewish Antiquities* 12:415). Four fragments of his history of the Jews are cited
by *Alexander Polyhistor and, subsequently, *Eusebius (and reflected as well in the
writings of *Clement of Alexandria). A fifth fragment is found as well in Clement's
Miscellanies; it is not clear whether Clement is citing via Polyhistor or some other
source. In addition to these five fragments, all conceded to be authentically the work of
Eupolemus, are two more fragments of an ancient historian. The first of these is
attributed by Eusebius to Eupolemus, but scholars are divided about its provenance,
many claiming that this passage is *not* the work of our Eupolemus; its author has

therefore come to be known as Pseudo-Eupolemus. Recently, R. Doran has argued forcefully that the passage is indeed the work of the first Eupolemus; I have therefore designated that fragment herein as the work of [Pseudo-]Eupolemus. The last fragment is attributed in Eusebius not to Eupolemus at all but to "anonymous works"; some scholars nonetheless likewise attribute this fragment to Pseudo-Eupolemus. (See further Doran in Charlesworth, OTP 2:873–878.) Text and translation: Holladay, *Fragments from Hellenistic Jewish Authors*, 1:93–187; also Fallon and Doran in Charlesworth, *OTP* 2:861–872, 873–882.

Eusebius (of Caesarea): Christian scholar, historian, and polemicist (c. 260-c. 340 C.E.). His *Ecclesiastical History* was a pioneering work that recounted the history of the church from the time of the Apostles to his own day. His *Preparation for the Gospel* (*Praeparatio Evangelica*) presented a spirited defense of Christianity against the background of Greek thought; in it he had occasion to cite from the writings of Hellenistic Jewish writers, including *Aristobulus, *Eupolemus, *Artapanus, *Demetrius the Chronographer, *Theodotus, and others. Text: Klostermann, *Eusebius Werke;* for *Praeparatio Evangelica* I also consulted the text and trans. by Guy Schroeder and Edouard des Places (*sources chrétiennes* 369) (Paris: Le Cerf, 1991). For fragments by Aristobulus and others, see those individual entries in this index.

exegesis: Interpretation, especially biblical interpretation.

exegetical motif: The underlying idea about how to explain a biblical text that becomes the basis, or part of the basis, for a *narrative expansion. Motifs tend to become more elaborate over time and often come to be joined with other motifs to form a new motif. A motif can thus exist in different variants or versions; the common source of two or more variants may be spoken of as the "basic motif." Motifs in this study are usually identified by the subheadings under which they are presented in each chapter, thus, "Wisdom Came First," "Death in a Day," and so forth.

(4Q) Exod.[b]: An Exodus scroll found at *Qumran and published in Ulrich and Cross, *Qumran Cave 4:VII* (*DJD* 12). All translations mine.

Exodus Rabba (also *Shemot Rabba*): A composite medieval midrash on the book of Exodus, whose first part consists of rabbinic comments on verses from Exodus, chapters 1–10, while the second is a series of sermons on Exodus 12–40 of the *Tanḥuma-Yelammedenu* type (see *Midrash Tanḥuma). Text: Shinan, *Midrash Shemot Rabba*, Chapters 1–14; *Midrash Rabba*. All translations mine.

(4Q464) Exposition on the Patriarchs: see (4Q464) *Apocryphon*[b]

Ezechiel the Tragedian: This Greek-speaking Jew of the second century B.C.E. probably authored other dramatic works, but all that survives of his writings are fragments of a retelling of the Exodus narrative, the *Exagōgē* ("leading out"). As has been demonstrated by various modern scholars (and in particular Jacobson, *The "Exagoge" of Ezekiel*), Ezekiel's retelling abounds in interpretive traditions about Moses and the Exodus, many of which are paralleled in other ancient texts. Text and translation: Holladay, *Fragments from Hellenistic Jewish Authors*, 2:301–529; Robertson in Charlesworth, *OTP* 2:803–819. (The latter translation is somewhat looser but I have generally favored it because of its attempt to reflect the metrical form of the original.)

4 Ezra (Fourth Book of Ezra): A recounting of various visions granted to Ezra (apparently Ezra the scribe of the biblical books of Ezra and Nehemiah—though *4 Ezra* 3:1 complicates the matter by identifying the author as "Salathiel, who am also called Ezra"). The visions, seven in all, contain much material relating to the interpretation of the Hebrew Bible and, more generally, to questions confronting Jews at the end of the Second Temple period. The book underwent a complicated history of transmission and came to be known by different names. The original version was apparently written in Hebrew, probably in the late first century C.E., but nothing of this Hebrew version survives; the text exists in Latin and other ancient versions. Translation: Stone, *Fourth Ezra,* with occasional slight modifications.

Fathers according to R. Nathan: see **Abot deR. Natan*

Firmicus Maternus (first half of fourth century C.E.): In his astronomical treatise *Mathesis,* written in Latin, Firmicus refers to the same tradition of "Abraham the Astrologer" found in **Pseudo-Orphica,* *Artapanus, and other earlier writings and writers. Text and translation: Stern, *Greek and Latin Authors,* 2.493–494.

(4Q174) Florilegium: A fragmentary text from *Qumran that interweaves biblical citations and interpretations, presenting some of them in an implied or explicit messianic sense. This text was first published by John Allegro in the 1950s and has been the subject of much speculation since then. Annette Steudel has suggested that another Qumran fragment, *(4Q177) Catena A,* is actually part of the same document, calling them respectively *MidrEschat a* and *b* (Steudel, *Der Midrasch zur Eschatologie aus der Qumrangemeinde*); while certainly possible, this hypothesis does not impose itself. All translations mine.

Galatians, Letter to the: A letter that is part of the New Testament, written around 53–54 C.E.; it is believed to be one of the authentic letters of Paul, which addresses in particular the issue of the Gentile Church, apparently in the face of pressure toward a more Judaizing Christianity (though the precise nature of Paul's opponents is still debated by scholars). See also: *Paul. Translation: Revised Standard Version, with occasional, slight modifications.

(1Q20 or 1Q apGen ar) Genesis Apocryphon: An Aramaic text found at *Qumran. The text as it stands is incomplete (although new technology is now making available readings of previously illegible portions). In its original form, this composition apparently presented a series of first-person narratives spoken by different figures from the book of Genesis (of these the Abraham section is the best preserved). These narratives frequently contain interpretive motifs, some of which are paralleled in other Jewish writings of the period (*Jubilees,* for example) or in later, rabbinic texts. It is likely that the *Genesis Apocryphon* was composed sometime in the first century B.C.E. Text: Beyer, *Die aramäischen Texte vom Toten Meer,* and Fitzmyer and Harrington, *A Manual of Palestinian Aramaic Texts,* 102–127; Greenfield and Qimron, "The Genesis Apocryphon Col. XII." All translations mine.

(4Q252–254a) Genesis Pesher: A fragmentary Hebrew text found at *Qumran and commenting on a number of distinct interpretive cruxes in the book of Genesis. The name is something of a misnomer, since this is not a *pesher* of the sort known from elsewhere in the Qumran library; indeed, the text is remarkable for its down-to-earth explanations and commentary-like tone. All translations mine.

Genesis Rabba (also *Bereshit Rabba*): A rabbinic anthology of comments on verses from the book of Genesis. It was probably compiled at the end of the fourth or in the early fifth century C.E., although much of its exegesis certainly goes back to an earlier period. In this book I have relied primarily on the critical edition of Theodor and Albeck, *Midrasch Bereschit Rabba*. (As Albeck recognized before completing the project, the best manuscript among those used in this edition was not the one chosen by Theodor as the basic text [MS. British Museum Add. 27169], but Ms. Vat. Ebr. 30. Where significant differences exist, I have therefore generally relied on the readings of that text, as well as those found in Sokoloff, *Geniza Fragments of Bereshit Rabba*. (It is to be noted that another ancient manuscript of *Genesis Rabba*, Ms. Vat. Ebr. 60, was not used by Theodor-Albeck in their edition.) All translations mine.

Gospel of Nicodemus: A pseudepigraphon also called the "Acts of Pilate" that relates the trial, crucifixion, and resurrection of Jesus, as well as his descent into hell, freeing the dead and seizing Satan. It was probably written in the third or fourth century C.E. Translation: Hennecke and Schneemelcher, *New Testament Apocrypha*.

Gospel of Philip (Gnostic): A Christian gnostic treatise and one of the texts of the *Nag Hammadi library. It was probably written in Syria in the second half of the third century C.E. Translation: *Coptic Nag Hammadi Library*.

Gospels, the Four New Testament (that is, the gospels of Matthew, Mark, Luke, and John): The word "gospel" comes from the Old English expression *gode spell* for "good news," corresponding to the Greek *euangelion*. In Paul's writings and elsewhere, the word refers to the message of Christianity, but the term later came to be used specifically of narrative accounts of the life and teachings of Jesus; the "four Gospels" are the four canonical books of this type contained in the New Testament, in addition to which other, noncanonical writings also bear the name "gospel."

The gospels of Matthew, Mark, and Luke are fundamentally similar, and much of New Testament scholarship has been devoted to unraveling their interrelationship as well as their possible dependence on other, still earlier, texts or traditions. Matthew was probably written around 90 C.E. by an unknown Christian living perhaps in the area of Antioch, Syria; Mark's gospel is earlier, closer to the time of the destruction of the Jerusalem Temple (70 C.E.), which he mentions (13:12). The author of Luke's gospel is also the author of *Acts; both were probably written around 80–85 C.E. Because these three gospels were at one point printed in parallel columns—an arrangement called a synopsis—in order to highlight their similarities and differences, they are sometimes called the synoptic Gospels. The gospel of John is of a different nature and some of its content stands in contrast to that of the first three gospels. It is generally dated later than the first three, no earlier than the end of the first century C.E. All four gospels contain frequent references (sometimes oblique) to texts from the Hebrew Bible; they often present or reflect interpretations of these biblical texts. Sometimes these interpretations, whether old or new, are only understandable fully by reference to the form in which the interpreted texts were transmitted in the *Targums or other bodies of ancient interpretation. Translation: Revised Standard Version, sometimes modified slightly.

Greatness of Moses: A Samaritan text of uncertain date translated by Moses Gaster in his *Studies and Texts*, 1:125–126.

Gregory of Nyssa (ca. 330–395 C.E.): Bishop of Nyssa (in Cappodocia), theologian, and biblical commentator. Text: *PG* 44. All translations mine.

halakhah: A general term common in rabbinic and later writings that refers to the manner in which the laws of the Bible are observed, extended, and applied to daily life. Different systems of *halakhah* were championed by different groups in Second Temple times; see *Rabbis, the. *Halakhah* was thus a major concern of ancient Jewish interpreters; it is sometimes paired with *aggadah* ("narrative"), a term usually referring to the interpretation of nonlegal parts of the Bible.

(4Q394–399) Halakhic Letter (or *Miqṣat Ma'asê ha-Torah*): One of the most recently published, and important, of the *Dead Sea Scrolls. It seems to be a kind of literary letter or manifesto. It speaks in the first-person plural ("We believe . . ." and "Here are some of our rulings") while it addresses—as a letter might—another group of people in the second-person plural ("We have written to you . . ."); at the same time, the fact that the text has been found in multiple copies would appear to indicate that this text, even if it originally was a real letter, eventually became an important statement of doctrine for the *Qumran community, defining some of the principal matters in which its *halakhah* differed from that of the (apparently Pharisaic) group to which its words are addressed. Text: Qimron and Strugnell, *Qumran Cave 4, V.* All translations mine.

halakhic midrashim: A group of individual rabbinic texts that interpret different books of the Pentateuch. The name reflects the fact that these books deal largely, though by no means exclusively, with matters of *halakhah, the interpretation and application of biblical laws. (It is apparently because of their concern with *halakhah* that these texts were compiled exclusively on the biblical books of Exodus, Leviticus, Numbers, and Deuteronomy; Genesis, because it contains little of an overtly legal character, was not included in the scope of the *halakhic midrashim.*) The *halakhic midrashim* include the *Mekhilta deR. Ishmael* and *Mekhilta deR. Shimon b. Yoḥai* (both on Exodus), *Sifra (on Leviticus), *Sifrei Numbers* and *Sifrei Zutta* (both on Numbers) and *Sifrei Deuteronomy* and *Midrash Tanna'im* (both on Deuteronomy). Because of the apparent doubling of *halakhic midrashim* on different books, David Hoffman and later scholars have pursued the possibility that the two different "sets" of *halakhic midrashim* derive from two ancient schools of rabbinic interpreters, those of R. Aqiba and R. Ishmael. While clear differences in content, approach, rabbinic scholars cited, and *halakhic* terminology do indeed characterize the different sets, Hoffman's brilliant thesis has nonetheless been shown by later scholars to oversimplify matters somewhat: non-*halakhic* material in the two sets does not seem to derive from the same putative sources as the *halakhic* material, and it is far from clear, moreover, which characteristics in the two sets reflect differences fundamental to the texts themselves and which may merely reflect preferences of the texts' final editors. With regard to date, since the rabbis cited in them are generally *tanna'im* along with some first-generation *'amora'im* (see *rabbis, the), the *halakhic midrashim* are generally assumed to have been compiled sometime in the third century C.E. (though some scholars have questioned this assumption as well). If this dating is correct, the *halakhic midrashim* represent, after the Mishnah, Tosefta, and perhaps one or two other texts, the earliest stage of rabbinic writings.

Hebrews, Letter to the: An anonymous New Testament letter whose precise addressees are unknown. It appears to be in fact a sermon or exhortation (and not a letter) addressed to an early Christian community, treating a number of doctrinal issues, including the issue of priesthood. Here, Melchizedek figures prominently in the argument. Some have suggested that this letter was written in opposition to teachings associated with the *Qumran community or the Essenes. Translation: Revised Standard Version.

Hecataeus of Abdera: The passage cited from Diodorus Siculus, *Bibliotheca Historica* 40:3 is attributed there to Hecataeus of Miletus, but scholars agree that the real author was the later (and lesser known) Hecataeus of Abdera, author of the *Aegyptiaca*, who lived in the third century B.C.E. See further Gager, *Moses in Greco-Roman Paganism*, 26. Text and translation: Diodorus Siculus LCL. See also Gauger, "Zitate in der Jüdischen Apologetik."

Hellenistic Synagogal Prayers: The last two books of the *Apostolic Constitutions* contain Christian liturgical works, among which survive a number of ancient Jewish prayers apparently composed in Greek for use in synagogue and subsequently adapted for Christian worship. The ancient, Jewish origin of these prayers was first proposed by Kaufmann Kohler and his thesis was taken up by later scholars, notably E. R. Goodenough. The date of the original prayers is still far from certain: the second century C.E. may be a good guess. For an overview of scholarship, see "Hellenistic Synagogal Prayers: One Hundred Years of Discussion," *JSP* 5 (1989), 17–27. Translation: Goodenough, *By Light, Light;* Darnell in *OTP* 2:677–697.

Hermas, Shepherd of: see *Shepherd of Hermas

Historical [Istoricheskaya] Paleya / Interpretive [Tolkovaya] Paleya: The various *Palei* that exist are all basically expansions and elaborations of the biblical text. The oldest manuscripts themselves are, from a biblicist's standpoint, very late, originating (like all Slavonic writings) well on in the Middle Ages; however, it is clear that behind these manuscripts themselves stand earlier Greek texts and arguably, in many instances, texts or traditions first formulated in Hebrew or Aramaic in the Second Temple period. Beyond this generalization there is little that can be said to characterize the whole of the *Paleya* literature, each text and manuscript tradition requiring its own treatment. (See further Istrin, *Ocherki istorii drevnorusskoy literatury;* Suminkova, *Izucheniye russkogo yazyka i istochnikovedeniye;* Tvorogov, *Drevnerusskiye khronografy.*)

For the purposes of this book I have cited from the printed editions of Popov, *Kniga Bytia Nebesi i Zemli (Paleya Istoricheskaya);* Tikhonravov, *Pamyatniki Starinnoy Russkoy Literatury;* Franko, *Apokrifi i Legendi;* and the Greek text of Vassiliev, *Anecdota Graeco-Byzantina.* All translations mine.

History of the Rechabites: A late (sixth-century C.E.?) Christian text, sections of which may, however, be based on an earlier Jewish work going back to before the second century C.E. (For more on this text, see Charlesworth, "A Study of the History of the Rechabites.") It survives in Syriac, Ethiopic, Greek, and other languages. Translation of the Syriac text: Charlesworth in *OTP* 2:443–461.

(1QH and 1Q35) Hodayot: see (1QH and 1Q35) *Thanksgiving Hymns

(11QPsª) Hymn to the Creator: A Hebrew hymn celebrating God's actions in creating the world. It was discovered in a psalms scroll from Cave 11 at *Qumran. Text: Sanders, *Psalms Scroll of Qumran Cave 11 (DJD* 4). Translation mine.

Hypostasis of the Archons: A treatise found in the gnostic *Nag Hammadi library containing an esoteric exposition of Genesis 1–6. The "archons" (rulers) in question are the enslaving authorities who hold temporary spiritual sway over all humanity. It may have been composed in the third century C.E. Translation: *Coptic Nag Hammadi Library.*

Irenaeus of Lyons (c. 130–c. 200): Theologian, bishop of Lyons, and the author of *Against All Heresies,* an important work for the history of gnosticism (see *Nag Hammadi library), one of the heresies prominently attacked therein. Although this treatise was written in Greek, it survives in Latin translation; all translations mine.

j.: Stands for *J(erusalem [or Palestinian] Talmud), just preceding the name of the tractate, thus j. *Pesaḥim.*

James, Letter of: A New Testament letter attributed to "James" (the English equivalent of the Hebrew name Jacob), possibly intended as a reference to the brother of Jesus; in fact the letter appears to be a collection of exhortations preserved by Christians living in the land of Israel and (hence) in close dialogue with Jewish ideas and practices. This letter's position on the performance of divine commandments (especially 2:18–26) seems to stand in contrast to the position articulated by Paul in *Romans. The date and circumstances of its composition are unknown. Translation: Revised Standard Version, sometimes modified slightly.

Jannes and Jambres: A book elaborating two figures identified as among Pharaoh's magicians or "wizards" at the time of the Exodus from Egypt. The text survives in fragmentary form: it appears to have been composed originally in Greek not later than the mid-third century C.E., though this composition may have been based on an earlier (Semitic) one on the same theme. Text and translation: Pietersma, *The Apocryphon of Jannes and Jambres the Magicians.*

Jerahmeel, Chronicles of: see *Chronicles of Yeraḥme'el*

Jeremiah, Letter (or *Epistle*) *of:* see *Letter of Jeremiah*

Jerome: An outstanding scholar and altogether fascinating figure, Jerome (Eusebius Sophronius Hieronymus, c. 345–420) was one of the most influential biblical scholars of the early Christian world. He traveled widely, lived for several years as a hermit in the Syrian desert, and served as secretary to Pope Damasus in Rome. The latter commissioned Jerome to revise the "Old Latin" (*Vetus Latina) version of the Bible, whose clumsy and occasionally ungrammatical prose had become a liability, particularly with regard to potential converts to Christianity. Jerome's mastery of classical style and his gift for languages made him an ideal translator. He began by seeking to revise the *Vetus Latina,* principally in the light of various Greek versions (the Septuagint and later translations). However, this work only led him to conclude that the Septuagint was itself corrupt: what was needed, he felt, was a new Latin version translated directly from the Hebrew. Jerome settled in Bethlehem and studied Hebrew and biblical interpretation with Jewish teachers, an act all the more remarkable when considered against the background of anti-Jewish polemics then popular among Christians. His translation of Scripture eventually supplanted the *Vetus Latina* and came to be called the Vulgate; Jerome referred to it proudly as a rendering of the *Hebraica Veritas* (the "Hebrew truth"). In addition to the interpretations embodied in the Vulgate itself, Jerome also transmitted much interpretive material in his *Hebrew Questions in Genesis,* his *Letters,* and his commentaries on various biblical books.

Texts: Vulgate: *Biblia Sacra Juxta Vulgatam Versionem; Quaestiones Hebraicae: PL* vol. 23; Antin, *Corpus Christianorum Series Latina,* vol. 72. All translations mine. (Too late for inclusion in this volume is a new English translation and commentary: Hayward, *Jerome's Hebrew Questions on Genesis.*)

Jerusalem Talmud: A compendium of Jewish learning and biblical exegesis compiled in the land of Israel in the late fourth or early fifth century C. E. Like the *Babylonian Talmud, it takes the form of a highly digressive commentary on the *Mishnah, but the Jerusalem Talmud is considerably shorter than the Babylonian. Because of the prestige and power of the Babylonian centers of Jewish learning (where the Babylonian Talmud was in use), the Jerusalem Talmud came to have less influence than the Babylonian within later Judaism. All translations mine.

John, Gospel of: see *Gospels

1, 2, and 3 John: Three New Testament letters traditionally attributed to John the son of Zebedee, who is also said to have written both the *gospel of John and the book of *Revelation. While the second and third are indeed formally letters, the first is not, and the salutations of 2 and 3 John refer to himself not as John but "the elder." The actual authorship and date of these texts is therefore disputed; arguably, they were written at the end of the first century C.E. or perhaps slightly later. Translation: Revised Standard Version, sometimes modified slightly.

(4Q371–373) Joseph Apocryphon: A brief text from *Qumran that mentions Joseph (apparently as a representative or embodiment of the Northern Kingdom of Israel and not as the biblical figure, the son of Jacob). Text: Schuller, "4Q 372: A Text about Joseph." All translations mine.

Joseph and Aseneth: A Greek romance elaborating the marriage of Joseph with Asenath (mentioned in passing in Gen. 41:45) and related events. This text was composed originally in Greek, presumably in or around Alexandria sometime near the turn of the era. Translation: Burchard in Charlesworth, *OTP* 2:202–247.

Josephus, Flavius (ca. 37 C.E.–c. 100 C.E.): Born of a priestly family in Jerusalem, Josephus was, by his own account, a gifted student who acquired a broad exposure to the different Jewish schools of thought existent in his own time. He served as a general in the great Jewish revolt against the Romans but was defeated and taken prisoner. (Josephus recounts that he prophesied that the Roman commander, Vespasian, would be made emperor; Vespasian spared Josephus' life and when, two years later, the prophecy came true, freed him.) After the war Josephus moved to Rome and composed, among other books, his multivolume *Jewish Antiquities.* The first four books of this massive work retell the events of the *Pentateuch with frequent additions and modifications that reflect the biblical interpretations he learned in his youth; they are a rich source of information about ancient exegesis. In addition, he wrote a lengthy account of the Jewish revolt against Rome (*The Jewish War*), a brief autobiography (*Life of Josephus*), and a spirited defense of Judaism (*Against Apion*). Texts and translations: Josephus, Works of, in LCL; Nodet, *Les Antiquités juives, 1–3.*

Jubilees: A book purporting to contain a revelation given to Moses by the "angel of the Presence," one of the angels closest to God, at the time of the Sinai revelation. It takes the form of a retelling of the book of Genesis and the first part of Exodus: the angel goes over the same material but fills in many details, sometimes shifting slightly the order of things, and occasionally skipping over elements in the narrative. The book was originally written in Hebrew, and fragments of it have been found among the *Dead Sea Scrolls. From Hebrew it was translated into Greek (parts of this translation still survive in quotations from Greek authors) and from Greek into Latin and Ge'ez. The (almost) complete text exists only in Ge'ez, though a substantial section is extant in Latin as well. Many scholars date the book to the middle of the second century B.C.E. or even later, but I favor an earlier date, perhaps at the beginning of the second century B.C.E. or even a decade or two before that.

The author of *Jubilees* was a bold, innovative interpreter in his own right—one might say, without exaggeration, something of a genius—and subsequent generations valued highly, even venerated, his book's insights into Scripture. In seeking to retell the book of Genesis and the beginning of Exodus, this author had a definite program: he wished to claim that this initial part of the Pentateuch, although it consists mostly of stories and does not contain any law code as such, had nonetheless been designed to impart legal instruction no less binding than the overt law codes found in the rest of the Pentateuch. In other words, by reading the stories of Genesis carefully, one could figure out all kinds of binding commandments that God had, as it were, hidden in the narrative. Reading in this fashion, the author of *Jubilees* was able to find a set of rules strictly defining what is permitted and forbidden on the Sabbath, regulations forbidding marriage between Jews and non-Jews, strictures against various forms of "fornication," and other subjects dear to this writer's heart. One interesting feature of the book is that it maintains that the true calendar ordained by God consisted of exactly 52 Sabbaths (364 days) per year and that the moon, whose waxing and waning determined the months and festivals for other Jews, ought rightly to have no such role in the true calendar. The author sought to show that this calendar, too, was implied by the stories of Genesis.

Apart from these pet issues, *Jubilees'* author ended up presenting a good deal more in the way of biblical interpretation. Some of these interpretations may likewise have been of his own creation, but others were certainly widespread traditions at the time of his writing. One way or another, the book is a treasure of ancient thinking about the Bible. The Dead Seas Scroll sect adopted the same calendar as that prescribed by *Jubilees*, and it is clear that the members of this group held this book in high esteem. Translations cited: (principally) VanderKam, *The Book of Jubilees*; Wintermute in Charlesworth, *OTP* 2:35–142; also consulted: Charles, *The Book of Jubilees, or, The Little Genesis*.

Jude, Letter of: A very brief New Testament "letter" (but really more of an exhortation) addressing various issues and invoking scriptural examples. Its date is unknown. Translation: Revised Standard Version.

Judith: One of the Old Testament *Apocrypha, a brief book that recounts the bravery of its fictional Jewish heroine in opposing the foreigners come to invade Judaea. It may well have come into existence in stages, an original tale going back to the early second century B.C.E. (or earlier) having undergone slight elaboration later on. Probably composed originally in Hebrew, it survives in Greek and other translations. While biblical interpretation is hardly a main item in the book, several passages do reflect an early stage of ancient biblical interpretation. Translation: Revised Standard Version of the Bible with Apocrypha, occasionally modified; also consulted: Grintz, *The Book of Judith.*

Julian (that is, Flavius Claudius Julianus, called in some Christian sources Julian the Apostate; 332–363 C.E.): A nephew of the emperor Constantine—whose adoption of Christianity had changed the course of history—Julian was of a different mind; when he himself became emperor in 361, he set about undermining the recent gains of the church and instituted a series of anti-Christian measures. He is the author of a now-lost treatise *Against the Galileans* (that is, the Christians), part of which may be reconstructed from a refutation of it written by Cyril of Alexandria. Julian shows a striking acquaintance with Scripture as well as Jewish practices and beliefs, which he clearly prefers to those of Christianity; he apparently intended to rebuild the temple in Jerusalem. Text and translation in Stern, *Greek and Latin Authors.*

Justin (Martyr) (c. 100–c.165 C.E.): Christian apologist and martyr, born in Flavia Neapolis (Shechem, Nablus) in Samaria. His *Dialogue with Trypho* consists of a lengthy debate with a certain learned Jew named Trypho (whom some have identified with R. Tarfon of the *Mishnah), in which the pair discuss numerous matters of biblical interpretation; the views of both discussants are most informative about the state of exegesis at this point. The dialogue is set in the wake of the Bar Kokhba revolt (132–135 C.E.; see *Dialogue* 1:3 and 9:3) but was probably written around 150 C.E. Text: Goodspeed, *Die ältesten Apologeten.* Translation: Williams, *The Dialogue with Trypho.*

Ladder of Jacob: An expansive retelling of Jacob's dream vision at Bethel. Surviving only in Slavonic, this text was apparently first written in Hebrew (or, less likely, Aramaic), arguably sometime in the first century C.E. or even B.C.E. (See further Kugel, "Ladder of Jacob.") Texts consulted: *Tolkovaya Paleya* of 1477, published in facsimile in *Obščestvo lyubitelei drevnorusskoy pis'mennosti* vol. 93 (Petersburg, 1893); Pipyn in G. Kušelev-Bezborodko, *Pamyatniki Starinnoy Russkoy Literatury;* Tikhonravov, *Pamyatniki Russkoy Literatury;* Franko, *Apokrifi i Legendi;* and several manuscript copies lent to me by Horace Lunt (see his "Ladder of Jacob" in Charlesworth, *OTP* 2:402–403). All translations mine.

Lamentations Rabba (or *Eikha Rabbati* or *Rabba*): A rabbinic midrashic compilation on the book of Lamentations, probably to be dated to the late fourth or early fifth century C.E., though obviously containing much earlier material. Text: Buber, *Midrasch Ekhah Rabbah* (though this text does not reflect all manuscripts and fragments now available). All translations mine.

Letter (or *Epistle) of Aristeas:* An apologetic tract in defense of Judaism, written in Greek, probably in the late second or first century B.C.E. This treatise, in the form of a letter from a certain Aristeas to his brother Philocrates, is notable for its account of the origins of the *Septuagint, its description of the Jerusalem Temple and its service, and its justification of various biblical laws and Jewish practices. Translation: Hadas, *Aristeas to Philocrates,* Shutt in Charlesworth, *OTP* 2:12–34.

Letter of Barnabas (or *Epistle of Barnabas*): A Christian work of the late first or early second century C.E. ascribed (probably falsely) to the disciple Barnabas. It was cited as Scripture by *Clement of Alexandria and *Origen. Despite a certain polemical, anti-Jewish character, the epistle frequently echoes Jewish traditions of biblical interpretation and contains other indications of close familiarity with Jewish practices and belief. Text and translation consulted: Prigent and Kraft, *l'Epître de Barnabé*. All translations mine.

Letter (or *Epistle*) *of Jeremiah:* A polemic against idolatry that was (or came to be) attributed to the biblical prophet Jeremiah. It is apparently referred to in 2 Macc. 2:2 and may thus be a rather ancient work, going back, according to some scholars, to the fourth century B.C.E. or earlier. It survives in Greek (including a Greek fragment found at *Qumran; see Baillet, *Petites grottes*, p. 143) but it may well have been translated from a Hebrew original. Text: Revised Standard Version with Apocrypha.

Leviticus Rabba (also *Vayyiqra [Wayyiqra] Rabba*): A homiletical midrash on the book of Leviticus, apparently redacted sometime in the fifth century C.E. in the land of Israel, but containing much earlier material. Text: Margulies, *Midrash Wayyikra Rabbah*. All translations mine.

Life of Adam and Eve: There exist in various languages and recensions different expansions of the Adam and Eve story in Genesis, all of which have certain common elements. Five principal versions of this narrative—the Greek *Apocalypse of Moses*, and the Latin, Armenian, Georgian, and Slavonic texts of the *Life of Adam and Eve*—have recently been presented synoptically in Anderson and Stone, *Synopsis of the Books of Adam and Eve*. As Anderson has demonstrated ("Penitence Narrative . . ."), the Armenian and Georgian versions of this text sometimes preserve more clearly than the others exegetical motifs from what was presumably the earliest form of this text; however, sometimes the opposite seems to be the case. In any event, I have indicated in citations herein from which of the various versions I am citing; for the more widely known Greek and Latin texts I have generally used Johnson's translations in Charlesworth, *OTP* 2:249–295, though sometimes I have translated them myself. (The Greek text is referred to herein as the *Apocalypse of Moses*, while in citing the latter I have referred to, specifically, the Latin text or the *Vita*.)

The interrelationship of these texts in their various recensions remains an unresolved question. However, all these texts arguably trace their ancestry back to an original Hebrew or Aramaic text of perhaps the first century C.E., which was subsequently modified more than once in the process of transmission. These "primary Adam writings" should be distinguished from the "secondary Adam literature," texts dealing with Adam and Eve that are generally of Christian authorship, though influenced by the primary Adam writings. This group includes, in Greek, the *Apocalypse of Adam*, *Penitence of Adam*, *Testament of Adam*, and the *Life of Adam*, as well as some of the Adam material contained in the Greek and Slavonic *Palei* and the Syriac *Cave of Treasures*; it also includes the *Conflict of Adam and Eve with Satan*, a work extant in Ethiopic and Arabic, and yet other writings. See further Stone, *History of the Literature of Adam and Eve*.

Luke, gospel of: see *Gospels

LXX: see *Septuagint

m.: Designates a tractate of the *Mishnah, thus m. *Abot* 3:14.

MT: Masoretic text. See traditional Hebrew text.

Maccabees, book of: The name given to four different books: see below. Translations: Revised Standard Version of the Bible with Apocrypha; also (for 3 and 4 Maccabees) Anderson in Charlesworth, *OTP* 2:509–564.

1 Maccabees: This book recounts the successful Jewish revolt against the Hellenized Syrians ruling their homeland. The revolt, which began in 167 B.C.E., was led by a group known as the Maccabees. The same book also contains a further chronicle of events to the end of the second century B.C.E. This book was apparently intended not only to celebrate the military victory but, as well, to legitimate the Hasmonean dynasty that this victory inaugurated. It was probably written early in the first century B.C.E.

2 Maccabees: Essentially a greatly abridged (and somewhat garbled) version of a now lost history of the Maccabean revolt written by a certain "Jason of Cyrene" (otherwise unknown), this abridgement was probably completed in the first half of the first century B.C.E.

3 Maccabees: A historical romance, this book was originally written in Greek in the first century B.C.E. and set in the third century B.C.E.

4 Maccabees: This book is a treatise devoted to the theme of reason's domination of the passions. Written in Greek in the first century C.E., it uses biblical people and incidents to illustrate its ideas.

(1QS or 1Q28) Manual of Discipline: see *Community Rule*

Mark, gospel of: see *Gospels*

Martyrdom and Ascension of Isaiah: A composite work whose first part (chapters 1–5) is now known as the *Martyrdom of Isaiah* (containing within it an independent unit, 3:13–4:22, which is sometimes called the *Testament of Hezekiah*); its second part, chapters 6–11, is called the *Vision of Isaiah*. The *Martyrdom* section (minus the *Testament of Hezekiah*, which appears to be a Christian interpolation) is the oldest part of the work, going back to the first century C.E. or earlier, arguably back even to the second century B.C.E. As for the *Testament of Hezekiah* section, it has been dated to the end of the first century C.E., while the *Vision of Isaiah* section may belong to the second or third century C.E. Translation: Knibb in Charlesworth, *OTP* 2:143–176.

Masoretic text (MT): see *traditional Hebrew text*

Matthew, gospel of: see *Gospels*

Megillat Ta'anit: A brief work written in Aramaic apparently about the time of the destruction of the temple by the Romans in 70 C.E. It is essentially a list of various holidays and remembrances established in Second Temple times and on which fasting and public mourning were forbidden. Some time after its composition, this text was supplemented by a scholion, written in Hebrew, explaining the contents of the list. The later date of the scholion notwithstanding, some of the information contained in it seems to be an accurate recording of ancient traditions. The text is, however, much in need of a new scholarly edition taking advantage of new manuscripts and linguistic information. An important new reckoning with this material is being made by Vered Noam, with some of her results already summarized in "The Scholion of *Megillat Ta'anit*—Toward an Understanding of its Stemma." She has argued that Lichtenstein's (eclectic) edition of the text is based on the false assumption that the two versions of it represented by mss. Parma and Oxford represent essentially a single work, the former being simply a shorter version of the latter. Noam's claim is that they were two quite different texts which were later supplemented by an expanded version that evolved in Europe in the twelfth to thirteenth centuries C.E. I have also used her unpublished Master's thesis (under the direction of Prof. Y. Sussman), "The Scholion to Megillat Ta'anit," Hebrew University, 1991. All translations mine. Edition: Hans Lichtenstein, "Die Fastenrolle," in the light of Noam, "The Scholion." Citations refer to page numbers in Lichtenstein's edition. See also Tabory, "When Was the Fast-Scroll Nullified?"

Mekhilta deR. Ishmael: A (rabbinic) collection of interpretations of verses in the book of Exodus. The *Mekhilta deR. Ishmael* is one of a group of texts known collectively as the *halakhic midrashim;* it would thus seem to belong to the third century C.E. In citing from the *Mekhilta deR. Rabbi Ishmael,* I have generally relied on the printed editions of Horovitz and Rabin, *Mekhilta of Rabbi Ishmael,* and that of Lauterbach. However, neither of these editions take into account the Eastern textual tradition, and there is need for a new critical edition: see Kahane, "The Critical Edition of the Mekhilta deR. Ishmael in the Light of Geniza Fragments." All translations mine.

Mekhilta deR. Shimon b. Yoḥai: One of the *halakhic midrashim,* a collection of interpretations of verses in the book of Exodus. For various reasons, scholars have suggested that it may in fact be somewhat later than the other *halakhic midrashim,* belonging therefore to the fourth or even fifth century C.E. Text: Epstein and Melamed, *Mekhilta deR. Šim'on b. Yoḥai,* though this edition is in need of updating in the light of new material. All translations mine.

(11Q13) Melchizedek Text: A *Qumran document centering on the figure of Melchizedek; its date is somewhat difficult to fix, but most scholars set it in the first century B.C.E. Translations mine.

(4Q521) Messianic Apocalypse: A brief, fragmentary text from *Qumran that twice seems to assert a belief in the resurrection of the dead. Published by Puesch, "Une apocalypse méssianique."

midrash: A Hebrew term meaning interpretation or exegesis. The term is used nowadays to designate specifically the sort of exegesis practiced by the *Rabbis and contained in such works as the *Babylonian and *Jerusalem Talmuds as well as various collections of rabbinic exegesis, such as the *Mekhilta deR. Ishmael, *Sifrei Deuteronomy, *Genesis (Exodus, Leviticus, etc.) Rabba, and dozens of others. *Midrash* is also often used as the title of such collections of exegesis, such as *Midrash ha-Gadol, Midrash Tanḥuma,* and so forth.

Midrash Abkir: A midrashic collection, now lost save for scattered excerpts in *Yalqut Shimoni and other works; a late medieval date appears likely. The name derives from the initial letters in the phrase "*Amen Beyamenu* [probably originally *Ba*] *Ken Yehi Raṣon*" ("He [the Messiah] is indeed coming, may it be [God's] will"), with which its homilies ended.

Midrash ha-Gadol: A late-medieval anthology of midrash on the Pentateuch. This collection, of Yemenite origin (generally attributed to David b. Amram of Aden, Yemen, who lived in the thirteenth or fourteenth century), often freely reworks its sources, sometimes interpolating material from Maimonides or other medieval scholars. At the same time, it also preserves much ancient material, some of it otherwise quite unattested or at least unknown in that particular form. Text: Margulies et al., *Midrash ha-Gadol.*

Midrash Konen: A midrash on the creation of the world, first printed in Venice, 1601. Text: Jellinek, *Bet ha-Midrasch,* 2:23–39. All translations mine.

Midrash Leqaḥ Tob: A late midrashic compilation on the Pentateuch and the five scrolls; it is attributed to Tubiah b. Eliʿezer, who lived in Bulgaria in the late eleventh and early twelfth centuries. Text: Buber, *Midrasch Lekach Tob.* All translations mine.

Midrash Petirat Moshe: see *Petirat Moshe

Midrash on Proverbs: A midrash on the biblical book of Proverbs that most scholars agree to have been compiled after the *Babylonian Talmud, some suggesting a date as late as the ninth or tenth century C.E. Text: Visotzky, *Midrash Mishle.* All translations mine.

Midrash on Psalms (or *Midrash Šoḥer Ṭob, Midrash Tehillim*): A composite midrash on the book of Psalms whose core probably goes back at least to Talmudic times; it was apparently compiled in some form in the land of Israel. Text: Buber, *Midrasch Tehillim,* and the *Midrash Šoḥer Ṭob;* also consulted: Braude, *The Midrash on Psalms.* All translations mine.

Midrash Sekhel Tob: A late midrashic compilation on the Pentateuch (only the Genesis and Exodus sections survive) written in 1139 by Menaḥem b. Solomon, possibly in Italy. Text: Buber, *Sechel Tob.* All translations mine.

Midrash Šoḥer Ṭob: see *Midrash on Psalms

Midrash Tanḥuma: An early medieval compilation of rabbinic midrash on the Torah extant in various forms. Because of a standard formula of opening, the midrashim in this collection are said to be of the *Tanḥuma-Yelammedenu* type, one found as well in other midrashic compilations and manuscripts including *Deuteronomy Rabba and parts of *Exodus Rabba, *Numbers Rabba, *Pesiqta Rabbati, and yet others. In addition to the standard ("printed") *Tanḥuma,* a significantly different text of this collection was published in the last century by Solomon Buber, who mistakenly believed his to be the "ancient" *Tanḥuma.* (This text is referred to herein as *Tanḥuma [Buber].*) Subsequently numerous *Tanḥuma* and *Tanḥuma*-like fragments have been published from manuscript. The various *Midrash Tanḥuma* texts and fragments may all stem back to a common type, but attempts to reconstruct any particular *Ur*-text have failed. Texts used herein: *Midrash Tanḥuma;* Buber, *Midrasch Tanḥuma;* fragments in Wertheimer, *Battei Midrašot,* 1:139–170; Urbach, "Fragments of Tanḥuma-Yelammedenu." All translations mine.

Midrash Tannaʿim: A reconstruction, made in the early twentieth century by David Hoffmann, of a lost *halakhic midrash on the book of Deuteronomy. Hoffmann derived most of his reconstruction from fragments preserved in *Midrash ha-Gadol as well as from some *Cairo Genizah fragments (see *Sirach) of this work published by Solomon Schechter; however, the actual content of the original work is still in dispute and a new edition, reckoning with Hoffmann's selections in the light of new information, is much to be desired. Text: Hoffmann, *Midrash Tanna'im Lesepher Debarim*. All translations mine.

Midrash on the Ten Commandments (or *Midrash 'Aseret ha-Dibberot*): A compilation of narratives and other material loosely connected to the Decalogue (see further Dan, *The Hebrew Story in the Middle Ages*, 79–85). Text: Jellinek, *Beit ha-Midrasch*, 1:62–90.

Midrash Tehillim: see **Midrash on the Psalms*

Midrash Wayyissa'u: An account of the wars of Jacob's sons that parallels the narratives in *Jubilees* 34 and the *Testament of Judah*; the relationship between these texts remains obscure. Text: Hyman, Lerrer, and Shiloni, *Yalquṭ Šim'oni*, 2:691–694.

Midrash Wehizhir: A medieval midrashic collection on the biblical books of Exodus-Numbers. Text: Freimann, *Midrash Wehizhir*.

MidrEschat a and *b*: see (4Q174) *Florilegium

(4Q394–399) Miqṣat Ma'asei ha-Torah: see *(4Q394–399)* *Halakhic Letter

Mishnah: A codification of Jewish law and practice put into its final form around 200 C.E. It fleshes out the details of many things treated only cursorily in biblical law in addition to addressing a number of entirely new matters. For the "traditions of the elders" that it transmits, see in greater detail Chapter 20 above and also **Rabbis, the*. Although not generally concerned with biblical interpretation as such, the Mishnah nonetheless contains much information about tannaitic and earlier Jewish biblical exegesis. All translations mine.

Moses, Armenian History of: See **Armenian Apocrypha*. This particular text is to be found in Issaverdens, *Uncanonical Writings of the Old Testament*, and Stone, *Armenian Apocrypha*, 109–116.

(1Q22) Moses, Words of (Dibrei Mosheh): see *Words of Moses

motif: see *exegetical motif

Nag Hammadi library: A collection of gnostic religious texts first discovered in December 1945 at Nag Hammadi in Egypt. The texts are written in Coptic but were originally composed in Greek. Although the texts are of diverse character, gnosticism appears to be the unifying element of the collection. Among the Nag Hammadi texts cited herein are: the **Apocalypse of Adam*, **Apocryphon of John*, **Concept of Our Great Power*, **Hypostasis of the Archons*, **On the Origin of the World*, *Sophia of Jesus Christ*, *Teaching of Sylvanus*, **Tripartite Tractate*, and **Valentinian Exposition*.

(4Q169) Nahum Pesher: A fairly well preserved text from *Qumran that presents a commentary on selected verses from the biblical book of Nahum, seeking to find referents to the prophet's words in the events of the commentator's own era. Text: Allegro, *Qumran Cave 4:I (DJD 5)*, 37–42; Strugnell, "Notes," 204–210. Translations mine.

narrative expansion: One of the most characteristic features of ancient biblical scholarship, whereby all manner of "extras" not found in the biblical text itself—additional actions performed by someone in the biblical narrative or words spoken by him—are inserted in a retelling of the text by some later author or in a commentary upon it. Such narrative expansions are, by definition, *exegetical* because they are ultimately based on something that *is* in the text—an unusual word or turn of phrase that sets off the imagination or the exegete, or simply some problem in the plot that requires resolution. Narrative expansions may be said to be based upon one or more *exegetical motif.

(4Q462) Narrative Fragment: A text from *Qumran that refers to events in the book of Genesis and elsewhere; the manuscript seems to date from the first century B.C.E., though the text itself may have been composed earlier. Text: M. Smith, "4Q462 (Narrative) Fragment." All translations mine.

Nash Papyrus: An ancient Hebrew manuscript purchased from an Egyptian dealer by W. L. Nash in 1903. This brief text dates from around 150 B.C.E. and contains the Decalogue followed by the beginning of the Shema (Deut. 6:4–9). The two passages may have been written together because they were intended to be recited together as part of the public liturgy, as specified in m. *Tamid* 5:1.

(2Q24, 4Q554–555, 5Q15, 11Q18) New Jerusalem: An Aramaic work found at *Qumran that appears to contain a detailed, first-person, account of a (visionary) tour of the city of Jerusalem. The relationship of the various fragments remains to be clarified. Translations mine.

Noah, (Armenian) Story of: Many ancient interpretive texts and traditions have been preserved only in Armenian; this (along with others) is to be found in Stone, *Armenian Apocrypha Relating to the Patriarchs and Prophets.*

(4Q380 and 381) Non-Canonical Psalms: A number of manuscripts from *Qumran contain psalmlike compositions that are not found in the present Jewish biblical canon (see, for example, *Hymn to the Creator*). The manuscripts numbered 4Q380 and 381 are fragments of collections of such texts. The manuscripts themselves have been dated roughly to the end of the second century B.C.E.; the texts may have been composed then or as much as a century or two earlier. Text: Schuller, *Non-Canonical Psalms from Qumran.* All translations mine.

Numbers Rabba (also *Bemidbar Rabba*): A composite medieval midrash on the book of Numbers, whose first part comments extensively on Numbers chapters 1–7, while the second part is a form of *Midrash Tanḥuma* on the rest of Numbers. Text: *Midrash Rabba.* All translations mine.

Numenius (of Apamea, Syria; second half of second century C.E.): An author cited by *Clement of Alexandria, *Origen, *Eusebius, and others, he was an admirer of Judaism and spoke of Moses favorably. Passages attributed to him are assembled in Stern, *Greek and Latin Authors,* 2:206–216.

Odes of Solomon: Much about these ancient hymnic compositions remains unresolved, including their original language (it seems to have been a Semitic one, though even this is not certain), the nature of the original community in which they were used (whether Jewish or Christian, and of what sort), and even whether the hymns represent a one-time composition or a later editorial reworking of earlier hymns. There are some striking similarities between them and the Qumran *Thanksgiving Hymns* (Hodayot), similarities in language, style, and ideas. An approximate date of 100 C.E. has been suggested by Charlesworth (*OTP* 2:727), but given the ambiguities mentioned, such a date must be regarded as only a broad approximation. Translation: Charlesworth in his *OTP* 2:735–771; Emerton in Sparks, *AOT* 683–732.

On the Origin of the World: A gnostic treatise (whose true title is unknown, the current one having been assigned to it by modern scholars), one of the texts of the *Nag Hammadi library. It was probably written, according to its editors, in Alexandria in the late third or fourth century C.E. Translation: *Coptic Nag Hammadi Library.*

Origen: Born in Alexandria around 185 C.E. into a family of Christians (his father died a martyr's death for his beliefs when Origen was seventeen), Origen received a full classical as well as Christian education. He was an extraordinary prolific and influential writer, the author of a systematic exposition of Christian belief, *First Principles* (*De Principiis*), as well as a refutation of a learned attack on Christianity, *Contra Celsum*, plus a ten-volume book of *Miscellanies* (*Stromata*), numerous biblical commentaries covering nearly all of the Old and New Testaments, and smaller treatises on specific subjects. In addition to all this, he was also the compiler of the *Hexapla* (see *Aquila), a work of remarkable biblical scholarship. As a commentator Origen championed the Alexandrian style of allegorizing that went back to Philo and his predecessors. Text of "Commentary on Matthew" from Klostermann and Benz, *Origenes Werke*, vol. 11. Translation of *First Principles* by G. W. Butterworth; translation of *Contra Celsum* by Henry Chadwick.

Orphica: see *Pseudo-Orphica

'Otiyot (or *Alphabet*) *deR. Aqiba:* A late Jewish mystical treatise written in Hebrew and of uncertain origin; it has been dated to around the seventh to ninth centuries C.E. Text: Wertheimer, *Battei Midrašot*, 2:333–477. All translations mine.

Paraleipomena Jeremiou (or *Things Omitted from Jeremiah*): see 4 *Baruch

(4Q422) Paraphrase of Genesis and Exodus: This document (like the much longer 4Q364–367 *Reworked Pentateuch) paraphrases parts of the Pentateuch. The script of this manuscript belongs to the earlier part of the first century B.C.E. It was published by Elgvin and Tov in Attridge et al., *Qumran Cave 4: VIII* (*DJD 13*), 417–442. All translations mine.

Passover Haggadah: A composite text traditionally read in conjunction with the festive evening meal on the Jewish holiday of Passover (*Pesaḥ*). The oldest parts of this text may arguably go back to before the common era, but there are also many accretions from Talmudic and even later times; the existence of traditions underlying the present *Passover Haggadah* is attested in the *Mishnah, *Tosefta, and elsewhere. Text: Goldschmidt, *The Passover Haggadah*. All translations mine.

Pastoral Letters (or *Pastoral Epistles*): Three New Testament letters, 1 and 2 *Timothy and the Letter to *Titus, are collectively known by this name because all three deal with matters of the congregation and pastoral care. The letters are attributed to Paul but this attribution is doubted by some scholars. Those who hold the latter view generally date them to the late first century C.E. See also *Paul. Translation: Revised Standard Version.

Paul (of Tarsus, a city in Cilicia, which was a Roman province along the southern coast of Asia Minor) (c. 10 C.E.–c. 62 C.E.): The great apostle of Christianity, indeed, its "second founder," Paul is the author of a good portion of the letters (or "epistles") collected in the New Testament. Thirteen letters in all are ascribed to him there, but modern scholars have generally concluded that some of these (*Ephesians, 1 and 2 *Timothy, and *Titus) were written by his followers, while the status of others (2 *Thessalonians, *Colossians) is in doubt. There is, however, general agreement that *Romans, 1 and 2 *Corinthians, *Galatians, *Philippians, 1 *Thessalonians, and *Philemon are authentically Paul's.

Paul was born, raised, and educated a Jew, "circumcised on the eighth day, of the people of Israel, of the tribe of Benjamin, a Hebrew born of Hebrews" (Phil. 3:5). He studied with the Jewish scholar R. Gamaliel (Acts 22:3, see also 5:34) and his letters attest to his acquaintance with Jewish traditions of biblical interpretation. After his conversion to Christianity (around 34 or 35 C.E.), Paul devoted himself to preaching and working on behalf of the new faith: he traveled widely along the eastern Mediterranean and beyond and corresponded with the newly founded churches. He was imprisoned and attacked for his beliefs and is said to have died a martyr's death. His letters articulate his own understanding of Christian belief, and in so doing they frequently rely on bold, new interpretations of ancient Hebrew Scripture to make their case. There was hardly a more significant biblical interpreter in the early church. Translations of Paul's (and other) New Testament epistles: Revised Standard Version, occasionally modified slightly.

Pentateuch: The first five books of the Hebrew Bible—Genesis through Deuteronomy—also known by the Hebrew word *Torah (understood as "teaching").

Pentateuchal Paraphrase: see *Reworked Pentateuch

(4Q252) Pesher on Genesis: see *Genesis Pesher

(4Q169) Pesher on Nahum: see *Nahum Pesher

(4Q 180–181) Pesher of the Periods: (also *Ages of Creation*): A Hebrew text from *Qumran that (according to J. T. Milik) may originally have contained a lengthy account of the "seventy generations" of human history mentioned in *1 Enoch* 10:12. The text as it survives is quite fragmentary; all translations mine.

Peshitta (or Pešiṭta): The name given to the Syriac (a very close relative of Aramaic) translation of the Old Testament widely used by Syriac-speaking Christians, including *Aphrahat and *Ephraem. Its origins (apparently composite) are unknown; some scholars have suggested that it may have started as an adaptation of one or more Jewish targums, since a number of interpretations otherwise known from rabbinic literature are to be found within it. Others have nonetheless maintained that it was from the start a Christian translation. See further Dirksen, "The Old Testament Peshitta." On the connection between the Peshitta and rabbinic exegesis, see also Maori, *The Peshitta Version;* this book appeared too late for systematic use in the present work. All translations mine.

Pesiqta deR. Kahana: A rabbinic collection of midrashic sermons designed for various Jewish festivals and other special occasions, apparently redacted sometime in the fifth century C.E. in the land of Israel, but containing much earlier material. Text: Mandelbaum, *Pesikta de Rav Kahana.* All translations mine.

Pesiqta Rabbati: A rabbinic collection of midrashic sermons designed for various Jewish festivals and other special occasions. It is patently a composite of originally separate compositions; these were combined into the present work sometime in perhaps the sixth or seventh century, though such a date says little about the age of the material contained within this work. Establishing a textual basis for *Pesiqta Rabbati* is particularly difficult; in the absence of a critical edition, I have generally used M. Friedmann's standard edition, comparing it with some of the extant manuscripts and duplicate passages in *Yalqut Shimoni*, as well as Braude, *Pesiqta Rabbati*. All translations mine.

1 and 2 Peter: Two New Testament letters ascribed to the apostle Peter but now generally agreed to be pseudonymous. Their dates are uncertain, but some time late in the first or early in the second century C.E. seems possible for both. Translation: Revised Standard Version.

Petirat Moshe: A medieval midrashic compilation dealing with the death of Moses, some of it based on much earlier material. Text cited from Jellinek, *Bet ha-Midrasch*, 6:71–78. Translation mine.

Pharisees: see the description of rival Jewish groups under *Rabbis, the.

Philemon, Letter to: A brief (authentic) letter of Paul found in the New Testament. See also: *Paul. Translation: Revised Standard Version, with occasional, slight modifications.

Philippians, Letter to the: A letter (or, possibly, a composite of two or three different letters) sent by Paul to the church in Philippi (Macedonia); it is part of the New Testament. Because of its possibly composite nature, its date is uncertain; see also: *Paul. Translation: Revised Standard Version, with occasional, slight modifications.

Philo (of Alexandria; c. 20 B.C.E.–c. 40 or 50 C.E.): This Greek-speaking Egyptian Jew is the author of a multivolume series of commentaries on the Pentateuch. Philo was heir to an already existing tradition of interpreting the Bible allegorically, a tradition that appears to have flourished in Alexandria, Egypt. Philo championed this approach; for him, although biblical stories recounted historical events, they likewise had an "under-meaning" (*huponoia*) by which Abraham, Jacob, and other biblical figures were understood to represent abstractions or spiritual realities whose truth applied to all times and places. Philo explained many biblical texts in keeping with then-current Greek philosophical ideas.

  Although Philo's allegorical explanations of Scripture were certainly widely known in the Jewish world, his works played almost no role in the later history of Jewish biblical interpretation. They were, however, extraordinarily important to Alexandrine Christianity, and through the writings of Clement of Alexandria, Eusebius, and other Christian scholars gained a place for his ideas and methods in much Christian biblical interpretation.

  When citing from Philo, I have used the translated names of treatises as found in the (standard) English translation by F. H. Colson and G. H. Whitaker, rather than the Latin abbreviations more commonly used in scholarly reference, since these are generally not familiar to the nonspecialist. Translation: Colson and Whitaker in LCL, sometimes slightly modified; also, where indicated, translations taken from Winston, *Philo of Alexandria*. The Loeb edition does not quite include all of Philo's writings, and since its publication some new texts have come to light. Note the Greek fragments of Philo's *Questions on Genesis* 2:1–7 published in Paramelle, *Philon d'Alexandrie*.

Philo the Epic Poet: A Jewish writer who must have lived sometime before the mid-first century B.C.E., since his poetry is cited by *Alexander Polyhistor, whence it found its way into the writings of *Eusebius. It is difficult to be more precise about the date of Philo's work; as for his place of origin, although he does describe Jerusalem in some of the passages preserved, the fact that he chose to write Greek epic might more likely point to the Greek city of Alexandria as his homeland. Translations: Attridge in Charlesworth, *OTP* 2:780–784; Holladay, *Fragments from Hellenistic Jewish Authors*, 2:205–299.

Pirqei deR. Eliezer (or *Pirqei R. Eli'ezer*): A midrashic work, written in rabbinic Hebrew, that retells much of the Pentateuch and discourses on other themes. Its allusions to Islamic culture and to Arab rule over the land of Israel certainly suggest that this work was put into its final form after the Arab conquest—according to some, as late as the eighth or ninth century C.E. At the same time, the text preserves many ancient traditions, including quite a few known only from the biblical *Apocrypha and *Pseudepigrapha. At times these traditions are presented by *Pirqei deR. Eliezer* in a form that suggests that their author had read these pseudepigraphic texts not in the Greek or other translations through which these texts have survived in Christian churches, but in a Hebrew or Aramaic version now lost. The midrashic material presented in *Pirqei deR. Eliezer* overlaps a good deal with that found in *Targum Pseudo-Jonathan*, but the precise relationship between these two texts remains the subject of conjecture. Text: *Pirqei deR. Eli'ezer*. All translations mine.

Pliny the Elder (23–24 C.E. – 79 C.E.): A Latin chronicler and geographer whose brief description of the *Essenes and their settlement has been connected with the site at *Qumran, home of the *Dead Sea Scrolls. Text: Pliny, *Natural History*, in LCL. Translation mine.

Pompeius Trogus (late first century B.C.E. to early first century C.E.): A classical historian whose *Historiae Philippicae* (a work that survived only via a later epitome) apparently focused on the history of the Macedonian-Hellenistic states, in the course of which he surveyed the history of the Jews and the geography of Judaea. Text and translation: Stern, *Greek and Latin Authors*, 1:334–343.

Prayer of Azariah and the Song of the Three Young Men: Two compositions, both of which arguably had existed previously as independent works, that came to be inserted in the book of Daniel between vv. 3:23 and 3:24 of the present traditional Hebrew text. They are preserved in the old Greek (*Septuagint) version of that book. Their insertion doubtless represents an attempt to have the book of Daniel conform to the pattern evidenced elsewhere in the literature of the Second Temple period, according to which humans in distress first pray to God for help and then offer words of thanksgiving after being saved. Both compositions draw heavily on the language of the Psalms and other biblical models. They probably were originally composed in Hebrew, perhaps in the first or second century B.C.E. Translation: Revised Standard Version with Apocrypha.

(4Q369) *Prayer of Enosh:* This text, addressed to God, has, to my mind, wrongly been identified both as a "prayer of Enosh" and a "messianic" text; in fact it deals with the biblical Jacob. The manuscript has been dated to the end of the first century B.C.E. or early first century C.E. Text: Elgvin et al., *Qumran Cave 4:VIII* (*DJD* 13), 353–362. All translations mine.

Prayer of Joseph: A fragmentary text bearing witness to the tradition that "Israel" was the name of the angel whose earthly correspondent was the patriarch Jacob. It was arguably written in the second, or possibly first, century C.E. Discussion and translation: Smith in Charlesworth, *OTP* 2:699–714.

Prayer of Manasseh: A short, penitential prayer attributed to the biblical king Manasseh. The existence of the text of such a prayer is mentioned in 2 Chron. 33:18–19. It is most unlikely, however, that our text is in fact the one being referred to in this passage; rather, the author of this text may have been inspired by 2 Chron. 33:18–19 to compose his own prayer and attribute it to Manasseh. (Alternately, our text may have merely been a stock liturgical piece that only later came to be attributed to Manasseh—a great sinner according to 2 Kings 21—because its anonymous speaker confesses to having committed sins that "are more in number than the sand of the sea; my transgressions are multiplied, O Lord, they are multiplied" [v. 9].) The text survives in Greek, Syriac, and other languages and is included among the *Apocrypha of the Hebrew Bible. The date of its composition is the subject of much speculation, but since the text appears to be a Jewish work without Christian embellishment, it may indeed have been a standard part of Jewish liturgy taken over unmodified into early Christian worship. If so, a date somewhere around the turn of the era would not be unreasonable. Text: Revised Standard Version with Apocrypha.

(4Q378–379) Psalms of Joshua (or *Joshua Apocryphon*): An apocryphal work found at *Qumran, parts of which were published in Newsom, "'Psalms of Joshua' from Qumran Cave 4." See also (4Q175) **Testimonia.*

Psalms of Solomon: These psalms are preserved in Greek and (partially) in Syriac, but most scholars agree that they were originally composed in Hebrew. They seem to reflect the political situation of the land of Israel, and at least some of them appear to refer to inner-Jewish strife; others refer as well to a conqueror who came "from the end of the earth" (8:15)—apparently the Roman emperor Pompey, who captured Jerusalem in 63 B.C.E. (Further details seeming to support this interpretation are to be found in 2:1–2, 26–27; 8:16–21; and 17:12.) *Psalms of Solomon* 17 and 18 further reflect expectation of the Davidic messiah. All these would suggest a first-century B.C.E. date for the psalms, although they need not all have been composed at the same time. Translations: Wright in *OTP* 2:630–670, and Brock in Sparks, *AOT* 649–682, occasionally modified slightly.

Pseudepigrapha (of the Hebrew Bible): A somewhat loose term to describe a group of texts, mostly written between the third century B.C.E. and the second century C.E., which, although generally not attributed the same sanctity as the Bible, were nonetheless studied and preserved by early Jews and Christians. They are called "Pseudepigrapha" ("falsely ascribed" writings) because many of them purport to be the pronouncements of this or that ancient worthy known from the Hebrew Bible—Enoch, Abraham, Jacob, and so forth. A great many of these books retell biblical stories or seek to comment on incidents or figures known from the Bible, and they can thus tell us much about how the Bible was read and interpreted from the third century B.C.E. on.

Among the Pseudepigrapha are various apocalypses, or revelations, given to this or that ancient figure, often "foretelling" events belonging to the time in which the apocalypse in question was actually written (*Apocalypse of Abraham, *Apocalypse of Adam, and so forth; see also *Sibylline Oracles); testaments, that is, the "last words" or spiritual wills of biblical figures standing at the threshold of death and imparting advice and recollections to their children (*Testament of Adam, *Testament of Abraham, *Testaments of the Twelve Patriarchs, and so forth); and interpretive retellings and expansions of biblical stories (the book of *Jubilees, *Pseudo-Philo, Book of Biblical Antiquities, and so forth). Current anthologies of the Pseudepigrapha in English include: Charles, APOT; Charlesworth, OTP; and Sparks, AOT.

Pseudo-Clementine Homilies: This text, probably written in Syria or Palestine in the late second century c.e., contains numerous allusions to exegetical traditions, many of which are paralleled in rabbinic texts. The text may have originated in an early Judeo-Christian community. (The Pseudo-Clementine Recognitions are a quite separate composition, probably written in the mid-fourth century c.e. in Palestine or Syria; they survive in the Latin translation of Rufinus.) See further Jones, "The Pseudo-Clementines: A History of Research." Text: Rehm and Strecker, Die Pseudoklementinen I: Homilien. All translations mine.

Pseudo-Eupolemus: see *Eupolemus

(4Q225–227) Pseudo-Jubilees: The name given to these fragments because, while they contain some features characteristic of the book of Jubilees (direct address by the text's speaker to "you, Moses," reference to the Satanic "Prince Mastema," and the reckoning of time by jubilees), they do not appear to be actual excerpts of that book. (The name Pseudo-Jubilees is somewhat unfortunate, since it might seem to imply a pseudepigraphon upon a pseudepigraphon, which is far from certain; indeed, even any direct connection with Jubilees is purely speculative.) The earliest copies at *Qumran belong to the late first century B.C.E.; the time of the texts' original composition is a matter of speculation. All translations mine.

(4Q390) Pseudo-Moses: The name given to a fragmentary text from *Qumran by D. Dimant in her preliminary edition of two large sections of it ("New Light from Qumran on the Jewish Pseudepigrapha"), but there is no clear indication that Moses is in fact its speaker; what is sure is that the text has something in common with the book of Jubilees—terminology and outlook—as well as other works discovered at Qumran. The manuscript has been dated to the end of the first century B.C.E. or so, but the text may well have been composed a century or so earlier. All translations mine.

Pseudo-Orphica: The name given to what appears to be original Greek poetry, attributed to the mythic figure Orpheus, which has undergone a complicated process of augmentation and editing. The poem cited is itself quite brief, forty-six lines in its longest form. It is presented as Orpheus' poetic instruction delivered to his son Musaeus. The poem survives in scattered quotations found among various early Christian writers, *Clement of Alexandria, *Eusebius of Caesarea, Pseudo-Justin, and others; using these passages, scholars have reconstructed what appear to be different recensions of the text. There is little agreement about how or when these recensions came into existence. In this volume I have followed the reconstruction of Carl Holladay. It seems likely to me that the earliest form of the poem (Recension A) goes back to the late third or second century B.C.E., while the second recension, with its Abraham material, may belong to the second or first century B.C.E., with recensions C and D belonging to still later times. Text and translation: Holladay, *Pseudo-Orphica* (forthcoming; vol. 4 of his *Fragments of Hellenistic Jewish Authors*); also LaFargue in *OTP* 2:799–801; Eusebius, *La Préparation Evangélique*, text and trans. Schroeder et des Places.

Pseudo-Philo: The author of the Latin *Book of Biblical Antiquities* was long presumed to be Philo of Alexandria; when it was demonstrated that Philo was not the author of this work, its anonymous creator came to be known as Pseudo-Philo. The book in question is a retelling of much of biblical history, from Adam to the death of Saul. Probably originally composed in Hebrew sometime before the middle of the second century C.E., it was subsequently translated into Greek and from Greek into Latin. It not only retells biblical stories but adds a wealth of interpretations, explanations, fanciful details, poems, and songs. Some of its interpretations are strikingly similar to those found in rabbinic writings. Translations are mine, though I have frequently been guided by Harrington's rendering in Charlesworth, *OTP.* Text of the original: D. Harrington et al., *Pseudo-Philon: Les Antiquités bibliques*, vol. 1.

Pseudo-Phocylides, Sentences of: A collection of metrical maxims and advice falsely attributed to the sixth-century B.C.E. proverbist Phocylides of Miletus; in fact this text was written sometime around the end of the first century B.C.E. by a Jewish poet bent on enshrining some of the laws and teachings of the Hebrew Bible—along with a certain amount of ancient biblical interpretation, as well as sage teaching not dependent on Jewish traditions—in Greek hexameters. Translation: Van der Horst in Charlesworth, *OTP* 2:565–582.

Qumran (or *Khirbet Qumrān*): A site near the Dead Sea, about eight and a half miles from Jericho, where, starting in 1947, a collection of ancient Jewish manuscripts, the *Dead Sea Scrolls, were found hidden away in various caves. Qumran was apparently the home-base of an ascetic Jewish community, probably to be identified with the Essene sect known from the writings of *Josephus and others, which flourished just before and on into the common era.

Qur'an (Koran): The sacred Scripture of Islam. Held by Muslims to have been dictated by God to Muḥammad, it belongs to the seventh century C.E. and contains various reflections of ancient biblical interpretation.

R.: see next entry

Rabbi: An honorific title (often abbreviated "R.") that means "my teacher" or "my master." See *Rabbis, the.

Rabbinic Judaism: The tradition of Judaism championed by the *Rabbis, which has survived, albeit with numerous modifications and innovations, in today's Judaism. Rabbinic Judaism is itself a descendant of the Judaism of the Pharisees, a group that existed in Second Temple times with its own distinctive style of interpretation and *halakhah.

Rabbis, the: A group of Jewish scholars that championed an approach to Scripture and to Judaism that came to bear their name (that is, *Rabbinic Judaism; see also *midrash). The Rabbis were so known because, starting in the first century C.E., the leaders and teachers of this group were addressed and spoken of as *"Rabbi" (that is, "my teacher," "my master"). A conventional distinction separates the Rabbis into two chronological groups: those before 200 C.E. (see *Mishnah) are called *tanna'im* and those after 200 C.E. are called *amora'im*. But as a school of exegetes and practitioners, the Rabbis are probably older than the use of their distinctive title might indicate: scholars of similar tendencies are known to us earlier as the "sages," "elders," *soferim* ("bookmen" or scribes), and Pharisees (possibly: "specifiers," "explainers"). The Pharisees are mentioned often in the New Testament, the writings of Josephus, the Mishnah, and elsewhere, but they are frequently presented as merely one of several rival Jewish groups that existed in Second Temple times. These groups disagreed on a number of fundamental issues; prominent among them was the matter of how and on what basis to interpret, extend, and apply biblical laws—that is, their systems of *halakhah*. (See on this issue Chapter 20 above.) It is clear that the Pharisees' *halakhah* was markedly different from that of another group, the Sadducees. Their two systems of *halakhah* had deep roots, perhaps going back early in the *Second Temple period. (At the same time, the overall Sadducean stance seems, to my mind, somewhat polemical, as if it originated in protest against a still older, already elaborate, system of *halakhah*.) There is some indication that the *Dead Sea Scrolls community basically followed the *halakhah* of the Sadducees, though they themselves seem to be connected (on the basis of other accounts in ancient writings) with yet a third group, the Essenes, a strict, somewhat ascetic Jewish sect that flourished in the same period.

Revelation, book of (also Book of the Apocalypse): A visionary book that is the last part of the New Testament; it contains cryptic images and revelations of the future, including the new Jerusalem. The book is attributed to "John," and tradition identified this John with the author of the fourth *Gospel and the "elder" who is the author of 2 and 3 *John, but modern scholars find scant reason to assert more than what the text itself says, that a certain John wrote this revelation. It has been dated to the late first century C.E. Translation: Revised Standard Version.

Revelation of Paul (or *Apocalypse of Paul*): Not the gnostic "Apocalypse of Paul" known from the *Nag Hammadi library but a New Testament apocryphon preserved in Latin, Greek, Syriac, Slavonic, and other languages. Translation: Hennecke and Schneemelcher, *New Testament Apocrypha*, 2:759–798.

Revised Standard Version: A popular modern translation of the Hebrew Bible, Apocrypha, and the New Testament undertaken under the sponsorship of the National Council of Churches. Because of its wide diffusion and familiarity I have tried to use this translation as much as possible, and I gratefully acknowledge its use. I have, however, more than occasionally diverged from it, usually to capture some particular nuance of the original text.

(4Q158 and 4Q364–367) Reworked Pentateuch (or *Pentateuchal Paraphrase*): The nature of these texts is still debated: Are they simply loose versions of the Pentateuch, which happen to change a word or two here or there but which only very rarely diverge from the biblical text for some purpose? Or are they instead explicative retellings that, while citing the text directly most of the time, nevertheless contain numerous slight deviations and additions intended to comment on or clarify the biblical text? In any case,

some of those deviations and additions do seem to conform with interpretive motifs attested elsewhere. The first group of manuscripts listed all seem to belong to the mid-first century B.C.E. Text: Attridge et al., *Qumran Cave 4 (DJD* 13), 187–353. 4Q158 was published in Allegro, *Qumran Cave 4: I (DJD* 5); see the remarks by Tov in *DJD* 13. All translations mine.

Romans, Letter to the: The longest and most important of Paul's authentic letters, this document systematically sets out much of Paul's theology. The letter was probably composed sometime between 55 and 58 C.E. See also: *Paul. Translation: Revised Standard Version, with occasional, slight modifications.

(1Q28b) Rule of the Blessings: A collection of various blessings preserved as an appendix to the *Community Rule* found at *Qumran. All translations mine.

(1Q28a) Rule of the Congregation: A text appended to (1QS) *Community Rule*, it consists of two full columns setting forth the "rule of the congregation of Israel in the final days." All translations mine.

Sadducees: see the description of rival Jewish groups under *Rabbis, the

Samaritan Pentateuch: The Hebrew text of the Pentateuch as preserved by the *Samaritans is slightly different from other forms of the Pentateuch text, such as the one apparently used by the *Septuagint translators or the Pentateuch as preserved by the *traditional (Masoretic) Hebrew text. Many of its differences may be attributed to the fact that the Pentateuch appears to have circulated in slightly different "editions" in late antiquity. See also *Septuagint. Text: von Gall, *Der Hebräische Pentateuch der Samaritaner.* All translations mine.

Samaritan Targum: This targum exists in widely divergent forms produced and revised over many centuries. The oldest form goes back to before the fourth century C.E. (its Aramaic is similar to that found in the Palestinian *targums), but greater precision as to the date is impossible, at least on linguistic grounds. I have used the critical edition of Tal, *The Samaritan Targum of the Pentateuch,* who suggests that the language of the earliest stratum of Samaritan targum texts may be "even older" than that of the Palestinian targums (vol. 3, p. 104). All translations mine.

Samaritans: Inhabitants of Samaria, a general name for the region north of biblical Judah or Judaea. When Samaria was conquered (along with the rest of the old Northern Kingdom of Israel) by the Assyrians in 722 B.C.E., the Assyrian king exiled the old, Israelite, inhabitants of Samaria's cities and repopulated the area with a conglomeration of different nations (2 Kings 17:24–31). Relations between the Jews—that is, the inhabitants of Judah—and the Samaritans in the *Second Temple period were often strained, and most Jews apparently regarded them as foreigners, although both groups worshiped the God of Israel and shared the Pentateuch as sacred Scripture (though the *Samaritan Pentateuch differs somewhat from the *traditional Hebrew text). In addition to the material preserved in the *Samaritan Targum, ancient Samaritan traditions of biblical interpretation are to be found in abundance in *Tibat Marqa; some scholars have suggested that *Theodotus, *(Pseudo)-Eupolemus, and the author of the *Aramaic Levi Document were Samaritans rather than Jews, but these attributions remain speculative and strong counterarguments have been advanced to each of them.

(4Q185) Sapiential Work: A work in praise of divine wisdom found at *Qumran. Text: Allegro, *DJD* 5, 85–87. All translations mine.

(4Q415) Sapiential Work A: An entirely different text from the preceding: quite fragmentary, it may have certain wisdom connections, though its character requires further exploration. (It may or may not be part of the same composition as found in another fragment 4Q416.) The text was published by Elgvin, "The Reconstruction of Sapiential Work A."

(4Q424) Sapiential Work C: Another composition of evident wisdom connections found at *Qumran; its advice is framed in a series of clauses beginning *"Do not . . ."*

(1Q22) Sayings of Moses (or *Dibrei Mosheh*): see *Words of Moses*

Second Temple period: The term basically referring to the entire span of history from the time of the Jews' return to their homeland after the Babylonian exile, starting in 538 B.C.E.—shortly after which (c. 520–515 B.C.E.) they rebuilt the Jerusalem Temple, which the Babylonians had destroyed—until the great revolt against the occupying Roman army in 66–70 C.E., at which time the Romans attacked Jerusalem and destroyed the temple once again. Although this entire time is technically covered by the phrase "Second Temple period," most scholars use the term to refer to the last few centuries thereof, as a more religiously neutral way of designating what Christian scholars had often called the "intertestamental period," that is, the time falling between the history recounted in the Old and New Testaments.

Secret Book according to John: see *Apocryphon of John*

Seder Eliahu Rabba (or *Tanna deBei Eliahu*): A midrashic compilation of uncertain date, certainly going back to before the ninth century. If its core is to be identified with the *Tanna deBei Eliahu* mentioned in the *Babylonian Talmud, then it must have existed before the latter was redacted (late fifth to early sixth century C.E.); some have even proposed a third-century C.E. date. Text: Isch-Schalom (Friedmann), *Seder Eliahu Rabba.* All translations mine.

Seder Olam: An ancient Hebrew chronography, traditionally ascribed to the *tanna* R. Yose b. Ḥalafta (second century C.E.), which retells biblical history in compressed form and supplies dates for major events. A critical edition of this text was published as part of a doctoral dissertation by Chaim Milikowsky, "Seder Olam: A Rabbinic Chronography," who is currently preparing an extensive commentary on the chronography. Milikowsky has argued that R. Yose b. Ḥalafta is cited more than any other authority in the book because he in fact transmitted it, his own comments later being incorporated into the work by his students; however, the text is in essence still older and may arguably be a "prerabbinic" document, its composition predating the destruction of the Jerusalem Temple in 70 C.E. (See further Milikowsky, "Seder Olam and Jewish Chronography," 124.) Text: Milikowsky (above); all translations mine.

Sefer ha-Yashar: A midrashic compilation in the form of an expansive retelling of biblical stories; composed in biblical Hebrew style probably no earlier than the thirteenth century. Its author is unknown, the place of its composition seems to be Italy. Text: *Sefer ha-Yašar.* All translations mine.

Septuagint: Starting in the third century B.C.E., Hebrew Scripture began to be translated into Greek, apparently for the use of Greek-speaking Jews in Hellenistic centers like Alexandria, Egypt. A legend eventually sprang up about this translation to the effect that seventy, or seventy-two, Jewish elders were commissioned to do the translation of the Pentateuch (Torah), each in an isolated cell; when the translations were compared, they all agreed in every detail, for the translators had been divinely guided. As a result, this translation came to be known as the *Septuaginta* ("seventy"). (Subsequently, the name "Septuagint" also came to include the old Greek translation of the other books of the Hebrew Bible, a translation made in stages from the third to the first century B.C.E.)

Any translation by nature contains a good bit of interpretation: ambiguities in the original text can rarely be duplicated in translation and, as a result, the translator must take a stand and render the ambiguity one way or another. Moreover, translators aware of this or that traditional interpretation will sometimes incorporate it (consciously or otherwise) into their translation. For both these reasons, the Septuagint, although a fairly close rendering, can frequently provide information about how a particular verse or phrase or single word was understood by Jews as early as the third century B.C.E.

However, there are great difficulties in using evidence from the Septuagint in an overall study of ancient interpretation of the Bible. To begin with, the biblical texts that were used by the Septuagint translators were often slightly, and in some cases, drastically, different from that of the *traditional Hebrew text; they bear witness to the coexistence of different text-forms of the Hebrew Bible in late antiquity. (The discovery of the *Dead Sea Scrolls has dramatically confirmed this fact.) No one of these text-forms can be said to be correct or "the best." Instead, there exists a whole branch of modern biblical scholarship, textual criticism, which is devoted to examining each and every verse of the Bible as preserved by various textual witnesses in order to understand the significance of any differences that might exist between different versions of that verse. Textual criticism is an art, not a science, and the conclusions of one textual critic are not necessarily shared by others. See further Jellicoe, *Septuagint and Modern Study;* Tov, *Text-Critical Use of the Septuagint.*

All this is of some consequence to the whole matter of ancient biblical interpretation. For example, it is often far from clear whether a particular difference between the Septuagint and the MT (the *Masoretic text, that is, the traditional Hebrew text of the Bible preserved by Jews through the ages) represents a case of the Septuagint translators *interpreting* in some nonliteral fashion the same Hebrew text as that found in the MT, or whether the difference between the Septuagint and the MT represents a difference in two different forms of the Hebrew text that were in circulation in late antiquity, the one having been used by the Septuagint translators and the other preserved in the MT. (The same is true, by the way, of differences between the Septuagint and other textual witnesses such as the *Samaritan Pentateuch* or ancient biblical manuscripts from *Qumran.) Nor, for that matter, is it often easy to establish which of various forms of a biblical verse attested in different sources represents the "most original" form of the verse (and which others, therefore, might represent some secondary, often simplified or *interpreted,* form of the same verse). Further complicating matters is the fact that the Septuagint itself underwent a complicated process of transmission and revision, so that in fact there is no one, single "Septuagint" to refer to.

I have not wished to impose all these complications on a book whose primary concern lies elsewhere and so, for example, I have only rarely referred in the body of this book to particular manuscripts of the Septuagint. Moreover, since numerous studies exist that seek to compare even minute differences between the Septuagint and other versions, I have not made such comparisons a major focus of this study, seeking instead to concentrate only on differences that seemed both significant and related to interpretive traditions witnessed in other ancient sources. All translations from Septuagint texts are my own. See also *Aquila, Symmachus, and Theodotion.

Shepherd of Hermas: A Christian apocalypse of possibly composite character; if it is a composite work, the earliest part seems to belong to the early second century c.e., the rest only slightly later. This text was apparently written in Rome and composed in a Greek sometimes marked by Latinisms as well as Semitisms, the latter apparently the result of an imitation of *Septuagint style. Text: *Apostolischen Väter: Neubearbeitung der Funkschen Ausgabe.* All translations mine.

Sibylline Oracles: A collection of oracular texts written in Greek in poetic form (hexameters) over a long period of time, from about the second century b.c.e. to the early Middle Ages. While some were apparently written in Alexandria, Egypt, others appear to stem from Syria or other locations. The unifying element of these diverse writings is their alleged authorship: they are ascribed to a "sibyl" or an aged woman prophet who speaks her metrical oracles (usual oracles of doom) in a state of ecstatic prophetic inspiration. Of the present collection of Sibylline books and fragments, some appear to have been written by Jews and to contain, in addition to various predictions and warnings, reflections of ideas and motifs found as well in the Hebrew Bible. The first three books of the *Sibylline Oracles,* which are those most frequently cited in the present work, are arguably ancient: book 3 seems to go back to the second century b.c.e.; books 1 and 2 may stem from a Jewish author living in the late first century b.c.e. or early in the common era, though this original text appears to have undergone augmentation by a Christian editor, possibly in the second century c.e. Translation: Collins in Charlesworth, OTP 1:317–472.

Sifra (also *Sifra debei Rab, Torat Kohanim*): A midrashic collection on the book of Leviticus. It is one of the *halakhic midrashim* and thus assumed to have been put into some preliminary form in the third century c.e. However, our present *Sifra* is a composite text. Thus, the *Mekhilta de Milluim* section of the book is a later addition, as is the section known as *Mekhilta de'arayot,* which is entirely absent from the first printed edition of the book (Constantinople, 1523) and is printed as a separate unit in ms. Assemani; while most of *Sifra* belongs to one of the two "sets" of *halakhic midrashim* (the Aqiba school), these two added sections seem to stem from the other (Ishma'el) set. There are apparently still other additions. Texts: *Sifra;* Weiss, *Sifra;* Friedman, *Sifra;* Finkelstein, *Sifra on Leviticus according to Vatican Ms. Assemani 66.* All translations mine.

Sifrei Deuteronomy (or *Sifrei Debarim*): A (rabbinic) collection of interpretations of verses found in sections of the book of Deuteronomy. It is one of the *halakhic midrashim* and thus assumed to have been put into some preliminary form in the third century c.e., though it certainly contains later additions. In citing from this text, I have consulted both the eclectic text of Finkelstein, *Siphre ad Deuteronomium* and mss. Margoliouth 341 and Bodleian Neubauer 151. See further Fraade, *From Tradition to Commentary,* xvii.

Sifrei Numbers (or *Sifrei Bemidbar, Sifrei deBei Rab*): A midrashic collection on the book of Numbers. It is one of the *halakhic midrashim* and thus assumed to have been put into some preliminary form in the third century C.E. *Sifrei* is apparently a composite text in its present form, and the sections numbered 78–106 and 134–141 in this text evidently derive from a different (though not necessarily later) source. Text: Horovitz, *Siphre d'Be Rab.* All translations mine.

Sifrei Zutta: A *halakhic midrash* on the book of Numbers which survived in fragments preserved in *Yalqut Shimoni, *Midrash ha-Gadol, *Numbers Rabba,* and various medieval quotations as well as manuscripts found in the Cairo *Genizah.

Sir. (abbreviation for Sira[ch]—see next entry)

Sira(ch): Yeshu'a ben El'azar ben Sira (or "Sirach," as his name appears in the Greek translation of his book) was a sage who wrote his book toward the beginning of the second century B.C.E., around the year 180 or so. From Hebrew the book was subsequently translated into Greek (by Ben Sira's own grandson) and became part of the Greek Bible of early Christianity; other ancient versions were made into Syriac and Latin (in which language it came to be known as "Ecclesiasticus"). Ben Sira's book was particularly beloved to the founders of rabbinic Judaism, but apparently because his identity was well known and the book was not attributed to some ancient worthy from the biblical past, they felt that it could not be included in the rabbinic canon of Scripture, and the original Hebrew version of it was therefore eventually lost.

Ben Sira saw in Scripture a great corpus of divine wisdom; he therefore made broad use of Scripture in writing his own book, including his lengthy catalog of biblical heroes mentioned earlier. But he was a conservative in all things—a "classicist," one might say—and this catalog contains relatively little that is not explicitly stated in Scripture itself. He certainly was aware of many interpretive traditions, which, for one reason or another, he chose not to include in his book. This notwithstanding, the book does contain a number of interpretations from a relatively early stage of development.

The textual problems connected with the book are notorious. Although composed in Hebrew, it was known for centuries only via its Greek and Syriac versions and secondary translations made from these. Medieval copies of portions of the Hebrew original were discovered at the end of last century in the *Cairo Genizah fragments, and these have been supplemented by further Hebrew finds at *Qumran and Masada, so that now slightly less than 70 percent of the Hebrew original is extant. Recent scholarship, however, has suggested that the original text-form in Hebrew was expanded at one point, and that both the original and expanded forms are represented in various manuscripts of the subsequent translations. To complicate matters further, the medieval copies of the Hebrew themselves frequently disagree or contain obvious errors; some scholars also suspect that the medieval Hebrew copyists may at times have sought to supplement their lacunary text(s) by retroverting from one of the ancient versions. I have been somewhat inconsistent in grappling with these difficulties. In cases where it seemed to matter little, I have simply reproduced (as with other books of the biblical apocrypha) the translation of the Revised Standard Version. Not infrequently, however, I have had to involve myself and the reader in the detailed work of textual criticism and reconstruction. I have generally given notice in such cases both in citing the work and, where appropriate, in explanatory footnotes. For such reconstructions I am frequently indebted to M. Z. Segal, *Complete Ben Sira* (Jerusalem: Mosad Bialik, 1958); Ziegler, *Sapientia Jesu Filii Sirach;* Skehan and Di Lella, *Wisdom of Ben Sira;* Wright, *No Small Difference.*

(4Q510–511) Songs of a Sage (or *Songs Against Demons*): A collection of psalmlike compositions that existed at *Qumran, they praise God and invoke His greatness to combat devils and alien spirits. The speaker refers to himself as a "sage" and his words have some connection to the world of biblical wisdom. Text: Baillet in *Qumran Grotte 4 III* (*DJD 7*), in 215–262. All translations mine.

(4Q400–407, 11Q17) Songs of the Sabbath Sacrifice: A collection of liturgical texts from *Qumran and Masada edited and translated by Newsom, *Songs of the Sabbath Sacrifice.* The texts are written in Hebrew; the oldest Qumran (Cave 4) material has been dated paleographically to the early or mid-first century B.C.E. See further E. Puech's review in *RB* 94 (1987), 604–608; idem, "Notes sur le manuscrit des Cantiques du Sacrifice du Sabbat." All translations mine.

Symmachus: see *Aquila, Symmachus, and Theodotion

Talmud, Babylonian and Jerusalem: see *Babylonian Talmud, *Jerusalem Talmud

Tanhuma-Yelammedenu: see *Midrash Tanhuma

Tanna deBei Eliahu: see *Seder Eliahu Rabba

tanna'im: see *Rabbis

Targum (in general): The name for a translation of the Hebrew Bible, or parts thereof, into Aramaic, a Semitic language related to Hebrew and spoken widely throughout the ancient Near East from the eighth century B.C.E. onward. Targums are not only interpretations in the sense that all translations involve interpretive decisions; some targums, notably *Targum Neophyti,* the *Fragment Targum,* and *Targum Pseudo-Jonathan* (all targums of the Pentateuch), contain frequent exegetical expansions of the biblical text, from a few words to entire paragraphs, not found in the original.

The dating and interrelationship of our various targums has been the subject of numerous classic studies, including Geiger, *Urschrift und Übersetzungen der Bibel;* Kahle, *Masoreten des Westens II;* idem, *The Cairo Geniza²;* Le Déaut, *Introduction à la littérature targumique;* and more recent studies through, as of this writing, the essays collected in Beattie and McNamara, *The Aramaic Bible: Targums in Their Historical Context.*

Despite the extensive research conducted over the last half-century in particular, scholars have still not reached consensus as to either the dating or interrelationship of the targums. Virtually all agree, however, that the process of translating biblical texts into Aramaic must have begun long before any of our extant targums was composed; such translation began perhaps as early as the time of the return from Babylonian exile. If so, then the various individual targum texts—*Onqelos, Neophyti,* and so forth—most likely do not represent the work of isolated translators "starting from scratch": their translations probably contain within them many translation *traditions* inherited from ages long past. In that sense, at least, any dating of a targum is likely to be misleading from the standpoint of ancient biblical interpretation, since at least some of the interpretations contained within that targum may go back to a period far earlier than the targum's own composition.

A particular affinity exists among the so-called Palestinian targums *Neophyti, Pseudo-Jonathan,* and the *Fragment Targums,* along with various snippets of targum texts discovered in the *Cairo Genizah, all of which arguably go back to a "Proto-Palestinian Targum." If, as some scholars have suggested, these various targums basically took shape late in the first or in the second century C.E., then their common ancestor should certainly be dated still earlier. Following is a brief description of the four main Jewish targums to the Pentateuch cited in this book: *Targum Onqelos, Targum Neophyti, Targum Pseudo-Jonathan,* and *Fragment Targums.* See also *Peshitta, *Samaritan Targum.

Targum Onqelos: This targum of the Pentateuch eventually acquired the status of *the* targum and was circulated widely in Jewish communities throughout the world. Some scholars now theorize that, although not descended from the "Proto-Palestinian Targum," *Targum Onqelos* was originally composed in the Land of Israel and subsequently transferred to the Jewish centers in Babylon, where its Aramaic underwent a process of "easternization." Onqelos, who was said to be a convert to Judaism (and whom some scholars have identified with *Aquila), translates the Torah in comparatively literal fashion, though frequently diverging from the literal in order to avoid anthropomorphisms or for other doctrinal reasons or when translating songs or highly metaphorical passages. Text: Hasid, *Sefer Keter Torah (ha-Tāj);* Sperber, *The Bible in Aramaic.* All translations mine.

Targum Neophyti: By "Targum Neophyti" is meant the main targum text elsewhere called more precisely "Targum Neophyti [or "Neofiti"] 1." This manuscript also contains numerous marginal and interlinear glosses, some of which I have also had occasion to cite. The manuscript itself is dated to the sixteenth century, but its original editor argued that the text it contains is one that goes back to pre-Christian times (Diez Macho, "The Recently Discovered Palestinian Targum"); however, this claim was soon disputed (York, "Dating of Targumic Literature"). The date and affiliations of *Targum Neophyti* have subsequently been much discussed and the arguments are too involved for review here; I agree with those who would fix its date roughly at the end of the first century C.E. On the relationship of this particular targum to others of the "Palestinian" tradition (and hence my preference for citing it over *Pseudo-Jonathan* and the *Fragment Targums),* see most recently Flesher, "Exploring the Sources of the Synoptic Targums to the Pentateuch." As is the case with other targums, this one obviously contains some material older than that, and despite the claims of some, the conflate character of this targum is not to be gainsaid. See further Kasher, "Targumic Conflations in Ms. Neofiti 1." Text: Diez Macho, *Neophyti 1: Targum Palestinense Ms. de la Biblioteca Vaticana.* All translations mine.

Targum Pseudo-Jonathan: Because of a (relatively late) misunderstanding, this targum was for a while wrongly attributed to Jonathan b. Uzziel (first centuries B.C.E.–C.E.); its present scholarly name reflects the consensus that it is not Jonathan's targum but an anonymous compilation (it is sometimes also called *Targum Yerushalmi* 1). This targum apparently took shape over a long period of time: while it is clearly related to the other "Palestinian" targums, it likewise has obvious affinities to *Targum Onqelos,* so that it might best be described as a hybrid of these two traditions to which a great deal of further material from rabbinic midrash has been added. For this reason, assigning any date to this work is likely to be misleading. There is little doubt that, despite the few, obvious post-Islamic references found in it, *Pseudo-Jonathan's* basis goes back far earlier. See (inter alia) Hayward, "The Date of Targum Pseudo-Jonathan"; Shinan, "Dating Targum Pseudo-Jonathan"; and Flesher, "Exploring the Sources," as well as the recent collection by Beattie and McNamara, *The Aramaic Bible: Targums in Their Historical Context.* All translations mine.

Targum(s), Fragment: There are in fact several similar but distinct fragment targums, most of which have been collected in an edition by Michael Klein, *The Fragment Targums of the Pentateuch.* Moreover, it is clear that these fragment targums were *not* originally complete targums of which only fragments survive, but that they were created (for reasons not yet understood) to be incomplete, that is, they are collections of translations of specific, isolated verses in the Pentateuch. These translations bear a close affinity to other "Palestinian" targums, in particular, *Targum Neophyti.* Where important, I have referred to specific manuscripts by letter as listed in Klein's edition. Some modern scholars refer to the *Fragment Targum(s)* as *Targum Yerushalmi* 2. All translations mine.

Targumic Tosefta: Alphabetical Acrostic on the Death of Moses: This Aramaic poem (like others incorporated into the targum reading cycle; see Ginsberger, "Les introductions araméennes à la lecture du Targoum") brings together different interpretive motifs. It was first published by Kasher, "Two Targum Toseftas on the Death of Moses"; see also Klein, "Corrections to the Song 'The Lord said to Moses . . . ,'" 451–453. Its date is not known; on the basis of its language, a fifth- or sixth-century date would not be inappropriate.

Targumic Tosefta to Exod. 15:2: This Aramaic poem (like others incorporated into the targum reading cycle; see preceding entry) brings together different interpretive motifs. It is found in (Parma) Codex dei Rossi 2887 (736) and was published by Klein, "The Targumic Tosefta to Exod. 15:2."

(11Q) Temple Scroll: The longest document found at *Qumran, this text presents itself as God's words to Moses on Mt. Sinai: in it, a variety of biblical laws are restated, often modified slightly or accompanied by some new material. The laws involved cover a range of topics: the temple itself and its environs, the sacrifices to be offered within it and the calendar of its ritual observances, the temple's physical layout, matters of ritual purity in general, laws governing the king and other officials, laws of warfare and other military matters, miscellaneous matters of civil law, and a good deal more. The date of the *Temple Scroll's* composition has been the subject of much speculation. The text has been preserved in copies by different hands, the oldest of which has been dated to the late second or early first century B.C.E., so that the actual composition of the work ought

probably to be dated still earlier; some have sugggested a date in the third century B.C.E. or even earlier. Text: Yadin, *The Temple Scroll*. All translations mine.

Tertullian (c. 160–c. 225 C.E.): An early Church Father and the author of various doctrinal and polemical works. Raised in Carthage, Tertullian converted to Christianity and came to exercise considerable influence. Text: *Opera,* ed. Reifferscheid and Wissowa; all translations mine.

testament (in general): see *Pseudepigrapha

Testament of Abraham: A brief narrative of the events preceding Abraham's death, when he is visited by the archangel Michael. Like Moses (see above, Chapter 25), Abraham is reluctant to surrender his soul—indeed, this pseudepigraphon may have originated as a transference of the motif "Moses Did Not Want to Die" back to Abraham. (See further Loewenstamm, "The Testament of Abraham and the Texts concerning Moses' Death," and Chazon, "Moses' Struggle for His Soul.") Michael then takes Abraham on a tour of this world and the next. The text exists in Greek in two recensions, designated A and B; despite certain obvious Christian insertions, this text remains essentially what it was to begin with, a Jewish work; its original composition should probably be dated late in the first century C.E. Text: Schmidt, *Le Testament grec d'Abraham.* Translation: Sanders, "Testament of Abraham," in Charlesworth, *OTP* 1:871–902.

Testament of Adam: A brief, composite text apparently composed originally in Syriac. Part of it appears to be dependent on earlier Jewish traditions and perhaps texts, and these may go back to pre-Christian times; however, the final editing of the text has been dated to the middle or late third century C.E. Text and translation: Robinson, *The Testament of Adam.*

Testament of ʿAmram: see **Visions of ʿAmram*

Testament of Asher, Benjamin, Dan, Gad, Issachar, Joseph, Judah, Levi, Naphtali, Reuben, Simeon, and Zebulon: see **Testaments of the Twelve Patriarchs*

Testament of Jacob: A testament that has survived in Coptic (Bohairic), Arabic, and Ethiopic. Its date and provenance are far from clear, these questions connected to that of its relationship to the **Testament of Abraham* and the *Testament of Isaac.* There is no direct evidence to suggest that the three were originally written as a trilogy, as some scholars have proposed; indeed, it may well be that the other two preceded the *Testament of Jacob* by some time, and that this last was consciously composed to fill out the picture with Israel's third and immediate ancestor. If the author of the *Testament of Jacob* was a Christian, he was certainly one acquainted with Jewish interpretive traditions, and not noticeably bent on turning Old Testament figures into advocates or forerunners of Christianity. Translation: (Bohairic text) Kuhn in Sparks, *AOT* 423, and (eclectic text, mostly based on Arabic) Stinespring in Charlesworth, *OTP* 1:913–918.

Testament of Job: This text, the pseudepigraphic "last words" of the biblical Job, was apparently composed originally in Greek; scholars disagree on whether its author was a Jew or a Christian, and hence on the time of its composition: dates from the first century B.C.E. to the second century C.E. have been proposed. Translation: Spittler in Charlesworth, *OTP* 1:829–868; Thornhill in Sparks, *AOT* 617–648.

Testament of Kohath: see * *Testament of Qahat*

Testament (or *Ascension*) *of Moses:* see * *Assumption of Moses*

(4Q542) Testament of Qahat: An Aramaic text from * *Qumran; it apparently presented itself as the last words of Levi's son Kohath (Qahat or Qĕhāt), since the speaker addresses "Amram my son" (2:9) and elsewhere refers to the "regulations of Abraham and the observances of Levi and myself" (1:8). The script of the manuscript has been dated to the end of the second century B.C.E. (though an accelerator mass spectrometry dating of the parchment has mysteriously yielded a considerably earlier date); the text's actual composition could conceivably be placed in the third century in keeping with Milik's suggestion that it is part of an early "trilogy" of priestly testaments (see Kugel, "Levi's Elevation," also * *Vision of 'Amram*, * *Aramaic Levi Document*). All translations mine.

Testament of Solomon: A text, apparently composed originally in Greek, that appears to be based on a kernel of Solomon traditions some of which are known from ancient Jewish sources. The text itself exists in several recensions, the earliest of which may go back to the late second or early third century C.E. Translation: Whittaker in Sparks, *AOT* 733–752, and Duling in Charlesworth, *OTP* 1:935–987.

Testaments of the Twelve Patriarchs: A series of spiritual last wills and testaments delivered in turn by each of Jacob's twelve sons at the time of their deaths. In these "testaments" Jacob's sons give advice and warnings of future events to their own descendants: what they have to say frequently reflects their own portraits as presented in biblical narratives (particularly details found in the Joseph story as well as in Jacob's blessings in Genesis 49). The date and provenance of the *Testaments* has been a particularly vexing subject for scholars. They survive in Greek and other translations, and it has been the position of M. De Jonge, a veteran *Testaments* scholar, that the *Testaments* were composed by a Greek-speaking Christian, who, however, may have loosely based his book on earlier, Semitic sources. An earlier Semitic source certainly stands behind at least one of the *Testaments,* that of Levi, which bears a striking resemblance to an Aramaic text found both in the * *Cairo Genizah (see * *Sirach) and in some * *Qumran fragments, (1Q21) *Aramaic Levi,* (4Q213) *Aramaic Levi*[a] and (4Q214) *Aramaic Levi*[b], and so on. This Aramaic text (now known to some scholars as the * *Aramaic Levi Document*) seems in one way or another to have supplied the Greek *Testament of Levi* with much of its material; however, the Greek text is not a straight translation of the Aramaic but represents a reworking and rearranging of its contents. What is more, the Greek *Testament of Levi* differs from the other testaments in some fundamental ways: it is a good hypothesis that, whoever first composed the twelve-testament book, he did not start from scratch but used an already-existing Levi text that he then modified and supplemented with eleven other testaments.

Many writers have expressed doubts about De Jonge's hypothesis that the Greek text of the *Testaments* is an original, Christian composition rather than merely a late, Christian edition of an earlier Jewish text. Quite apart from the *Testament of Levi,* there is evidence elsewhere within the *Testaments* that the Greek text was created by someone who had a written, Semitic (that is, Aramaic and/or Hebrew) text in front of him. A

Hebrew fragment found at Qumran and dealing with Naphtali (4Q215) further supports the hypothesis of an original, Semitic version of the *Testaments*, as do smaller Aramaic fragments tentatively identified as part of the testaments of Judah (3Q7, 4Q484, 4Q538) and Joseph (4Q539). (See Milik, "Écrits préesséniens de Qumran.") If so, it is likely that such a Hebrew, twelve-testament text was itself based on earlier, Semitic sources such as the *Aramaic Levi Document*. A Hebrew original of the *Testaments* might plausibly go back to before the common era, though the dependence of such a text on both the *Aramaic Levi Document* and the book of *Jubilees* does not allow too early a dating. Text of the Greek *Testaments*: De Jonge, *The Testaments of the Twelve Patriarchs: A Critical Edition*. Also consulted, translations of Hollander and De Jonge, *The Testaments of the Twelve Patriarchs: A Commentary*, and Kee, "Testaments of the Twelve Patriarchs," in Charlesworth, *OTP* 1:775–828. All translations mine.

(4Q175) Testimonia: A chain of citations from biblical books (Numbers, Deuteronomy, and Joshua) and apparently as well as from the apocryphal work (4Q378–379) *Psalms of Joshua*. First published in Allegro, *Qumran Cave 4: I (DJD 5)*, 57–60; see also Strugnell, "Notes en marge," 225–229.

Testimony of Truth: This Christian gnostic treatise is one of the texts of the *Nag Hammadi library. Its original composition in Greek has been dated to either the late second or possibly the late third century C.E. Translation: *Coptic Nag Hammadi Library*.

(1QH and 1Q35) Thanksgiving Hymns (or *Hodayot*): A group of hymns found at *Qumran; they are so called because of their characteristic opening formula, "I thank You, O Lord . . ." Text: I have followed the order of Licht, *The Thanksgiving Scroll*, although Puech, "Quelques aspects," has proposed a new arrangement. All translations mine.

Theodoret (c. 393–c. 466 C.E.): Christian exegete, theologian, and polemicist, he served for a time as bishop of Cyrrhus, in Syria. Like other Syrian Christians, Theodoret avoided excessively allegorical interpretation in his exegetical writings. He was also the author of *Against the Heresies*, in which are reflected the church's battles against gnosticism and other condemned beliefs. All translations mine.

Theodotion: see *Aquila, Symmachus, and Theodotion

Theodotus: A Greek-speaking epic poet of the second century B.C.E. All that survives of Theodotus' poetry are eight fragments cited by *Eusebius of Caesarea (he quotes them from the writings of *Alexander Polyhistor). Because these fragments show a certain interest in Shechem, some scholars have suggested that Theodotus was a Samaritan, but there is little to justify such a conclusion; the fragments all seem to bear on the biblical story of Dinah (Genesis 34), which is set in Shechem. Theodotus' retelling of the story preserves many exegetical motifs otherwise found in ancient Jewish sources and has much in common in particular with the treatment of the story in the *Testament of Levi*. (See further Kugel, "Story of Dinah.") Text and translation: Holladay, *Fragments from Hellenistic Jewish Authors*, 2:51–204, Fallon in Charlesworth, *OTP* 2:785–794.

Theophilus of Antioch: Bishop of Antioch in the late second century C.E. and, along with Justin Martyr, Athenagoras, Tertullian, and others, one of the Christian "apologists" who flourished between approximately 120 and 220 C.E. and who sought to present a rational and attractive picture of Christianity to non-Christians. Theophilus' tract "To

Autolycus" (cited here from *PG* vol. 92) is an important repository of early interpretive traditions. All translations mine.

1 and 2 Thessalonians: Two letters attributed to Paul found in the New Testament. The first is believed to be authentically Paul's and is thought to be the oldest of his letters (and, hence, the oldest New Testament text); it has been dated to 50 C.E. The second letter's authenticity is doubted by some scholars but maintained by others. See also: *Paul. Translation: Revised Standard Version, with occasional, slight modifications.

Tibat Marqa (or *Tibat Marqe*; also *Memar Marqa*): A Samaritan work commenting upon various biblical passages and principally concerned with the events of the life of Moses. The work is apparently a composite, the first two books datable on linguistic grounds to the third or fourth century C.E., the time of their reputed author Marqa, whereas the latter four books were either composed or edited at a later period. Text: Ben-Ḥayyim, *Tibat Marqe.* All translations mine.

1 and 2 Timothy: see *Pastoral Letters

Titus, Letter to: see *Pastoral Letters

Tobit, book of: A pious Jewish tale recounting the trials of its eponymous hero, his son Tobias, and his future daughter-in-law Sarah; all's well that ends well. This story, included among the *Apocrypha of the Hebrew Bible, may show some influence of the *(Aramaic) Sayings of *Ahiqar.* It was apparently originally composed in Aramaic, and fragments of the Aramaic text have been found at *Qumran. It survives in its entirety in ancient Greek, Latin, Syriac, and other versions. The date of its composition is difficult to fix, but it certainly preceded the revolt of the *Maccabees; a date in the third century B.C.E. seems a reasonable guess. Translation: Revised Standard Version with Apocrypha.

Torah (understood as "teaching"): A Hebrew word used in the Bible to describe, inter alia, a particular statute or procedure, or a collection thereof; the phrase "Torah of Moses" or "Torah of God" that appears in later biblical books may designate the contents of the *Pentateuch as a whole. In any case, the term *Torah* was used in postbiblical Hebrew to designate (1) the *Pentateuch (in this sense the word *torah* was translated into Greek as *nomos* [law, way of life] and appears in the New Testament phrase, "the Law and the Prophets," meaning [more or less] the Bible); (2) somewhat more loosely, the Bible as a whole; and (3) still more loosely, the entire corpus of rabbinic learning, including Bible, *Mishnah, *Talmud, *midrash.

Tosefta (also Tosephta): A rabbinic compilation of teachings apparently intended as a supplement (its name in fact means "supplement") to the *Mishnah and thus containing much that is relevant to the study of early *rabbinic interpretation of the Bible, particularly in the domain of *halakhah.* Presumably, its compilation dates back to the early third century C.E., though much of the material presented in it goes back to still earlier times. Texts: Zuckermandel, *Tosephta Based on the Erfurt and Vienna Codices;* Lieberman, *Tosefta.* All translations mine.

traditional Hebrew text (of the Hebrew Bible): I have generally used this expression instead of "Masoretic text" (the latter more accurate but generally unknown to nonspecialists). One form of the Hebrew text of the Bible, standardized in its basics sometime around

100 C.E., became *the* Bible for Jews and has been preserved and handed down by them from generation to generation ever since. (Another, somewhat different, form of the Hebrew text has been preserved by the Samaritans; other Hebrew textual witnesses have been found at *Qumran and elsewhere.) In the Middle Ages, the Masoretes—a group of Jewish Bible scholars who gave this text-form its current scholarly name—pinned down and promulgated the last details of this form, having developed a sophisticated system of annotation and punctuation in order to preserve the subtlest nuances in the text's traditional pronunciation, meaning, and conventions of public reading.

Tripartite Tractate: The name given by scholars to a treatise found in the *Nag Hammadi library: it deals with the biblical account of the creation as well as the story of Adam and Eve, then moves to the subject of redemption. Translation: *Coptic Nag Hammadi Library.*

(4Q473) Two Ways, The: A brief fragment from *Qumran, so called because it evokes the theme of the two ways popular in Second Temple times. Translation mine.

typological interpretation (also *typology*): An approach to Scripture whereby earlier things are held to foreshadow or represent later ones. Although it has analogues in early Jewish exegesis, the typological reading of Scripture became particularly characteristic of early Christian interpreters, who saw in the Old Testament a host of "types" or "figures" (that is, foreshadowings) of New Testament people, events, and ideas. Thus Adam, Isaac, Jacob, Moses, Joshua, etc., are all held to prefigure Jesus; the crossing of the Red Sea is a *type* of baptism; and so forth.

Valentinian Exposition: This gnostic treatise is one of the texts of the *Nag Hammadi library. It expounds the creation and process of redemption through Sophia, divine wisdom. Translation: *Coptic Nag Hammadi Library.*

Vettius Valens (fl. latter half of second century C.E.): In an astrological work written in Greek, this author refers to the same tradition of "Abraham the Astrologer" found in *Pseudo-Orphica, *Artapanus, and other earlier writings and writers. Text and translation: Stern, *Greek and Latin Authors* 2:174–175

Vetus Latina ("Old Latin"): An early Latin Bible translation or group of different translations (it is not clear which) that was ultimately displaced by Jerome's Vulgate. This old translation, reconstructed by scholars from numerous citations and snippets in ancient manuscripts, was largely a rendering of the Septuagint into Latin rather than a translation made from a Hebrew text. Its awkward style, elegantly apologized for by *Augustine and other writers, was nevertheless a liability in the Roman church. Text: Fischer: *Vetus Latina.* All translations mine.

(4Q545–548) Visions of 'Amram (or *Testament of 'Amram*): An Aramaic text from *Qumran in which Amram, the father of Moses, recounts a vision he has had. J. T. Milik, who published part of it in his "4Q Visions de 'Amram et Une Citation d'Origène," suggested that it might well be a "testament" of Amram, part of a trilogy of priestly testaments along with the Aramaic *Testament of Qahat and the *Aramaic Levi Document. The Qumran fragments have been dated by Milik to the first half of the second century B.C.E., and he has suggested that the putative trilogy was composed still earlier. All translations mine.

Vulgate: see *Jerome

(1QM and 1Q33, 4Q491–496) War Scroll (or War Rule): A text found in multiple copies at *Qumran; the differences among the manuscripts indicate at the least that the text underwent considerable editing or rewriting in the course of its transmission. The text recounts, or rather predicts, the great final conflict between the "sons of light" and the "sons of darkness," a great setting aright of Israel's fortunes and the final defeat of the Kittim (Romans). Along with this account are sections of divine praise, details concerning the battle formations and weapon to be used, descriptions of the role of priests and Levites, and so forth. All translations mine.

Wisd.: see *Wisdom of Solomon

Wisdom of Solomon: A book written in Greek, probably late in the first century B.C.E. or early in the first century C.E. by a Greek-speaking Jew from, most likely, Alexandria. The book presents itself as the wise writings of the biblical king Solomon; it contains a lengthy praise of, and exhortation to follow, the path of wisdom. It also summarizes a good bit of Scripture in brief, gnomic sentences that reflect many of the interpretive traditions then current. The author may have inhabited Egypt, but he was well versed in interpretive traditions otherwise known to us in Hebrew or Aramaic, traditions that seem to stem, in other words, from the Jewish homeland.

The Wisdom of Solomon, or Book of Wisdom, was part of the Greek Bible of early Christianity and has remained, along with Ben Sira, Judith, and other books, as part of the Old Testament in many churches (although these books are classified by some as biblical Apocrypha or "Deutero-canonical" works). Translations: Revised Standard Version of the Bible with Apocrypha; also Winston, *The Wisdom of Solomon.*

(1Q22) Words of Moses (or Dibrei Mosheh): A brief, fragmentary text from *Qumran, much of it a paraphrase of passages from Deuteronomy in which Moses speaks in the first person. Here and there elements of an explicative or expansive nature have been interwoven with the biblical citations. All translations mine.

(4Q504–506) Words of the Luminaries (Dibrei ha-Meʿorot): One of several collections of regular prayers and other liturgical compositions from *Qumran. The three Qumran manuscripts of this text were published in Baillet, *Qumran Grotte 4 III (DJD 7)*; the oldest, 4Q504, has been dated to the mid-second century B.C.E. A number of scholars have suggested that these prayers originated in a "proto-Qumranic group." All translations mine.

Yalquṭ Shimoni: A late (thirteenth-century?) medieval collection of midrashic material on the entire Hebrew Bible compiled by Shimʿon ha-Darshan from earlier sources, many of them now lost. Text: Hyman, Lerrer, and Shiloni, *Yalquṭ Šimʿoni; Yalquṭ Šimʿoni* (Saloniki, 1526–27 edition).

Yannai: An early Hebrew liturgical poet, many of whose works have been recovered thanks to discoveries from the *Cairo Genizah. Yannai's precise time period and biographical data are unknown; dates from the fifth to seventh century C.E. have been proposed. Texts are cited from the editions of Zulay, *Piyyuṭ Yannai,* Rabinowicz, *Maḥzor Piyyuṭei Yannai lattorah velammoʿadim.* All translations mine.

Bibliography

Aberbach, M., and B. Grossfeld, *Targum Onkelos to Genesis* (New York: KTAV, 1982).

Adler, W., "Jacob of Edessa and the Jewish Pseudepigrapha in Syriac Chronography," in J. Reeves, ed., *Tracing the Threads* (Atlanta, Ga: Scholars Press, 1994) 143–171.

Albeck, H., *Mabo la-Mishnah* (Jerusalem: Mosad Bialik, 1967).

————, *Shisha Sidre Mishnah* (Jerusalem: Mosad Bialik, 1959).

Alexander, P., "The Fall into Knowledge: The Garden of Eden/Paradise in Gnostic Literature," in Paul Morris and Deborah Sawyer, *A Walk in the Garden* (JSOTSS 136) (Sheffield: JSOT Press, 1992) 92–105.

————, "Notes on the 'Imago Mundi' of the Book of Jubilees," *JJS* 33 (1982) 197–213.

————, "The Rabbinic Lists of Forbidden Targumim," *JJS* 27 (1976) 177–191.

————, "The Targumim and Early Exegesis of the 'Sons of God' in Genesis 6," *JJS* 23 (1972) 60–71.

————, "3 Enoch," in Charlesworth, *OTP* 1:223–315.

Alexandre, M., "L'épée de flamme (Gen. 3, 24): textes chrétiens et traditions juives," in A. Caquot et al., eds., *Hellenica et Judaica: Hommage à Valentin Nikiprowetzky* (Leuven-Paris: Peeters, 1986) 403–442.

Allegro, J. M. *DJD* 5, 85–87, with corrections of Strugnell, "Notes en Marge."

Allegro, John M., *Qumran Cave 4: I* (*DJD* 5) (Oxford: Clarendon, 1968).

Allon, G., "The Halakhah in Epistle of Barnabas," *Tarbiz* 11 (1940) 23–38.

Altmann, A., *Jewish Medieval and Renaissance Studies* (Cambridge, Mass.: Harvard University Press, 1967).

Andersen, F. I., "2 Enoch," in Charlesworth, *OTP* 1:102–221.

Anderson, G., "Celibacy or Consummation in the Garden? Reflections on Early Jewish and Christian Interpretations of the Garden of Eden," *HTR* 82 (1989) 121–148.

————, "The Cosmic Mountain: Eden and Its Early Interpreters in Syriac Christianity," in G. A. Robbins, ed., *Genesis 1–3 in the History of Exegesis: Intrigue in the Garden* (Lewiston, N.Y.: Mellen, 1988) 187–224.

————, "Intentional and Unintentional Sin in the Dead Sea Scrolls," in D. P. Wright et al., eds., *Pomegranates and Golden Bells: Studies in Biblical, Jewish, and Near Eastern Ritual, Law, and Literature in Honor of Jacob Milgrom* (Winona Lake, Ind.: Eisenbrauns, 1995) 49–64.

————, "The Interpretation of Gen. 1:1 in the Targums," *CBQ* 52 (1990) 21–29.

————, "The Life of Adam and Eve," *HUCA* 63 (1992) 1–38.

————, "The Penitence Narrative in *The Life of Adam and Eve*," *HUCA* 63 (1992) 1–38.

————, "The Status of the Torah Before Sinai," *DSD* 1 (1994) 1–29.

Anderson, G., and M. E. Stone, *A Synopsis of the Books of Adam and Eve* (SBL EJL 5) (Atlanta, Ga.: Scholars Press, 1994).

Anderson, H., "3 and 4 Maccabees," in Charlesworth, *OTP* 2:509–564.

Antin, P., ed., *Corpus Christianorum Series Latina*, vol. 72 (Tournai: Berpholt, 1959).

Aptowitzer, V., "Asenath, the Wife of Joseph: A Haggadic Literary-Historical Study" *HUCA* 1 (1924) 239–306.

———, "The Heavenly Temple according to the Haggadah," *Tarbiz* 2 (1931) 137–153, 257–287.

———, *Kain und Abel in der Agada* (Vienna: R. Loewit Verlag, 1922).

———, "Malkizedek. Zu den Sagen der Agada," *MGWJ* 70 (1926), 3/4, 93–113.

———, *Parteipolitik der Hasmonäerzeit im rabbinischen und pseudepigraphischen Schrifttum* (Vienna: Verlag der Kohut-Coundation, 1927).

———, "The State of the Embryo in the Jewish Law of Punishment," *Sinai* 6 (1942) 9–32.

Arnold, W. R., "The Passover Papyrus from Elephantine," *JBL* 31 (1912) 1–33.

Ashton, J., "The Transformation of Wisdom: A Study of the Prologue of John's Gospel," *NTS* 32 (1986) 321–343.

Athanasius of Alexandria, *Contra Gentes*, ed. and trans. by Robert W. Thomson (Oxford: Clarendon, 1971).

Attridge, H., *The Epistle to the Hebrews* (Philadelphia: Fortress Press, 1989).

Attridge, H., et al., *Qumran Cave 4: VIII* (*DJD* 13) (Oxford: Clarendon, 1995).

Attridge, H., John. J. Collins, and Thomas Tobin, *Of Scribes and Scrolls* (Lanham, Md.: University Press of America, 1991).

Attridge, H., John Strugnell et al., *Qumran Cave 4 VIII: Parabiblical Texts Part I* (*DJD* 13) (Oxford: Clarendon, 1994).

Augustine, *The City of God against the Pagans*, in LCL (Cambridge, Mass.: Harvard University Press).

Aune, D. E., *Prophecy in Early Christianity and the Ancient Mediterranean World* (Grand Rapids, Mich.: Eerdmans, 1983).

Bacher, W., "Lilith, Königen von Smargad," *MGWJ* 19 (1870) 187–189.

Baer, R. A., *Philo's Use of the Categories Male and Female* (Leiden: Brill, 1970).

Baillet, M., *Les "petites grottes" de Qumran* (*DJD* 3) (Oxford: Clarendon, 1962).

———, "Songs of a Sage," in Baillet, *Qumran Grotte 4 III* (*DJD* 7) (Oxford: Clarendon, 1982), 215–262.

Bamberger, B. J., "Philo and the Aggadah," *HUCA* 48 (1977) 153–185.

Bandstra, A. J., "A Kingship and Priests: Inaugurated Eschatology in the Apocalypse [Rev. 1:5–6]," *CTJ* 27 (1992) 10–25.

Barrett, C. K., *From First Adam to Last: A Study in Pauline Theology* (New York: Scribner's, 1962).

Barth, L. M., "Genesis 15 and the Problem of Abraham's Seventh Trial," *Maarav* 8 (1992) 245–263.

Barthélemy, D. "Est-ce Hoshaya Rabba qui censura le 'commentaire allégorique'?" in R. Arnaldez, *Philon d'Alexandrie* (Paris: C.N.R.S., 1967) 45–78.

Bassler, J., "Cain and Abel in the Palestinian Targums," *JSJ* 17 (1986) 56–64.

Baumgarten, A. I., "Myth and Midrash: Gen. 9:20–29," in J. Neusner (ed.), *Christianity, Judaism, and other Greco-Roman Cults*, part 3 (Leiden: Brill, 1975) 55–71.

————, "The Pharasaic *Paradosis*," *HTR* 80 (1987) 63–77.

————, "Unwritten Law," *JSJ* 3 (1972) 7–29.

Baumgarten, J. M., "A Fragment on Fetal Life and Pregnancy in 4Q270," in David Wright et al., *Pomegranates and Golden Bells: Studies in Biblical, Jewish, and Near Eastern Ritual, Law, and Literature in Honor of Jacob Milgrom* (Winona Lake, Ind.: Eisenbrauns, 1995) 445–448.

————, "Does TLH in the TS Refer to Crucifixion?" *JBL* 91 (1972) 472–481, reprinted in his *Studies in Qumran Law*, ed. J. M. Baumgarten (Leiden, 1977).

————, "Hanging and Treason in Qumran and Roman Law," *Eretz Yisrael* 15 (1982) 7–16.

————, "Purification and the Garden in 4Q265 and Jubilees," in G. Brooke, ed., *New Qumran Texts and Studies* (STJD 15) (Leiden: Brill, 1994) 3–10.

————, "Recent Qumran Discoveries and Halakhah in the Hellenistic-Roman Period," in S. Talmon, ed., *Jewish Civilization in the Hellenistic Roman Period* (Sheffield: JSOT Press, 1991) 147–158.

————, *Studies in Qumran Law* (Leiden: Brill, 1977).

Baumstark, A., "Die Zitate des Mt.-Evangeliums aus dem Zwölfprophetenbuch," *Biblica* 37 (1956) 296–313.

Beattie, D. R. G., and M. J. McNamara, *The Aramaic Bible: Targums in Their Historical Context* (JSOTSS 166) (Sheffield: Sheffield Academic Press, 1994).

Beckwith, R. T., "The Solar Calendar of Joseph and Aseneth," *JSJ* 15 (1984) 90–111.

Beer, M., "The Riches of Moses in Rabbinic *Aggada*," *Tarbiẓ* 43 (1974) 70–87.

Belkin, S., *Philo and the Oral Law* (Cambridge, Mass.: Harvard University Press, 1940).

————, *Philo's Midrash* (New York: Yeshiva, 1989).

Belleville, Linda, *Reflections of Glory: Paul's Polemical Use of the Moses-Doxa Tradition in 2 Cor. 3:1–18* (JSNT 42) (Sheffield: JSNT, 1991).

Ben-Ḥayyim, Z., "The Book of Asatir," *Tarbiẓ* 14 (1942–43) 71–87.

————, *Tibat Marqe* (Jerusalem: Israel Academy of Sciences, 1988).

Berger, D., *Nitzaḥon Yašan: The Jewish-Christian Debate in the High Middle Ages* (Philadelphia: Jewish Publication Society, 1979).

————, "Three Typological Themes in Early Jewish Messianism: Messiah Son of Joseph, Rabbinic Calculations, and the Figure of Armilus," *AJS Review* 10 (1985) 141–164.

Berger, K., *Die Gesetzauslegung Jesu* (Neukirchen: Neukircher Verlag, 1972).

Bernstein, M. J., "Deut. 21: 23: A Study in Early Jewish Exegesis," *JQR* 74 (1983–84) 21–45.

————, "4Q252 i 2 . . . Biblical Text or Biblical Interpretation?" *RQ* 16 (1994) 421–428.

————, "4Q252: From Rewritten Bible to Biblical Commentary," *JSJ* 45 (1994) 1–27.

Bertrand, D. A., *La Vie grecque d'Adam et Eve* (Paris: A. Maisonneuve, 1987; New York: Doubleday, 1983) 605–613.

Betz, Hans Dieter, *Galatians* (Philadelphia: Fortress Press, 1979).

Beyer, K., *Die aramäischen Texte vom Toten Meer* (Göttingen: Vanderhoeck und Ruprecht), vol. 1 (1984), vol. 2 (1994).

Bezold, C., *Die Schatzhöhle* (Leipzig: J. C. Hinrichs, 1883, 1888).

Bickerman, E., *The Jews in the Greek Age* (Cambridge, Mass.: Harvard University Press, 1988).

Bienaimé, G., *Moïse et le don de l'eau dans la tradition juive ancienne* (Rome: Biblical Institute Press, 1984).

Bihlmeyer, K., *Die Apostolischen Väter: Neubearbeitung der Funkschen Ausgabe* (Tübingen: Mohr, 1924).

Birnbaum, Ellen, *The Place of Judaism in Philo's Thought* (Brown Judaica Series 290) (Atlanta, Ga.: Scholars Press, 1996) 61–127.

Blenkinsopp, J., "The Oracle of Judah and the Messianic Entry" *JBL* 80 (1961) 55–64.

———, "Prophecy and Priesthood in Josephus" *JJS* 25 (1974) 239–262.

Bockmuehl, M., "The Noachide Commandments and New Testament Ethics," *RB* 102 (1995), 72–105.

Bogaert, P., *Apocalypse de Baruch* (Paris: Le Cerf, 1969).

Bohlen, R., *Die Ehrung der Eltern bei Ben Sira* (Trierer Theologische Studien 51) (Trier: Paulinus, 1991) 82–139.

Bohlig, A., and F. Wisse, eds., *Nag Hammadi codices III,2 and IV,2* (Nag Hammadi Studies 4) (Leiden: Brill, 1975).

Bonsirven, J., *Le divorce dans le Nouveau Testament* (Paris: Desclée, 1948).

Borgen, P., *Bread from Heaven: An Exegetical Study of the Concept of Manna in the Gospel of John and the Writings of Philo* (Leiden: Brill, 1960, rev. ed. 1981).

———, "Logos Was the True Light," *Novum Testamentum* 14 (1972) 115–130.

———, " 'There Shall Come Forth a Man': Reflections on Messianic Ideas in Philo," in J. H. Charlesworth, ed., *The Messiah* (Minneapolis: Fortress, 1992) 341–361.

Borst, A., *Der Turmbau von Babel: Geschichte der Meinungen über Ursprung und Vielfalt der Sprachen und Völker* (Stuttgart: Hiersemann, 1957–1959).

Bottrich, C., "Recent Studies in the Slavonic Book of Enoch," *JSP* 9 (1991) 35–42.

Bousset, W., *Judischchristlicher Schulbetrieb in Alexandria und Rom* (Göttingen: Vandenhoeck und Ruprecht, 1915).

Bowker, J., *The Targums and Rabbinic Literature* (Cambridge: Cambridge University Press, 1969).

Boyarin, Daniel, "The *Dôrĕšê Rĕšûmôt* Said . . . ," in M. Cogan, *Moshe Held Memorial Volume* (Beer Sheba: Ben Gurion University, 1988), 23–35.

———, "Inner Biblical Ambiguity, Intertextuality, and the Dialectic of Midrash," *Prooftexts* 10 (1990) 29–48.

———, "On the Identification of the *Dôrĕšê Rĕšûmôt*: A Lexigraphical Study," *Beer-Sheva* 3 (1988) 23–25, reprinted in M. Cogan, ed., *Linguistic Studies in Memory of Moshe Held* (Jerusalem: Magnes, 1988).

———, "On the Status of the Tannaitic Midrashim," *JAOS* 112 (1992) 455–465.

Braude, W. G., *The Midrash on Psalms* (New Haven, Conn.: Yale University Press, 1959).

———, *Pesiqta Rabbati* (New Haven, Conn.: Yale University Press, 1968).

Braun, F. M., "Le sacrifice d'Isaac dans le quatrième évangile d'après le Targum," *NRT* 101 (1979) 481–497.

Bray, G. "The Significance of God's Image in Man," *TB* 42 (1991) 195–225.

Bregman, M., "The Depiction of the Ram in the Aqedah Mosaic at Beith Alpha," *Tarbiz* 51 (1982) 306–309.

Brewer, D. Instone, "1 Cor. 9:9–11: A Literal Interpretation of 'Do Not Muzzle the Ox,'" *NTS* 38 (1992) 554–565.

Brin, G., "Biblical Prophecy in the Dead Sea Scrolls," in M. A. Fishbane, ed., *Shaare*

Talmon: Studies in the Bible, Qumran, and the Ancient Near East Presented to She-maryahu Talmon (Winona Lake, Ind.: Eisenbrauns, 1992) 101–112.

Brock, S. P., "Abraham and the Ravens," *JSJ* 9 (1978) 135–152.

———, "Clothing Metaphors as a Means of Theological Expression in Syriac Tradition," in Margot Schmidt, *Typus, Symbol, Allegorie bei den östlichen Vätern und ihren Parallelen im Mittelalter* (Eichstatt: F. Pustet Regensburg, 1981) 11–40.

———, "Genesis 22 in Syriac Tradition," in P. Casetti et al., *Mélanges Dominique Bathélemy* (Fribourg: Editions Universitaires; Göttingen: Vandenhoeck und Ruprecht, 1981) 1–30.

———, "Jewish Traditions in Syriac Sources," *JJS* 30 (1979) 212–232.

———, *The Luminous Eye: The Spiritual World Vision of St. Ephrem* (Rome: C.I.I.S., 1985).

———, "Some Syriac Legends," *JJS* 33 (1982) 237–255.

———, "To Revise or Not to Revise," in G. Brooke et al., *Septuagint, Scrolls, and Cognate Writings* (Atlanta, Ga.: Scholars Press, 1990) 301–338.

———, "The Two Ways and the Palestinian Targum," in P. R. Davies and R. T. White, eds., *A Tribute to Geza Vermes* (JSOTSS 100) (Sheffield: JSOT Press, 1990), 139–152.

Brod, M., *The Biography of Franz Kafka*, tr. G. H. Roberts (London: Secker and Warburg, 1947).

Brooke, G., *Exegesis at Qumran: 4Q Florilegium, Its Jewish Context* (Sheffield: JSOT Press, 1985) 203–204, 302–304.

———, "The Kittim in the Qumran Pesharim," in L. Alexander, ed., *Images of Empire* (Sheffield: JSOT Press, 1991) 135–159.

———, "The Messiah of Aaron in the Damascus Document," *RQ* 15 (1991) 215–230.

———, "The Temple Scroll and the NT," in his *Temple Scroll Studies* (JSP Supplement Series 7) (Sheffield: JSOT Press, 1989) 181–199.

———, *Temple Scroll Studies* (JSP Supplement Series 7) (Sheffield: JSOT Press, 1989).

Brooke, G., et al., *Septuagint, Scrolls, and Cognate Writings* (Atlanta, Ga.: Scholars Press, 1992).

Broshi, M., et al., *Qumran Cave 4: XIV (DJD* 19) (Oxford: Clarendon, 1995).

Brown, R. N., "And the Elder Shall Serve the Younger: A Midrash About Jesus," *HTR* 87 (1994) 363–366.

Buber, S., *Aggadat Bereschit* (Cracow: J. Fischer, 1902).

———, *Midrasch Ekhah Rabah* (Tel Aviv: s.n. 1963).

———, *Midrasch Lekach Tob* (Wilna, 1884).

———, *Midrasch Tanḥuma* (Jerusalem: H. Vagshal, 1964).

———, *Midrasch Tehillim* (Jerusalem: H. Vagshal, 1977).

———, *Sechel Tob* (Berlin, 1900).

Budge, E. A. W., *Book of the Bee* (Oxford: Clarendon, 1886).

———, *The Book of the Cave of Treasures* (London: Religious Tract Society, 1927).

Burchard, C. "Joseph and Aseneth," in Charlesworth, *OTP* 2:202–247.

Burstein, S., *The "Babyloniaca" of Berossus* (Malibu: Undena, 1978).

Butler, H. E., *The Apologia and Florida of Apuleius* (Oxford, 1901).

Campbell, D. A., *The Rhetoric of Righteousness in Romans 3:21–26* (JSNT 65) (Sheffield: JSOT Press, 1992).

Caquot, A., "Le livre des Jubilés, Melkisedeq et les dîmes," *JJS* 33 (1982) 257–264.

———, "Siméon et Levi sont frères," in J. Doré, P. Grelot, and M. Carrez, *De la Torah au Messie: Mélanges H. Cazelles* (Paris: Desclée, 1981) 113–119.

Carmignac, J., "Le document de Qumran sur Melkisedeq," *RQ* 7 (1970) 343–378.

Catchpole, D., "The Synoptic Divorce Material as a Traditio-Historical Problem," *BJRL* 57 (1974–75) 92–127.

Charles, R. H., *The Apocrypha and Pseudepigrapha of the Old Testament* (Oxford: Clarendon, 1903).

———, *The Assumption of Moses* (London: Black, 1987) 105–110.

———, *The Book of Jubilees, or, The Little Genesis* (1902, reprinted Jerusalem: Makor, 1972).

Charlesworth, J. H., "History of the Rechabites" in his *OTP* 2:443–461.

———, "The Messiah in the Pseudepigrapha," in H. Temporini and W. Haase, eds., *Aufstieg und Niedergang der Römischen Welt* (Berlin: de Gruyter, 1979) II.19.1 188–218.

———, *Pseudepigrapha and Modern Research* (Chico, Calif.: Scholars Press, 1981).

———, "A Study of the History of the Rechabites," in A. Caquot et al., *Hellenica et Judaica: Hommage à Valentin Nikiprowetzky* (Leuven-Paris: Peeters, 1986) 219–243.

———, ed., "Hellenistic Synagogal Prayers: One Hundred Years of Discussion," *JSP* 5 (1989).

———, ed., *John and Qumran* (London: Geoffrey Chapman Publishers, 1972).

———, ed., *The Messiah: Developments in Earliest Judaism and Christianity* (Minneapolis: Fortress, 1992).

———, ed., *The Old Testament Pseudepigrapha* (London: Darton, Longman and Todd, 1983–1985).

Chazon, E., "Moses' Struggle for His Soul: A Prototype for the *Testament of Abraham*, the Greek Apocalypse of Ezra, and the Apocalypse of Sedrach," *SC* 5 (1985–86) 151–164.

Chernus, "The Rebellion at the Reed Sea: Observations on the Nature of Midrash" (Chico, Calif.: Scholars Press, 1981).

Chiesa, B., "La Promessa di Una Profeta (Dt. 18:15–20)," *BO* 15 (1973) 17–26.

Chilton, Bruce, "Aramaic and Targumic Antecedents of Pauline Justification," in D. R. G. Beattie and M. J. McNamara, *The Aramaic Bible: Targums in Their Historical Context* (JSOTSS 66) (Sheffield: JSOT Press, 1994) 379–399.

———, "A Comparative Study of Synoptic Development," *JBL* 101 (1982) 553–562.

Clarke, E. G., "Jacob's Dream at Bethel," *SR* 4 (1974–75) 367–377.

Cogan, M., *Linguistic Studies in Memory of Moshe Held* (Jerusalem: Magnes, 1988).

Cohen, G., "Esau as a Symbol in Early Medieval Thought," in Altmann, *Jewish Medieval and Renaissance Studies*, 19–48.

Cohen, J., *"Be Fertile and Increase, Fill the Earth and Master It": The Ancient and Medieval Career of a Biblical Text* (Ithaca, N.Y.: Cornell University Press, 1989).

Cohen, N. G., "*Agraphos Nomos* in Philo's Writings," *Da'at* 5 (1985), 5–20.

———, "'*Al Taseg Gevul 'Olim* (Peah 5:6, 7:3)," *HUCA* 56 (1985) 145–166.

———, "The Jewish Dimension of Philo's Judaism," *JJS* 38 (1987) 165–186.

———, "Taryag and Noahide Commandments," *JJS* 43 (1992) 46–57.

Collins, A., "Ezekiel, the Author of the Exagoge: His Calendar and Home," *JSJ* 22 (1991) 201–211.

Collins, A. Y., "Aristobulus," in Charlesworth, *OTP* 2:831–842.

Collins, John J., "Artapanus," in Charlesworth, *OTP* 2:897–903.

———, *The Scepter and the Star: the Messiah of the Dead Sea Scrolls and Other Ancient Literature* (New York: Doubleday, 1993).

Collins, John J., and G. W. Nickelsburg, *Ideal Figures in Ancient Judaism* (SCS 12) (Missoula, Mont.: Scholars, 1980).

Connolly, R. H., *Didascalia Apostolorum* (Oxford: Clarendon, 1929).

Coptic Nag Hammadi Library (Nag Hammadi Studies Series) (Leiden: Brill, 1975-).

Cothenet, E., "L'arrière-plan de l'allégorie d'Agar et Sara (Gal. 4:21–31)," in J. Doré et al., *De la Torah au Messie* (Paris: Desclée, 1981) 457–465.

Couliano, I. P., *The Tree of Gnosis* (San Francisco: HarperCollins, 1992).

Cresson, B., "The Condemning of Edom in Postexilic Judaism," in James M. Efird, *The Use of the Old Testament in the New and Other Essays* (Durham, N.C.: Duke University Press, 1972) 125–148.

Cryer, F. H., "The Interrelationship of Gen. 5:32, 11:10–11 and the Chronology of the Flood," *Biblica* 66 (1985) 241–261.

Dahl, N. A., "Die Erstegeborene Satans und der Vater des Teufels," in W. Eltester, ed., *Apophoreta: Festschrift Ernst Hänchen* (Berlin: Topelmann, 1964) 70–84.

Dan, J., *The Hebrew Story in the Middle Ages* (Jerusalem: Keter, 1974).

———, review of E. Yassif's *The Tales of Ben Sira in the Middle Ages* (Jerusalem: Magnes, 1984), in *Qiryat Sefer* 60 (1984) 294–297.

Daniélou, J., *Études d'exégèse judéo-chrétienne* (Paris: Beauchesne, 1966) 53–75.

———, *Sacramentum Futuri: Etudes sur les origines de la typologie biblique* (Paris: Beauchesne, 1950).

———, *Les symboles chrétiens primitifs* (Paris: Le Seuil, 1961).

Darnell, D. R., "Hellenistic Synagogal Prayers," in Charlesworth, *OTP* 2:677–697.

Davidson, *Angels at Qumran: A Comparative Study of I Enoch 1–36, 72–108, and Sectarian Writings from Qumran* (Sheffield: JSOT Press, 1992).

Davies, P. R., "Calendrical Change and Qumran Origins," *CBQ* 45 (1983) 80–89.

Davies, P. R., and B. D. Chilton, "The Aqedah: A Revised Tradition History," *CBQ* 40 (1978) 514–546.

Davies, W. D., *Paul and Rabbinic Judaism: Some Elements in Pauline Theology* (London: SPCK, 1955).

———, *The Setting of the Sermon on the Mount* (New York: Cambridge University Press, 1964).

De Jonge, M., "Jewish Expectations about the 'Messiah' according to the Fourth Gospel," *NTS* 19 (1973) 246–270.

———, "The Testament of Levi and 'Aramaic Levi,'" *RQ* 13 (1988) 369–385.

———, *The Testaments of the Twelve Patriarchs: A Critical Edition of the Greek Text* (Leiden: Brill, 1978).

Delcor, M., "Le mythe de la chute des anges et l'origine des géants comme explication du mal dans le monde dans l'apocalyptique juive: Histoire des traditions," *RHR* 190 (1976) 3–53.

———, "Melchizedek from Genesis to the Qumran Texts and the Epistle to the Hebrews," *JSJ* 2 (1971) 115–135.

Delling, G., "The 'One Who Sees God' in Philo," in F. Greenspahn et al., *Nourished with*

Peace: Studies in Hellenistic Judaism in Memory of Samuel Sandmel (Chico, Calif.: Scholars Press, 1984) 27–41.

DeLubac, H., *Exégèse médiévale: Les quatres sens de l'Ecriture* (Paris: Aubier, 1959–1964).

Derrett, J. D. M., "*Beḥuqei hagoyim*," *RQ* 11 (1983) 379–389.

———, "The Bronze Serpent," *EB* 49 (1991) 31–49.

Dexinger, F., "Die Taheb Vorstellung als politische Utopie," *Numen* 37 (1990) 1–23.

———, "Der Prophet 'Wie Mose' in Qumran und bei der Samaritanern," in A. Caquot et al., *Mélanges bibliques et orientaux en honneur de M. Mathias Delcor* (Heukirchen-Vluyn: Butzon und Bercker, 1985) 97–111.

Didyme l'Aveugle, *Sur la Genèse: texte inédit d'après un papyrus de Toura,* ed. P. Nautin (Paris: Le Cerf, 1978).

Diez Macho, A., *Biblia Polyglotta Matritensia* Series 4, *Targum Palaestinense in Pentateuchum* vol. 1 Genesis (Madrid: Consejo Superior de Investigaciones Cientificas, 1988).

———, *Neophyti 1: Targum Palestinense Ms. de la Biblioteca Vaticana* (Madrid-Barcelona: Consejo Superior de Investigaciones Científicas, 1968–78).

———, "The Recently Discovered Palestinian Targum: Its Antiquity and Relationship with the Other Targums," *VTS* 7 (1959) 222–245.

Dimant, D., "The Biography of Enoch and the Books of Enoch," *VT* 33 (1983) 14–29.

———, "The Fallen Angels in the Dead Sea Scrolls, Apocrypha and Pseudepigrapha, and Related Writings" (PhD. diss., Hebrew University, 1974).

———, "New Light from Qumran on the Jewish Pseudepigrapha," in J. Trebolle Barrera and L. Vegas Montaner, *Proceedings of the International Congress on the Dead Sea Scrolls, Madrid, 18–21 March 1981,* 405–447.

———, "Qumran Sectarian Literature," in M. E. Stone, *Jewish Writings of the Second Temple Period* (Philadelphia: Fortress Press, 1984) 483–550.

———, "The Pesher on the Periods 4Q180 and 4Q181," *Israel Oriental Studies* 9 (1979) 77–102.

Dimant, D., and U. Rappaport, *The Dead Sea Scrolls: Forty Years of Research* (Leiden: Brill, 1992).

Diodorus Siculus, *Library of History,* in LCL (Cambridge, Mass.: Harvard University Press).

Dirksen, P. B., "The Old Testament Peshitta," in M. J. Mulder, *Mikra* (CRJANT 2) (Minneapolis: Fortress, 1990) 255–297.

Dodd, C. H., *According to the Scriptures: The Substructure of New Testament Theology* (New York: Scribner's, 1953) 129–142.

Doran, R., "Pseudo-Eupolemus," in Charlesworth, *OTP* 2:873–882.

Dorival, G., and M. Harl, *La Bible Grecque des Septante* (Paris: C.N.R.S., 1988) 39–82.

Doukhan, J., "The Seventy Weeks of Daniel 9: An Exegetical Study," *Andrews University Seminar Studies* 17 (1979) 1–22.

Duling, D., "'Do Not Swear By Jerusalem . . .' (Matt. 5:35)," *JBL* 110 (1991) 291–330.

Dunn, J. D. G., "Yet Once More, 'The Works of the Law'—a Response," *JSNT* 46 (1992) 99–117.

Elgvin, T., "The Reconstruction of Sapiential Work A," *RQ* 16 (1995) 559–590.

Elgvin, T., and E. Tov, "Paraphrase of Genesis and Exodus," in H. Attridge et al., *Qumran Cave 4: VIII* (*DJD* 13) (Oxford: Clarendon, 1994) 417–442.

Elior, R. "Mysticism, Magic, and Angelogy," *Jewish Studies Quarterly* 1 (1993).

Ellis, E. E., *Paul's Use of the Old Testament* (Grand Rapids: Baker, 1991).

Emerton, J. A., "The Site of Salem, The City of Melchizedek (Genesis XIV 18)," in J. A. Emerton, *Studies in the Pentateuch* (Leiden: Brill, 1990) 45–71.

Enns, P., "Exodus Retold: Ancient Exegesis of the Departure from Egypt in Wis 10:15–21 and 19:1–9" (Ph.D. diss., Harvard University, 1994).

Epstein, J. N., *Mavo le Nusaḥ ha-Mishnah* (Jerusalem: [n.p.], 1948).

Epstein, J. N., and E. Z. Melamed, *Mekhilta deR. Šimʿon b. Yoḥai* (Jerusalem: Mekitse Nirdamim, 1979).

Eshel, E., and M. Stone, "The Holy Tongue at the End of Days in the Light of a Qumran Fragment" (Hebrew), *Tarbiz* 62 (1993) 169–178.

Eusebius, *La Préparation Evangélique*, text and trans. Guy Schroeder and Edouard des Places (Sources Chrétiennes 369) (Paris: Le Cerf, 1991). *Livres XII-XIII* ed. Edouard des Places (Sources Chrétiennes 307) (Paris: Le Cerf, 1983).

Evans, C. A., *Early Jewish and Christian Exegesis* (Atlanta: Scholars, 1987).

———, "A Note on the 'First-Born Son' of 4Q369," *DSD* 2 (1995) 185–201.

Falk, Zeev, "*Šôpeṭ* and *Šēbeṭ*," *Leshonenu* 30 (1966), 243–247.

Fallon, F., "Eupolemus," in Charlesworth, *OTP* 2:861–872.

Fassberg, S., *Studies in Biblical Syntax* (Jerusalem: Magnes, 1994).

Feldman, L., "Abraham the Greek Philosopher in Josephus," *TAPA* 99 (1968) 145–149.

———, "Josephus' Version of the Binding of Isaac," in *SBL Seminar Papers* 17 (Chico, Calif.: Scholars Press, 1982) 113–128.

———, "Prophets and Prophecy in Josephus," *JTS* 41 (1990) 402–411.

———, "Use, Authority, and Exegesis of Mikra in the Writings of Josephus," in M. J. Mulder, *Mikra: Text, Translation, Reading, and Interpretation of the Hebrew Bible in Ancient Judaism and Early Christianity* (Assen: Van Gorcum; Minneapolis: Fortress, 1988) 455–518.

Fiedler, Johannes, "*Dikaiosunē* in der Diaspora-jüdischen und Intertestamentarischen Literatur," *JSJ* 1–2 (1970) 120–143.

Field, F., *Origenis Hexaplorum quae supersunt*, vols. 1 and 2 (Oxford: Clarendon, 1867–1871).

Fiensy, D., "Hellenistic Synagogal Prayers: One Hundred Years of Discussion," *JSP* 5 (1989) 17–27.

Finkelstein, L., *Sifra on Leviticus according to Vatican Ms. Assemani 66* (4 vols.; New York: JTS, 1983–1990).

———, *Siphre ad Deuteronomium* (New York: JTS, 1969).

Firestone, R., "Difficulties in Keeping a Beautiful Wife," *JJS* 42 (1991) 196–214.

Fischer, B.. *Vetus Latina: Die Reste der altlateinischen Bibel* (Freiburg, 1951).

Fishbane, M.A., *Biblical Interpretation in Ancient Israel* (Oxford: Clarendon, 1985).

———, "The Well of Living Water: A Biblical Motif and Its Ancient Transformations," in Fishbane and Tov, *Shaʿarei Talmon: Studies in the Bible, Qumran, and the Ancient Near East Presented to Shemaryahu Talmon* (Winona Lake, Ind.: Eisenbrauns, 1992) 3–16.

Fitzmyer, J. A., "Crucifixion in Ancient Palestine, Qumran Literature, and the New Testament," *CBQ* 40 (1978) 493–513.

———, "Glory Reflected on the Face of Christ (2 Cor. 3:7–4:6) and a Palestinian Jewish Motif," *TS* 42 (1981) 630–644.

———, "4QTestimonia and the New Testament," in Fitzmyer, *Essays on the Semitic Background of the New Testament* (Missoula, Mont.: Scholars Press, 1974) 59–89.

———, "The Matthean Divorce Texts and Some New Palestinian Evidence," *JTS* 37 (1976) 197–226.

———, *Romans: A New Translation* (New York: Doubleday, 1993).

Fitzmyer, J. A., and D. J. Harrington, *A Manual of Palestinian Aramaic Texts* (Rome: Biblical Institute Press, 1978).

Fleischer, E., *Hebrew Liturgical Poetry in the Middle Ages* (Jerusalem: Keter, 1975) 104–107.

Flesher, Paul V. M., "Exploring the Sources of the Synoptic Targums to the Pentateuch," in Flescher, ed., *Targum Studies: Textual and Contextual Studies in the Pentateuchal Targums* (South Florida Studies in the History of Judaism 55) (Atlanta, Ga.: Scholars Press, 1992) 101–134.

Flusser, D., "The Decalogue in the New Testament," in B. Z. Segal and Gershon Levi, *The Ten Commandments in History and Tradition* (Jerusalem: Magnes, 1990) 219–246.

———, "Melchizedek and the Son of Man," in his *Judaism and the Origins of Christianity* (Jerusalem: Magnes, 1988) 186–192.

———, *Sefer Jossipon* (Jerusalem: Mirkaz Zalman Shazar, 1978).

———, "There Are Two Ways," in his *Judaism and Christian Origins* (Hebrew) (Tel Aviv, 1979) 235–252.

Flusser, D., and S. Safrai, "Das Aposteldekret und die Noachitischen Gebote," in E. Brocke et al., *Wer Torah vermehrt, mehrt Leben* (Neukirchen-Vluyn: Neukirchener Verlag, 1986) 173–192.

———, "Nadab and Abihu in the Midrash and in Philo's Writings," *Millet* 2 (1985) 79–84.

Fore, A., "The Beginnings of Sects in Post-Exilic Judea," *Cathedra* 49 (1988).

Fossum, J., "Gen. 1,26 in Judaism, Samaritanism, and Gnosticism," *JSJ* 16 (1985) 202–239.

Fraade, S. D., *Enosh and His Generation* (Chico, Calif.: Scholars Press, 1984).

———, *From Tradition to Commentary* (Albany: SUNY Press, 1991).

Frankemölle, H., "Mose in Deutungen des Neuen Testaments," *KI* 9 (1944) 70–86.

Franko, I., *Apokrifi i Legendi* (Lvov: Pamyatniki ukrains' ko-rus' koi mory i literature, 1899).

Freimann, I., *Midrash Wehizhir* (Warsaw, 1880, reprinted Jerusalem: n.p., 1973).

Freudenthal, J., *Hellenistiche Studien von J. Freudenthal* (Breslau: H. Skutsch, 1875–1879).

Friedmann, M., *Pesiqta Rabbati* (Vienna, 1880).

———, *Sifra* (Jerusalem: n.p., 1968).

Funk, F. X., *Didascalia et Constitutiones Apostolorum* (Paderborn, Libraria Ferdinandi Schoeningh, 1905).

Funk, S., *Die Haggadischen Elemente in den Homilien des Aphraates, des persischen Weisen* (Frankfurt: J. Kaufmann, 1915).

Gager, J. G., *Moses in Greco-Roman Paganism* (Nashville, Tenn.: Abingdon, 1972).

Garcia Martinez, F., "Las Tablas Celestas en el Libro de los Jubileos," *MC* 78–79 (1983) 333–349.

Gartner, Y., "Fasting on Rosh ha-Shanah," *Ha-Darom* 36 (1973), 125–165.

Gaster, M., *The Chronicles of Jerahmeel* (New York: KTAV, 1971).

———, *Studies and Texts in Folklore, Magic, Mediaeval Romance, Hebrew Apocrypha, and Samaritan Archaeology*, 3 vols. (New York: KTAV, 1971).

Gauger, J. D., "Zitate in der Jüdischen Apologetik und die Authentizität der Hekataios Passagen bei Josephus und im Pseudo-Aristeas-Brief," *JJS* 13 (1982) 6–46.

Gaylord, H. E., "Book of Baruch," in Charlesworth, *OPT* 1:653–679.

———, "How Satanael Lost His '-el'," *JJS* 33 (1982) 303–309.

Geiger, A., *Urschrift und Übersetzungen der Bibel in ihrer Abhängigkeit von den inneren Entwicklung des Judentums* (Breslau: Verlag Julius Hainauer, 1875); Hebrew translation: *Hammiqra Vetargumayv* (Jerusalem: Mosad Bialik, 1949).

Georgi, D., *Die Gegner des Paulus im 2. Korintherbrief: Studien zur religiösen Propaganda in der Spätantike* (Neukirchen-Vluyn: Nekirch. Verlag, 1964).

Gianotto, Claudio, *Melchisedek e la sua Tipologia* (Brescia: Paideia, 1984).

Gil, M., "Enoch in the Land of Eternal Life," *Tarbiz* 38 (1969) 322–337.

Gilat, Y., "Fasting on the Sabbath," *Tarbiz* 52 (1982) 1–15.

———, "On the Antiquity of Some Sabbath Prohibitions," *Bar-Ilan* 1 (1978) 104–106.

Ginsberger, M., "Les introductions araméennes à la lecture du Targoum," *REJ* 73 (1921) 14–26, 186–189.

Ginzberg, L., *Die Haggada bei den Kirchenvätern* (Berlin: S. Calvary, 1900).

———, *Legends of the Jews* (Philadelphia: Jewish Publication Society, 1968).

———, *An Unknown Jewish Sect* (New York: JTS, 1976).

Goldberg, J., "Kain: Sohn des Menschen oder Sohn der Schlange?" *Judaica* 25 (1969) 203–221.

Goldin, J., *The Fathers according to Rabbi Nathan: A Translation and Commentary*, trans. from Hebrew (New Haven, Conn.: Yale University Press, 1955).

Goldschmidt, D., *Mahzor leyamim nora'im* (Jerusalem: Koren, 1970).

Goldschmidt, E. Daniel, *The Passover Haggadah: Its Sources and History* (Jerusalem: Mosad Bialik, 1981).

Goldstein, J., "The Origins of the Doctrine of Creatio Ex Nihilo," *JJS* 35 (1984) 127–135.

———, *II Maccabees* (Anchor Bible 41A) (Garden City, N.Y.: Doubleday, 1983).

Goldstein, N., "The Strip of Scarlet-Dyed Wool in the Day of Atonement Ritual," *Tarbiz* 49 (1980) 237–245.

Goodenough, E. R., *By Light, Light* (New Haven, Conn.: Yale University Press, 1935; Amsterdam: Philo Press, 1969).

Goodman, D., "Do Angels Eat?" *JJS* 37 (1986) 160–175.

Goodspeed, E. J., *Die ältesten Apologeten* (Göttingen: Vandenhoeck und Ruprecht, 1914).

Goshen-Gottstein, A., "The Body as Image of God in Rabbinic Literature," *HTR* 87 (1994) 171–195.

Goshen-Gottstein, M., "Humanism and the Flowering of Jewish Studies—From the Christian to the Jewish Renaissance," *Newsletter of the World Union of Jewish Studies* 19 (August 1981) 1–8.

Goulder, M. D., "Exegesis of Genesis 1–3 in the NT," *JJS* 43 (1992) 226–229.

Grabbe, L. L., "The End of the Desolation of Jeremiah," in C. A. Evans et al., *Early Jewish and Christian Exegesis* (Atlanta, Ga.: Scholars Press, 1987) 67–72.

———, "Philo and Aggada," *Studia Philonica Annual* 3 (1991) 153–166.

————, "The Scapegoat Tradition: A Study of Early Jewish Interpretation," *JSJ* 18 (1987) 152–167.

Grabbe, L., "Social Setting of Early Jewish Apocalypticism," *JSP* 5 (1989) 27–47.

Greene, J. T., "The Balaam Figure and Type," *JSP* 9 (1991) 67–110.

Greenfield, J. "A Touch of Eden," in *Orientalia J. Duchesne-Guillaume Emerito Oblata* (Leiden: Brill, 1984) 219–224.

————, "The Meaning of PḤZ," in Y. Avishur and J. Blau, *Studies in the Bible and the Ancient Near East Presented to Samuel E. Loewenstamm, on His Seventieth Birthday* (Jerusalem: E. Rubinstein, 1978) 35–40.

————, "The Words of Levi Son of Jacob in *Damascus Document* IV 15–19," *RQ* 13 (1988) 319–322.

Greenfield, J. C., and Elisha Qimron, "The Genesis Apocryphon Col. XII," *Abr Nahrain Supplement* 3 (1992) 70–77.

Greenfield, J. C., and Michael Stone, "Aramaic Levi," *RB* 86 (1979) 216–230.

————, "The Prayer of Levi," *JBL* 112 (1993) 247–266.

————, "Two Notes on the Aramaic Levi Document," in Attridge, H., John J. Collins, and Thomas Tobin, *Of Scribes and Scrolls* (Lanham, Md.: University Press of America, 1991) 153–161.

Greenspahn, F., "Why Prophecy Ceased," *JBL* 108 (1989) 37–49.

Grelot, P., "La géographie mythique d'Hénoch et ses sources orientales," *RB* 65 (1958) 33–69.

————, "La légende d'Hénoch dans les apocryphes et dans la Bible: Origine et signification," *Recherches de Science Réligieuse* 46 (1958) 5–26, 181–210.

————, "Quatre cent trente ans (Ex. XII, 34) [*sic*]: Du Pentateuque au Testament araméen de Lévi," in A. Caquot et M. Philonenko, *Hommages à Dupont-Sommer* (Paris: Librairie de l'Amérique et de l'Orient, 1971) 384–394.

————, "Quatre cents [*sic*] trente ans (Ex 12,40)," in L. Alvarez Verdes et al., *Homenaje a Juan Prado: Miscelanea de Estudíos Bíblicos y Hebraicos* (Madrid: Instituto Arias Montano, 1975) 559–570.

————, "Soixante-dix semaines d'années," *Biblica* 50 (1969) 169–186.

————, "Les Targums de la Pentateuque," *Semitica* 9 (1959) 59–88.

Grintz, J. M., *The Book of Judith* (Hebrew) (Jerusalem: Mossad Bialik, 1986).

Grünbaum, M., "Zu Jussuf und Suleicha," in his *Gesammelte Aufsätze zur Sprach- und Sagenkunde* (Berlin: S. Calvary, 1901) 515–551.

Grünwald, I., *Apocalyptic and Merkavah Mysticism* (Leiden: Brill, 1980).

Grünwald, I., et al., *Messias and Christos: Studies in the Jewish Origins of Christianity Presented to David Flüsser* (Tübingen: Mohr, 1992).

Haberman, H., "Phylacteries in Antiquity," *Eretz Yisrael* 3 (1954) 174–177.

Hadas, M., *Aristeas to Philocrates* (New York: Columbia University Press, 1951).

Hadas-Lebel, M., "L'évolution de l'image de Rome auprès des juifs en deux siècles de relation, judéo-romains," *ANRW* II 20, 715–856.

————, "Jacob et Esaü ou Israël et Rome dans le Talmud et le Midrash," *RHdR* 20 (1984) 369–392.

Halkin, A. S., "Samaritan Polemics against the Jews," *PAAJR* 7 (1935) 28–30.

Halperin, D. J., "Crucifixion, the Nahum Pesher, and the Rabbinic Penalty of Strangulation," *JJS* 32 (1981) 32–46.

Hammer, R., *Sifre: A Tannaitic Commentary on the Book of Deuteronomy* (New Haven, Conn.: Yale University Press, 1986).

Hanhart, R., "The Translation of the Septuagint in the Light of Earlier Traditions and Subsequent Influences," in G. Brooke et al., *Septuagint, Scrolls, and Cognate Writings* (Atlanta, Ga.: Scholars Press, 1992) 339–379.

Hanson, A., "The Treatment in the LXX of the Theme of Seeing God," in G. Brooke et al., *Septuagint, Scrolls, and Cognate Writings* (Atlanta, Ga.: Scholars Press, 1992) 557–568.

Hanson, J., "Demetrius the Chronographer," in Charlesworth, *OTP* 2:843–854.

Hanson, P., "Rebellion in Heaven, Azazel, and Euhemeristic Heroes in 1 Enoch 6–11," *JBL* 96 (1977) 195–233.

Haran, M., "The Conception of the 'Taheb' in the Samaritan Religion," *Tarbiẓ* 23 (1952) 96–111.

Harl, M., "La 'ligature' d'Isaac (Gen. 22, 9) dans la Septante et chez les pères grecs," in A. Caquot et al., *Hellenica et Judaic: Homage à Valentin Nikiprowetzky* (Leuven-Paris: Peeters, 1986) 457–472.

Harl, M., "La prise de conscience de la 'nudité' d'Adam," *SPat* 92 (1966) 486–495.

Harrington, D., et al., *Pseudo-Philon: Les Antiquités bibliques,* vol. 1 (Paris: Le Cerf, 1976).

Hartman, T. C., "Some Thoughts on the Sumerian King List and Genesis 5," *JBL* 91 (1972) 25–32.

Hasid, Y., *Sefer Keter Torah (ha-Tāj)* (Jerusalem: n.p., 1978).

Hayward, C. T. R., "The Date of Targum Pseudo-Jonathan," *JSJ* 20 (1989) 280–281.

———, "Inconsistencies and Contradictions in Targum-Pseudo-Jonathan: The Case of Eliezer and Nimrod," *JSS* 37 (1992) 49–52.

———, *Jerome's Hebrew Questions on Genesis* (Oxford: Clarendon, 1995).

———, "Phinehas—The Same Is Elijah: The Origins of a Rabbinic Tradition," *JJS* 29 (1978) 22–34.

———, "Pirqei deRabbi Eliezer and Targum Pseudo-Jonathan," *JJS* 42 (1991) 215–246.

———, "The Present State of Research into the Targumic Account of the Sacrifice of Isaac," *JJS* 32 (1981) 127–150.

Hecht, R. D., "Patterns of Exegesis in Philo's Interpretation of Leviticus," *SP* 6 (1979–80) 77–155.

———, "Philo and Messiah," in J. Neusner et al., *Judaisms and Their Messiahs* (Cambridge: Cambridge University Press, 1987) 139–168.

Heinemann, I., *Altjüdische Allegoristik* (Breslau: Marcus, 1936).

———, "Die Lehre vom Ungeschriebenen Gesetz im jüdischen Schrifttum," *HUCA* 4 (1930–31), 149–161.

———, *Methods of Aggadah* (Jerusalem: Magnes, 1970).

———, *Philons griechische und jüdische Bildung* (Breslau: Marcus, 1932).

Heinemann, J., *Aggadah and Its Development* (Hebrew) (Jerusalem: Keter, 1974) 98–102.

———, "The Messiah of Ephraim and the Premature Exodus of the Tribe of Ephraim," *HTR* 68 (1975) 1–16.

———, "My Creatures Are Drowning . . ." (Hebrew), *Bar Ilan Annual* 7 (1969–70) 80–84.

Hengel, M., *Crucifixion in the Ancient World* (Philadelphia: Fortress Press, 1977).

———, *Judaism and Hellenism* (Philadelphia: Fortress Press, 1974).

———, *The Zealots* (Edinburgh: T and T Clark, 1989).

Hennecke, E., and W. Schneemelcher, *New Testament Apocrypha*, trans. R. McL. Wilson (Philadelphia: Westminster Press, 1963).

Henning, W. B., "The Book of Giants," *Bulletin of the School of Oriental and African Studies* 11 (1943–1946) 52–72.

Herr, M. D., "Realistic Political Messianism and Cosmic Eschatological Messianism," *Tarbiz* 54 (1985) 331–346.

Himmelfarb, M., "A Report on Enoch in Rabbinic Literature," *SBL Seminar Papers* 13 (Missoula, Mont.: Scholars Press, 1978) 259–269.

———, "Some Echoes of Jubilees in Medieval Hebrew Literature," in J. C. Reeves, *Tracing the Threads: Studies in the Vitality of Jewish Pseudepigrapha* (Atlanta, Ga.: Scholars Press, 1994) 115–412.

Hirshman, Marc, "The Preacher and His Public in Third-Century Palestine," *JJS* 42 (1991) 108–114.

Hoffman, D. H., *Midrash Tanna'im Lesepher Debarim* (Jerusalem: Book Exports, 1977).

Hoffman, Y., "Edom as a Symbol of Evil in Prophetic Writings," in B. Uffenheimer, *The Bible and Jewish History: Studies in Bible and Jewish History, Dedicated to the Memory of Jacob Liver* (Tel Aviv: Tel Aviv University, 1972) 76–89.

Holladay, C. R., *Fragments from Hellenistic Jewish Authors*, 3 vols. (SBLPS 12) (Atlanta, Ga.: Scholars Press, 1983–).

———, *Theios Anēr in Hellenistic Judaism: A Critique of the Use of This Category in New Testament Christology* (SBLDS 40) (Missoula, Mont.: Scholars Press, 1977).

Hollander, H. W., and M. de Jong, *The Testaments of the Twelve Patriarchs: A Commentary* (Leiden: Brill, 1985).

Holstein, J. A., "The Case of *'iš hā'elōhīm* Reconsidered . . .," *HUCA* 48 (1977) 69–81.

Horovitz, H. S. *Siphre de'Be Rab* (Jerusalem: Wahrmann, 1966).

Horovitz, H. S., and I. A. Rabin, eds., *Mekhilta of Rabbi Ishmael* (Frankfurt: Kauffmann, 1931).

Horowitz, W., "The Babylonian Map of the World," *Iraq* 50 (1988) 147–163.

Horsely, R. A., "Spiritual Marriage with Sophia," *VC* 33 (1979) 30–54.

Horsely, R. H., "Like One of the Prophets of Old," *CBQ* 47 (1985) 135–163.

Horton, F. L., *The Melchizedek Tradition* (Cambridge: Cambridge University Press, 1976).

Huffmon, Herbert, "The Fundamental Code Illustrated: The Third Commandment," in David P. Wright, *Pomegranates and Golden Bells* (Winona Lake, Ind.: Eisenbrauns, 1995) 363–372.

Hyman, D., D. N. Lehrer, and I. Shiloni, *Yalquṭ Šim'oni* (Jerusalem: Mossad ha-Rav Kook, 1973–1991).

Idel, M., "Enoch Is Metatron," *Immanuel* 24–25 (1990) 220–240.

Isch-Schalom (Friedmann), M., *Seder Eliahu Rabba* (Vienna, 1902).

Isenberg, "Anti-Sadducee Polemic," *HTR* 63 (1970) 433–444.

Issaverdens, Jacques, *The Uncanonical Writings of the Old Testament* (Venice: Armenian Monastery of St. Lazarus, 1901).

Isser, Stanley, "Two Traditions: The Law of Exodus 21:22–23 Revisited" *CBQ* 52 (1990) 30–45.

Istrin, V. M., *Ocherki istorii drevnorusskoy literatury* (Petrograd: Nauka i shkola, 1922).

Jacobson, H., "Biblical Quotation and Editorial Function in Pseudo-Philo's *Liber Antiquitatum Biblicarum*," *JSP* 5 (1989) 47–64.

———, *The "Exagoge" of Ezekiel* (Cambridge: Cambridge University Press, 1983).

James, M. R., *The Apocryphal New Testament* (Oxford: Clarendon, 1969).

Jansen, H. L., *Die Henochgestalt: Eine vergleichende religionsgeschichtliche Untersuchung* (Oslo: Dybwad, 1939).

Japhet, S., *The Ideology of the Book of Chronicles* (Frankfurt: Peter Lang, 1989).

———, "Sheshbazzar and Zerubbabel," *ZAW* 94 (1982) 89–105.

Jaubert, A., "Le calendrier des Jubilés et de la secte de Qumran," *Vetus Testamentum 3* (1953) 250–264.

———, *Clément de Rome, épitre aux Corinthiens* (Sources Chrétiennes 167) (Paris: Le Cerf, 1971).

———, *La Date de la Cène: calendrier biblique et liturgie chrétienne* (Paris: Gabalda, 1957); translated as *The Date of the Last Supper* (Staten Island, N.Y.: Alba House, 1965).

———, "Symboles et figures christologiques dans le Judaïsme," *RSR* 47 (1973) 373–390.

Jellicoe, S., *The Septuagint and Modern Study* (Oxford: Clarendon, 1968).

Jellinek, A., *Bet ha-Midrasch* (Jerusalem: Wahrmann, 1967).

Jerome (Eusebius Sophronius Hieronymus), *Biblia Sacra Juxta Vulgatam Versionem* (Stuttgart: Deutsche Bibelgesellschaft, 1969).

———, *Quaestiones Hebraicae*, in Migne, *PL* vol. 23 (Paris, 1865), also in P. Antin, ed., *Corpus Christianorum Series Latina*, vol. 72 (Tournai: Berpholt, 1959).

Jervell, J., *Imago Dei* (Göttingen: Vanderhoeck und Ruprecht, 1960).

Johnson, L., "The Use of Leviticus in the Epistle of James," *JBL* 101 (1982) 391–401.

Johnson, M. D., "Apocalypse of Moses," in Charlesworth, *OTP* 2:249–278.

Jones, F. Stanley, "The Pseudo-Clementines: A History of Research," *SC* 2 (1982) 1–33, 63–96.

Jonson, B., *The Alchemist*, ed. E. Cook (London: A. and C. Block, 1991).

Josephus, *Works*, in LCL (Cambridge, Mass.: Harvard University Press, 1956–65).

Kahane, M., "The Critical Edition of the Mekhilta deR. Ishmael in the Light of Geniza Fragments," *Tarbiz* 55 (1986) 489–524.

Kahle, P. *The Cairo Geniza*[2] (Oxford: Oxford University Press, 1959).

———, *Masoreten des Westens* (Stuttgart: W. Kohlhammer Verlag, 1930).

Kahn (Cohen-Yashar), J. G., "Did Philo Know Hebrew?" *Tarbiz* 34 (1965) 337–345.

———, "Israel—Videns Deum," *Tarbiz* 40 (1971) 285–292.

Kampen, John, "The Eschatological Temple(s) of 11QT," in Kampen and J. C. Reeves, *Pursuing the Text* (JSOTSS 184) (Sheffield: Sheffield Academic Press, 1994).

Kampers, F., *Mittelalterliche Sagen von dem Paradiesbaum und das Holz des Kreuzes Christi* (1897).

Kannengiesser, C., "Philon et les Pères sur la double création de l'homme," in *Philon d'Alexandrie* (Colloques Nationaux du Centre National de Recherche Scientifique) (Paris: C.N.R.S., 1967) 277–296.

Kasher, R. "Targumic Conflations in Ms. Neofiti 1," *HUCA* 57 (1986) Hebrew section, 1–20.

———, "Two Targum Toseftas on the Death of Moses," *Tarbiz* 54 (1985) 217–24.

Kim, S., *The Origin of Paul's Gospel* (Tübingen: Mohr, 1981).

Kippenberg, H. G., *Garizim und Synagogue* (Berlin and New York: de Gruyter, 1971).

Kirschner, "The Rabbinic and Philonic Exegesis of the Nadab and Abihu Incident (Lev.. 10:1–6)," *JQR* 73 (1983) 375–393.

Kister, M., "A Contribution to the Interpretation of Ben Sira," *Tarbiẓ* 59 (1990) 303–379.

———, "Different Versions of Aggadot," *Tarbiẓ* 60 (1991) 179–224.

———, "Observations on Aspects of Exegesis, Tradition, and Theology in Midrash, Pseuepigrapha, and Other Jewish Writings," in J. C. Reeves, *Tracing the Threads: Studies in the Vitality of Jewish Pseudepigrapha* (Atlanta, Ga.: Scholars Press, 1994).

———, "Some Aspects of Qumran Halakhah," in J. Barrera and L. Montaner, eds., *The Madrid Qumran Congress: Proceedings of the International Congress on the Dead Sea Scrolls* (Leiden: Brill, 1992) 571–588.

Klaasen, W., "Jesus and the Messianic War," in C. A. Evans, *Early Jewish and Christian Exegesis* (Atlanta, Ga.: Scholars Press, 1987) 155–175.

Klausner, J., *The Messianic Idea in Israel* (London: Allen and Unwin, 1956).

Klein, Michael, "Corrections to the Song 'The Lord Said to Moses . . . ,'" *Tarbiẓ* 55 (1986) 451–453.

———, *The Fragment Targums of the Pentateuch* (AB 76) (Rome: Pontifical Biblical Institute, 1980).

———, "The Targumic Tosefta to Exod. 15:2," *JJS* 26 (1975) 61–67.

Klijn, A. F. J., "Book of Baruch," in Charlesworth, *OPT* 1:615–652.

———, *Seth in Jewish, Christian, and Gnostic Literature* (Leiden: Brill, 1977).

Klostermann, E., *Eusebius Werke* (Leipzig: J. C. Hinrichs, 1902).

Klostermann, E., and R. Ernst Benz, *Origenes Werke*, vol. 11 (Leipzig: J. C. Hinrichs, 1933).

Knibb, M. A., *Ethiopic Book of Enoch* (Oxford: Clarendon, 1978).

———, "The Interpretation of Damascus Document VII,9b-VII,2a and XIX.5b-14," *RQ* 15 (1991) 243–251.

———, "Messianism in the Pseudepigrapha in the Light of the Scrolls," *DSD* 2 (1995) 165–184.

Knohl, I., "A Parashah Concerned with Accepting the Kingdom of Heaven," *Tarbiẓ* 53 (1983) 11–31.

Kobelski, P., *Melchizedek and Melchireša* (CBS Monograph Series 10) (Washington, D.C.: Catholic Bible Association, 1981).

Kraft, R. A., and A. E. Purintun, *Paraleipomena Jeremiou* (Missoula, Mont.: Scholars Press, 1972).

Kronholm, T., *Motifs from Genesis 1–11 in the Genuine Hymns of Ephrem the Syrian* (Lund: Liber Laromede/Guerup, 1978).

Kugel, J. L. "'The Bible as Literature' in Late Antiquity and the Middle Ages," *HSL* 11 (1983), 20–70.

———, "The Bible in the University," in W. H. Propp, B. Halpern, and David N. Freedman, *The Hebrew Bible and Its Interpreters* (Winona Lake, Ind.: Eisenbrauns, 1990) 143–165.

———, "Cain and Abel in Fact and Fable," in R. Brooks and John J. Collins, *Hebrew Bible or Old Testament?* (Notre Dame, Ind.: University of Notre Dame, 1989), 167–190.

———, "David the Prophet," in Kugel, ed., *Poetry and Prophecy* (Ithaca, N.Y.: Cornell University Press, 1990), 45–55.

———, "The Holiness of Israel and Its Land in Second Temple Times," in Michael Fox et al., *Texts, Temples, and Traditions: A Tribute to Menahem Haran* (Winona Lake, Ind.: Eisenbrauns, 1996).

————, *The Idea of Biblical Poetry* (New Haven, Conn.: Yale University Press, 1981).

————, *In Potiphar's House: The Interpretive Life of Biblical Texts* (San Francisco: Harper-Collins, 1990; 2d ed., Cambridge, Mass.: Harvard University Press, 1994).

————, "Is There But One Song?" *Biblica* 63 (1982) 329–350.

————, "The *Jubilees* Apocalypse," *DSD* 1 (1994) 322–337.

————, "The Ladder of Jacob," *HTR* 88 (1995) 209–219.

————, "Levi's Elevation to the Priesthood in Second Temple Writings," *HTR* 86 (1993) 1–64.

————, "On Hidden Hatred and Open Reproach: Early Exegesis of Lev. 19:17," *HTR* 80 (1987), 43–61.

————, "Reuben's Sin with Bilhah in the Testament of Reuben," in D. P. Wright et al., *Pomegranates and Golden Bells: Studies in Biblical, Jewish, and Near Eastern Ritual, Law, and Literature in Honor of Jacob Milgrom* (Winona Lake, Ind.: Eisenbrauns, 1995) 525–554.

————, "The Story of Dinah in the Testament of Levi," *HTR* 85 (1992) 1–34.

————, "Two Introductions to Midrash," *Prooftexts* 3 (1983); reprinted in G. Hartman and S. Budick, *Midrash and Literature* (New Haven, Conn.: Yale University Press, 1985), 77–103.

————, "Why Was Lamech Blind?" *HAR* 12 (1990) 91–104.

Kugel, J. L., and Rowan Greer, *Early Biblical Interpretation* (Philadelphia: Westminster Press, 1986).

Kuiper, J. G., "Targum Pseudo-Jonathan: A Study of Gen. 4:7–10, 16," *Augustinum* 10 (1970) 533–570.

Kutsch, E., "Der Kalender des Jubiläenbuches und das Alte und das Neue Testament," *VT* 11 (1961) 36–47.

Laato, "The Seventy Yearweeks in the Book of Daniel," *ZAW* 102 (1990) 212–225.

Lambden, Stephen, "From Fig Leaves to Fingernails: Some Notes on the Garments of Adam and Eve," in Paul Morris and Deborah Sawyer, *A Walk in the Garden* (JSOTSS 136) (Sheffield: JSOT Press, 1992) 74–91.

Lang, B., *Frau Weisheit: Deutung einer biblischen Gestalt* (Düsseldorf: Patmos, 1975).

Laporte, Jean, "The High Priest in Philo of Alexandria," *SP Annual* 3 (1991), 71–82.

————, "Philo in the Tradition of Biblical Wisdom Literature," in R. Wilken, ed., *Aspects of Wisdom in Judaism and Early Christianity* (Notre Dame, Ind.: University of Notre Dame, 1975) 103–141.

Larson, G., "The Chronology of the Pentateuch: A Comparison of the MT and the LXX," *JBL* 102 (1983) 401–409.

Lauterbach, J. Z., *Mekhilta of Rabbi Ishmael* (Philadelphia: Jewish Publication Society, 1933–1935).

Layton, B., *The Gnostic Scriptures* (Garden City, N.Y.: Doubleday, 1987).

Le Déaut, R., "Une aggadah targumique et les 'murmures' de Jean 6," *Biblica* 51 (1970) 80–83.

————, *Introduction à la littérature targumique* (Rome: Pontifical Biblical Institute, 1966).

————, *La Nuit pascale: Essai sur la signification de la Pâque juive à partir du Targum d'Exode XII 42* (AB 22) (Rome: Pontifical Biblical Institute, 1963).

Lee, A. L., A *Lexical Study of the LXX Version of the Pentateuch* (SCS 14) (Chico, Calif.: Scholars Press, 1983).

Leiman, S. Z., *The Canonization of Hebrew Scripture* (Hamden, Conn.: Academy for Archon Books, 1976).

Levenson, J. D., *Death and Resurrection of the Beloved Son* (New Haven, Conn.: Yale University Press, 1993).

Levine, D. B., "*Hubris* in Josephus' *Jewish Antiquities* 1–4," *HUCA* 64 (1993) 51–87.

Levison, J. R., "The Exoneration of Eve in the *Apocalypse of Moses*," *JSJ* 20 (1989) 135–150.

———, *Portraits of Adam in Early Judaism: from Sirach to 2 Baruch* (JSP Supplement Series 1) (Sheffield: JSOT Press, 1988).

Levy, B. B., *Targum Neophyti 1: A Textual Study* (Lanham, Md.: University Press of America, 1986).

Lewis, J. P., "The Offering of Abel (Gen. 4:4): A History of Interpretation," *Journal of the Evangelical Theology Society* 37 (1944) 481–496.

———, "The Woman's Seed, (Gen. 3:15)," *JETS* 34 (1991) 299–319.

Licht, J. *The Scroll of the War of the Sons of Light against the Sons of Darkness* (Jerusalem: Mosad Bialik, 1957).

———, *The Thanksgiving Scroll: A Scroll from the Wilderness of Judah* (Jerusalem: Mosad Bialik, 1957).

Lichtenstein, Hans, "Die Fastenrolle," *HUCA* 8–9 (1931–32) 317–351.

Lieberman, S., *Hellenism in Jewish Palestine* (New York: JTS, 1962).

———, *Midrash Debarim Rabba* (Jerusalem: Shalem, 1992).

———, *Tosefta* (Jerusalem: Sifre Wahrmann, 1970).

———, *The Tosefta* and *Tosefta Kifshuto* (New York: JTS, 1955–1973).

Lim, T. H., "The Chronology of the Flood Story in a Qumran Text," *JJS* 43 (1992) 288–298.

Lindenberger, J. M., "Sayings of Ahiqar," in Charlesworth, *OTP* 2:494–507.

Liver, Jacob, "The Doctrine of the Two Messiahs in Sectarian Literature in the Time of the Second Commonwealth," *HTR* 52 (1959) 149–185, esp. p. 157 n.

Loader, J. A., "The Model of the Priestly Blessing in IQS," *JSJ* 14 (1983) 11–17.

———, *A Tale of Two Cities* (Kampen, Netherlands: Kok, 1990).

Loewenstamm, S., "The Death of Moses" *Tarbiz* 27 (1958) 142–157, translated in G. W. E. Nickelsburg, *Studies in the Testament of Abraham* (SCS 6) (1972) (Missoula, Mont.: Scholars Press, 1976) 185–217.

———, "*Šôpeṭ* and *Šebeṭ*," *Leshonenu* 32 (1968) 272–275.

———, "The Testament of Abraham and the Texts concerning Moses' Death," in G. W. E. Nickelsburg, Jr., *Studies on the Testament of Abraham* (Missoula, Mont.: Scholars Press, 1976) 219–225.

Lövestam, E., "Divorce and Remarriage in the New Testament," *JLA* 4 (1981) 47–65.

Lowy, S., *The Principles of Samaritan Bible Exegesis* (Leiden: Brill, 1977).

Lucas, E. C., "The Origin of Daniel's Four Empires Scheme Reexamined," *TB* 40 (1989) 185–202.

Lull, David J., "'The Law Was Our Pedagogue': A Study in Galatians 3:19–25" *JBL* 105 (1986) 481–498.

Lunt, H., "Ladder of Jacob," in Charlesworth, *OTP* 2:402–403.

Luther, M., "Assertio Omnium Articulorum M. Lutheri per Bullam Leonis X, Novissimam Damnatorum," in his *Werke*, vol. 7 (Weimar: H. Böhlau, 1898).

Maccoby, H., "Neusner and the Red Cow," *JSJ* 21 (1990) 60–75.

———, *Paul and Hellenism* (London: SMC, 1991).

Mach, Michael, *Entwicklungstadien des jüdischen Engelsglaubens in vorrabinischer Zeit* (Tübingen: Mohe, 1992).

Mack, B. L., *Logos und Sophia: Untersuchungen zur Weisheitstheologie im hellenistischen Judentum* (Göttingen: Vanderhoeck und Ruprecht, 1973).

———, "Wisdom and Apocalyptic in Philo," *The Studia Philonica Annual Studies in Hellenistic Judaism* 3 (1991) 21–39.

MacRae, G., "Apocalypse of Adam," in Charlesworth, *OTP* 1:707–719.

Malina, B. J., *The Palestinian Manna Tradition* (Leiden: Brill, 1968).

Mandel, P., "Birah as an Architectural Term in Rabbinic Literature," *Tarbiz* 61 (1992) 195–217.

———, "The Call of Abraham: A Midrash Revisited," *Prooftexts* 14 (1994) 267–284.

Mandelbaum, Bernard, *Pesikta de Rav Kahana* (New York: JTS, 1962).

Maori, Y. "Methodological Criteria for Distinguishing between Variant *Vorlage* and Exegesis in the Peshitta Pentateuch," in P. B. Dirksen and A. van der Kooij, *The Peshitta as a Translation* (Leiden: Brill, 1995).

———, *The Peshitta Version of the Pentateuch and Early Jewish Exegesis* (Jerusalem: Magnes, 1995).

Marcus, R. "Tree of Life in Essene Tradition," *JBL* 74 (1955) 274.

———, "Tree of Life in Proverbs," *JBL* 62 (1943) 117–120.

Margulies, M., *Midrash Wayyikra Rabbah: A Critical Edition* (New York: JTS, 1993).

Margulies, M., and A. Steinsaltz, S. Fisch, Z. M. Rabinowitz, *Midrash ha-Gadol* (Jerusalem: Mossad haR. Kook, 1975–76).

Mason, S., *Flavius Josephus on the Pharisees: A Composition-Critical Study* (Leiden: Brill, 1991).

Matthews, E. G., Jr., and J. P. Amar, *St. Ephrem the Syrian: Selected Prose Works* (Washington, D.C.: Catholic University Press, 1994).

McHugh, M. P., *Saint Ambrose: Seven Exegetical Works* (Fathers of the Church 65) (Washington, D. C.: Catholic University Press, 1972).

McNamara, Martin, *The New Testament and the Palestinian Targum to the Pentateuch* (AB 27) (Rome: Pontifical Biblical Institute, 1966) 168–82.

McVey, K. E., *Ephrem the Syrian: Hymns* (Mahwah, N.J.: Paulist Press, 1989).

Meeks, W. A., "Image of the Androgyne," *History of Religions* 13 (1974) 165–208.

———, "Moses as God and King," in J. Neusner, *Religions in Antiquity* (Leiden: Brill, 1968) 354–371.

Mellinkoff, R. *The Horned Moses in Medieval Art and Thought* (Berkeley: University of California Press, 1970).

———, *The Sign of Cain* (Berkeley: University of California Press, 1981).

Mendelson, A., "Did Philo Say the Shema? And Other Reflections on E. P. Sanders' Judaism: Practice and Belief," *SP Annual* 6 (1994) 160–170.

———, *Philo's Jewish Identity* (Atlanta, Ga.: Scholars Press, 1988).

Meynet, R., "Le cantique de Moise et le cantique de l'Agneau (Ap. 15 et Exod. 15)," *Gregorianum* 73 (1992) 19–55.

Midrash Rabba (Vilna ed., reprinted Jerusalem, 1986).

Midrash Šoher Ṭob (Lemburg, 1851 ed., reprinted Jerusalem: Books Export Enterprises, n.d.).

Midrash Tanḥuma (Jerusalem: Merkaz ha-Sefer, 1987).

Migne, J. P., *Patrologiae cursus completus: Patrologia Graeca-Latina et Patrologia Latina* (Paris: Migne, 1857–1866).

Milgrom, J., "The Qumran Cult: Its Exegetical Principles," in G. Brooke, *Temple Scroll Studies* (JSP Supplement Series 7) (Sheffield: JSOT Press, 1989) 165–180.

Milik, J. T. "4Q Visions de 'Amram et Une Citation d'Origène" *RB* 79 (1972) 77–97.

———, *The Books of Enoch* (Oxford: Clarendon, 1976).

———, "Écrits préesséniens de Qumran: d'Hénoch à Amram," in M. Delcor, *Qumran: sa piété, sa théologie et son milieu* (Louvain: Université de Louvain, 1978), 91–106.

———, "Hénoch au pays des Aromates," *RB* 65 (1958) 70–79.

Milikowsky, C., "Again: *Damascus* in Damascus Document and in Rabbinic Literature," *RQ* 41 (1982) 97–106.

———, "The End of Prophecy and the End of the Bible in the View of *Seder 'Olam*, Rabbinic Literature, and Related Texts," *Sidra* 10 (1994) 83–94.

———, "Seder Olam: A Rabbinic Chronography," Ph.D. diss., Yale University, 1981.

———, "*Seder Olam* and Jewish Chronography," *PAAJR* 52 (1985) 115–139.

———, "*Seder Olam* and the *Mekhilta of R. Šim'on b. Yoḥai* on the Enslavement of Israel in Egypt," *Bar Ilan* 26–27 (1995) 221–225.

———, "Which Gehenna? Retribution and Eschatology," *NTS* 34 (1988) 238–249.

Millard, Alan, "The Etymology of Eden," *VT* 34 (1984) 103–106.

Mirsky, Aaron, "Beginnings of the Qerobah," *Sinai* 57 (1965) 127.

Moberly, R. W. L., "Abraham's Righteousness (Genesis XV 6)," in J. A. Emerton, *Studies in the Pentateuch* (Leiden: Brill, 1990) 103–130.

Moreno-Martinez, J. L., "El Logos y la Creacion," *ST* 15 (1983) 381–419.

Mowinckel, S., *He That Cometh: The Messianic Concept in the Old Testament and in Later Judaism* (Nashville, Tenn.: Abingdon, 1955).

Muñoz-León, D., "Un reino de sacerdotes y una nacion santa (Ex 19,6): La interpretación neotestamentaria a la luz de los Sententa y de las traducciones targúmicas," *EB* 37 (1978), 149–212.

Murphy, R. E., "*Yeṣer* in Qumran Literature," *Biblica* 39 (1958) 334–344.

Murphy-O'Connor, J., "*Pneumatikoi* and Judaizers in 2 Cor. 2:14–4:6," *AusBR* 34 (1986) 42–58.

Murray, R., *Symbols of Church and Kingdom* (Cambridge: Cambridge University Press, 1975).

Neudecker, R., "And You Shall Love Your Neighbor as Yourself," *Biblica* 73 (1992) 496–517.

Neugebauer, O., "Astronomy of the Book of Enoch," *Orientalia* 33 (1964) 48–61.

Neusner, J., *History of the Mishnaic Law of Purities, Part 22* (Leiden: Brill, 1977).

Neusner, J., et al., *Judaisms and Their Messiahs* (Cambridge: Cambridge University Press, 1987).

Newman, Judith, "Praying by the Book: The Scripturalization of Prayer in the Postexilic Period" (unpublished Ph.D. dissertation, Harvard University, 1996).

Newsom, C., "4Q374: A Discourse on the Exodus/Conquest Tradition," in D. Dimant and U. Rappaport, *The Dead Sea Scrolls: Forty Years of Research* (Leiden: Brill, 1992) 40–52.

——, "An Apocryphon on the Flood Narrative," *RQ* 13 (1988) 23–41.

——, "The Development of 1 Enoch 6–19: *Cosmology and Judgment*," *CBQ* 42 (1980) 310–329.

——, "The 'Psalms of Joshua' from Qumran Cave 4," *JJS* 39 (1988) 56–73.

——, *Songs of Sabbath Sacrifice* (HSM 27) (Atlanta, Ga.: Scholars Press, 1985).

Neyrey, J. H., "Without Beginning of Day or End of Life," *CBQ* 53 (1991) 439–455.

Nickelsburg, G., "Apocalyptic and Myth in 1 Enoch 6–11," *JBL* 96 (1977) 383–405.

Niditch, S., "Cosmic Man as Mediator in Rabbinic Literature," *JJS* 34 (1983) 137–146.

Niehoff, M. R., "Philo's Mystical Philosophy of Language," *JSQ* 2 (1995) 220–252.

Nikiprowetzky, V., *Le Commentaire de l'Ecriture chez Philon d'Alexandrie* (Leiden: Brill, 1977).

——, "Sur une lecture démonologique de Philon d'Alexandria, *De gigantibus* 6–11," in G. Nahon and C. Touati, eds., *Hommage à Georges Vajda: Etudes d'histoire et de pensée juives* (Leuven-Paris: Peeters, 1980) 43–71.

Noam, Vered, "The Scholion of *Megillat Ta'anit*—Toward an Understanding of Its Stemma," *Tarbiẓ* 62 (1993) 55–99.

Nodet, E., *Les Antiquités juives* vols. 1–3 (Paris: Le Cerf, 1990).

Novak, D., "Before Revelation: The Rabbis, Paul, and Karl Barth," *JR* 71 (1991) 50–66.

——, *The Image of the Non-Jew in Judaism: An Historical and Constructive Study of the Noachide Laws* (Toronto Studies in Theology) (New York: E. Mellen Press, 1983).

Olyan, S., "The Israelites Debate Their Options at the Sea of Reeds," *JBL* 110 (1991) 75–91.

——, *A Thousand Thousands Served Him* (Tübingen: Mohr, 1993).

Origen, *Contra Celsum*, trans. Henry Chadwick (Cambridge: Cambridge University, 1953).

——, *First Principles*, trans. by G. W. Butterworth (Gloucester, Mass.: Peter Smith, 1973).

Otzen, B., "Old Testament Wisdom Literature and Dualistic Thinking," *VTS* 28 (1974) 146–157.

Paramelle, J., *Philon d'Alexandrie: Questions sur la Genèse* (Geneva: P. Cramer, 1984).

Patai, R., *The Hebrew Goddess* (Detroit, Mich.: Wayne State University Press, 1990) 221–225.

Pearson, B. A., *Gnosticism, Judaism, and Egyptian Christianity* (Minneapolis: Fortress, 1990).

——, "Introduction to IX, 1: Melchizedek," in B. A. Pearson, *The Coptic Gnostic Library*, vol. 9 (Leiden: Brill, 1981) 19–40.

Petit, M. "Le contenu de l'Arche de l'alliance: Génération et addition de thèmes," in A. Caquot et al, eds., *Hellenica et Judaica* (Leuven-Paris: Peeters, 1986) 335–346.

Philo, ed. and trans. F. H. Colson and G. H. Whitaker, in LCL (Cambridge, Mass.: Harvard University Press).

Philonenko, M., "Philon d'Alexandrie et l'Instruction sur les Deux Esprits," in A. Caquot et al., eds., *Hellenica et Judaica* (Leuven-Paris: Peeters, 1986) 61–68.

Philonenko-Sayar, B., and M. Philonenko, *L'Apocalypse d'Abraham* (Paris: Maisonneuve, 1981).

Piattelli, D., "The Marriage Contract and Bill of Divorce in Ancient Hebrew Law," *JLA* 4 (1981) 66–78.

Pietersma, A., *The Apocryphon of Jannes and Jambres the Magicians: P. Chester Beatty XVI* (Religions in the Graeco-Roman World 119) (Leiden: Brill, 1994).

Pipyn, A. N., "Paleya," in G. Kuŝelev-Bezborodko, *Pamyatniki Starinnoy Russkoy Literatury* (St. Petersburg, 1862).

Pirqei deR. Eli'ezer (Warsaw, 1852 edition with commentary of David Luria, reprinted Jerusalem, n.p., 1970).

Pliny the Elder, *Natural History*, in LCL (Cambridge, Mass.: Harvard University Press).

Popov, A., *Kniga Bytia Nebesi i Zemli* (*Paleya Istoricheskaya*) (Moscow: Imperial Society of Russian History and Antiquities at Moscow University, 1881).

Prigent, P., and R. A. Kraft, *L'Epître de Barnabé* (Paris: Le Cerf, 1971).

Prijs, L., *Jüdische Tradition in der Septuaginta* (Hildesheim: G. Olms, 1987).

Puech, E., "Une apocalypse méssianique," *RQ* 60 (1992) 475–522.

———, "Fragments d'un apocryphe de Lévi et le personnage eschatologique," in J. Trebolle Barrera and L. Vegas Montaner, *The Madrid Qumran Congress: Proceedings of the International Congress on the Dead Sea Scrolls* (STJD 11) (Leiden: Brill, 1992) 449–501.

———, "Les deux derniers psaumes davidiques du rituel d'exorcisme," in D. Dimant and U. Rappaport, *The Dead Sea Scrolls: Forty Years of Research* (Leiden: Brill, 1992), 64–89.

———, "Notes sur le Manuscrit de XI Melkisedeq," *RQ* 12 (1985–1987) 483–513.

———, "Notes sur le manuscrit des Cantiques du Sacrifice du Sabbat trouvé à Masada," *RQ* 12 (1987) 575–583.

———, "Quelques aspects de la restauration du rouleau des hymnes," *JJS* 39 (1988) 38–55.

Purvis, J. D., "Ben Sira and the Foolish People of Shechem," *JNES* 24 (1965) 88–94.

Qimron, E., "Terminology for Intention Used in the Legal Texts of the Dead Sea Scrolls," in *Proceedings of the Tenth World Congress of Jewish Studies* (Jerusalem: World Union of Jewish Studies, 1990) 103–110.

Qimron, E., and M. Broshi, eds., *Damascus Document Reconsidered* (Jerusalem: Israel Exploration Society, 1992).

Qimron, E., and J. Strugnell, *Qumran Cave 4: V* (*DJD* 10) (Oxford: Clarendon, 1994).

Quispel, G., "Der gnostische Anthropos und die jüdische Tradition," *Eranos Jahrbuch* 22 (1953) 195–234.

———, "Origins of the Gnostic Demiurge," in Patrick Granfield and J. A. Jungman, *Kyriakon: Festschrift Johannes Quaesten* (Münster: Aschendorff, 1970) 252–271.

Rabello, A. M., "Divorce of Jews in the Roman Empire," *JLA* 4 (1981) 79–102.

Rabinowicz, Z. M., *Maḥzor Piyyuṭei Yannai lattorah velammo'adim* (Jerusalem: Mosad Bialik, 1985).

Rad, Gerhard von, *Problem of the Hexateuch and Other Essays* (London: SCM Press, 1984) 125–130.

Rajak, T., "Moses in Ethiopia, Legends and Literature" *JJS* 29 (1978) 111–122.

Reeves, J. C., *Jewish Lore in Manichaean Cosmogony: Studies in the "Book of Giants" Traditions* (Cincinnati, Ohio: Hebrew Union College Press, 1992).

Rehm, Berhard, and Georg Strecker, *Die Pseudoklementinen I: Homilien* (*Die Griechischen Christlichen Schriftsteller der Ersten Jahrhunderte*) (Berlin: Akademie Verlag, 1992).

Reiterer, F. V., *"Urtext" und Übersetzungen: Sprachstudie über Sir. 44:16–45:26 als Beitrag zur Siraforschung* (St. Ottilien: EOS Verlag, 1980).

Robertson, R. G., "Ezechiel the Tragedian," in Charlesworth, *OTP* 2:803–819.

Robinson, S. E., "The Apocryphal Story of Mechizedek," *JSJ* 18 (1987) 26–39.

———, *The Testament of Adam: An Examination of the Syriac and Greek Traditions* (SBL DS 52) (Chico, Calif.: Scholars Press, 1982).

Rodriguez-Carmona, A., "La figura de Melquisedec en la literatura targúmica," *EB* 37 (1978) 79–102.

Rofé, A., "The Beginnings of Sects in Post-Exilic Judea," *Cathedra* 49 (1988) 13–22.

———, "The Editing of the Book of Joshua in the Light of 4QJosh^a," in G. J. Brooke, *New Qumran Texts and Studies: Proceedings of the First Meeting of the International Organization for Qumran Studies, Paris 1992* (Leiden: Brill, 1994) 73–80.

———, "The End of the Book of Joshua in the Septuagint," *Henoch* 4 (1982) 17–36.

———, "Moses' Mother and Her Servant according to an Exodus Scroll from Qumran," *Beit Miqra* 40 (1995) 197–202.

———, "Qumran Paraphrases, the Greek Deuteronomy, and the Late History of the Biblical *Nāsî*," *Textus* 14 (1988) 163–174.

Rokeach, D., "Philo of Alexandria, Midrash, and Ancient Halakhah," *Tarbiz* 55 (1986) 433–439.

Rook, J., "The Names of the Wives from Adam to Abraham in the Book of Jubilees," *JSP* 7 (1990) 105–117.

Rorsdorf, W., and A.Tuilier, *La Doctrine des douze apôtres* (Sources Chrétiennes 248) (Paris: Le Cerf, 1978).

Rosenfeld, M., *Der Midrasch Deuteronomium Rabba par. IX und XI, 2–10 über den Tod Moses verglichen mit der Assumptio Mosis* (Berlin: H. Itzkowski, 1899).

Rosso, L., "Deut. 21:22: Contributo del Rotolo del Tempio alla Valuazione di una Variante Medievale dei Settanta," *RQ* 9 (1977–78) 231–236.

Rubinkiewicz, R., *L'Apocalypse d'Abraham en Vieux Slave* (Lublin: Société des Lettres et des Sciences de l'Université Catholique de Lublin, 1987).

Runia, D. T., *Exegesis and Philosophy: Studies on Philo of Alexandria* (Brookfield, Vt.: Gower, 1990).

———, "God and Men in Philo of Alexandria," *JThS* 39 (1988) 48–75.

———, *Philo in Early Christian Literature* (Minneapolis: Fortress, 1993).

Russell, W., "Who Were Paul's Opponents in Galatia?" *BS* 147 (1990) 329–350.

Safrai, S., *The Literature of the Sages* (CRJANT) (Philadelphia: Fortress Press, 1987).

———, "Midrash Wayyisa'u—The War of the Sons of Jacob in Southern Samaria," *Sinai* 100 (1987).

Saldarini, A. J., *The Fathers according to Rabbi Nathan: A Translation and Commentary* (Leiden: Brill, 1975).

Salveson, A., *Symmachus in the Pentateuch* (Manchester: University of Manchester, 1991).

Sanders, E. P., *Judaism, Practice, and Belief 63 B.C.E.–66 C.E.* (Philadelphia: Trinity, 1992) 421–448.

Sanders, J. A., *The Psalms Scroll of Qumran Cave 11 (DJD 4)* (Oxford: Clarendon, 1965).

Sandmel, S., "Parallelomania," *JBL* 81 (1962) 1–13.

———, *Philo's Place in Judaism: A Study of Conceptions of Abraham in Jewish Literature* (New York: KTAV, 1971).

Scarpat, G., "La torre di Babele in Filone e nella Sapienza," *RiB* 98 (1991) 199–221.

Schäfer, P., "Berešit Bara' 'Elohim. Zur Interpretation von Genesis 1,1 in der rabbinischen Literatur," *JJS* 2 (1971) 161–166.

———, *Rivalität zwischen Engeln und Menschen* (Berlin: de Gruyter, 1975).

Schechter, S., *Abot de Rabbi Nathan* (New York: Feldheim, 1967).

———, *Fragments of a Zadokite Work* (Cambridge: Cambridge University Press, 1910).

Scheiber, A., "La fumée des offrandes de Caïn et d'Abel: Histoire d'une légende," *REJ* 115 (1956) 9–24.

Schiffman, L. H., *Halakhah at Qumran* (Leiden: Brill, 1975).

———, "Pharasaic and Sadducean Halakhah in Light of the Dead Sea Scrolls: The Case of Tevul Yom," *DSD* 1 (1993), 285–299.

———, *Sectarian Law in the Dead Sea Scrolls: Courts, Testimony, and the Penal Code* (Brown Judaica Series 33) (Chico, Calif.: Scholars Press, 1983).

Schlecht, J., *Doctrina XII Apostolorum* (Freiburg: Herder, 1901).

Schmidt, F., *Le Testament Grec d'Abraham: Introduction, Édition Critique, Traduction* (Tübingen: Mohr, 1986).

Schneemelcher, W., *New Testament Apocrypha* (Louisville, Ky.: Westminster John Knox, 1991).

Schneider, G., "Jesu Wort über die Ehescheidung in der Überlieferung des Neuen Testaments," *Trierer Theologische Zeitschrift* 80 (1971) 65–87.

Scholem, G., *The Messianic Idea in Judaism and Other Essays on Jewish Spirituality* (New York: Schocken, 1971).

Schuller, E. M., *Non-Canonical Psalms from Qumran* (Harvard Semitic Studies 28) (Atlanta, Ga.: Scholars Press, 1986).

———, "4Q 372: A Text about Joseph," *RQ* 14 (1989–90) 349–376.

Schulz, S., "Die Decke des Moses: Untersuchungen zu einer vorpaulinischen Überlieferung in II Cor. 3:7–18," *ZNW* 49 (1958) 1–30.

Schürer, E., *The History of the Jewish People in the Age of Jesus Christ*, vol. 3 (revised by G. Vermes and F. Millar) (Edinburgh: T. and T. Clark, 1986).

Schwarzbaum, H., "Prolegomenon" to M. Gaster, *Chronicles of Jerahmeel* (New York: KTAV, 1971).

Schwenk-Bressler, Udo, *Sapientia Salomonis als ein Beispiel frühjüdischer Textauslegung* (Frankfurt a. M.: Peter Lang, 1993).

Scott, R. B. Y., "A Kingdom of Priests," *OS* 8 (1950) 213–219.

Scroggs, R., *The Last Adam: A Study in Pauline Anthropology* (Oxford: Blackwell, 1966).

Sefer ha-Yašar (Tel Aviv: Alter-Bergman, n.d.).

Segal, Alan F., *Two Powers in Heaven: Early Rabbinic Reports about Christianity* (Leiden: Brill, 1977).

———, *Paul the Convert: The Apostolate and Apostasy of Saul the Pharisee* (New Haven, Conn.: Yale University Press, 1990).

Segal, M. Z., *Sefer Ben Sira Hashalem* (Jerusalem: Mosad Bialik, 1958).

Seitz, O. J. F., "Love Your Enemies," *NTS* 16 (1969) 39–54.

————, "Two Spirits in Man," *NTS* 6 (1959–60) 82–95.

Seligmann, I. L., "The Beginnings of Midrash in the Book of Chronicles," *Tarbiz* 49 (1979–80) 14–32.

————, "Voraussetzung der Midraschexegese," *VTS* 1 (1973) 150–181.

Sharpe, J. L., "The Second Adam in Romans 5 and 1 Corinthians," *CBQ* 35 (1973) 35–46.

Shinan, A., "Dating Targum Pseudo-Jonathan," *JJS* 41 (1990) 57–61.

————, "*Dibrei ha-Yamim shel Mosheh Rabbenu*," *Hassifrut* 24 (1977) 100–116.

————, *Midrash Shemot Rabba, Chapters 1–14* (Tel Aviv: Debir, 1984).

————, "Midrashic Parallels to Targumic Traditions," *JSJ* 8 (1977) 185–191.

————, "Moses and the Ethiopian Woman," *Scripta Hierosolymitana* 27 (1978) 66–78.

————, "On Targum Pseudo-Jonathan to Gen. 4:15," *Tarbiz* 45 (1976) 148–150.

————, "The Sins of Nadab and Abihu in Rabbinic Literature," *Tarbiz* 48 (1978–79) 201–214.

Shinan, A., and Y. Zakovitch, *Abram and Sarai in Egypt* (Jerusalem: Hebrew University, 1983).

————, "*And Jacob Came Shalem*" (Jerusalem: Hebrew University, 1984).

————, *Story of Judah and Tamar* (Jerusalem: Hebrew University, 1992).

Shotwell, W. A., *The Biblical Exegesis of Justin Martyr* (London: SPCK, 1965).

Shutt, R. J. H., "Letter of Aristeas," in Charlesworth, *OTP* 2:12–34.

Siegert, F., *Drei hellenistisch-jüdische Predigten* (Wissenschaftliche Untersuchungen zum Neuen Testament 20) (Tübingen: Mohr, 1980).

Siegfried, C. G. A., *Philo von Alexandria als Ausleger des Alten Testaments* (Jena: Hermann Dufft, 1875).

Sifra (Venice, 1545, reprinted Jerusalem: Maqor, 1971).

Sigal, P., *The Halakhah of Jesus of Nazareth According to the Gospel of Matthew* (Lanham, Md.: University Press of America, 1986).

Siker, J., "Abraham in Greco-Roman Paganism," *JSJ* 18 (1987) 188–208.

Skehan, P. W., "*Jubilees* and the Qumran Psalter," *CBQ* 37 (1975) 343–347.

Skehan, P. W., and A. A. Di Lella, *The Wisdom of Ben Sira* (New York: Doubleday, 1987).

Sloley, R. W., "Primitive Methods of Measuring Time," *JEA* 16 (1930) 172–173.

Slomovic, Eliezer, "Toward an Understanding of the Exegesis in the Dead Sea Scrolls," *RQ* 7 (1969) 3–15.

Smith, J. Z., "Introduction" to the "Prayer of Joseph" in Charlesworth, *OTP* 2:699–714.

Smith, M., "4Q462 (Narrative) Fragment: A Preliminary Edition" *RQ* 15 (1991) 55–77.

————, "Hate Thine Enemy," *HTR* 45 (1952) 71–73.

————, "The Image of God: Notes on the Hellenization of Judaism," *BJRL* 40 (1958) 473–512.

Smolar, L., and M. Aberbach, "The Golden Calf Episode in Postbiblical Literature," *HUCA* 39 (1968) 91–116.

Sokoloff, M., *The Geniza Fragments of Bereshit Rabba* (Jerusalem: Israel Academy of Sciences and Humanities, 1982).

Sparks, H. F. D., *The Apocryphal Old Testament* (Oxford: Clarendon, 1984).

Sperber, A., *The Bible in Aramaic*, vol. 1 (Leiden: Brill, 1959).

Sperber, D., "Varia Midrashica IV," *REJ* 137 (1978) 149–157.

Spiegel, S., *The Last Trial* (New York: Random House, 1967).

Spiro, A., "The Ascension of Phinehas," *PAAJR* 22 (1953) 91–114.

Stadelmann, Helge, *Ben Sira als Schriftgelehrter* (*Wissenschaftliche Untersuchungen zum Neue Testament–2. Reihe*) (Tübingen: Mohr, 1980).

Stählin, O., *Clemens Alexandrinus*, vols. 2 and 3 (GCS 15 and 17) (Leipzig: J. C. Hinrichs, 1906, 1909).

Stein, E., *Philo und der Midrasch* (Beihefte ZAW 57) (Giessen: A. Topelmann, 1931).

Steinhauser, M. G., "Gal. 4:25a: Evidence of Targumic Tradition in Gal. 4:21–31?" *Biblica* 70 (1989) 234–240.

Stendahl, K., "Hate, Non-Retaliation, and Love," *HTR* 55 (1962) 345–355.

Stern, D., "Interpretatio Hominis: Anthropomorphism and the Character[s] of God in Rabbinic Literature," *Prooftexts* 12 (1992) 151–174.

Stern, M., ed., *Greek and Latin Authors on Jews and Judaism*, 3 vols. (Jerusalem: Israel Academy of Sciences, 1974–1984).

Steudel, A., *Der Midrasch zur Eschatologie aus der Qumrangemeinde* (STJD 13) (Leiden: Brill, 1994).

Stone, M. E., *Armenian Apocrypha Relating to the Patriarchs and Prophets* (Jerusalem: Israel Academy of Sciences, 1982).

———, "Enoch, Aramaic Levi, and Sectarian Origins," *JSJ* 19 (1988) 159–170.

———, *Fourth Ezra* (Hermeneia) (Philadelphia: Fortress Press, 1990).

———, *A History of the Literature of Adam and Eve* (Atlanta, Ga.: Scholars Press, 1992).

———, *Jewish Writings of the Second Temple Period* (Philadelphia: Fortress Press, 1984).

———, "Paradise in 4 Ezra," *JJS* 17 (1966) 85–88.

———, *Scriptures, Sects, and Visions* (Philadelphia: Fortress Press, 1980).

Stone, M. E., and Esther Eshel, "An Exposition on the Patriarchs (4Q464) and Two Other Documents," *Le Muséon* 105 (1992) 243–264.

Stone, M. E., and J. Greenfield, "The First Manuscript of the *Aramaic Levi Document* from Qumran," *Le Muséon* 107 (1944) 257–281.

Strack, H. L., and P. Billerbeck, *Kommentar zum Neuen Testament aus Talmud und Midrasch* (Munich: C. H. Beck, 1956).

Stroumsa, G. G., *Another Seed: Studies in Gnostic Mythology* (Nag Hammadi Studies 24) (Leiden: Brill, 1984).

———, "Form[s] of God: Some Notes on Metatron and Christ," *HTR* 76 (1983) 269–288.

Strugnell, J., "The Angelic Liturgy at Qumran," *VTS* 7 (1960) 318–345.

———, "Notes en Marge du volume 5 des DJD," *RQ* 7 (1976) 163–276.

Suminkova, T. A., *Izucheniye russkogo yazyka i istochnikovedeniye* (Moscow: Nauka, 1969).

Su-Min Ri, *La Caverne des Trésors: Deux Recensions Syriaques* (Leuven-Paris: Peeters, 1987).

Sussman, J., "Study of the History of Halakhah," *Tarbiẓ* 59 (1990) 11–76.

Swetnam, J., *Jesus and Isaac: A Study of the Epistle to the Hebrews in the Light of the Aqeda* (AB 94) (Rome: Pontifical Biblical Institute, 1981).

Tabory, J., "When Was the Fast-Scroll Nullified?" *Tarbiẓ* 54 (1985) 261–265.

Tal, Abraham, *The Samaritan Targum of the Pentateuch*, 3 vols. (Tel Aviv: Tel Aviv University, 1980–1983).

Talmon, S., "The Calendar Reckoning of the Sect from the Judean Desert," *Scripta Hierosolymitana* 4 (1958) 162–199.

Ta-Shema, I., "Tosefet Shabbat," *Tarbiẓ* 52 (1982) 309–323.

Tertullian, Quintus Florens, *Opera*, ed. A. Reifferscheid and G. Wissowa (Corpus Scriptorum Ecclesiasticorum Latinorum) (Vindobanae: F. Tempsky, 1890).

Teshimah, Isaiah, "The Order of Things: Contradictions in Narrative Order in Ancient Biblical Interpretation" (unpublished Ph.D. dissertation, Harvard University, 1996).

Theodor, J., and H. Albeck, *Midrasch Bereschit Rabba* (Jerusalem: Wahrmann, 1965).

Thomas, J. C., "The Fourth Gospel and Rabbinic Judaism," *ZNTW* 82 (1991) 159–182.

Tigay, J. H., "On the Term Phylacteries (Matt. 23:5)," *HTR* 72 (1979) 45–54.

Tikhonravov, N. S., *Pamyatniki starinnoy russkoy literatury* (Moscow, 1863).

Tobin, T. H., *The Creation of Man, Philo, and the History of Interpretation* (Washington, D.C.: Catholic Biblical Association, 1983).

———, "The Prologue of John and Hellenistic Jewish Speculation," *CBQ* 52 (1990) 252–269.

Tomson, Peter J., *Paul and the Jewish Law: Halakha in the Letters of the Apostle to the Gentiles* (Assen: Van Gorcum, 1990).

Tonneau, R. M., "Moïse dans la tradition syrienne," in H. Cazelles et al., *Moïse: Homme de l'Alliance* (Paris: Desclée 1955) 247–265.

———, *Sancti Ephraem Syri in Genesim et in Exodum Comentarii* (Corpus Scriptorum Christianorum Orientalium 153, Scriptores Syri 72) (Leuven: Imprimerie Orientaliste, 1955).

Tov, E., "The Exodus Section of 4Q422," *DSD* 1 (1994) 197–209.

———, "The Rabbinic Tradition concerning the 'Alterations' Inserted into the Greek Pentateuch," *JSJ* 15 (1984) 65–89.

———, "Reworked Pentateuch," in H. Attridge et al., *Qumran Cave 4 VIII* (*DJD* 13) (Oxford: Clarendon, 1994) 187–353.

———, *Text-Critical Use of the Septuagint in Biblical Research* (Jerusalem: Simor, 1981).

Treitel, L., "Agada bei Philo," *MGWJ* 53 (1909) 28–45.

Tromp, J., *The Assumption of Moses: A Critical Edition with Commentary* (VTS 10) (Leiden: Brill, 1993).

Tvorogov, O. V., *Drevnorusskiye khronografy* (Leningrad: Nauka i shkola, 1975).

Ubigli, L. R. "Alcuni aspetti della concezione della 'porneia' nel tardo-giudaismo," *Henoch* 1 (1979) 201–245.

———, "La Fortuna di Enoc nel giudaismo antico," *Annali di storia dell'esegesi* 1 (1984) 13–63.

Ulrich, E., and F. M. Cross, *Qumran Cave 4: VII* (*DJD* 12) (Oxford: Clarendon, 1994).

Urbach, E. E. "Fragments of *Tanḥuma-Yelammedenu*," *Qobeṣ 'al Yad* 6 (1966) 1–54.

———, "Halakhah and Prophecy," *Tarbiẓ* 18 (1947) 1–27.

———, "Homilies of the Rabbis on the Prophets of the Nations and the Balaam Stories," *Tarbiẓ* 25 (1956) 272–289.

———, "The Role of the Ten Commandments in Jewish Worship," trans. G. Levi in *The Ten Commandments in History and Tradition* (Jerusalem: Magnes, 1990) 161–189.

———, *The Sages* (Cambridge, Mass.: Harvard University Press, 1987).

———, "When Did Prophecy Cease?" *Tarbiẓ* 17 (1946) 1–27.

Vaillant, A., *Le Livre des Secrets d'Hénoch: Texte Slave et Traduction Française* (Paris: Institut des Etudes Slaves, 1952).

Van den Hoek, A., *Clement of Alexandria and His Use of Philo in the Stromateis: An Early Christian Reshaping of a Jewish Model* (Leiden: Brill, 1988).

Van der Horst, P. W., "The Interpretation of the Bible by the Minor Hellenistic Jewish Authors," in M. J. Mulder, *Mikra: Text, Translation, Reading, and Interpretation of the Hebrew Bible in Ancient Judaism and Early Christianity* (Assen: Van Gorcum; Minneapolis: Fortress, 1988) 519–546.

———, "Moses' Throne Vision in Ezekiel the Dramatist," *JJS* 34 (1983) 21–29.

———, "Nimrod after the Bible," in his *Essays on the Jewish World of Early Christianity* (Göttingen: Vandenhoeck und Ruprecht, 1990) 220–232.

———, "Some Notes on the Exagoge of Ezekiel," *Mnemosyne* 37 (1984).

Van der Osten-Sacken, P., *Gott und Belial* (Göttingen: Vanderhoeck und Ruprecht, 1969).

Van der Ploeg, J., *Le Rouleau de la Guerre* (Leiden: Brill, 1959).

Van der Woude, A. S., "Melchisedek als himmlische Erlösergestalt in den neugefundenen eschatologischen Midraschim aus Qumran Höhle 11," *Oudtestamentliche Studien* 14 (1965) 354–373.

———, *Die messianischen Vorstellungen der Gemeinde von Qumran* (Assen: Van Gorcum, 1957).

Van de Sandt, "Didache 3:1–6," *JSJ* 23 (1992) 21–41.

Van Unnik, M., "With Unveiled Faces: An Exegesis of 2 Cor. 3:12–18," *NT* 6 (1963) 153–169.

VanderKam, J. C., "The Birth of Noah," in Z. J. Kapera, ed., *Intertestamental Essays in Honour of Jozef Tadeusz Milik* (Krakow, Poland: Enigma Press, 1992) 213–237.

———, *The Book of Jubilees* (Corpus Scriptorum Christianorum Orientalium 511) (Leuven-Paris: Peeters, 1989).

———, *Enoch and the Growth of an Apocalyptic Tradition* (CBQ Monograph Series 16) (Washington, D.C.: Catholic Biblical Association, 1984).

———, "I Enoch 77:3 and a Babylonian Map of the World," *RQ* 11 (1982) 271–278.

———, "Genesis 1 in Jubilees 2," *DSD* 1 (1993), 300–321.

———, "The Granddaughters and Grandsons of Noah," *RQ* 16 (1994) 457–461.

———, "The Origin, Character, and Early History of the 364-Day Calendar," *CBQ* 41 (1979) 390–411.

———, "Righteousness of Noah," in John J. Collins and G. W. Nickelsburg, *Ideal Figures in Judaism* (SCS 12) (Missoula, Mont.: Scholars, 1980) 4–22.

———, "The Temple Scroll and the Book of Jubilees," in G. Brooke, ed., *Temple Scroll Studies* (JSP Supplement Series 7) (Sheffield: JSOT Press, 1989).

Vander Kam, J. C., and J. T. Milik, "First Jubilees Manuscript from Qumran Cave 4," 110 (1991) 243–270.

Vassiliev, A., *Anecdota Graeco-Byzantina* (Moscow: Moscow University, 1893).

Vermes, G., "The Archangel Sariel," in J. Neusner, *Christianity, Judaism, and Other Greco-Roman Cults* (Leiden: Brill, 1975) 159–166.

———, "Bible and Midrash: Early Old Testament Exegesis," in *The Cambridge History of the Bible*, vol. 1 (Cambridge: Cambridge University Press, 1970) 199–231.

———, "Genesis 1–3 in Post-Biblical Hebrew and Aramaic Literature before the Mishnah" *JJS* 43 (1992) 221–225.

———, "La figure de Moïse au tournant des deux testaments," in H. Cazelles et al., *Moïse, l'Homme de l'Alliance* (Paris: Desclée, 1955).

———, *Jesus the Jew* (Philadelphia: Fortress Press, 1973).

———, "Leviticus 18:21 in Ancient Bible Exegesis," in E. Fleisher and J. J. Petuchowski, eds., *Studies in Aggadah, Targum, and Jewish Liturgy in Memory of Joseph Heinemann* (Jerusalem: Magnes, 1981) 108–124.

———, *Post-Biblical Jewish Studies* (Leiden: Brill, 1975).

———, *Scripture and Tradition* (Leiden: Brill, 1973).

Visotzky, B., *Midrash Mishle* (New York: JTS, 1990).

Vivian, A., "I Movimenti che si oppongono al Tempio," *Henoch* 14 (1992) 97–112.

Von Gall, August Freiherrn, *Der Hebräische Pentateuch der Samaritaner* (Giessen: A. Töpelmann, 1918).

Wacholder, B. Z., *The Dawn of Qumran: The Sectarian Torah of the Teacher of Righteousness* (Cincinnati, Ohio: Hebrew Union College, 1983).

———, "'Pseudo-Eupolymos' Two Greek Fragments on the Life of Abraham," *HUCA* 34 (1963) 83–113.

———, "The 'Sealed' Torah vs. the Revealed Torah: An Exegesis of Damascus Covenant 5:1–6 and Jer. 21:10–14," *RQ* 12 (1986) 351–368.

Wan, Sze-Kar, "Charismatic Exegesis: Philo and Paul Compared," *Studia Philonica Annual* 6 (1994) 54–82.

Weinfeld, M., "God versus Moses in the Temple Scroll," *RQ* 15 (1991) 175–180.

———, "Killing an Embryo . . ." *Zion* 42 (1978) 129–142.

Weiss, H., "The Sabbath in the Synoptic Gospels," *JSNT* 38 (1990) 13–27.

Weiss, I., *Sifra* (Vienna, n.p. 1862).

Weiss, R., "Fragments of a Midrash on Genesis from Qumran Cave 4," *Textus* 7 (1969) 132–134.

Wernberg-Møller, P., "A Reconsideration of the Two Spirits in 1QS 3:13–4:26," *RQ* 3 (1961–62) 413–441.

Wertheimer, S. A., *Battei Midrašot* (Jerusalem: Ktab Wasepher, 1968).

Wevers, J. W., *Notes on the Greek Text of Exodus* (Atlanta: Scholars, 1990).

White, S. A., "All Souls Deuteronomy and the Decalogue," *JBL* (1990) 193–214.

———, "A Comparison of the 'A' and 'B' Manuscripts of the Damascus Document," *RQ* 48 (1987) 537–553.

Wieder, N., "The 'Law Interpreter' of the Sect of the Dead Sea Scrolls," *JJS* 4 (1953) 158–175.

Wilcox, M., "'According to the Pattern . . .' Exod. 25,40 in the New Testament and Early Jewish Thought," *RQ* 13 (1988) 647–656.

———, "The Bones of Joseph: Hebrews 11:2," in B. P. Thompson, ed., *Scripture: Meaning and Method* (Hull, Quebec: Hull University Press, 1987) 114–130.

———, "Upon the Tree—Dt. 21:22–23 in the NT," *JBL* 96 (1977) 85–99.

Willi, T., *Der Chronik als Auslegung* (Göttingen: Vanderhoeck und Ruprecht, 1972).

Williams, A. L., *The Dialogue with Trypho* (London: SPCK, 1930).

Williamson, R., *Philo and the Epistle to the Hebrews* (Leiden: Brill, 1970).

Wilson, A. M., and L. Wills, "Literary Sources of the Temple Scroll," *HTR* 75 (1982) 275–288.

Wilson, R. M., "The Early Exegesis of Gen. 1:26," in K. Aland and F. L. Cross, *SPat* vol. 1 (Berlin: Akademie Verlag, 1957) 420–437.

Winston, D., "Aspects of Philo's Linguistic Theory," in *SP* vol. 3 (Atlanta, Ga.: Scholars Press, 1991).

——, "Creatio Ex Nihilo Revisited," *JJS* 37 (1986) 88–91.

——, s.v. "Moses," *Encyclopedia Judaica*, vol. 12 (Jersualem: Keter Publishing House, 1972) col. 389.

——, *Philo of Alexandria: The Contemplative Life, the Giants, and Selections* (New York: Paulist Press, 1981).

——, "Philo's Doctrine of Free Will," in Winston and J. Dillon, eds., *Two Treatises of Philo of Alexandria* (Chico, Calif.: Scholars Press, 1983) 181–197.

——, "Philo's *Nachleben* in Judaism," *Studia Philonica Annual* 6 (1994) 103–110.

——, "Theodicy and the Creation of Man in Philo of Alexandria," in A. Caquot et al., *Hellenica et Judaica* (Leuven-Paris: Peeters, 1986) 105–111.

——, "Two Types of Mosaic Prophecy according to Philo," *JSP* 4 (1989) 49–67.

——, *The Wisdom of Solomon: A New Translation with Introduction and Commentary* (New York: Doubleday, 1979).

Winter, P., "Sadoqite Fragments 4:20–21 and the Exegesis of Gen. 1:27 in Late Judaism," *ZAW* 6 (1956) 79–81.

Wintermute, O. S., "Apocalypse of Elijah," in Charlesworth, *OTP* 1:721–753.

——, *The Book of Jubilees*, in Charlesworth, *OTP* 2.

Wolfson, H. A., "Patristics Arguments against the Eternity of the World," *HTR* 59 (1966) 351–367.

——, *Philo, Foundations of Religious Philosophy in Judaism, Christianity, and Islam*, 2 vols. (Cambridge, Mass.: Harvard University Press, 1947, 1962).

Wright, *No Small Difference: Sirach's Relationship to its Hebrew Parent Text* (Atlanta: Scholars, 1989).

Yadin, Y., *The Ben Sira Scroll from Masada* (Jerusalem: Israel Exploration Society, 1965).

——, "The Dial of Ahaz," *Eretz Yisrael* 5 (1958) 91–96.

——, *The Scroll of the War of the Sons of Light against the Sons of Darkness* (Oxford: Oxford University Press, 1962).

——, "Tefillin (Phylacteries) from Qumran," *Eretz Yisrael* 9 (1969) 60–85.

——, *The Temple Scroll* (Jerusalem: Israel Exploration Society, 1977–1983).

Yadin, Y., J. C. Greenfield, and A. Yardeni, "Babatha's *Ketubba*," *IEJ* 44 (1994) 75–101.

Yalquṭ Šimʻoni (Saloniki, 1526–27; reprinted Jerusalem: Makor, 1968–1973).

Yassif, E., *The Tales of Ben Sira in the Middle Ages* (Hebrew) (Jerusalem: Magnes, 1984).

York, Anthony, "The Dating of Targumic Literature," *JSJ* 5 (1974) 49–62.

Zani, A., "Tracce di un[a] . . . esegesi midrašica," *BO* 24 (1982) 157–166.

Zeron, A., "Critical Note: The Martyrdom of Phineas-Elijah," *JBL* 98 (1979) 99–100.

Ziegler, J., *Sapientia Iesu Filii Sirach* (Göttingen: Vandenhoeck and Ruprecht, 1965).

Zimmern, H., "Urkönige und Uroffenbarung," in Eberhard Schrader, *Die Keilinschriften und das Alte Testament*, vol. 2 (Berlin: Reuther und Reichard, 1903) 530–543.

Zipor, M. A., "Notes sur les chapitres 1 à 17 de la Genèse," *ETL* (1994) 385–393.

Zuckermandel, M., *Tosephta Based on the Erfurt and Vienna Codices: New Edition* (Jerusalem: Wahrmann, 1970).

Zulay, M., *Piyyuṭ Yannai* (Berlin: Schocken, 1938).

Illustration Credits

century, Ms. gr. 139, fol. 419v. Courtesy of the Bibliothèque Nationale de France, Paris.

Chapter 19   Moses, Aaron, and Hur. Miniature from a Hebrew Pentateuch, before 1300, Ms. 11639, fol. 525v. British Museum, London. By permission of the British Library.

Chapter 20   Illuminated manuscript, Bible of Moutier Grandval, Tours, 834–843, Ms. 10546, fol. 25v. By permission of the British Library, London.

Chapter 21   Moses. Detail of a painting by Jan Gossaert, ca. 1520. Kunsthistorisches Museum, Vienna.

Chapter 22   Moses expounding the law of the unclean beasts from the Bury Bible. Executed at Bury St. Edmunds by Master Hugo between 1130 and 1140. Parker Library, Corpus Christi College, Cambridge, Ms. 2, fol. 94r. By permission of the Master and Fellows of Corpus Christi College, Cambridge.

Chapter 23   The messengers from Canaan. German miniature, ca. 1260–1270. Staatsbibliothek, Munich.

Chapter 24   God speaks to Balaam. French miniature, ca. 1250, Ms. Bodl. 270b, fol. 82r. The Bodleian Library, Oxford.

Chapter 25   Luca Signorelli, The Angel shows Moses the Promised Land. Sistine Chapel, Vatican Palace, Vatican State. Courtesy of Alinari/Art Resource, New York.

Index

SUBJECTS

Aaron, 299–300, 364, 441–444, 463, 498; tried to discourage rabble, 424; took fright, 424; staff of, 475–476; messiah son of, 509

Abel, 87–89; the righteous, 90–93; was killed with a stone, 92–93. *See also* Cain

Abezethibou (demon), 292

Abimelech, 148n

Abraham, 225, 229–300, 306, 465, 497; toured heaven, 80; the monotheist, 134–135, 140, 556; an astronomer, 139–140; rescued from Chaldea, 141–142; was saved from fire, 143–144; wept about Sarah, 146; had prophetic dream, 147–148; was called "prophet," 148, 169; was blessed by Melchizedek, 151, 161–162; underwent many tests, 166, 167–168; was found faithful, 166–167; foresaw future of Israel, 169–170; informed Isaac about sacrifice, 176; famous for hospitality, 189–190; saw two paths, 531

Adam, 67–69, 92, 530, 538; added an extra proviso, 76–78. *See also* Adam and Eve

Adam and Eve, 406; lived only one day, 68–69; were punished with mortality, 69–71; passed on sinfulness, 71–72

Afterlife, 531–532

Agag, 203, 490–491

Amalek, 203, 364–365, 491; was the devil, 366

Ammonites and Moabites, 182, 412, 483

Amos, 251

Animals, justifiable death of, 118, 322

Angel, 532; tried to kill Moses, 305–306; of death, 307, 539–540; concealed in pillar of cloud, 336–338. *See also* Belial; Gabriel; Mastema; Michael; Satan

Angels, 190, 224–229; creation of, 58–61;

caused the flood, 108n, 109, 111–112; challenged God about Abraham, 171; ascending and descending, 211–213; wanted to see Jacob, 213; eat manna, 358–359; rule over Gentile nations, 408; buried Moses, 542. *See also* "Sons of God"; Watchers

Aquinas, Thomas, 551

Arpachshad, 112

Artaxerxes, 10

Atonement, Day of, 448; requires repentance, 449–450; does not effectuate forgiveness for all sins, 450–451

Augustine, 551, 552

Babel, Tower of. *See* Tower of Babel

Babylon, 213, 276; conquered Judah, 2–3, 5

Balaam, 94, 140, 474; a sage, 293; the wicked, 483; loved money, 485–487; foresaw the messiah, 488–493; urged that Moabite women seduce Israelites, 494–496

Balak, 244n, 484–487

Baptism, 119, 346–347, 356, 362, 509

Bathsheba. *See* David

"Beginning," a name for wisdom, 55–56

Belial, 155. *See also* Satan

Bible, deemed cryptic, 18–19; fundamentally relevant, 19–20; considered perfect, 20–22; divinely inspired, 22–23; in the Renaissance, 552–553; became "ancient" and "oriental," 553

Biblical interpretation in antiquity, beginnings of, 1–2; four assumptions of, 17–23; ideological motivations in, 25–26; "legendization" of, 46; was itself canonized, 550; decisive role of, 559–560. *See also* Modern biblical scholarship

649

HEBREW BIBLE

NEW TESTAMENT

ANCIENT BIBLICAL TEXTS and VERSIONS

DEAD SEA SCROLLS and RELATED TEXTS

PSEUDEPIGRAPHA and OTHER ANCIENT TEXTS CITED
(in alphabetical order; authors or sources with fewer than three citations
have not been listed)